Date Due

Date Due			
Apr 14 '47			
OCT 1 8 '60			

DUKE UNIVERSITY PUBLICATIONS

AMERICAN STATE DEBTS

AMERICAN STATE DEBTS

by

B. U. RATCHFORD

Associate Professor of Economics, Duke University

DUKE UNIVERSITY PRESS

DURHAM, NORTH CAROLINA

1941

PRINTED IN THE UNITED STATES OF AMERICA BY THE SEEMAN PRINTERY,
DURHAM, N. C., AND BOUND BY L. H. JENKINS, INC., RICHMOND, VA.

TO

MY FATHER AND MOTHER

AS AN AFFECTIONATE, ALTHOUGH BELATED,

TRIBUTE TO THEM, ON THEIR

GOLDEN WEDDING

ANNIVERSARY

PREFACE

PUBLIC CREDIT plays an important and expanding role in modern industrial societies. The proper control and management of this vital force is essential to the efficient functioning of the industrial economy. We know comparatively little about the proper use and control of credit, either private or public. During the past two centuries the states of the American Union have had a wide and varied experience with debts. A comprehensive analysis of their experience should yield some principles and conclusions which would be valuable as guides to the proper use of public credit.

The complete story of the debt of even one of the states would require a volume in itself. Only a few such stories have been written. In the absence of such complete histories, with their detailed description of political and economic background, one can never be sure, in dealing with the debt of a given state, that he has obtained the proper perspective or placed the correct interpretation upon a particular phase of debt history. In this work attention has necessarily been focused upon general trends except in the few instances where particularly important or significant situations warranted a more detailed description of developments. This procedure excludes much of the color and detail of debt developments in individual states, but it does not, I believe, distort the general picture nor affect the conclusions which should be drawn.

In view of the large amount of factual material which is presented it is, perhaps, too much to hope that all mistakes have been avoided or that all facts have been presented in their true perspective. It is hoped, however, that such mistakes as have crept in are neither numerous enough nor large enough to distort the general outline of the story or invalidate the conclusions. Since I have attempted to cover developments in forty-eight states, it has been necessary to rely heavily upon the data collected for all states by the

Bureau of the Census and upon secondary works where they have proved to be trustworthy.

This work is presented, then, as a comprehensive general survey and evaluation of the debt experience of our forty-eight states. It should be particularly useful to three major groups of readers: first, those who are interested in the investment aspects of state securities; second, those who formulate and administer state financial policies; and, third, students of public finance generally.

In the collection of material and the preparation of the manuscript I have become indebted to a great many people, to most of whom I must here express my thanks *en masse*. Among them are many state officials who have generously responded to my requests for data and information, and various members of the staff of the Duke University Library who have cheerfully assisted in locating and obtaining material. Mr. Walter Hargreaves served on two occasions as my research assistant and in that capacity rendered highly satisfactory service. He also gave much helpful advice and criticism in the preparation of the manuscript. Professor Wilford J. Eiteman, Dr. William M. Gibson, Professor Malcolm McDermott, Professor J. J. Spengler, Professor Charles S. Sydnor, and Dr. Weldon Welfling, all of Duke University, and Professor A. M. Hillhouse of the University of Cincinnati, have read parts of the manuscript and have offered many valuable suggestions. Others of my colleagues who have given generously of their time to discuss particular phases of the work include Professor R. Taylor Cole, Professor Calvin B. Hoover, and Professor Herbert von Beckerath. While all of these have saved me from many errors, they, naturally, are not responsible for any that remain.

The following publishers have given their permission to use quotations from the works named, which are more definitely identified in footnotes to the quotations: *The American Political Science Review;* Dun and Bradstreet, Inc., *Resources and Debts of the Forty-eight States, 1937,* and *Borrowing for Highways,* both by Edna Trull; The Johns Hopkins Press, *Money and Transportation in Maryland, 1720-1765,* by C. P. Gould; The Macmillan Company, *Foreign Bondholders and American State Debts,* by Reginald C.

McGrane; Prentice-Hall, Inc., *Revenue Bonds and the Investor,* by Laurence S. Knappen; The University of Chicago Press, *The Journal of Political Economy;* The Yale University Press, *The Readjuster Movement in Virginia,* by C. C. Pearson.

I am indebted to the Research Council of Duke University and to the Southern Regional Committee of the Social Science Research Council for grants-in-aid which greatly facilitated the collection of material.

Finally, I am most indebted to my wife for the uncounted hours which she has devoted to the preparation of the manuscript. Without her encouragement and assistance the task would have been much longer and harder, if not indeed impossible.

Durham, North Carolina   B. U. R.
February, 1941

CONTENTS

[xi]

CONTENTS

CONTENTS

CONTENTS

TABLES

AMERICAN STATE DEBTS

INTRODUCTION

DURING THE past twenty-five years the total of state debts in the United States has increased approximately fivefold. This phenomenal increase, starting from the highest point reached by state indebtedness up to that time, added an eventful chapter to the record of the preceding two centuries during which the states had experimented widely in borrowing operations. It is true that even after this great increase the total of state debts was still small in comparison with the debt of the Federal Government or with the total of local government debts. Yet the increase was significant because it indicated profound changes taking place in the field of state finances and because it gave rise, in several states, to critical problems, many of which remain to be solved. During the depression of the past ten years one state defaulted on its obligations, while several others avoided that embarrassment only by the narrowest of margins. For approximately half of the states, debts are a major problem, to be added to other financial worries. The problem is of ancient, if not entirely honorable, origin.

For more than one hundred years—roughly from 1700 to 1815— the colonies and states experimented with debts, mainly in the form of paper money, for a variety of purposes. Some of the experiments were successful, others were partial failures, while still others were disastrous. The Federal Constitution deprived the states of the power to issue money; so when they began to borrow for internal improvements around 1820, they incurred their first bonded or funded debt. For nearly one hundred years after 1820 the total of state debts rose and fell in response to various developments but never exceeded $400,000,000. Then came the events of the past quarter century which have raised the total gross indebtedness to more than $3,000,000,000 and the net indebtedness to more than $2,500,-000,000.

State Functions

Before we begin a study of the causes and effects of state borrowing it may be well to note the position of the states in the scheme of governmental organization in the United States. The functions of the states have varied widely with changing social and economic conditions. During most of our national life there has been a trend toward centralization. With respect to certain functions, the states have been merely way-stations for governmental functions en route from local governments to the national government. In the beginning, for example, the function of defense rested in large part upon the state and local governments. In the Revolutionary War and in the Civil War both groups made heavy contributions for war purposes. Several Northern states, after the Civil War, assumed local debts which had been incurred by local governments to pay bounties. In more recent years local governments have made no such contributions, and the states have almost entirely discontinued their efforts, although after the World War many states succumbed to veterans' lobbies and paid large amounts in bonuses. Before 1930 the relief of the poor and unemployed was almost entirely a local function, but so severe was the depression that that function, in a matter of months, passed in large measure from the hands of the local governments first to the states and then to the Federal Government. In recent years states have been taking over from local governments more and more of the responsibility for financing road maintenance and the operation of public schools. The Federal Government is granting subsidies for both of these functions, and there is considerable sentiment favoring increased federal aid for the latter; whether these will ultimately become federal functions remains to be seen. The function of aiding early railroads was shared by state and local governments. This function, too, passed to the Federal Government before the railroads finally were able to stand alone.

This shifting of functions provides an important clue to the variations in state borrowing. When a state is forced suddenly to assume an important new function it may resort to borrowing in order to provide the capital facilities necessary for the performance of that function and to adjust its finances to the new and higher level of expenditures. It may be asked why the shifting of functions has occurred. For that there are at least three answers. First, the function may become primarily state-wide or nation-wide in scope. Highways and railroads provide good examples of such transitions. Second, the function may become so costly that local governments are financially unable to carry it. In the 1930's the local governments were so heavily indebted and their current resources so limited that they could not finance unemployment relief. Third, democratic sentiment in favor of "equalization of opportunities" may demand that wealthier communities help to finance certain functions in poorer communities. This is the argument most often advanced in favor of state or federal financing of public education.

Several factors indicate that, instead of the trend toward centralization being reversed in the future, it is likely to continue. First, constant improvements in communication and transportation make the nation more and more one large community. The different parts become more interdependent, and conditions in one area affect the whole. Second, local governments are nearing the limit of their financial effort. Their debts have, in many instances, reached or passed the limits of safety; and the property tax, on which they have depended heavily, will no longer yield additional revenues by the mere act of raising rates. Indeed, local governments are becoming more and more dependent upon state and federal subsidies.

Whether the Federal Government will continue to assume or subsidize additional functions is more problematical. The trend in that direction has been strong in recent years, but as the federal debt increases and as it becomes more difficult to find new sources of federal revenue we may find the Federal Government more reluctant to take on new responsibilities. If so, the states may well be caught between the upper and the nether millstones; they may be forced to finance those functions which cannot be financed elsewhere.

Purposes of Borrowing

The one purpose which has dominated state borrowing since 1820 has been the financing of transportation. Before the Civil War the bulk of state borrowing was for the purpose of aiding the building of canals and railroads. The canals soon became obsolete and the railroads were taken over by private finance. Thereafter, except for the Civil War and Reconstruction borrowing (and a large part of the latter was nominally for some form of transportation), state debts declined steadily until nearly the end of the century. With the development of the automobile came the demand for more and better highways. Nearly one half of all state debts incurred since 1900 have been for the purpose of building roads and bridges.

The second most important cause of state borrowing has been war. Most of the borrowing during the Colonial and Revolutionary periods was for this purpose. During the Civil War, states borrowed some $200,000,000 for war purposes, and since the World War about one half of the states have borrowed approximately $450,000,000 to pay bonuses to, or to create loan funds for, veterans.

Perhaps the third most important reason for state debts has been the relief of the unemployed. Borrowing for this purpose made its appearance only after 1930, but since that time sixteen states have borrowed more than $400,000,000 for that purpose.

Another persistent reason for state borrowing has been the creation of loan funds. Many of the Colonial issues of paper money were authorized for this purpose. Often there was a double motive for such issues; to augment the money supply (and thus to lower the rate of interest) and to accommodate a favored few who wished to speculate in land. The chronic shortage of capital funds and the correspondingly high rate of interest, which are characteristic of a new country, often resulted in an acute shortage of circulating medium. If all of these experiments had been properly managed and protected from favoritism, as some of them were, they might have made an outstanding contribution to monetary theory and practice. Shortly after 1800 New York and Missouri established small loan funds which failed. The debts which several states incurred after 1825 to establish banks were essentially for the same purpose as the loan funds. Several such projects were complete failures, while none was an outstanding success. Within the past twenty-five years the loan funds established by Minnesota and the

Dakotas have entailed state borrowing to the extent of more than $125,000,000 and have been disastrous to the states concerned.

From the beginning, colonies and states have borrowed at frequent intervals to fund current deficits. When not abused, this form of borrowing is most useful to the states in that it provides a convenient and desirable element of elasticity in adjusting revenues to meet expenditures. Some states, however, have abused it by using it as the easy way out of difficult financial situations and have thereby delayed and made more difficult the ultimate solution.

The purposes enumerated above have accounted for a large majority of all state borrowing. The remainder has been distributed among a variety of purposes, including the construction of public buildings, the development of harbors and wharves, the creation of parks, and others. Thus far the states have borrowed very little for public schools. Even in those states which have assumed responsibility for the operation of such schools, local governments are still responsible for the construction and equipment of buildings. Whether this will change in the future remains to be seen.

Constitutional Limitations

States are the only governmental units which have imposed upon themselves constitutional limitations curbing their borrowing power. These have been voted by the electorate only after legislatures have borrowed recklessly and brought financial embarrassment to the state. The first limitations were imposed after the numerous defaults of the 1840's, while others were voted after the Reconstruction abuses in the South. Subsequently most states which entered the Union placed such provisions in their constitutions. After a limitation has been imposed there are usually many attempts to evade or circumvent it. As the conditions which prompted the limitation recede into the background, there is frequently a tendency for these efforts to increase while the defense of the limitation weakens. In a few states the courts have been so lenient—not to say lax—in their construction of constitutional provisions that the limitations have lost much of their effectiveness. The most usual method of evasion is for the state to issue revenue or limited obligation bonds based upon certain designated funds. The courts have, over the past fifty years, developed the special fund doctrine which justifies the exclusion of such borrowing from constitutional limitations. Unless some method is found to control this type of borrowing, it may become a serious threat to state finances.

Conclusion

Perhaps the greatest need in the field of state debts today is intelligent and comprehensive planning and administration. When debts are small, the lack of such features is not fatal, but as the debts increase, careful planning and management become more and more essential. This record of the states' experiences with their debts and the generalizations drawn therefrom should provide some guidance in the formulation and administration of such plans.

CHAPTER I

THE COLONIAL PERIOD

AMERICAN STATE debts had their beginnings in the Colonial period. Since most of the obligations issued by the colonies were in the form of circulating notes, studies in this field heretofore have usually been concerned with the debts in their capacity as money. In this survey the principal emphasis will be placed upon the debt aspect, although, of course, the two aspects cannot be divorced completely.

Since this must be a brief and summary chapter and because it would be a herculean task to delve into the primary sources for each colony, the facts here presented are gathered largely from secondary sources. There has been at least one monograph devoted entirely or partly to the paper issues of each of the colonies except Georgia, Rhode Island, and South Carolina.[1] We shall discuss the facts uncovered by these studies, supplementing them wherever necessary and possible, and appraise them as data on public debts rather than as statistics on the money supply. An attempt is also made to compile in one table a list of the obligations issued by the different colonies.

Purposes of Issues

Did the colonies issue bills of credit primarily to raise funds or to supply a circulating medium? An often quoted remark of a contemporary regarding the first issue of bills by Massachusetts in 1690 is that the bills were issued not "for want of money, but for want of money in the treasury."[2] That was probably true for that particular case and for initial issues in several other colonies, but those issues were continued and enlarged, and in some colonies the issues were initiated, principally to increase the money supply. Pre-

1. See the works cited below in this chapter.
2. Andrew McF. Davis, *Currency and Banking in the Province of Massachusetts Bay* (New York, 1900), Part I, "Currency," p. 8.

ambles to authorizing acts frequently stated that one purpose of the issues was to supply a circulating medium. Thus at the very outset the public credit was inextricably tied up with the money question. In recent years the close connection between bank credit and public debts has tended to emphasize this relationship once more.

Undoubtedly the basic reasons for the colonial issues were to create money and to raise funds for the treasury. There were, however, at least four immediate purposes or occasions which were the proximate causes of the issues. They were: (1) to create loan funds or "banks" to be loaned out on mortgages, (2) to supply funds to cover the costs of wars, (3) to cover deficits in ordinary operating expenses of the colonies, and (4) to supply funds for capital outlays. The latter category was of minor importance and did not appear except in a few colonies between 1760 and 1775.

Let us first examine the outstanding developments and events in the years (arbitrarily divided into six periods) between the first issue of bills and the Revolutionary War. Then we shall discuss some of the more important topics affecting the whole period.

HISTORICAL SURVEY

1690-1702

Massachusetts emitted the first issue of bills in 1690, to pay soldiers who had returned from an unsuccessful expedition against Quebec. It had been expected that the soldiers would be rewarded largely by their plunder. But there was no plunder, the treasury was empty, and the soldiers were threatening mutiny. After an unsuccessful attempt to borrow money, the colony issued £7,000 in bills of credit.[3] The next year additional bills were issued to pay other costs of the war, and almost immediately the colony began the vicious practice of issuing bills to cover ordinary expenditures. By 1702 a total of £82,000 had been issued. The bills, certificates of indebtedness bearing no interest, were not legal tender, but were receivable for taxes. Since adequate measures were taken to call them in promptly, they were, in effect, tax-anticipation notes. Only £5,000 were outstanding at the end of 1702.

3. *Ibid.,* pp. 8-11.

When first issued, these bills depreciated as much as 20 or 30 per cent, but in the second issue it was provided that they should be received by the government in the payment of taxes at a 5 per cent advance or premium. This feature and their prompt redemption kept them near par thereafter for the next twenty years.[4] No other colony issued bills before 1703.

1703-1717

Seven other colonies joined Massachusetts in its paper money experiment during this period; in all of them the bills depreciated, although at different rates. In 1703, and again in 1707, 1708, and 1711, South Carolina issued bills to cover the costs of Indian wars. North Carolina emitted issues for the same purpose in 1712 and 1713. In 1709, Connecticut, New Hampshire, New York, and New Jersey, and in 1710, Rhode Island issued small sums to pay debts incurred in Queen Anne's War. Massachusetts continued to issue bills for both emergency and ordinary expenditures. The other colonies were not long in following its lead, though none except Rhode Island was quite so reckless. Also, Massachusetts began to postpone the levy of taxes for the retirement of the bills, and soon was four or five years behind. Then depreciation began, and after about 1717 it became serious. The bills of all the New England colonies were affected alike in this, for there was more or less of a common circulation in the four colonies until 1749. Each colony made efforts to keep out the bills of others but without success.

The other New England colonies and New York followed the lead of Massachusetts in receiving bills for taxes at a premium. This feature was abolished and restored several times, but was finally abolished permanently. South Carolina agreed to allow 12 per cent interest on its bills when they were used in paying taxes, but this feature was repealed in 1707.[5] North Carolina paid interest on the bills of 1712 and 1713, but not on those issued in 1715. The New Jersey bills bore no interest. As a general rule, there were no more

4. *Ibid.*, pp. 88-92.

5. Curtis P. Nettels, *The Money Supply of the American Colonies Before 1720* (Madison, 1934), pp. 263-264. One of the principal objections to this feature, expressed in several colonies, was that it caused hoarding and thus reduced the money supply. This is another indication of the principal reason for the issuance of the bills.

interest-bearing notes until after 1750. The legal tender provision now made its appearance, and almost all of the bills issued during this period contained this feature.

Refunding and exchange issues also featured this period. When a colony fell behind in the redemption of its bills, it would emit an issue to refund all old bills. The reasons assigned for these issues were that the old bills had become dirty and mutilated or were widely counterfeited. New emissions frequently accompanied these refunding issues; this was true of the issues of 1711 and 1712 in New Hampshire, of 1712 in South Carolina, and of 1715 in North Carolina.

Another significant development of the period was the loan issues, or "banks" as they were called. The first was established in South Carolina in 1712, when £32,000 were set aside to be loaned at interest. Borrowers were to give security in the form of land, slaves, or other personal property equal in value to twice the amount of the loan and were to pay 12½ per cent a year for twelve years to cover both principal and interest. The state would thus receive "a gain of Fifty Pounds . . . on each Hundred Pounds So lent out. . . ." The interest rate was thus 8⅓ per cent. The preamble to the act of 1712 stated:

Whereas the Publick Debts occasioned by the vast charges to which this Province for these Several years past hath been Subject and Liable . . . are become at least [sic] So great Burthensome and considerable that there is no hopes or Probability the Same can be discharged in any Tolerable time by the Publick Duties and Incomes of this Province, And that it is also impracticable . . . to discharge and defray the same by the Ordinary method of imposeing a Tax on the Estates, Stocks and abilities of the Inhabitants of this Province without Pressing too hard upon them. Therefore, . . . following the Example of many great and Rich countries who have helped themselves in the like Streights and Exigencies with funds of Credit which have Effectually answered the Ends of money and thereby given a Quick Circulation and Encouragement to Trade and Commerce, Be it Enacted. . . .[6]

In Massachusetts there had been a long and persistent campaign to charter a private bank of issue. To forestall such a move, the

6. The law is quoted in W. A. Clark, *The History of the Banking Institutions Organized in South Carolina Prior to 1860* (Columbia, 1922), pp. 13-19.

colony issued, in 1714, £50,000 to be loaned on real property for five years at 5 per cent interest. Another issue of £100,000 followed in 1716.[7] Rhode Island emitted a loan issue of £40,000 in 1715. In the other colonies the demand for such issues became more and more insistent, the principal argument being that a larger money supply was needed. These issues were particularly attractive to the states because the interest on the loans promised to provide an income without the necessity of levying taxes.

1718-1739

Between 1718 and 1739, Pennsylvania, Delaware, and Maryland joined the paper money group, leaving only Virginia and Georgia free of debts. The principal issues were for loans, refunding, and current expenditures. Rhode Island ran wild with loan issues, issuing £100,000 in 1721, £40,000 in 1728, £60,000 in 1731, £100,000 in 1733, and £100,000 in 1738; a total of £400,000 in twenty-two years for a colony of probably eighteen thousand inhabitants. Massachusetts emitted two issues to towns to be loaned on mortgages: £50,000 in 1720 and £60,000 in 1727. The towns were allowed to keep all interest on the first issue and two thirds of the interest on the second. Other loan issues were made by Connecticut in 1733, New York in 1737, New Jersey in 1723, 1730, and 1733, Delaware in 1723, 1729, and 1734, Pennsylvania in 1723, North Carolina in 1729, and South Carolina in 1736 and 1746. Three prominent citizens entered a formal protest against the 1736 issue in South Carolina, stating that the local currency had already depreciated to such an extent that the exchange rate was then upwards of £740 for £100 sterling, and that the "bills are made to be a perpetual bank, and are to be perpetually current."[8] After a seven-year controversy, Maryland issued its first bills in 1733. Of the total issue of £90,000 a part was loaned at 4 per cent, but over £48,000 was given away at the rate of 30s. to each taxpayer. In return, however, and in order to raise the price of tobacco, the law required the burning of 150 pounds of "the most ordinary Sorts of Tobacco" for each taxpayer.[9] Thus it appears that

7. Davis, *op. cit.*, pp. 22-23, 56-57.
8. Clark, *op. cit.*, p. 28.
9. Kathryn L. Behrens, *Paper Money in Maryland, 1727-1789* (Baltimore, 1923), p. 44; Richard A. Lester, "Currency Issues to Overcome Depressions in Delaware,

the A.A.A. was not the first agency to pay farmers for destroying a part of their crops.

Depreciation proceeded apace with the reckless issues in New England and the Carolinas and caused acute monetary disturbances. The Middle Colonies started later with their paper issues and seem to have displayed more discretion in managing them so that depreciation was never a serious problem in that area. In Massachusetts silver was quoted at 8s. per ounce in 1710, 12s. in 1720, 16s. in 1727 and 27s. in 1737.[10] In North Carolina exchange, which had been £210 to £100 sterling in 1716, moved steadily up until it reached £1,000 in 1739.[11] In an effort to maintain the value of its bills, Massachusetts emitted a "new tenor" issue in 1737. The old bills had stated merely that they were "equal in value to money," but the new bills were labeled as being worth a certain amount of gold or silver. One shilling in the new bills was to be worth three in the old.[12] In spite of this move the new bills depreciated.

The English Government became alarmed at the monetary abuses practiced in the colonies, and took energetic steps to stop them. Beginning about 1720, the governors sent over from England received increasingly severe instructions not to assent to any laws authorizing the emission of bills until such laws should be approved in England. Exceptions were made, however, of war issues in order to encourage colonial aid in the conduct of the wars. This restraint provoked the colonists, and legislators frequently refused to pass appropriation bills unless governors would permit paper issues. On innumerable occasions governors had to dismiss obstreperous legislatures, but more often than not this procedure did not secure the desired result. In South Carolina not a single law was enacted between 1727 and 1731, and for a time civil war threatened, because of a violent disagreement between the governor and the legislature over paper money.[13] When other means failed, legislators

---

New Jersey, New York, and Maryland, 1715-37," *Journal of Political Economy,* XLVII (April, 1939), 211.　　　　　10. Davis, *op. cit.,* pp. 90, 140.

11. B. U. Ratchford, *A History of the North Carolina Debt, 1712-1900* (an unpublished dissertation in the Duke University Library, Durham, N. C.), p. 32.

12. Davis, *op. cit.,* pp. 126, 140.

13. David Ramsay, *History of South Carolina* (2 vols.; Newberry, S. C., 1858), II, 93-94; D. D. Wallace, *The History of South Carolina* (3 vols.; New York, 1934), I, 318-322.

sometimes resorted to bribes in the form of outright grants of money to secure the consent of governors.[14] The controversy over the right to issue bills remained a sore point in the relations between England and her colonies, and was undoubtedly one of the important factors which led to the Revolution.[15]

1740-1751

This period marked the complete breakdown of the paper money system in New England, and continuing depreciation in the South. Heavy outlays for the Spanish War, especially in New England, caused large new issues, which were piled upon the large amounts already outstanding. Depreciation continued at a rapid rate, and by 1748 silver was quoted at 60s. per ounce in New England. Massachusetts emitted two additional new tenor issues; Rhode Island, three; and Connecticut and New Hampshire, one each. North Carolina effected a conversion of its old bills into new ones at the rate of seven and one half to one, the new bills having a nominal value 25 per cent less than sterling. One table often quoted gives the following as the rates, in colonial currency, for £100 sterling in this period:[16]

	1740	1748
New England	525	1100
New York	160	190
New Jersey	160	180 to 190
Pennsylvania	170	180
Maryland	200	200
North Carolina	1400	1000
South Carolina	800	750
Virginia	—	120 to 125

These figures were given by contemporary writers and probably are fairly accurate, although it is doubtful if sterling exchange in North Carolina ever rose above 1,150 or 1,200.[17]

As Massachusetts had led the way into paper money issues, so it led the way out. At the close of King George's War, England made

14. Charles J. Bullock, *The Monetary History of the United States* (New York, 1900), p. 44.   15. *Ibid.*, pp. 58-59.

16. William M. Gouge, *A Short History of Paper Money and Banking in the United States* (2 vols.; Philadelphia, 1833), II, 10.

17. Ratchford, *History of North Carolina Debt*, p. 32.

an appropriation to the colonies to cover a part of their expenses in that war. Massachusetts received the net sum of £175,240 in silver and copper. After considerable debate as to policies and methods, the colony finally voted in 1749 to use this specie to retire its bills. This was done and the specie was sufficient to retire £50,708 old tenor, £38,431 middle tenor, and £1,703,100 new tenor, at a rate of one in specie to ten in paper, or at a rate of seven and one half to one, New England money.[18] But since this did not account for all the bills, the colony levied taxes to retire the remainder. In the meantime two small issues of interest-bearing notes, payable in silver, were sold to provide current funds and to retire bills as they came in. At first these notes suffered a slight depreciation, but when the colony redeemed them promptly according to specifications they rose to par. From time to time thereafter Massachusetts negotiated loans and issued treasury notes, but until 1775 its obligations were worth face value. The last of the old bills was finally retired in 1758.[19] Other colonies received money from England at this time, too, but in most cases it became a bone of contention between governors and legislatures. More frequently it was used for current expenses than for the retirement of bills.

The English attitude on paper money became more determined during this period, and in 1751 Parliament prohibited any further issues or reissues of legal tender bills by the New England colonies, and required them to retire outstanding bills according to schedule. After September 29, 1751, the old bills would no longer be legal tender. Treasury notes, for not more than two years, might be issued to meet current expenses and emergencies.[20]

1752-1764

During these years Connecticut, New Hampshire, and Rhode Island made progress in the stabilization of their currencies. Forbidden to make further legal tender issues or to extend the life of those already in circulation, they were aided in the redemption of

---

18. Henry Bronson, *A Historical Account of Connecticut Currency, Continental Money, and the Finances of the Revolution* (New Haven, 1865), p. 66. All these sums are computed, as was the practice, in terms of old tenor.

19. Charles H. J. Douglas, *The Financial History of Massachusetts* (New York, 1897), pp. 132-134.   20. Davis, *op. cit.*, pp. 251-252.

bills by specie payments from England as reimbursement of war costs. In 1755 Connecticut followed the example of Massachusetts, and in the 1760's New Hampshire and Rhode Island took steps to retire their bills. Connecticut redeemed its bills at the rate of one ounce of silver to 58s. of paper, or a ratio of about nine to one, New England money.[21] As each colony stabilized its currency, it had difficulty in keeping out the depreciated bills of other colonies.

The New England colonies were greatly handicapped in their efforts to retire their bills by the French and Indian War. All of the colonies borrowed to provide funds for this war, as can be seen from Table 1. Since the New England colonies could no longer issue legal tender bills, their obligations took the form of interest-bearing treasury notes, which, however, were receivable for taxes. Other colonies, especially the Carolinas, used this same form. These notes served in some degree as money, although it is impossible to say to what extent.[22] The small denominations in which they were issued indicate that the legislators hoped they would circulate. Depreciation of the old bills continued at varying rates, and in New Hampshire silver was quoted at 120s. per ounce, old tenor, in 1758.[23]

Virginia made its first issue of bills in 1755, and in the following years emitted several large issues. Its delay in following the other colonies was due in part to the tobacco notes which it issued from time to time, and which functioned as money. These notes "were not liable to the abuses of paper bills, and they never suffered depreciation." Together with "a fair amount of coin" they satisfied the demand for a circulating medium.[24]

On the whole, the experience of the colonies with the treasury notes showed a distinct improvement in financial practices. Massachusetts kept its obligations at par throughout the period. By 1764 Connecticut had retired more than half of its £192,000 of notes ahead of schedule, and its obligations were at par.[25] In 1764 the New Hampshire legislature concluded that another issue of money would "be fruitless and attended with mischievous consequences"

21. Bronson, op. cit., p. 75.
22. Ibid., p. 82.　　　　　　　　　23. Bullock, op. cit., p. 251.
24. William Z. Ripley, The Financial History of Virginia, 1609-1776 (New York, 1893), pp. 147-153.　　　　25. Bronson, op. cit., p. 83.

and took definite steps to retire its obligations.[26] In the same year Rhode Island called in the last of its old tenor bills and established their value at seven pounds for a silver dollar. Sterling exchange was then reported at par.[27] South Carolina retired its treasury notes within four or five years,[28] while North Carolina displayed more diligence in collecting taxes and retiring notes than it had shown in connection with any of its issues of bills.[29] On the other hand, the Middle Colonies, during this period, continued to issue legal tenders.

After the return of peace in 1763 Parliament determined to put a definite and permanent stop to the issues of legal tenders by the colonies. An act of 1764 prohibited all such issues as well as the postponement of the redemption of issues then in circulation. Any governor or council member who assented to any law to the contrary would be fined £1,000, be dismissed from office, and be forever disqualified to hold any public office or place of trust in the kingdom.[30] This caused much resentment in many of the colonies and was the occasion of many disputes between governors and legislatures. There were many ingenious attempts to circumvent the law, and bills were not always retired according to schedule, but the law was responsible for much of the improvement which took place in the following ten years.

1765-1775

The issues during this period were scattered and, with a few exceptions, small, as a glance at the table will show. Pennsylvania and Virginia continued to emit small issues for current expenses. Strong agitation for new loan issues continued in New York, New Jersey, Pennsylvania, and Maryland. In 1771 New York issued £120,000 for loans, and in 1769 and 1773 Maryland emitted $318,000 and $480,000, respectively, for this purpose. The 1769 issue was secured by state-owned stock in the Bank of England, a peculiar feature which, after the outbreak of the Revolution, caused some unusual legal complications.[31] A part of the 1773 Maryland issue

26. Bullock, op. cit., p. 255.
27. Samuel G. Arnold, History of the State of Rhode Island (2 vols.; New York, 1860), II, 250.
28. Wallace, op. cit., I, 459; Ramsay, op. cit., II, 93-94.
29. Ratchford, History of North Carolina Debt, pp. 18-19.
30. Bullock, op. cit., p. 168; Behrens, op. cit., p. 49.
31. Behrens, op. cit., pp. 53, 88-94.

was loaned to counties and a part to "supervisors" to build a road. The £162,000 issued by Pennsylvania in 1773 probably was a loan issue. A New Jersey act to issue £100,000 on loan was approved in England on February 20, 1775, but the Revolution started before the act became effective. The North Carolina issues were made to cover the costs of a governor's "palace" and the expenses of the War of the Regulators—an internal rebellion. South Carolina issued £70,000 to assist the counties in building courthouses and jails.

The rigid ban on legal tenders did much to improve the financial condition of the colonies during this period. In Rhode Island old tenor bills were not allowed to circulate after January 1, 1771;[32] in New Hampshire paper money disappeared in the same year.[33] In North Carolina exchange rates improved, and were quite steady around £160 to £100 sterling from 1770 to 1775.

Georgia

Very little information is available concerning colonial finance in Georgia. It was the last colony formed and never had a large debt. Under the Trustees from 1735 to 1752, the principal circulating medium was the "sola" bills. These were bills of exchange issued only in the original by the Trustees. A total of over £135,000 of them was issued, of which only £1,149 were unredeemed in 1752. They were not legal tender, but they did not depreciate; they circulated freely and nearly supplanted every other form of currency in the colony.[34]

After it became a Crown colony in 1752, Georgia emitted at least two issues of bills: one of £3,000 in 1756 and one of £7,410 in 1761. There may have been others. In the latter year there were about £5,500 in circulation.[35]

CHARACTERISTICS OF DEBTS

The Monetary Unit

Many aspects of colonial borrowing invite attention at this point, but only a few may be considered. Space is lacking for a full con-

---

32. Arnold, *op. cit.*, II, 304.   33. Bullock, *op. cit.*, p. 257.

34. W. B. Stevens, *A History of Georgia* (2 vols.; New York, 1847), I, 314-316, 402.   35. *Ibid.*, II, 20-21.

sideration of colonial monetary values,[36] but it is essential that we note the basis upon which colonial currencies were valued. The standard of value in England at this time was the silver pound. The most important coin which circulated in the colonies, however, was the Spanish milled dollar or "piece of eight," the metallic content of which was equal to approximately 4s. 6d. In order to attract this coin and to lighten debt burdens, the colonies developed the practice of officially "rating" the dollar at 5, 6, and even 8s., thus officially establishing pars of approximately 111, 133, and 177 in relation to sterling. Thus the value of a currency which was "at par" with sterling depended upon the rating which had been established. An official proclamation of the English Government in 1704 set 6s. as the maximum at which a colony might rate the dollar, but the indications are that this was not always observed. It can be seen, then, that the exchange rate between colonial currency and sterling depended upon the rating given the dollar, the weight of the dollar itself (which varied somewhat), the conditions of transportation and communication, and the balance of payments between the colonies and England.

Nettels states that the official ratios of colonial money to sterling after 1708 were: New England and New York, 155: 100; Pennsylvania, 178: 100; Maryland, 133: 100; Virginia, 120: 100; South Carolina, 161: 100.[37] New York's first issue of bills, however, rated silver at 8s. per ounce, which is equivalent to a ratio of approximately 145: 100. The same rate prevailed in New Jersey in 1711.[38] The North Carolina bills issued in 1715 were made legal tender at a ratio of £150 to £100 sterling.[39] It is necessary to keep these ratios in mind when considering exchange rates on sterling.

Form of Debt

Very few of the colonial loans were floated on a voluntary basis. Between 1750 and 1775, it is true, several acts of New England colonies authorized officials to "hire" money. Thus in 1755 Massachusetts borrowed £23,000 sterling in London, and the following

---

36. For good discussions on this point see Bullock, op. cit., chap. iii, and Nettels, op. cit., chap. ix.   37. Nettels, op. cit., p. 248.

38. Horace White, "New York's Colonial Currency," Sound Currency, V, 53; Nettels, op. cit., p. 247 n.   39. Bullock, op. cit., pp. 130-131.

year, £30,000. There are other references to such borrowing, but we do not know the amounts. These, however, were the exceptions; the great bulk of the borrowing was done by means of legal tenders and treasury notes of small denominations. In other words, they were forced loans, usually without interest. In the earlier issues it was the usual practice to issue only bills of large denominations; but later, when depreciation set in and specie was driven out, the denominations became quite small. Thus in South Carolina the denominations for certain issues were:[40] issue of 1703, from 50s. to £20; issue of 1707, from £1 to £20; issues of 1712 to 1731, from 5s. to £20; issue of 1746, from 2s. 6d. to £20.

The Loan Issues

The loan issues or "banks" were apparently successful in Pennsylvania and Maryland. "In Pennsylvania a public loan bank was managed with success and won the praise of English officials, who in general were not partial to issues of paper money."[41] In Maryland the

office seems to have been a decided benefit to the colony. A list of loans standing in 1755 contains the names of the most prominent men in the colony, including a surprising number of those engaged in mercantile affairs. The borrowed funds must, therefore, have been largely used in productive investments. From the banker's point of view the success of the office was remarkable. We have no means of knowing how many foreclosures were necessary, but only one appears in the records at hand. In 1765 it was reported that principal money still out amounted to only £222. Thus, losses through bad loans were almost negligible, while interest paid in amounted to thousands of pounds. Both as a business venture for the public and as a stimulus and aid to private industry the loan-office seems to have been an unqualified success.[42]

In New England and the Carolinas, however, there were frequent complaints of interest payments in default and in many cases both interest and principal were lost.[43] The borrowers constituted a

40. Clark, op. cit., pp. 9-29.
41. Davis R. Dewey, Financial History of the United States (12th ed.; New York, 1934), p. 26.
42. C. P. Gould, Money and Transportation in Maryland, 1720-1765, in "Johns Hopkins University Studies," XXXIII (1915), 109.
43. Arnold, op. cit., p. 56; Davis, op. cit., p. 352; Bullock, op. cit., pp. 34-37.

large and frequently influential group of citizens who were interested in postponing the redemption of the bills; their arguments
were strengthened by the fact that, since the bills had driven out
specie, redemption would cause deflation and precipitate a painful
crisis. Allied with this group, of course, were others who were
interested in paper money for other reasons, and this alliance was
frequently successful in preventing redemption and in bringing out
new issues. This was the cause of the severe depreciation which
occurred in several colonies.

Finally, there was the problem of political "pull" or favoritism
in the distribution of the loans. Rhode Island, having emitted more
loan issues than other colonies, experienced more than ordinary
abuses along this line. The "sharers" flourished in that colony.
These were a favored few who secured large amounts of the loan
funds and reloaned them at higher rates or sold their participation
rights; they constituted the "preferred list" of their day. One contemporary estimate was that they could make a profit of £150,000
on every £100,000 issue.[44]

Economic Effects

Economists have generally damned all colonial issues of paper
money as excessive and unsound and as the cause of ruinous inflation. There was certainly justification for such judgment in New
England and the Carolinas, but that the Middle Colonies fared much
better in their experience has usually been overlooked when general
conclusions were drawn. Professor Lester has made a new and careful study of the issues emitted by these colonies and has arrived at
the conclusion that they were generally successful attempts to prevent deflation, to stimulate business and trade, and to stabilize prices.
Thus he states:

. . . all the middle colonies had surprisingly successful experience
with monetary expansion as a method for stimulating the return of
prosperity, and in all of them, except Maryland for the first few years,
the exchange value of the currency seems not to have fallen more
than about 30 per cent in terms of gold and silver for any year during

44. William Douglas, *A Discussion Concerning the Currencies of the British Plantations in America,* in "Economic Studies of the American Economic Association,"
Vol. III, No. 1 (New York, 1897), pp. 308-309.

the period of fifty or sixty years that these colonies were on a paper standard prior to the Revolutionary War. . . . In Pennsylvania a little currency inflation did not lead to extreme currency inflation, and the price level during the fifty-two years prior to the American Revolution that Pensylvania was on a paper standard was more stable than the American price level has been during any succeeding fifty-year period.[45]

In regard to the New Jersey issues he writes: ". . . the currency experience of New Jersey represents a worthy record of achievement. From the first issue in 1709 to the last issue in 1786, all the paper money circulated by the colony was punctually and faithfully redeemed."[46] Similarly about New York:

New York's experience with paper money over a seventy-five year period was highly satisfactory and from all accounts the currency issues of 1715, 1717, and 1737 aided considerably in the colony's recovery from economic depressions. . . . In 1768 the governor of New York wrote to England of the colony's currency: ". . . They had allways [sic] kept up the credit of their paper Currency and taken particular care it should not be depreciated."[47]

The same general conclusion would apply to Delaware, while in the case of Maryland, Lester agrees with the conclusion already quoted from Gould. Georgia and Virginia, too, were apparently successful with their colonial issue of bills of credit. This means that seven colonies, altogether, had successful experience with the bills. It should be noted, however, (and Lester probably does not give this point sufficient weight in his conclusion) that the constant and increasingly stringent supervision exercised by the English Government was an important factor in preventing abuses in these colonies. It may have been that these colonies had stronger administrators who adhered more faithfully to their instructions or that their citizens were not so persistent or unruly in demanding more issues of paper money.

In New England and the two Carolinas there can be no doubt that the issues were excessive and that harmful inflation resulted.

45. Richard A. Lester, "Currency Issues to Overcome Depressions in Pennsylvania, 1723 and 1729," *Journal of Political Economy*, XLVI (June, 1938), 325.
46. Richard A. Lester, "Currency Issues to Overcome Depressions in Delaware, New Jersey, New York, and Maryland, 1715-37," *ibid.*, XLVII (April, 1939), 199.
47. *Ibid.*, p. 207.

The final count of seven favorable to six unfavorable experiences would seem to indicate that the success or failure of the paper money device was due more to the discretion with which it was employed than to any inherent characteristic. In view of the natural attitude of the taxpayers, the novelty of the device, and the poor guidance which economic theory could afford at the time, it is remarkable that the successful colonies fared as well as they did.

The Eve of Revolution

When the Revolution broke, New England was practically free of paper money. So far as can be determined, there was none in Massachusetts, New Hampshire, and Rhode Island.[48] An issue of small denomination notes amounting to £27,000 was in circulation in Connecticut.[49] New York had a circulation of £120,000,[50] Maryland approximately £295,000,[51] and North Carolina about £80,000.[52] Delaware probably had no bills outstanding, since its last issue of £4,000 in 1760 was to have run for five years. New Jersey had £190,000 outstanding in 1769.[53] Since there were no later issues, this could not have increased, and it probably was reduced to some extent. As an estimate, we may place the amount at £150,000. Pennsylvania had about £421,709 of bills outstanding in 1774.[54] In 1772 Virginia had outstanding £88,189[55] and thereafter reissued £36,384. An estimate of £75,000 would not be far wrong here. South Carolina bills and notes amounted to £497,653 in 1770.[56] Since a considerable part of these were short-term notes issued in anticipation of taxes, and since there were complaints of the scarcity

48. C. H. J. Douglas, *op. cit.*, p. 132; Bullock, *op. cit.*, p. 257. In Rhode Island a tax of £10,000 was laid to retire treasury notes in each of the years 1770, 1771, and 1772, but was discontinued in 1773. Arnold, who lists in great detail the acts of the legislature, makes no other mention of bills or notes from 1770 to 1775. Since the state treasurer had been directed to exchange his two-year notes for all bills and since there is no record of the postponement of the redemption of these notes,—or new issues—we may assume that all were retired (Arnold, *op. cit.*, II, 254, 304, 307, 322, 328, 341).   49. Bronson, *op. cit.*, p. 84.

50. White, *op. cit.*, p. 58.   51. Behrens, *op. cit.*, p. 32.

52. Ratchford, *History of North Carolina Debt*, p. 32.

53. Henry Phillips, Jr., *Historical Sketches of the Paper Currency of the American Colonies* (Roxbury, 1865), p. 76.

54. Lester, "Currency Issues in Pennsylvania," *op. cit.*, p. 353.

55. Ripley, *op. cit.*, p. 161.   56. Wallace, *op. cit.*, I, 459.

of bills between 1770 and 1775,[57] we may assume that considerable sums of them were retired. Let £350,000 suffice as an estimate. The amount in Georgia could not have been large enough materially to affect the total, but it may be placed at a nominal £10,000.

The sum of the estimates for the individual colonies as given above is £1,549,000. The maximum that could have been outstanding, according to figures available, is £1,730,025. With the dollar rated at 6s., the estimated total would be $5,163,333 and the maximum, $5,766,750. In 1779 Pelatiah Webster estimated the total "circulating cash" of the colonies in 1774 at $12,000,000. He thought that one half or three fifths of the currency of Pennsylvania was made up of paper, and believed that this proportion was not exceeded in other states.[58] Considering the fact that very little paper circulated in New England, the estimated amount given above is in keeping with Webster's estimate.

In addition to the bills and notes, some of the colonies owed varying amounts in other forms, but we know very little about these. In 1772 Virginia owed £150,000 in addition to bills, and the New England colonies were usually in debt for small amounts at short term. It is not likely, however, that the total of debts other than circulating bills and notes was large enough to be significant. Our final estimate is that the total indebtedness of the colonies at the outbreak of the Revolution was between $6,000,000 and $7,000,-000. Sumner, basing his figures on data quoted by Adam Smith, estimated the annual civil expenses of the colonies at $300,000.[59] If this was correct, colonial debts were equal to from twenty to twenty-three times their civil expenditures.

SUMMARY

The colonies borrowed primarily to supply a circulating medium and to provide revenue. Frequent wars were often responsible for empty treasuries, although borrowing to meet ordinary current ex-

57. *Loc. cit.;* Ramsay, *op. cit.,* II, 95.
58. Pelatiah Webster, *Political Essays* (Philadelphia, 1791), p. 142. This was evidently the estimate Dewey had in mind when he stated that "in 1774 it was estimated that $12,000,000 (of notes and bills) were in current use" (Dewey, *op. cit.,* p. 30).
59. William G. Sumner, *The Financier and the Finances of the American Revolution* (2 vols.; New York, 1891), I, 25.

TABLE 1

A Partial List of the Issues of Bills of Credit and Treasury Notes Emitted by the American Colonies, 1703-75

(In thousands of Colonial pounds except where dollars ($) are indicated)

Year	Mass.	Conn.	N.H.	R.I.	N.Y.	Pa.	N.J.	Md.	Del.	Va.	N.C.	S.C.
1703	32											6*
1704	32											
1705	18											
1706	44											
1707	32											8
1708	32											8
1709	46	19*	3*	7*	13		3*					
1710	44	5	2.5	7*								
1711	95†	10	4	6.3	10*		5*					7*
1712	25		1.5‡								4*	52†
1713	14	21.5‡									8*	
1714	50†		1.2		27.7							
1715	44		0.5	40†							24‡	35*
1716	111†		1.5			4.7						15*
1717	9		15†		16.7							
1718	11											
1719	15	4										
1720	65†											34
1721	17			100†								
1722	45	4	10.2‡								12‡	
1723	40			2	2.1	45†	40†		11†			
1724	55	4	2*									63
1725	70		2*		6.6							
1726	25		2.5	49.6‡								
1727	88†	4	2		3‡		24.8‡					20‡
1728	36	4		48†								
1729	20	6	1.8‡			30†			12†		40†	
1730	13		1.3		3‡		20†					
1731	23.7			60†								106.5‡
1733	79.2	30†		104†			40†	90				
1734	29.6			2.1	12				12†			
1735	39.3										52.5‡	
1736	48							1‡				210†
1737	81		9.5	30	48.3†							
1738	26.4			110†								
1739					10‡	80‡			6‡			
1740	80	49*§	2*	30†§				7.6‡				
1741	120			16				0.9‡				
1742	117		29.7§									
1743	85.4		1.3					6.1†				
1744	344.1*	19*		50†§		10‡		0.5‡				
1745	1040*	40*	27†	8.7*								
1746	661.6*	23*	60*	11.2*	53*	5	16*	5.6‡	20			210†
1747	348*		15*	28*								
1748	400*			30							21.3‡§	106.5‡
1751				25†§								
1752												20‡
1753									3‡			
1754	10							4‡			40*	
1755		62*	40*	240*	63*	15‡	40*			60*		33.6
1756			35.7*	14*§	62*	85*	17.5*	40.2*	2*	35*	3.6*	
1757			20*			100*	40*			180	14.8*	229.3*

TABLE 1 (*Continued*)

Year	Mass.	Conn.	N.H.	R.I.	N.Y.	Pa.	N.J.	Md.	Del.	Va.	N.C.	S.C.
1758....		30*	20.5*	20.9	100*	100*	60*		12*	88.6	11*	
1759....		70*	13*§	20*	100*	100*	50*		27*	62		
1760....		70*	15*	27*	60*	100*	45*		4*	52	12*	391.7*
1761....	70*	45*	20*				25*				20*	
1762....	60*	65*	20	13*			30*	0.5		19.7		
1763....		10*					10*					
1764....		7*			55		25*					
1766....				0.7				65.1				
1767....				2	20							
1768....										20		
1769....						30		$318†		10		106.5‡
1770....												70
1771....			1.5		120†	15				30	66*	
1772....						25						
1773....					162..			$480†		36.4‡		
1775....				60		6						

Sources: See text.

NOTE. An effort has been made to list in this table all issues of bills of credit and treasury notes emitted by the colonies between 1703 and 1775. (Massachusetts issued £82,000 in bills between 1690 and 1702.) It is quite likely, however, that the list is incomplete and that many of the issues listed were not made at the time nor in the exact amount stated. In some cases the only source of information is a law authorizing issue, with no further supporting documents to indicate how, when, or to what extent the issue was actually made. No figures are given for Georgia for reasons indicated in the text.

The figures for Massachusetts, through 1748, are taken from Davis, *op. cit.*, p. 443, and run from May 1 to April 30. For the years 1737-48, Davis expressed all issues in terms of old tenor. This procedure has not been followed for other colonies, because the author does not feel sufficiently well acquainted with the circumstances in each case to make the conversion with assurance.

In order to increase the usefulness of the table for reference purposes, an attempt has been made to indicate the principal purposes for which the larger issues were made. This procedure is limited by the fact that one figure must be given for each year, which sometimes included several issues for different purposes. Only those years are marked, however, in which a majority of the notes or bills were issued for one purpose. With these qualifications, the purposes of the different issues are indicated by the following symbols: (*) war costs; (†) loans; (‡) reissues or exchanges. The symbol (§) indicates years in which there were issues of different tenor or on a different basis from previous issues.

penses was all too common. A third purpose of borrowing was to establish loan funds or "banks." Favoritism and other forms of fraud frequently marked the administration of these funds, in New England and the Carolinas, while in the Middle Colonies the funds were generally successful. The establishment of the funds created a class of debtors opposed to the retirement of the bills and in favor of new issues. This class naturally allied itself with other easy money groups.

An overwhelming proportion of the debts was evidenced by circulating bills, the excessive issue of which, in several colonies, caused great depreciation amounting to from 80 to 90 per cent of their face value. Two special results of this depreciation should be noted. First, a great part of the loss was borne by British subjects— merchants, public officials, and other creditors—while American

TABLE 2

STATEMENTS AND ESTIMATES OF AMOUNTS OF PAPER MONEY OUTSTANDING IN THE
AMERICAN COLONIES AT SELECTED DATES, 1705-75

(In thousands of colonial pounds)

Year	Mass.	Conn.	N.H.	R.I.	N.Y.	Pa.	N.J.	Del.	Md.	Va.	N.C.	S.C.
1705....	28											
1710....	89	20	......	7	7							
1715....	170	26.5	8.2	51	36.3	......	4.7			......	24	74
1720....	229.5		22							12		
1725....	350.7		26.6			38.9	36.9	11[a]				116[b]
1730....	311.3		26.8	320.4[c]		68.9	17.6				40	106.5
1735....	309.4		22.4			68.9	22.7	20.2[d]	90		52.5	
1739....	243	60	22.6	340[e]	79.8[f]	80	60	17.2	90		52.5	250
1744....	304.8		29.9			85		14	90			
1748....	2135.3	281	113.8	550		85	37.8[g]		60		21.3	133[g]
1752....		340.2[b]	113.8			83.5			60			
1760....			212.2[i]			485.8	155.2[i]				50[j]	
1765....					260[k]	432.2	247.5[l]			302.6[m]	75[l]	
1770....						343.5	190[n]			88.2[o]	78.5	497.7
1775....		27			120	421.7[p]			295		80	

[a]1723   [b]1724   [c]1728   [d]1734   [e]1741   [f]1740   [g]1749   [h]1751   [i]1758   [j]1759   [k]1766   [l]1764   [m]1763
[n]1762   [o]1772   [p]1774.

NOTE. In this table an attempt is made to bring together estimates and statements of the amounts
of paper money in circulation in the colonies at different times as recorded in the various monographs
mentioned in the text. Many of the authors of these monographs did not concern themselves with
this question, neither giving statements or estimates of others nor attempting to make estimates themselves. Contemporary estimates were usually made by legislative committees or public officials; less
often by contemporary writers. Many of the estimates for 1739 and 1748 were made by William
Douglas, concerning whom see Bullock's introduction in *Economic Studies of the American Economic
Association*, Vol. II, No. 1. The only estimate for Georgia is £5,500 for 1761.

debtors profited. This naturally stimulated ill feeling and encouraged the colonists to demand new issues. Secondly, since each
colony had its own paper money which had driven out most specie,
trade between the colonies was hampered by the lack of a common
currency. As a rule, outside New England, the bills of one colony
were not acceptable in another except at heavy discounts. In money
matters the colonies had to deal with each other practically as
foreign countries.

Finally, it should be noted that a very dangerous psychological
attitude was built up in the colonies during their seventy-year experience with paper money. As a result of many conflicts with the
mother country the colonists had developed a very strong antipathy
to taxes of all kinds. They had seen the colonies, year after year,
issue large amounts of paper money, levy few taxes to retire that
money, and finally repudiate a large part of the debt by retiring the
bills at a fraction of their face value. This procedure had hurt

principally the British merchants, moneylenders, and officials, while large numbers of colonists—such as the debtors, political favorites, and farmers—had been benefited. Perhaps this was partly responsible for the strength shown by the cheap money sentiment throughout our national life.

CHAPTER II

THE REVOLUTIONARY DEBTS

INTRODUCTION

MANY FACTORS influenced the financial policy—or lack of policy—
pursued by the states during the Revolution, but perhaps three
may be distinguished as of major importance. The first was the
penchant of the people for paper money, developed during the
Colonial period. The second was their aversion to taxes, which
had been aggravated and quickened by the long quarrels with the
mother country. Perhaps these two factors are, in a sense, opposite
sides of the same proposition, since much of the enthusiasm for
paper money was undoubtedly due to the fact that it obviated
taxes. The third factor was the lack of organization in the newly
founded governments. Even under the most favorable circumstances it is difficult to levy and collect the taxes necessary to
finance a war; the task is much greater for governments set up by
rebels under pressure. The lack of organization also accounts, to a
considerable extent, for the fact that information concerning the
debts of this period is incomplete and often inaccurate. Many
different commissions, agencies, and individuals issued state obligations; in many cases the few and inadequate records which they
kept have been destroyed; and, finally, counterfeiting and official
fraud increased the difficulty of determining the true debts. For
these reasons most of the figures given in this chapter are little
better than estimates; they are derived, as were those in the previous
chapter, from the works of those who have made careful studies
of the finances of this period.

Continental Finances

The Continental Congress was given no power to levy taxes,
yet it was expected to provide funds for carrying on the war. As

Bolles writes, it "was weak and without credit; nevertheless every eye was turned toward it for aid. The singular spectacle was presented of the retention of nearly all the power by the States, and of a refusal on their part to exercise it, preferring to trust a weak and inefficient General Government rather than to rely upon stronger local organizations."[1] Congress made repeated requisitions on the states for funds, but the states were very slow in responding and rarely paid more than a small fraction of the amounts requested. Under these circumstances Congress could obtain funds only by borrowing or by issuing paper money. For more than a year no attempt was made to obtain domestic loans, and then the rate of interest offered was too low to attract funds. Further, large amounts of paper money had been issued and depreciation had begun; this greatly increased the difficulty of borrowing. In spite of these handicaps, however, some loans were made. Dewey places the specie value of domestic loans made during the war at $11,585,506. The value of foreign loans he places at $7,830,517.[2] The first and main reliance of Congress, however, was placed on paper money issues. Beginning with an issue of $6,000,000 in 1775, the stream of paper grew at a rapid rate until approximately $140,000,000 had been issued by 1779. The specie value of the continental emissions is estimated at from $36,000,000 to $38,000,000, contrasted with less than $6,000,000 of taxes received by the general government. Paper money provided the continental treasury with about one half of the funds it spent.

STATE FINANCES

In spite of the fact that the states had all the power which Congress lacked, they followed a policy very similar to the one described above. In discussing the finances of the states during this period it will be necessary to consider the following points: tax policy, paper money issues, domestic borrowing, foreign borrowing, and the various types of certificates issued. These will now be considered in turn.

1. Albert Sidney Bolles, *The Financial History of the United States* (2d ed., 3 vols.; New York, 1884-86), I, 44-45.
2. Dewey, *op. cit.*, p. 35.

Tax Policy

In view of their record during the Colonial period, it is not surprising that the states taxed themselves rather lightly, once they had thrown off British rule. All those who have studied the finances of this period agree that the states were very slow in levying taxes to finance the war.[3] Bullock asserts: "Like the other states, Massachusetts suspended the collection of taxes, and set the printing presses at work, relying upon the Congress at Philadelphia to find some ultimate solution of financial problems. No state tax was levied in 1776, and not until 1777 did the legislature awake to the real needs of the situation."[4] In some states practically no taxes at all were levied during the first three or four years of the war, while the general practice was to tax only for the retirement of paper money; in some cases even these taxes were not payable for two or three years. According to Bolles, "There is no weaker spot in the financial history of these times than the unwillingness or failure of the States to tax at once and deeply, as soon as the first issues of paper money were sent forth by Congress."[5] Writing to Washington in 1780, Joseph Reed stated: ". . . in my opinion we have miscalculated the abilities of the country, and entirely the disposition of the people to bear taxes in the necessary extent. The country not immediately the seat of either army is richer than when the war began, but the long disuse of taxes and their natural unpalatableness have embarrassed the business exceedingly."[6]

In his essays written during the war, Pelatiah Webster insisted on the necessity for heavier taxation, which he thought the country was well able to bear.[7] Franklin and others commented from time to time on the prosperity of the people and the display of luxury to be seen in some of the cities, even during the worst period of the war.[8] Yet Congress, for more than two years, did not even

3. Cf., for example, Bolles, *op. cit.*, I, 53, 83, 194-195; Sumner, *op. cit.*, I, 23-24; II, 137, 180-181; Bronson, *op. cit.*, p. 148.

4. Charles J. Bullock, *Historical Sketch of the Finances and Financial Policy of Massachusetts from 1780 to 1905* (cited hereinafter as Bullock, *Finances of Mass.*), in "Publications of the American Economic Association," Third Series, Vol. VIII, No. 2 (New York, 1907), pp. 5-6.

5. Bolles, *op. cit.*, I, 195.   6. Quoted in Sumner, *op. cit.*, II, 137.

7. Pelatiah Webster, *op. cit.*, first four essays.

8. Horace White, *Money and Banking* (New Ed.; New York, 1935), p. 62.

recommend that the states levy taxes, and it was not until paper money had depreciated greatly that the states began to think seriously of taxation. But by that time the currency was in such disorder that it was impossible to develop a fair and adequate tax system. In fact, by 1781 the currency system had broken down completely, and the states were compelled to resort to the cumbersome and awkward practice of levying taxes "in kind."

PAPER MONEY

Issues

Almost without exception, the first constitutional or legislative body which met in each of the new states authorized the emission of paper money to meet the expenses of setting up a new government and preparing for war. Some of these issues were made even before the first issue made by the Continental Congress in 1775. Table 3 lists the various issues of state money in so far as it has been possible to compile them. This table is based largely on a similar table by Schuckers.[9] Additional details have been inserted and several changes made, chiefly on the basis of data drawn from the monographs cited in the previous chapter. Often the amounts given here are only approximate, since it is frequently impossible to determine the exact amount of bills issued. This is particularly true with regard to the issues of North and South Carolina and Virginia; in those states there are very few reliable records of the amounts of bills actually issued, and so the amounts authorized by the legislature must usually be taken as guides. But in several instances the amounts which might be issued were dependent on certain contingencies, and in one case the governor and council of North Carolina were empowered to issue as many bills as they thought necessary.[10] The figures for Virginia in 1780 and 1781 are indeed fantastic, and it is doubtful whether all of them were ever issued, but the amounts shown were authorized by the legislature.[11] On the other hand, it is probable that the figure for

9. J. W. Schuckers, *A Brief Account of the Finances and Paper Money of the Revolutionary War* (Philadelphia, 1874), p. 127.

10. 10 *Hening's Statutes* 347, 399; Wallace, *op. cit.*, II, 328; James Iredell, *Laws of the State of North Carolina* (Edenton, 1790-1817), p. 397.

11. 10 *Hening's Statutes* 279-280, 347, 399, 430.

TABLE 3

STATE ISSUES OF PAPER MONEY DURING THE REVOLUTIONARY WAR

(In thousands of dollars)

State	1775	1776	1777	1778	1779	1780	1781	1783	Total
N. H.	$ 133	$ 145	$ 100	$ 120	$.....	$ 145	$......	$.....	$ 643
Vt.	......	......	......	......	......	......	84	......	84
Mass.	1,000	667	......	667	......	1,534	......	......	3,868
Conn.	500	367	17	......	......	633	......	......	1,517
R. I.	200	567	182	......	133	67	......	......	1,148
N. Y.	112	637	......	......	......	......	411	......	1,161
Pa.	420	227	532	......	......	1,516	1,330	300	4,325
Del.	80	......	66	......	......	......	......	......	146
N. J.	......	467	......	681	......	600	800	85	2,632
Md.	535	535	......	......	......	320	533	......	1,924
N. C.	125	1,250	......	2,125	1,250	3,100	......	250	8,100
S. C.	1,120	942	615	1,062	5,000	......	......	......	8,739
Va.	1,167	1,667	2,700	2,300	3,300	40,000	116,700	......	167,834

Source: See text.

South Carolina is too small. Schuckers gives a total of $33,458,926 for that state, but gives no distribution by years. His figure of $33,325,000 for North Carolina is entirely too large because he includes an issue of $26,250,000 of certificates of the nature described below. It is probable that there were some issues in Georgia of which no record is found. A study of the table and all other relevant data would seem to indicate that Jefferson's estimate of $200,-000,000 as the amount of state issues during this period was a reasonable one. He placed the specie value of the bills, at the time of issue, at $36,000,000.[12]

Characteristics

Bills were usually issued in terms of pounds, shillings, and pence, although the equivalent value in Spanish milled dollars was frequently stated. It was not unusual for the same state to issue bills in terms of dollars one year and in terms of pounds the next. The same nominal relationships between pounds and dollars prevailed as in the Colonial period except for South Carolina. That state recognized the pound "currency" which was equal to 0.6138 of

12. Agnes P. Dodd, *History of Money in the British Empire and the United States* (London, 1911), p. 253. For details of the issues in various states, see Allan Nevins, *The American States during and after the Revolution, 1775-1789* (New York, 1924), pp. 478-492.

a Spanish dollar. In other words, the dollar was worth "thirty-two shillings and six pence currency" or 1.625 pounds.[13]

Almost without exception the issues were legal tender. A few, especially those in New England after 1776, bore interest. Death was the usual penalty for counterfeiting, while drastic punishments were prescribed for any who refused to accept the bills as equivalent in value to gold and silver. As a rule, the states planned to retire these bills within a comparatively short period of time, and for this purpose often pledged the yield of a special tax, the confiscated estates of Tories, or some other similar fund.

Depreciation

During the latter part of 1775 and all of 1776 the states poured forth large amounts of paper money to augment the steadily growing issues of continental money. Under such conditions depreciation was, of course, inevitable. In December, 1776, a committee representing New England states recommended that the states issue no more bills unless it was absolutely necessary. It was suggested that funds be raised by taxation and borrowing, and that if it was necessary to issue bills they should be at 4 per cent interest and be payable in three years.[14] Finally, in order to preserve some semblance of value in the bills, Congress, in February, 1777, recommended that the states should "stop issuing bills, recall those already emitted, and rely wholly upon the paper money which Congress should provide for the country. . . . All of the States ceased to emit any more paper money; and some of them remained true to the recommendation of Congress nearly four years."[15] From the table it is evident that most of the states except those in the South did refrain from further issues until 1780, when Congress changed its recommendation.

The natural tendency towards depreciation caused by the large issues of continental and state money was augmented by two other factors. The first was extensive counterfeiting. In spite of drastic penalties, this practice flourished. One writer observes, concerning

13. See Clark, *op. cit.,* pp. 34-37, for reproductions of these bills with values stated in terms of both pounds and dollars. See also 4 *Statutes at Large of S. C.* 360, 445.

14. Phillips, *op. cit.,* p. 115. 15. Bolles, *op. cit.,* I, 148.

the situation in North Carolina: "Counterfeits . . . were soon abundant, and the only means of distinguishing the difference was said to lie in the superior execution of the spurious bills."[16]

The second factor was the tendency of the people, after the first few years of the war, to use the certificates described below as money. These were not intended to circulate in most instances; they were not legal tender, they were not in small or even denominations, and they usually bore interest. But when the currency had depreciated to only a small fraction of its face value, these factors were of little importance, and many certificate holders were glad to dispose of them at any price. In the latter stages, the depreciation of both continental and state issues was speeded by the reversion to barter. State issues generally depreciated faster than continental money. The scales of depreciation adopted by the Continental Congress and by the various states indicate the extent to which the depreciation progressed.[17]

The continental scale shows depreciation as starting in September, 1777, and reaching a maximum of 40 to 1 in March, 1780. On the North Carolina scale depreciation began in March, 1777, and reached a maximum of 800 to 1 in December, 1780; while in Virginia the starting date was January, 1777, and the maximum of 1,000 to 1 was attained in December, 1780.[18] The South Carolina scale is unique. In the first column it shows depreciation in terms of rice, indigo, and Negroes; in the second column, depreciation "by the British specie depreciation table"; and in the third column, "Value of £100 specie in the depreciated paper currency, taken from the average of the two foregoing tables. . . ."[19] According to this table, depreciation began in April, 1777, and reached its maximum on May 10, 1780, when £100 specie was worth £5,248 10s. paper currency. The first two columns start approximately together, but soon the depreciation in terms of specie goes much the faster so that by January, 1779, it is more than four times as great as in terms of the commodities. After that, the deprecia-

16. J. W. Moore, *History of North Carolina from the Earliest Discoveries to the Present Time* (2 vols.; Raleigh, 1880), I, 216.

17. See *State Papers*, Finance, V, 772-774, for these scales.

18. Iredell, *op. cit.*, p. 453; 10 *Hening's Statutes* 472-473.

19. 4 *Statutes at Large of S. C.* 564.

tion shown by the first column increases the faster, and by May, 1780, the specie series is only about 60 per cent above the commodity series.

It is true that these scales are all notoriously inaccurate in that they greatly understate the depreciation, but this is probably as true of one state as of another, so that the relation between them may be taken as reasonably accurate. The states usually provided that bills might be redeemed or exchanged for some form of state security at the rate of the maximum depreciation. Thus in 1781 Virginia provided that the bills would continue to be received for taxes and might also be exchanged for loan office certificates at the ratio of 1,000 to 1.[20] In North Carolina the bills were receivable in payment for confiscated estates and for taxes at 800 to 1.[21]

Joint Issue with the United States

When the continental currency had become almost completely worthless and the credit of the Continental Congress had almost disappeared, Congress made a desperate attempt to restore the currency system by basing it upon state credit. By the act of March 18, 1780, the total of the continental currency then outstanding was apportioned among the different states; they were expected to retire their quotas within twelve months, taking the bills at a ratio of 40 to 1 for gold and silver. "All bills which came in in this way were to be destroyed, and other bills were to be issued for not more than one-twentieth of those destroyed, to be redeemable in specie in six years, and to bear interest at five per cent in specie."[22] These bills were to be redeemed in specie or in sterling bills of exchange; they were payable by the United States if the issuing state was not able to redeem them. "As fast as they were signed the state was to have six-tenths of them, and the remainder was to be at the disposition of the United States, but credited to the States on their requisitions."[23] The states were to provide funds to retire one sixth of them annually, beginning in 1781.

Since there was approximately $200,000,000 of continental money outstanding, this plan, if it had succeeded, would have reduced this

20. 10 *Hening's Statutes* 456.   21. Iredell, *op. cit.*, pp. 426-445.
22. Sumner, *op. cit.*, I, 85.   23. *Ibid.*, p. 86.

amount to about $10,000,000. But the plan was not a success. Bronson gives the best summary of the results:

The new scheme for reforming the currency, restoring the government credit, and controlling prices, was a conspicuous failure. The taxes recommended by Congress were but partially collected; the old tenor nuisance was not abated, and the new tenor bills did not secure the confidence of the public.

The new currency rapidly declined in value. The agents of Congress paid it out at different rates, but by average at three for one of specie, no account being taken of the accrued interest. At length, it became worth, in the general market, no more than five or six for one, and Congress advised that the states should stop the supply. Connecticut (and I might add Delaware, North and South Carolina and Georgia) emitted none of the new bills.[24]

It was in general a repetition of the experiences of the Colonial period; depreciation continued, and prices and computations generally were made in terms of the old tenor bills. According to one writer, $4,468,625 of the new bills were put into circulation.[25] In 1781 Congress officially rated them at 75 to 1, and they continued to depreciate after that, eventually reaching a value of about 1,000 to 1 in relation to specie.[26]

Reasons for the Use of Paper Money

It is evident from the foregoing that the states placed their main reliance upon paper money in financing the war. Bronson's explanation is that "they were governed by false notions of economy, by popular clamor and the debtor interest. They wished to wage a cheap war—one which should provide an economical method of discharging debts."[27] Undoubtedly their ignorance of the inevitable results of this policy, in spite of the experiences of the Colonial period, was an important reason for the use of paper money. In addition, the poor governmental organization and the aversion of the people to taxation made this the easiest way out—and in a war the easiest way is usually taken. In any case, we of the present are hardly free to criticize our Revolutionary fathers, for every

24. Bronson, *op. cit.*, pp. 125-126.
25. R. V. Harlow, "Aspects of Revolutionary Finance, 1775-1783," *American Historical Review*, XXXV (1929), 62.
26. *Ibid.*, p. 61.   27. Bronson, *op. cit.*, p. 148.

major war in which we have participated since then has been
financed in the same basic way—by an excessive use of credit—and
if another major war should come, it, too, would probably be
financed in the same way. Perhaps the reason is that those who
shape financial policies in time of war are dominated by the concepts and ideas of those classes which profit by this method of
finance.

OTHER DEBTS

Domestic Loans

There was, especially during the early years of the war, opposition to borrowing by the states for two reasons; one, economic
and the other, political. The economic reason was that the state
would have to pay interest on the loans, while funds might be
raised by paper money issues without the necessity of paying interest. The political opposition was based on the belief that borrowing would create a bondholding class which might exert an un-
healthy influence on the government. For these and other reasons
the states made few attempts to borrow during the first two years
of the war. By October, 1777, Massachusetts had borrowed £956,-
400 on "treasury securities";[28] whether these were true short-term
securities such as the state frequently sold before the war or
whether they were certificates forced upon state creditors, it is impossible to say. The other states did not give serious attention to
this matter until they were asked by Congress to stop issuing paper
money in 1777. By that time the currencies had begun to depreciate,
and the credit of both the states and Congress had fallen considerably. Under these conditions the 5, 6, or 7 per cent interest
which was offered could hardly attract large amounts of funds.

The first attempts at borrowing were usually authorizations by
legislatures directing the proper persons to receive any money
which might be offered on loans and to give certificates in return.
Later most of the states set up loan offices to solicit loans, giving in
exchange "loan office certificates" according to specified terms. In
South Carolina the first authority to receive loans up to £500,000
was enacted in October, 1776, the interest rate being fixed at 6

28. Felt, *op. cit.*, p. 175.

per cent. This authority was repeated several times, and in August, 1777, the interest rate was raised to 7 per cent. In September, 1779, the governor was authorized to borrow up to £6,000,000 current money at 10 per cent interest, and the rate on all outstanding loans was increased to 10 per cent.[29] Frequently, in other states as well as in South Carolina, the authority to borrow was followed by the authority to issue the stated amount in paper money if the loans were not offered; the language often indicated that the legislators did not entertain much hope of seeing the loans made. Thus this preamble:

> Whereas it is necessary for the public service of this State, that one million of dollars should be immediately issued, and that the Governor . . . should be empowered . . . to print or stamp and issue a further sum, not exceeding four millions of dollars, if the same cannot be borrowed on loans in due time to supply the exigencies of the State. . . .[30]

North Carolina's first real efforts to borrow were made in 1780. Stating that "emitting further sums of bills would have a tendency to increase the price of necessities," the legislature authorized the issue of two-year, tax-exempt, 5 per cent certificates in return for "such sums of money as any of the good people of this State shall be willing to supply."[31] These loan office certificates were to be paid, principal and interest, on May 1, 1782, plus any depreciation they might have suffered.

In the very few statements of debts for this period which are now extant, the analysis is not usually sufficient to show the loan-office debt separate from the other debt. Consequently, we have little means of knowing the extent to which the states borrowed from their own citizens to finance the war. One statement for Rhode Island shows borrowing, between December, 1776, and February, 1779, of $533,333, which was somewhat less than one half of the total war debt incurred by the state. Virginia's total debt was £1,104,223 in 1790, of which £119,382 was loan-office debt. It seems safe to conclude that only a minor part—probably not more

29. 4 *Statutes at Large of S. C.* 360, 392, 398, 444, 485.
30. *Ibid.*, p. 461.   31. *S. R.*, XXIV, 347-348.

than 20 to 30 per cent—of the states' debts was represented by loans voluntarily made by their citizens.

Foreign Loans

There are indications that several of the states attempted to borrow funds or otherwise to obtain aid abroad during the war. Franklin on several occasions complained that his efforts to obtain loans in behalf of the Continental Congress were hindered by the actions of individual states "which were trying to borrow money . . . on their own account, often offering higher rates of interest than Congress." Three states had applied to the French Government for loans and expected him to help negotiate them. "The States, by attempting to borrow money in Europe, have hurt our credit and produced nothing." European lenders were confused regarding the power of the states to contract loans, and were generally of the opinion that Congress should do the borrowing.[32] In 1779 William Lee succeeded in negotiating a loan for Virginia in Holland, but the contract was later abandoned. In 1781 representatives of Connecticut and Pennsylvania failed in their attempts to borrow money in Holland. In the following year a representative of Maryland succeeded in negotiating a loan of £40,500 in Holland, although the legislature ordered the contract annulled and the money refunded because of the disadvantageous terms specified. Repayment, however, was not made until 1793.[33] There is mention of a loan which Virginia secured from the King of France in 1782, while "Beaumarchais had also an account with the state of Virginia for supplies furnished. It was liquidated in 1785, by the state authorities, at 973,023 pounds of tobacco."[34] This latter account was probably similar to one maintained by North Carolina with one Marquis de Bretigney for supplies ostensibly purchased from merchants in the French Island of Martinique, but which in reality came from the King's storehouses. After the state had paid the Marquis and he had absconded with the funds, the French Government requested payment from the state. The state's efforts to extinguish the debt,

32. Dodd, op. cit., p. 246; Sumner, op. cit., I, 292; II, 60-61.
33. H. S. Hanna, A Financial History of Maryland, 1789-1848 (Baltimore, 1907), pp. 22, 30.
34. Sumner, op. cit., I, 180, 292; II, 60.

which amounted to only about $6,000, extended over almost twenty years and included some unique financial transactions.[35]

Of the states which reported their debts in 1789-90, only two showed foreign debts; these were Virginia with £40,826, or $136,087, and South Carolina with £115,810, or $495,667.[36]

Certificate Debt

The major portion of the states' debts consisted of certificates issued for almost every purpose for which the states spent money. The most important purposes were as follows:

(1) To pay soldiers of the "state line." In addition to the Continental Army or "line" each state had its own militia or "line." Frequently the states were not able to pay these men, and gave them certificates representing the amount due to them.

(2) To supplement the pay, or to cover the depreciation of the pay, of soldiers in the Continental line. Some states supplemented the pay of their citizens serving in the Continental Army; most of them attempted to make good the losses sustained by soldiers because of depreciation. Lacking funds, the states often gave the soldiers certificates.

(3) To pay bonuses to soldiers. States offered these to stimulate enlistment, both in the state militia and in the Continental Army. In 1779 South Carolina offered those who would enlist for twenty-one months a bounty of $500 to be paid at the date of enlistment, and $2,000 plus 100 acres of land to be paid at the completion of the term. In 1782, after the currency system had collapsed, the bounty was offered in a new medium; those who would enlist for three years or for the war should receive "for each and every year's service, the bounty of one sound negro between the age of ten years and forty. . . ." The same bounty was offered to anyone who would procure twenty-five enlistments within two months. On another occasion General Pickens allowed his men "a cow and a calf per month, in lieu of pay."[37]

35. This incident is related in some detail in B. U. Ratchford, "An International Debt Settlement: The North Carolina Debt to France," *American Historical Review*, XL (1934), 63-69.
36. *American State Papers*, Finance, I, 28.
37. 4 *Statutes at Large of S. C.* 502, 513-515, 599.

(4) To pay benefits to soldiers and dependents. Congress, in 1776, had made provisions for pensions to disabled veterans and their dependents. In 1778 commissioned officers who would serve until the end of the war were promised half pay for seven years; this was extended for life in 1780.

These promises of pensions were made to encourage enlistments in the Revolutionary Army and to prevent desertions and resignations from the Army at critical times. They probably prevented the dissolution of the Army and the loss of the Revolutionary War.

In all these cases, however, the administration and payment of the pensions were necessarily left to the several states, as the Continental Congress had no real executive power and had no money to make such payments.[38]

Such obligations were responsible for the issuance of a large number of state certificates, both during the war and for several years thereafter.

(5) To pay for supplies and equipment. The states required large amounts of food, clothing, livestock, and other materials for the use of their own militia, and later, to meet their quota of "specifics" requested by Congress. When these goods were purchased, impressed, or otherwise acquired, the usual payment was in certificates. It was here that much of the confusion concerning the debts arose, for quartermasters, purchasing agents, treasurers, and various other agencies were authorized to issue these certificates. It would be too much to expect all of these to keep complete records and preserve them through the rigors of a campaign.

(6) To pay for damages and losses caused by the war. In some cases where property had been destroyed to keep it from falling into the hands of the enemy, or where enemy troops had caused heavy losses, the states issued certificates to reimburse the owners.

(7) To pay bills of the Continental Army. After 1781:

The public contracts still continued to be turned over to the several States for settlement, a course which was not only a relief, but a necessity to a government with an empty treasury. The main obliga-

38. Weber and Schmeckebier, *The Veterans Administration* (Washington, 1934), p. 5.

tions thus undertaken by the States were that they should settle the arrears of pay of their respective lines of the army, as well as the claims of their own citizens, many of whom already held the certificates of the commissioners or other officers of the United States for supplies furnished or services rendered. Now, these obligations the States either paid in their own bills of credit, or substituted their own state certificates for the certificates of the United States. Such creditors, therefore, not only had never been asked to consent to this transfer of their claims from the United States, but had besides received no actual payment, but only promises of payment, which remained still unredeemed.[39]

(8) To discharge liens on confiscated Tory estates. The states usually seized the property belonging to Tories; often this property was encumbered by claims held by Patriots. To discharge these claims and to free the property for sale, certificates were often issued.

(9) To pay claims of various kinds. It was the usual practice, in the years immediately after the war, for states to set up commissions to hear all kinds of claims against the states arising out of the war. When allowed, these claims were usually paid in certificates.

(10) In addition, there were the loan-office certificates already described.

The above, together with a great many other kinds of certificates, made up the states' debts. The terms and conditions of the different issues varied widely. Most of them bore interest at rates from 5 to 8 per cent, and were payable in from two to ten years. Some were transferable and others were not. Special issues were sometimes payable in specie or equivalent. The certificates were in all sizes and shapes; they were for various odd amounts and bore many different signatures. Paper and printing were often of the poorest quality. Under such circumstances counterfeiting was inevitable, and the detection of counterfeits was thus added to the other debt problems. One North Carolina commission which settled a great many army accounts and issued certificates therefor was convicted of fraud and collusion. The certificates it issued were disallowed until they could be examined by another commission in order to separate the good from the bad.

39. J. W. Kearny, *Sketch of American Finances, 1789-1835* (New York, 1887), pp. 20-21.

From this it is easy to see why the states usually did not know what their debts were at the end of the war. In order to ascertain the amount of certificates outstanding, to detect counterfeits, and to reduce all claims to a specie basis, it was the usual practice to require that all certificates be presented for registration or exchange for new ones at some certain time. In some states this was done two or three times between the end of the war and 1790. At such times efforts were made to consolidate all certificates into one uniform issue. Frequently special certificates were issued for accumulated interest.

Debts at Close of War

For the reasons given above, it is impossible to give any statement of the debts of all the states outstanding at the end of the war. The New England states, however, kept better records than did the others, and for them we have fairly good estimates. Below are the amounts for these states as given by various students.

Massachusetts (1785) $5,000,000
New Hampshire (1784) 500,000
Rhode Island (1783) 479,175
Connecticut (1783) 3,783,840

In 1786 South Carolina's interest on its debt was estimated at £93,960. If the average interest rate was 7 per cent, the principal would be approximately £1,342,300, or $5,705,000. At the same time Georgia's debt was estimated at $1,000,000. For the other states the figures are too scant to warrant an estimate of the debt before 1789 or 1790.

POST-WAR DEBTS

Trends of Debts, 1783-90

Since exact figures are not available for the debts of most states in 1783, it is impossible to say whether the debts generally increased or decreased between the end of the war and 1790. In most of the states there was probably some reduction; in a few the debt increased, perhaps because of accruing interest. The Massachusetts debt was about $5,000,000 in 1783 and $5,226,801 on November 1, 1789. The Rhode Island debt probably increased too;

it was quoted at £153,048 in 1787, compared with £143,752 in 1783. The New Hampshire debt was estimated at $500,000 in 1784, although Bullock questioned this figure. By 1790 it had been reduced to $300,000.[40] In Connecticut, "by a most stringent system of taxation—a system once suspended but never abandoned—the state debt was so diminished that, on the first day of November, 1789, it amounted to only £605,043."[41] In seven years the state had reduced its debt by more than $1,700,000. Virginia, too, reduced its debt in this period; in 1790 the legislature, in a message to Congress, referred to a "large proportion of the debt . . . having already been redeemed by the collection of heavy taxes." North Carolina and Maryland also reduced their debts, but it is impossible to give amounts. The South Carolina debt changed very little. In the other states debts were reduced little, if at all.

Taxpayers were irritated by the necessity of providing funds to pay interest on the debts. After the return of peace, state governments performed only a few basic, elementary functions and their budgets were quite small. For most of the states interest on the debt, if paid, constituted from 50 to 90 per cent of all expenditures. Thus in 1786 South Carolina's interest amounted to £93,-960, while total expenditures were only £114,919. The situation must have been somewhat similar in Massachusetts, for Sumner reports that in 1785 the debt was £1,400,000 and taxes amounted to £100,000. The debt was only $13.97 per capita, and taxes only 93 cents per capita, but interest represented such a large proportion of expenditures that the debt burden seemed excessively heavy. These conditions were ideal for stimulating a demand for paper money, and the demand soon appeared.

Post-War Paper Money

When in 1781 continental and state paper money became worthless, trade reverted to a specie basis, and for a few years gold and silver were plentiful. This is usually ascribed to the fact that both French and British troops brought considerable coin with them. After experiencing the exhilarating effects of paper money, the people could not long be content with the drab, monotonous effects

40. Bullock, *op. cit.*, p. 271.   41. Bronson, *op. cit.*, p. 161.

of specie. It is probable that the demand for easy money was the factor primarily responsible for the issues of 1783, although the states could claim the necessity of closing out war expenses. But soon after peace returned, there arose complaints about heavy taxes, especially for interest on the debt, when there had been no adjustment of the debts between Congress and the states. In every state there was a strong political movement for paper money, and in some places the movement developed into riots and small rebellions. Thus Shays' Rebellion in Massachusetts "was occasioned by the burden of taxes necessarily imposed on the people of that State, to pay a debt incurred merely for national purposes."[42]

The Carolinas and Pennsylvania led the way in this issue of money in 1785. South Carolina had made a gradual approach to the problem by authorizing, in March, 1785, the issue of £83,184 of "special indents" "to facilitate the payment of the taxes." These were receivable for taxes levied in 1785 and other dues to the state, and were redeemable in gold or silver on May 1, 1786.[43] This measure evidently did not produce the effects desired, because in October of that year the legislature, stating that "the citizens of this State are reduced to great and general distress by the scarcity of money to answer the calls of internal trade; and therefore to afford a speedy and effectual relief to the general calamity, by introducing a paper medium of circulation upon solid foundations," authorized the issue of £100,000 in bills, to be loaned on real estate mortgages or gold and silver plate for five years at 7 per cent interest.[44] The issue was not retired in five years; in fact, in 1808 the state was still receiving $9,000 per year in interest on these loans, compared with the $30,000 it received at first, and it was estimated that the state had cleared $300,000 on the issue.[45] North Carolina and Pennsylvania issued £100,000 and £150,000, respectively, in this year, while issues were defeated in Maryland and Virginia, by narrow margins. The North Carolina issue was partly to cover current expenses and partly to finance a program of tobacco purchases by the state, mainly speculative in nature.

42. Bronson, *op. cit.*, p. 169 n. For a good account of the paper money movement at this time, see Nevins, *op. cit.*, pp. 515-543.

43. 4 *Statutes at Large of S. C.* 690.

44. *Ibid.*, pp. 712-716.   45. Ramsay, *op. cit.*, II, 104.

In 1786 there were the following paper money issues: Georgia, £30,000; New Jersey, £100,000; New York, £200,000; and Rhode Island, £100,000. In Rhode Island a paper money party championed both paper money issues and states' rights. After a campaign which "awakened fierce passion and bitter strife, and ended in mobs and riots" this party was elected to power in May, 1786. It proceeded immediately to issue a "bank" of £100,000, "to be loaned to the people according to the apportionment of the last tax, upon a pledge of real estate of double their value, and to be paid into the treasury at the end of fourteen years."[46] The bills began to depreciate as soon as they were issued, and a forcing bill was necessary. This act "subjected any person who should refuse to receive the bills on the same terms as specie . . . to a penalty of one hundred pounds, and the loss of the rights of a freeman."[47] It also provided a source of revenue to the state, since if bills were tendered and refused, they became the property of the state. There was much opposition to the bills, and a riot occurred in Newport when merchants refused to sell corn for paper money. Many owners of notes and other negotiable instruments endorsed them and sent them to friends outside the state to prevent their being paid in paper money. Soon another forcing act was necessary, illustrating the extent to which fanaticism of this kind may go:

This act suspended the usual forms of justice in regard to offenders against the bank law, by requiring an immediate trial, within three days after complaint entered, without a jury, and before a court of which three judges should form a quorum, whose decision should be final, and whose judgment should be instantly complied with on penalty of imprisonment . . . the act was to be in force until all complaints that should be made within ten days after the rising of the Assembly had been tried.[48]

When this act came before the Rhode Island Supreme Court it was declared unconstitutional, whereupon the legislature summoned the court before it to justify its actions. After hearing the defense offered by the justices, the legislature could find no

46. Samuel G. Arnold, *History of the State of Rhode Island* (2 vols.; New York, 1860), II, 520.
47. *Ibid.*, p. 521.   48. *Ibid.*, p. 523.

grounds for impeachment, but since "no satisfactory reasons had been rendered by them for their judgment" the justices were dismissed. The bills continued to depreciate, and by June, 1787, were passing at 8 for 1.

The paper money advocates now determined to pay a part of the state debt in the depreciated money. A law was enacted requiring holders of certain claims against the state to present them and to take payment in paper money. The payments were made in instalments, the amount paid being stamped on the obligations each time. By the time the last instalments were paid the new money was passing at about 12 to 1. Under this arbitrary and unjust act some £48,000 in state claims were surrendered and the holders lost from 80 to 90 per cent of the value of their holdings. "The immorality of this proceeding was so glaring, that many churches of different denominations excommunicated their members for tendering paper money."[49] The bills eventually depreciated to a ratio of 15 to 1.

If this action was grossly unfair and highly irregular, the state, by another most unusual and unique act, moved to alleviate, at least in part, some of the worst of its effects a few years later. After the United States had assumed the state debts, the state provided that those evidences of debts which had been retired by the paper money should be returned to the original holders with the specie value of the payments made by the state stamped thereon. The United States refused to accept them as evidences of state debt in payment for federal obligations, but Rhode Island provided for them at a later date when it received the balance due on the final settlement of state claims.[50]

Adoption of Constitution

When the new Federal Constitution was proposed to the states, it was found to affect state debts at two points; it prohibited the states from emitting legal tender bills of credit, and it was generally understood that the new Federal Government would assume the

49. *Ibid.*, p. 538.
50. John W. Richmond, *Rhode Island Repudiation: or the History of the Revolutionary Debt of Rhode Island* (Providence, 1855), pp. 29-31.

Revolutionary debts of the states. Both of these factors aroused opposition and were partly responsible for the delay of certain states, especially North Carolina and Rhode Island, in ratifying the Constitution.[51] The fondness of the states for paper money is shown by their delay in retiring the amounts in circulation after the adoption of the Constitution; in several states it was twenty to thirty years before it was all removed from circulation. In North Carolina the tax which was levied to retire the bills was repealed immediately after the Constitution was ratified, and very few bills were retired for the next twenty years. In 1799 the state treasurer reported that many of the bills were unfit for circulation, but that he was undecided as to the wisdom of destroying them, since the state could issue no more. He then proposed an ingenious scheme whereby new bills would be issued against old ones held in deposit; the new bills would not be legal tender, but merely receipts for the old ones. In this way "the amount of paper money the state now has might long be kept in circulation, and possibly without impairing its credit. . . ."[52] This plan was not adopted, but some of the old bills remained in circulation until 1830.

The total of state debts in January, 1790, was estimated by Alexander Hamilton at about $25,000,000. He had received reports from six states giving their debts as follows:

Massachusetts	$5,226,801.29	New Jersey	$ 788,680.66
Connecticut	1,951,173.34	Virginia	3,680,743.03
New York	1,167,575.25	South Carolina	5,386,232.05
		Total	$18,201,205.61

He estimated the debts of three other states as follows: New Hampshire, $300,000; Pennsylvania, $2,200,000; and Maryland, $800,-000.[53] Rhode Island had not yet ratified the Constitution, and there were no reports from Delaware, Georgia, and North Carolina. Approximate figures for three of these states were: Rhode Island, $510,000; North Carolina, $3,480,000; and Georgia, $950,000.[54] Delaware had only a nominal debt—probably between $50,000 and

51. Bullock, *op. cit.,* p. 197.
52. *Journal of the House of Commons,* 1799, p. 16.
53. *State Papers,* Finance, I, 28-29.   54. Nevins, *op. cit.,* p. 542.

$60,000. The figures for these four states, added to Hamilton's estimates for the other nine, give a sum of approximately $26,-500,000. This figure corresponds very closely with Hamilton's figures given in his report on the progress of funding made to Congress in January, 1792, and may be taken as fairly accurate.

CHAPTER III

FEDERAL ASSUMPTION OF STATE DEBTS

FUNDING AND ASSUMPTION

Hamilton's Plan

ONE OF THE most difficult tasks which Alexander Hamilton set for himself when he became Secretary of the Treasury was the rehabilitation of public credit. He rightly perceived that to bring order out of the chaos which prevailed in state and national finances, he must make definite and permanent provision for the millions of dollars of public debts, a major portion of which was in the chaotic state described in the previous chapter. To Hamilton's genius for organization this problem was a challenge; in response to it he produced one of his famous reports—the Report on Public Credit delivered to Congress on January 9, 1790.[1]

As a political document intended to convince and guide a legislative body, this report is indeed a great document; it is persuasive in its arguments and it outlines a definite program of action without appearing to dictate. But as an exposition in economics it contains several glaring flaws. For instance, Hamilton contended that funding the debt would benefit merchants by increasing capital and so enable them to operate at a lower profit; that it would benefit agriculture and manufacturing by making capital more abundant; and, finally, that it would benefit everyone by lowering the interest rate. It is difficult, if not impossible, to determine the extent to which Hamilton really believed these things and the extent to which he used them because they fitted in with the ideas prevalent at the time, and thus were likely to meet with the approval of legislators.

After discussing the national debt, Hamilton considered the state debts. He recommended that they should be assumed by

1. *State Papers,* Finance, I, 15-37.

the Federal Government for the following reasons: (1) it was necessary to insure orderly and stable national finances; (2) it would be more convenient for the national government to raise the funds and to care for all the debts since the principal source of revenue (the tariff) was vested exclusively in the United States, while the states were limited in the revenues which they could raise, "from the want of power to extend the same regulation to the other states, and from the tendency of partial duties to injure its industries and commerce"; and (3) it would not be fair to discriminate between creditors of the individual states, since all contributed to the same cause.[2]

Previous Attempts at Settlement

This was not the first effort to bring about a settlement between the Federal Government and the states. From the first it had been understood that there would be a settlement of some kind. Thus Sumner states: "March 19, 1777, Congress advanced to New Jersey and to Pennsylvania each $100,000, each State 'to be accountable.' During that and the following year Congress went on making advances to the States, and also to various officers in enormous amounts, the phrase being always added that the recipient was 'to be accountable.'"[3]

Article 8 of the Act of Confederation, which was proposed by Congress in 1777 and finally became effective in 1781, provided that "All charges of war, and all other expenses that shall be incurred for the common defence or general welfare, and allowed by the United States in congress assembled, shall be defrayed out of a common treasury, which shall be supplied by the several states in proportion to the value of all land within each state granted to or surveyed for any person. . . ."

When Morris assumed his post as financier in 1781, he strove hard to bring about a settlement with the states, believing that it would stimulate them to better efforts. "Some States went so far as to say that, having contributed beyond their proportion, they would not furnish anything more until there was a final settlement."[4] Morris did not succeed, however, in getting the states

2. *Ibid.*, p. 18.   3. Sumner, *op. cit.*, I, 36.   4. Bolles, *op. cit.*, I, 290.

to report to him on their accounts with the central government. Congress appointed commissioners in 1782 to adjust the state accounts and in 1786 renewed their authority and increased their number. In June, 1784, an act was passed governing the accounting methods to be followed.[5] Apparently no reports or recommendations concerning the state debts were ever made by these commissioners. The finances of the central government were in such shape that it could not pay the interest on the debt which it had contracted; it would have benefited no one to have it assume additional indebtedness.

Objections to Funding

In his report Hamilton stated that obligations of the United States had advanced in price 33⅓ per cent from January to November, 1789, and 50 per cent from the latter date to January, 1790. To some, this was damning evidence, for there were rumors of "leaks" and "tips" given out by Hamilton to his speculator friends. There were charges on the floor of Congress that, about the time Hamilton made his report, "expresses with very large sums of money" and two fast-sailing vessels, chartered by a member of Congress, were on their way south to speculate in public obligations. The reason for this commotion was that in the years before the adoption of the Constitution, the price of federal and state obligations had fallen to very low levels—as low as 12 or 15 per cent of their face value in some cases. The obligations had, to a considerable extent, been given to soldiers and others in discharge of claims for services and supplies. According to a contemporary, it was "a matter of public notoriety and general belief, that almost the whole of the widows, orphans, soldiers, and other distressed public creditors, have sold their certificates, which are now in the hands of the speculators."[6]

Webster and many others like him were bitter on this point. They contended that, pressed for funds, the original holders had been forced to dispose of the certificates for what they would bring, and in this way had lost from one half to seven eighths of their pay. Now Hamilton proposed to pay these obligations at face value,

5. *Ibid.*, pp. 327, 334. 6. Webster, *op. cit.*, p. 277.

together with all accrued interest. Webster contended that this would give the speculators a return of 48 per cent on their money and return them, in principal, eight times what they had invested. At the same time the funds to make the payments would come from taxes paid, in part, by those who had lost a major part of their pay. Further, it was contended that payment at face value was unreasonable because the obligations were already greatly depreciated at the time of issue. The scaling down of claims which followed the depreciation during the war was so fresh in the minds of the people that the speculators, if they were rational, must have expected such a reduction.

James Madison was a leader of the group in Congress which opposed payment in full. This group proposed to "discriminate" between original holders and present holders. One proposal would have paid present holders "at a scale of value founded on their original value when they were issued" and the remainder to original holders. Another would have paid present holders "the mean exchange at which they have passed for two or three years back" and the remainder to original holders.[7] The plan to discriminate was hotly debated in the House of Representatives, but was defeated on February 23, 1790. Hamilton had won his first point. The defeat, however, seemed only to increase the opposition: "the public interest had been awakened. The tongue of criticism had been loosened. The man in the street began to hold forth. It was all beyond him . . . but he could understand that a policy had been adopted that would be advantageous to the rich, profitable to the speculator, and mean loss to the common soldier."[8] As time passed and the remote districts were heard from, the opposition grew. When the time came to consider the next item on Hamilton's program—the assumption of state debts—all the bitterness against the speculators was turned against assumption, for it was claimed that assumption would only increase the scope of the speculators' operations. Hamilton and his followers lobbied in favor of the bill, but perhaps were overconfident as a result of their victory on the

7. *Ibid*.
8. Claude G. Bowers, *Jefferson and Hamilton* (New York, 1928), pp. 56-57. Chapter III gives a detailed and vivid account of this episode.

first point. "Party feeling ran high and the fate of the infant American republic hung in the balance as Congress sharply debated the merits and demerits of the bill."[9] The first vote on the measure came in April; the bill was defeated by two votes. Jefferson later declared that "So high were the feuds excited by this subject, that, on its rejection, business was suspended. Congress met and adjourned from day to day without doing any thing, the parties being too much out of temper to do business together."[10]

Opposition to Assumption

In addition to the fact that some felt that assumption would favor speculators, there were other reasons for the opposition. Many, especially in the South, opposed it because it would necessitate heavy national taxation and thus promote a strong central government. It would strengthen the central government also in that it would create a bondholding group dependent on the United States for the safety of its investment. Another factor that aroused opposition in the South was the method by which the costs of the war were to be apportioned. The Articles of Confederation had proposed to distribute war costs according to the value of surveyed lands. But it was now proposed to make the distribution on the same basis used for direct taxation and representation in Congress; that is, population. Southerners felt that this plan gave too much weight to the slave population. Then, too, records and accounts of Southern states were in much worse shape than those of Northern states; many of their claims would never be allowed by the Federal Government because they could not be properly supported. Another important reason, although not openly urged by Southern states, was the fact that a large part of the obligations were now held by Northern speculators. Finally, Virginia opposed the move because it had already paid a large part of its debt.[11]

In spite of the strong opposition widespread in the South, South Carolina favored assumption because of its large debt. On the

9. Reginald C. McGrane, *Foreign Bondholders and American State Debts* (New York, 1935), p. 1.

10. *House Report No. 296,* 27th Congress, 3d Session, p. 484.

11. Communication from Virginia legislature to Congress, *State Papers,* Finance, I, 90.

other hand, Rhode Island in the North opposed assumption. Its representatives had not been seated in Congress when the bill was passed, and they felt that the amount allotted to Rhode Island was too small. Massachusetts strongly favored assumption because of a large debt. Several states sent petitions or protests to Congress. North Carolina instructed its delegates "to exert their endeavors to prevent as far as possible the evil operations of such acts to the interests and liberties of this country."[12] The state proposed a constitutional amendment to prohibit assumption.

The Case for Assumption

In his report Hamilton had offered good reasons for desiring assumption. Moreover, it had been promised. As Bolles puts it: "Obvious justice required the assumption of all the debts thus contracted. Congress, under the Confederation, had repeatedly promised to do full justice to all the creditors and States; and their successors had no right to repudiate the promise. The assumption of the claims of State creditors . . . was not so much an act of expediency as an act of open and express obligations. There was no honest way of escaping the fulfillment of it."[13] Hamilton, however, was undoubtedly influenced by two other reasons. In his attempt to form a strong central government it was necessary that the propertied class—the bondholders in this instance—should have their interests placed in the safekeeping of the Federal Government rather than of the states.[14] In the second place—and this explains the refusal to compromise on the matter of discrimination—the speculators were Hamilton's friends and he desired their support.

Assumption Adopted

Hamilton did not give up after the first defeat of assumption; rather, he began to plan and scheme in earnest. There was another question before Congress at this time on which the alignment was almost the reverse of that on assumption—this was the question of the permanent location of the national capital. There were great differences on this question, the Southern states being strongly in

12. S. R., XXI, 1055-1056.   13. Bolles, op. cit., II, 36.
14. Henry Cabot Lodge, Alexander Hamilton (Boston, 1899), pp. 90-91.

favor of placing the capital near Baltimore or on the Potomac. Hamilton was indifferent as to the location of the capital, but he saw a chance to drive a bargain. With patience and finesse he bargained; he was all the more anxious now, for it appeared that the fate of the whole funding bill hinged on assumption. Washington himself was concerned and exerted himself in favor of assumption. Charles Carroll of Carrollton later claimed that "the only time that he knew General Washington to wish to effect an arrangement was on the occasion alluded to, and that he was strongly importuned by General Washington to vote for the assumption bill."[15] Finally Hamilton was able to strike a bargain with Jefferson,[16] and the fight was soon won. The manner in which the bill was passed indicates that definite bargains had been made in advance. On a matter so important, one would certainly have expected much debate, yet in the weeks preceding passage the matter was barely mentioned on the floor of Congress. The funding bill became law on August 4, 1790.[17]

Provisions of Assumption

To accomplish assumption, the United States offered a new loan of $21,500,000, subscriptions to which were "payable in the principal and interest of the certificates or notes, which, prior to the first day of January last, were issued by the respective states, as acknowledgments or evidences of debts by them, owing, . . . provided, that no such certificate shall be received, which, from the tenor thereof, or from any public record, act, or document, shall appear, or can be ascertained, to have been issued for any purpose, other than compensations and expenditures for services or supplies towards the prosecution of the late war, and the defence of the United States, or some part thereof, during the same."[18] The maximum amounts which could be subscribed in each state were prescribed as shown in Table 4; if those amounts were oversubscribed, subscriptions were to be filled pro rata. If the amount allotted to any state was not subscribed in full, that state was to receive interest on the

---

15. *House Report No. 296*, 27th Congress, 3d Session, p. 484.
16. Bowers, *op. cit.*, pp. 66-68.
17. 1 *Statutes at Large* 34.   18. *Ibid.*, sec. 3.

deficiency, "in trust for the nonsubscribing creditors of such state
... until there shall be a settlement of accounts between the United
States and the individual states." Subscriptions were to be made
by October 1, 1791, but by successive extensions the time limit was
finally placed at December 31, 1797. Subscriptions were to be filled
by issuing United States bonds in the following proportions: four
ninths in 6 per cent bonds, two ninths in bonds bearing 6 per
cent after 1800, and three ninths in 3 per cent bonds. Interest on
state obligations was to be computed until December 31, 1791. The
obligations of each state received in this way were to be "a charge
against such state, in account with the United States."

There is nothing to indicate the method used in determining
the amounts to be assumed in each state. Gallatin later said that
the amount for each state was "limited to a certain sum fixed at
random, each State trying to make the best possible bargain."[19]
Evidently Hamilton had fixed the sums arbitrarily, with some
rough relation to the indebtedness of the states. Of course, in
theory the amounts designated here did not make a great deal of
difference, since there was to be a settlement of accounts later, but
many did not understand the latter provision and were much concerned about the fairness of the apportionments. Rhode Island
protested vigorously that the amount assigned to it was far too
small, while Southern states had received liberal treatment, presumably as an inducement to get their approval of assumption.
Rhode Island spokesmen charged that the amount for Georgia was
so liberal that its representatives had to go home and "manufacture debt" in order to be able to make the subscriptions.

Progress of Assumption

In January, 1792, Hamilton reported to Congress on the amount
of state obligations converted up to the expiration of the first time
limit, September 30, 1791, giving the figures shown in Table 4.
The total amount was $17,072,334.39 (the total amount subscribed—
$18,328,186.21—less oversubscriptions in certain states—$1,255,851.82),
which was $4,427,665.61 less than the amount authorized. He at-

19. Henry Adams (ed.), *The Writings of Albert Gallatin* (3 vols.; London,
1879), III, 130.

TABLE 4

SUBSCRIPTIONS TO LOANS PAYABLE IN STATE OBLIGATIONS,
OCTOBER 1, 1790-SEPTEMBER 30, 1791

State	Amount Assumed by Act	Amount Unsubscribed [sic]	Remaining Unsubscribed to Complete Amount Assumed	Subscribed beyond Amount Assumed	Estimated Amount of Remaining Debt of State
N. H...	$ 300,000	$ 242,501.25	$ 57,468.75	$	$ 100,000
Mass...	4,000,000	4,447,013.81	....	477,013.81	1,838,541
R. I....	200,000	344,259.49	....	144,259.49	349,260
Conn. ..	1,600,000	1,455,331.81	144,668.19	....	458,437
N. Y...	1,200.000	1,028,238.75	171,761.25	....	195,640
N. J....	800,000	599,703.56	200,296.44	....	207,648
Pa......	2,200,000	675,101.33	1,524,898.67	....	500,000
Del.....	200,000	53,305.84	146,694.16	....	None
Md.....	800,000	299,225.40	500,744.60	....	430,000
Va......	3,500,000	2,552,570.88	947,429.12	....	1,172,555
N. C....	2,400,000	*1,666,355.57	733,644.43	....	713,192
S. C....	4,000,000	4,634,578.52	....	634,578.52	1,964,756
Ga.....	300,000	300,000.00	....	....	400,000
Totals..	$21,500,000	$18,328,186.21	$4,427,665.61	$1,255,851.82	$8,331,028

*This figure was 1,166,355.57 in the original, but this was evidently a typographical error; it must be 1,666,355.57 if the amounts in the second and third columns are to add up, as they should, to the amount shown in the first column.
Source: *State Papers*, Finance, I, 150.

tributed this deficiency to three factors: (1) in some cases the amounts apportioned to states were greater than the amount of debt outstanding; (2) in other instances certain parts of the debt were excluded, such as certificates issued after January 1, 1790, in exchange for certificates issued before that time; and (3) "ignorance of, or inattention to, the limitation of time for receiving subscriptions." He had received complaints about assumption and many strong pleas for its extension to cover *all* state debts. He advocated such an extension, estimating that the total would not be more than $25,403,362.71, or an addition of $3,903,362.71 to that already authorized. He also recommended the extension of the time limit for subscriptions.[20] Congress readily granted the extension of time, but refused to authorize the assumption of any more debt. The amount finally assumed was $18,271,814.74, distributed among the states as shown in the last column of Table 5. Of the

20. *State Papers*, Finance, I, 147.

1010

total amount assumed, $12,181,254.07 represented principal, while $6,090,560.67 represented accumulated interest.[21]

Generally state creditors were not only willing but eager to exchange state for federal obligations, in spite of the reduction in the nominal interest rate. But there was some hesitation in Maryland. There

The state credit was practically as good as that of the United States; and the exchange of the securities of the former for those of the latter under the complicated interest arrangement, meant a surrender of a 6 per cent. investment for one of 4 per cent. or less. For the state to force its creditors to make the exchange would be on the state's part a virtual repudiation of so much of its just debt. An act of the Legislature was passed which attempted to supply the necessary inducement, and, at the same time, maintain the faith of the state. By this act the state agreed to receive from all subscribers under the assumption provision of the Funding Law their proportions of 3 per cent. and deferred stock (i.e., stock to bear no interest until 1801 and thereafter 6 per cent.) and to give in exchange an equal amount of United States 6 per cent. stock bearing immediate interest.[22]

The state held a certain amount of the 6 per cent United States stock in its treasury as an investment and hence was able to make this offer. No statement is available showing the amount which the state exchanged in this way.

THE SETTLEMENT OF STATE ACCOUNTS
The Problem

Mention has already been made of the fact that the assumption of the state debts by the Federal Government was only one step in the larger problem of the adjustment of the accounts between the states and the United States. Kearny gives the best description of this adjustment:

A board of three commissioners was appointed for the settlement of the accounts between the United States and the individual states. The States were charged with all advances made to them by the United States including the amount of assumed debt with interest to the last day of 1789. Bills of credit were liquidated according to established scale on a specie value at the date of each of the advances. States were credited with their expenditures, whether money or supplies

21. *Ibid.*, p. 483.　　　　　　　　22. Hanna, *op. cit.*, p. 29.

furnished to the United States. This was computed on a specie basis also with interest to the last day of 1789. Expenditures by the United States exceeded the advances from the United States by over seventy-seven and a half million dollars. This excess was apportioned among the States according to the rule for apportioning representatives and direct taxes.[23]

Table 5, which is a reproduction of a statement issued by the Register's Office of the Treasury Department in 1831, shows certain computations made in the adjustment. When all computations had been made and the balances struck, seven states were found to be creditors of the United States to the amount of $3,517,584, while the other six states were debtors to the same amount. The creditor states were entitled to have the balances due them "funded upon the same terms with the other part of the domestic debt of the United States; but the balances so credited to any state shall not be transferable." The terms of the funding were: two thirds of the principal of the original claims was payable in stock bearing 6 per cent at once; one third, in stock bearing 6 per cent after 1800; and accrued interest was payable in 3 per cent stock. These states received the balances due them in 1795. Several of them wished to use this payment to discharge debts which they owed; and, on request, Congress permitted the states to transfer the 6 per cent stocks.[24] In addition to the balance shown here, "each state received 3 per cent stock to cover interest on balances due from December 31, 1789 to December 31, 1794; this amounted to $703,-516.80." The total debt assumed by the United States on behalf of the states was thus $22,492,915.43.[25]

Balances Due by Debtor States

Although the United States settled with the creditor states promptly, the debtor states never settled their accounts. Those states made no move to pay, and by January 1, 1797, interest to the amount of $984,924 had accrued, making the total owed by the six states $4,502,208.[26] Representatives of debtor states, particu-

---

23. Kearny, *op. cit.*, p. 24; the act authorizing the settlement, approved Aug. 5, 1790, is found in 1 *Statutes at Large* 178.

24. 1 *Statutes at Large* 409-533.

25. Kearny, *op. cit.*, pp. 26-27.   26. *State Papers,* Finance, I, 479.

TABLE 5

ABSTRACT OF THE BALANCES DUE TO AND FROM THE SEVERAL STATES ON THE ADJUST-
MENT OF THEIR ACCOUNTS WITH THE UNITED STATES, BY THE GENERAL BOARD OF
COMMISSIONERS FOR THAT PURPOSE, UNDER THE SEVERAL ACTS OF CONGRESS, FOR THE
FINAL SETTLEMENT OF THE STATE ACCOUNTS, PER THEIR REPORT OF JUNE 27, 1793

State	Sums Allowed to the Credit of the Several States with Interest to January 1, 1790	Advances Made by the United States to the Several States together with the Assumption of the State Debts and Interest to January 1, 1790	Balance Due to the Several States	Population of the United States Answering to the Rule Prescribed in the Constitution of the United States	Proportion of the Several States of $77,666,678, the Aggregate Amount of the Balances
New Hampshire .	$ 4,278,015.02	$ 1,082,594.02	$ 3,198,061	141,722	$ 3,120,006
Massachusetts...	17,964,613.03	6,258,880.03	11,705,733	475,327	10,456,932
Rhode Island....	3,782,974.46	1,977,608.46	1,805,366	68,446	1,505,755
Connecticut.....	9,285,737.92	3,456,244.92	5,829,493	236,841	5,210,372
New York.......	7,179,982.78	1,960,031.78	5,219,951	331,590	7,294,797
New Jersey......	5,342,770.52	1,343,321.52	3,999,449	179,569	3,050,419
Pennsylvania....	14,137,076.22	4,690,686.22	9,446,390	432,879	9,523,099
Delaware.......	739,319.98	229,898.98	609,421	55,540	1,221,849
Maryland.......	7,568,145.38	1,591,631.38	5,975,514	278,514	6,127,154
Virginia.........	19,085,981.51	3,803,416.51	15,282,565	699,265	15,383,444
North Carolina..	10,427,586.13	3,151,358.13	7,276,228	353,523	7,777,310
South Carolina ..	11,523,299.00	5,780,264.29	5,743,035	206,235	4,537,057
Georgia.........	2,993,800.00	1,415,328.86	1,578,472	70,842	1,558,484
Totals......	$114,409,303.10	$36,742,625.10	$ 77,666,678	3,530,393	$ 77,666,678

State	Sums Due to Creditor States	Sums Due by Debtor States	Proportion of the Several States' Debts Authorized to Be Funded by the Thirteenth Section of the Act of August 4, 1790	Amount of Debt Funded by Each State under the Said Section
New Hampshire..................	$ 75,055	$	$ 300,000	$ 282,595.51
Massachusetts..................	1,248,801	....	4,000,000	3,981,733.05
Rhode Island...................	299,611	....	200,000	200,000.00
Connecticut....................	619,121	....	1,600,000	1,600,000.00
New York......................	....	2,074,846	1,200,000	1,183,716.69
New Jersey....................	49,030	....	800,000	695,202.70
Pennsylvania..................	....	76,709	2,200,000	777,983.48
Delaware......................	....	612,428	200,000	59,262.65
Maryland......................	....	151,640	800,000	517,491.08
Virginia.......................	....	100,879	3,500,000	2,934,443.29
North Carolina.................	....	501,082	2,400,000	1,793,803.85
South Carolina.................	1,205,978	....	4,000,000	3,999,650.73
Georgia.......................	19,988	....	3,000,000*	246,030.73
Totals.....................	$ 3,517,584	$ 3,517,584	$ 21,500,000	$10,271,814.74†

(Signed) T. L. Smith, Treasurer
Treasury Department, Register's Office, February 9, 1831.
*This should read $300,000.
†This should read $18,271,814.74.

larly of New York, complained that the method of settlement had
not been fair, and some even claimed that it was understood at
the time of assumption that debtor states would never be asked to
pay. Gallatin denied the latter statement, saying that the point had
been considered but voted down. Several times between 1796 and
1804 resolutions were introduced into Congress calling for the collection of the amounts due the Federal Government. Such occasions always provoked heated and bitter debates and provided
opportunities that were seldom missed, to air local patriotism and to
draw invidious distinction between states. To judge from the
language of these debates, the Union was about to be broken up
and the states were ready to fly at each other's throats.[27]

Attempts to Collect

At first the measures proposed in Congress for the collection of
the balances were mild. Even a resolution asking the President to
inform the debtors of the amounts due and to request payment provoked much debate, and led congressmen from debtor states to as-
sert that the move was an insult to the dignity of their "sovereign"
states. Later, other proposals were made: one would have prohibited the transfer of United States bonds in the debtor states;
one would have seized United States bonds held by such states
(whereupon the New York legislature immediately ordered the
sale of all such bonds held by that state); another would have required the United States to equalize accounts by issuing additional
bonds to the creditor states; still another would have levied a direct
tax on all states and remitted it to the creditor states. But none
of those steps was taken. On several occasions Congress provided
that if the debtor states would erect fortifications within their
bounds and cede them to the United States, the costs of such outlays would be allowed on the balances.[28] Congress made a special
concession to New York in 1799 by providing that balances might
be discharged if states paid or expended on fortifications an amount
equal to the balances due *or to the sum assumed by the United
States in the debt of such state*￼ (italics mine).

27. *Annals of Congress,* VI, 1747-1817; X, 1039-1040; XIV, 888-938.
28. 1 *Statutes at Large* 521-522, 554-555, 616-617.

As the difference between the New York debt and the amount assumed by the nation in 1790 was $891,129, the act in itself released the state of an appreciable share of her obligations. The state chose the method of expending money on fortifications, and the federal committee, reporting to Congress in 1801, stated that New York had spent $222,810 for that purpose. This was all of this debt to the federal government ever paid by the state.

The operation of the federal act caused wide discontent, particularly since New York had been freed from a portion of its obligation. Other states also were tardy in making their payments.[29]

New York expended only $136,533.82; the $222,810.06 allowed was credited because the amount spent would have bought that amount, par value, of United States bonds at that time. The other states were, indeed, discontented, for none of them except Delaware had benefited by the provision which released New York from almost $900,000 of its debt. No one of the debtor states was willing to pay anything unless all the others paid; on one occasion Pennsylvania "appropriated the amount of the balance . . . to be paid as soon as the other states . . . should pay the balances so reported against them."[30]

A special committee reported to the House of Representatives on these balances in 1801. After a review of the developments, it arrived at the conclusion that, since none of the states had "manifested any disposition to pay the balances reported against them . . . and none of them have assented to the justice or equity of the claim of the United States, and no means exist of exacting payment it seems unwise to keep alive a claim which cannot be enforced, and may have the effect of producing irritation, and exciting discontent."[31] The committee recommended that the balances should be extinguished; another committee reached a similar conclusion in 1802. In 1805 Gallatin reported that no other states had made any outlays on fortifications.

Here the trail of the balances seems to end. Bolles declares that the debtor states "were relieved of their indebtedness to the government by Congress," and a New York study claims that in 1815

29. State of New York, Special Joint Committee on Taxation and Retrenchment, *The Debt of the State of New York, Past, Present, and Future* (Albany, 1926), Legislative Doc. No. 70, p. 15.

30. *State Papers*, Finance, I, 734-735.   31. *Ibid.*, p. 697.

the New York account "was wiped off the books."[32] The acts and resolutions of Congress, however, mention no action on the matter. As a matter of fact, the only evidence uncovered points in the opposite direction; for, in a law enacted in 1841, Congress specified that when sums of money became due to the states because of the sale of public lands, any debts due to the United States should first be deducted. This was not, however, to apply to "any sums apparently due to the United States as balances of debts growing out of the transactions of the Revolutionary War."[33] This would seem to indicate that the states were never formally released from the balances. Thus almost at the very beginning of our national life there was established a tradition or precedent which may be summarized in these words: when the Federal Government owes the states, it pays liberally; when the states owe the United States, they seldom pay.

EVALUATION OF ASSUMPTION

Gallatin's Views on Assumption

Albert Gallatin was a critic of many of Hamilton's policies, including the method used in assuming the state debts. Thus he states:

But it was unexpectedly proposed, without waiting for the adjustment of the accounts, without knowing which of the States had really advanced more than their proportion, without examining whether the debts they then owed arose from the greatness of their exertions during the war, or from their remissness in paying taxes; it was proposed that the Union should at once, indiscriminately, assume the payment of all the debts then due by the several States in their individual capacity. A measure so little expected even by the creditors of those States, that the evidence of the debts of some of them had not appreciated in value since the establishment of the present government. . . .[34]

He indicates that this hasty action was due, first, to "the impatience of those States who labored under a heavy weight of debt" and, second, to "an idea that government would be strengthened by rendering all the creditors of the individual States dependent upon the Union." He adds that "suspicions have been entertained that

32. Bolles, *op. cit.*, II, 41; N. Y. Spec. Joint Comm., *op. cit.*, p. 16.
33. 5 *Statutes at Large* 454.   34. *Writings*, III, 129.

private interest and speculation were amongst the most powerful causes of the measure."[35]

Concerning the results of this method of assumption he writes:

Thus, had the United States waited to assume State debts till the accounts had been finally settled, instead of assuming at random before a settlement had taken place, the very same result which now exists might have been effected, the accounts of the Union with the individual States might have been placed in the same relative situation in which they now stand by assuming eleven millions instead of twenty-two. The additional and unnecessary debt created by that fatal measure amounts, therefore, to dollars $10,883,628 58/100.[36]

Hamilton was supremely confident of his ability to legislate wisely; he brooked neither advice nor delay. In the matter of assumption he was only partially successful. His plan did restore some degree of order to the field of state finances and it improved the standing of public credit, but it also permitted speculators to make unreasonable profits and, in view of the fact that the debtor states never paid the balances which they owed, it probably accomplished nothing toward equalizing the costs of the war, which was originally the primary purpose of the action. On the other hand, Gallatin's plan would probably have resulted in a slower recovery of state credit, but this would not have been an unmixed evil.

Aside from the problem of method, the question may be asked whether assumption was, in itself, desirable and expedient at the time. It probably was, but we must recognize one strong argument against it. "Though assumption was justified on grounds of national expediency and the national purpose for which the debts were created, the effect was to relieve the states of the necessity of working out a plan for debt redemption. Failure to experience the inevitable difficulty of retiring debt undoubtedly made the state hasty in embarking upon improvement programs entailing the extensive use of credit."[37] Fifty years after this first assumption, Congress was to hear its first action held up as a precedent, with

---

35. *Ibid.*, p. 130.

36. *Ibid.*, p. 133. In an appendix to the third volume of his *Writings*, and printed also in the *Annals of Congress*, VI, 1814-1815, there is a long computation by Gallatin showing how he arrived at the above conclusion.

37. N. Y. Spec. Joint Comm., *op. cit.*, p. 16.

the most urgent pleas for another assumption, which was barely averted.

Remaining Debts of States

In 1792 Hamilton estimated (see Table 4) that the debts of the states remaining after the amounts subscribed to United States bonds up to that time, amounted to $8,331,028. After that time more than $1,000,000 of obligations were exchanged for United States securities, and the creditor states received more than $4,000,-000 in payment of balances due them in 1795. These latter payments were, as a rule, used to pay debts owed by the states. When these transactions had been completed, the remaining debts of the states should have amounted to between $3,000,000 and $4,000,000, plus such interest as had accrued since 1792. Delaware and Connecticut were entirely free of debt, while New Hampshire, Massachusetts, New York, and New Jersey could hardly have had more than nominal debts. The debts of the other states were so small that they could be managed easily, and for the most part they were reduced quickly.

North Carolina's debt in 1796 was approximately $600,000, about equally divided between certificates and circulating bills. By 1810 practically all of the certificates had been retired; some had been bought by the treasurer at 15s. on the pound, while others had been received in payment for public lands. After 1800 there were several years in which treasury surpluses were used to retire certificates. Retirement of the bills had been stopped after the ratification of the constitution and was not resumed until 1813. Shortly after 1810 the state assisted in the establishment of three banks, which were required to retire the state bills out of dividends accruing on the state-owned stock. The banks were so prosperous that between 1813 and 1824 practically all of the bills were retired.[38]

Between 1791 and 1802 South Carolina retired and burned £41,933 of bills issued in 1785; it was then receiving £4,065 or $17,420 per year as interest on the remaining £58,067 out on loan.

38. *Treasurer's Reports, passim.*

The state had retired, from 1796 to 1802, obligations to the total amount of $668,462.[39]   Between 1792 and 1796 Massachusetts retired about $300,000 of its debt, and "by 1801 Governor Strong could report that the debt was on the way to extinction without levying taxes for that purpose.   In 1812 only $550,000 of the old script was outstanding, an amount which was largely exceeded by the productive funds in the treasury."[40]   Connecticut retired all of its debt out of the payment received from the United States and had a balance left over:

That part of the United States stock not required to meet the state indebtedness remained to the credit of the state; but as the principal was being paid off from year to year, the Comptroller was authorized, in May, 1803, to subscribe the money thus received to the several banks of the State, they consenting thereto.

The Comptroller, in his annual report, continued to make a statement of the nominal public debt till 1842, at which time it amounted to $2,390.76.[41]

Interest Payments and Methods of Retirement

Aside from circulating bills, the debts of the states were composed mainly of certificates which bore no definite maturity date. Usually they bore interest, but it was a general practice to pay the interest only when the certificates were retired.   Thus in 1797 Rhode Island paid two years' interest on outstanding certificates, but paid no more until they were bought in.   A North Carolina law enacted in 1801 provided that the treasurer was to pay cash only for the principal of certificates; for the accumulated interest he was to give non-interest-bearing certificates.   All certificates ceased to bear interest after 1803.[42]

There was little order or method to be found in the retirement of certificates.   When the legislature felt disposed or when there was a surplus in the treasury, certain sums might be paid into a sinking fund, which was to be used to retire certificates.   This was accomplished either through a call for tenders or by purchases in the open market.   Since the payment of interest was very sporadic and

39. John Drayton, *A View of South Carolina* (Charleston, 1802), pp. 189-191.
40. Bullock, *Finances of Massachusetts,* pp. 6, 25.
41. Bronson, *op. cit.,* pp. 189-190.   42. *Laws,* 1801, c. 1; 1802, c. 7.

uncertain, the certificates were usually quoted well below par. The Treasurer of North Carolina was not allowed to pay more than 15s. per pound for certificates. Between 1796 and 1802 South Carolina retired obligations amounting to $668,462 at a cost of only $448,919 to effect a saving of $219,543, while Massachusetts, up to 1795, paid only $111,892 to retire securities with a face value of $147,011.[43] Rhode Island sinking fund committees, between 1804 and 1819, purchased obligations with a par value of more than $90,000 at prices ranging from 75 cents down to 57½ cents on the dollar.[44]

The Rhode Island Debt

The retirement of Rhode Island's debt was sufficiently unique to warrant a more detailed study of events in that state. Up to about 1840 developments were about the same as in other states. In 1795 the state, having received $420,000 from the United States as payment of the balance arising out of the settlement of accounts, called upon creditors to present their claims and to receive United States stock in payment. The $420,000, however, was not sufficient to pay all claims; so 446 "balance certificates," bearing 4 per cent interest and amounting to $83,892.93, were issued.

In 1797 certain old certificates and other claims were recognized and new certificates were issued therefor. A precedent having been established, additional claims were presented at almost every session of the legislature. Many were claims for pay by veterans or their dependents. By 1819 a total of 802 certificates, with a face value of $138,676.05, had been issued for such claims.

In 1797 the state paid two years' interest on the certificates then outstanding. No further interest was paid after that except upon the issuance of new certificates, in which case it was the custom to pay two years' interest at the time of issuance. During this period the state made several appropriations to the sinking fund for the retirement of the certificates, the first in 1803. By 1820 it had

43. Drayton, op. cit., p. 191; Bullock, Finances of Massachusetts, p. 22.
44. Anonymous, The Plough and the Sickle: or Rhode-Island in the War of the Revolution of 1776 (Providence, 1846), pp. 22-24.

retired $94,759 at prices ranging from 57 to 75, leaving $43,917 outstanding.

No certificates were redeemed after 1820, and soon the legislature ceased to honor claims and old certificates. Charges were made that many of the claims were fraudulent and that certain groups were using veterans' claims as a means of robbing the state. A Dr. John W. Richmond, who had been a successful businessman before his retirement, became interested in the holders of old claims. He was convinced that they were suffering a serious wrong and that the state was repudiating a just and legal obligation. He tried without success to persuade the legislature to honor certain of the old certificates. He purposely became indebted to the state and offered some of the disputed certificates in payment, but the state refused to accept them and started suit to collect. The legislature then ordered the attorney-general to discontinue the suit.[45] Dr. Richmond made much of this legislative act, claiming that it was proof that the state's contention would not stand the scrutiny of a court. Defeated in all his efforts to make the state pay, Dr. Richmond began, through the newspapers and through tracts, to call attention to the state's action, which he held was repudiation. A large number of those publications were brought together to form the book cited above. Finally he shook the dust of the state from his feet, saying that he would not live in a repudiating state. On his tombstone at Stonington, Connecticut, where he died in 1857, he caused these words to be inscribed: "When Rhode Island, by her legislature from 1844 to 1850, repudiated her Revolutionary debt, Dr. Richmond removed from that state to this Borough and selected this as his family burial place."

Many years later a member of the Rhode Island Historical Society claimed that the whole plan of Richmond and others to enforce the claims against the state was a corrupt plot of speculators to enrich themselves.[46] No attempt was made to answer the definite and convincing statement made by Richmond. Further,

45. Richmond, *op. cit.,* pp. 59-60.
46. Amos Perry, *Rhode Island Revolutionary Debt,* in "R. I. Historical Society Publications" (Providence, 1897), IV, 234-243.

the charge that a group was trying to enrich themselves should not be given much weight, since only a few thousand dollars were involved. However, since almost a century has passed and since there were probably other angles to the question which do not appear on the surface, no attempt can be made here to pass judgment on the episode. So far as is known, the state never made any further payment on claims or certificates arising out of the Revolutionary War.

CHAPTER IV

THE FIRST BOOM AND COLLAPSE

PRIOR TO 1800 state debts were represented almost entirely by paper money or certificates, and many were, in effect, forced loans. Those debts were incurred to meet war costs or to cover operating deficits. After 1820 states began to borrow for internal improvements. These loans were voluntary; the states "funded" their debts, and state bonds made their appearance in the investment markets. This marked the beginning of state debts as we know them today.

MISCELLANEOUS DEBTS

Early New York Borrowing

Before the era of internal improvement debts, however, there were several isolated instances of state borrowing for miscellaneous purposes, which should be noted here. The first of these occurred in New York: "Beginning with an initial loan of $73,000 in 1797, the state borrowed for the general fund every year until 1820 except for 1801 and 1817. The total loans aggregated $5,378,917.79 for the period and were not far below the amount borrowed for the construction of the Erie Canal."[1] Occasionally the loans were to cover operating deficits, but more often they were for the purpose of purchasing bank stocks or making loans to farmers, businessmen, and counties. Although the bank stocks proved to be good investments, the loans were unfortunate ventures for the state. In 1808 the state contracted its first loan of any considerable size—$450,000—in order to make loans to new manufacturers. "Loans to individuals proved to be the least secure investment of the funded assets. Though the acts of 1803 and 1805 were intended to safeguard the state's interest, enforcement of the state lien against farmers or

1. N. Y. Spec. Joint Comm., *op. cit.*, p. 18.

business men was often financially impossible and frequently politically inexpedient."[2] In the years since that time the story has seldom been different. The total debt of the general fund, contracted for the various purposes mentioned, reached $3,103,685 in 1815.

A few years later New York contributed to the rise of the Astor fortune by issuing $500,000 of bonds to John Jacob Astor. About 1810 Astor's lawyers found that the state had, during the Revolutionary War, illegally confiscated a large Tory estate comprising nearly one third of Putnam County. For $100,000 Astor secured options from the heirs of the original owner and started proceedings to evict those then in possession of the property and to confiscate their improvements. This created such an uproar that the state was forced to intervene. Astor offered to settle for $667,000, but finally compromised for $500,000 of 5 per cent bonds.[3]

Borrowing for War of 1812

During the War of 1812 the military organization and the finances of the Federal Government were in such shape that the states frequently had to make heavy outlays for their own defense. This was especially true of Massachusetts, Pennsylvania, Maryland, Virginia, and South Carolina. Because funds had to be raised quickly and because they expected to be reimbursed, the states financed their activities by borrowing from banks or by liquidating investments which they held. Altogether the states borrowed more than $5,000,000 from banks; the Federal Government reimbursed them to the amount of approximately $3,710,000. After the war the states began to request adjustments for the interest which they had paid on the loans. Between 1824 and 1826 Congress authorized the payment of interest to five states and the City of Baltimore. But the states were not satisfied with the method used in computing the interest and, led by Maryland, they campaigned for a more liberal interest allowance. Finally, in 1857, Congress acceded to Maryland's request, and ordered a re-audit of its account under

2. *Ibid.*, p. 17.
3. Gustavus Myers, *History of the Great American Fortunes* (New York, 1936), pp. 111-113.

what came to be known as the Maryland Rule. Maryland received an interest adjustment of $275,770, although the original principal was only slightly more than that. From time to time, after long intervals, other states succeeded in obtaining re-audits of their accounts according to the Maryland Rule. In 1902 the accounts of Baltimore, South Carolina, and Virginia were settled; in 1906 those of Delaware, Pennsylvania, and New York were re-audited and paid, although it seems that the New York account is not yet finally settled. In 1928 North Carolina secured an adjustment. In all these cases the recomputations showed small balances due in the 1820's, but the accumulation of interest for eighty or one hundred years multiplied these small sums several times. Connecticut, New York, and Vermont still have claims before Congress.[4] The liberality of the Federal Government in paying these claims contrasts sharply with the procedure of the debtor states in regard to the balance due under the settlement of 1793.

North Carolina Treasury Notes

In 1814, 1816, and 1823, when banks were retiring the last of the state paper money issued in 1783 and 1785, North Carolina issued $262,000 of treasury notes in order to purchase bank stocks and thus relieve the banks in a period of distress. An important reason for the issue of the new notes was the demand for a circulating medium to replace the notes then being withdrawn. The new notes were in denominations from 5 to 75 cents, bore no interest, were receivable for debts and taxes due the state, and were redeemable by the state treasurer on presentation, but might be paid out again. They were not legal tender since the state lacked the power to give them that characteristic. The first two issues were put into circulation by the banks, which received them in payment for stock. The $100,000 issue of 1823 was exchanged for specie, which was used to purchase bank stocks directly from the banks in an attempt to aid them at a time when they were experiencing a heavy demand for specie to redeem their notes.

4. For a detailed discussion of these settlements see B. U. Ratchford, "The Settlement of Certain State Claims against the Federal Government," *Southern Economic Journal*, IV (1937), 54-75.

Redemption began in 1819, and most of the notes were retired between 1825 and 1833, when retirements frequently amounted to more than $20,000 per year. After 1849 the $48,826 which had not been presented for redemption ceased to appear in the state reports as a liability; it was assumed that those notes had been lost or destroyed. This was quite reasonable in view of the fact that they were bills for less than one dollar and had been in continuous circulation for more than twenty-five years. Although the state followed a dangerous policy in the issue of these notes, this particular experience proved profitable. The state received a loan of $262,000 without interest; it was relieved of the redemption of some $49,000 because the notes were never presented; and it made a handsome profit on the bank stocks which were bought with the notes.[5] The whole transaction, however, was unconstitutional since it violated the provision of the Federal Constitution forbidding states to issue bills of credit. This is clearly indicated by the decision in the Missouri case cited below. In North Carolina no one brought the matter before the courts.

Missouri's Loan Office

In June, 1821, Missouri authorized the establishment of loan offices and the issue of $200,000 in certificates bearing 2 per cent interest and ranging in value from 50 cents to $10. The certificates were to be loaned to citizens "in proportion to county population." The loans were to bear 6 per cent interest, to be secured by a mortgage, and were not to exceed $1,200 to one person. "In the cases of worthy and needy borrowers, two years' interest might be refunded." The certificates were receivable for all salaries and fees of civil and military officers, for salt, and for taxes and debts due to the state. Ferrymen were compelled to accept them as fare, and the state treasurer was empowered to pay warrants with them.

About $185,000 of the certificates were issued, principally in the payment of warrants rather than through the loan procedure. In November, 1822, the first steps were taken to abolish the loan office system. The issue of certificates was stopped, they were declared to be no longer legal tender for fees, the treasurer thereafter was

5. Ratchford, *History of North Carolina Debt*, pp. 76-80.

not allowed to redeem warrants with certificates, and debtors to the loan offices were permitted to discharge their debts by paying 80 per cent thereof. In May, 1824, the Supreme Court of Missouri held that the certificates were "bills of credit" and that their issue violated Article 1, Section 10, of the Federal Constitution, but ruled also that the invalidity of the bills did not free debtors from the responsibility of repaying their loans.[6] The Supreme Court of the United States, however, held that the invalidity of the bills made the whole transaction invalid and that the state could not recover from the debtors.[7] This decision left the state of Missouri holding uncollectible notes to the amount of $42,896; estimated interest brought the total to approximately $63,000. In 1831 Missouri contracted its first funded debt by borrowing $70,000 to redeem these outstanding certificates.[8]

BORROWING FOR INTERNAL IMPROVEMENTS

State Finances Around 1820

A brief survey of state finances around 1820 will give perspective to a study of their debts. During the first part of the twenties the states, with the exception of New York, had only nominal debts; some had none at all. State activities were strictly limited and budgets were quite small compared with present-day figures. Most states had annual expenditures ranging between $100,000 and $200,000; Pennsylvania, with one of the largest budgets, had total revenues of $440,802 in 1820. With these limited expenditures, the states were able to raise sufficient revenues with few taxes and almost no direct taxation. For several years North Carolina accumulated a surplus, which reached $90,000 in 1828; in 1824 Ohio had a surplus of $40,000. In Massachusetts the old funded debt was practically wiped out by 1821, and for several years the state was free of debt. The proceeds of land sales, which had been used for the sinking fund, were turned into the ordinary revenues.[9] In Pennsylvania, "Before the year 1826, with the exception of the tax

6. *Mankser* v. *The State,* 1 Mo. 452 (1824).
7. *Craig* v. *The State of Missouri,* 4 Peters 410 (1830).
8. Albert J. McCulloch, *The Loan Office Experiment in Missouri,* in "The University of Missouri Bulletin," Vol. XV, No. 24.
9. Bullock, *Finances of Massachusetts,* p. 26.

on bank dividends and on certain court officers, there was no taxation whatever except in the way of licenses."[10]

The states were able to dispense with taxes to this extent because they had come into possession of numerous investments and other sources of income. Frequently banks, when chartered, were required to give the state a block of stock or to pay an annual bonus. Several states held public lands, the sale of which brought funds to the state. Balances received from the United States in 1795 had been invested. About this time North Carolina owned bank stocks which had cost $700,000 and on which it eventually realized a gross profit of more than $1,000,000. In 1813 Maryland held investments valued at $1,475,922,[11] yielding an annual return of over $90,000, or an amount equal to two thirds of its expenditures. In 1822 various states held 3 per cent stock of the United States as follows: New Hampshire, $95,134; Massachusetts, $249,760; Connecticut, $55,303; New Jersey, $10,144; and Maryland, $335,105.[12] In 1820 Pennsylvania's return from investments amounted to $127,027, as compared with $122,272 from taxes. In 1827 a legislative committee reported "that there had been a steady increase in the various permanent sources of revenue, that they would suffice for the general expenses of government, and that the surplus in a few years would redeem the public debt, which had increased in 1826 to $2,457,915.44. To offset these liabilities, the committee claimed that the vested capital of the state (bank, turnpike, and bridge stocks) was worth $4,522,134.40."[13]

Evidently the states at this point were in a fair way to realize the Cameralist ideal—a situation in which the state derives a major part of its income from state-owned properties rather than from taxation. This factor is important because it undoubtedly influenced borrowing during the next twenty years. To the state official, borrowing offered the possibility of participating in larger financial operations, enlarging the permanent income of the state

10. T. K. Worthington, *Historical Sketch of the Finances of Pennsylvania*, in "Publications of the American Economic Association," Vol. II, No. 2 (Baltimore, 1888), p. 61.

11. These were divided as follows: bonds of the United States, $934,822; stocks of local banks, $516,100; and other stocks, $25,000.

12. Elliott, *Funding System*, p. 785.   13. Worthington, *op. cit.*, p. 35.

and freeing himself still further from the taxpayer. To the taxpayer it offered the prospect of the complete elimination of taxes.

The years from 1825 to 1843 were packed with important developments affecting state debts. Eighteen states were involved, which means that at one time or another eighteen different stories were unfolding. In a brief survey, such as this must be, it is impossible to follow each of these. Special monographs and general works, many of which are listed in the Bibliography, relate the development of internal improvements and the growth of debts in the different states. Here consideration will be given only to general trends and lines of development which affected all the states, together with a few special features.

Course and Extent of Borrowing

Table 6 shows the progress of borrowing through the year 1838. Until 1830 the borrowing was orderly and was indulged in

TABLE 6

STATE BORROWING, 1820-41

(In thousands of dollars)

State	AMOUNTS BORROWED					Debt, 1841
	1820–25	1825–30	1830–35	1835–38	Total	
Ala......	$ 100	$......	$ 2,200	$ 8,500	$10,000	$15,400
Ark......	......	......	......	3,000	3,000	2,676
Fla.......	......	......	1,500	......	......	4,000
Ga.......	......	......	......	......	......	1,310
Ill.......	......	......	600	11,000	11,600	13,527
Ind......	......	......	1,890	10,000	11,890	12,751
Ky.......	......	......	.. ...	7,369	7,369	3,085
La.......	1,800	.....	7,335	14,000	23,135	23,985
Me.......	......	......	555	......	555	1,735
Md......	58	577	4,210	6,648	11,493	15,215
Mass.....	......	......	......	4,290	4,290	5,424
Mich.....	......	......	......	5,340	5,340	5,611
Miss.....	......	......	2,000	5,000	7,000	7,000
Mo......	......	......	......	2,500	2,500	842
N. Y.....	6,873	1,624	2,205	12,229	22,931	21,797
Ohio.....	......	4,400	1,701	......	6,101	10,924
Pa.......	1,680	6,300	16,130	3,167	27,277	36,336
S. C......	1,250	310	......	4,000	5,560	3,691
Tenn.....	......	......	500	6,648	7,148	3,398
Va.......	1,030	469	686	4,133	6,318	4,037
Wis......	......	......	......	......	......	200
Totals..	$12,791	$13,680	$41,513	$107,824	$174,307	$192,945

Source: *Tenth Census*, VII, 523.

mainly by the older states of the East and South. After that year, however, the movement got out of hand. The older states increased their rate of borrowing, and the sparsely settled states of the Middle West began to join in the movement with an enthusiasm untempered by experience. As one writer puts it, "Of all the states that launched out upon the sea of internal improvements prior to 1840, Indiana, Illinois, and Michigan had the most canvas spread and the least ballast; and of these three Illinois drew the least water."[14] The totals for the different periods show the familiar boom pattern, in which series tend to increase in arithmetic progression. In spite of temporary difficulties in selling bonds during the panic of 1837, the states incurred more debts during the three years 1836-38 than they had during the previous half century. Bond sales reached a peak during 1838 and remained heavy until the fall of 1839. Then they practically ceased except for emergency borrowing. Debts continued to increase after that time, but the increase was due largely to accumulating interest, unpaid warrants, and other forms of floating indebtedness. The gross debt figures for 1841, as given in Table 6, are taken from reports made by state officials to the Secretary of the Treasury of the United States and show the debts as of September 2, 1841. These statements were not uniform in their arrangement of material, especially of contingent liabilities. It is probable that the correct amount was somewhat greater than is shown here; another tabulation given by the Tenth Census for approximately the same time gives a total, including $1,316,030 for the District of Columbia, of $207,894,613. The congressional committee which studied the question of federal assumption placed the total in 1843, including floating liabilities, at $231,642,111.[15]

Causes of the Boom

There were many possible reasons for the overborrowing in this period. In fact, there were so many factors to encourage borrowing that it would have been surprising if there had not been an inflation

14. John W. Million, *State Aid to Railways in Missouri* (Chicago, 1896), pp. 20-21.

15. *House Report No. 296*, 27th Congress, 3d Session, p. 117.

of credit. Many of those factors were so interrelated that their significance can be realized only if they are discussed together. For purposes of analysis these may be classified into three groups; i.e., political, economic, and financial. In many cases, of course, the dividing line is rather arbitrarily drawn.

Political Causes

Adams believed that one of the most important causes of state borrowing in this period was the shift in the relative political powers of the states and of the Federal Government as manifested by the advent of Jacksonian Democracy. Jackson's political creed called for a curtailment of federal activities at a time when the demand and the need for governmental services were increasing. Consequently, the states had to supply the services.[16] Since current funds were limited, it was natural that the states should consider borrowing, especially as a large part of the planned expenditures were for projects which were expected to be self-supporting.

In this connection the attitudes of politicians and taxpayers were no doubt of much importance. It can readily be imagined that the politicians were not averse to seeing the state embark upon large projects which would give them a large field for "self-expression," much patronage to distribute to loyal party workers, and perhaps eventually make them entirely independent of the taxpayers. On the other hand, the taxpayers could hardly be expected to protest. They were paying few taxes to the state, and were offered a plan which would eliminate even those. At the same time they would get the banks, canals, and railroads for which they were clamoring. It seemed as though they had everything to gain and nothing to lose.[17] After early successes had apparently demonstrated the soundness of this philosophy, almost everybody was in favor of more borrowing. For example, Alabama's state bank, established by the proceeds of state borrowing, was so successful that in 1836 it yielded a return of $100,000 to the state treasury, allowing the state to abolish practically all direct taxation. The following year

16. H. C. Adams, *Public Debts* (New York, 1887), pp. 317-331.
17. Cf. Worthington, *op. cit.*, p. 26.

the state borrowed an additional $7,500,000 for the bank, and in 1837 and 1838 started work on several railroads.[18]

Another important political cause was the rivalry between the different states. State boundaries do not, as a rule, mark off distinct economic areas. But under state leadership and control, each state had to develop a complete system of canals, railroads, and banks. In fact, facilities were often purposely duplicated in order to prevent a rival state from obtaining a monopoly. The boom was definitely under way when, after New York had successfully put the Erie Canal into operation, Philadelphia and Baltimore merchants insisted that their states should build competing systems to divert some of the traffic into those cities. In a similar way the locations of many of the state railroad systems were determined by political boundaries rather than by natural lines of communication and transportation.

Economic Causes

Behind those political factors were real and substantial economic causes for the growth of state debts. Probably the most basic and fundamental of these was the westward movement of population. As soon as the fertile lands beyond the Alleghenies were settled there was a real need for communication and transportation between the Middle West and the eastern seaboard and between the Great Lakes and the tributaries of the Mississippi. Private enterprise was not able to raise the large amounts of capital necessary to provide such facilities, so the burden was passed to the state. New York was the first to tackle the problem when, in 1817, it started the construction of the Erie Canal. The canal was completed in 1825 at a cost of approximately $7,000,000. One writer sums up the ensuing developments as follows:

The success of the Erie Canal was immediate and sensational. Before the work was finished the tolls exceeded the interest charges and within ten years the bonds issued for its construction were selling at a premium. The cost of freight from Buffalo to New York dropped from $100 to $15 per ton, and the time from twenty days to eight. Villages and cities sprang up along the route; the price of farm products in

18. *Tenth Census,* VII, 591.

western New York doubled in value, and that of the states north of
the Ohio River was increased with a corresponding rise in land values.
New York City became the emporium of western trade.[19]

These results demonstrated the possibilities of a program of
internal improvements, and other states were quick to follow the
lead set by New York. The success of the Erie Canal "was the
signal for rival states to embark on similar improvement schemes.
. . . [It] was the lever used by propagandists in every state to
secure the adoption of bills for similar improvements."[20] Considering the large number of people affected—merchants, brokers,
land speculators, farmers, and others—and the large stakes which
they had, it is no wonder that they were able to persuade legislatures to act. By 1830 Maryland, Ohio, and Pennsylvania were
busily engaged in borrowing money to build canals.

In the midst of this enthusiasm for canals the railroad appeared
as a new and revolutionary device. For several years its eventual
success was problematical, but from the first it was a factor to be
reckoned with. Here again large amounts of capital were needed
to build lines and to develop the possibilities of the steam engine.
In some cases states were so skeptical of the success of the railroads
that both railroads and canals were built to serve the same areas.

One other important economic cause of state borrowing was the
scarcity of capital and the consequent high rates of interest in the
young and rapidly growing country. Capital was so scarce that
if the country had been forced to depend entirely upon its own
resources the banks, canals, and railroads would have come much
more slowly than they did. The need was for some means whereby
to tap the capital markets of Europe. Since few private concerns
in this country had credit standing abroad and since the enterprises to be undertaken were hazardous by nature, it was evident
that private organizations were unequal to the task. It was a task
either for the Federal Government or for the states; since the
Federal Government was barred by political considerations, the
states had to assume the burden.

19. McGrane, *op. cit.*, p. 5. Chapter I of this work is an excellent discussion
of the whole topic.
20. N. Y. Spec. Joint Comm., *op. cit.*, pp. 33-34.

Financial Causes

Several financial factors swelled the demand for state borrowing. The Second Bank of the United States, together with its many branches, had provided banking facilities for almost every section of the country and, of equal importance, had served as a check on the state banks by requiring them to redeem their notes on presentation. After Jackson had weakened the Bank by his refusal to keep the government deposits in it, the Bank was forced to curtail its activities sharply. Then arose a clamor for more banking facilities. Although state banks were multiplying on every side so that there were soon too many *banks,* it was probably true that there was a scarcity of banking *capital,* since many institutions were established with almost no capital. In any event, several states, especially in the South, issued large amounts of bonds in order to subscribe to bank stocks or even to found state banking systems. Indiana, Alabama, Louisiana, Arkansas, and Mississippi were leaders in this movement.

Aside from the direct demand for state borrowing which it created, this change in the banking situation exerted an indirect influence on state borrowing. The rapid multiplication of state banks and the flood of paper money which they issued added to the general inflation. Prices of commodities, land, and securities were all rising. Profits were high, and it seemed that a great and permanent prosperity had come at last. The people, more than ever, demanded banks, canals, and railroads, and felt more able than ever before to pay for them.

The rapid repayment of the debt of the United States encouraged borrowing in two ways. First, it freed certain funds which were normally invested in public securities and made them available for investment in state bonds. When the federal debt had been entirely repaid, even the Federal Government had to seek investments for trust funds under its direction, so that by 1842 it held bonds of ten states to the amount of $2,546,547.[21] In the second place, the psychological attitude created by the rapid retirement of the federal debt

21. Elliott, *Funding System,* p. 1042. Many of these bonds were later defaulted or scaled down. The efforts of the Federal Government to collect them constitute a long and involved story, part of which is related in Chapter IX.

was favorable to state borrowing. It was reasoned that if the Federal Government could repay a debt of more than $130,000,000 within less than twenty years following the War of 1812, the states, now that they were much more populous and more prosperous than ever before, could easily repay a much larger debt.

The Federal Government not only repaid its debt but was embarrassed by a growing surplus in its treasury. This surplus was the subject of long and heated debates. When Congress finally voted to "loan" this surplus to the states, it added the climax to a long series of events which had raised the enthusiasm for borrowing and spending to a fever pitch.[22] Even those states which did not wish to borrow were having funds thrust upon them; they could hardly be blamed if they regarded the federal funds as manna from heaven. Also, if Uncle Sam was so generous in prosperous times surely he would not desert them if they incurred a debt and later found repayment difficult.

One other financial factor influenced borrowing. Most of the bonds issued in this period bore either 5 or 6 per cent interest; during the years immediately before 1837 many of these bonds commanded handsome premiums. It was the general practice to use such premiums to pay interest, thus concealing the real burden of the debts which were being created. Worthington states in regard to Pennsylvania: "It seems so evident at the present time that the state could not go on indefinitely paying interest on its debt with the premiums realized on new loans, that we are surprised when the governor seriously protests against such a financial method. When the wild folly of repealing the state tax laws, and chartering the United States Bank of Pennsylvania was perpetrated, we are almost convinced that it was not childishness, but wilful criminality; it closed every possible loophole from financial disgrace."[23]

22. This distribution of surplus federal funds was made in the form of a loan because it was thought that an outright gift would be unconstitutional. But it was understood by all concerned that repayment would never be demanded. The United States Treasury, however, still carries these "loans" on its books, and within recent years Comptroller McCarl, in reporting on the claims of certain states against the United States, has made reference to them as a factor which might be used to offset the states' claims. *Senate Document No. 304,* 67th Congress, 4th Session, p. 6; *Senate Document No. 325,* 67th Congress, 4th Session, p. 3; *Senate Document No. 52,* 70th Congress, 1st Session, p. 4.   23. Worthington, *op. cit.,* p. 38.

If we take all of the causes listed above—political, economic, and financial—and mix them with a liberal dash of the traditional American optimism, we can understand something of the strength of the movement for state borrowing. One writer has summed it up in these words: "In their few years of independence the United States had prospered beyond all precedent. It seemed that nothing could ultimately fail, that a special Providence was in charge of all things American. Each new generation saw the population more than doubled; each year saw the limits of civilization pushed farther and farther westward, into a land of seemingly inexhaustible wealth. Every line of business shared in this prosperity—agriculture, manufactures, and commerce."[24]

Borrowing after 1837

The severe panic of 1837 should have served as a warning to the states, but they continued to borrow heavily for two years after that event. In the first place, the states were in the midst of their programs of internal improvements. Generally the canal and railroad systems were not completed, and brought in little, if any, revenue. The states had to complete those projects or lose everything. Secondly, there were many who refused to accept the panic at its true value; they regarded it as merely a financial phenomenon which would not affect the economic situation. As in 1929, there were many who believed that business was still "fundamentally sound." One contemporary writer lays much of the blame in this connection on the United States Bank of Pennsylvania:

. . . it seems to have adopted the bold measure of attempting to bring back the unnatural state of things which had existed before May, 1837; hoping that, by means of high prices and unlimited credit, it might be able gradually to withdraw itself from its dangerous position. It entered largely into the purchase of State stocks, speculations in cotton, and other transactions. It was impossible in the nature of things that this scheme should succeed; but it did have some effect. Many began to think that the reverses of 1837 were small affairs, and that they were already overcome; that the disease was cured, and the patient restored to a sound state and ready for action. Our foreign commercial

24. H. S. Hanna, *A Financial History of Maryland, 1789-1848* (Baltimore, 1907), pp. 70-71. See also "Debts of the States," *North American Review*, LVIII (1844), 110-118.

debt had been paid with so much promptness, that European capitalists formed a very high opinion of both our resources and our honor, and they took the stocks of the States as freely as if they had been gold and silver.[25]

A third reason for continued borrowing was that, after the depression did manifest itself unmistakably, there was a demand that the projects be carried through to help business and relieve unemployment.

Nonborrowing States

In view of the above considerations we might well inquire why the New England states, North Carolina, and Georgia did not participate in the borrowing of this period. In the case of New England there were at least three good reasons: (1) the inherent conservatism of the region; (2) those states had no hinterland demanding communication systems; and (3) time, nature, and a more liberal supply of local capital had supplied these states with fairly good systems of internal communications.

North Carolina and Georgia were kept out of the procession by bitter political divisions between the eastern and western parts of the states. This deadlock was partly broken in North Carolina by the constitution of 1835. The state then prepared to embark upon a program of borrowing, but the distribution of federal funds in 1837 and the ensuing panic delayed the movement for another decade. In Georgia the impasse was ended by a series of constitutional amendments beginning in 1833, the most important of which abolished the property qualification for voting in 1834.[26]

Purposes of Borrowing

Table 7 shows the purposes for which debts outstanding in 1838 had been incurred. The Southern states had diversified programs of borrowing with banking, however, a heavy favorite. The largest amount borrowed by any state for a single purpose was Louisiana's $22,950,000 for banks. The Northern and Western

25. Benjamin R. Curtis (ed.), *A Memoir of Benjamin Robbins Curtis, LL.D., with Some of His Professional Writings* (2 vols.; Boston, 1879), II, 106.

26. Fletcher M. Green, *Constitutional Development in the South Atlantic States, 1776-1860* (Chapel Hill, 1930), pp. 228-240.

TABLE 7

STATE DEBTS OUTSTANDING IN 1838 AND PURPOSES FOR WHICH
THEY WERE CONTRACTED

(In thousands of dollars)

State	Banking	Canals	Railroads	Turnpikes	Miscellaneous	Total
Ala......	$ 7,800	$......	$ 3,000	$......	$......	$10,800
Ark......	3,000	......	......	......	......	3,000
Fla.......	1,500	......	......	......	......	1,500
Ill.......	3,000	900	7,400	......	300	11,600
Ind......	1,390	6,750	2,600	1,150	......	11,890
Ky.......	2,000	2,619	350	2,400	......	7,369
La.......	22,950	50	500	......	235	23,735
Me.......	......	......	......	......	555	555
Md......	......	5,700	5,500	......	293	11,493
Mass.....	......	......	4,290	......	......	4,290
Mich.....	......	2,500	2,620	......	220	5,340
Miss.....	7,000	......	......	......	......	7,000
Mo.......	2,500	......	......	......	......	2,500
N. Y.....	......	13,317	3,788	......	1,158	18,262
Ohio.....	......	6,101	......	......	......	6,101
Pa.......	......	16,580	4,964	2,596	3,167	27,307
S. C......	......	1,550	2,000	......	2,204	5,754
Tenn.....	3,000	300	3,730	118	......	7,148
Va.......	......	3,835	2,129	355	343	6,662
Totals....	$54,140	$60,202	$42,871	$ 6,619	$ 8,475	$172,306

Source: *Tenth Census*, VII, 526.

states were interested mainly in transportation. The total for all
forms of transportation—canals, railroads, and turnpikes—was
$109,691,503, or approximately two thirds of the total. In the cen-
tury which has passed since state borrowing began in earnest this
trend has continued except in abnormal times, and transportation
in its various forms has accounted for more state borrowing, by far,
than any other single purpose.

Maine's Experience

Developments in Maine provided a variation from the above
pattern. The governor believed that, because of the rigorous cli-
mate, agriculture should be encouraged by public subsidies. Accordingly, the legislature, in 1838 and 1839, provided bonuses for
all corn and wheat grown in the state. These acts cost $76,946
in 1839 and $153,982 in 1840; they were hastily repealed. Previ-
ously, however, the state, stimulated by receipts from public land

sales which in 1835 a most equaled total expenditures, had repealed all state property and poll taxes. Receipts from the sale of public lands dropped sharply in 1836, and a deficit appeared; by 1840 expenditures had risen to $654,000, and revenues had dropped to $52,000, leaving a deficit of $602,000. In six years the funding of deficits raised the debt from $55,000 to $1,734,000. The legislature came back to earth, levied new taxes, reduced expenditures, and began slowly to pay off the debt, which by 1860 had been reduced to about $700,000.[27]

MANAGEMENT OF THE DEBTS

Methods of Financing

Three principal methods were used by the states in extending aid to the various projects. The first, and the one most generally used, was for the state to sell its bonds for cash and use the proceeds to buy the stocks or bonds of private companies. Frequently this was accompanied by a prerequisite that certain amounts should be subscribed and paid in by private subscribers, a stipulation that was probably modified or disregarded more often than it was observed. The second method was for the state to exchange its obligations directly for the stocks or bonds of private companies. This method was used, as a rule, only when the state bonds could not be sold for par. Most of the acts authorizing the sale of bonds specified that they should not be sold below par. By this method the state bonds could be exchanged for a like amount, face value, of stocks or bonds of the private company, and it was generally considered that this fulfilled the legal requirements. The private companies could then sell the bonds for what they would bring on the market. The third method was for the state to guarantee the bonds of private companies. This enabled the companies to sell bonds which otherwise could not be sold on reasonable terms. This method was used principally by Southern states in aiding railroads.

Probably the most dangerous and most inequitable use of state credit was found in Southern states in connection with the estab-

27. F. E. Jewett, *A Financial History of Maine* (New York, 1937), pp. 30-41.

lishment of banks. A legislature would charter a bank with a capital of, say, $5,000,000 and provide that property owners could subscribe and pay for this stock by giving mortgages on their property. The state would then provide the actual capital of the bank by issuing to it $5,000,000 of bonds. In Mississippi the subscribers were required to pay 10 per cent of their subscriptions in cash, but this was to be refunded with interest when the state loan was floated. This method was used extensively in Alabama, Arkansas, Louisiana, and Mississippi; it gave to the stockholders the right to receive all the profits of the bank without having advanced any money at all. Of course, in theory, they took some risk by giving their mortgages. In practice, however, it was probably true that the mortgages were seldom enforced when the banks failed, as almost all of them did. A later governor of Arkansas observed that "Perhaps never before in the history of banking operations was such a system adopted—a system whereby a few favored individuals were created stockholders by the act, and enjoyed the special privilege of bank ownership without contributing anything themselves."[28] It was an astonishing example of the special-privilege doctrine of the use of governmental powers—of the use of the state's credit for the benefit and profit of a privileged group.

Bond Sales

In this period most states were selling their first bonds, and the methods of sale were quite different from those in use today. The usual procedure was for the legislature to authorize an issue of bonds, which the governor and treasurer would sign and turn over to a committee to be disposed of in accordance with the terms stipulated in the enabling act. This committee would then go to New York or Philadelphia to find a buyer. The enabling act usually specified the rate of interest and prohibited the sale of the bonds below par. The latter provision frequently caused trouble because of misunderstandings or open violations. The misunderstandings arose in two ways. First, the bonds were often made payable in sterling, frequently at the rate of $4.44 per pound. This

28. Powell Clayton, *The Aftermath of the Civil War in Arkansas* (New York, 1915), p. 251. See also Curtis, *op. cit.*, II, 126.

was not the exact ratio between the amounts of gold in the two monetary units, and of course the actual rate of exchange constantly varied. As a result, there were many misunderstandings as to whether the bond sales had been made in compliance with law.[29] The other factor which created confusion on this point and also caused heavy losses to the states was the practice of selling bonds on credit. The contract of sale would specify that interest should begin immediately on the full amount of bonds sold, but in some cases the bankers would be allowed as much as a year in which to complete payment. This raised the question as to whether the legislature meant, by forbidding sales below par, to prohibit this practice. Even if it is assumed that they did, however, there remained a nice question as to whether there had actually been a sale below par in any sense. When premiums were paid for bonds sold on credit, it required intricate calculations to determine just when the state had received the equivalent of par.

Aside from the legal aspect, this practice of instalment sales was dangerous and costly to the states. Both Michigan and Indiana lost heavily by the failure of banks after bonds had been delivered. Michigan had contracted with the Morris Canal and Banking Company to sell bonds to the amount of $5,000,000, the contract being guaranteed by the United States Bank: "Under the two contracts the state received pay in full for $1,387,000 of bonds; for the remainder but a small portion of the amount was paid to the state when the Morris Canal and Banking Company failed. A further small amount was paid by the United States Bank of Philadelphia as sureties, when that bank also failed."[30] The bonds had been transferred to the United States Bank, which, although it knew they were not paid for, had pledged them to European bankers as security for a loan. Indiana lost $3,559,791 in the same way,[31] and it is probable that other states lost smaller amounts.

In addition to these troubles there were irregularities, financial manipulations, and other forms of dishonesty on the part of state agents. Thus in Indiana, "the negotiation of the railway bonds was affected by a system in which there was the 'most

---

29. See McGrane, *op. cit.*, p. 7, for a discussion of this point.
30. *Tenth Census*, VII, 126-127.   31. *Ibid.*, p. 619.

fearful jobbing.' . . . One of the fund commissioners whose duty it was to sell the bonds of the state to the best advantage possible was one of the largest stockholders in the two banks, and one whaling company, through which the bonds were negotiated. In this transaction the state lost $2,275,000. Further losses were traceable to the perfidious conduct of this particular fund commissioner."[32]   Again, considering the methods, or lack of methods, that prevailed generally in the handling of bonds, it is probable that if all the facts were known many other similar incidents would be revealed.

McGrane sums up these practices admirably in the following words:

> In disposing of their stocks . . . American agents frequently disregarded and openly flaunted state statutes. Bonds were sold on credit and below par; and the signed contracts often specified that the interest should begin at once. Michigan bonds were given to the Morris Canal and Banking Company in advance of their payment, and negotiators of Indiana bonds received numerous favors in the way of stock and commissions from this company. Thus agents of the states violated state statutes in negotiating the loans, and American bankers aided and abetted them. These acts were unknown to foreign investors when they purchased the bonds; but they were often later the basis of the state's contention that the contracts were illegal and, therefore, the state was relieved of all obligation to meet the demands of foreign creditors.[33]

According to one statement, Indiana disposed of bonds with a face value of $14,057,000 for only $12,303,989.[34]   Such practices were an important factor in creating the demand for repudiation which later arose.

Sources of Funds

Most of the state bonds were handled by a small group of New York and Philadelphia bankers and brokers. The more important of these were: the United States Bank; Thomas Biddle and Company; the Morris Canal and Banking Company; The Phoenix Bank of New York; Prime, Ward and Company; and August Bel-

32. Million, *op. cit.*, p. 223.
33. McGrane, *op. cit.*, p. 8.   34. *Tenth Census*, VII, 619.

mont. The latter two were the agents, respectively, of the Barings and the Rothschilds. Many state bonds were sold in Europe, where, for several reasons, they found a ready market. First, the interest rates on the bonds were attractive in comparison with the lower rates prevailing in Europe. Second, the European investors felt that these public debts were incurred for productive purposes rather than for war, as was usually the case in Europe. Third, those investors had profited from their investments in the stocks of the First and Second Banks of the United States and in the bonds of the Federal Government. The English and the Dutch purchased the majority of state bonds sold abroad.

By 1839 it was estimated that British subjects held between 110 and 165 millions of dollars of American stocks. . . . Between 1830 and 1836 the total value of imports into the United States rose from $71,-000,000 to about $190,000,000 or an increase of 270 per cent in six years. During the same period the total value of American Exports increased only from about $74,000,000 to about $129,000,000, or about 174 per cent.[35]

These figures show the great extent to which funds were being drawn from Europe. Some elements in England, especially the London *Times,* were critical of the rapidly mounting debts of the states and frequently warned of trouble to come.

Until 1837 the large European bankers transacted business in this country only through old and established banks and agents. In this way they tried to keep in close touch with the situation here and to weed out some of the more highly speculative bonds. Their confidence in their American agents was not entirely justified, but it was a far better arrangement than that which prevailed after 1837. In that year three English firms which had been handling large amounts of state bonds found themselves in financial difficulties and were forced to appeal to the Bank of England for aid. The Bank finally decided to give the aid, but only on condition that the houses give up their American business. Subsequently the houses failed in spite of the aid. About the same time other English firms sharply curtailed their American business. The European market was almost completely closed to the American

35. McGrane, *op. cit.,* pp. 9-13.

states at a time when the financial system of this country was paralyzed by panic. This chaotic condition gave to Nicholas Biddle, smarting under his recent defeat at the hands of Jackson, an opportunity to enlarge his sphere of operations. As president of the United States Bank of Pennsylvania, he determined to establish agencies in England to handle state bonds. In doing this he necessarily became heavily involved in foreign exchange operations and soon he found his position threatened by falling cotton prices. His next step was to advance funds to cotton planters to enable them to hold their crops for higher prices.

Biddle was indeed in deep water now, but for a time was quite successful. American commercial debts were rapidly paid off, and American credit was restored in England. Biddle and his bank were quickly accepted by English bankers: "The best recommendation for an American loan was to have the indorsement of the United States Bank. . . . With the possible exception of the Barings, few entertained any doubt of the financial stability of the United States Bank. English bankers were willing to trust it as they trusted the Bank of England. . . ."[36]

The states began to pour forth bonds in larger volume than ever; few checks were imposed by the bankers, and some of the wildest schemes now appeared. Some states sent their agents direct to Europe to negotiate loans. "This increased the difficulty of the European financiers, for it deprived them of the salutary discrimination of their American correspondents. . . ." These agents used "high pressure" tactics and presented copious statistics to show that the bonds were safe. "Attention was also called to the investments by the United States government in state stocks as proof that the security of 'even the newest and smallest states, such as Arkansas, for instance,' was satisfactory to the Government in Washington."[37] Thus the mad race of bond selling continued; in the summer of 1839 "There was nearly $100,000,000 of American stocks and bonds for sale in the London money market." But an acute depression was developing, its intensity becoming more evident every day. Biddle kept his bank afloat as long as he could, but in October, 1839, it went down for the second time, carrying

36. *Ibid.*, p. 18.   37. *Ibid.*, pp. 18-19.

with it several millions of dollars of state bonds. With this blow state borrowing stopped, not to start again for several years.

Interest Rates

Almost all bonds bore interest at the rate of either 5 or 6 per cent; other rates were rare. Amounts issued were rather evenly divided between these two rates, giving an average rate of about 5½ per cent. The prevailing rates were: 6 per cent in Arkansas, Florida, Illinois, Kentucky, Maine, Michigan, Ohio, and Virginia, and 5 per cent in Alabama, Indiana, Louisiana, Massachusetts, Mississippi, New York, Pennsylvania, and Tennessee. South Carolina's issues were about evenly divided between the two rates. Small Maryland issues bore 3 and 4½ per cent, while Pennsylvania had issues at 4 and 4½ per cent. New York had one small issue at 4½ per cent. On the other hand, one Florida issue bore 8 per cent, and one Virginia issue, 7 per cent.

Since legislatures usually set the interest rate some time in advance of the date of sale and frequently without knowing in what market the bonds would be sold, it was impossible, even if fractional interest rates had been employed, to adjust the nominal interest rate closely to the prevailing rate. The result was that the bonds frequently were sold at large premiums or discounts; if the latter was prohibited, the bonds could not be sold except by resort to subterfuge. An Ohio issue of $2,000,000 of 6 per cent bonds sold at a premium of 9.6 per cent in 1838, but the following year $2,500,000 of similar bonds commanded only 3 per cent premium, and in 1842, $1,300,000 were sold at a discount of 33.6 per cent.[38]

Debts in the District of Columbia

Although cities in the District of Columbia are not, strictly speaking, within the scope of this study, they are of sufficient interest to justify brief consideration. Acting under authority granted by Congress, Washington, in 1829, borrowed $1,000,000 to pay for stock in the Chesapeake and Ohio Canal; Alexandria and Georgetown each borrowed $250,000 for the same purpose. The sale of

38. E. L. Bogart, *Internal Improvements and State Debt in Ohio* (New York, 1924), pp. 166-167, 175.

these bonds abroad was facilitated by a forceful prospectus which stressed the connection of the cities with the Federal Government. It was stated that the cities were "under the peculiar care, as well as exclusive legal and political jurisdiction of Congress"; the nation owned much of the real estate in Washington, which was the permanent seat of the government and "its infant but cherished metropolis." Funds to service the debt were to be handled by the Treasury of the United States, and if the cities should fail to provide sufficient funds, "THE PRESIDENT OF THE UNITED STATES" could "cause the money to be raised, by directing a levy upon property" within the towns. "Substantially, the funded debt proper of the United States stands upon no higher [ground]."[39] In 1834 Congress appropriated $70,000 to pay interest on the Washington debt, and in May, 1836, the Federal Government assumed the $1,500,000 debt and took over the canal stocks.[40]

DEVELOPMENT OF THE CRISIS

Financial Difficulties

The year 1840 was a year of reckoning for the borrowing states. The second banking collapse in the autumn of 1839 revealed the seriousness of the depression and the weakness of the financial structure. The collapse not only shut off all borrowing, but, as we have seen, caused heavy losses to several states. Work on extensive canal and railroad projects came to a stop because of lack of funds. Partly completed works were producing no income, although the debt service requirements had mounted to large figures. Banks which had been established by state borrowing failed completely or were so heavily involved that they could not pay interest on the bonds which had been issued for their benefit. State revenues, meager enough at best, fell off sharply because of the paralysis which pervaded all business and commerce. Revelations of the irregularities which had prevailed in the marketing of state bonds, together with the failure of the projects for which the money had been spent, quickly brought demands for repudiation.

39. Richard Rush, *Remarks on the Loan of a Million and a Half of Dollars* (London, 1829), pp. 5-11.   40. McGrane, *op. cit.*, p. 37.

In an effort to quiet the growing alarm of British bondholders, British bankers prevailed upon Daniel Webster, in December, 1839, to issue a reassuring statement. Considerable doubt had arisen concerning the constitutional powers of the states to contract loans. Webster asserted that the states had full legal powers to contract debts, and would scrupulously observe the moral obligations implied by the bonds.[41]

Devices to Avert Default

During 1840 and 1841 legislatures of the borrowing states wrestled with the problem of providing funds to pay interest on their debts. They hardly dared to levy taxes; taxpayers were already talking repudiation, and additional taxation would be a powerful stimulus to the movement. Further, many of the states had practically no revenue system, and to attempt to raise funds by taxation at such a time as this would be a slow, difficult, and expensive task. So the states used any available funds, confiscated trust funds, liquidated investments, issued treasury notes, hypothecated bonds for bank loans, and made use of any other device which promised temporary relief. Illinois did levy an additional tax of 10 cents per $100, but, on the other hand, Indiana reduced its tax from 30 cents to 15 cents per $100 in order to relieve the taxpayers. Illinois pledged $804,000 of state bonds to secure a bank loan of $321,000 in order to meet interest payments due in July, 1841. Between 1840 and 1842 Indiana issued $2,222,640 in treasury notes and $419,355 in other scrip. Maryland used first the income from, and later the principal of, a trust fund which had been set up for public schools out of the federal funds distributed in 1837.

Because of its large debt and old established position, Pennsylvania's struggle to avert default attracted special attention. Governor Porter told the 1840 legislature that in the previous year the state had incurred a deficit of over $1,000,000, and that during the past five years the state's average annual revenues from public works had been only $139,697 while interest charges on the debts contracted for them had been over $1,200,000. Since the state could

41. *Ibid.*, pp. 22-23. The charge that Webster received £1,000 for making this statement was never proven.

no longer borrow, this deficit had to be met from taxes or the state would default. This was a rude awakening to those who had expected public works to pay their own way and also to contribute to state revenues. The legislature adjourned without taking any action to meet the critical situation, and the state was forced to default temporarily on the interest due in February, 1840.

In a special session in June of that year the legislature made a half-hearted attempt to meet the situation by enacting a tax bill estimated to yield $600,000, which actually brought in only $33,000. Another tax bill in the following year also proved inadequate, and the state resorted to "relief notes."[42] The state "authorized" state banks to subscribe to these notes which bore interest at the rate of 1 per cent. The banks could pay for them by issuing their own notes to the state. Notes were issued to the amount of $2,220,265, and quickly depreciated. Since the notes were receivable for taxes, the state's receipts soon consisted primarily of depreciated notes. As the next step the state sold, for $1,395,000, bank stocks which had cost it $4,200,000. When these funds were exhausted, banks were required to make loans to the state up to 5 per cent of their capital.[43] This exhausted the state's bag of tricks; as one writer said of Maryland, "Every expedient had been resorted to short of taxation, and this or repudiation was the alternative now presented."[44] Another writer stated that "Speculation and hatred of all forms of direct taxation were the causes of the downfall of Pennsylvania's credit."[45]

Defaults

One after another, as their juggling of funds came to an end without success, the states defaulted. Florida and Mississippi were first, in the early part of 1841; they were followed by Arkansas and Indiana in July of that year. In January, 1842, Illinois, Maryland, and Michigan, joined the ranks. In August, 1842, Pennsylvania, the mightiest of them all, after twice delaying payment, was humbled by having to pay its creditors in scrip. Louisiana, in December, 1842, brought the number of defaulting states to nine.

42. *Ibid.*, pp. 67-69.
44. Hanna, *op. cit.*, p. 104.

43. *Tenth Census,* VII, 541-545.
45. Worthington, *op. cit.*, p. 38.

The effects of Pennsylvania's default were especially marked because of its position and because over two thirds of its $36,000,000 debt was held abroad. A veritable deluge of bitter protests, recriminations, and accusations came back across the Atlantic when this news reached the other side. Letters of the Rev. Sydney Smith to a London newspaper were reprinted, and received wide circulation in this country as well as in England. In one of his letters he asserted that Americans "prefer any load of infamy however great, to any pressure of taxation however light. . . . I repeat again, that no conduct was ever more profligate than that of the State of Pennsylvania. History cannot pattern it: and let no deluded being imagine that they will ever repay a single farthing—their people have tasted of the dangerous luxury of dishonesty, and they will never be brought back to the homely rule of right."[46] Several other statements of the Rev. Mr. Smith relative to the character of Pennsylvanians received wide circulation. It is true that there was some reason for his rantings, since he owned a Pennsylvania bond, but as a wearer of the cloth he might have set a better example of temperance.

While only nine states defaulted, several others barely avoided it. Alabama was "on the verge of financial ruin, and repudiation was favored by a considerable minority." But several branches of the State Bank were liquidated, the law abolishing taxes was repealed, a portion of the debt was refunded, and the state managed to pull through. New York's credit declined greatly, and its bonds sold as low as 78. "Virtual bankruptcy forced a reconsideration of the entire financial policy of the state. . . ." Under considerable difficulties $5,422,136 of bonds were sold, and the proceeds were used to protect the credit of the state. Then the legislature enacted the "Stop and Tax Law" of 1842, which was "one of the milestones in the financial history of the state. It balanced the budget and ended the headlong rush toward bankruptcy."[47] In Ohio the deficit in the interest fund for the six years ending with 1844 was nearly $1,600,000. "This was partly supplied . . . by transfer of

46. *The Works of the Rev. Sydney Smith* (2 vols.; London, 1859), II, 327.

47. N. Y. Spec. Joint Comm., *op. cit.*, pp. 30-31; Don C. Sowers, *The Financial History of New York State from 1789 to 1912* (New York, 1914), pp. 69-71.

money from other funds and irregular sources, and by adding
nearly $900,000 to the state debt. This was the case notwithstanding
that the rate of taxation reached a high figure."[48]   In Tennessee
the tax rate was increased by 50 per cent to enable the state to meet
interest requirements on its debt of a little more than $2,000,000.

THE MOVEMENT FOR FEDERAL ASSUMPTION

Origin

As soon as serious trouble loomed on the horizon, there arose
a movement for a second federal assumption of state debts. Although it was popularly believed that this idea originated with
foreign bankers, McGrane states that it "owed its inception to the
necessities of the United States Bank."   Ten days before the
Bank closed in 1839 a close friend of Biddle's made the suggestion
to a member of the Barings firm.   However, the idea persisted
that this was a plan of the foreign bankers to foist the debt burden
on the Federal Government in order to recoup their funds.   In
any case it made good ammunition for political campaigns and
was a powerful factor against the movement.   In favor of assumption it was argued that it would enable the states to complete their
improvement programs and that the Federal Government could
refund the bonds at a much lower rate of interest and thus save
nearly half of the ten or twelve million dollars per year which the
states were paying in interest, much of it to foreigners.   Against
assumption it was argued that it was unconstitutional, that it would
establish a dangerous precedent, that it would make the non-
indebted states bear part of the burdens of the states which had
borrowed, that it would cause higher tariffs, that it would promote
a stronger central government, and that it would yield large profits
to foreign bondholders.[49]   The opponents of assumption, by clever
strategy, put through Congress in January, 1840, a resolution con-
demning assumption.   The question was an issue in the election of
1840, the Democrats appealing to national prejudice to condemn
it as a move on the part of foreign bankers to dictate the internal
affairs of this country.   Strength was lent to this charge by a letter

48. Bogart, *op. cit.,* p. 169.
49. Much of the material in this section is drawn from McGrane, *op. cit.,* chap. ii.

from an English banker to the governor of Missouri intimating that assumption would be necessary before any more state bonds could be sold in Europe.

Growth of the Movement

As state after state defaulted and the financial situation became progressively worse, the assumption movement gained strength. In 1842 European bankers joined in refusing to bid for a loan offered by the United States. One English firm told the United States commissioners that they could expect no assistance unless the Federal Government assumed the debts of the states. This revived the hopes of the assumptionists, and there were rumors of a possible war with Great Britain unless the debts were assumed. In the House a committee was appointed in December, 1842, to consider the matter. The committee headed by William Cost Johnson of Maryland, made its voluminous report of nearly six hundred pages in March, 1843.[50]

The report contained numerous economic fallacies and over-statements, clearly showing its bias in favor of assumption. The principal arguments offered were: (1) there were precedents for this action in that Congress in 1790 and 1836 had assumed debts of the states and of the cities of the District of Columbia; (2) the United States could replace the 6 per cent state bonds with 3 per cent bonds; the saving could be put into a sinking fund which would soon retire the principal; (3) the states' right to levy tariffs was taken away by the Constitution and without it they could not pay their debts except by direct taxation, which was "most inconvenient and onerous"; (4) the states had donated the public lands to the Federal Government as a public trust for the payment of the public debt; the federal debt had been retired and now the Federal Government was morally bound either to assume the debts or to return the public lands to the states. This latter argument was stressed most by the committee. A major part of the long report was devoted to detailed statistics on land sales and to elaborate arguments to show that the grant of public lands to the Federal Government had not been unconditional.

50. *House Report No. 296*, 27th Congress, 3d Session.

Proposed Plan of Assumption

The committee proposed that assumption should be effected as follows: the United States should issue bonds to the amount of $200,000,000 and allocate them among the states and territories on the basis of $1,000,000 for each senator and $651,982 for each representative. To the extent that a state had bonds outstanding, these bonds of the United States would be given to the bondholders in exchange; they should not be turned over to the states lest they should be used for some other purpose. Those states which had no debts "might be credited on the books of the Department, and the

TABLE 8

PROPOSED FEDERAL ASSUMPTION OF STATE DEBTS, 1843

State	Share of $200,000,000	Amount of State Debt Which Will Be Retired	Amount of State Debt Which Will Remain Unpaid
Maine.................	$ 6,563,877	$ 1,734,861	$ ....
New Hampshire........	4,607,930	....	....
Massachusetts..........	8,519,824	5,424,137	....
Connecticut..........	4,607,930	....	....
Vermont.............	4,607,930	....	....
Rhode Island..........	3,303,965	....	....
New York.............	24,167,400	21,797,268	....
New Jersey...........	5,259,912	....	....
Pennsylvania..........	17,647,578	17,647,578	18,688,466
Delaware.............	2,651,982	....	....
Maryland.............	15,911,894	5,911,894	9,302,867
Virginia.............	11,779,736	6,994,308	....
North Carolina........	7,867,841	....	....
South Carolina........	6,563,877	5,691,234	....
Georgia.............	7,215,859	1,309,750	....
Kentucky.............	8,519,824	3,085,500	....
Tennessee.............	9,171,806	3,198,166	....
Ohio.................	15,691,630	15,691,630	4,308,370
Louisiana.............	4,607,930	4,607,930	19,377,070
Indiana.............	8,519,824	8,519,824	4,231,176
Mississippi............	4,607,930	4,607,930	2,392,070
Illinois................	6,563,877	6,563,877	6,963,416
Alabama.............	6,563,877	6,563,877	8,836,123
Missouri.............	5,259,912	842,261	....
Arkansas.............	2,651,982	2,651,982	24,018
Michigan.............	3,955,947	3,955,947	1,655,053
Florida.............	651,982	651,982	3,348,018
Wisconsin.............	651,982	....	....
Iowa.................	651,982	....	....
District of Columbia....	651,982	651,982	664,048
Totals...........	$200,000,000	$128,103,918	$ 79,790,696

Source: House Report No. 296, 27th Congress, 3d Session, pp. 120-121.

States might draw their semiannual interest on the same, and their proportion of the principal when finally liquidated. . . . no stock need be issued but such as might be applied on the books of the Treasury to the liquidation of the outstanding debts of the States." In this way it was argued that nonborrowing states would not be treated unjustly. The last sentence quoted above illustrates the naïveté of the committee: it assumes that the debt would not be so large if the nonborrowing states merely had a balance to their credit on the books of the treasury, on which they received interest, instead of actually having bonds. Table 8 gives the proposed distribution of the bonds to the different states, together with the amount of debts which would be retired and the amounts which would remain after the assumption, according to the calculations of the committee. It shows that nine states had no debts at that time. Nine others would be entirely relieved of their debts by the assumption, while twelve would be left with debts ranging from a nominal $24,000 in Arkansas to over $18,000,000 in Louisiana and Pennsylvania.

The Plan Defeated

In spite of the earnest recommendations of the committee and in spite of the undoubted enthusiasm for assumption in parts of the country, the movement came to naught. McGrane is of the opinion that the sentiment for assumption was strong in Pennsylvania and Maryland but that elsewhere it was not popular. "In the south and west the great mass of the people were not interested in the subject. . . . The moral force of sustaining the public faith weighed lightly with those who were overwhelmed by their own personal indebtedness and in the legislatures there were few who had the moral courage or political honesty to urge the maintenance of state credit. . . . There was no chance for assumption being adopted."[51] Neither of the major parties would advocate assumption, and when Johnson made his report in the House it was tabled. It is surprising that the movement did not develop more strength, for there must undoubtedly have been influential men behind it: bankers; bondholders, both domestic and foreign; state politicians; pri-

51. McGrane, op. cit., pp. 38-40.

vate owners of banks, canal and railroad securities; as well as the taxpayers in some of the more heavily burdened states. Then, too, the tender solicitude which the Federal Government has always displayed for the financial welfare of the states would normally have been enough to put the measure through. But regardless of causes, the result was most fortunate, for a second assumption would almost certainly have converted a precedent into a habit, the results of which are not pleasant to contemplate.

CHAPTER V

REPUDIATIONS, READJUSTMENTS, RECOVERY, AND THE SECOND BOOM

THE PRECEDING chapter traced the developments in state credit up to the critical years 1842-43, when state indebtedness totaled about $230,000,000, when nine states with debts of approximately $122,-000,000 were in default, and when others were having difficulty servicing their debts. The purpose of this chapter is to describe the steps taken by the states to extricate themselves from this difficult situation, to trace the recovery in state credit, and to present the details of the second wave of borrowing which developed around 1850.

REPUDIATIONS

Mississippi

In 1830 Mississippi chartered the Planters' Bank with a capital of $3,000,000, of which the state subscribed two thirds. Bonds to the extent of $2,000,000 were sold at a premium, and the proceeds were used to pay for this stock. For several years the bank was successful, stimulating demands for more banks. When the Second Bank of the United States closed, the demands were intensified.

In 1837 the legislature passed for the first time the charter of the Union Bank with a maximum authorized capital of $15,500,-000, all to be raised by the issue of 5 per cent state bonds. Subscribers to the stock were to give mortgages on property for the amount of their subscriptions and to pay in 10 per cent thereof, which was to be refunded with interest when the state loan was floated. In compliance with the constitution of 1833, the essential portions of this act were published and the charter was re-enacted by the next session of the legislature. In the fall of 1837 McNutt, the successful candidate for governor, waged a campaign marked

by intense hatred for banks. In spite of the governor's attitude
the legislature, on February 5, 1838, re-enacted the Union Bank
Charter. Ten days later it passed a supplementary act which had
not been passed the previous year, and which changed several
details of the plan for establishing the bank. The most important
of those permitted the governor to issue the bonds without waiting
for the deposit of mortgages by the stockholders. The mortgages
were never deposited. A formal protest alleging the unconstitu-
tionality of the supplementary act was recorded in the *Senate
Journal*.

Bonds to the amount of $5,000,000 were issued, signed, and, on
August 18, 1838, sold to Nicholas Biddle's Bank of the United
States. Interest started at once, but the bank paid for the bonds in
five equal instalments at intervals of two months. The coupons
were payable in London at the rate of 4s. 6d. a dollar. The
governor continued to castigate the banks and to stir up hatred
against them; nevertheless, he declared that the state was pledged
for the payment of the bonds and he allowed the banks to receive
the instalment payments. Because of the criticism which had been
aroused, the legislature, in 1839, appointed a committee to investigate the sale of the bonds. This committee reported that "the
proceeds of the sale of the State Bonds in reality amount to more
than their par value" and that the sale was "highly advantageous to
the State and in accordance with the injunctions of the charter
requiring them to be sold at par value; a sale . . . bringing timely
aid to an embarrassed community." This report was concurred in
by the House and Senate.[1] It was later revealed that the payments
for the bonds were made at New Orleans in gold, against which the
bank sold exchange at a premium. The premiums amounted to
more than the interest on the bonds during the time the instalment payments were being made.

In the meantime the banks were being conducted in a most
reckless manner. Heavy loans of a capital nature were made on
land and slaves. The Union Bank issued large amounts of post
notes and speculated in cotton. Both banks refused to allow the

1. *Senate Journal*, 1839, p. 134.

bank commissioners to examine their books.[2]   In a short time they were hopelessly insolvent. Governor McNutt first hinted at repudiation in 1840, when he issued a warning against accepting the bonds as collateral for loans. In 1841 he openly advocated repudiation, claiming that the bonds were invalid because: (1) the charter of the United States Bank prohibited it from buying bonds; and (2) the bonds were sold on credit and thus below par. A committee of the House of Representatives made a thorough study of the question and arrived at the conclusion that "To refuse now to recognize the State's liability upon these bonds . . . would . . . amount to positive dishonesty. It would . . . cast a stigma upon the sovereignty and fair name of the State of Mississippi, and justly make her a by-word and a reproach amongst all her sister States. . . . To make the claim binding on our honor and public faith it is enough to know that we received and used the money . . . to disapprove and refuse now to pay and carry out the contract, would be nothing short of skilful plundering."[3]

The committee then reported a resolution stating the intention of the state to pay the bonds and declaring "That the insinuation that the State of Mississippi would repudiate her Bonds and violate her plighted faith is a calumny upon the justice, honor, and dignity of the State." On January 27, 1841, the legislature passed these resolutions and defeated a proposed repudiation amendment by a large majority. The governor vetoed the resolutions and returned them with a profane and abusive message.[4]   This action aroused the indignation of bondholders; British bondholders requested the British Foreign Secretary to present the matter at Washington, but he refused. Newspapers, both British and American, were violent in their castigation of Mississippi, but this only intensified the issues within the state. In the fall of 1841 Tucker, who favored repudiation, was elected governor, although the wealthier counties voted against him. He interpreted his election as a mandate to repudiate the Union Bank bonds but not the Planters' Bank bonds. On February 26, 1842, the legislature formally declared that the Union Bank

2. McGrane, *op. cit.*, p. 199. Much of the material here is based on Chapter X of his book, which gives an excellent account of the whole affair.

3. *House Journal*, 1841, p. 416.   4. *Ibid.*, p. 502.

bonds were not valid claims against the state, because the supplemental act of February 15, 1838, "was a fundamental change of said original charter passed contrary to the letter and spirit of the constitution of the State and adopted without the assent of her citizens as required thereby."[5]

Bondholders were eager to take such steps as they could to protect their interests, but for some years they did not consider conditions propitious for starting action. After a few years, high cotton prices brought prosperity and state help was desired in the building of railroads. About 1850 the bondholders began to agitate for a resumption of interest on the Planters' bonds which had been in default since 1841. In the election of 1852 the question of paying these bonds was submitted to the people and defeated, although the wealthier counties again voted for payment. About the same time a suit against the state was brought on one of the Union Bank bonds. The lower court decided in favor of the bondholder, and the case was appealed to the High Court of Errors and Appeals, which, after extensive arguments on both sides covering some two hundred printed pages, delivered its momentous opinion. It found that the supplementary act "was not void in consequence of not having been passed in conformity with the . . . constitution," and that "the liability of the State . . . would attach, so soon or whenever the bonds were legally executed to the bank, and that the execution of the mortgages was neither a condition precedent to the pledge of the faith of the State, nor the conditions on which the State bonds were to be executed and delivered." It declared, further, that the bonds were not sold "for less than their par value; consequently, the sale was neither illegal nor void."[6] The court then upheld the decision of the lower court and declared that the state was liable for the payment of the bonds. Petitions of the state for re-argument were denied.

This fearless, honest, and well-reasoned decision cost the judges their political lives and availed the bondholders nothing. McGrane points out that the bondholders were not prepared to follow up the decision with a publicity campaign to influence public opinion, and

5. *Laws*, 1842, c. 127, pp. 260-262.
6. *State* v. *Johnson*, 25 Miss. 625, 755, 769 (1852).

no further action was taken.   Shortly after the Civil War attempts
were made to persuade the Reconstruction government to ac-
knowledge these bonds, but they came to naught.   In 1875 the
voters of the state adopted a constitutional amendment prohibiting
the payment of both the Union and the Planters' bonds.[7]   Representatives of the bondholders, particularly the British Council of
Foreign Bondholders, kept the issue alive through the years.
Finally, in 1934, the Principality of Monaco asked leave to bring suit
against Mississippi on these bonds in the Supreme Court of the
United States.   This permission was refused in a decision which
is discussed in a later chapter.

Florida

From 1822 to 1845 Florida existed as a territory.   Between 1831
and 1835 the territorial government chartered three banks and
provided for public aid.   In two cases aid took the form of guarantees of bank certificates, but territorial bonds were sold to provide
the $3,000,000 capital of the Union Bank of Florida.   Stockholders
gave mortgages on property, as in Mississippi, and they could receive
loans equal to two thirds of the value of such property. For this
purpose land was valued at the arbitrary figure of $5.00 per acre,
although it had cost from $1.25 to $5.00. After the bank had been
operating for some time the stockholders desired larger loans, so
appraisals were increased to $15.00 per acre and the loan value thus
rose to $10.00.   Florida got an early start in juggling land values.
The first $1,000,000 of state bonds were sold in 1834-35; the others
were sold in Europe by a state agent in 1839 at prices between 90
and 95, in violation of the enabling act which prohibited sales
below par.   The liability of the stockholders on their mortgages
was repealed by an act secretly passed in 1838.

The affairs of the territory were under the supervision of Congress, which could set aside any act of the legislature.   The constitutional power of the territorial government to make contracts which
would bind the later state government was challenged, and to settle
this point a group of four eminent lawyers, including Daniel Webster, in 1835 issued a statement unanimously declaring that such

7. McGrane, *op. cit.,* pp. 217-220.

contracts would be binding.[8] Congress did not set aside the laws authorizing borrowing, and this point was used as an argument to facilitate the sale of the bonds; it was implied, though never stated, that Congress would see that the bonds were paid.

In February, 1840, the legislative Committee on Banks reported on the conduct of the Union Bank. It was the story all too common for that period; the bank had engendered a reckless spirit of extravagance by its profuse loans; it had "not only distributed all its borrowed capital among shareholders and others, upon terms which precluded the possibility of its being repaid within any reasonable time," but it had also "extended these imprudent loans upon the capital based on circulation and floating deposits."[9] The committee severely criticized the sale of bonds below par and implied that those bonds were null and void. A month later the Senate Judiciary Committee reported that the legislature of the territory did not have the power to bind "the sovereign people of Florida" and that the bonds were invalid. In 1841 Governor Reid also announced a doctrine of repudiation. He did not question the power of the territorial legislature to make the contracts, but he contended that the bondholders would have to look to the stockholders of the defunct banks for payment. Bondholders were quick to protest against these expressions of opinion, but to no avail. In February, 1842, the legislature formally declared that it "does not possess, nor was it ever invested with the authority to pledge the faith of the Territory," and thus repudiated the bank debt.[10]

Bondholders brought this matter before Congress several times in an effort to secure federal action. They contended that there was at least a moral, if not a legal, obligation resting on Congress to see that the bonds were paid, since they had been issued with the tacit consent of that body. But in 1847 the Senate Judiciary Committee, although admitting that it had not made a full investigation, reported that it was inclined to believe that "neither the United States nor the State of Florida was in anywise responsible

8. *Ibid.*, p. 226. Chapter XI of McGrane's work gives a full account of the Florida troubles.

9. *Ibid.*, pp. 234-235, quoting from *Senate Journal*, 1840, pp. 7-8.

10. *Laws*, 1842, p. 53.

for these bonds."[11]   In 1853 British bondholders presented claims
based on these bonds to the Anglo-American Claims Convention
which met that year.   The British and American representatives on
that Convention disagreed, and the decision was made by the um-
pire, Joshua Bates, an Englishman.   He found that there was no
federal liability but that the bondholders had "a just claim on the
State of Florida . . . and the State is bound by every principle of
honor to pay interest and principal; and it is to be hoped that
sooner or later the people of Florida will discover that honesty is
the best policy; and that no State can be called respectable that
does not honorably fulfill its engagements."[12]   Bondholding groups
have tried to keep the issue alive by retelling the story, but no
further action has been taken.   Although in all essential respects the
Florida action was as inexcusable as that of Mississippi, the latter
has received much more publicity.[13]

Arkansas

Shortly after becoming a state in 1836, Arkansas chartered two
banks—The State Bank of Arkansas and The Real Estate Bank
of Arkansas and authorized the sale of $4,500,000 of state bonds
to provide their capital.   Bonds to the amount of $2,827,000 were
eventually sold, although much difficulty was encountered in disposing of them during 1837 and 1838.   Both banks were in liquidation by 1842.   In the meantime, the Real Estate Bank had, in
1840, pledged $500,000 of bonds to the North American Trust and
Banking Company of New York as collateral for a loan; it expected
to receive $250,000 but actually got only $121,337.   Shortly before
it became insolvent in the following year, the North American
Company pledged the bonds to James Holford, a private banker
of London, for a loan of $325,000.   This was one of several flagrant

11. *Senate Document No. 163,* 29th Congress, 2d Session, p. 1.
12. Quoted in McGrane, *op. cit.,* p. 244.
13. One interesting side light on the Florida case is afforded by resolutions sent
by the Georgia legislature to the Governor of Florida which read in part: "There is
a moral obligation upon every government to discharge its pecuniary obligations, and
any state refusing to do so, or to provide the means of payment, is false to the
principles of common honesty, and an enlightened civilization, and is unworthy of
the confidence of its sister states" (quoted in *ibid.,* p. 243).

violations of laws and instructions by the bank, for the charter of the Real Estate Bank prohibited sale of the bonds below par. When the North American Bank became insolvent, Holford became the owner of the bonds, which came to be known as the "Holford Bonds." In 1841 the state defaulted on the interest payments on its debt of $2,676,000. In the fall of 1841 Governor Yell wrote to Holford that the state was neither morally nor legally bound to pay the bonds which he held, since they had been illegally sold. This position was sustained by the Arkansas Supreme Court in a case decided in 1862, although the court added that "the bank, having thought proper to receive and appropriate to its use the money advanced to its agents by the New York banking company upon a pledge of the bonds, it is just and reasonable to conclude that the bank became bound in equity and good conscience to repay the money so advanced to it."[14] In 1884 the people of the state, by constitutional amendment, repudiated the Holford bonds along with several issues of Reconstruction bonds.

Arkansas remained in default on all its bonds until after the Civil War. In the late 1840's some degree of prosperity returned to the state, but the legislature refused to levy taxes to pay the interest. About 1850 the state considered plans to aid railroad building, and this necessitated some thought for the debt. The movement failed, however, apparently because of the opposition of large landowners and land speculators to increased taxes. In 1856 Governor Conway declared that the mortgaged lands held by the Real Estate Bank were sufficient to pay the whole state debt and recommended action to this end, but the legislature refused to act.[15] The debt at that time, with accumulated interest, was about $4,500,000.

Michigan

When Michigan was admitted to the Union in 1836, a section in its constitution imposed upon the legislature the duty of providing a system of internal improvements. In 1837 the legislature authorized loans of $5,200,000 for this purpose—a very large amount in view of the population and resources of the state. Difficulty was

14. *Whitney* v. *Peay*, 24 Ark. 26 (1862).
15. McGrane, *op. cit.*, p. 262.

experienced in selling the bonds in 1838, but the Morris Canal and Banking Company, acting as agents for the state, sold about $1,000,-000. This arrangement was changed, and $4,194,250 of bonds were sold to the Morris Company and the United States Bank in return for their unsecured notes. The banks soon hypothecated most of the bonds in Europe. Banking difficulties of 1839 made Michigan officials uneasy about the unsecured notes, and they tried to obtain collateral. At one time the banks offered to return a large part of the bonds, but political differences in the legislature caused the offer to be refused. Shortly afterward the banks failed. Although the state made many attempts, it was never able to collect much on the bank notes, on which more than $2,000,000 were owing.

In 1842 the legislature declared that the state would recognize its debts only to the extent that payment had been received. It then passed an act requiring all bondholders to present their bonds and to receive new bonds to the extent that payments had been made, less damages sustained by the state due to the failure of the banks to meet their instalment payments. The damages were later set at 25 per cent. The same act authorized the governor to sell the public works and a part of the public lands of the state.[16] The bond-holders protested against this law and engaged Charles Butler as lobbyist. By diplomatic strategy he was able to persuade the legislature, in 1843, to pass the so-called Butler Act, which provided for funding the interest accrued on the $1,387,000 of full-paid bonds up to July 1, 1845, into 6 per cent bonds. It also authorized the governor, when all the part-paid bonds had been returned to the state, to issue new bonds in exchange to the amount the state had received payment, less 25 per cent damages.[17] Because of the requirement that *all* bonds be returned before any exchanges could be made, none of the old bonds were offered.

In 1846 the state sold two railroads, which had cost it $3,363,881, for $2,500,000 and agreed to accept state bonds in payment; full-paid bonds at face value and part-paid bonds at the rate of $403.88 per $1,000. This latter amounted to reducing the damages for

16. *Laws*, 1842, Act No. 60, pp. 260-262.
17. *Laws*, 1843, Act No. 73, pp. 150-153.

failure to pay instalments to 3 per cent.[18] In 1848 the state agreed
to accept *any part* of the part-paid bonds and to issue in exchange
new bonds at the rate of $403.88 per $1,000 plus interest to January
1, 1846, and a slightly lower interest until the exchange was made.[19]
An act of 1855 required holders of bonds to present them for exchange within six months or to lose interest after that date. This
act had the desired effect, and within a short time almost all of
the bonds had been exchanged. By these steps and by small payments from revenues, Michigan reduced its debt to only a little more
than $2,000,000, where it stood at the outbreak of the Civil War.

Total Repudiations

The four states mentioned above repudiated bonds with a principal value of approximately $13,770,000. The amounts were dis-
tributed as follows:

Arkansas	$ 500,000
Florida	4,000,000
Michigan (approximately)	2,270,000
Mississippi	7,000,000

Mississippi received face value for its bonds, Florida received more
than 90 per cent of face value, Arkansas received less than 25 per
cent, while Michigan repudiated only that part of its bonds which
represented payments on which the purchasers of the bonds defaulted. Aside from legal and constitutional technicalities, there
was some justification for the action taken by Michigan, and, to a
less extent, by Arkansas, although the latter should unquestionably
have repaid the amount of money it actually received. With Florida
and Mississippi, it is difficult to see that there was any justification
for their drastic action; the states merely forced bondholders to
bear the losses arising from extremely speculative and very poorly
managed state enterprises.

Bondholders' Activities

Bondholders did not remain idle in the midst of these moves
which affected their interests. They were frightened, and justly so,

18. *Laws*, 1846, Act No. 113, sec. 4.
19. *Laws*, 1848, Act No. 173, pp. 228-232.

by the spreading movement for repudiation and by the reluctance of legislatures to take effective action to meet debt problems. But the situation was a delicate one; the temper of the people was such that too much aggression on the part of bondholders would do more harm than good. Bankers and bond dealers, both here and abroad, were willing to contribute money for the protection of bondholders' rights, but they were anxious to see that the contributions were kept secret and to see that the funds were so used that they would not create scandals.

Thousands of dollars were contributed, mostly by English banking firms, to pay writers, speakers, and lobbyists in Pennsylvania, Maryland, Mississippi, Illinois, Indiana, and Michigan. In general the policy was to secure the services of outstanding and influential men in the particular states involved. In addition bankers carried on extensive correspondence with legislators and public officials of the states. Their efforts to secure diplomatic aid failed. The best and most widely circulated contemporary study of the general question was written by B. R. Curtis at the suggestion of, and from materials furnished by, a representative of the Barings.[20] Curtis was a prominent lawyer who later served as a justice of the Supreme Court of the United States.

Charles Butler and John H. B. Latrobe were two colorful characters who did skillful, effective work with legislators. In regard to his work in Michigan, Butler wrote, none too modestly: "The Senate by a vote of 14 to 1 have passed a bill which I had prepared *in the very form in which I had prepared it* . . . [italics in original]. I am confident that I say but the simple truth, and what is apparent, that it would not have been settled if I had not come; and that no one else could probably have effected it in the same way."[21] In Indiana he worked with legislators steadily for a month, frequently meeting with a committee two or three times a week for hours at a time. Finally, he was able to write: "My labors have been crowned with complete success. The public credit of

20. McGrane, *op. cit.*, p. 163. The article, entitled "Debts of the States," appeared in the *North American Review* for Jan., 1844.

21. F. H. Stoddard, *The Life and Letters of Charles Butler* (New York, 1903), pp. 198-199.

Indiana is restored and her bondholders protected."[22] Latrobe represented the Barings in Maryland and did much to defeat threatened repudiation. Instead of the modest fee of $1,000 which he requested, the company paid him £500.[23]

DEBT ADJUSTMENTS

Pennsylvania

Pennsylvania was the last state save one to default and the first to resume interest payments. Scrip bearing 6 per cent interest had been issued to bondholders in payment of interest in 1843 and 1844. After all other expedients had failed, the state levied a tax in 1844 to raise funds necessary to pay interest. By 1845 the debt amounted to $40,703,866, on which the annual interest charge was $1,789,990. The regular revenues of the state in that year were more than $3,000,000. An act of April 16, 1845, authorized the governor to issue ten-year, 5 per cent bonds in exchange for scrip. Interest on the scrip, however, was computed at 4½ per cent instead of the 5 and 6 per cent which had been promised. By December 3, 1845, $2,481,398 of the new bonds had been issued.[24] Pennsylvania maintained interest payments regularly after that time, but was able to make little progress in reducing its debt before the Civil War. In 1858 the state paid $1,989,244 in interest and redeemed relief notes to the amount of $421,378—a total debt service payment of $2,410,622, which was approximately 64 per cent of total expenditures of $3,775,857.

Maryland

Maryland's debt was over $15,000,000, with an annual interest charge of about $600,000. Resumption of interest payments was delayed by widespread opposition to the taxes levied for that purpose. Repudiation was never a serious threat in Maryland, but a move was made to distribute the state's interest in public works to the bondholders in settlement of their claims. In the face of much opposition, taxes were levied to meet interest requirements. Oppo-

22. *Ibid.*, p. 264.
23. John E. Semmes, *John H. B. Latrobe and His Times, 1803-1891* (Baltimore, 1917), pp. 457-463. McGrane cites many other instances of activities of this nature.
24. Worthington, *op. cit.*, pp. 64-65.

sition to the taxes was so strong that it was often impossible to find competent men to act as tax collectors, and local governments frequently did not make the appointments. Finally the governor was empowered to make the appointments. Difficulties were increased by an act of 1843 which permitted taxpayers to offer coupons from state bonds in payment of taxes. In 1846 all but about $50,000 of the $523,000 received from income and property taxes were in this form. In 1845 stamp and collateral inheritance taxes were levied, and the governor prevailed upon a number of influential citizens to accept positions as tax collectors.[25] These measures sharply increased revenues. An act of March 8, 1847, authorized the funding of accrued interest into 6 per cent bonds. Interest payments were resumed January 1, 1848, and the funding bonds were all retired by 1851. The relative importance of debt service payments is illustrated by expenditure figures for 1849: $170,818 were spent for general or ordinary expenditures, $715,556 for interest on the public debt, and $260,118 for the redemption of funding bonds. Thus, debt service payments constituted approximately 85 per cent of total expenditures. After the funding bonds had been retired, the state did little to reduce its debt before the Civil War.

Illinois

In 1842 Illinois, with a population of about 476,000, had a debt of $15,178,340, incurred mainly for railroads and canals. Annual interest requirements amounted to nearly $900,000. In 1842 the tax rate was reduced from 30 to 20 cents per $100. A proposal to reduce the debt by offering public land in exchange for bonds failed to receive legislative approval. In order to complete the Michigan and Illinois Canal, the state's largest enterprise, the legislature, in 1843, authorized a loan of $1,600,000 with only the revenues of the canal and canal lands as security. Much difficulty was experienced in placing the loan, and it was not sold until the legislature, in 1845, levied a tax to pay the interest on the remainder of the debt. The canal and canal lands were deeded to a group of trustees, to be administered for the benefit of the bondholders. "The loan was effected, and the work pushed to completion. The lands, on being

25. McGrane, *op. cit.*, p. 99.

sold, more than realized the estimated values on which the trust was based, and the revenues equaled expectations."[26]   In the meantime the state had reduced its debt by more than $3,000,000 by exchanging bank stock which it owned for state bonds held by the banks.   An act of 1847 authorized the refunding of the entire debt and the funding of accrued interest into certificates bearing interest after 1856.   Another act provided for the funding of interest accrued on the canal bonds into certificates receivable for certain lands.   Interest payments were partly resumed in 1847 and shortly thereafter resumed in full.   By 1860 the debt had been reduced to $10,277,161.

Indiana

Indiana's debt in 1845 was around $16,000,000, incurred mainly for canals.   The state defaulted in 1841 after failing in an effort to raise funds by the sale of 7 per cent bonds.   In the same year the tax rate was reduced from 30 to 15 cents per $100.   In 1845-46 the diplomatic Butler worked long and hard with the legislature to prevent repudiation.   He persuaded the legislature to pass a bill whereby the state would assume one half of the debt and deed the Wabash and Erie Canal to the bondholders in payment of the other half, provided they would supply $2,500,000 to complete construction.   The plan was to become effective only on acceptance by the bondholders.   Butler was unable to secure the approval of the bondholders; so in January, 1847, a supplementary act was passed. The state assumed one half of the debt, to be refunded into 5 per cent bonds paying 4 per cent in cash and 1 per cent in bonds until 1853; after that date all interest was payable in cash.   For the accrued interest on this half the state issued bonds bearing 2½ per cent interest after 1853.   For the other half of the principal, 5 per cent canal stock was issued, and for accrued interest, canal stock bearing 2½ per cent after 1853.   The bondholders were required without option to raise $800,000 for the completion of the canal. They protested against this act, but to no avail.   It is estimated that they lost $998,100 by failure to receive interest on the interest certificates from 1847 to 1853.[27]

26. Tenth Census, VII, 265.   27. McGrane, op. cit., p. 139.

The state had cut its liabilities in half and now resumed interest payments. In the ensuing years the state did not reduce its debt but rather increased it to over $10,000,000 by 1860. The bonds resting on the canal funds met with disaster. It is claimed that the state broke faith with the holders of these bonds. While it had promised to do everything possible to insure the success of the canal, it had chartered several competing railroads. Soon the bonds were in default and attempts were made to secure state aid. "But politicians waged war against them, and succeeded in getting law after law, from 1852 onward, passed, declaring the determination of the State not to pay the debt. Finally, in 1873, by an amendment to its constitution, Indiana prohibited itself from ever fulfilling its moral—and as many thought its legal—obligations, by resolving that no law or resolution should ever be passed by the General Assembly of the State that should recognize any liability for these bonds."[28]

Louisiana

In 1840 Louisiana's debt was $23,309,246, almost all of which had been borrowed for banks. The management of these banks was considerably better than that found in Mississippi and Florida. About half of the Louisiana banks survived this period, and the others yielded substantial amounts when placed in liquidation. The state repudiated none of its obligations, although in 1843 it provided that stockholders might secure the release of mortgaged property by paying the face amount of the mortgage in state bonds. Since the bonds were selling at heavy discounts, this favored the stockholders at the expense of the bondholders, who protested vehemently. One English paper stated that this was "a more heinous breach of faith than repudiation," and Curtis believed that the act was unconstitutional.[29] The state sold the bank stocks which it owned, and in this way reduced its debt by more than $3,000,000. By 1848, $5,854,616 of the bonds issued on behalf of the banks had been retired by the liquidation of pledged mortgages, and the remaining $12,395,384 were funded. In 1902 a part of these bonds was funded into direct obligations of the state at the rate of 60

28. Stoddard, op. cit., p. 277.   29. McGrane, op. cit., pp. 184-187.

per cent of par value after the courts had ruled that they were a part of the state debt.[30]

RECOVERY

As the states increased tax rates and refunded their debts, conditions gradually improved. In 1843, the year which marked the turning point, New York 5 per cent bonds and Ohio 7 per cent bonds sold at par. In the following year Ohio sold $210,000 of 6 per cent bonds at par, and in 1847 enjoyed a surplus for the first time in eleven years.[31] By 1849 Pennsylvania 5 per cent bonds, which had sold as low as 32½, were quoted in London at 80. Other quotations in the London market about this time were: New York 5's and Ohio 6's, 93 to 95; Massachusetts 5's, 100; Virginia 6's, 91 to 93. The Mississippi repudiated bonds were quoted at 50.[32] In addition to improved state finances resulting from rising commodity prices, increasing business, and heavier taxes, conditions in Europe also helped to strengthen the market for these bonds. The revolution of 1848 and the constant threat of war were driving capital funds to America.

Sale of Public Works

We have already noted that certain states disposed of bank stocks and public works in efforts to meet interest charges on their debts during the period of stress. These included Alabama, Illinois, Indiana, Louisiana, and Pennsylvania. In 1841 New York also foreclosed on certain railroad holdings, at a great loss, when the roads defaulted on payments. Ten years later Pennsylvania voters authorized the sale of the state's railroad holdings which was finally accomplished in 1858. The holdings cost the state originally about $29,600,000. The total investment was increased several millions by the excess of interest payments over receipts from the investment. The properties were sold for $11,000,000 and eventally became parts of the Pennsylvania and Erie systems. Receipts from the sale constituted the only return of the state from a gross outlay

30. S. A. Caldwell, *A Banking History of Louisiana* (Baton Rouge, 1935), pp. 105-110.

31. Bogart, *op. cit.,* pp. 177-181.   32. McGrane, *op. cit.,* pp. 270-271.

of some $64,400,000 on its system of internal improvements.[33] Ohio's great system of canals declined in earning power during the 1850's and before the Civil War became a financial burden to the state. "Finally, in 1861, the public works of the state were leased to a private company for a term of ten years, at the nominal rental of $20,075 a year . . . and ceased to be a burden, except to a slight extent, upon state revenues."[34]   After the war the canals were given back to the state, and all except two or three of the principal ones were abandoned.   The other states retained their holdings for a time, but none of them realized more than nominal amounts from them. Many investments were completely lost when the companies became bankrupt. New York poured many millions more into its canal system during the next hundred years. Tolls were reduced several times and finally, in 1882, abolished entirely. After that date the taxpayers carried the debt alone.

CONSTITUTIONAL DEBT LIMITATIONS

Many taxpayers were rudely disillusioned by the developments of the 1830's and early 1840's. They saw how the abuse of state credit increased tax burdens at the most inopportune time and led to overexpansion, waste, extravagance, and fraud. It was not surprising that they should demand safeguards to prevent the repetition of such events. Previous to 1840 no state constitution limited the debt which the legislature might incur, but within a period of fifteen years thereafter the constitutions of nineteen states were amended to include such limitations.   These acts were part of a general movement by the voters to curtail the liberal powers granted to legislatures by early constitutions. As one writer expresses it, "Criticism centered now upon the excess of government activity, which had brought debt and disaster, and especially upon the legislators who had been the agents of this expansion. Especially bitter and universal did this criticism become in the crisis years of the forties, when, in both East and West, discredited legislatures and governments were denied the prestige and powers granted so freely in the first frames."[35]

33. Worthington, *op. cit.*, pp. 27-31.   34. Bogart, *op. cit.*, p. 401.

35. Bayrd Still, "An Interpretation of the Statehood Process," *Mississippi Valley Historical Review*, XXIII (1936), 190-191.

Rhode Island led the way in 1842 by adopting an amendment forbidding the legislature, without the consent of the people, to pledge the faith of the state for the payment of obligations of others or to incur debts amounting to more than $50,000 except in time of war, insurrection, or invasion. Two years later New Jersey adopted a provision which was widely copied. It provided that the legislature should not incur debts which "singly or in the aggregate . . . at any time exceed $100,000 except for purposes of war or to repel invasion or to suppress insurrection, unless the same shall be authorized by a law for some single work or object, to be distinctly specified therein." The authorizing act must provide ways and means to pay interest and to discharge the principal within thirty-five years and was not to take effect until approved by the people at a general election. As illustrated by these provisions, three elements were commonly present in the limitations: (1) a nominal debt was allowed to cover casual deficits; (2) beyond this, the consent of the people was required; and (3) the state might not endorse obligations of others.

In some states all borrowing beyond the nominal amount was absolutely prohibited; in such cases the constitution had to be amended before the state could borrow. Constitutional limitations were adopted as follows: 1842, Rhode Island; 1843, Michigan; 1844, New Jersey; 1845, Louisiana and Texas; 1846, Iowa and New York; 1848, Illinois, Maine and Wisconsin; 1849, California; 1850, Kentucky; 1851, Indiana, Maryland, and Ohio; 1855, Kansas; 1857, Minnesota, Oregon and Pennsylvania. New states admitted after the Civil War usually included debt limits in their constitutions.

THE SECOND ERA OF BORROWING

The improvement in business conditions and the recovery of state credit after 1845 brought renewed demands for state aid to internal improvements. The states which had not borrowed earlier were generally deficient in railroad facilities, and some believed, in spite of the object lesson which they had just witnessed, that the use of state credit was the proper means whereby to obtain those facilities. Improved conditions in the capital market, both here and abroad, permitted a renewal of borrowing, and by 1850 a second, though smaller, boom was under way. Several characteristics of this period are worthy of note: (1) none of the states which defaulted in the 1840's participated; (2) except for New York, only Southern and Western states borrowed; (3) borrowing was predominantly for railroads; and (4) the pace was slower and more cautious than in the preceding period.

New York

New York, the only state with a large debt in 1841 which increased its debt in this period, borrowed to finance the widening and deepening of the Erie Canal. After 1845 the canal produced a net profit of over $900,000 per year, and these sums, less deductions for sinking funds, were used to finance the enlargement of the canal. It was desired to speed up the work, and, since the constitutional amendment of 1846 prohibited borrowing without a vote of the people, the practice of anticipating revenues developed. Money was borrowed on the sole security of future revenues. In 1849 the legislature authorized the comptroller to sell $3,000,000 of canal revenue certificates annually for three years. These certificates, which were not guaranteed in any way by the state, probably marked the beginning of the so-called "special fund" theory, which will be discussed later.

After $1,500,000 of the certificates had been sold, the constitutionality of the authorizing act was challenged. The court, in a long and carefully reasoned decision, rejected the special fund theory and declared the certificates invalid.[36] Shortly afterward the people approved a bond issue to refund the invalid certificates and also an appropriation of $200,000 of the canal revenues annually to the general fund. Any amounts remaining were to be used to enlarge and complete the canal. Such funds could not be anticipated for more than one year in advance. Loans not to exceed $2,250,000 per year for four years were also authorized.[37] The canal debt of the state, which stood at $20,302,324 in 1843, rose to $27,107,321 by 1860.

36. *Newell* v. *People,* 7 N. Y. 9 (1852).
37. Sowers, *op. cit.,* p. 77.

Virginia

Virginia borrowed most in this period. The state was starting an extensive system of canals and railroads when the depression halted operations. Its strategic location between the South and the North Atlantic region made it a natural highway. Also, demands for transportation facilities came from the region which is now West Virginia. These two factors impelled the state to resume work on internal improvements as soon as conditions permitted. About half of the debt of $33,248,141 in 1860 was incurred for railroads and the other half for canals and turnpikes. The James River and Kanawha Canal, the largest single undertaking, received $10,400,000 of state funds.

Of Virginia's program one writer has declared: ". . . the results obtained were distinctly creditable. For the thirty-five millions which the state had invested down to 1861, it had secured, besides smaller improvements, a canal from Richmond to the Valley and a railroad system which cost nearly seventy millions and which was nearly half as long as that of all New England."[38] The total length of the railroad system was 2,483 miles, of which 1,805 miles were in operation. Interest and sinking fund requirements for the year 1860 were $2,183,001, of which interest accounted for $1,782,165.

Missouri

Next to Virginia, Missouri was the heaviest borrower in this period. The railroad movement in Missouri started before 1840, but for several reasons the state took no definite action before the 1839-44 depression. By 1849-50 the rapid settlement of the Middle West and the discovery of gold in California increased traffic to such an extent that the state felt impelled to act.[39] The first railroad-aid law was passed in February, 1851, and the state embarked on a program of matching private investors' funds dollar for dollar in building a railroad system radiating south and west from St. Louis. Construction progressed rapidly until temporarily halted by the panic of 1857. By 1860 the state had aided in the building of eight hundred miles of railroad at a cost of about $22,000,000. On January

38. C. C. Pearson, *The Readjuster Movement in Virginia* (New Haven, 1917). pp. 3-4.   39. Million, *op. cit.*, pp. 53-63.

1, 1859, two of the roads defaulted on interest payments to the state, and soon were followed by all others except one; they paid no more interest until after the Civil War. For a time the state paid the interest on its bonds, raising part of the funds by short-term loans at high rates of interest, but after the outbreak of the war no interest was paid on the railroad-aid bonds until 1866.

By January 1, 1867, total railroad mileage amounted to 914, for which the state had borrowed $23,701,000. Accumulated interest raised this part of the debt to $31,855,940, and interest which the state had paid on the bonds brought the total cost of the roads to the state to $33,417,887.[40] In order to provide for the completion of the roads the state, in 1868, sold its railroad holdings to private interests for $6,131,496, leaving taxpayers to pay the remaining debt of $25,604,344. This debt was slowly reduced during the ensuing thirty-five years, reaching $4,365,000 in 1902.

Tennessee

Like Virginia, Tennessee was in a strategic position. Traffic from the Great Lakes to the Gulf and from the mountains to the Mississippi had to traverse the state. The first move to aid railroad building was made in the 1830's, but after an outlay of more than $2,000,000 not a single mile of railroad was in operation at the beginning of 1850. This early fiasco made the people wary of further commitments, but as adjoining states completed lines to the state border, sentiment slowly changed. In 1852 and 1854 laws were enacted authorizing state aid to the extent of $10,000 per mile of road, and construction was soon under way. The state also made considerable outlays for turnpikes, but these enterprises were failures almost from the beginning. In 1857 it held turnpike stocks which had cost $992,717 and which had an estimated value at that time of only $294,827. In the same year Governor Andrew Johnson recommended that the state sell all its investments in bank and internal improvement stocks and apply the proceeds to reducing its debt.[41] Although halted by the panic of 1857, construction was soon resumed, and by 1860 some twelve hundred miles had been

40. *Ibid.*, p. 139.   41. *Message,* Oct. 6, 1857, p. 5.

built. The state contributed some $15,000,000 and in 1860 had a total debt of $20,898,606.

North Carolina

The first attempts to gain state support for railroads in North Carolina failed, chiefly because of sectional differences in the state. After the constitutional convention of 1835 had brought about a shift in the political control of the legislature, a different attitude was apparent, but the depression developed before any effective action was taken. In 1848-49 the first state aid was provided for railroads, principally to divert traffic from Virginia ports to the north. A state system of roads, comprising two lines from the mountains to the sea and cutting across the north-south lines of travel which took traffic out of the state, was the main under-taking.[42]

At the outbreak of the Civil War the state had a debt of approximately $9,700,000, almost all of which had been incurred for railroads; plankroads had accounted for $180,000, and small amounts had been spent for river navigation. During Reconstruction the state issued some $15,000,000 more bonds for railroads, most of which were dissipated. Except for two investments totaling $4,-466,600, both made before the Civil War, the state eventually lost all the money spent for railroad aid. Of these two roads, one is now under lease and brings the state an annual income of $210,000. The other road was leased for a long time and brought the state a small income, but recently the lease payments were defaulted and the state-controlled company is again operating the road.

Summary

The states discussed above were responsible for the bulk of the borrowing in this period. South Carolina and Georgia borrowed for railroads to a less extent. Table 9 shows the debts of the different states in 1841, 1853, and 1860. It will be noted that almost all of the increase came in the eight years from 1853 to 1860. The actual borrowing was somewhat more than the increase in the totals shown here, because several states, including Alabama, Illinois, and

42. Cf. C. K. Brown, *A State Movement in Railroad Development* (Chapel Hill, 1928). This is an excellent and complete story of North Carolina's aid to railroads.

TABLE 9
STATE DEBTS, 1841-60

State	1841	1853	1860
Alabama	$ 15,400,000	$ 4,497,666	$ 3,445,000
Arkansas	2,676,000	4,103,056	3,092,622
California	....	3,267,300	3,824,000
Connecticut	....	....	....
Delaware	....	....	....
Florida	4,000,000	....	383,000
Georgia	1,309,750	2,802,472	2,670,750
Illinois	13,527,292	17,000,000	10,277,161
Indiana	12,751,000	7,712,880	10,179,267
Iowa	....	55,000	351,932
Kentucky	3,085,500	5,571,297	5,479,244
Louisiana	23,985,000	9,589,207	4,561,108
Maine	1,734,861	471,500	699,500
Maryland	15,214,761	15,356,224	14,876,958
Massachusetts	5,424,137	6,445,000	7,132,637
Michigan	5,611,000	2,359,551	2,316,328
Minnesota	....	....	318,636
Mississippi	7,000,000	7,271,000	5,753,413
Missouri	842,261	802,000	25,952,000
Nebraska	....	....	52,960
New Hampshire	....	74,899	50,087
New Jersey	....	....	....
New York	21,797,267	24,323,838	33,570,238
North Carolina	....	2,224,000	9,129,505
Ohio	10,924,123	15,218,129	16,927,834
Pennsylvania	33,301,013	40,272,235	37,969,847
Rhode Island	....	....	....
South Carolina	3,691,234	1,925,893	4,046,540
Tennessee	3,398,000	3,653,856	20,898,606
Texas	....	5,341,528	....
Vermont	....	....	199,636
Virginia	4,037,200	12,089,382	33,248,141
Wisconsin	200,000	100,000	....
Totals	$189,910,399	$192,527,913	$257,406,950

Source: *Tenth Census*, VII, *passim*.

Louisiana, reduced their debts substantially in these years. The reductions in Alabama and Louisiana were accomplished mainly by the liquidation of banks, while Illinois realized its reduction partly by giving bondholders canal property and partly through taxation. On the whole, however, debt reduction through taxation was insignificant; the states were not yet willing to assume the unpleasant task of debt repayment.

Bogart points out that in Ohio four different attempts to establish and maintain sinking funds failed. "The most striking feature in the entire history of the state debt of Ohio was the

complete disregard of all sinking fund provisions. Four times . . .
laws were solemnly enacted . . . to levy taxes for the purpose of
accumulating a sinking fund with which to redeem the debt at an
accelerating pace. Each time these laws were evaded, disregarded,
or utterly forgotten."[43] The Virginia law required the appropriation each year of "a sum exceeding by one per cent the aggregate amount of annual interest agreed to be paid" on the debt,
the excess to go into a sinking fund which was calculated to retire
the debt in thirty-four years. It seems that this law was observed,
and by 1859 the sinking fund amounted to $1,083,657.

The Texas Debt

The Republic of Texas began its existence in 1836 with a debt
of about $1,250,000. One of the first acts of its legislature authorized
a $5,000,000 issue of 10 per cent bonds. Attempts to sell these in the
United States failed. In the fall of 1839 the Bank of the United
States purchased $457,380 of 10 per cent sterling bonds. On the
strength of this the Republic attempted to sell bonds in several
European countries, but these efforts also failed.[44]

A part of the debt was incurred to build a navy. On at least
two occasions contracts were made for the purchase or building
of ships at stated prices, payment to be made at the end of one year,
but with the proviso that the amounts should be doubled if payment were not made at maturity. Payments were defaulted, causing liabilities equal to twice the contract prices. The total naval
debt in 1850 was $1,622,405.

Most of the Republic's debt was incurred originally in the form
of treasury orders, audited drafts, and treasury notes to cover operating deficits arising, to a great extent, out of the war with Mexico.
Audited drafts and claims were issued in large amounts in the early
period, and amounted to $7,681,782 by 1846. Some of these were
paid, others were received in payment of taxes and dues, and many
were refunded into bonds after 1840. They depreciated rapidly, and
in 1837 were quoted as low as 15 cents on the dollar. In most

43. Bogart, op. cit., p. 253.
44. The materials in this section are taken largely from E. T. Miller, A Financial
History of Texas, in "Bulletin of the University of Texas," No. 37 (Austin, 1916),
Part II, chap. iii, and Part III, chap. v.

cases the value received by the Republic for these claims was only
a fraction of their face value.

Beginning in 1837 the Republic issued several kinds of paper
money; the total to September, 1840, not including reissues, was
$3,945,500. The money depreciated rapidly and in 1841-42 was
quoted in New Orleans as low as 8 to 12 cents. The amount outstanding in 1850 was placed at $2,716,645. According to Miller, the
Republic's experience with paper money illustrated "Excessive issue, depreciation to the point of worthlessness, old and new tenors,
varying tender qualities, and in fact, every phase except that of a
legal tender between individuals. . . ."[45] In 1840, issues of 8 and
10 per cent bonds were authorized for the purpose of funding claims
against the state. These bonds were receivable for dues, and their
interest was secured by a pledge of revenues, principally customs.
The total debt secured by revenues amounted, in 1850, to $10,-
078,703, but proceeds realized in specie from this total amounted to
only $524,370. Interest had been long in default, and the high
rates of interest caused accrued interest to increase rapidly.

When Texas was annexed as a state, an attempt was made to
persuade the United States to assume its debt, but the resolution
of annexation specifically disclaimed this responsibility, specifying
that the state should retain its public lands for the payment of the
debt. On January 1, 1850, the Auditor of Texas reported that the
total debt of the state was $11,055,695. Scaled according to the value
received by the state at the time of issue, the amount due was about
$5,600,696. An act of February 11, 1850, provided for payment
of the debt in land at the rate of 50 cents per acre. Bondholders
refused this settlement, and the debt question became troublesome.
It was complicated by the fact that the state had relinquished to the
United States the right to collect customs, the revenue from which
had been an important element in the security of the bonds.

In establishing the territory of New Mexico the United States
desired certain lands claimed by Texas. A dispute arose, and in
order to settle it, the United States voted to pay $10,000,000 in 5
per cent bonds if the latter would relinquish certain claims against
the United States for ships, forts, and other armaments. Texas

45. *Ibid.*, p. 67.

was to use the bonds for the retirement of its own debt. One half of the payment was to be paid immediately on the acceptance of the terms by Texas, but the other half was not to be paid "until the creditors of the State holding bonds and other certificates of stock of Texas for which duties on imports were specifically pledged, shall first file at the treasury of the United States releases of all claims against the United States for or on account of said bonds or certificates."[46] The state accepted the terms and in February, 1851, received $5,000,000, of which $1,257,605 was used to discharge debts, $2,800,000 turned over to a school fund, and the remainder used for current expenses. By the end of 1851 the total debt was $12,435,982, composed of $8,700,306 principal and $3,735,676 accrued interest. The scaled or specie value of the whole was $6,847,322.

Further troubles regarding payment developed. Bondholders did not wish to take payment at the low rates provided by the Texas scale. A Texas law provided for payment of the debt not secured by revenues, but allowed payment of the revenue debt only provided the United States would pay over the remaining $5,000,000 in proportion as releases were secured from creditors. Federal officials ruled that the payment could be made only in one sum after *all* creditors had signed releases. The latter was practically impossible of attainment, so Congress, in February, 1855, voted an additional $7,750,000 in lieu of the second $5,000,000. This amount was to be paid to creditors pro rata. After long and heated debate and in spite of an adverse vote of the people, the Texas legislature accepted these terms. Creditors were finally paid at the rate of 76.9 cents per dollar. Most of the claims had been rated at from 20 to 70 cents on the dollar by the Texas scale, while three claims totaling a little over $1,000,000 were rated above the rate received. The holders of those claims lost $123,218 in the settlement, but the state made no move to pay them. By 1860 the state had only a nominal debt—probably about $110,000.

The California Debt

California entered the Union without a probationary period as a territory and found it necessary at the very beginning to borrow

46. 9 *Statutes at Large* 446-447.

funds for current expenses until a tax system could be established. An act of February 1, 1850, authorized an issue of $300,000 of bonds payable in six months and bearing interest at the rate of 3 per cent per *month*. Although the constitution of 1849 limited the state debt without a vote of the people to $300,000, an act of February 27, 1850, authorized an issue of $1,000,000 of 10 per cent, ten-year bonds. Other issues, exclusive of refunding issues, between 1851 and 1856 amounted to $3,200,000, all for current expenses (to be exchanged for state warrants), and all bearing 7 per cent interest.[47] In 1856 the supreme court of the state held that all bonds above $300,000 were unconstitutional. In 1857 and 1860 the people approved the issue of $4,100,000 of refunding bonds to pay off these invalid bonds. Before 1853 the bonds were quoted at about 50 cents on the dollar in spite of the high interest rate.

Beginning in 1851 the state issued about $1,278,000 in bonds to finance campaigns against Indians. A first issue of $200,000 bore 12 per cent interest; the others, 7 per cent. The United States reimbursed the state for most of these expenditures; in fact, it is stated that "As the Indian War issues were considered to be obligations of the United States and not the State, they were never recorded in early records as state bonds."[48] The debt of the state in 1860 was $3,824,000.

The Kansas Debt

Kansas, during its troubled existence as a territory, accumulated a debt of some $381,000, which it later repudiated. The state recognized and paid about $100,000 of warrants which the territorial government had issued for current expenses, but refused to pay warrants and bonds issued to adjust claims.

In the early days of the Territory a great many claims were presented to the legislature for indemnity for money spent in maintaining the laws of the Territory, suppressing rebellion, furnishing military supplies, and for loss of property by depredations. Provision was made for fully and correctly ascertaining these losses. . . .

The territorial statute of 1859, covering these claims was ambiguous, implying that they were to be paid by Congress, but stating that the

47. MS prepared in the office of the State Treasurer of California.
48. *Ibid.*

auditor was to issue his warrant on the treasurer for each claim allowed by the Claims Commission. The auditor accordingly drew warrants for $380,774.13. The treasurer issued territorial bonds on the face of these warrants to the amount of $95,700, the law limiting the funded debt to $100,000. The last territorial legislature took up the matter, and enthusiastically voted to repudiate the whole debt, both warrants and bonds. And almost in the next breath, both Houses in a concurrent resolution, voted to memorialize Congress for a grant on these claims, either of 500,000 acres of land, or $500,000 in money. To settle the fate of these claims, so far as their payment by Kansas was concerned, the incoming State legislature promptly made their repudition [sic] definite and absolute. Congress ignored the subject entirely, and so the holders of the claims were doomed to complete disappointment.[49]

Bond Features and Methods of Sale

Most of the bonds sold in this period bore 6 per cent interest and matured in thirty or forty years. Certain issues of Texas and California bore 8, 10, 12, and even 36 per cent as already noted, but Missouri, North Carolina, and Tennessee regularly paid 6 per cent. New York and Virginia sold small issues at 5 per cent but paid 6 per cent on the major part of their debts. Because of the almost complete dominance of the 6 per cent rate, the average rate paid in this period was probably higher than before 1840.

A peculiar feature of the North Carolina bonds issued to aid the construction of the North Carolina Railroad was their security. The act authorizing the bonds gave them a statutory first lien on the $3,000,000 of stock in that road owned by the state, although the state's ownership of that stock was not, until many years later, evidenced by a stock certificate. The road was profitable, and its stock usually sold at a substantial premium. Shortly after the Civil War the state "traded on its equity" by issuing bonds to aid in the construction of the Western North Carolina Railroad, giving as security a second mortgage on the North Carolina Railroad stock. In this instance a formal mortgage was executed, each bond being given a second mortgage on ten shares of stock. These were the bonds which later figured in the South Dakota suit, discussed below.

49. James E. Boyle, *The Financial History of Kansas*, in "Bulletin of the University of Wisconsin, Economic and Political Science Series," Vol. V (Madison, 1908), pp. 22-23.

Table 10 shows variations in prices of the bonds of different states from 1854 to 1860. The bonds of all borrowing states except New York were selling below par throughout these years. The panic of 1857 caused a drastic decline in the prices of state bonds, as shown by the quotations for October 13, 1857—the climax of the panic. Prices recovered quickly, however, and by the end of 1858 were at or near their highest level of the decade. During most of the time the average price of state 6 per cent bonds ranged from 15 to 20 points below United States 6's.

TABLE 10
PRICES OF STATE BONDS, 1851-60

State and Issue	1851 Oct.	1852 Oct.	1853 Oct.	1854 Dec.	1855 Dec.	1856 Dec.	1857 Oct. 13	1857 Dec.	1858 Dec.	1859 Dec.	1860 Dec.
Calif. 7's	......	......	......	86	87½	82¼	54	65	85	85½	87
Ga. 6's	......	......	......	96	97	98	80	90	102½	102	99
Ill. 6's	61	......	......	81	105	114	70	87	102	101	100
Ind. 5's	78	98	99	80	81½	83	65	79	91	87	90
La. 6's	......	......	......	86	93⅜	90⅝	67	85	95¼	94	78
Mo. 6's	......	......	......	93½	88¾	89¼	60¼	80	90¼	83	70
N. Y. 6's '67	......	......	......	108	114	111	89	105	110	103	101
N. C. 6's	......	......	......	96	96¼	96½	80	90	98	96	77
Ohio 6's, '70	109	110	107	101½	110	105	83	100	107	107	100
Pa. 5's, '77	91	96	100	84	84¼	84⅜	82¾	84½	95¼	[illegible]	89¾
Tenn. 6's, '90	......	......	......	92½	95⅞	94	55	82½	94¾	[illegible]	75
Va. 6's	100	......	......	96¾	96½	94⅜	67	88½	99½	94	78
U. S. 6's, '67-8	......	......	......	118¾	115¾	116	117¾	112	114	108½	99
Average, State 6's	......	......	......	94.6	99.6	99.2	72.4	89.8	99.9	96.7	86.4

Source: *Hunt's Merchants Magazine and Commercial Review.*

The fact that bonds were usually quoted at discounts is at least partly responsible for the fact that many, if not most, of the bonds were exchanged directly for railroad obligations. This was a way of evading the provisions which prohibited the sale of bonds below par. In a similar way, many of the states' obligations were incurred by guaranteeing railroad bonds.

European purchases of state bonds were comparatively small in this period. New York and Virginia sold some bonds abroad, but there is nothing to indicate that any substantial amounts of Missouri, North Carolina, or Tennessee bonds found their way to Europe. It is true European investors were attracted by the high yields in the United States, but they were turning more toward the securities

of railroads and other private companies. Two estimates in 1854
placed the amount of state bonds held in Europe at $72,931,507
and $110,972,108 respectively. In 1850 Virginia reported that of its
total debt of $7,541,294, $2,281,099 were held in Europe, $4,703,268
in Virginia, and only $556,927 in other states of the Union. For
Missouri, North Carolina, and Tennessee the pattern was probably
considerably different; much smaller relative amounts were held in
Europe and within the issuing states, while more were held in other
states. The Eastern states had become more important financial
centers by this time and were absorbing more investment securities.
Also, states were beginning to require banks to hold collateral—
usually public bonds—against note issues. This practice created a
considerable demand for state bonds.

Summary

The developments of the fifteen years before the Civil War
may be summarized briefly as follows: the states which were in default in the early 1840's, except . rkansas, resumed interest payments
before 1850, some by liquidating banks and selling bank stocks,
others by turning over internal improvements to bondholders, and
most of them by raising tax rates. Several states took steps to
dispose of their internal improvement projects and those which
succeeded lost heavily. Most of the states in this group amended
their constitutions to limit the borrowing power of the legislature.
None of them repaid any substantial part of its debt from tax revenues before 1860.

Another group of states—the most important of which were
Missouri, New York, North Carolina, Tennessee, and Virginia—
borrowed more than $90,000,000, mainly to finance railroad con-
struction. They borrowed less in Europe and paid a slightly higher
rate for their money than the states which had borrowed earlier.
They were a little more cautious in their borrowing and undertook no enterprises as speculative as some which had marked the
earlier period, but on the whole their operations were still far
from sound and involved heavy losses.

CHAPTER VI

CIVIL WAR BORROWING

THE OUTBREAK of the Civil War brought to a halt the internal improvement projects then under way and presented to the states another need for borrowing. The indications are that the states borrowed, during the period 1861-70, more than $200,000,000 for war purposes, the Northern states accounting for somewhat more than one half of the total. These funds were of considerable importance in financing the war, but are frequently overlooked by students of state finance. This is especially true as regards the Northern states. In the following discussion the borrowing of the Union and Confederate states will be considered separately.

UNION STATES

Amounts Borrowed

Table 11 shows the amounts borrowed by the various Union states for war purposes. In so far as possible these figures have been compiled to show the total long-term or funded indebtedness incurred. For some states the data are so scant that the figures are subject to considerable error. All temporary borrowing has been excluded; the difficulty of compiling those data from widely scattered sources and the absence of data for many states make it impossible to present accurate figures on that point. In a few states, such as Massachusetts, short-term borrowing reached significant proportions, while in many others it was negligible.

Delaware, New Jersey, and the New England states, except Massachusetts, had not borrowed since the Revolution, but now they incurred substantial debts. Generally the states which had borrowed heavily in earlier periods—such as Maryland, Ohio, and Pennsylvania—borrowed comparatively little for the war. New York had no war debt until 1865, when it assumed local war debts.

TABLE 11

Union States: Funded Debts Incurred for Civil War and Reimbursements Received from the United States

(In thousands of dollars)

State	War Debt Incurred	Reimbursements*	State	War Debt Incurred	Reimbursements*
Calif.	$ 2,800	$......	Mo.	$ 7,547	$ 8,057
Colo.	......	55	Nev.	......	595
Conn.	10,000	2,710	N. H.	6,375	1,258
Del.	1,100	32	N. J.	3,395	2,226
Ill.	2,000	4,087	N. Y.	27,644	4,267
Ind.	2,000	4,378	Ohio	2,627	3,775
Iowa	300	1,500	Ore. (est.)	400	......
Kan.	131	812	Pa.	3,000	4,617
Ky.	2,412	4,876	R. I.	4,000	879
Me.	7,666	1,387	Vt.	1,650	1,121
Md.	4,132	136	Va.	......	48
Mass.	17,614	5,581	W. Va.	......	471
Mich.	2,555	1,228	Wis.	2,801	2,245
Minn.	......	139			
			Totals	$112,149	$ 55,481

*House Report No. 1162, 74th Congress, 1st Session, pp. 6-7.

Tax policies varied greatly from state to state. In the beginning taxes were not levied because it was felt that the emergency was temporary; later some states hesitated to impose heavy taxes on the ground that their citizens were already paying heavy taxes to the Federal Government, while others disregarded this consideration and raised large amounts from taxes. Connecticut borrowed $10,000,000 or more and spent about $12,500,000 for war purposes; Maine borrowed $7,666,400 and spent $11,254,046; Wisconsin raised only $674,659 from taxes and borrowed $2,245,480. On the other hand, Ohio spent a total of $10,410,240 while borrowing only $2,627,039, and Vermont spent $4,736,780 while borrowing only $1,650,000. In other words, Connecticut borrowed about four times, Wisconsin more than three times, and Maine about twice the amounts they raised from taxes for war purposes, while Ohio raised from taxes three times, and Vermont about twice as much as they borrowed. Complete figures are not available for other states, but those given are probably typical of the great variation in policies which prevailed.

Purposes of Borrowing

The states assisted in the conduct of the war in several different ways, each of which gave rise to borrowing. In the rush to get soldiers into the field in the early days of the war, many states borrowed to equip troops. They were encouraged in this by an act of Congress which authorized payments to states to cover "the costs, charges, and expenses properly incurred by such state for enrolling, subsisting, clothing, supplying, arming, equipping, paying, and transporting its troops employed in aiding to suppress the present insurrection."[1] Borrowing for those purposes was dominant in 18'1 and the early part of 1862, but after that it practically disappeared as the Federal Government's war organization took over the raising and equipping of troops. Almost all the states engaged in borrowing during this first wave of patriotic endeavor. After it had passed, about one half of them continued to borrow for other purposes, and those were the states which built up large debts.

Debts were incurred also to assume and pay the direct war tax imposed by Congress, to supplement soldiers' pay, and to aid soldiers' families. Connecticut, Kansas, and Kentucky issued bonds to pay their shares of the tax, while the New England states led in aid to the soldiers and their families. Vermont spent some $3,350,000, or about two thirds of its total war expenditures, for extra pay, while Massachusetts paid out $9,442,000, Maine, $1,963,000, and Connecticut, $2,109,000, to aid soldiers' families.

The most important single cause of borrowing was the payment of bounties. Borrowing for this purpose first became general in 1863 and in several instances continued for several years after the war, as claims were settled and as states assumed bounty debts of local units. The purpose of the bounties was to stimulate enlistment and thus to fill state and local quotas, but near the end of the war and afterwards something of the bonus or pension element entered the question. Discussions arose concerning "equalization" as between men who had enlisted early without the bounty and those who had enlisted after receiving it, or between volunteers and conscripts. In Massachusetts there was a long and bitter discussion

1. 12 *Statutes at Large* 276.

of this question, and the matter was not finally settled until after 1900. In Michigan final action was not taken until 1919, when $50,000 was appropriated to pay the last claims.

Bounties gave rise to many problems and abuses. Thus in New York by 1864 "the bounty system had become highly objectionable in certain respects. Both the counties and the municipalities were offering bounties, the localities bidding against each other in order to fill their quotas promptly. Naturally the recruits held back until competition had forced up the offers. . . . In consequence it was decided that the state must assume responsibility for all bounties. Accordingly a proposal was submitted in 1865 for a bond issue, . . . the proceeds to be used for offering new bounties and for refunding the local bounties."[2] Similar competition prevailed in Maine, and "The passage of the draft act in 1862 did not, as might have been supposed, eliminate the bounty system, because of the practice of allowing a drafted man to furnish a substitute. . . . Actuated by a spirit of justice, many cities and towns attempted to offer bounties sufficiently large to enable every drafted man to hire a substitute."[3]

In his report for 1862 the Adjutant General oi Maine had these observations to make on the question: "Some . . . volunteers were members of our earlier regiments, who reentered the army at this time, only to secure the enormous gratuities so insanely proffered. . . . A large amount of money has gone into the pockets of agents and brokers. . . . Deceptions and frauds in all forms . . . characterized the details of so much of this work."[4]

In spite of this condemnation, the bounty system was continued in Maine; in fact, in 1862 a bounty of $100 was voted for every *drafted* man. In 1864 the amount of all bounties was raised to $300. In 1870 Maine assumed the bounty debt of local units on the basis of $100 for every man furnished for three years of service, and in the same proportion for shorter periods of time, provided

2. N. Y. Spec. Joint Comm., *op. cit.,* pp. 54-55.
3. Jewett, *op. cit.,* p. 49.
4. *Report of Adjutant General,* 1862, pp. 6-7, quoted in Jewett, *op. cit.,* pp. 49-50. For a comprehensive discussion of the bounty question see F. A. Shannon, *The Organization and Administration of the Union Army, 1861-1865* (2 vols.; Cleveland, 1928), II, 42-102.

war. By 1866 Illinois had reduced its $2,000,000 debt to $945,000, and Indiana had paid down a similar debt to $309,000. By 1880 Illinois and New York had completely paid off their war debts, and all except the New England states had reduced their debts to nominal proportions. In that year the total of all Civil War debts outstanding was approximately $32,000,000, or less than one third of the amount incurred.

CONFEDERATE STATES

South of the Potomac the pattern of war finances was very similar to that found in the states during the Revolution. The individual states, unaccustomed to waging war, hastened to raise and equip troops, to foster essential war industries, and to care for soldiers' families. They raised money by borrowing from banks, by issuing treasury notes, or by selling bonds. Like their Revolutionary predecessors, they hesitated to levy taxes. Above the states, the Confederate Government slowly took shape. Its financial powers and policies were almost identical with those of the Continental Congress. True, it had the power to tax, but this power was used very sparingly and very irregularly at first. During the first year or two it was able to borrow comparatively small sums by the sale of bonds, but its main reliance was upon note issues, which depreciated rapidly and ultimately became worthless.

The basic causes of these developments were the penchant of the people for easy money and the fallacy still fondly cherished by an overwhelming majority of citizens and politicians that the cost of a war can be shifted to some far distant future by borrowing. While these were the causes, the situation was further complicated by two additional factors. First, the position of the states in relation to the Confederacy was uncertain. During the first half of 1861 the states had to carry on practically all war activities, for the Confederacy was in process of organization. After that there was considerable dispute as to whether the states should continue to operate their war machines and be reimbursed by the Confederacy, or whether all war activities should be turned over to the Confederacy. Some of the states—Georgia and North Carolina in particular—insisted upon a large share of state control over troops and war activities in general and continued to spend heavily through 1862 and a part of 1863. Since the states expected to be reimbursed by the central government (as they were in considerable amounts), they naturally thought it proper to borrow the funds. These relations were a constant source of friction between states and the Confederacy, and after a time the states gradually retired in favor of the central government.

The second factor adding to the confusion was the fact that in most states financial and other legislation was enacted by two separate bodies. In every state a constitutional convention met to decide on the question of secession. Usually the conventions remained in existence for a year or more and held several sessions. To meet the initial emergency, they freely authorized bond and note issues and bank loans; less frequently they considered tax levies. In addition, the regular legislative bodies continued functioning with many special sessions and were as free as the conventions with bond and note issues. With two such bodies acting separately under emergency conditions, it is little wonder that the finances lacked plan and system.

Bank Loans

In the early months of the war the states relied heavily upon the banks. One reason for this is obvious: it was the quickest method of raising funds. Another important reason in Alabama and Virginia, and probably in the other states too, was that the banks held much specie which the states wanted and needed. Many banks were reluctant to make large loans or to give up their specie, but the states were able to exert pressure by making the suspension of specie payments dependent upon such loans. Since no bank could maintain specie payment, all were forced to make the loans and to give up their specie.[10] In several states the banks were required to loan to the state amounts equal to one fifth of their capital; actually the loans were often larger.

The states continued to incur and repay bank loans throughout

10. J. C. Schwab, *The Confederate States of America* (New York, 1901), pp. 128-129, 142; Walter L. Fleming, *Civil War and Reconstruction in Alabama* (New York, 1905), p. 163.

the war, but it is impossible to give any figures as to the total amount of such financing. The indications are, however, that these loans declined sharply after the first year of the war, both in relative importance and in absolute amounts. Often the loans were discharged, or rather refunded, by the issuance of long-term bonds. In North Carolina, at least, the making and funding of bank loans became one of the principal methods by which state bonds were sold.[11] In the Alabama and Virginia loans mentioned above, the banks made the loans by purchasing long-term bonds. Up to October, 1861, Alabama had sold $975,067 of bonds, all but $28,500 of them to banks.[12] After the states began to issue paper money it was very easy to discharge bank loans with such paper, and this was evidently done, for in the statements of the debts at the close of the war, bank loans are conspicuous by their absence. North Carolina, with a total of $471,368, was the only state to show such loans separately.

Paper Money

The most widely and most frequently used method of raising funds was the issue of paper money. Apparently the issues began as early as January, 1861, when Mississippi authorized an issue of one million dollars of three-year "certificates" bearing 10 per cent interest.[13] They continued throughout the war, but the heaviest issues seem to have come in 1861 and 1862. In the last two years of the war two factors operated to reduce the size of issues: first, the states had lost much of their enthusiasm and looked more to the Confederacy to finance the war; and, second, depreciation had become so great that it was obvious that further heavy issues would make the paper completely worthless. It is impossible to estimate with any degree of accuracy the total amount of the various issues of paper money. Table 12 shows that the amount outstanding at the end of the war was over $40,000,000. The total issue must have been considerably larger than this, for large amounts were funded

11. *Treasurer's Report,* 1863, p. 39; *Public Laws,* First Extra Session, 1861, c. 4, sec. 3.   12. Fleming, *op. cit.,* p. 163.

13. John K. Bettersworth, *Confederate Mississippi* (a dissertation in the Duke University Library, Durham, N. C., 1937), p. 62. Much of the material on Mississippi in this section is from his study.

into bonds,[14] or were reissued after being redeemed. Curiously enough, Virginia, in which most of the fighting took place, seems to have been the state which retired the greatest portion of its paper money. The amounts of notes issued and redeemed by Virginia for three years, according to the Treasurer's reports, were:

	Issued	Redeemed
1861	$6,726,468	$1,726,492
1862	2,212,424	3,032,782
1863	3,718,119	3,175,555

On September 10, 1863, a total of $4,939,016 of notes was outstanding. By October 1, 1864, the amount had been reduced to $3,860,-392.[15] North Carolina authorized a total of $20,170,000 in notes, issued $8,507,847.50, refunded $3,050,540.75 into bonds, redeemed $210,970.50, leaving $5,246,336.25 in circulation at the end of the war. Georgia, with $14,727,275, had the largest amount of notes outstanding in 1865.

The notes of the different states varied greatly in form and text. Some were called treasury warrants, some treasury notes, while others bore no title but merely embodied the promise of the state to pay. Florida issued one series of notes which stated merely that they were "receivable as one hundred dollars by the State of Florida."[16] Some of the early issues bore interest, but this feature was soon discontinued. Often, however, so-called "bonds" were issued in denominations as low as five dollars, with the obvious intention that they should circulate. As the interest on them was defaulted, and as depreciation created a demand for the larger denominations, these bonds were very easily used as money. The deposed Jackson administration in Missouri issued "Defence Bonds" ranging from $1.00 to $4.50, and "Requisitions for Defence Bonds" in denominations from $10 to $100, all of which circulated.[17] With one or two exceptions the denominations of the treasury notes ranged from $500 down to the fractional "change bills," which

14. A great many of the issues were fundable into bonds bearing interest at rates from 5 to 8 per cent. One Alabama issue was payable in 5 per cent bonds at the option of the state. See William West Bradbeer, *Confederate and Southern State Currency* (Mt. Vernon, N. Y., 1915), p. 107.

15. *Special Report of the Auditor of Public Accounts*, Oct. 3, 1864, p. 182.

16. Bradbeer, *op. cit.*, p. 115.   17. *Ibid.*, pp. 134-135.

Legal Tender Powers

Although the matter was the subject of long and bitter debate, the notes issued by the Confederate Government were never made legal tender. The individual states, under the Confederate constitution, were not prohibited from issuing bills of credit, but they could not make anything but gold and silver a legal tender. Thus state legislatures could not meet the strong demand frequently made upon them to make both Confederate notes and their own paper legal tender. But what they could not accomplish directly was done almost as effectively—in some cases perhaps more effectively —by indirection. If the notes were "bankable"—that is, if the banks would accept them—they were assured of good circulation. The states therefore exerted pressure on the banks to make them accept state and Confederate papers. Banks which refused to accept were subject to one or more of the following handicaps: (1) they suffered discriminatory taxes; (2) their notes would not be received in payment of taxes; or (3) they would be required to resume specie payment. Under such circumstances, all banks accepted the notes, and this, together with the fact that they were receivable for all dues to the government, gave them a wide circulation.

Additional forcing devices were applied indirectly. In October, 1863, the Virginia legislature provided that every contract made after that date for the payment of money should be deemed to be for the currency receivable in payments to the state when the contract fell due, unless the contrary was specified. In Arkansas creditors who refused to accept state paper could not proceed against debtors until two years after the close of the war, while an Alabama act provided that the suit of any creditor refusing Confederate or state notes should be dismissed.[25] In addition to these legal provisions, those who refused the notes had to face public opinion, which was frequently harsher and more direct than legal action; they were called enemies of the country and threatened with having their names published or even with physical harm. However, "The most effective threat was enrollment in the army."[26] These devices, together with the fact that metallic money had completely disap-

25. Schwab, *op. cit.*, pp. 100-101.   26. *Ibid.*, p. 101.

peared from circulation, gave the state and Confederate notes about the same status as if they had been legal tender.

Depreciation

In addition to the large amounts of notes issued by the states and the Confederacy, many cities, banks, railroads, and even private business organizations issued bills, especially fractional "change bills." All these of course brought rapid and inevitable depreciation. Space forbids a consideration of this interesting problem here, but it is ably discussed in many histories of this period.[27] An official scale of depreciation adopted by North Carolina after the war showed the following as the value of a gold dollar in terms of Confederate currency at selected dates:[28]

	1862	1863	1864	1865
January	$1.20	$ 3.00	$21.00	$ 50.00
April	1.50	5.00	20.00	100.00
July	1.50	9.00	21.00	
October	2.00	14.00	26.00	

As is usual in such cases, the official scale did not recognize depreciation as soon as, nor to the extent that, it actually developed.[29]

Our particular interest, however, is with the depreciation of state obligations. The general, if not unanimous, testimony here is that state obligations did not depreciate as rapidly as Confederate obligations and hence were always at a premium in terms of Confederate notes. We have already seen that this was true in Florida and Mississippi. Fleming reports that Alabama sold bonds in 1862 "at a premium of from 50 per cent to 100 per cent." In North Carolina the state treasurer reported in 1863 that state notes were at a "substantial premium over confederate notes," and during the

27. See, for example, Schwab, *op. cit.*, pp. 165-185; Fleming, *op. cit.*, pp. 178-183; and Bettersworth, *op. cit.*, pp. 74-86.

28. *Public Laws*, 1866, c. 39.

29. For example, the Comptroller General of Georgia in October, 1862, after quoting the prices of a great many articles, concluded that "$2,000 will not go as far now as $500 a year or two back in the purchase of the common necessaries of life . . ." (*Report*, 1862, pp. 19-20). In other words, he was of the opinion that Confederate notes at that time were not worth more than one fourth what gold coins had been worth a few years before. Of course, there were some changes in *gold* prices, but not enough to account for the discrepancy between his figure and the figure given in the above table.

last months of that year state bonds sold at premiums considerably above 100 per cent.[30]   There must have been a considerable premium on state notes in Virginia, for the governor stated in 1863 that "We have no state bank circulation, we have no state treasury note circulation, both of these descriptions of note having been hoarded as fast as they could be collected by moneyed men."[31]   Georgia notes were, in 1862, "eagerly sought after by all classes, and the Banks and others that hold them, will not pay them out if they can possibly avoid it"; the Comptroller doubted "if fifty persons outside of the banks have ever seen the $100 and $50 issue."[32]

The preference for state obligations was undoubtedly caused by the feeling that the states were more permanent than the Confederacy, but the premiums were accentuated by two other factors. First, hoarding made the notes scarcer and hence more desirable. Second, state officials paid out Confederate notes whenever possible and kept the volume of state issues down. The North Carolina Treasurer stated in 1863 that he "deemed it inexpedient to increase the indebtedness of the state by the issue of these notes, excepting where required to do so . . ." and that "This policy will be continued in future unless your Honorable body shall otherwise direct."[33]   As the result of this policy he issued only $8,507,847 out of an authorized total of $20,170,000.

Bonds

The third method of raising funds was to sell bonds. As already indicated, it would be difficult to indicate definitely where circulating paper ended and true bonds began, since many of the bonds were in small denominations and circulated as money, especially after interest payments ceased. The methods used to sell the bonds encouraged their circulation, since buyers frequently bought under pressure. Banks, which were subject to pressure in several ways, were the principal buyers, often taking the bonds in payment of loans. We have already seen that they bought most of the first Alabama issue. In Georgia they bought $2,000,000 of

30. *Treasurer's Reports,* 1863, p. 40, and 1864, p. 4.
31. *Message,* Sept. 7, 1863, p. ix.
32. *Comptroller General's Report,* 1862, p. 15.
33. *Treasurer's Report,* 1863, p. 40.

the $2,441,000 sold in 1862 to pay the state's share of the war tax. The North Carolina Treasurer reported in October, 1863, that he had sold, since the preceding January, $2,665,500 of 6 per cent bonds to banks "in payment of this amount due to them for temporary loans." In the same period he had sold $979,500 to the Commissioners of the Sinking Fund, and $126,000 to others.[34] The general procedure of the states was to convert all assets of trust and sinking funds under their control into Confederate and state war bonds.[35] The bonds which were sold in this way, together with those forced upon the banks, accounted for a large majority of all bonds sold. In other words, individual purchases of bonds were comparatively small.

Most of the war bonds ran for short periods—ten to twenty years—and bore interest at from 6 to 8 per cent. A little more than one half of North Carolina's large issue bore 6 per cent, and the remainder, 8 per cent. Georgia's largest issue paid 7 per cent. Usually no specific collateral was pledged, but in Florida and Arkansas the public lands were so pledged.

No attempt is made here to compile the total of borrowing during the war period; in view of the state of public records during the war, that would be a most formidable, if not impossible, task. Table 12, however, presents the amounts of the Rebel or

34. *Treasurer's Report*, 1863, p. 38. The Governor of Tennessee reported that, of the three banks in the state, only the Bank of Tennessee bought bonds in the amount he thought proper. He declared that, after extensive conferences with the officials of the other two banks, he "made those Gentlemen clearly understand that if they did not cooperate with the Bank of Tennessee in meeting these financial necessities, that I would compell them to do so, or take the assets of the Banks out of their hands and place them in the hands of a receiver who was friendly to the Confederate Cause . . . the next morning I was informed by the officers of both the Union and Planters Banks that they would take the bonds. . . . I was resolved that the assets of these Banks should not be used against Tennessee or the Confederate Cause, but to the extent necessary, should be used in support of that cause, and should not have hesitated to order the seizure of their assets at any time that I should have become satisfied that it was the only means of securing this result" (R. H. White, *Development of the Tennessee State Educational Organization, 1796-1929*, in "George Peabody College for Teachers, Contributions to Education," No. 62, Nashville, 1929, pp. 276-278).

35. For example, the North Carolina sinking fund in 1865 consisted of state bonds amounting to $2,372,500, "all issued under Ordinances or Acts, passed since May 20th, 1861"; Confederate bonds, $226,200; balance due the fund, $740,012.20; profit and loss, $437,070.32; a total of $3,775,782.52 (*Treasurer's Report*, Sept. 4, 1865, pp. 2, 12).

TABLE 12

CIVIL WAR DEBTS OF CONFEDERATE STATES AT OR NEAR
THE END OF THE WAR

State	Bonds	Treasury Notes and Other Paper Money	Other Debt	Total Debt
Alabama......	$ 5,929,500	$ 7,165,232	....	$13,094,733
Arkansas......	2,000,000	....	....	2,000,000
Florida........	300,000	1,800,000	....	2,100,000
Georgia.......	3,308,000	14,727,275	....	18,035,775
Louisiana.....	....	....	....	13,562,500
Mississippi....	815,680	6,800,460	....	7,616,140
North Carolina.	12,871,000	5,246,336	$ 508,423	18,626,259
South Carolina.	2,241,840	612,142	....	2,835,982
Tennessee.....	5,791,000	....	....	5,791,000
Texas.........	911,929	1,150,000	4,805,091	6,867,019
Virginia.......	630,200	4,901,950	....	5,532,150
Totals......	$34,799,149*	$42,403,395*	$ 5,313,514	$96,061,558

*Incomplete.
Sources: state documents and general works.

war debts outstanding in 1865 in, so far as they can be ascertained.
These figures include only bonds and paper money of one kind
or another; they do not, except for Texas, include claims for supplies, services, and other items which may have been outstanding.
More than one half of the total for Texas is made up of such claims.
For this reason this figure is not strictly comparable with the other
figures; undoubtedly the other states owed sums for such purposes
but never entered them as part of their debts. At the close of the
war, with public records in a most deplorable state and often
scattered or destroyed by federal troops, it was difficult to ascertain
even the amount of the debts represented by bonds and notes.
The amounts of the unaudited claims could have been ascertained
only after extensive investigations, and there was really no motive
to ascertain the amount of any part of the debt since it was all to
be repudiated. Except for Arkansas and Tennessee the figures
given in Table 12 have been obtained from reliable sources and are
fairly accurate; for those two states no accurate figures can be
found.

In addition to the debts shown here, there was the large debt of
the Confederacy. The amount of that debt at the close of the war

is not definitely known. On October 1, 1864, it amounted to $1,149,896,108, of which $541,340,090 was funded and $608,556,018 was represented by circulating notes. In the last six months of the war the total was raised somewhat, mostly by note issues, and the total at the time of the surrender was probably near $1,500,000,000.

Purposes of Borrowing

As a rule the loans contracted by the states were not designated for any special purpose, but were labeled "Ways and Means for Defence" or "For Defence of the State." One important cause of borrowing was the direct war tax levied by the Confederate Congress in August, 1861, on all property at the rate of ½ per cent. A state could assume the portion due from its citizens and was entitled to a 10 per cent discount if payment was made before April 1, 1862. All of the states except Mississippi and Texas assumed the tax and borrowed funds to make payment. South Carolina contracted a short-term loan and proceeded to collect the tax for repaying the loan; it was the only state to make the tax effective in this way. The total amount borrowed by the states for this purpose was approximately $15,000,000.

Other instances of loans labeled for specific purposes are rare. In January, 1861, the North Carolina legislature authorized a loan of $300,000 to purchase arms and ammunition. In 1862 Alabama sold $2,000,000 of bonds to provide for indigents. Undoubtedly many other states borrowed to care for soldiers' dependents and the poor. Several states borrowed for the specific purpose of buying ships and engaging in blockade-running. All of the states raised and equipped troops, especially in the first year of the war; North Carolina and Georgia probably continued this practice longer and borrowed more to finance it than other states. The establishment of essential war industries, especially those to produce ammunition and salt, was another function which gave rise to borrowing.

There was no clear division of functions between the states and the Confederacy, but the latter was expected to reimburse the states for most of their war expenditures, especially those connected with the furnishing of supplies to the troops. Up to October, 1864, North

Carolina had received $8,091,892 as a reimbursement, but was claiming $13,831,515 more. As the states received these funds and paid them out again, they had a turnover of funds which was much larger than the financial burden they bore.

European Loans

Although it is unlikely that any of the states borrowed any substantial amount in Europe, there are indications that a few of them tried to raise funds there in connection with their blockade-running activities. Probably they succeeded to a very limited extent; the facts are not available except, in a very incomplete way, for North Carolina. In July, 1863, the legislature of that state ratified a contract between John White, special agent of the state in England, and Alexander Collie and Co. of Manchester, England, for a loan of money to the state.[36] "According to this [contract] the State issued cotton and rosin bonds, which were promises to deliver cotton and naval stores within thirty days after the end of the war. These bonds were given a ready market value by redemption in cotton and naval stores which were shipped through the blockade, and by the deposit of $1,500,000 of State bonds."[37]

A statement accompanying the *Treasurer's Report* of May 17, 1864, showed that £119,700 had been raised on cotton bonds and £47,500 on rosin bonds. In August, 1865, White estimated that the net amount owed by the state in England at that time was about £30,000.[38] Concerning the $1,500,000 of state bonds which were deposited in England as collateral, the treasurer said: "I have uniformly understood that the cotton bonds were negotiated without this security, and that these bonds were deposited for safe keeping in some Banking House in England to be returned when a cessation of hostilities should make it safer to return them."[39] The fact that even this small amount of financing could be managed under the difficulties which threatened, indicates that millions might have been raised in this way had the channels of trade been kept open.

36. *Acts of the General Assembly Passed in Secret Session* (bound with *Laws,* 1864-1865), c. 1, p. 1.

37. W. K. Boyd, "Fiscal and Economic Conditions in North Carolina During the Civil War," *North Carolina Booklet,* XIV (1915), 206.

38. *Treasurer's Report,* Sept. 4, 1865, pp. 3, 14-16.   39. *Ibid.,* p. 3.

Proposed State Guarantee of Confederate Bonds

One development strongly reminiscent of the Revolutionary period was a movement to have the states guarantee the bonds of the Confederacy, quotas to be determined on the basis of congressional representation. During the latter part of 1862 there was considerable agitation favoring such a move, and in January, 1863, Secretary of the Treasury Memminger formally proposed such action. In March of that year the Confederate Congress passed a funding act providing for the sale of 6 per cent bonds in exchange for treasury notes on the guarantee of the states. The legislatures of Alabama, Florida, Mississippi, and South Carolina approved the idea and expressed their readiness to guarantee their respective quotas. Georgia and North Carolina, however, opposed the scheme. While the plan was being considered, the serious military reverses suffered by the Confederate troops in the summer of 1863 changed the whole outlook. In the fall of that year the Mississippi legislature refused to take the final action necessary to make its approval effective. The other states had lost their enthusiasm, and the whole plan was abandoned.[40]

Interest Payments

A majority of the bonds issued by Southern states before the war were held in the North. Naturally the states felt that they were not obligated to pay the interest on these bonds during the war; in fact, quite the contrary. As one official expressed it, ". . . it could not be paid during a state of war . . . without subjecting the whole to the risk of confiscation, and without giving aid and comfort to the public enemy."[41] Virginia was the first state to

40. Schwab, *op. cit.*, pp. 49-52.

41. *Report of the Commissioner of the Sinking Fund* (Va.), 1863, p. 9. This statement applied to the payment of interest during the war; there were some who went further and argued after the war that the interest which accrued during the war period should not be paid on the ground that a state of war and nonintercourse suspended the accrual of interest. John L. T. Sneed, *Tennessee and Her Bondage: A Vindication and a Warning* (Memphis, 1881), p. 8. This was answered, however, by the contention that the states themselves were responsible for the state of rebellion which prevented payment, and that they could not plead the result of their own actions as a defense for inability to pay (Jordan Stokes, *State Debt of Tennessee,* Nashville, 1880, pp. 12-15). Regardless of the legal points involved, it was most unpleasant for Southerners, in the bleak, calamitous Reconstruction days, to pay to

take formal action on this point when the state convention, on June 26, 1861, prohibited the payment of interest on bonds "now the property of the government of the United States, or held by it in trust, or which are now the property of a citizen or corporation of said government or of any state adhering thereto." Tennessee took similar action on July 1. There is no record of official action by other states, but undoubtedly they followed the same policy.

Released from the necessity of paying interest on the bonds held in the North, the states, for a time, paid interest promptly on the locally held debt. In fact, in 1863, a Virginia official complained that the bondholders who were entitled to receive interest were not collecting it, and that "a large amount of money must be kept idle in the treasury to satisfy creditors who are unwilling to receive it, or who will not apply for it when due."[42] The Treasurer of North Carolina reported in 1864 that many of the bondholders within the state were not presenting their coupons as they came due, and offered one explanation: the coupons were being paid in Confederate notes, and many bondholders preferred to hold on to the coupons rather than accept the notes.[43] Regarding the foreign debt, Virginia, in the early years of the war, made earnest efforts to arrange for payments of interest due in London; but payments were defaulted beginning in July, 1862, "not for the want of means or the will to pay, but from the impossibility to make remittances." Fleming reports that Alabama shipped gold "through the blockade at Mobile to pay the interest on the state bonded debt held in London";[44] the state maintained interest payments on its English debt until January, 1865.

At the close of the war all states had accumulated unpaid interest, but it is difficult to find any reliable figures for the amounts. On the whole, however, it seems that the amount of unpaid interest was small considering the circumstances.[45] In Virginia the Auditor

their former enemies interest which had accrued during the struggle. This explains why bonds which were issued to fund this interest received rather drastic treatment when the debts were adjusted several years later.

42. Report of the Commissioner of the Sinking Fund, 1863, p. 8.
43. Treasurer's Reports, May 17, 1864, p. 6.
44. Fleming, op. cit., p. 167.
45. In November, 1865, it was unofficially estimated that the interest would amount to about $35,000,000 (The Commercial and Financial Chronicle, cited here-

of Public Accounts reported unpaid interest on July 1, 1865, at $5,071,337,[46] while another official reported the amount due on the same date at $6,091,918.[47] The larger figure seems more logical in view of the fact that Virginia had a debt of approximately $34,000,000 in 1861, held mostly out of the state and requiring an annual interest payment of about $2,000,000. In October, 1865, the accrued interest on Tennessee's debt amounted to $5,169,740. In September, 1865, the Treasurer of North Carolina estimated that accrued interest on the prewar debt amounted to $2,500,000, but this was considerably too high; when bonds were authorized in 1866 to fund all interest accruing *through* 1866 as well as some $311,000 of maturing bonds, the total issue amounted to only $2,-439,900. Unless a great many coupons were lost or destroyed so that they could not be presented, this would indicate that the amount accrued at the end of the war was only about $1,500,000. Other Southern states authorized funding bonds to take care of the interest which accrued during the war, but the amounts were smaller than in these three states.

Other Uses of Credit

The above discussion has given some indication of the extent to which the states made use of their credit through the formal devices of bonds, notes, and bank loans. It is impossible, however, to say to what extent they used their credit by such means as diverting income and assets from trust and sinking funds without giving formal obligations in return, incurring floating, unaudited obligations for services and supplies, and other similar methods. Tennessee stopped all appropriations for public schools, including the proceeds of a trust fund, and Virginia, in the two years up to 1863, diverted $1,348,524 from the sinking fund to war expenditures. There is no way accurately to estimate the unaudited claims, which probably amounted to several millions. In addition to these forms of debt, there were the debts of local governmental units, banks,

inafter as *Chronicle*, I, 643, Nov. 18, 1865). This was far too high; one half of that sum would have been nearer the truth.   46. *Report*, Nov., 1865, p. 7.

47. William Luster Grenoble, *A History of the Virginia State Debt* (a thesis in the University of Virginia Library, Charlottesville, Va., 1937), p. 49.

railroads, insurance companies, and others which had issued paper
money and otherwise incurred debts for war purposes. Again there
are no records available, but the amounts must undoubtedly have
been large. For example, it was estimated that the counties in
North Carolina had borrowed approximately $20,000,000 for the
relief of families and dependents of soldiers, and in Georgia "each
county . . . issued bonds and levied extra taxes to equip volunteers
and to support indigent families of volunteers."[48] Taking all these
things into consideration, it would not seem unreasonable to assume
that the unrecorded debts of the states and the debts of local units
and business organizations were as large as the state debts shown
in Table 12. If this is correct, the total indebtedness incurred for
war purposes was near $200,000,000.

Taxation

While the states were raising huge sums by borrowing, their
attitude toward taxation was apathetic. During the first two years
of the war they made almost no effort to increase tax revenues, and
borrowed to absorb the tax levied by the Confederate Congress.
The governor of Alabama in October, 1861, recommended that no
tax be levied to pay the war tax, since the state's finances were in
good shape. Fleming states that "there was a relaxation in taxation
during the war; paper money was easily printed and the people
were opposed to heavy taxes."[49] In Georgia the tax rate on property was not increased until the end of 1862; for 1863 the tax levy
was increased from $1,000,000 to $1,500,000.[50] The North Carolina
tax rate remained at 20 cents per $100 for 1861 and 1862; it was
raised to 40 cents in 1863.

The most extreme cases are afforded by Arkansas and Florida.
Arkansas levied extra taxes of ⅙ per cent and ⅓ per cent for
1861 and 1862 respectively, and also an income tax of 10 per cent.
However, in December, 1862, it gave "the remarkable example of
suspending the collection of state taxes until further notice and
ordered the refunding of those already paid."[51] In Florida "the

48. C. Mildred Thompson, *Reconstruction in Georgia* (New York, 1915), p. 31.
49. Fleming, *op. cit.*, p. 164.   50. Thompson, *op. cit.*, pp. 29-30.
51. David Y. Thomas, *Arkansas in War and Reconstruction* (Little Rock, 1926),
pp. 105-106.

property tax rate, one-sixth of one per cent, was not increased during the war, and the assembly in December, 1861, suspended payment of taxes for the year 1860-61 until the next year."[52] It is almost incredible that legislators could proceed to spend heavily for two years without making a move to increase tax revenues, but this seems to have been the case in most of the states.

Texas was an exception to the practice described above. There the general property tax rate in 1861 was 12¼ cents plus a special 4 cents tax to pay interest on a war loan. In 1862 the rate was increased to 25 cents; in 1863, to 50 cents. In January, 1862, the poll tax was raised from 50 cents to $1.00, an extensive system of business taxes was started, and a small income tax was levied. In 1863 and 1864 the rates on these taxes were increased and still other taxes were levied, including a gross receipts tax on wholesale and retail merchants, so that during the war period the state collected from taxes more than $8,000,000, which was considerably more than it borrowed.[53] Surprisingly enough, Virginia, too, seems to have kept its finances in good shape in spite of the fact that its territory was the theater of war. Between 1861 and 1863 it increased tax revenues by more than 50 per cent, and in the latter year the governor was able to report that "The finances of the state are in a highly prosperous condition—much more prosperous indeed than could have been anticipated, under the circumstances which surround us. The numerous demands made upon the treasury have been promptly met and satisfied. Our revenue is increasing, and the people . . . cheerfully pay their taxes, and thus maintain the credit and uphold the character of the commonwealth."[54]

By the latter part of 1863 all states were facing a desperate financial situation and all began a frantic search for tax revenues. Property and poll tax rates were increased sharply, numerous license taxes were imposed upon business and professional men, and certain lines of business, such as insurance and the making and selling of liquor, came in for heavy taxes. Excise and stamp duties were levied on all kinds of transactions, some of the states tried inheritance taxes, and almost all of them experimented with income and

52. Brevard, op. cit., p. 78.
53. Miller, op. cit., pp. 140-144.   54. Message, Sept. 7, 1863, p. xvi.

profits taxes, aimed principally at speculation and excessive profits. For example, in Georgia profits above 8 per cent were taxed at from 5 to 25 per cent, while in North Carolina profits above 75 per cent were confiscated. But these measures had been delayed too long; it was too late now to realize much from taxes. The Confederate Government had begun to levy heavy taxes and was soon to impose taxes in kind. The currency was depreciating so rapidly that taxes lost a large part of their value between the levy and the collection. In many states large and important areas were occupied by federal troops. The assessed value of property had increased little in spite of the fantastic rise in prices. Tax collection systems were demoralized, and taxpayers delayed as long as possible in paying taxes in order to realize the profit from depreciation. The people had been led to believe that the war could be fought without taxes, and the numerous and high rates now met with intense opposition. The new taxes increased nominal receipts, but not in proportion to the decline in the value of the currency. Even though the states reduced their military expenditures sharply, they could not maintain interest payments on their large debts. It was another display of the familiar pattern of war finance which has prevailed almost exclusively since the inception of large scale borrowing.

Repudiation of the War Debts

At the end of the war the states which had participated in the rebellion found that, although their efforts to withdraw from the Union had been unsuccessful, their constitutions still declared that they were independent of the United States. To correct this situation, constitutional conventions were called to undo the work of the secession conventions. In four of the states—Arkansas, Louisiana, Tennessee, and Virginia—this had been done during 1864 and the early part of 1865 by loyal conventions acting under the protection of the Federal Government. One of the chief problems of these conventions, which met in the latter part of 1865 or the early part of 1866, concerned the action to be taken on war debts. All conventions took general action invalidating all acts and laws directly or indirectly aiding the rebellion, but there was considerable doubt as to whether this amounted to a repudiation of the war debts. Since the states were in no condition to make payments on any debts for some time, the conventions generally were inclined to let the matter rest and take no definite action.[55] The Florida convention at first decided to submit the matter to a vote of the people. But in his directions to the conventions, President Johnson emphatically directed that the debts be repudiated.[56] All conventions except those of Mississippi and South Carolina followed those directions; in those states, opposition to repudiation—or resentment against federal dictation—was so strong that the conventions took no action on the debts, leaving the matter to be dealt with by conventions which met in 1868 under the program of congressional reconstruction.

The loyal conventions which had dealt with the matter in 1864 and early 1865 repudiated by constitutional amendments.[57] The conventions of 1865-66 repudiated by ordinances.[58] Mississippi and South Carolina repudiated by constitutional amendments in 1868.[59] Those provisions all declared the debts void and forbade the respective legislatures ever to assume them or to provide for paying them. The Tennessee provision also repudiated notes of the Bank of Tennessee issued after May 6, 1861.[60] The repudiations left the Southern states with prewar debts of approximately $105,000,000 and the accrued interest mentioned above.

Opinion was sharply divided over repudiation, and many champions of the Lost Cause were bitter in their denunciation of the acts. One North Carolina paper commented: "One of the last acts of the Convention, and certainly the most humiliating act

55. Arguments for this course of action are given in the (N. C.) *Treasurer's Report*, Sept. 4, 1865, pp. 5-7.

56. Walter L. Fleming, *Documentary History of Reconstruction* (2 vols.; Cleveland, 1906), I, 180-181, and Thompson, *op. cit.*, p. 152.

57. For these amendments see the constitutions of 1864 or 1865 as follows: Ark., preamble; Louisiana, Title VII, Art. 129; Tenn., sec. 6 of "Schedule," *Laws*, 1865, p. xi; Va., Art. IV, sec. 27.

58. See: Ala., Shepherd's *Constitution and Ordinances 1865*, pp. 53-54; Fla., Ordinance No. 6; Ga., *Journal of the Convention*, p. 234; N. C., *Ordinances*, p. 66; Texas, *Laws of Texas*, V, 887.

59. Miss., Art. XII, sec. 21; S. C., Art. 9, sec. 16.

60. Later, however, the United States Supreme Court held that the notes had not been issued to aid the rebellion and required Tennessee to redeem them. *Keith v. Clark*, 106 U. S. 464 (1882).

ever performed by a body claiming to be the embodiment of the sovereignty of the people of a state . . . was the passage of the ordinance repudiating for all time the war debt of the state."[61]

We have seen that the banks invested heavily in the war bonds and notes of the states and of the Confederacy. Coming after four trying years of war, the repudiations administered the coup de grâce to these tottering institutions. In North Carolina the banks held $4,000,000 of state war bonds and $3,500,000 of Confederate bonds; all of them were forced into liquidation. In Georgia, "Those that survived the crisis . . . had only part of their capital in banking operations" and the "banking business had to start practically from the beginning."[62] In December, 1865, the banks of Louisiana held $4,627,833 of state war bonds; nevertheless, many of them remained solvent. Generally, however, the banking systems were completely wrecked and had to be rebuilt from the foundations.

Conclusions

In the Northern states borrowing was due in part to the unpreparedness—financial and military—of the central government and in part was a reflection of the fact that the states still thought that waging war lay partly within their domain. In the South those two factors were much more important, and as an added factor there was the desperation that goes with a losing fight. On both sides the excessive use of credit was due both to lack of planning and to the ubiquitous fallacy that borrowing is the proper and best method of financing a war. The borrowing of the Southern states, however, more directly affected the monetary system and thus contributed substantially to bringing on the evils of a deranged currency which were added to the horrors of war. Perhaps abuse of credit is inevitable in time of war. Nevertheless, it is pertinent to note that the states flagrantly abused their credit during the Civil War and that this abuse was followed, as is usual, by financial confusion and economic chaos.

61. *Raleigh Sentinel*, Oct. 26, 1865.   62. Thompson, *op. cit.*, p. 110.

CHAPTER VII

RECONSTRUCTION

LANGUAGE IS not adequate to picture the desperate plight of the Southern states in the years immediately following Appomattox, but a few salient facts will suggest the magnitude of their debt problems.

In 1860 the assessed value of property in the Southern states was $4,363,030,347, including $1,634,105,341 for slaves. By 1865 the slaves had been emancipated, and other assessed values had declined from $2,728,825,006 to $1,603,402,429. The total decline of assessed values in the five years was thus $2,917,005,731, or 67 per cent. The decline in assessed values other than slaves was 41 per cent. Property losses due to the war have been estimated at more than $5,000,000,000.[1] But these figures do not show the full extent to which the economic system of the South was crippled. Thousands of its best young men had been killed and other thousands maimed; thousands more were soon to migrate to escape intolerable economic and political conditions, their places often to be taken by corrupt and vicious soldiers of fortune. Livestock and industrial equipment had been stolen, destroyed, or ruined by overwork and undermaintenance. The banking system was almost a complete wreck, and the currency system had collapsed, forcing a return to barter in many sections.

Agents of the federal treasury were moving in to collect more than $5,000,000 of the war tax of 1861 which had been apportioned to the South. They collected over $2,000,000, in some cases resorting to land sales, before collection was suspended. The agents were never kind; some were dishonest and took more than was legally due, while others were outright impostors. A part of their duty was to seize cotton which had belonged to the Confederate Government. "But since they were allowed 25 per cent of the return of their

1. *Senate Report No. 41, 42d Congress, 2d Session, Part I, pp. 214-215.*

catches, they took full advantage of the confusion of the times and the difficulties of establishing titles, seizing much cotton which belonged to private persons."[2] Further, the Federal Government, from 1865 to 1868, collected over $66,000,000 from a special tax on cotton production—a sum several times the amount of all taxes collected by Southern states in those years.[3] Partial crop failures in 1865 and 1866 added to the distress.

State governments were badly crippled. Any funds remaining in state treasuries at the end of the war were usually in the form of worthless state and Confederate notes. Movable state property, including large amounts of cotton acquired during the war, was seized whenever found by federal troops or treasury agents. In 1860 debts of Southern states amounted to about $90,000,000, against which the states held approximately $70,000,000 in trust funds, sinking funds, and other earning assets. By 1865 the debts had increased, chiefly through the accumulation of unpaid interest, to about $112,-000,000, while the assets had declined to an estimated $33,000,000. Revenue systems had collapsed, and it was only with the greatest difficulty that states obtained the funds necessary to provide the most essential services.

There was great need for state aid to internal improvements. Some projects had been halted short of completion by the war. Those which had been completed suffered greatly. The rolling stock of railroads had been stolen, destroyed, or worn out. Rails had been confiscated to meet military needs, or had been ruined by enemy troops; ties had been used for fuel; and even roadbeds were damaged. Levees and canals also were damaged.

Complete political and social chaos added the final touches to the tragic picture. Deserters and irresponsible ex-soldiers from both armies, together with the newly freed Negroes, provided a constant threat to life and property. Civil authority was impotent while federal troops, when they did not instigate abuses, did little to stop them. Loyal Southerners differed bitterly as to whether they should

2. F. B. Simkins and R. H. Woody, *South Carolina During Reconstruction* (Chapel Hill, 1932), p. 32.

3. For a good discussion of the cotton tax see J. W. Garner, *Reconstruction in Mississippi* (New York, 1901), pp. 131-133.

submit peaceably to their fate or continue their resistance. It was against this turbulent background that the notorious Reconstruction debts were incurred and repudiated.

PRESIDENTIAL RECONSTRUCTION

In attempting to restore the Southern states to their place in the Union, President Johnson favored a policy of fair and lenient treatment.[4] In general, he wished them to take constitutional action to repeal the secession acts, to repudiate war debts, and to forbid slavery. With those changes made and state governments in the hands of responsible citizens, he believed the states would be ready to resume their proper place in the Union. Against constant and growing opposition in Congress, he tried to put this program into operation. Congress first decided that it would not seat representatives from any Southern state until it decided that the state was entitled to representation,[5] and finally took the whole matter out of the hands of the President by the drastic Reconstruction Act of March 2, 1867.[6] This act declared all existing civil governments in the South provisional, set up military government, and required the states to rewrite their constitutions and to elect new state officials thereunder. When all this was done, Congress would consider seating Southern representatives. This program was followed, and representatives of seven states—Arkansas, North Carolina, South Carolina, Louisiana, Georgia, Alabama, and Florida—were admitted to Congress in June, 1868, subject to the ratification of the Fourteenth Amendment by those states. Representatives of Virginia, Mississippi, and Texas were not admitted until 1870.

Technically, presidential reconstruction ended with the Reconstruction Act of March 2, 1867, but since legislators and officials elected under that act did not gain possession of the state governments until Congress recognized them in 1868 or 1870, the latter dates are usually recognized as the end of presidential, and the beginning of congressional, reconstruction. Similarly, although those

4. See article on "Reconstruction," by Howard K. Beale, *Encyclopedia of the Social Sciences*, XIII, 168-172.   5. Resolution of Feb. 20, 1866.

6. 15 *Statutes at Large* 428. Tennessee, the only state to be restored under the President's program, regained its representation July 24, 1866, and thus escaped the Reconstruction horrors which befell the other Southern states.

dates legally marked the end of Reconstruction, they are usually regarded as the beginning of congressional reconstruction, which lasted until the states were restored to the control of native whites in the years from 1872 to 1876. During presidential reconstruction, native whites were in control in the South. They were, in the main, fairly honest, sincere, and moderate. They had some regard for state credit and made an effort, even though feeble, to cope with the formidable problems facing them.

Funding and Refunding Bonds

Not only were the states faced with large amounts of matured principal and accrued interest on their debts in 1865, but they could not pay current interest. Neither Alabama nor Louisiana collected any revenues in 1865 and 1866 except a few license taxes.[7] North Carolina's tax revenues were reduced to about $200,000 per year, and total revenues were not sufficient to pay current expenses. The same general condition prevailed in other states, and accrued interest continued to mount. North Carolina issued $2,231,000 to fund accrued interest and matured principal in 1866, and $2,301,249 more in 1868. For the same purpose Tennessee issued about $2,800,000 and Georgia, $1,630,000 in the same years. Alabama authorized an issue of $1,500,000 in 1865 to meet current expenses.

New Issues

Only three states borrowed appreciable amounts of new funds between 1865 and 1868. Georgia borrowed $1,500,000 for the rehabilitation of a state-owned railroad, and Louisiana, $5,000,000 for levees. Bonds were sold with great difficulty and at low prices.[8] Tennessee resumed its railroad-building program in 1866, and in about three years issued over $14,000,000 in bonds. The borrowings of these three states, together with accruing interest, account for practically all of the increase in debts between 1865 and 1868, as shown in Table 14.

Several states made unsuccessful attempts to dispose of bonds during 1865 and 1866. Alabama authorized $500,000 and Georgia $800,000 to pay their parts of the federal war tax, but federal treasury

7. McGrane, op. cit., pp. 285, 312. 8. Ibid., pp. 312-313.

officials refused to accept the bonds and ruled that the states could not assume the tax.[9] Alabama tried to borrow $500,000 and South Carolina, $300,000, to buy corn for the needy and destitute, but could not sell the bonds. Georgia was apparently successful in selling $200,000 for this purpose.

At least two states attempted to aid internal improvements by a new procedure. Tennessee gave to a turnpike company $425,000 of railroad stock previously acquired. North Carolina exchanged $1,000,000 of the bonds of one railroad for a similar amount of stock of another, and accepted $800,000 of the stock of two other roads in payment of debts owed to the state.

In three years, debts of Southern states increased about $33,000,-000. While this was a significant sum to the poverty-stricken states, it was small compared with additions made in the next six years.

CONGRESSIONAL RECONSTRUCTION

The Plan

The plan of congressional reconstruction, in brief, was as follows: Military districts were set up covering the South, the commanders to supervise the registration of voters, including Negroes, who were to vote on the question of calling constitutional conventions and at the same time to elect delegates to the conventions. The conventions were to formulate new constitutions in accordance with the views of Congress. If the voters approved the new constitutions and if the states ratified the Fourteenth Amendment, Congress would then consider seating Southern members.[10] Congress not only laid down the rules as to who should vote, but issued elaborate regulations interpreting them, thus taking the matter out of the President's hands and infringing upon his executive powers. The military commanders were given considerable discretion in revising registration

9. H. E. Smith, *The United States Federal Internal Tax History from 1861 to 1871* (New York, 1914), pp. 32-36. According to one statement, all Southern states offered to assume this tax.

10. See John W. Burgess, *Reconstruction and the Constitution* (New York, 1902), pp. 118-156, for an excellent description of the Reconstruction plan and its execution. Randall summarizes the plan even more succinctly: "Temporary military rule under Northern Radical control and drastic reorganization of state governments on the basis of negro suffrage, were the main features of the bill" (J. G. Randall, *The Civil War and Reconstruction*, New York, 1937, p. 753).

lists. The result was that "A large majority of the old leaders were disfranchised completely . . . while negroes, 'poor white trash,' 'carpetbaggers' and a few self-denying respectables formed the new electorate for recreating 'State' governments."[11] In five of the ten states the newly freed Negroes constituted a majority of the registered voters. These illiterate ex-slaves were to decide whether new constitutions were needed, and, if so, who was to frame them.

Constitutional Conventions

Conventions were called in all the states. The delegates elected were largely Negroes and carpetbaggers. Burgess comments: "No such hideous bodies of men had ever been assembled before upon the soil of the United States for the purpose of participation in the creation of a 'State' of the Union, and but for the control exercised over them by the military commanders and the cooperation between the commanders and the small conservative white element in these bodies, the result of their work would have been the most ghastly travesty of justice, common-sense, and common honesty which the republic had ever been called upon to witness."[12] As it was, however, the conventions produced very good constitutions except for several vicious and vengeful provisions regarding suffrage and the qualifications for holding office.[13] The North Carolina delegates were so thirsty for loot that they could not wait to gain control of the state government; the convention authorized the issue of state bonds and indorsements to the amount of $3,860,000, including $510,000 to cover expenses of the convention.[14]

Debt Limitations

Most of the new constitutions set limits on state debts and on the use of state credit. In North and South Carolina there were no definite limits, but bills authorizing borrowing had to specify some single object and to receive a recorded two-thirds vote in each house. In South Carolina the bills had to levy a tax to pay interest, while in North Carolina the same was true if state bonds were selling

11. Burgess, op. cit., p. 147.
12. Ibid., p. 150.   13. Ibid., pp. 150-151.
14. Ordinances of the Convention, pp. 44, 57, 62, 64, 69, 71. The latter loan was never made.

below par. The North Carolina legislature was required to provide for "the prompt and regular payment of the interest" and, after 1880, to levy a tax for the retirement of the principal; it was forbidden to lend the credit of the state except to complete railroads then unfinished.[15] The Georgia constitution prohibited any law making the state a stockholder in a private corporation and forbade the extension of state credit to any company except in return for a first lien on all property of the company and unless private investment was at least equal to the state aid.[16] The Florida constitution prohibited the extension of state credit in aid of any corporation. The Texas constitution merely required the legislature to provide for current interest and a 2 per cent sinking fund.

During the winter and spring of 1868 the new constitutions were ratified by the voters in seven states—North and South Carolina, Georgia, Florida, Alabama, Louisiana, and Arkansas.[17] Only in Mississippi was ratification defeated. Tennessee had already been readmitted to the Union, and constitutions were not yet ready in Texas and Virginia.

New Legislators and State Officials

In several states military commanders had ordered voters to choose new state legislators and officials in the same election in which they voted on the constitutions. This meant that all those disqualified by Congress from voting on the constitutions were also barred from voting for state and local officials, regardless of the franchise provisions of the constitutions. Burgess states that this procedure

. . . violated the law and practice under the constitution of the United States. . . . Such officers and legislators could have been constitutionally elected only by the electors designated in the constitution

15. Art. V, secs. 4 and 5.   16. Art. III, sec. 6.

17. Not, however, without some juggling of the election laws by Congress. Originally Congress had specified that the constitutions should be approved by a majority of registered voters. In Alabama conservatives organized considerable opposition and refrained from voting in such large numbers that the constitution received the approval of less than a majority of the registered voters. Congress hastily passed an act "providing that the approval of a majority of those voting, no matter what the proportion of the vote to the registration might be, should be regarded as a sufficient ratification of the proposed 'State' constitutions . . ." and applied it retroactively to Alabama (Burgess, op. cit., pp. 152-153).

submitted for adoption. The qualifications of the electors who vote upon the question of the adoption of the first "State" constitution are necessarily fixed by Congress, but Congress has no constitutional power to fix the qualifications of the electors of "state" officers and legislators. Neither has the constitutional convention, which frames the first "State" constitution any such power, for the constitution which it frames is only a proposition, and ratification by the electors designated by Congress is necessary to its validity.[18]

In a similar vein, Congress, to hasten ratification of the Fourteenth Amendment, authorized the governors-*elect* to summon the legislatures to meet in special session.[19] Even before this law was passed the governor-elect of North Carolina issued his call. One newspaper of the state commented on this move: "This is the first time in the history of the country—perhaps of any country—that an officer-*elect,* and one who is indeed, at present ineligible, performs the function of the officer *de facto."* It further pointed out that the governor-elect derived any powers he had from the United States and not from the people or constitution of North Carolina.[20] Most of the legislatures met in special session in July, 1868. The legality of all such sessions might be questioned on the grounds that there was no proper summons.

These were serious errors and cast a shadow upon the status of the legislatures elected at that time and thus upon all their work. Doubts on this point were strengthened by charges of widespread and general bribery and fraudulent voting.

Lack of words and space prevents an adequate description of the legislators elected at this time. Negroes and carpetbaggers predominated. These were the most ignorant, corrupt, and venal lawmakers ever to hold office in this country. State officials were of the same caliber.[21] Those in control were out to loot and plunder. The credit of the states was the vehicle whereby much of the stealing was accomplished. As soon as Congress readmitted the states the military authorities relinquished their powers,[22] and these bands of

18. Burgess, *op. cit.,* pp. 151-152.
19. Act of June 25, 1868.   20. *Raleigh Sentinel,* June 17, 1868.
21. For brief typical descriptions see McGrane, *op. cit.,* pp. 286, 300, 305, 313, 335-336, 344.
22. The North Carolina civil governor who had remained in office during the military regime, in giving up his office to the Reconstruction governor, stated that he

thieves were free to plunder. The groups controlling Louisiana and South Carolina were the worst of the lot, although those in Florida and North Carolina were little better. Four states—Georgia, Mississippi, Texas, and Virginia—escaped the worst effects of misrule. For special reasons, military government was reimposed upon Georgia for a time, and the Reconstruction government did not have a free hand.[23] The other three states were not readmitted until 1870. In the meantime, more ex-Confederates had been pardoned, had received the franchise, and were thus able to exert some influence.[24] Mississippi's credit had been so badly damaged by earlier repudiation that it would have been difficult to find buyers for its bonds, while Virginia's debt was so large that it was obvious to all that the state could not endure a greater debt. Tennessee, as already noted, had no Reconstruction government.

Because of general inefficiency and dishonesty among state officials, it is often impossible to speak with assurance concerning financial figures during this period. Officials frequently admitted that it was impossible to give accurate figures on debts. Later, when investigating committees tried to find out what had happened, they frequently had to resort to estimates. An Alabama commission had to arrive at the amount of the debt by asking all holders of state obligations to report their claims. Figures for Louisiana and South Carolina are most conflicting and unreliable. All data for this period must be interpreted with these reservations and qualifications.

Political Organization

As soon as the military authorities were removed, the Reconstruction governments rushed to plunder public treasuries. Since those treasuries were usually empty and since the possibilities of taxation were severely limited, the only alternative was to despoil the public credit. This the Negroes and carpetbaggers proceeded to do with alacrity. In most states there was a well-organized "Ring"

---

did not recognize the validity of the recent election, that he regarded the new state officers as appointees of the military powers of the United States, and that he surrendered his office only under military duress (Ratchford, *History of North Carolina Debt*, p. 174).

23. Burgess, *op. cit.*, pp. 238-244.   24. *Ibid.*, pp. 247-249.

comprising most or all state officials, leaders in the legislature, and the officials of banks and internal improvement companies. Such groups usually maintained, in or near the capitols, a "Third House," in which money, liquor, and tobacco were freely dispensed to legislators. They passed such financial legislation as they desired for themselves, and levied a toll on all such legislation for others. In North Carolina the usual toll was 10 per cent of the bonds authorized, while in South Carolina there was "a well-settled tariff for legislative action of this kind most accurately graduated."[25] Only in Arkansas did the voters have a chance to pass on bond legislation. In that state a bill to issue bonds in aid of railroads was approved in 1868, only 4,134 votes being cast against it. "As soon as the law became operative a general scramble began to secure the bonds. New railroad companies sprang up over night, the number reaching 86 by the end of 1871, all of them controlled by fewer than twenty men. The aid was to be in the nature of a loan, repayable by taxes levied on the road."[26]

Bonds Authorized

Legislatures were exceedingly liberal in authorizing bond issues, but in most instances it is impossible to state total amounts authorized. Laws were conflicting and overlapping, and bonds to aid railroads were usually authorized at so much per mile, with no statement or limitation as to the number of miles. For four states, however, there are estimates that may be taken as fairly accurate. They are: Arkansas, $15,750,000; Georgia, $32,000,000; Louisiana, $38,691,000; North Carolina, $29,210,000. These total more than $115,000,000, and show the gigantic proportions assumed by the frauds. In no case were all the authorized bonds issued, and in at least two cases some that were issued were later returned. North Carolina courts prevented the issue of nearly $10,000,000 on the grounds that authorizing acts were unconstitutional. Later, railroads were made to return $4,343,000 of bonds before they were sold. In Arkansas one railroad relinquished $3,000,000 of bonds.

25. James S. Pike, *The Prostrate State* (New York, 1874), p. 210.
26. Thomas, *op. cit.,* p. 425.

Purposes of Issue

Although the primary purpose of almost all the Reconstruction bonds was to provide money for members of the "Rings," some other nominal purpose had to be given. In most cases this nominal purpose was the aid of railroads. With minor exceptions the Florida and North Carolina bonds were exclusively for railroads, while issues for that purpose were dominant in Alabama, Arkansas, and Georgia, and were important in Louisiana and South Carolina. Some roads received flat sums, while others received certain amounts, usually from $10,000 to $16,000 per mile. Arkansas gave $10,000 per mile if the road received federal aid and $15,000 if it did not. Usually some minimum private investment in the roads was required as a prerequisite for state aid, but such provisions were rarely observed.

Other purposes for bond issues were numerous, but comparatively unimportant. Levee construction was aided in Arkansas and Louisiana. Several states issued bonds to fund accrued interest and to refund matured principal. Florida, Georgia, South Carolina, Texas, and probably other states sold bonds to meet current expenses. South Carolina issued over $1,500,000 to fund the bills of a state bank and $700,000 for the use of a land commission, which had been formed to assist those who wished or were forced to sell their lands and also to aid Negroes and settlers to acquire lands. It proved to be a "gigantic folly" and an instrument of fraud. In 1874 Texas authorized the issue of 10 per cent bonds to fund pensions due to veterans of the Texas Revolution. Ultimately over $1,100,000 of such bonds were issued.

Fraud

Gross fraud and corruption attended the authorization and sale of the Reconstruction bonds. First, legislators were bribed to pass the authorizing acts. The Alabama legislature granted $2,000,000 to the Alabama and Chattanooga Railroad as the result of bribery.[27] It was generally understood in Louisiana that "anyone who wanted to get a bill through had to pay for it," and Governor Warmoth

27. Fleming, *Civil War and Reconstruction in Alabama*, p. 594.

publicly declared that he had offered bribes.[28] In North Carolina, G. W. Swepson paid $241,713 in cash plus some bonds to secure legislation aiding one road. Every road in the state except one paid for legislation.[29] In South Carolina it was stated that "No act was passed there, other than of a purely legal character, that the Legislature was not bribed to pass ... the members of the Senate and the House of Representatives, as well as the officials do not hesitate openly to charge each other with fraud and corruption."[30]

Second, there was fraud in the issuing of the bonds. In both Alabama and Georgia the records were in such shape that it was impossible to tell how many bonds had been issued to the financial agents of the states or what disposition had been made of them. Bonds which could not be sold were hypothecated for loans of a small fraction of their face value. Governor Bullock of Georgia issued bonds to railroads before a mile of line was completed, although the law required the completion of 20-mile sections for indorsements. The American Bank Note Company printed South Carolina bonds in an amount far exceeding amounts authorized; it was charged that the overissue amounted to $6,314,000.[31]

Third, there were fraud and criminal carelessness in disposing of the proceeds of bond sales. Bonds intended for railroads were frequently given to the presidents of those roads personally instead of to treasurers or other proper financial officials. Several of the presidents formed a pool, using state bonds as margin, and speculated on the New York Stock Exchange. It is reported that they lost between $300,000 and $400,000 in the gold panic of Black Friday. Some bonds were used to buy chips in New York gambling houses, and it was reported that some were used to pay New York prostitutes. Two investigating committees found that North Carolina railroads had disposed of approximately $13,000,000 of state bonds for $4,049,063, of which only $1,904,272 had been spent on the roads.[32] The $4,000,000 of railroad bonds indorsed by Florida were sold in Holland for about $2,800,000.

28. McGrane, op. cit., p. 313.
29. Greensboro (N. C.) Patriot, Sept. 20, 1876.
30. Pike, op. cit., pp. 207-210.
31. Simkins and Woody, op. cit., p. 160.
32. Ratchford, History of North Carolina Debt, p. 195.

Only a small part of the proceeds went to the improvement of the railroads. Littlefield's expense account as agent in England for a few months was in round numbers $24,000, while a fourth as much was paid to agents of Hopkins and Company; $200,000 to Bayne and Company, London; $50,000 to Swepson; $350,000 to the Western Division of the Western Carolina Railway Company [controlled by Swepson]; $48,600 to the commissioners of that company; and $223,-750 to Governor Reed: these were some of the items accounted for, while the amount said to have been spent for bettering the Florida roads was only about $308,000.[33]

In Alabama, Georgia, and South Carolina state officials and financial agents received large sums for which they never accounted.[34]

Such flagrant abuses and glaring frauds did not pass unnoticed by the decent elements in the South. Though helpless politically, Southern leaders and newspapers gave notice to the world that these debts would never be honored. While Florida was trying to sell its bonds, "there appeared in the New York *World* of June 15, 1870, an article written to the editor from Florida, stating that the $4,000,-000 worth of bonds were a fraud and would be repudiated by the people of Florida." The writer pointed out that the bonds were unconstitutional and that their issue was procured by "corruption on the part of both the legislative and executive branches of the state government."[35] Louisiana taxpayers printed a pamphlet in French, German, and English and circulated it in this country and abroad, proclaiming that parts of the debts of that state were illegal and void.[36] A bold North Carolina Senator, on the floor of the Senate in 1868, stated that "one of the most gigantic swindles is on

33. Brevard, *op. cit.*, II, 156-157.

34. The firm of Henry Clews and Company, of New York, acted as financial agents for Alabama, Georgia, and North Carolina and figured in many shady deals. Their reports were always meager and incomplete and often gave evidence of fraud. In one case the Governor of Alabama gave the firm twelve notes amounting to $299,-660, with $650,000 of state bonds as collateral. Clews and Company made a "fictitious sale" of the bonds and a year later presented to the state the $299,660 in notes, and a claim for "balance due" of $235,039 plus interest. These with the $650,-000 of bonds which were still outstanding, made a total of $1,184,689 (*Report of the Commissioners to Adjust and Liquidate the Indebtedness of the State of Alabama*. Montgomery, 1876, pp. 15-16).

35. C. K. Brown, "The Florida Investments of George W. Swepson," *North Carolina Historical Review*, V (1928), 281.

36. McGrane, *op. cit.*, pp. 316-317.

foot that men were ever made victims to . . ." and warned that the
bonds would not be paid. Newspapers of the state protested long
and bitterly, and warnings were printed in current New York
papers.[37] South Carolina newspapers protested and issued solemn
warnings; even then the bonds were sold.[38]

Debt Service

When Reconstruction governments took charge, Southern states
were paying only a part, if any, of the interest due on their debts.
If large amounts of bonds were to be sold, some provision must be
made for current interest. The usual procedure was to issue funding
bonds to clear up accrued interest and then, by some device or other,
to raise cash for current interest payments. In Arkansas the first
move was to authorize conversion bonds to fund the state debt,
including the Holford bonds, and accrued interest since 1841. In
Florida it was conveniently rumored that the state would recognize
the territorial bonds repudiated in the 1840's. The Governor of
Louisiana was authorized to negotiate a loan to provide any funds
needed to pay interest in 1870. The Treasurer of North Carolina
was authorized to borrow at 8 per cent for this purpose, pledging
the first money received from 1869 taxes as security, but he was
unable to find a lender, and the state defaulted on January 1, 1869,
only three months after resuming interest payments. Railroads receiving state bonds were required to pay to the state, at the different
interest dates, the full amount of interest due on such bonds for the
first year and one half that amount for the second year. The treasurer was to withhold bonds to the amount of twice the payments.[39]
The carpetbaggers knew how to sell wildcat securities! A South
Carolina act of 1869 required the payment of interest on state
obligations in gold or silver coin.[40]

Revenue possibilities were limited. Many of the debts were sup-
posedly self-supporting in that the states received railroad securities
in return for bonds, but the roads were not in a condition to pay

37. Ratchford, *History of North Carolina Debt*, pp. 186-187.
38. Simkins and Woody, *op. cit.*, p. 164.
39. Ratchford, *History of North Carolina Debt*, pp. 182, 187.
40. *Tenth Census*, VII, 570.

interest or dividends. North Carolina received dividends from one railroad, and South Carolina received a total of 3 per cent in dividends from one road during this whole period. The Western and Atlantic Railroad returned a fair profit to Georgia. But these were exceptions; as a rule, the state investments were total losses. The prospects for tax revenues were not much better, but the legislatures did their best by raising rates. Debts were increasing so rapidly, however, that interest requirements grew faster than revenues.

Although tax revenues were doubled or trebled in Alabama, total revenues in 1874 were only about one half enough to pay interest.[41] The tax rate in Louisiana increased from 37½ cents per $100 in 1865 to $2.15 in 1871. In North Carolina, revenues increased from about $200,000 in 1867 to nearly $900,000 in 1870, but were still less than one half enough to meet all interest payments. In Mississippi the tax rate rose from 10 cents per $100 in 1867 to $1.40 in 1874. Tax revenues increased about fourfold in South Carolina and Texas.

Forms of Obligations

Most state obligations were in the form of direct state bonds or state guarantees of railroad company bonds. Practically all of the debts of Arkansas, Florida, North Carolina, and Texas were represented by direct bonds, while the debts of Alabama, Georgia, Louisiana, and South Carolina included many contingent liabilities in the form of indorsed bonds. The debt of Georgia, for example, was made up of $12,450,000 of state bonds and $5,733,000 of indorsed railroad bonds. In several instances Louisiana indorsed the second mortgage bonds of railroads. Frequently no accurate records were kept of the amounts of bonds indorsed.

Except for approximately $5,000,000 of Georgia gold bonds, and one issue of $1,192,000 of Alabama bonds in 1873, all of the bonds were apparently currency bonds. One issue of South Carolina sterling bonds to the amount of £1,200,000 was printed but never sold.

The prevailing nominal rate of interest was from 6 to 8 per cent, although this meant little in view of the large discounts at which most of the bonds were sold. An Alabama law of 1865 authorized 8

41. Fleming, op. cit., p. 191.

per cent if dollar bonds were issued, or 6 per cent if they were sterling bonds. Georgia paid 7 per cent on several issues, and Texas issued some 10 per cent bonds. Most authorizing acts set 8 per cent as the limit for interest.

Scrip and warrants of various kinds made up unfunded debts, which reached substantial size in several states. Florida issued $50,000 in scrip to pay the expenses of the constitutional convention of 1867. It circulated and "encouraged speculation and graft and enormously decreased the revenues of the state."[42] South Carolina issued $1,800,000 of scrip in exchange for $4,000,000 of state bonds which had been issued to the Blue Ridge Railroad and which the road could not sell. It was receivable for all taxes and dues to the state, and the treasurer could pay it out on all claims except interest on the debt. In 1872 the state supreme court held the scrip void because it violated the section of the Federal Constitution forbidding the emission of bills of credit. Shortly thereafter the legislature repealed the act levying a tax for the redemption of the scrip, thus, in effect, repudiating the issue.[43] Years later the Supreme Court of the United States ruled the scrip invalid on the grounds that it had been issued in contravention of the state constitution and that it was a bill of credit within the prohibition of the Federal Constitution.[44]

In most states, especially in Arkansas, Georgia, Louisiana, and Texas, there were large amounts of warrants outstanding at different times. These usually depreciated, and in Texas were quoted as low as 50 cents on the dollar. Speculation in warrants, sometimes with public funds, was a frequent source of profit for state officials. In South Carolina members of the "Ring" organized a bank, secured the custody of state funds, and then charged a liberal discount for cashing state warrants.[45] It was charged that in Georgia and South Carolina the overissue of warrants for the payment of salaries was a common form of fraud, and that in the latter state it amounted at one time to almost $1,000,000. In Ar-

42. W. W. Davis, *The Civil War and Reconstruction in Florida* (New York, 1913), p. 679.
43. Simkins and Woody, *op. cit.*, pp. 208-221.
44. *Lee* v. *Robinson*, 196 U. S. 64 (1904).
45. Simkins and Woody, *op. cit.*, pp. 160-161.

kansas, treasury certificates and warrants amounted to $1,100,000 in 1873, and in Louisiana the total was $1,922,593 in 1874.

Bond Prices

After the war the bonds of Southern states were naturally selling below par, and as the Reconstruction governments piled up additional debts, prices went lower. Alabama's credit was good at the beginning, and its bonds were sold for fairly good prices. As late as 1873 its bonds were quoted at 60.[46] Georgia, too, maintained its credit fairly well and sold many bonds at prices between 80 and 90. In Louisiana conditions were worse, and by 1872 bonds of that state were selling below 50. But bonds of North and South Carolina fell to the lowest levels. Many North Carolina bonds were sold in 1869 for prices ranging from 60 to below 25, and by April, 1870, they were as low as 21; in New York they were "for sale on almost every corner of the streets . . . hawked about the streets like stale fish from the market."[47] When the Reconstruction government took charge in South Carolina, bonds were selling at about 60. By the end of 1872 they were down to 25, and eventually were quoted as low as 15. The proceeds realized from the sale of $8,057,500 of bonds were only $3,442,127.[48] Table 13 has been constructed to show the price movements of certain Southern bonds as quoted in New York. The figures show, for each year, the average price for an issue of prewar bonds and an issue of Reconstruction bonds. Quotations on New York and Ohio bonds are given for comparison.

Foreign Bond Sales

In spite of their unfavorable experience with state bonds before the Civil War and in spite of frequent warnings by London newspapers, European investors bought considerable amounts of Reconstruction bonds. Because of its favorable record of interest payments, Alabama enjoyed better credit, both here and abroad, than any other Southern state. In 1869 an 8 per cent Alabama issue for £1,040,000 was sold in London at 81, and the following year

46. McGrane, op. cit., p. 287.
47. Ratchford, History of North Carolina Debt, pp. 189-190.
48. Simkins and Woody, op. cit., pp. 152-153.

TABLE 13

PRICES OF STATE BONDS, 1866-76

(Averages of prices quoted on or near March 15, June 15, September 15, and December 15 of each year, as given in the *Commercial and Financial Chronicle*)

State and Issue	1866	1867	1868	1869	1870	1871	1872	1873	1874	1875	1876
Alabama.......Old 5's.	....	....	....	64	71	66	60	45	34	33	32
New 8's.	....	....	....	94	99½	100½	89	63	47	33	31
Georgia........Old 6's.	103½	71	79½	82	82	85	77	71	76	90	93½
Louisiana......Old 6's.	....	....	....	70	73½	70	57	44	22	35	42
New 7's.	....	....	....	60	70	60	47	41	22	35	42
North Carolina.Old 6's.	70	53	70	53	48	43	37	27	22½	18½	16
Special Tax	....	....	....	39	23	18	14½	11½	7	3	1
South Carolina.Old 6's.	....	....	....	71	88	70	50½	26	26	31	34
New 6's.	....	....	....	67½	76	56	28	15	16	30	34
Tennessee......Old 6's.	81	66	70	60	61	69	72	80	61	64	44
New 6's.	....	....	....	47	58	69	72	80	61	64	43
Virginia........Old 6's.	61½	47	56	56	68½	65	49½	41	32	36	29
New....	....	....	....	55½	66	69	55	68	33	36	29
New York General Fund 6's.	....	99½	101	103	106	107	106	106	103	101½	103
Ohio.............. 5's.	98½	102	101	101½	101½	105	102½	101½	103	100½	105½

another 8 per cent issue of £400,000 was sold at 94½, a total of approximately $7,000,000.[49] In 1874 an Arkansas representative tried to sell Arkansas bonds in London, attempting to win the confidence of English investors by a series of letters in the London *Times*. "None of the Arkansas loans were favorably received in London, although some of them were floated in Amsterdam."[50]

A large block of Florida bonds was sold in Holland: "Endeavors were made to sell them in London, Paris, Brussels, Frankfort and Vienna. Everywhere the story of fraud preceded the salesmen. Finally, John Collinson, of London, succeeded in disposing of $2,800,000 worth of them in Holland, by forming a Dutch syndicate to take them over. . . . It seems obvious that the syndicate took the bonds as a speculative venture, for the story of fraud and corruption

49. Cleona Lewis, *America's Stake in International Investments* (Washington, 1938), p. 58.

50. McGrane, *op. cit.*, p. 293.

was circulated in Holland as in other countries of Europe."[51] Later 206 more bonds were sold to the Dutch, making a total of $3,006,000.

Georgia bonds were admitted to dealings on the London, Berlin, and Frankfort exchanges. Henry Clews claimed that when the bonds of the Brunswick and Albany Railroad, indorsed by Georgia, were offered at 104 in Berlin and Frankfort the subscriptions were so heavy that it was necessary to allot the bonds pro rata among the bidders. A Georgia investigating committee in New York in 1872 received sworn statements from European investors that they held about $4,000,000 of Georgia bonds.[52] No figures were given to show what part of these were post-war bonds, but elsewhere it was stated that $1,716,000, par value, of Georgia bonds were sold in Europe between January, 1870, and October, 1871, for $1,459,583.[53] There are scattered references to Louisiana bonds held in Holland, but no figures are available. The face value of bonds sold abroad was probably in the neighborhood of $12,000,000.

The Tennessee Debt

Although spared from some of the worst phases of Reconstruction, Tennessee still had plenty of debt troubles. At the end of the war the debt, including contingent liabilities and accrued interest, was $25,277,000, and ranked second only to Virginia's in the South. Undaunted, the state entered upon a vigorous campaign to complete its railroad program. By 1870 the debt reached $43,052,625. An act of February 25, 1869, allowed the railroads to cancel their obligations to the state under the indorsed bonds by offering, at face value, state bonds *of any issue*. The roads were allowed to issue first mortgage bonds to the amount of the bonds so offered, transferring the first liens held by the state to the holders of the railroad bonds. Since post-war state bonds were selling at 65 or lower, solvent railroads quickly accepted this opportunity to reduce their liabilities, and in a short time paid to the state over $14,000,000 in bonds, about $10,000,000 of which were post-war issues. In this way the debt of the state was reduced to $27,920,386 by 1874.[54]

51. Brown, *op. cit.*, p. 282.   52. McGrane, *op. cit.*, p. 306.

53. *Report of the Committee of the Legislature to Investigate the Bonds* (Atlanta, 1872), pp. 65-67.

54. *Biennial Report of the Treasurer of the State*, 1930, p. 9.

The railroads engaged in a campaign to cast doubts on the validity of the post-war issues and thus to drive down the price; ". . . at least one newspaper was paid to cast suspicion on, and depreciate the post-bellum bonds."[55] Many citizens of the state opposed the act, feeling that each road should have been required to offer the same bonds issued for its benefit. The deliberate attempt of the roads to depreciate state bonds for their own profit greatly intensified this opposition, and soon the state was seething over the debt issue. In 1872 the legislature authorized the sale of roads delinquent in their payments to the state. Eleven roads, which had received state aid to the amount of $14,648,000, were sold for a total of $6,698,000, the state taking a loss of $7,950,000.

The state defaulted on interest payments in 1870 and thereafter paid interest only intermittently. In 1873 the legislature passed a funding bill providing for funding *all legally issued bonds* and all unpaid interest coupons up to January 1, 1874, into 6 per cent, 40-year bonds, but failed to levy taxes to meet interest requirements. Since revenues were not sufficient to service the debt, only about one fourth of the bonds was converted. Thus the matter remained for some time. On December 19, 1879, the total debt was $24,274,017, including over $4,000,000 of accrued interest.[56]

Debts at End of Reconstruction

Table 14 shows the debts of the Southern states: (1) in 1865, as near the close of the war as possible; (2) at the time the Reconstruction governments took control; and (3) at the time the Reconstruction governments were driven out. There is so much doubt and uncertainty concerning the correct figures for several states at the latter date that it is necessary to give some brief explanations and to indicate the sources of the data. All of the figures represent gross debt and include, so far as possible, accrued interest.

The figures for Alabama and Georgia are those arrived at by committees appointed to investigate the debt.[57] The figure for

55. J. W. Caldwell, *Studies in the Constitutional History of Tennessee* (Cincinnati, 1907), p. 251.

56. McGrane, *op. cit.,* pp. 360-361.

57. Alabama, *Report of the Commissioners to Adjust and Liquidate the Indebtedness,* 1876, p. 21; Ga., *Report of the Committee to Investigate the Bonds,* 1872, p. 14.

Arkansas is dated January 6, 1873;[58] the Democrats did not regain power until 1874, when the debt was somewhat larger than the amount indicated. The Florida figure was found by adding $4,000,-000, the amount of the debts repudiated by that state, to the debt of the state in January, 1874, as reported by the Comptroller.[59] The figure for Mississippi is the gross debt on January 1, 1875, as given by the auditor.[60] The North Carolina figure is that given by the State Treasurer.[61] The figure for Texas is that given by Miller.[62] There is no dispute concerning the figures for Tennessee and Virginia; they are taken from official sources.

It is much more difficult to secure satisfactory figures for Louisiana and South Carolina. It is well established that the state debt proper of Louisiana on January 1, 1874, was $24,356,339, and that the state was contingently liable for $4,803,083 of bonds issued to banks before the war.[63] Beyond this the state was contingently liable for a large amount of the bonds, but it is impossible to state the exact amount. In 1874 a citizens' investigating committee put the total at about $30,000,000,[64] but that included bonds which the state might be called upon to issue. A careful study of all available data seems to indicate that the debt on January 1, 1874, was: state debt proper, $24,356,339; contingent liability on bank bonds, $4,803,-083; other contingent liabilities, $7,200,000, making a total of approximately $36,356,000.

The figure most frequently quoted for South Carolina is that stated by a legislative committee in 1872—$29,158,914. But this sum included the $6,000,000 of sterling bonds which were never issued.[65] Pike states that the debt was possibly as much as $33,900,000.[66] The correct amount seems to be $23,158,914, including $6,787,608 of contingent liabilities, but exclusive of floating debt in the form of warrants and scrip.[67]

58. W. C. Evans, The Public Debt of Arkansas: Its History from 1836 to 1885 (an unpublished thesis in the Library of the University of Arkansas, Fayetteville, 1928), p. 81.
59. Tenth Census, VII, 589.   60. Garner, op. cit., p. 321.
61. Ratchford, History of North Carolina Debt, p. 332.
62. Miller, op. cit., p. 238.
63. Stephen A. Caldwell, A Banking History of Louisiana (Baton Rouge, 1935), pp. 104-107.   64. McGrane, op. cit., p. 318.
65. Pike, op. cit., p. 130.   66. Ibid., p. 125.
67. The railroad scrip mentioned above was not issued until after this time.

If these figures are correct, the total of all debts in 1874 was $247,578,000, an increase of $101,232,000 over the total of $146,346,000 for 1868. Included in this, however, is the decrease of about $12,000,000 by Tennessee; so the actual increase in the other states was about $113,209,000. This was a part of the price for six years of misrule.

TABLE 14

DEBTS OF SOUTHERN STATES, 1865-74

(In thousands of dollars)

State	Debt, 1865	Debt at Beginning of Reconstruction (1868-70)	Debt at End of Reconstruction (1872-74)
Alabama.........	$4,065	$ 6,848	$ 30,038
Arkansas........	4,528	4,821	13,612 (1873)
Florida..........	1,371	1,524	5,446
Georgia..........	2,800	6,544	18,183
Louisiana........	11,182	17,347	36,356
Mississippi.......	1,100	1,177 (1870)	3,750 (1875)
North Carolina...	13,869	15,345	38,922
South Carolina...	5,160	5,841	23,159
Tennessee........	25,277	39,897 (1869)	27,920
Texas............	1,000	1,129	3,167
Virginia.........	41,061	45,873	47,025
Totals......	$111,413	$146,346	$247,578

Sources: See text.

REPUDIATION AND REFUNDING

When the Democrats had succeeded, slowly and painfully, in wresting control from the carpetbaggers, they proceeded to make good their warnings that the Reconstruction debts would not be paid. In several instances they went farther and scaled down the debt incurred before Reconstruction. The usual procedure was, as soon as the Reconstruction government was overthrown, to stop all issues of bonds and to appoint an investigating committee in order to determine the extent of the frauds and to find out the amount of the debt, if possible. North Carolina disposed of its governor by the impeachment route, and a similar proceeding was threatened in South Carolina, but came to naught. The Governor of Georgia fled the state, and the Governor of Mississippi resigned rather than face charges. The exact procedure followed in repudiating or scaling down the debt was different in each state as described below.

North Carolina

North Carolina was first to take steps toward repudiation, but one of the last to complete the process. The Reconstruction legislature in its second session (1869-70) was so impressed by the popular reaction to the excesses of its first session that it undid a part of its own work. The usual committee was appointed, and the treasurer was directed to stop interest payments on bonds authorized in the previous session. Railroad officials were required to render a complete report on state bonds received and to return any bonds or proceeds thereof then in their possession. Finally, all acts of the previous session making appropriations to railroads (which were the acts authorizing bonds) were repealed. The total effect of these acts was practically equivalent to repudiation.[68]

In 1870 the Democrats gained a majority in the legislature. They impeached and convicted the governor, but did nothing about the debt, on which interest was accruing. In 1872 there was a political reaction and a Republican governor was elected. In 1874 the Democrats gained strength again, and in 1876 restoration was completed by the election of a Democratic governor.

In 1879 the legislature passed an act to fund the debt, which by that time amounted to nearly $45,000,000, including accrued interest. The prewar debt, amounting to $5,477,400, was funded at 40 cents on the dollar; bonds for internal improvements issued during and after the war, amounting to $3,261,045, were funded at 25 cents; and funding bonds issued in 1866 and 1868, amounting to $3,888,600, were funded at 15 cents. Accrued interest on these bonds, amounting to $7,586,394, was disregarded. The total principal of old 6 per cent bonds amounted to $12,627,045, for which $3,589,511 of 4 per cent funding bonds were to be exchanged—an average settlement of 28.5 per cent. All bonds issued by the Reconstruction government, amounting to $12,655,000, were repudiated by a constitutional amendment ratified in 1880.[69]

Bonds in the amount of $2,795,000, issued before the war for the construction of the North Carolina Railroad and secured by state-

68. Ratchford, *History of North Carolina Debt*, pp. 191-192.

69. B. U. Ratchford, "The Adjustment of the North Carolina Public Debt, 1879-1883," *North Carolina Historical Review*, X (1933), 158-167.

owned stock in that road, were outstanding. In 1874 a federal court allowed the bondholders to sue on the pledge, and awarded them the decision, appointing a receiver to receive the dividends from the stock for the benefit of the bondholders.[70] The bondholders were thus in a strong position and were threatening to sell the stocks if the principal of the bonds was not paid at maturity, in 1883-85. Rather than face this contingency the state authorized the refunding of the bonds into new 6 per cent bonds, the bondholders sacrificing only three years' interest. The action of the court in this case was most unusual, since it allowed individuals, in effect, to sue a state. If the case had been carried to the Supreme Court, the decision would probably have been reversed, for a short time later that court decided against the bondholders in an essentially similar case.[71]

Georgia

Georgia Democrats were next to regain control of their state in 1872. An investigating committee found that certain bonds had been fraudulently and illegally issued. The legislature declared the bonds null and void. In 1875 and 1876 additional bonds were added to the list.[72] It is difficult to determine the amount of bonds and indorsements thus repudiated, but the best estimate that can be made from available data is $7,746,000.[73] In 1877 the voters of the state ratified a constitutional amendment confirming the repudiations. The state did not scale down any part of the valid debt.

South Carolina

In December, 1873, the South Carolina legislature passed the Consolidation Act, repudiating $5,965,000 of bonds and providing for funding the remainder of the debt. The report of the treasurer on which the act was based showed the total direct debt of the state at $15,851,627. The $9,886,627 of valid bonds were to be funded into new 6 per cent consolidated bonds at 50 cents on the dollar. The

70. B. U. Ratchford, "The North Carolina Public Debt, 1870-1878," North Carolina Historical Review, X (1933), 6-7.
71. Cunningham v. Macon and Brunswick Railroad Company, 109 U. S. 446 (1883). 72. McGrane, op. cit., pp. 310-311.
73. McGrane states that the amount "is estimated at $9,352,000," but no data can be found in the state reports and laws to substantiate this sum.

coupons on the new bonds were receivable for all taxes except school taxes. No record is found of any action on the $6,787,608 of contingent liabilities, which, it is said, existed in 1872.

Refunding proceeded, but after a few years there were charges that illegal bonds and coupons were being funded. After an investigating committee had reported, the legislature, in 1878, set up a court of claims to hear cases dealing with the validity of the consolidated bonds. Several cases were appealed to the state supreme court, which found that many of the original bonds had been illegally issued, and held consolidated bonds invalid to the extent that they had been exchanged for such bonds. A special commissioner was appointed to determine the extent of such invalidity. He reported in 1880, setting the figure at $1,126,763. All bondholders were then required to exchange their bonds for new ones, taking a reduction to the extent that any old bonds were invalid.[74]

Among the contingent liabilities of the state were $4,000,000 of bonds issued to the Blue Ridge Railroad. On the request of the road, these were exchanged for $1,800,000 of state scrip which ultimately became worthless when the tax to retire it was repealed, as noted above. Presumably the remainder of the contingent liabilities were repudiated, since no record of any action on them is found. Thus repudiations for South Carolina were $5,965,000 of direct liabilities and $4,587,608 of contingent liabilities, or a total of $10,552,608.[75]

Florida

During Reconstruction, Florida issued to two railroad companies $4,000,000 of state bonds in exchange for bonds of the roads. The latter promised that the road would make interest and principal payments at the time and in the amounts such payments were due on the state bonds. In a short time the roads defaulted on their payments, and the state took possession of them. Although the legislature never repudiated the state bonds, payments thereon were

74. McGrane, *op. cit.*, pp. 352-354.

75. Here, as elsewhere, the figures for contingent liabilities are very uncertain. It should be noted, also, that such repudiations did not necessarily mean complete losses to bondholders, since they still had claims against the railroads. See the Florida case, below.

refused. In 1876 the state supreme court held that the bonds were illegal because they were issued in violation of the state constitution.[76] This decision was repeated in at least two other cases, and the Supreme Court of the United States gave its tacit approval by saying that the question was "one it was eminently proper the courts of Florida should determine."[77] In 1880 the same court held that, although state bonds were illegal and "steeped in fraud," the innocent Dutch holders should have some redress. It accordingly gave the bondholders liens against the roads, holding that the roads were not released from liability because the state bonds were illegal.[78] The two roads were sold for a total of $355,000.[79]

Alabama

The Alabama commission appointed in 1874 made a detailed report in January, 1876, in which it attempted to separate valid from invalid claims. The funding act was based on this report. For $7,416,800 of direct bonds, bearing 5, 6, and 8 per cent interest, the state issued new "Class A" 30-year bonds bearing 2 per cent for five years, 3 per cent for five years, 4 per cent for ten years, and thereafter 5 per cent until maturity. The 7 per cent bonds issued to railroads in 1873, amounting to $1,192,000, were scaled to 50 cents on the dollar and funded into "Class B" bonds bearing 5 per cent. For the state's indorsements of $5,300,000 of Alabama and Chattanooga bonds, $1,000,000 of new "Class C" bonds were issued, bearing 2 per cent for five years and 4 per cent for twenty-five years. For $2,000,000 of state bonds issued to the same road, the act gave the bondholders a large tract of land. State certificates and certain bonds held by the Educational Fund were left undisturbed. Other obligations amounting to $3,705,000, consisting principally of indorsements of railroad bonds, were not provided for and were thus repudiated.[80] Accrued interest was disregarded in all cases. In this way the state repudiated $3,705,000 of bonds, scaled down its recognized debt by about $5,185,000, paid off $2,000,000 by a grant of land, and eliminated $4,574,000 of interest which had accrued on the valid debt.

76. *Holland* v. *Florida,* 15 Fla. 455 (1876).
77. *Florida* v. *Anderson,* 91 U. S. 667 (1875).
78. *Railroad Companies* v. *Schutte,* 103 U. S. 118 (1880).
79. Brown, *op. cit.,* p. 288.   80. McGrane, *op. cit.,* pp. 290-291.

Louisiana

On January 1, 1874, Louisiana's direct debt amounted to $24,356,-339. The legislature passed a funding act limiting the state debt to $15,000,000 and providing for funding the direct debt into 7 per cent, 40-year bonds at 60 cents on the dollar. In 1875 the legislature designated some $14,320,000 of bonds as questionable, and not to be funded until their validity was passed upon by the courts. Under this act $3,191,602 of bonds were ultimately held not to be fundable and were thus repudiated.[81]

After most of the bonds had been converted, the people of the state became dissatisfied, feeling that the 7 per cent interest was excessive. An ordinance of the Constitutional Convention of 1879 provided for exchanging the consolidated bonds into new 40-year bonds bearing 2 per cent for five years, 3 per cent for fifteen years, and 4 per cent thereafter; as an option, holders could convert into 4 per cent bonds at 75 cents on the dollar. Very few bondholders accepted the terms, and some tried to sue the state. Finally, in 1882 the legislature accepted a proposal from the bondholders and provided for new bonds bearing 2 per cent for five years and 4 per cent thereafter.[82]

The amount of Louisiana's contingent debt is not definitely known. It was estimated at $30,000,000 in 1874, but this included large amounts of bonds which the state might be called upon to issue. The funding act of that year canceled all such pledges which, it was said, consisted of "bonds not issued and stock not subscribed amounting to over $18,000,000.[83] This would leave about $12,000,000 as the amount outstanding. Of this, $6,653,683 was itemized in 1871, composed principally of bonds loaned to banks. The funding act made no provision for any of these liabilities, but the state was required by its courts to pay a part of the bank bonds later.[84] This liability, amounting to $743,500, was funded at 60 per cent into $446,102 of state bonds.

Louisiana's repudiations were thus about $11,250,000 of contingent liabilities and $3,191,602 of direct bonds held not to be

81. Caldwell, *Banking History of Louisiana*, p. 110.
82. McGrane, *op. cit.*, pp. 318-322.   83. *Chronicle*, XVIII (1874), 87.
84. *Hope and Co.* v. *Board of Liquidation*, 43 La. Ann. 741 (1891).

fundable, or a total of $14,441,602. By scaling, the state reduced the recognized debt by approximately $8,606,000. In 1880 accrued interest amounted to $1,381,300; to pay it, the state issued non-interest-bearing bonds. These bonds were more nearly tax warrants, since the only security pledged for their payment was taxes delinquent in 1878. By 1914, $470,570 of them had been paid, and the state disclaimed responsibility for the remaining $910,727. The amount of consolidated bonds issued up to 1914 was $12,378,622.[85]

Arkansas

During Reconstruction, Arkansas issued $5,350,000 bonds to aid railroads and $3,005,846 to aid levee construction, and funded its prewar debt with accrued interest, including the much disputed Holford bonds. In answer to charges that the railroad and levee bonds were illegally issued, suits were brought in the state courts to test their validity. In 1877 the state supreme court held the railroad bonds invalid on the ground that the act of the legislature authorizing a vote of the people in 1868 was not in force at the time of the vote. The constitution of 1868 provided that if no effective date was mentioned, acts of the legislature were to become effective ninety days after adjournment. The authorizing act was passed July 21, 1868, and mentioned no effective date. The legislature adjourned July 23 to meet again on the third Tuesday of November. The people voted on the act in November, 1868. The court held that the act did not become effective until ninety days after the adjournment of the *last session* of the legislature (which was in April, 1869) and hence the authorizing act was not in force when the people voted on it. The bonds were held to be "utterly void."[86] In the following year the court held the levee bonds to be unconstitutional because "the names of those voting for and against the bill in the legislature had not been entered in the journals" as required by the constitution.[87] These two decisions invalidated bonds to the amount of approximately $7,097,000.

In 1879 a constitutional amendment was proposed to repudiate

85. Caldwell, *op. cit.*, pp. 108, 110.
86. *Arkansas* v. *L. R., Miss R., and Tex. R. R. Co.*, 31 Ark. 712 (1877).
87. *Smithee* v. *Garth*, 33 Ark. 17 (1878).

the railroad, levee, and Holford bonds. In September, 1880, the voters favored the amendment by a count of 64,497 to 41,049, but the favorable votes were not a majority of the 132,985 votes cast in the election, and the amendment was not ratified. In 1884 the measure was submitted to the voters again, and was ratified by a vote of 119,806 to 15,492.[88] The principal of the debt thus repudiated was $8,365,000, leaving the state with a debt, in 1884, of $8,085,981, including $2,576,100 of bonded debt, $2,722,938 of floating debt, and $2,786,943 of accrued interest.[89]

Tennessee

Tennessee also found it necessary to adjust its debt in the postwar period. The funding act of 1873 was a failure because the bondholders were reluctant to convert their bonds, and it was charged that state officials funded all bonds presented, making no effort to separate legal from illegal issues. Representatives of bondholders attempted to secure a compromise, proposing that the debt be funded into new 6 per cent bonds at from 50 to 60 cents on the dollar. The question became a political issue, and the mass of the people were thoroughly aroused. In 1879 the legislature proposed to fund the debt into new 4 per cent bonds at 50 cents on the dollar, subject to the approval of the voters and two thirds of the bondholders. The voters rejected it by a large majority. An act of 1881 proposed to fund the debt at 100 cents into 3 per cent, 99-year bonds, the coupons of which were to be receivable for taxes. The state supreme court declared the act unconstitutional on the ground that the legislature could not contract away the state revenues for such a time or make a contract which subsequent legislatures could not modify.[90] A special session of the legislature in the same year enacted a law to fund the debt at 60 cents into bonds bearing interest at a rate rising from 3 per cent to 6 per cent. A large portion of the debt was funded under this act, but before the process was completed a new funding act was passed in 1883.

The 1883 act provided for funding the state debt proper into new

88. Evans, op. cit., pp. 95, 102.
89. Eleventh Census, "Wealth, Debt, and Taxation," Part I, p. 151.
90. Lynn v. Polk, 8 Lea's Tenn. 121 (1881).

bonds bearing the same interest as the old bonds—5 and 6 per cent—with the deduction of four years' accrued interest. The bulk of the debt—the railroad aid bonds—was funded, principal and accrued interest, at 50 cents into 3 per cent bonds. Bonds issued under the 1882 act were adjusted to this basis.[91] The bonded debt and accrued interest at that time were estimated at $28,786,066. This act provided for reducing it to $15,784,608—a reduction of approximately $13,-000,000.

About this time the United States Supreme Court increased the state's liabilities by ruling that the state was liable for notes of the Bank of Tennessee issued during the war. These notes had been repudiated by a constitutional amendment in 1865, but the court ruled the amendment invalid because it impaired the obligation of the contract contained in the notes.[92] To fund the notes, the state issued over $500,000 of non-interest-bearing certificates receivable for taxes. All were retired before 1890.

Summary of Adjustments

In Texas there was much dispute concerning the validity of certain obligations, but the amount involved was small. The story is too long and complicated to justify consideration here.[93] Mississippi neither repudiated nor scaled down any debt in this period. The story of Virginia's adjustment is told in the next chapter.

Table 15 shows the amounts of bonds repudiated by the different states, the amounts by which they scaled down their debts, and the amounts of accrued interest written off on the debts which were scaled. No figures are given for accrued interest on repudiated bonds, for by their repudiations the states indicated that they were never liable for such interest. In several cases the figures are open to question; they are estimates based on the best available information. They should be interpreted only in the light of the explanations and qualifications given in the text above. In addition to the

91. *Eleventh Census, op. cit.,* pp. 128-129.

92. *Keith* v. *Clark,* 97 U. S. 454 (1878). The notes had been made receivable for taxes, and the court held that this was a contract on the part of the state. Although Chief Justice White dissented, the court held that the notes had not been issued in aid of the rebellion.

93. See Miller, *op. cit.,* pp. 180-195, 229-238.

reduction of approximately $116,000,000 in principal and accrued interest, there should be added an indefinite amount to represent the savings of the states because of lower interest payments on the refunding bonds. If this sum is included, it would seem that the Southern states reduced their total and ultimate liabilities by not less than $150,000,000. The table also shows, for comparative purposes, the gross debts of these states in 1890 after the adjustments were fairly well completed. Few states reduced their debts before 1890 by redeeming bonds. Rather, some allowed their debts to increase by an accumulation of floating debts.

TABLE 15

REDUCTION OF DEBTS OF SOUTHERN STATES BY REPUDIATION AND
SCALING DOWN, AND GROSS DEBTS IN 1890
(In thousands of dollars)

State	Principal of Repudiated Debts	Reduction of Principal by Scaling Down	Accrued Interest on Scaled Debt Not Paid	Total	Gross Debt, 1890
Alabama.......	$ 3,705	$ 5,185	$ 4,574	$13,464	$12,413
Arkansas.......	8,365	......	......	8,365	8,681
Florida........	4,000	......	......	4,000	1,275
Georgia........	7,746	......	......	7,746	10,450
Louisiana......	14,442*	8,606	911	23,959	16,009
North Carolina.	12,655	9,037	7,586	29,278	7,703
South Carolina.	11,553*	4,943	......	16,496	6,993
Tennessee......	......	13,000	......†	13,000	19,696
Totals......	$62,466	$40,771	$13,071	$116,308	$83,220

*Includes both direct and contingent liabilities.
†Included in previous column.
Sources: See text.

Debt Limitations Revised

After their experience with debts during Reconstruction, several Southern states revised their constitutions to prevent a repetition of such experience. Amendments to the Georgia constitution adopted in 1877 forbade the state to assume the debts of other governmental units, prohibited any increase in the bonded debt except for defense, limited the debt which could be incurred for casual deficits to $200,000, and specified that proceeds from the sale of railroads or other state-owned property should be applied to debt retirement.[94]

94. *Tenth Census*, VII, 586.

The Louisiana constitution of 1879 limited the debt of the state to $15,000,000.[95] In 1873 the people of South Carolina, "out of sheer desperation," ratified a constitutional amendment forbidding the creation of any state debt, "either by the loan of the credit of the state, by guaranty, indorsement, or otherwise, except for the ordinary or current business of the state" unless the question should be approved by two thirds of the qualified voters.[96] That constitution thus became, as it remains today, the only constitution to limit the debt without exception for defending the state. The Texas constitution of 1876 prohibited the state from lending or giving the credit of the state to any private corporation or individual, and forbade any direct debt except to defend the state and to cover casual deficits up to an aggregate of $200,000.[97]

Appraisal of Debt Adjustments

These adjustments have been the subject of long and heated controversy in the sixty years or more since they were enacted, and it would be presumptuous to attempt to write the final verdict at this time. Even if all the facts were definitely known and if the data were available for an exhaustive survey of the political, legal, and economic conditions in the South in 1875 or 1880, space would not permit of such an analysis here. Instead, a few general remarks must suffice.

On the whole the repudiations can be defended. Let us consider first the legal and constitutional aspects of the question. No state has ever been called upon to defend itself before the United States Supreme Court regarding these repudiations, but if such a case ever developed the state could offer some or all of the following arguments in its defense. (1) The Reconstruction acts were unconstitutional. A majority of constitutional authorities would probably sustain this proposition today, although the question has never been definitely settled. The Supreme Court has held several features of the various acts to be unconstitutional.[98] Burgess states that the

95. Constitution of 1879, Art. III.
96. *Tenth Census*, VII, 574.   97. *Ibid.*, p. 602.
98. *U. S.* v. *Cruikshank*, 92 U. S. 542 (1876); *U. S.* v. *Reese*, 92 U. S. 214 (1876); *U. S.* v. *Harris*, 106 U. S. 629 (1882); *The Civil Rights Cases*, 109 U. S. 3 (1883).

acts were "a very serious stretching of its power by Congress, if not a distinct usurpation." Congress showed its doubts and fears on the point by hastily repealing the act of February 5, 1867, while the *McCardle* case was before the court.[99] This argument would apply especially in those cases where military commanders were allowed to determine the suffrage at the election of state officials. If the Reconstruction acts were unconstitutional, the state governments established under them were illegal.

(2) Delegates to the constitutional convention of 1867-68 were improperly elected. Charges of fraud and corruption in the voting have been noted above. If these bodies were not properly elected, their work is open to question. (3) There were gross fraud and corruption in the election of state legislators and state officials. This charge has been substantiated in almost every state and casts grave doubt on the legality of all Reconstruction legislation. The North Carolina legislature betrayed its doubts on this point in 1868, when, after reciting many charges made concerning the legality of the constitutional convention and the legislature, it resolved that the state government as then organized was "the legitimate, rightful, legal, and constitutional government of the State of North Carolina" and that the recently adopted constitution was "the rightful and valid constitution of this State."[100] A most unique act indeed!

(4) Passage of the acts authorizing the bonds was procured by bribery. This, too, has been substantiated in almost every state, as noted above. (5) The bills authorizing bonds did not follow the course specified by the constitutions in their passage through the two legislative houses. The two Arkansas acts were held invalid on this ground, and similar charges have been made in other states. With conditions as they were, this was almost inevitable. Constitutions were new, usually containing detailed specifications for the passage of finance bills. In the legislative halls chaos reigned. Ignorant, inexperienced, and careless legislators knew little and cared less about the constitutions. (6) There were fraud and criminal carelessness in the issue and sale of the bonds. This has been substantiated beyond question in all the repudiating states. Other

99. Burgess, *op. cit.,* p. 197.   100. *Public Laws,* 1868, p. 105.

more detailed and technical counts could be added, but enough has been said to show that the states could present a strong case in any court.

In the broader fields of ethics and economic justice the issues are not so precise nor the answers so definite. The following arguments, however, may be presented in favor of the repudiating states. (1) A majority of the citizens did not favor the bonds, and many gave adequate warnings that they would not be paid. (2) Prudent, intelligent investors should have been put on guard by these warnings, by the low prices at which the bonds were sold, and by the general knowledge of conditions existing in the South. (3) The states derived very little, if any, benefit from the sale of bonds. Bonds were sold far below par, and the proceeds frequently were stolen, spent extravagantly, or invested in railroads which soon failed. The latter would not be valid argument, had the states been acting in good faith; but when the same band of adventurers authorized the bonds and turned over the proceeds to their own projects to be mismanaged, it is a different matter. (4) By the end of Reconstruction several states had debts larger than they could service, and some of the holders had to take a loss. With economic conditions and tax systems as they were, the states were having difficulties with their debts incurred before Reconstruction. The added burdens imposed during Reconstruction often could not be handled. It was only fair that the holders of the bonds last issued, and which had been issued through fraud, should be called upon to take the inevitable loss.

While repudiation may be defended, it must be admitted that Arkansas, Florida, and North Carolina acted drastically in repudiating all Reconstruction bonds without discrimination. It would have been more in keeping with justice if they had dealt with each issue of bonds on its merits, as did Alabama and Georgia.

The action of the states which scaled down their pre-Reconstruction debt cannot be justified so easily. It is true that a few of these bonds had been sold for depreciated Confederate money and a few for depreciated greenbacks. Others had been issued, principally to Northern bondholders, to fund interest which accrued during the war. Naturally Southerners were not too tender in dealing with bonds in the latter category. But several states, especially North Carolina, drastically scaled down their prewar debts. With the possible exception of Tennessee and Virginia, all Southern states could and should have paid their prewar debts in full. Alabama and Georgia did substantially this. But as one writer has observed about repudiation, scaling down "was to the southern people a weapon of defense and retaliation against what they considered corrupt and hostile governments supported by outside military force."[101] One argument frequently heard in North Carolina was that most of the bonds were held in the North by those who were responsible for the enormous destruction of life and property which had been security for the debt, and that those people had no moral right to demand payment in full.[102] The passions aroused by war do not subside overnight.

After their repudiations and fundings, the Southern states made little progress in reducing their debts, while other states made substantial reductions. As a result, the South Atlantic and South Central states, in 1890, had per capita debts considerably above the national average. They were, respectively, $10.12 and $6.04 compared with $3.66 for the country as a whole, $1.44 for the North Atlantic states, $1.86 for the North Central states, and $2.07 for the Western states. The difference in per capita annual interest charges was even greater, being 96 cents for the South Atlantic states, and 58 cents for South Central states compared with 16 cents for the nation.[103] The fact that per capita wealth and income were much lower in the Southern states than elsewhere made these differences even more significant.

101. B. C. Randolph, "Foreign Bondholders and the Repudiated Debts of the Southern States," *American Journal of International Law*, XXV (1931), 74.
102. Ratchford, *History of North Carolina Debt*, p. 207.
103. *Eleventh Census*, op. cit., pp. 146, 857-858.

CHAPTER VIII

THE VIRGINIA DEBT SETTLEMENT AND THE
WEST VIRGINIA SUITS

FIFTY YEARS after the Civil War, Virginia was still struggling to arrive at a final settlement of its prewar debt. That debt, which on January 1, 1861, amounted to $33,897,074 plus some $2,500,000 of bonds held by state funds, had been incurred mainly for railroads, canals, and turnpikes. On August 20, 1861, a Union convention, which claimed to be a constituent assembly acting for all of Virginia, met at Wheeling and passed an ordinance providing for the formation of West Virginia. Article 9 of the ordinance provided: "The new State shall take upon itself a just proportion of the public debt . . . prior to the first day of January, 1861, to be ascertained by charging to it all the state expenditures within the limits thereof and a just proportion of the ordinary expenses of the State government since any part of said debt was contracted, and deducting therefrom the moneys paid into the treasury of the Commonwealth from the counties included within the said State during said period."[1]

The constitution of West Virginia, which was framed in November, 1861, and ratified in April, 1862, bound the new state to assume an "equitable proportion" of the debt as of January 1, 1861, and directed the legislature to ascertain the amount "as soon as possible" and to provide for its liquidation. The loyal or "restored" legislature of Virginia, in May, 1862, accepted the constitution and consented to the creation of the new state. Congress, on December 31, 1862, sanctioned this agreement by admitting West Virginia into the Union. "This action by Congress sealed

1. Quoted in James G. Randall, "The Virginia Debt Controversy," *Political Science Quarterly*, XXX (1915), 557.

the contract between the states by which West Virginia was bound to pay an 'equitable proportion' of the debt."[2]

By the end of the war Virginia's debt, including accrued interest, was approximately $41,000,000. Nearly a third of the state's area and population had been included in West Virginia. The state, ravaged by four years of war, was in the direst poverty.[3] It was estimated that the revenue potentialities of the state had been reduced by at least two thirds. State-owned assets, which in 1861 had been worth about $35,000,000, were now worth only a small part of that sum. The debt burden had been considered heavy in 1860, but now it was immeasurably greater.

Presidential Reconstruction

The first post-war legislature of Virginia met in December, 1865, and continued in office until the establishment of military rule in 1867. The legislators who composed this body were representatives of the old regime, proud of the state's honors and traditions, and determined to uphold them at all costs. On March 2, 1866, they assumed full responsibility for the prewar debt and provided for funding all accrued interest.[4] In the same session they appointed a commission to attempt to bring about a reunion with West Virginia. If unsuccessful, the commissioners were to treat for a division of the public debt and assets.[5] A large part of the accrued interest was funded, and on January 1, 1867, the debt was $43,383,679.

By the autumn of 1866 West Virginia had taken no action on reunion or division of the debt. Crops had been poor, and economic conditions had not improved. There was talk of repudiation or a scaling down of the debt. The legislature, however, took no drastic action. Declaring that the state was unable to pay the full rate of interest, it ordered that on January 1 and July 1, 1867, 2 per cent interest should be paid, "that being the interest which this State feels obliged to pay, until there is a settlement of accounts between this State and West Virginia."[6] This was two thirds of

2. *Ibid.*, pp. 557-558.
3. For a vivid description of post-war conditions see William L. Royall, *History of the Virginia Debt Controversy* (Richmond, 1897), pp. 10-15.
4. *Acts*, 1865-66, p. 79.   5. *Ibid.*, p. 453.   6. *Ibid.*, 1866-67, c. 35.

the interest due, and the act "expressed the settled conviction of the people that Virginia ought equitably to pay two-thirds of the debt, and West Virginia ought to pay one-third of it."[7] To quiet current fears and rumors, the legislature emphatically resolved that there would be no repudiation.[8]

With the ending of this session of the legislature, native white rule ended, and Virginia soon passed under military control. The prescribed interest payments were made in 1867, and 2 per cent was paid in 1869. By January 1, 1870, the debt amounted to $45,-872,778, including nearly $5,000,000 of accrued interest.[9] There was much uncertainty as to the future of the debt, and many native bondholders were selling their bonds to outsiders.[10] Several more attempts were made to reach an agreement with West Virginia, but nothing was accomplished for many years because of a pending boundary suit between the two states and because Virginia had not been readmitted to the Union. In 1870 commissioners from the two states met, but accomplished nothing. In 1871 Virginia proposed arbitration by citizens from other states, but West Virginia would not agree. Virginia, in turn, refused to appoint commissioners to meet with West Virginia representatives, and there the matter rested for many years, while Virginia wrestled with the problems of internal debt adjustment.[11]

THE ADJUSTMENT OF VIRGINIA'S DEBTS

Congressional Reconstruction

The Reconstruction government in Virginia initiated many democratic reforms and for a time seemed to favor scaling down the debt or repudiating a part of it. Sentiment changed, however, before any such action was taken. Charters for new railroads and permissions to consolidate existing roads were freely granted. At the same time the state began to dispose of its assets, consisting

7. Royall, *op. cit.*, p. 17.

8. *Acts,* 1866-67, p. 499.   9. *Tenth Census,* VII, 556.

10. C. C. Pearson, *The Readjuster Movement in Virginia* (New Haven, 1917), p. 12.

11. Randall, *op. cit.*, pp. 558-559. It was charged that Virginia railroad interests "blocked a settlement with West Virginia lest the latter demand a share of Virginia's assets and so delay railroad consolidation; and the opinion became fixed in West Virginia that no settlement would ever be demanded" (Pearson, *op. cit.*, p. 30 n.).

mostly of railroad securities. It was charged that party leaders frequently bought those securities at very favorable prices. Perhaps this practice was a substitute for the large bond issues found in other Southern states. In a few years the state had disposed of practically all of its holdings except the stock of one road, which it still holds and which pays a liberal return. In 1870 the state sold its holdings in two railroads for $1,610,324, which sum was applied to the reduction of the debt. Only $3,400,000 had been received from such sales up to 1874, when the governor estimated that $2,600,000 would be "immediately," and $10,000,000 more remotely, available.[12]

Funding Act of 1871

Carrying out Governor Walker's "restoration of credit" policy, the legislature on March 30, 1871, passed the epoch-making Funding Act,[13] which was to block every attempt to adjust the debt in the next twenty years. The act provided for refunding the whole debt, including accrued interest, except $1,818,375 of sterling bonds and certain other small debts. Bondholders were to receive new 6 per cent, 10-34 year bonds, later to be known as "consols," to an amount equal to two thirds of the principal and accrued interest of old bonds. For the other third they were to receive interest-bearing certificates, the payment of which was to be provided for "in accordance with such settlements as shall hereafter be made between the states of Virginia and West Virginia." Similar certificates were to be given in payment of one third of the interest on sterling bonds as it accrued, Virginia paying two thirds. Expressed on the face of the coupons of the new bonds was the state's promise to receive them, at and after maturity, for all "taxes, debts, dues, and demands due to the state." This constituted a contract which the state later tried in vain to break. To create a sinking fund for the new bonds, the act pledged the proceeds from all sales of state-owned securities and real estate, and from any state claims against the United States. Also, after 1879 a tax of two cents per $100 was to be levied for the sinking fund.

There was much opposition to the act, and many charged that

12. *Tenth Census*, VII, 558; Pearson, *op. cit.*, p. 31 n.
13. *Acts*, 1870-71, p. 378.

the state had been sold out to the brokers and bondholders. "The governor himself was known to be financially interested, directly or indirectly, in state bonds. Men said, and no one took the trouble to deny the rumor, that the negroes had been bought."[14] It was argued, also, that the act favored the rich, who could realize large savings by buying coupons below par and using them to pay their taxes, while the poor would not be able to use this device. Railroad and other special interests were active in support of the measure.

The act recognized $47,090,867 as the fundable debt. Interest on Virginia's part of the new debt was estimated at $1,865,451, which would "about equal the estimated revenue under the new tax law less the minimum appropriated by the constitution for public education, leaving nothing for government expenses, which the auditor estimated at over one million dollars. . . . Expenses could be reduced only by undoing the democratic features of the constitution just put into effect; but at best this would require years. Any considerable increase in revenue depended upon economic improvement, which could come only gradually, or upon the always slow process of finding new subjects and new methods of taxation."[15] This estimate proved to be correct, and the state at once defaulted on interest payments on the new bonds.[16] In the meantime, the exchange of bonds under the act proceeded rapidly, and by December, 1871, the state had issued $21,610,691 of the new bonds,[17] which meant that $32,416,036 of the old obligations had been surrendered.

Popular opposition to the Funding Act was an important factor in the decisive victory which the Conservatives scored in the 1871 election. Of the 132 members of the lower house which passed the Funding Act, only 26 were re-elected. After this, the Radicals, or Republicans as they were soon to become, declined rapidly in power and soon ceased to be an important political factor.

Issue of Consols Stopped

The new legislature immediately voted to stop the issue of bonds with tax-receivable coupons. The governor vetoed the bill on the ground that it was contrary to public policy and discriminated

14. Pearson, *op. cit.*, p. 32.   15. *Ibid.*, p. 31.
16. Royall, *op. cit.*, p. 22.   17. *Tenth Census*, VII, 558.

against those who had not offered their funds for funding, but it was passed over his veto. The act prohibited the issue of any more "consols" and forbade tax-collectors to receive anything except gold, silver, greenbacks, or national bank notes in payment of taxes.[18] Bondholders immediately attacked the latter provision, and the state supreme court upheld their contention on the ground that the promise to receive the coupons in payment of taxes was a contract between the state and the bondholder which the state could not repudiate without violating the Federal Constitution.[19]

Funding continued for a time at a much reduced rate, the new bonds being issued without tax-receivable coupons. These bonds came to be known as "peelers," while those which were never funded were known as the "unfunded" debt. Thus the debt structure began to grow more complex. Another act of 1872 ordered the auditor to pay into the treasury so much of the public revenues as was necessary to pay interest on the debt, and provided for the payment of 4 instead of 6 per cent on the debt in 1872.[20] The first provision was significant because there had been some agitation for keeping the proceeds separate from the special tax levied for public schools.

The 1872-73 session of the legislature enacted the first of a long series of acts designed to discriminate against the tax-receivable coupons and to discourage holders from presenting them in payment of taxes. One act prohibited collecting officers from dealing in coupons and imposed a broker's license tax on others dealing in them.[21] Another imposed upon all bonds an annual tax of 50 cents per $100 of market value, provided that the tax should be

18. *Acts*, 1871-72, p. 141.

19. *Antoni* v. *Wright*, 22 Grattan 833 (1872). This decision was reaffirmed in *Wise* v. *Rogers*, 24 Gratt. 169 (1873), and *Clarke* v. *Tyler*, 30 Gratt. 134 (1878). In the latter case Mr. Justice Staples, in a dissenting opinion, succinctly stated an argument frequently used to justify the state's action: ". . . if the legislature, under no circumstances, has for the next thirty years, the power to diminish the rate of taxation, whatever may be the conditions or necessities of the people; if, during that time, whatever may be the public exigencies, the revenues of the state are irrevocably dedicated to the creditor; if, to such an extent and for such a time the legislature has surrendered all control of the revenues and resources of the state beyond recall, then, indeed, has the government abdicated its function, and the state is stripped of one of the most essential attributes of sovereignty" (p. 146).

20. *Acts*, 1871-72, p. 218.   21. Pearson, *op. cit.*, p. 51.

deducted from interest payments, and made it the duty of tax collectors to deduct it from any matured coupons presented in payment of taxes.[22] In 1880 the United States Supreme Court held this act, as amended in 1876, to be unconstitutional because it impaired the contract in the bonds, and also approved the state court's decision invalidating the 1872 act.[23]

The tax-receivable coupons were widely used for the payment of taxes, and "almost all of each annual crop was regularly redeemed thus." Between January 1, 1873, and October 1, 1878, the state received $5,404,789 of coupons in this way—an average of almost $1,000,000 per year.[24] "They were redeemed, however, at the expense of other demands upon the State, as the revenue was not sufficient for all, the deficiency fell principally upon the provision for public free schools."[25] When Governor Kemper took office January 1, 1874, he faced a most difficult financial problem. The country had just suffered the severe panic of 1873, and "the large surplus which had existed at the beginning of Governor Walker's administration was gone. Nearly a million dollars in authorized cash payments and half a million in tax-receivable coupons were outstanding, the current year would show a deficit of almost another million, the bulk of the state's assets had been bargained away, and general economic conditions demanded a decrease rather than an increase, in taxes."[26] A conference between a state commission and representatives of the holders of the "consols" failed to produce relief, and thus "two attempts at undoing the Funding Act . . . had failed." Then there "began a united and truly heroic attempt on the part of almost all the upper classes to meet the state's obligations as they stood."[27]

Rise of the Readjusters

After the Radical or Republican party had declined to impotence, many dissatisfied elements were left without a means of

22. *Acts,* 1872-73, p. 207.
23. *Hartman* v. *Greenhow,* 102 U. S. 672, 685 (1881).
24. William L. Grenoble, *A History of the Virginia State Debt* (an unpublished thesis in the Library of the University of Virginia, Charlottesville, 1937), p. 65.
25. Royall, *op. cit.,* p. 23.
26. Pearson, *op. cit.,* p. 51.   27. *Ibid.,* p. 53.

political expression. These included many from the southwestern part of the state, the Negroes and most of the poor whites. They opposed the funding of the interest which had accrued during the war, and favored an "adjustment" in the principal of the debt. They argued that, since Virginia had been treated as "conquered territory," its debts, according to the law of nations, devolved upon the conquerors.[28] This group also favored increased state expenditures for public schools, for care of the sick and insane, and for the other democratic measures initiated by the Reconstruction government.

Opposed to these "Readjusters" were the "Debt Payers" or "Funders." They came mainly from the middle and upper classes and included the leaders of the "Conservatives" or Democrats. They had never been enthusiastic about the democratic reforms, and now that the issue was sharply drawn between increased state activities and payment of the debt, they took their stand for the latter. Extremists even contended that "it would be better to burn the schoolhouses than to permit the state to default in interest payment on the debt." This nearly happened, for while the school system was growing in popularity, "teachers were going unpaid and schools were closing."[29] Although the auditor had been directed to pay to the schools their constitutional quota of state funds in cash, he failed to do this, and by 1877 the amount due to schools was $850,000.

The Conservatives made desperate attempts to reduce expenditures and to increase revenues, although keeping within the bounds of political expediency. "Capital, notwithstanding its demand for an honest debt policy, availed itself of every constitutional safeguard, of old charter exemptions, and of the strong railroad contingent in the legislature; not until 1879 did it pay as much as $120,000. Great efforts were made to reach the masses."[30]

Since there was no effective Republican organization in the state, the situation was ripe for a division within the "Conservative" or Democratic party. About 1875 the Readjuster movement began to take shape under the leadership of William Mahone,

28. *Ibid.*, pp. 53-67.
29. *Ibid.*, pp. 62-63.　　　　　30. *Ibid.*, pp. 56-57.

"Parson" Massey, and others who had the ability to arouse the masses. This party stood for "forcible" readjustment of the debt, the extension of state activities, and strong measures to prevent the receipt of tax-receivable coupons. In 1877 the party elected several members of the state legislature. In 1879 the party held a state convention, waged an intensive campaign, and captured control of the legislature. By even a larger margin it swept the field in 1881, electing a governor and a large majority of state and local officials. At one time both federal senators from the state belonged to this party.

More Funding Acts

The strength of the Readjuster movement, even in 1878, is shown by the passage of the Barbour Bill, which declared that the state was unable to bear any financial burden heavier than what then existed, and that the income of the state was inadequate to service the debt as funded under the 1871 act, after the necessary general governmental expenses had been met. It proposed to allocate 50 per cent of all revenues to the support of general government, 20 per cent to schools, and 30 per cent to interest, the amounts going to government and the schools to be paid in cash.[31] The governor vetoed the bill. In the following month the legislature passed a compromise funding act which provided for converting all bonds issued under the 1871 act at par into new 10-50 year bonds bearing 3 per cent for eighteen years and 4 per cent thereafter. Holders of unfunded bonds were to receive new bonds equal to two thirds of the old, West Virginia certificates being issued for the other third. No exchange was to be made until holders of $15,000,000 of "consols" signified their acceptance of the terms.[32] This condition was never met, no bonds were issued, and the act was repealed the following year. Since the holders of "consols" had a decided advantage over other bondholders, one of the major aims of the legislature at this time was to fund the debt into uniform bonds bearing the same rate of interest. Heretofore "consol" holders had stoutly refused to give up their advantage.

By the end of 1878 creditors of the state had taken notice of

31. *Ibid.*, p. 79.   32. *Acts*, 1877-78, p. 230.

the growing demand for debt adjustment, and were in a mood to compromise. In December the governor transmitted to the legislature two propositions, one from London and the other from New York, both pledging the efforts of bondholders "to secure from all creditors a readjustment of the debt on the basis of equity to all and a rate of interest not exceeding four per cent."[33] The outcome of these two propositions was the McCulloch Bill, which became law on March 28, 1879.[34] It provided for funding the debt into new 10-40 year bonds bearing 3 per cent for ten years, 4 per cent for twenty years, and 5 per cent thereafter. The bonds were to bear tax-receivable coupons and to be exempt from all taxation in Virginia. The old debt was divided into two classes: Class I included "consols" and registered bonds convertible into "consols," while Class II included all other bonds issued under the 1871 act and two thirds of the face value and interest accrued up to July 1, 1871, of all unfunded bonds, including sterling bonds. The proportion of Class II bonds funded could not exceed one third of the total until $18,000,000 of Class I bonds had been retired. Interest accrued since 1871 was to be funded at 50 per cent.

The terms of the act were to become a contract if accepted by The Corporation of Foreign Bondholders (London) and The Funding Association of the United States (New York) by May 1, 1879, and if they funded at least $8,000,000 by January 1, 1880, and at least $5,000,000 each six months thereafter. Otherwise a contract might be made with other responsible parties to conduct the funding. Accompanying the new bonds were certificates representing West Virginia's third of the original debt, the acceptance of which completely and finally released Virginia from all liability therefor, although the state promised to endeavor to secure for the bondholders an amicable settlement with West Virginia. After 1884 a tax of two cents per $100 was to be levied for a sinking fund, to be used for retiring the new bonds. If revenues should be insufficient to cover interest requirements, the auditor might incur short-term loans, or, if necessary, sell special non-interest-bearing, tax-receivable certificates at not less than 75. At about the same time the legislature passed an act to protect the public school funds.

33. Pearson, *op. cit.*, p. 85.   34. *Acts*, 1878-79, p. 264.

Pearson states that the McCulloch Act "represented the triumph of that moderate move for readjustment which had manifested itself in 1871 and 1874. It discarded on the one hand the ideas of 'state sovereignty,' 'will of the people,' and antagonisms to 'money rings'; on the other hand, it recognized the actual fiscal situation and the existence of new popular necessities."[35]   Slightly over $8,000,000 of the new bonds were issued up to October 1, 1879, when the state debt stood at $29,667,305 exclusive of $15,239,371 designated as West Virginia's portion.[36] Accrued interest was reduced $835,415 by the funding, and annual interest requirements were reduced by $227,150, of which $168,587 were represented by tax-receivable coupons.

The Riddleberger Act

When the Readjusters gained control of the legislature in 1879 they proceeded to put into effect their program of "forcible readjustment" of the debt. To this end they enacted, in 1880, the Riddleberger Bill, but it was vetoed by the "Funder" governor who still held office. The governor asserted that the bill defied both state and federal courts and was contrary to "the spirit which has ever moved and inspired the traditions of the Commonwealth."[37] Two years later, with a Readjuster governor in office, the bill was remodeled and became a law.[38]

The act "to ascertain and declare Virginia's equitable share of the debt before and actually existing at the time of partition of her territory and resources, and to provide for the issuance of bonds covering the same" was very complex. The underlying purpose was to adjust the debt in such a way as to eliminate bonds which had been issued to fund interest which had accrued during the Civil War and Reconstruction, and also to scale down certain issues because they had, for a number of years, received interest at a higher rate than was considered just and equitable. In other words, the holders of "consols" were to pay now for the advantage they had been enjoying. A long preamble declared that the state was not able to pay more than 3 per cent

35. Pearson, op. cit., p. 88. 36. Tenth Census, VII, 559.
37. Quoted in Pearson, op. cit., p. 142. 38. Acts, 1881-82, p. 88.

on its equitable share of the old debt, which was taken to be the debt of $39,095,929 existing on July 1, 1863, the approximate date of the formation of West Virginia.

The act provided for the issue of new 3 per cent 18-50 year bonds in exchange for all old bonds. Each group of old bonds was to be exchanged at a different rate, calculated in such a way as to effect the adjustments described above. The amounts of these bonds to be funded and the rates of exchange are shown in Table 16.

TABLE 16

REFUNDING PROVISIONS OF RIDDLEBERGER ACT

Class	Class of Securities and Obligations	Amount to Be Funded	Per Cent of Face Value Allowed in Exchange
A	"Consol" bonds	$14,369,971	53
B	10-40 bonds (issued under McCulloch Act, 1879)	8,517,600	60
C	"Peeler" bonds	2,394,305	69
D	Interest on "Peelers"	1,072,546	80
E	Dollar and sterling bonds ($\frac{2}{3}$)	3,773,494	69
F	Interest on dollar and sterling bonds ($\frac{2}{3}$)	2,862,854	63
G	Literary fund securities	1,428,245	69
	Interest on literary fund securities	602,017	63
	Total	$35,021,032	

Source: *Eleventh Census*, "Wealth, Debt, and Taxation," Part I, p. 135.

No bonds other than those authorized in the act were to be issued, and interest payments on all other bonds were forbidden. Annual payments equal to 2¼ per cent of the new bonds outstanding were to go into a sinking fund to be used to retire those bonds by lot. The act declared the correct debt of the state to be $21,035,377, including $16,843,034 of principal and $4,192,343 of accrued interest. Allowing for West Virginia's third of the dollar and sterling bonds and interest thereon, the act would have reduced the debt, if all obligations had been promptly funded, from $32,808,916 to $21,035,377, or a reduction of $11,773,539.

The legislature paved the way for the funding act by enacting two "Coupon-Killers." These acts[39] prohibited tax-collectors, under heavy penalties, from receiving any coupons except for "identifica-

39. *Acts*, 1881-82, pp. 10, 37.

tion and verification." Taxpayers offering coupons were required
to pay taxes in cash, and to file their coupons, together with a
petition, to be considered by a jury of the county court. If the coupons were found to be genuine, the money would be refunded.
There was "no other remedy," and no writ to prevent or hinder the
collection of revenue should "in anywise issue, either injunction,
supersedeas, mandamus, prohibition or any other writ or process
whatever." A fee of five dollars was charged against the plaintiff,
to be paid to the state's attorney. "The remedy offered for the
breach of contract would, it was thought, satisfy the courts; the
difficulty and cost of proving the genuineness of coupons, clipped
from bonds held abroad perhaps would prevent their deluging
the treasury and tend to encourage conversion of consols and ten-
forties into Riddlebergers."[40]

The philosophy upon which the Readjusters were operating is
admirably summed up by Royall, one of the outstanding attorneys
for the bondholders:

> It was argued that if a political party should take possession of the
> State in all its departments—legislative, judicial, and executive—and
> fill every office in the State with a person determined to destroy the
> coupon as a tax-paying instrument, its value as such would disappear
> even though it had behind it the guarantee of the Constitution of the
> United States.
> They relied on the judges with whom they had filled the corporation
> and county courts to make the suit to recover the money a farce, and
> the complexion of the judiciary which they had established in Virginia
> gave every encouragement to the hope that they entertained.[41]

Readjusters Overthrown

In their rise to power the Readjusters had catered to the Negro
vote, which had helped them greatly. This action, however, rankled
in the minds of many white party members. In the 1883 campaign
the Conservative-Funders adopted a more lenient view toward the
adjustment of the debt and came around finally to an approval of
the Riddleberger Act. They were impelled in this direction by the
decision of the United States Supreme Court in March of that
year sustaining "Coupon-Killer Number One" and, by implication,

40. Pearson, *op. cit.*, pp. 143-144.   41. Royal, *op. cit.*, pp. 29-30, 60.

the Readjuster debt settlement.[42]   This decision was, according to
Royall, "to the dismay of the creditors and the unbounded astonish-
ment of the white people of Virginia. . . ."[43]

Royall contends, further, that the decision produced a profound
change in the attitude of the people toward the debt: "From desiring to pay it, they became absolutely indifferent as to whether it
was paid or not. . . . They unanimously resolved that they would
never more allow it to be used by demagogues, as a text by which
their own vote could be divided. . . . They resolved that the
formation of a pure government for their State was of first importance; considerations affecting the public debt of second."[44]   This
analysis seems to be essentially correct, for in 1883 the Conservatives
subordinated the debt question, raised the issue of white rule, and
swept the Readjusters from power.   Thereafter the Readjusters
ceased to be an important factor in state politics.   Some of the
leaders had already returned to the Democratic party, while Mahone
and others joined the Republicans, with whom they had long been
closely associated.

Perhaps the most remarkable feature of this political upheaval
was the fact that the Democrats accepted the Readjuster debt
settlement and proceeded to enforce it with as much determination
as had Mahone and his followers.   The next session of the legislature declared that the people of Virginia accepted the Riddleberger Act as the final and ultimate settlement of the debt, and
called upon creditors to fund their bonds and to cease the controversy.   But the fight had only begun.

42. *Antoni v. Greenhow,* 107 U. S. 769 (1883). The Court held that the remedy
offered by the state for breach of contract was "substantially equivalent to that in
force when the coupons were issued," and that this remedy was the "one which
the state has chosen to give, and the only one therefore which the courts of the
United States are authorized to administer."

43. Royall, *op. cit.,* p. 74. Royall implies that the Court was not impartial in
this case: "The court consisted exclusively of Republican judges except one, who
dissented.   The Republican President and Senators had just entered into their
contract with Senator Mahone, whereby he was to be allowed to control all federal
appointments in Virginia, in consideration of voting with the Republicans in the
United States Senate. The people of Virginia jumped to the conclusion that a Republican court had become part of the bargain with Mahone, and had sustained his
legislation in opposition to their preceding decisions, in order that his hands might
be held up" (*ibid.,* p. 75).   44. *Ibid.,* p. 76.

Litigation by Bondholders

There now began a most remarkable fight between bondholders and taxpayers on one side and the state on the other—a veritable endurance contest which has been called a "period of legal warfare." Since they could not trust the state courts, bondholders sought to bring their suits in the federal courts, while the state endeavored to give its courts exclusive jurisdiction. In 1883, however, the United States Supreme Court ruled that a federal question was involved and allowed the cases to be heard in federal courts.[45] Taxpayers started another suit to test the validity of the "Coupon-Killers" and continued to offer large amounts of coupons in payment of taxes, since they could be bought as low as forty cents on the dollar. One method of enforcing their rights was for taxpayers to ask a federal court for a mandamus compelling state and local collectors to receive the coupons. Another was for the taxpayer to tender coupons, to refuse to pay money, and then, when collectors seized property in satisfaction of delinquent taxes, to bring suit in federal court against the collector for trespass and illegal seizure of property.

Additional Legislation

Actions by bondholders and taxpayers against collectors became so numerous that the legislature of 1884 enacted several additional measures against the troublesome coupons. Coupons could not be received in payment of license taxes. No action of trespass on the case could be maintained against any collecting officer for levying upon the property of any taxpayer who had tendered coupons. Attorneys for the state should, under penalty, appeal to a higher court "as a matter of right" if defeated in tax cases. A "tax-receivable coupon bond sinking fund" was established. When the state was compelled to accept coupons, the auditor was to enter in this fund the difference between the face value of the coupons and the amount which would have been payable on the bond if it had been funded. This amount was later to be deducted from the principal of the bond when it was presented for payment.[46]

45. *Smith* v. *Greenhow*, 109 U. S. 669 (1883).
46. *Acts*, 1883-84, pp. 120, 504, 527, 721.

Employees of the auditor and treasurer could not be required to leave their duties to testify concerning the genuineness of bonds or coupons, and depositions could be taken only after office hours. This was to hamper taxpayers in establishing the validity of coupons, as they were required to do. Persons selling coupons were required to have a special license, which was taxed $1,000 per year plus 20 per cent of the face value of all coupons sold. Lawyers bringing suits on coupons were required to pay a special tax of $250.[47]

The Virginia Coupon Cases

Bondholders and taxpayers scored a victory in April, 1885, when the United States Supreme Court handed down its decision in eight cases. The Court, by a vote of five to four, held that the coupons should be received for taxes as though they were money and that when a taxpayer had tendered coupons he, "in legal contemplation has paid the debt he owed the State. . . . He is free from all further disturbance, and is securely shielded by the constitution in his immunity."[48] Any collector who attempted to collect the tax after such a tender was stripped of "his official character" and was personally liable for any damages to the taxpayer. Of the Riddleberger Act, the "Coupon-Killers," and the Act of 1884 prohibiting action for trespass, the Court said: "The whole legislation, in all its parts, as to creditors affected by it and not consenting to it, must be pronounced null and void."[49]

Three other cases were determined on the basis of the Poindexter case, while three others were dismissed because no federal question was involved. In the last case, the Court refused to issue a mandamus to compel the Treasurer of the City of Richmond to receive coupons, and stated that this reaffirmed the decision in *Antoni* v. *Greenhow*.[50] In these cases the Court did not exactly reverse itself, but the taxpayers had secured the advantage they desired, provided they brought their action in the correct way.

47. See *Eleventh Census*, "Wealth, Debt, and Taxation," Part I, pp. 136-138, for a summary of these acts.
48. *Poindexter* v. *Greenhow*, 114 U. S. 270, 300-301 (1885).
49. *Ibid.*, pp. 305-306.
50. *Moore* v. *Greenhow*, 114 U. S. 338 (1885).

In 1886 and 1887 Royall won two cases in which the Court held that coupons could be used to pay license taxes, and that if, after a tender of coupons, the proper official refused to issue the license, a person otherwise qualified could practice his profession without liability for damages.[51]

More Coupon Legislation

The 1886 legislature attempted to destroy the advantages which bondholders and taxpayers had won. Taxpayers tendering coupons had previously been required to offer them for "verification." They were now required to assume the burden of proving them valid and were not allowed to introduce expert testimony in doing so. They were also required to produce the bonds from which the coupons were clipped. Collectors were to be indemnified for liabilities or damages resulting from attempts to collect taxes. Coupons were not to be accepted unless proved genuine within one year of maturity. Any person, not a lawyer, soliciting or inducing action on coupons should be guilty of champerty and subject to fines and imprisonment. Any lawyer who solicited or induced suits against the state should be guilty of barratry and should be disbarred. New regulations were provided concerning the payment of license taxes, designed to delay the issue of the license when coupons were tendered.[52] An act of 1887 provided that if a taxpayer tendered coupons and refused to pay cash, the state's attorney should, within ten days, bring suit in the proper state court to collect the taxes, and "the burden of proving the tender and the genuineness of the coupons shall be on the defendant." But, "If the defendant fails in his defence . . . any coupon filed by him . . . [and not spurious] shall be returned to him. . . ." In other words, if he failed to prove the coupons valid they should be returned to him, if they were valid! If the state obtained judgment and the taxpayer offered coupons to satisfy the judgment, the process could be repeated indefinitely.[53] These added regulations placed insuperable

51. Royall v. Virginia, 116 U. S. 572 (1886); Royall v. Virginia, 121 U. S. 102 (1887).
52. Acts, 1885-86, pp. 36, 40, 249, 266, 384.
53. Acts, Special Session, 1887, p. 257.

obstacles upon the taxpayers and threatened to break their resistance.

More Litigation

Taxpayers secured an injunction prohibiting the attorney-general from enforcing the act requiring suits against taxpayers who tendered coupons. The attorney-general disregarded the injunction, contending that it was a suit against the state, which could not be maintained. A federal circuit court found him guilty of contempt, fined him $500, and committed him to jail until the fine should be paid. He applied to the United States Supreme Court for a writ of habeas corpus, which was granted.[54] "This decision relieved the officers of the State from all embarrassment, and placed those who had tendered coupons at their mercy. Suits were prosecuted against them all over the State; the State courts refused to allow them to make any defence; judgments with costs were entered against them; second judgments on these with second costs were added; third judgments with third costs were added to these, and so the iniquity went on."[55]

Another series of cases was carried to the United States Supreme Court, and again the taxpayers were victorious.[56] In these cases the Court held the following acts to be unconstitutional: the act requiring that the bond from which the coupons were clipped be produced to establish the validity of the coupons; the act prohibiting expert testimony in establishing the validity of coupons; the act requiring a special license for the right to sell coupons; and the act requiring that coupons be offered within one year of maturity. In addition, the Court questioned "very much whether" the acts

54. *In re Ayers,* 123 U. S. 443 (1887).

55. Royall, *op. cit.,* p. 95. Royall, deeply impressed by the unfairness of the law and convinced that "each grand juror knew very well that he was giving his aid to enforcing statutes forbidden by the Constitution," sued the members of a state grand jury in a federal court for damages and publicly announced that he would continue this policy when he or his clients were indicted under the law. For a time he stopped the indictments, and the grand jury declined to take action against him for suit, but the attorney-general filed a complaint against him for intimidating grand jurors. For this he was tried, fined $150, and placed in jail until the fine should be paid. From a federal court he obtained a writ of habeas corpus and refused to pay the fine (*ibid.,* pp. 103-106).

56. Royall, *op. cit.,* pp. 103-106; *McGahey* v. *Virginia,* 135 U. S. 662 (1890). This case gives an excellent summary of the various laws and cases involving the coupons.

requiring suits against taxpayers who tendered coupons and acts requiring that coupons be rejected, "are not themselves laws impairing the obligation of the contract." Finally, the Court added a postscript to the last case: "It is certainly to be wished that some arrangement may be adopted which will be satisfactory to all the parties concerned, and relieve the courts as well as the Commonwealth of Virginia, whose name and history recall so many interesting associations, from all further exhibitions of a controversy that has become a vexation and a regret."[57]

Thus, it appeared that the bondholders, at great expense, were winning most of the battles but losing the war. "Business men refused to use the old coupons, lawyers to take coupon cases." After the Supreme Court had expressed its impatience with the continued litigation, the creditors decided that it would be best to come to an agreement with the state. Negotiations followed, ending with the final settlement in 1892.

Coupons Paid to State

The varying success of bondholders and taxpayers is reflected partly by the amount of coupons which they forced the state to accept for taxes. Up to September 30, 1879, $6,676,632 of coupons had been received. Between 1880 and 1890 the amount of tax-receivable coupons maturing each year varied between $1,300,000 and $1,400,000. The amounts received by the state in fiscal years ending September 30 were:[58]

Year	Received for Taxes	Received on Judgments
1880	$1,125,285	
1881	876,718	
1882	724,260	483
1883	49,741	41,023
1884	172,997	172,997
1885	50,164	50,164
1886	56,186	56,186
1887	81,620	81,620
1888	258,938	258,938
1889	214,580	214,580
	$3,610,491	$ 875,993

57. *Ibid.*, p. 721.
58. *Eleventh Census,* "Wealth, Debt, and Taxation," Part I, p. 133.

The Final Settlement

Under a joint resolution of March 3, 1890, a commission was appointed to receive propositions for funding the debt not funded under the Riddleberger Act. A bondholders' committee reached an agreement with the state commission, which was later embodied in the Act of February 20, 1892, known as the "Olcott Settlement."[59] Under this act the commissioners of the sinking fund were empowered "to such an extent as may be necessary to issue nineteen millions of dollars of bonds in lieu of the twenty-eight million dollars of outstanding obligations, not funded under" the Riddleberger Act. The new "Century" bonds were to be dated July 1, 1891, and to run for one hundred years. Interest was to be paid at the rate of 2 per cent for the first ten years and 3 per cent thereafter. New bonds were to be issued in exchange for the principal of old bonds, plus any unpaid coupons maturing up to and including July 1, 1891, in the proportion of 19 to 28. By July 1, 1892, the bondholders' committee was to present in bulk $23,000,000 of old obligations and to receive in exchange new bonds which were to be apportioned among the several classes of creditors by a tribunal appointed by the creditors. Creditors not represented by the bondholders' committee were allowed to refund their obligations, receiving new bonds at the same ratio as holders of similar obligations under the distribution made by the creditors' committee.

As in previous funding acts, certificates were to be issued representing West Virginia's share of the debt, on which Virginia assumed no liability. Coupons which had previously been tendered in payment of taxes were to be accepted in payment of such taxes, and any judgment secured thereon was to be discharged, provided the taxpayer paid, in money, the costs of the judgment. Provisions were made for a sinking fund for the new bonds and also for the canceling, as soon as $15,000,000 of the new bonds had been issued, of the Riddleberger bonds then held by the sinking fund.

Progress of Funding.

Because of a delay in issuing the new bonds, the state gave to the bondholders' committee a manuscript bond for $16,359,860 on which

59. *Acts,* 1891-92, p. 533.

interest was paid until July 1, 1893. The manuscript bond was surrendered and canceled July 21, 1893, and engraved bonds were issued therefor. Up to September 30, 1902, bondholders had surrendered obligations amounting to $27,193,001, including $19,741,738 of principal and $7,451,273 of interest, and had received in exchange $18,042,707 of century bonds. Thus the state's obligations were reduced by $9,150,304.[60] In 1892 the state's funded debt was $31,-469,054, and the annual interest requirements thereon were approximately $1,500,000. By 1902 the funded debt had been reduced by 15 per cent to $27,044,310, while the annual interest charge had been reduced by approximately 43 per cent to $877,397. Table 17 shows the composition of the debt at selected dates.

TABLE 17

COMPOSITION OF THE VIRGINIA DEBT AT SELECTED DATES

(In thousands of dollars)

Class of Obligation	1881	1891	1893	1902
Prewar bonds............	$ 4,333	$ 1,935	$ 780	$ 129
"Consols"*............	14,370	14,150	757	53
"Ten-forties"*........	8,517	5,728	312	21
"Peelers".............	2,394	719	336	6
"Riddlebergers"........	......	8,613	6,331	6,330
"Centuries"...........	......	......	16,641	18,039
Obligations to trust funds..............	1,428	516	2,460	2,466
Total funded debt......	$31,043	$31,660	$27,618	$27,044
Accrued interest........	4,977	9,387	2,722	304
Gross debt.............	36,020	41,048	30,340	27,348
Sinking fund...........	2,047	5,205	2,923	3,802
Net debt..............	33,974	35,842	27,416	23,546

*Coupons receivable for taxes.
Source: Bureau of the Census.

It will be noticed that little progress was made in funding the bonds with tax-receivable coupons into "Riddlebergers" in the nine years after 1882. Almost none of the consols and comparatively few of the ten-forties were funded. Less than $9,000,000 of the "Riddlebergers" were issued, mainly in exchange for prewar bonds and "Peelers." The extent to which the holders of the "consols"

60. Bureau of the Census, *Wealth, Debt and Taxation* (Washington, 1907), p. 175.

and "ten-forties" accepted the final agreement of 1892 is shown by the heavy conversion reflected in the 1893 figures.

By the various funding acts scattered over twenty years, Virginia had scaled its obligations, exclusive of the amount assigned to West Virginia, by about $13,650,000. This was realized by funding under the different acts as follows: under the McCulloch Act, $836,000 (50 per cent of accrued interest funded); under the Riddleberger Act, $3,664,000; and under the final settlement, $9,150,000.

THE WEST VIRGINIA SUITS

During the twenty years or more in which Virginia struggled with its internal debt problem, it gave little attention to working out a division of the old debt with West Virginia. Not until after 1892 was it able to give attention to the interstate problem. Let us notice the positions taken by the two states.

West Virginia's Position

West Virginia argued that the debt was a local, and not a general, debt. It had been incurred, it was contended, almost entirely for the benefit of the eastern counties. In support of this contention it was pointed out that the Baltimore and Ohio Railroad was not permitted to extend its lines westward beyond Winchester and that the Cleveland and Pittsburgh road was not allowed to extend its lines through Virginia territory to Wheeling, but had to enter that city from Ohio. Moreover, not a single public building was completed within the limits of the new state between 1823 and 1861. It was also argued that the east had greater proportionate representation in the legislature and that eastern landlords and slaveowners received concessions in the levying of taxes.[61] For these reasons the state claimed that it should assume only an amount equal to outlays within the new state plus "a just proportion of the ordinary expenses of the State Government" since the first debt was incurred, less state taxes paid from western counties during the same period.

61. Randall, *op. cit.*, pp. 555-556.

Virginia's Position

In answer, Virginia contended that the program of internal improvements had been designed for the benefit of the whole state and that the development of the resources of western counties was one of the principal purposes of that program. Although the program was not complete in 1861, several million dollars had been spent for railroads and canals within the new state, and other projects were of great benefit, although not touching the area directly. That the new state profited by these works was shown by the remarkable increase in property values in the years immediately following the war. It was also pointed out that representatives from western counties had consistently voted in favor of incurring the debt and that many projects could not have been undertaken without their votes. West Virginia had also received from Virginia over $600,000 in bank stocks and other assets worth several million dollars.[62] For these reasons Virginia believed that the debt should be divided according to area and population. This was the basis of the provisions in the various funding acts which assigned one third of the debt to West Virginia.

Attempts at Negotiation

In 1894 the Virginia Debt Commission was created to represent the holders of the certificates issued by Virginia. It could not enter into any negotiation "except upon the basis that Virginia is bound only for two thirds of the original debt." This limitation weakened the commission in its negotiation; so an act of 1900 provided that, with the consent of certificate holders, "the commission was to be invested with control of the certificates with the understanding that the holders would accept the amount realized from West Virginia as a full settlement of all their claims."[63] The commission might bring suit if certificate holders would agree that costs thereof might be deducted from any proceeds realized. There were $15,-481,692 of the certificates outstanding. The holders of $13,173,-435 deposited them with the commission and agreed to the terms of the act, but the commission was unable to reach an agreement.

62. *Virginia* v. *West Virginia*, 206 U. S. 290, 291-299 (1907).
63. Randall, *op. cit.*, p. 564.

West Virginia still insisted upon a settlement on the basis of calculated expenditures, and at different times presented various computations on this basis. Some of those showed West Virginia's part of the debt as high as $3,000,000 or $4,000,000, while others showed that Virginia owed West Virginia "from $769,000 to $3,123,000, the exact amount varying according to the different ways of construing the [Wheeling] ordinance."[64]

In 1906 the West Virginia legislature resolved that that state did "not owe any part of the so-called debt of Virginia, and that this legislature is opposed to any negotiations on that subject." The Virginia Debt Commission reported that similar resolutions had been passed at nearly every session since 1896, "Thus showing a persistent and determined refusal on the part of West Virginia to pay any portion of what they are bound for on account of the debt of the original state, or to enter into any accounting or negotiation whatsoever on the subject."[65]

The First Case

In 1906 Virginia asked the United States Supreme Court to determine West Virginia's part of the debt and to issue an order requiring its payment. West Virginia argued that the Court had no jurisdiction because it could not enforce a final decree and because Virginia had "no interest in these certificates, nor can her interests be in any manner affected by a decree in relation to these certificates." Virginia, it was claimed, was prosecuting the suit for the benefit of the individuals holding the certificates and was thus attempting to circumvent the Eleventh Amendment. The Court cited several cases in answer to the first argument, but gave no answer to the second except to state that "We are satisfied that as we have jurisdiction, these questions ought not to be passed upon on demurrer."[66] By a decree of May 4, 1908, the case was referred to a master for the ascertainment of the facts necessary for the settlement.[67]

64. *Ibid.*, p. 566.
65. Quoted in Grenoble, *op. cit.*, p. 107.
66. *Virginia* v. *West Virginia*, 206 U. S. 290, 317-322 (1907).
67. 209 U. S. 514, 534.

The master found that the debt on January 1, 1861, was $33,-897,074, and that on June 20, 1863, the date of separation, West Virginia had one third of the free population and 23.5 per cent of total population. His most difficult problem was to ascertain the value of property on June 20, 1863. The prevalence of Confederate currency and great fluctuations in value due to the war forced him to resort to estimates in an effort to find true values. His final estimates were that total property values, including slaves, were $551,000,000 in Virginia, and $98,000,000 in West Virginia. Without slaves, the figures were: Virginia, $300,000,000, and West Virginia, $92,000,000.[68]

The Second Case

The matter was again brought before the Supreme Court in January, 1911, to be decided on the basis of the master's findings. Virginia, after some preliminary disagreements, agreed to the amount of the debt as stated, but took exceptions to some of the other findings in the master's report. Virginia attorneys estimated that West Virginia was liable for $9,652,769 of the original debt and interest thereon from January 1, 1861.

West Virginia repeated its former arguments and added new ones. It contended that the constitutional mandate to assume "an equitable proportion" of the debt must be interpreted in accordance with the special agreement embodied in the Wheeling ordinance of 1861 requiring division according to calculated expenditures. It disclaimed liability for interest from 1861, arguing that it had agreed to pay "accruing interest" from the transfer of the debt.[69]

Considering the case "in the untechnical spirit proper for dealing with a quasi-international controversy," Mr. Justice Holmes, speaking for the Court, first determined that the division of the debt should not be made on the basis of calculated expenditures. He held that "All the expenditures had the ultimate good of the whole State in view" and that the contract was "not modified or affected in any practical way by the preliminary suggestions of the

68. Randall, *op. cit.*, pp. 567-568.   69. *Ibid.*, pp. 569-571.

Wheeling ordinance."[70]   Regarding Virginia's right to sue, he declared that West Virginia's liability was "a deep-seated equity, not discharged by changes in the form of the debt nor split up by the unilateral attempt of Virginia to apportion specific parts to the two States," and that Virginia was a party to the contract with West Virginia, "in the performance of which the, honor and credit of Virginia is concerned."

As the basis for the settlement he specified property values, exclusive of slaves, as of June 20, 1863, which required Virginia to pay 76.5 per cent of the total debt, or $25,931,261. But Virginia had assumed only two thirds of the debt, which was $22,598,049, or $3,333,212 less than its part as stated above. The Justice then subtracted the $3,333,212 from the total debt and stated West Virginia's just part as 23.5 per cent of the remainder, or $7,182,507. Regarding interest, there was "a serious controversy in the record, . . . concerning which there is room for a wide divergence of opinion. . . . As this is no ordinary commercial suit, but . . . a quasi-international difference . . . we think it best at this stage to go no farther. . . . Great States have a temper superior to that of private litigants, and it is to be hoped that enough has been decided for patriotism, the fraternity of the Union, and mutual consideration to bring it to an end."[71]

Although the West Virginia legislature was meeting in special session in May, 1911, the governor maintained that it was called for another purpose and could not consider the debt. He refused to amend the call or to call another special session. Discouraged by these delays, Virginia asked the Supreme Court to proceed at once to a final decree since there, was "no reasonable hope for an amicable settlement," but the motion was overruled.[72]   In its regular 1913 session the West Virginia legislature created a debt commission, but denied it the power to make a final settlement. Commissions from the two states met in Washington in July, 1913, but since neither had any proposal to submit, nothing was accomplished. Again Virginia moved for a final decree by the Court, claiming that the futile negotiations made it "indisputably certain that no

70. *Virginia* v. *West Virginia*, 220 U. S. 1, 27-30 (1911).
71. *Ibid.*, pp. 35-40.   72. 222 U. S. 17 (1911).

hope of an adjustment exists." West Virginia asked for more time while its commission completed certain investigations. The Court continued its lenient attitude and set the final hearing for April, 1914.[73]

In March, 1914, the two commissions met again, and West Virginia, after eight years of litigation, finally put in a claim for its proportionate share of the assets held by Virginia and pledged for the retirement of the debt as of January 1, 1861. The total value of such assets was placed at $20,810,358, and West Virginia's portion (23.5 per cent less minor adjustments) at $4,855,312, which, subtracted from the $7,182,507 stated by the Supreme Court as West Virginia's part of the debt, left $2,327,195. The West Virginia commission offered to recommend the immediate payment of that sum.[74] Virginia refused the offer, and in the following month West Virginia asked the Court to be allowed to file a "supplemental answer" containing the material concerning the newly discovered credits. The Court held that in a case between "ordinary litigants" the request would not be granted, but again special recognition was given to the status of the parties, and the master was ordered to consider and report to the Court on West Virginia's claims and any counter claims Virginia might make.[75]

The Third Case

The master recommended that the credits be allowed, setting the value of all the assets at $14,511,946 and West Virginia's share at $3,410,307. Attorneys for the two states and for the bondholders took exception to the findings, and the Court, in June, 1915, gave its decision, setting the total value of the assets at $14,929,161 and West Virginia's portion, adjusted, at $2,966,885. This reduced West Virginia's part of the debt to $4,215,622.[76]

Before it could enter a final decree the Court had to decide the troublesome question of interest. It held that West Virginia was definitely bound to pay interest from January 1, 1861, on its part of the debt, and, since no rate was specified, at approximately the same

73. 231 U. S. 89 (1913).   74. Randall, op. cit., pp. 573-574.
75. Virginia v. West Virginia, 234 U. S. 117, 122 (1914).
76. Virginia v. West Virginia, 238 U. S. 202, 206, 233 (1915).

rate as Virginia paid on its share. Of course, it was impossible accurately to determine the average effective rate paid by Virginia in those years, but the Court finally decided upon 4 per cent from January 1, 1861, to July 1, 1891, and 3 per cent thereafter until the date of judgement. Calculated to July 1, 1915, the amount assessed against West Virginia was: principal, $4,215,622; interest, $8,178,307; total, $12,393,929. Interest on the judgment was to be paid at the rate of 5 per cent.[77]

During the remainder of 1915 the Virginia Debt Commission made several attempts to arrange a meeting with the West Virginia Commission but to no avail. In June, 1916, Virginia asked the Supreme Court to issue a writ of execution directing the federal marshal to levy on property owned by West Virginia to satisfy the judgment, but the Court refused on the ground that a state should have ample time to act.[78] A special session of the West Virginia legislature in November, 1916, took no action on the matter, and when the regular session opened in January, 1917, the governor mentioned the possibility of a rehearing and made other suggestions for delaying the case. Finally, Virginia, in February, 1917, asked the Court for a mandamus ordering the speakers and members of the West Virginia legislature to levy a tax to pay the judgment. In response to the Court's show-cause order, West Virginia argued that the Court could not constitutionally issue such an order, and interposed another claim. It contended that Virginia had a claim against the United States arising out of the cession of the Northwest Territory in 1783, amounting to over $80,000,000, and that West Virginia's portion of that amount would discharge its liability.[79] The Court overruled these objections and proceeded to hear the case on its merits.

The Final Case

The issues at stake in the case[80] were the power of the Court to enforce a judgment against a state and the methods of such enforcement. The Court held that it had this power in spite of the

77. *Ibid.*, p. 242.
78. 241 U. S. 531 (1916).   79. 246 U. S. 567-579 n. (1918).
80. *Virginia* v. *West Virginia*, 246 U. S. 565 (1918).

Tenth Amendment and in spite of the underlying assumption of the Constitution requiring the preservation of the states: ". . . when the constitution gave original jurisdiction to this court to entertain at the instance of one State a suit against another, it must have intended to . . . bring the States and their governmental authority within the exceptional judicial power which was created. No other rational explanation can be given for the provision."[81]

Regarding methods of enforcement, the Court ruled that "the powers to render the judgment and to enforce it . . . are federal powers and . . . are sustained by every authority of the federal government, judicial, legislative, or executive, which may be appropriately exercised." Thus, Congress, since it had the right "to refuse or to assent to a contract between States," had the power "to see to its enforcement." Furthermore, this power did not violate the rights of the states under the Tenth Amendment, but was necessary to the maintenance of the Constitution; to deny it would be to "disregard and overthrow the doctrines irrevocably settled by the great controversy of the Civil War. . . ."[82]

The Court also believed that it had the power to issue the mandamus asked, but it preferred not to do so because "if we refrain now from passing upon the questions stated, we may be spared in the future the necessity of exerting compulsory power against one of the States of the Union to compel it to discharge a plain duty resting upon it under the Constitution." Thus, because of the status of the litigants, it reserved "further action in order that full opportunity may be afforded to Congress to exercise the power which it undoubtedly possesses."[83] If the matter was not settled, the Court suggested that the case be put on the docket for the next term for argument on methods of enforcing judgment including "such other and appropriate equitable remedy, by dealing with the funds or taxable property of West Virginia or the rights of that State, as may secure an execution of the judgment." The Court also reserved the right to appoint a master to study "the amount and method of taxation essential to be put into effect . . . to secure the full execution of the judgment. . . ." Having thus displayed its

81. *Ibid.*, pp. 595-596.
82. *Ibid.*, pp. 601-603.   83. *Ibid.*, pp. 604-605.

assortment of clubs, the Court hoped West Virginia would take the hint.

The Final Payment

When the West Virginia legislature met in January, 1919, neither the debt commission nor the governor made any definite recommendation for action on the debt. Interest to the extent of $2,168,938 had accrued on the original judgment of $12,393,925, making the total $14,562,867. The legislature desired more information and also recommendations as to whether the debt should be paid; if so, in what manner; and if not, "why not and how can the payment thereof be avoided?"[84] Shortly thereafter a representative of the Virginia Debt Commission addressed the legislature and made an offer. The only obstacle to agreement theretofore was the matter of allowing West Virginia to hold in escrow enough bonds to represent certificates lost or unrepresented. The above offer was to accept $1,062,876 plus interest at 5 per cent after January 1, 1919, in cash, and $13,500,000 in 3½ per cent, 20-year bonds, West Virginia to hold about $1,100,000 of bonds in escrow. This offer was accepted,[85] and shortly thereafter the legislature authorized payment.[86]

The bonds were to be issued according to the above specifications. As soon as Virginia filed a list of the certificates deposited, $12,366,500 of the bonds were to be paid over, the other $1,133,500 were to be placed in escrow with the West Virginia Board of Public Works. This board was to deliver to Virginia all bonds not needed to cover outstanding certificates not deposited with the Virginia Debt Commission; thereafter bonds were to be delivered on order of the Virginia commission as outstanding certificates were deposited. Any bonds not claimed by January 1, 1939, were to be destroyed. The board was directed to levy annual taxes sufficient to pay interest on the new bonds and to retire one twentieth of them each year.

On April 18, 1919, West Virginia deposited $1,070,663 in a Wash-

84. Senate Joint Resolution No. 6, Jan. 24, 1919, *Acts,* 1919, p. 499.
85. *Acts,* 1919, p. 507.
86. *Acts, Extraordinary Session,* 1919, p. 19. Effective April 1, 1919.

ington bank to the account of such agency as might be appointed to distribute the funds. Virginia asked the Supreme Court to appoint a receiver for this purpose, but the request was denied. On July 2, 1919, West Virginia delivered to the Virginia Debt Commission $12,366,500 of bonds.[87] When those payments had been made, Virginia notified the Supreme Court that the judgment had been satisfied and instituted an action in the Circuit Court for the City of Richmond "for the purpose of convening all parties in interest and having said court take charge of the fund in said cause, determine and adjudicate the rights of all parties in interest and distribute the said fund under its authority and direction."[88] The Court took jurisdiction, designated a depository, and appointed a master to report on the matter. The master made a comprehensive report. On July 22, 1920, the Court confirmed the report and ordered the distribution of the cash and bonds in accordance therewith.

Certificates representing West Virginia's part of the debt had been issued to the amount of about $18,223,000, of which approximately $1,250,000 bore no interest. Virginia state funds held $2,745,462 of certificates, which the Court had held might not participate in the award. This left $15,477,530 outstanding in the hands of the public. Of these, $14,368,843 had been deposited with the Virginia Debt Commission and were held by Brown Brothers and Company, of New York, as depository, leaving $1,108,687 undeposited. By the time the court decree was issued, the West Virginia Board of Public Works had delivered to the Virginia Debt Commission additional bonds (from those held in escrow) to the amount of $272,275, making the total $12,638,733. The original deposit of cash had increased, by interest on itself and by the deposit of maturing interest on the bonds, to $1,776,798. The total of cash and bonds was thus $14,415,531.

This sum was distributed according to the court order. In accordance with the agreement of the certificate holders with Virginia, the expenses of the debt commission, amounting to $1,144,-

87. *Chronicle,* CVIII (1919), 1741, 1846; CIX (1919), 301.
88. *Report of the Virginia Debt Commission* (Va.), *House Document No. 10,* 1922, p. 4.

017, were paid first in cash. Next, Virginia received in its own right $470,244—$22,426 in cash and $447,818 in bonds. The remainders—$610,356 of cash and $12,190,857 of bonds—were delivered to Brown Brothers and Company for distribution to certificate holders. That firm levied an assessment of 5 per cent of the face value of the certificates as a service charge, which took all the remaining cash and about $30,000 of the bonds. After the deduction of the service charge, the holders of interest-bearing certificates received, in bonds, the following percentages of the face value of their certificates; certificates of 1871, 90.895; certificates of 1879, 87.695; certificates of 1882, 75.254; certificates of 1892, 66.812. Non-interest-bearing certificates, or scrip, were redeemed at 16.868 per cent of par.[89] Thus, after fifty years in which they had received no interest, the holders had their certificates redeemed at a discount.

By July 16, 1921, $381,747 of additional certificates had been deposited with Virginia, and $288,084 of West Virginia bonds had been released from escrow, leaving $573,132 still thus held.[90] Very few certificates appeared thereafter, for on June 30, 1936, $450,800 of the bonds were still held in escrow. The West Virginia Board of Public Works regularly levied the tax for interest and principal as directed. The rate at first was ten cents per $100, but soon this was reduced to five cents, and later to four cents. In 1920 and 1921 the Board purchased $2,030,000 of the bonds for retirement at an average price of 81. In 1922-23, $3,200,000 were bought at about 84. By 1935 the issue had been reduced to $2,240,000, which was then refunded into 1.4 per cent notes maturing in 1936-39. These notes were redeemed according to schedule, thus bringing to a close this long and troubled episode.

SUMMARY

An unbearable debt burden forced Virginia into a most unusual political struggle wherein one group of contestants held that the state's contract should remain inviolate while the other believed that it should be subject to the pressing needs of the state. The latter view denied the existence of any ironclad contract which deprived

89. *Chronicle*, CXI (1920), 1390.
90. *Report of Virginia Debt Commission*, p. 8.

the legislature of its constitutional control over public revenues; it held that public funds should be used in such ways as would subserve true democracy rather than the interests of bondholders. Before the final settlement was reached, however, this line of cleavage between parties and groups had all but disappeared, and the necessity of debt adjustment was generally accepted. It was democracy against rigid constitutionalism, and democracy won. The sanctity of contract was subordinated to certain social values of the time.

While Virginia struggled to adjust its debt, West Virginia, by inaction, sought to avoid the assumption of any part of the debt of the old state. Apportionment between the two states was not accomplished without a severe legal test which challenged the power of the United States Supreme Court to hear such cases or to enforce its decisions. Even before the beginning of litigation the court had established the joint liability of the two states for the old debt. All things considered, the court could not well recede from this position, and, if it did not, it had to face the delicate problem of coercing West Virginia to assume its just portion.

What might have happened had West Virginia not yielded to pressure from the high court is an interesting subject for speculation. This case and others to be described in the following chapter reveal problems peculiar to a federal system of government. In spite of the recalcitrance which some states have shown to court orders, it is significant and gratifying that all have finally acceded to the court's authority without resort to violence.

CHAPTER IX

FROM RECONSTRUCTION TO THE WORLD WAR

CERTAIN MISCELLANEOUS developments, in addition to those already described, affected state debts between the Reconstruction period and the World War. These, together with a general view of the trend of state indebtedness during these years, are the subject of this chapter.

REPUDIATION IN MINNESOTA

Minnesota repudiated an issue of bonds and later rescinded the repudiation and compromised the bonds, in peculiar legal fashion. In 1857 Minnesota voters amended their constitution, by a vote of 25,023 to 6,733, to allow the state to issue $5,000,000 in 7 per cent bonds to aid railroad construction. The railroad companies were to give the state first mortgage bonds as security. The governor demanded that the roads should give the state a closed issue of bonds, but the roads desired to issue other bonds with equal priority to those given to the state, and won a court order to that effect.[1] The reaction on public sentiment, however, was unfavorable to the roads. After the state had issued $2,275,000 of bonds, work was stopped with the roads uncompleted. In 1859 all the roads defaulted on interest payments, and in 1860 the governor foreclosed the mortgages and bought in the roads for a nominal $1,000 each, later selling the properties and franchises to other companies. In 1860 the legislature proposed, and the people ratified by a vote of about 19,000 to 700, two constitutional amendments, forbidding the legislature to levy a tax to pay principal or interest of the bonds without the approval of the voters, and prohibiting further issue of bonds under the 1858 amendment, which was "expunged

1. *Minn. and Pac. Railroad Co.* v. *H. H. Sibley,* 2 Minn. 13 (1858).

from the Constitution."[2]   It was charged that the bonds had been sold at from 17½ cents to 50 cents on the dollar.

Between 1860 and 1880 many proposals were advanced for settling the debt. Several involved the use of public lands to retire the bonds, but none won the approval of both voters and bondholders. In 1876 the United States Supreme Court stated, as an *obiter dictum,* that the bonds were "legal obligations of the state, and binding upon it in law, honor, and justice . . . if the state were suable in the courts, there can be no doubt that the bonds would be legally enforcible against it."[3]   Several governors urged legislators to provide for the debt, but without success. Finally, in 1881, Governor Pillsbury persuaded the legislators to pass an unusual law. It made provision for funding the debt, but was to be submitted to a vote of the people only in case a special tribunal, composed of the five justices of the state supreme court, held that the repudiating amendment of 1860 was valid. If the tribunal held the amendment invalid, the state was to proceed with the funding without a vote of the people.[4]

The supreme court justices declined to serve, and the governor, in keeping with the act, appointed five district judges to compose the tribunal, which met in St. Paul on July 26, 1881. The attorney-general objected to the jurisdiction and competency of the tribunal and petitioned the state supreme court for a writ of prohibition to prevent it from considering the case. The court issued a show-cause order, and the tribunal adjourned to await the court's decision.[5]   The court had to decide two questions: first, whether the 1881 act was unconstitutional because it violated the 1860 amendment; and, second, whether it was unconstitutional in that it attempted to delegate legislative power to the judges by leaving it for them to decide which part of the act should become law; i.e., whether the act should be submitted to the people.

After a lengthy and erudite discussion on the impairment of the obligation of contracts, the court decided that the 1860 amendment

2. *General Laws,* 1860, p. 297. See McGrane, *op. cit.,* pp. 322-328, for a fuller account of these transactions.

3. Quoted in McGrane, *op. cit.,* p. 331.

4. *General Laws,* 1881, pp. 117-123.

5. *State* v. *Young,* 29 Minn. 474, 485 (1881).

impaired the contract in the bonds and was therefore "repugnant to the constitution of the United States and void. Being void, it cannot affect the validity of the act of March 2, 1881; for it is still in the power, and is still the duty of the legislature to provide for the payment of the bonds."[6] The court held further, however, that the act was void because it attempted to delegate legislative power to the judges. But the justices had been forced to decide the principal question in the case which they, as a special tribunal, had refused to consider!

After this decision, the legislature met in special session and re-enacted the essential portions of the previous act, omitting provision for a referendum. The debt, principal and interest, was to be funded into new 5 per cent bonds at 50 cents on the dollar.[7] Before the governor could issue the funding bonds, a writ of injunction was obtained and served on him, yet he proceeded to issue the bonds. When the first interest payment on the bonds came due, a suit was brought to restrain the state treasurer from making payment, on the ground that the authorizing amendment of 1858 was void because Minnesota was then a territory and not a state. It was contended that "the constitution was not yet in force . . . therefore, there was no constitution to be amended."[8] The court rejected this argument and refused to issue the injunction, thereby ending twenty-four years of controversy over the state debt in Minnesota.

SUITS AGAINST SOUTHERN STATES

The repudiation or scaling down of debts by Southern states in the years following Reconstruction aroused intense opposition on the part of bondholders. Barred by the Eleventh Amendment from bringing direct actions against the states, creditors sought by various expedients to exert pressure upon the states indirectly. Several of the suits which arose in this way are discussed below.

Louisiana v. Jumel

Under the funding act of 1874 Louisiana issued 7 per cent, 40-year consolidated bonds in exchange for old bonds at the rate of

6. *Ibid.*, p. 550.   7. *General Laws*, Extra Session, 1881, p. 13.
8. *Secombe* v. *Kittelson*, 29 Minn. 555, 558 (1882).

60 cents on the dollar. Section 7 of the act levied a tax of 5½ mills to pay interest and principal, the revenues from the tax being "set apart and appropriated to that purpose, and no other." It was made a felony for any fiscal officer to divert any of the funds to any other purpose. The tax was to be "a continuing annual tax until the said consolidated bonds shall be paid or redeemed," and the appropriation of the revenues was to be "a continuing annual appropriation during the same period." The auditor, treasurer, and the Board of Liquidation were to "collect said tax annually, and pay said interest and redeem said bonds until the same shall be fully discharged."[9]

The act was declared to be a contract between Louisiana and the bondholders, and no court or judge could enjoin the collection of the tax nor the payment of interest and principal. Shortly after the act was passed, its terms were embodied in a constitutional amendment, which further provided that "the judicial power shall be exercised when necessary" to secure the levy and collection of taxes and the payment of interest, and that "no further legislation or appropriation" would be required to attain those ends.[10]

Louisiana found it difficult to pay interest at the rate of 7 per cent. In 1880 a new constitution was adopted, including the so-called "Debt Ordinance," which reduced the rate to 2 per cent for five years, 3 per cent for fifteen years, and 4 per cent thereafter. The ordinance also reduced the interest tax to three mills, remitted the interest coupons due January 1, 1880, and declared that "any interest taxes collected to meet said coupons are hereby transferred to defray the expenses of the State Government."[11] Over $300,000 of the taxes had been collected and were held in the state treasury; they were later invested in United States bonds.

Soon after the new constitution was adopted private bondholders started two suits in the federal courts. One was a suit in equity "to prevent, by injunction, officers of the State from using the proceeds of taxes already raised . . . for any purpose other than that for which they were collected and paid to the State treasurer." The other asked for a mandamus "against the State officers com-

9. Quoted in *Louisiana* v. *Jumel*, 107 U. S. 711, 713 (1883).
10. *Ibid.*, p. 714.   11. *Ibid.*, p. 715.

pelling the application of the moneys so collected to the payment
of their coupons, and also the collection of taxes to meet future
interest as it becomes due."[12] The circuit court denied the petitions on the ground that they were actions against a state and that
they involved political questions, and the cases were taken to the
United States Supreme Court.

Decision of the Court

The Court admitted that Louisiana had made a contract and
had "violated its contract, and, if it could be sued, might perhaps
be made to set aside its wrongful appropriation of the money
already in hand. . . ." But the requested relief would "require the
officers against whom the process is issued to act contrary to the
positive orders of the supreme political power of the State, whose
creatures they are, and to which they are ultimately responsible in
law for what they do."[13] The Court held that the taxes already
collected were not held as a trust fund for the bondholders, and
that "The remedy sought . . . would require the court to assume
all the executive authority of the State, so far as it related to the
enforcement of this law, and to supervise the conduct of all persons
charged with any official duty in respect to the levy, collection and
disbursement of the tax in question. . . ." For these reasons the
Court decided against the bondholders, although it was forced to
resort to English court records for a precedent. A dissenting justice
questioned the applicability of the case so cited.

Dissenting Opinions

Two justices filed long dissenting opinions. Citing an impressive
array of cases to substantiate their opinions, the justices argued as
follows: Louisiana admittedly had made a contract and then had
attempted to break it. If the constitution of 1880 had not been
adopted, the courts, without question, could have given the bondholders the relief which they wanted. But the parts of that constitution in question were null and void and hence of no more effect than
if they had never been enacted. The two justices argued convincingly
that the duties which the bondholders wished state officers to per-

12. *Ibid.*, pp. 750-751.   13. *Ibid.*, pp. 719-721.

form here were "purely ministerial" and clearly marked out and ordered by the act and amendment of 1874. They berated their colleagues on the bench for holding "that the judicial arm of the nation is hopelessly paralyzed in the presence of an ordinance . . . passed in admitted violation of the constitution of the United States," and contended that "The books are full of cases where executive and administrative officers of a State have been required by the judiciary to do certain acts, or been enjoined from doing them."[14] Certainly the Court was cautious and hesitant in asserting its power in this case.

New Hampshire v. Louisiana

In 1879 the New Hampshire legislature enacted a law permitting citizens who held defaulted state bonds to assign them to the state. If the assignment were accompanied by a deposit of funds to cover the costs of a suit, the attorney-general, if he decided that the bonds were "a valid claim which shall be just and equitable to enforce," should bring suit in the name of the state. No state funds were to be spent, and "the assignor of such claim may associate with the attorney-general in the prosecution thereof . . . such other counsel as the said assignor may deem necessary. . . ." All funds recovered, less any unpaid expenses, were to be paid to the depositing bondholders.[15] In 1880 New York passed a substantially similar law.[16] In 1881 suits were started by both states against Louisiana. Both were based upon the same type of bonds involved in the *Jumel* case, and asked for the same relief. The two cases were heard together.

New Hampshire and New York advanced several of the arguments made in the *Jumel* case and also argued that, since they were the lawful owners of the bonds, they could bring suit on them regardless of the method by which they gained possession. New York advanced an unusual argument to the effect that it, "having been a sovereign, and with powers to make war, issue letters of marque and reprisal, and otherwise to act in a belligerent way,

14. *Ibid.*, pp. 735, 748.
15. *New Hampshire* v. *Louisiana*, 108 U. S. 76, 77 (1883).
16. *Ibid.*, pp. 78-79.

resigned those powers into the control of the United States, to be held in trust, and therefore this court must make decrees in the cases in favor of the plaintiff. . . . "[17] Louisiana's principal defense was that the suit was not a controversy between states, but "a vicarious controversy between individuals."

Decision of the Court

The Court described the steps by which individuals had been deprived of their original right to sue states, and stated that the real question to be decided was "whether a State can allow the use of its name in such a suit for the benefit of one of its citizens." There could be no doubt that these cases "were in legal effect commenced, and are now prosecuted, solely by the owners of the bonds and coupons." Since the purpose of the Eleventh Amendment "was to prohibit all suits against a State by or for citizens of other States . . . one State cannot create a controversy with another State . . . by assuming the prosecution of debts owing by the other State to its citizens."[18] For this reason the cases were dismissed.

Baltzer v. North Carolina

In 1895 a suit was brought against North Carolina to test the validity of the constitutional amendment of 1880 which repudiated the Reconstruction bonds. It was contended that the amendment violated the Federal Constitution by impairing the obligation of the bond contract. The Court, however, held that before the adoption of the amendment the Supreme Court of North Carolina had only the power to hear claims against the state based on the bonds; that its decisions could be only recommendatory and that it could issue no process in the nature of an execution. Since the power was "in no way a remedy, its removal could not be an impairment of the obligation of a contract."[19] A second case was decided on the same grounds.[20]

South Dakota v. North Carolina

In 1901 a New York firm—Schafer Brothers—held 252 North Carolina bonds issued in 1867 and known as Western North Caro-

17. *Ibid.*, p. 85.   18. *Ibid.*, pp. 89-91.
19. *Baltzer* v. *North Carolina*, 161 U. S. 240, 245 (1896).
20. *Baltzer and Taaks* v. *North Carolina*, 161 U. S. 246 (1896).

lina ten-share bonds, because they had been issued to aid the Western North Carolina Railroad and because each had a *second* mortgage on ten shares of state-owned stock in the North Carolina Railroad.[21] After some questionable dealings with the Republican Governor of North Carolina,[22] Schafer Brothers asked the state for permission to bring suit to recover the full principal and about $400,000 of accrued interest on their bonds.[23] The permission was refused. In 1900 a Republican senator from North Carolina visited South Dakota and suggested that it might be possible to arrange for a donation of some of the bonds in question to the University of South Dakota. In 1901 the South Dakota legislature specified that all gifts tendered to the state should be accepted and, if necessary, suits should be brought to collect on any securities so given. The attorney-general could employ counsel to aid him in such suits, to be paid from the proceeds realized. On September 10, 1901, Simon Schafer donated ten bonds to South Dakota, declaring that if that state could enforce payment, "it would be the inclination of the owners of a majority of the total issue now outstanding to make additional donations to such governments as may be able to collect from the repudiating state, rather than accept the small pittance offered in settlement."[24]

Without having made a demand for payment, South Dakota asked the United States Supreme Court for permission to bring suit against North Carolina and two private individuals. The permission was granted, and on November 18, 1901, the complaint was filed. The two individual defendants were Simon Rothschild, a holder of bonds secured by a first mortgage on the stocks in question, and Charles Salter, a holder of bonds similar to those on which the suit was being brought, "the two individuals being made defendants as representatives of the classes of bondholders to which they severally belonged" in order to define and fix the relationships

21. The first mortgage on this stock was security for the Construction Bonds, concerning which see above, pp. 184-185. The bonds here in question were not "Reconstruction" bonds, but were issued before the Reconstruction government came into power.

22. Ratchford, *History of North Carolina Debt*, p. 257.

23. Under the funding act of 1879 these bonds were fundable into 4 per cent bonds at 25 cents on the dollar.

24. *South Dakota* v. *North Carolina*, 192 U. S. 286, 291 (1904).

between the holders of the bonds in question and others who had claims on the stock.

The South Dakota petition asked that, in default of payment, so many of the shares of stock "as might be necessary to pay off and discharge *the entire mortgage indebtedness* be sold and the proceeds . . . be applied in satisfaction of the bonds and coupons secured by such mortgage. . . ."[25] Thus, it was an attempt, indirectly, to benefit the private bondholders.

The case was heard in April, 1903. South Dakota stated the facts and argued that it had a valid claim against North Carolina and that the suit was within the jurisdiction of the Court. North Carolina's arguments were: first, the Court did not have jurisdiction because this was an attempt to circumvent the Eleventh Amendment; second, individuals whose interests were adverse to those of the state were named as co-defendants, and their presence would oust the jurisdiction of the Court; third, South Dakota gained possession of the bonds under conditions which prevented it from invoking the jurisdiction of the Court; fourth, the bonds were illegally issued; and fifth, the mortgage was never legally executed, and hence the only right of action was for breach of contract for failure to deliver the mortgage.[26]

Decision of the Court

After a rehearing, requested by the Court, a five-to-four decision was announced February 1, 1904. The Court held that the bonds were valid obligations and that South Dakota had a good title, the motive of the donor not affecting validity of title. But it was held that the individuals were not necessary parties to the suit, and that South Dakota could not ask for a foreclosure on all the bonds; "So far as these individual defendants are concerned, the suit will be dismissed with costs against South Dakota." After asserting that it had jurisdiction over the case, the Court then ordered North Carolina to pay South Dakota $27,400, the principal and unpaid

25. *Ibid.*, p. 291. Italics are mine.

26. *Ibid.*, pp. 295-309. Each bond declared that ten shares of North Carolina Railroad stock were thereby mortgaged as collateral security. The enabling act specified that this provision should have the effect of a registered mortgage without being registered.

coupons of the ten bonds. If payment were not made by January 1, 1905, one hundred shares of the stock held as collateral should be sold at the east door of the Capitol in Washington to satisfy the claim. The time limit was later extended to April 1, 1905, in order to allow the legislature to act on the matter. Four justices, including the Chief Justice, joined in a dissenting opinion which upheld the arguments advanced by North Carolina.

The decision met a hostile reception in North Carolina, but after considerable discussion the legislature authorized the payment of the judgment. Since the bondholders had threatened further litigation, it was deemed best to effect a settlement with them. After some negotiations, the state finally agreed to pay Schafer Brothers 25 per cent of the bonds held by them plus interest thereon from 1879, amounting to $892 per bond, or a total of $215,864 for the 242 bonds. To meet the two payments, $250,000 of bonds were sold.[27] A few more bonds of the same issue were redeemed at the same rate in later years.

Attempted Suits

Although several suits were brought on bonds which the states had scaled down, bondholders scored no great victories, and gradually these bonds were funded, thus eliminating the possibility of future suits. But the repudiated bonds remain outstanding to this day, constituting a potential source of litigation if and when parties with the power to sue can be found. North Carolina repudiated

27. *Public Laws,* 1905, p. 550. South Dakota received payment on the judgment, but its governor, in 1907, earnestly recommended that the legislature return the payment. The following are some excerpts from his *Biennial Message:* "We took it [the money] away from our sister state, North Carolina, simply because the law said we could. . . . Morally we have no right to one cent of this money and we ought to be brave enough and true enough to give it back. The money was clearly intended for our University. She can use it but it is tainted money. . . . It is entirely plain that ingenious schemers are using our state for private ends. . . . It is clear to me that our state ought not to become a collecting agency neither ought it to forget the doctrine of 'comity between states'. . . . North Carolina does not owe South Dakota anything and never did, at least in this transaction. Let us balance the account by giving back to her that which is hers and not ours." He reported that he had refused another offer of $50,000 of North Carolina bonds ([South Dakota] *Senate Journal,* 1907, pp. 31-33). A bill to authorize repayment to North Carolina was introduced in the Senate, but received an unfavorable committee report, which was sustained by a roll-call vote (*ibid.,* pp. 152, 1141, 1226).

more bonds than any other Southern state, and its bonds have been the basis of many attempted suits. These attempts, all abortive, are listed below.[28] No doubt a detailed study of other states would reveal many other similar attempts. So far as can be found, no federal court has ever passed on the validity or constitutionality of the Reconstruction bonds of any Southern states.

Inspired by the decision in the South Dakota case, holders of North Carolina Reconstruction bonds made many efforts to persuade states to accept bonds and to bring suit. In 1905 and 1906 bonds were offered to Venezuela and Colombia, but the offers were refused. In this country the usual procedure was quietly to persuade some state to enact a law requiring the acceptance of all gifts and the institution of litigation, if necessary, to collect on any securities included in such donations. Then an offer of bonds would be made. This procedure was followed with North Carolina bonds in New York and Michigan in 1905 and in Rhode Island and Nevada in 1909. New York and Michigan refused the bonds. Rhode Island demanded payment, but dropped the claim when the facts became known. The Governor of Nevada refused to receive the bonds, and when the court issued a mandamus to compel him to accept them, the legislature repealed the law. An unsuccessful offer of bonds was made to Missouri in 1916.

In November, 1916, Cuba asked the United States Supreme Court for permission to bring suit against North Carolina on bonds received through the Corporation of Foreign Bondholders of London. The claim for principal and interest amounted to over $2,000,000. North Carolina senators brought diplomatic pressure upon Cuban officials, and the petition was withdrawn just before the date of the hearing.[29] In 1928 Connecticut filed a similar petition, but withdrew it after the governors of the two states had conferred. Over $500,000 of North Carolina bonds were given to Colorado for the use of the state university in 1932. The state made some inquiries concerning the status of the bonds, but later returned

28. For additional details, see B. U. Ratchford, "The Conversion of the North Carolina Public Debt after 1879," op. cit., pp. 268-272.

29. In the Matter of the Republic of Cuba vs. The State of North Carolina (Raleigh, 1917).

them to the donor. As the years pass, it becomes more unlikely that any federal court will ever pass upon these bonds.

Monaco v. Mississippi

The most recent decision of the Court in this field, although not involving post-war bonds, was rendered in 1934. The Principality of Monaco had received as a gift fifty-five Mississippi bonds which were issued in 1833 and 1838 and repudiated in 1841. Monaco asked for permission to sue Mississippi. Mr. Chief Justice Hughes pointed out that the Constitution was not explicit on the right of a foreign power to sue a state. He held that the states are immune from suit without their consent, save where there has been "a surrender of this immunity in the plan of the Convention." By adopting the Constitution the states waived this immunity in relation to other states and the United States, but a foreign state "lies outside the structure of the Union." Since a state could not sue a foreign power without its consent, it was only fair that the rule should work the other way. Permission to sue was denied.[30]

STATE BONDS OWNED BY THE UNITED STATES

Before the Civil War the United States entered into numerous treaties with Indian tribes and paid them large amounts for lands.

TABLE 18

DEFAULTED STATE BONDS OWNED BY INDIAN TRUST FUNDS, DECEMBER, 1867

State	Amount of Bonds	Accrued Interest
Florida	$132,000	$ 60,060
Georgia	3,500	1,365
Missouri	158,000	59,772
North Carolina	205,000	82,290
South Carolina	125,000	52,500
Tennessee	334,667	64,350
Virginia	796,800	310,742
Louisiana	37,000	15,540
Indiana	210,000	40,653
Arkansas	90,000	not reported
Railroad bonds guaranteed by Tennessee	512,000	not reported
Railroad bonds guaranteed by Virginia	100,000	not reported
Totals	$2,703,967	$687,172

Source: *House Executive Doc. No. 59*, 40th Congress, 2d Session, p. 2.

30. *Monaco v. Mississippi*, 292 U. S. 313, 322, 330 (1934).

In many cases the payments were placed in trust funds to be administered by federal officials, the United States guaranteeing a return of 5 per cent on the investments. Since there were few federal obligations outstanding at that time, many of the funds were invested in state bonds. In 1842 the total of state bonds held in this way was $2,440,217.[31]

In December, 1867, the Attorney-General of the United States reported that total investments of the trust funds amounted to $4,291,808, of which over one half were in default, as shown in Table 18.[32]

Concerning the defaulted bonds the Attorney-General said:

So far as the States are liable upon these bonds, . . . I see no grounds upon which that liability can be enforced by proceedings either at law or in equity. A State can be sued only by its own consent . . . whether we regard these bonds as belonging to the United States or to the respective Indian tribes, the right to bring an original suit upon them . . . does not exist . . . for neither the United States nor any Indian tribe is a foreign state within the meaning of the constitutional provision. But if any of these States hold claims against the United States, it may be deemed expedient to exercise the right of retention and application in the nature of a set-off. . . .[33]

These were indeed strange words coming from the Attorney-General of the United States just after the Civil War, but his recommendation was adopted, and in 1870 Congress directed that the Secretary of the Treasury should withhold funds due from the United States to the defaulting states and apply them to the principal and interest of the defaulted bonds.

Some funds were sequestered in this way, but the amounts are not available. In 1876 the Treasurer of the United States was made custodian of the bonds. In 1884 he reported that investments of the funds amounted to $1,808,016 and that Indiana and Maryland had paid all interest on their bonds, while seven Southern states were still in default. Bonds of Arkansas, North Carolina, and Virginia in the amount of $688,800 had become the property of the United States by payment of principal and interest to the trust

---

31. Elliot, *Funding System*, p. 1042.
32. *House Executive Document No. 59*, 40th Congress, 2d Session, p. 2.
33. *Ibid.*, p. 4.

funds for which they were originally purchased.[34] Presumably this amount represented sequestered funds. Included in the above were $538,000 of Arkansas bonds, which formerly belonged to the Smithsonian Institute. In 1885 the United States owned $1,757,800 of the bonds, including $545,000 of Louisiana bonds captured by federal troops during the Civil War, and held by the Treasurer for the Secretary of War. Of the original amount captured, $21,000 had been surrendered to Louisiana in 1884.[35]

North Carolina Sued for Interest

Among the trust fund investments were $147,000 of North Carolina Construction Bonds. The state had provided for refunding these bonds at par, requiring the bondholders to relinquish $240 per bond in accrued interest. The bonds matured in 1884 and 1885. After the United States had refused to waive interest as required in the funding act, North Carolina, in 1889, paid the bonds and interest coupons in full—a total of $193,590. But the United States demanded that interest accruing after the maturity of the bonds— amounting to $41,280—should be paid. The state refused, and an agreed case was brought before the United States Supreme Court. In 1890 the Court gave its decision in favor of North Carolina, holding that "Interest . . . is not to be awarded against a sovereign government unless its consent to pay interest has been manifested by an act of legislature, or by a lawful contract of its executive officers . . . it is equally well settled, by judgments of the Supreme Court of North Carolina, that the State, unless by or pursuant to an explicit statute, is not liable for interest even on a sum certain which is overdue and unpaid."[36]

Attempts to Collect

In 1894 Congress transferred title to all state bonds held by Indian trust funds to the United States. In 1897 the Attorney-General reported that the total of state bonds held—all issued by Southern states—was $2,075,467. For years he had been trying without success to negotiate with the states and also to obtain from

34. *Report of the Treasurer of the United States*, 1884, pp. 24-25.
35. *Ibid.*, 1885, p. 38.
36. *United States* v. *North Carolina*, 136 U. S. 211, 221 (1890).

Congress a statement of the policy to be pursued. He did not wish to start suits without specific authority, and he did not feel free to compromise claims of the United States by funding the bonds at the rates specified by the various state funding acts.[37] In the midst of a long act passed in 1899 to provide for the settlement of state claims arising out of the Spanish-American War, Congress inserted a seven-line paragraph directing the Secretary of the Treasury to start proceedings in the collection of defaulted state bonds. An equally well-hidden paragraph of the following year repealed the above provision and dismissed all proceedings.[38] Again Congress showed the tender solicitude with which it handles financial claims against states.

Settlements with Three States

For many years South Carolina and Virginia had asserted claims against the Federal Government for interest on state advances made during the War of 1812.[39] The United States held $125,000 of South Carolina bonds and $594,800 of Virginia bonds, on all of which there were large interest arrearages. Balances struck between federal and state claims in 1901 showed South Carolina owing $6,807, and Virginia, $338,641. Again Congress was lenient and, by an act of 1902 directing the settlement of the claims, specified that state bonds held by the United States were to be credited as offsets "as of the dates, respectively, at which the accounts will be completely or most nearly balanced, and the balance found due on such date, after deducting the principal and interest on said bonds . . . shall be paid to or by said States. . . ." In the settlement which followed, the United States paid $89,138 to South Carolina and $5.50 to Virginia.

A similar interest claim by North Carolina was "discovered" in 1922.[40] The state claim amounted to $264,176, including $96,836 for cotton seized by federal troops at the close of the Civil War. The United States held $58,000 of North Carolina bonds with $88,140 of

---

37. *House Document No. 263*, 54th Congress, 2d Session.
38. 30 *Statutes at Large* 1358; 31 *Statutes at Large* 612.
39. For details of these claims see B. U. Ratchford, "The Settlement of Certain State Claims. . . ," *op. cit.*, pp. 66-68.   40. See *ibid.*, pp. 68-70.

unpaid coupons attached, making a total of $146,140. The balance of $118,036 was paid to North Carolina in 1928. Congress disregarded Comptroller McCarl's note that the state owed the Federal Government $1,433,757 on account of the "deposits" of 1837.

The Treasurer of the United States still holds $37,000 of Louisiana bonds, $335,667 of Tennessee bonds, and, for the Secretary of War, the $545,480 of captured Louisiana bonds. Political expediency has indeed had fantastic results and placed the financial practices of the Federal Government in a most unfavorable light.

THE DEBT OF THE DISTRICT OF COLUMBIA

Before the Civil War the area within the District of Columbia was governed by three municipal corporations, all of them "too weak financially to improve the territory they occupied."[41] Very little had been done to improve the District, which was "a most unsightly place . . . disagreeable to pass through in summer in consequence of the dust . . . and almost impassable in the winter from the mud. . . ."[42] Water and sewer systems were inadequate, and there were few parks. The increased population and the expanded activities incident to the war accentuated the need for improvement and brought demands for changes. In 1871 Congress prescribed a consolidated government for the district, closely resembling a territorial government.

The most powerful organ of the new government was the Board of Public Works, which had charge of all public improvements. The board immediately entered upon an ambitious program for paving streets and establishing water and sewer systems. The original plan called for an outlay of about $6,500,000, one third of which was to be assessed against adjoining property owners, but several times this amount was soon spent. The 1871 act limited the debt, without a vote of the people, to 5 per cent of assessed value, but the board paid little attention to the limit. In 1872 Congress passed a special act setting the limit at $10,000,000, but it, too, was disregarded.[43]

41. W. F. Dodd, *The Government of the District of Columbia* (Washington, 1909), p. 93.

42. President's *Annual Message*, 1873, quoted in L. F. Schmeckebier, *The District of Columbia: Its Government and Administration* (Baltimore, 1928), p. 33.

43. Dodd, *op. cit.*, pp. 45-46.

Growth of the Debt

The new government took over, at its inception, a debt of $4,350,190. In a little more than three years the energetic board had increased this, mostly in the form of floating debt, to $23,360,700, which was equal to nearly 25 per cent of the assessed value of property.[44] Property owners were aroused by the heavy assessments on property and by the extravagance and waste of the board. "The arbitrary conduct of the Board toward individuals, the rapidly increasing debt of the District, and the undeniable jobbery prevalent in the letting of contracts at last aroused the people to petition Congress for another investigation into the affairs of the District of Columbia."[45] The investigation was held in 1874 and showed, for the first time, the extent and scope of the board's work.

There were charges of graft and corruption on the part of board members, but none was proven. The board had done much work, and many commended it. President Grant gave it high praise in 1873. Dodd states that it "had done a tremendous amount of work within a short time; it had changed the whole appearance of the city of Washington—in fact it had practically created a beautiful city out of a straggling, dirty, and mean-looking town."[46] But it had incurred obligations far beyond its legal powers and beyond the ability of the District to handle at the time. Its business management was poor, and it was guilty of lax practices in the letting of contracts.

The investigating committee found the finances in a chaotic state. The treasury was empty and there was a huge mass of floating obligations. "The District of Columbia was bankrupt," and the committee "recommended what was practically the appointment of receivers to conduct its affairs and to settle its financial obligations."[47]

Funding of the Debt

Congress adopted the recommendation of the committee, abolished the territorial government, and established a temporary com-

44. Schmeckebier, *op. cit.*, p. 42. The debt statement of 1874 showed only $22,106,650, but $1,254,050 of floating debt outstanding at that time were later verified and funded.   45. Dodd, *op. cit.*, p. 46.
    46. *Ibid.*, p. 48.   47. *Ibid.*, p. 49.

missioner government of the kind which has since ruled the District.[48] The commissioners were forbidden to incur, without the specific consent of Congress, any new obligations except those necessary to carry out existing contracts and to complete improvements under way. The first and second comptrollers of the United States Treasury were constituted an auditing board to examine and audit all floating and unfunded debts, which were then to be funded into 3.65 per cent, 50-year bonds. The United States pledged its faith to see that taxes would be levied and appropriations made to pay the interest and principal of these bonds. Shortly thereafter the Federal Government began the practice of paying one half of the expenses of the District, and thus, in effect, paid one half of the debt. An act of 1878 abolished the District Board of Sinking Fund Commissioners and transferred their duties to the Treasurer of the United States.

The new government established in 1874 "had the difficult task of carrying out all unfinished contracts and of settling the debts of an administration the accounts of which had not been well kept." In its early years it incurred considerable disfavor, probably resulting "from a lack of knowledge as to the state of the outstanding contracts of the territorial government when it was abolished, and from uncertainty regarding the real indebtedness of the District."[49] But it survived and was made permanent in 1878. The auditing board finished its work and was dissolved in 1876. At the completion of its work the bonded debt stood at $22,106,650, of which

TABLE 19

NET DEBT OF THE DISTRICT OF COLUMBIA FOR SELECTED YEARS

(In thousands of dollars)

Year	Net Debt	Year	Net Debt
1871	$ 4,350	1900	$15,095
1874	22,107	1905	14,991
1880	22,498	1910	12,766
1885	21,279	1915	6,223
1890	19,781	1920	2,153
1895	18,465		

48. 18 *Statutes at Large* 116 (Act of June 20, 1874).
49. Dodd, *op. cit.*, p. 50.

$13,743,250 represented 3.65 per cent bonds. Thereafter no additional bonds were issued except $1,254,050 of 3.65 per cent bonds authorized by Congress in 1880-94 to fund claims incurred before 1874, and $3,892,300 of refunding bonds issued between 1879 and 1894. Appropriations for interest and principal were made regularly, and the debt declined steadily, as shown in Table 19.

Borrowing from the United States

Between 1880 and 1890 the finances of the District were in good shape and there were frequent surpluses. But soon after 1900 a number of large improvement projects were undertaken, and the District experienced difficulties in paying its half of the expenditures. In 1901 Congress authorized the Secretary of the Treasury to advance to the District such sums as might be necessary to meet local expenses authorized by Congress. The advances bore 2 per cent interest and were repayable within five years. By 1908 these advances amounted to $3,650,563.[50] Total advances, made between 1902 and 1910, amounted to $4,144,696 and were repaid, with $586,703 of interest, between 1910 and 1916.[51] By 1925 the debt of the District had been paid in full.

THE NEW YORK DEBT

New York has had a varied debt experience. The debt, which had fluctuated between $30,000,000 and $35,000,000 for a number of years, was sharply increased by the issuance of over $27,000,000 of bounty debt in 1865-66. The peak of nearly $52,000,000 was reached in 1866. Aside from the bounty debt, the principal components at that time were the $18,248,000 canal debt and the $5,-643,000 general fund debt.

Redemption of the Canal Debt

The canal building program begun in 1847 was completed in 1862. The closing of the Mississippi River and Southern ports during the Civil War gave a great impetus to canal traffic, and canal tolls reached their high mark of $5,028,431 in 1863. Since canal construction ended in 1862, large amounts of funds were available

50. *Ibid.*, pp. 116-117.   51. Schmeckebier, *op. cit.*, p. 52.

for debt redemption, and the debt was reduced from $27,107,321 in 1860 to $11,966,580 in 1870. But the canal prosperity was short-lived, and after the war the railroads began to take more and more of the canal traffic. By 1870 tolls were down to $3,000,000, and in another ten years, below $1,000,000. Tolls were reduced in an unsuccessful attempt to recapture traffic. In 1870 the people rejected a constitutional amendment levying a tax to aid in the redemption of the canal debt. But tolls continued to decline and soon were inadequate to cover operating costs. Finally a constitutional amendment in 1882 abolished canal tolls and authorized general taxation for canal maintenance and debt service. At that time the debt was nearly $9,000,000. Regular appropriations from tax revenues reduced it steadily and finally wiped it out in 1893.[52]

Redemption of Other Debts

The general fund and bounty debts amounted to approximately $33,000,000 in 1866. The constitution of 1846 required the legislature to levy annual taxes sufficient to pay interest and to retire the debts within eighteen years. But for many years revenues which should have gone into the sinking fund were used for other purposes. In 1872 Governor Dix found that nearly two thirds of the $15,600,000 in the sinking funds "existed only on paper and that the moneys belonging to them had been consumed in defraying the current expenses of government in direct violation of the constitutional requirement."[53] The legislature levied a special tax to rebuild the fund, and the constitution of 1874 prohibited the use of sinking funds "in any manner, other than for the specific purpose for which it shall have been provided." The amendment "was faithfully observed and the process of debt redemption was completed without further scandal."

In spite of this trouble with the sinking fund, the debt was rapidly reduced. "The period from 1866 to 1877, inclusive, was distinctly one of rapid retirement. . . . Not only the general fund debt, but the contingent debt as well, and all but $11,000 of the

52. N. Y. Spec. Joint Comm., *op. cit.,* pp. 47-51; Sowers, *op. cit.,* pp. 336-338.
53. New York State Constitutional Convention Committee, *Problems Relating to Taxation and Finance* (Albany, 1938), pp. 126-127.

Civil War bounty debt was retired during these eleven years, while the canal debt was halved. Altogether, a total debt of $51,753,082 was reduced to only $9,154,055."[54] This was truly a remarkable achievement.

Redemption Completed

In 1885 the state incurred a debt of $1,000,000 for the Niagara State Reservation, but it was retired in a few years. By 1893 the state was free of debt except for $660 of obligations which had not been presented for payment. Of approximately $99,000,000 devoted to debt retirement between 1846 and 1893, about $43,000,000 came from canal tolls, about $45,000,000 from taxes, and the remainder from miscellaneous sources.

The New Canal Debt

The state remained free of debt for only a short time. For some years the canal system had been poorly maintained and by 1894 was badly in need of repairs. In 1895 voters authorized the issue of $9,000,000 of bonds for this purpose. An annual tax of 0.13 mill was levied to service them. It soon developed that the amount authorized was insufficient to finance the project planned, and there were charges of incompetency and dishonesty on the part of certain state officials. Rather than appropriate the additional $7,000,000 or $8,000,000 necessary to complete the project, the legislature left it uncompleted.

For some time there had been agitation in favor of enlarging the Erie Canal to a size suitable for 1,000-ton barges and for the deepening of the Champlain and Oswego canals. After numerous surveys and estimates, the legislature, in 1903, submitted to the people an act allowing the issue of $101,000,000 of 18-year bonds for those purposes. It was ratified by a substantial majority. Not more than $10,000,000 of bonds were to be issued at one time, and a tax of 0.012 of a mill for each million of bonds outstanding was levied. Using the permission extended in a 1905 amendment, the state thereafter issued bonds running for fifty instead of eighteen years. In 1906 the special tax was suspended, and for five years

54. N. Y. Spec. Joint Comm., *op. cit.,* p. 53.

appropriations to the sinking fund were made from the general fund. An additional $7,000,000 of bonds were authorized by the people in 1909 for the Cayuga and Seneca canals.

Under these acts bonds were issued in amounts increasing from about $1,000,000 in 1906 to about $20,000,000 in 1914, most of them bearing 4 or 4½ per cent interest. In 1916 the total outstanding canal bonds amounted to $118,000,000, and by 1936 the total was over $150,000,000.

The Highway Debt

New York was one of the first states to borrow for highway construction. In 1898 the state established a highway department, provided for state aid and supervision for road construction, and encouraged local governments to participate in the program. Under this plan the counties, by 1902, had constructed only 456 miles of road, and the people were becoming impatient.[55] In 1905 they approved a constitutional amendment to permit the issue of $50,-000,000 of bonds for roads.[56] By 1912 these bonds had been sold and the proceeds spent, but the state's program of roadbuilding was hardly more than half completed. In that year another $50,000,000 of 50-year bonds were authorized by the voters, this time by a regular referendum vote. Two fifths were allocated to state roads and the other three fifths, to county roads. By 1916 highway bonds outstanding amounted to $65,000,000. Before 1905 the state had appropriated considerable sums from general revenues for highway purposes, but after the bonds were authorized these appropriations practically disappeared.

Other Debt Factors

The state sold two small bond issues for the Adirondack Park in 1896 and 1898. Beginning in 1910 the state extended its activities along this line and by 1915 had borrowed an additional $3,450,000. Park bonds outstanding in 1916 amounted to $3,000,000.

55. N. Y. Spec. Joint Comm., *op. cit.*, p. 67.
56. Instead of the usual referendum on a bond proposal this was an amendment to the constitution. The $50,000,000 maximum "did not refer to the total sums to be authorized but to the amount outstanding at any given time." Thus new bonds could be issued as old ones were retired. They ran for fifty years (*ibid.*, p. 68).

During the Spanish-American War, New York invoked its constitutional power to borrow for defense without a vote of the people and issued $900,000 of bonds to cover war costs. All were redeemed by 1906 from general taxes.

The constitution which was proposed in 1915 and which failed of ratification, contained several significant provisions relating to the debt. It would have required the state to issue only serial bonds divided into equal annual instalments and running for not longer than the life of the improvement for which issued and in no event longer than fifty years. Sinking fund contributions would have been computed on the basis of interest earnings at the rate of 3 per cent. A unique provision would have required the comptroller, in case the legislature failed to make an appropriation for the sinking fund, to set aside the necessary amount from the first general fund revenues received. Bondholders could bring suit to compel him to do this.[57] This would indeed have been the strongest protection ever afforded a sinking fund in a state constitution and "was tantamount to a surrender by the State of its sovereign right of repudiation of its debts. . . ."

Conclusion

The gross debt of New York State in 1916 was $195,525,895, made up largely of canal and highway bonds. The net debt—$148,740,465—was by far the largest state debt in the country and was approximately 32 per cent of the total of all state debts—$459,661,269. The per capita net debt of $14.81 was more than three times the national average of $4.59 and was exceeded only by the $23.52 figure for Massachusetts.[58]

After a century of debt, New York, in 1893-96, was free of debt for a short time. But within twenty years thereafter it incurred a debt larger than it or any other state had ever owed before. It is easy to understand why the people approved the highway bonds, but considering the status of canals and the experiences of the state with the canal debt in the past, it is difficult to explain why they favored the enormous borrowing program for canals. The canal

57. New York State Constitutional Convention Commission, *op. cit.*, p. 132.
58. *Financial Statistics of States,* 1916, pp. 120-121.

debt, in 1916, was equal to nearly one fifth of the total gross debt of all states and was almost equal to the total highway debts of all the states.

The canal system has been and remains a source of considerable expense to the state in the form both of debt service and of current maintenance, while its traffic, although increasing in recent years, is almost negligible. Debt service on the canal amounts to more than $5,000,000, while in recent years the state has expended from $1,500,000 to $3,000,000 per year on current maintenance. Traffic on the barge canal amounted to only about 1,250,000 tons in 1919, but increased thereafter, especially after 1930. In 1928 it was approximately 3,000,000 tons, and by 1935 had reached 4,500,000 tons. In the latter year the Federal Government made a grant of $5,000,000 for the improvement of the canal.[59]

In spite of its heavy costs, the people of New York insist that the state shall retain and operate the canals. A constitutional amendment ratified in 1921 prohibited the legislature from selling or leasing the principal canals, which are to "remain the property of the state and under its management forever." The same paragraph specifies that any funds derived from the lease or sale of other canals shall be applied to the improvement or repair of remaining canals.[60] Tolls are prohibited, and the legislature is charged to provide for maintenance and repairs by taxation. It seems unlikely that water transportation has justified the enormous subsidies it has received from New York State.

THE GENERAL TREND OF STATE INDEBTEDNESS, 1870-1916

Table 20 shows the net debts of the states for selected dates between 1870 and 1916, as given by the Bureau of the Census. At best, the census figures for this period contain many inaccuracies, and many of the figures for Southern states in 1870 and 1880 are far from the truth, as will be seen by comparison with the material in Chapter VII. No attempt has been made to correct them, however, since the necessary data are not available for making computation comparable with those made by the Bureau. In spite of large

59. *Annual Report of the Superintendent of Public Works,* 1935 (New York Leg. Docs. 1936, Vol. 16), p. 3.

60. New York Constitution, Art. VII, par. 8.

TABLE 20

NET DEBTS OF THE STATES, 1870-1916

(In thousands of dollars)

State	1870	1880	1890	1902	1912	1916
Alabama	8,478	12,371	12,413	12,727	13,132	13,564
Arizona	......	......	757	3,099	3,065	844
Arkansas	3,600	6,789	8,672	1,101	1,236	1,239
California	3,429	3,133	2,522	2,955	10,223	33,376
Colorado	......	146	600	3,797	3,174	3,753
Connecticut	9,807	4,968	3,740	1,678	7,110	13,064
Delaware	......	905	888	762	763	796
District of Columbia	......	22,498	19,781	14,540	9,002	5,470
Florida	1,289	1,174	1,032	1,032	619	602
Georgia	6,544	9,918	10,450	7,876	6,934	6,322
Idaho	......	83	218	324	2,143	1,712
Illinois	4,891	1,446	1,185	2,155	2,273	2,067
Indiana	4,168	4,996	8,538	2,914	1,350	768
Iowa	534	545	245	50	357	......
Kansas	1,593	994	1,120	632	243	......
Kentucky	3,892	1,094	1,671	2,291	4,442	2,607
Louisiana	25,022	23,438	16,009	13,593	13,546	13,479
Maine	8,068	5,512	3,471	2,785	1,255	2,638
Maryland	13,317	11,119	8,434	4,942	7,334	16,575
Massachusetts	28,271	20,785	7,267	65,964	79,551	86,043
Michigan	2,385	3,253	5,308	6,566	7,089	6,915
Minnesota	350	5,417	2,239	1,755	1,345	1,516
Mississippi	1,796	3,324	3,503	2,877	4,461	5,127
Missouri	17,866	19,509	11,760	4,366	4,671	7,033
Montana	......	70	168	1,204	1,513	1,186
Nebraska	247	440	254	2,005	374	......
Nevada	643	375	510	624	608	680
New Hampshire	2,818	3,630	2,691	1,551	1,956	1,951
New Jersey	2,996	649	1,023	......	642	116
New Mexico	......	......	870	999	1,218	2,562
New York	32,409	7,659	2,308	8,187	86,205	148,740
North Carolina	29,900	15,422	7,703	6,755	8,058	8,884
North Dakota	......	......	704	968	820	511
Ohio	9,732	10,023	7,136	4,685	5,142	5,341
Oklahoma	......	......	......	510	6,930	6,447
Oregon	107	511	2	236	31	......
Pennsylvania	31,112	13,883	4,069	389	......	473
Rhode Island	2,913	1,701	423	2,620	5,127	6,391
South Carolina	7,666	7,478	6,954	6,730	6,190	5,387
South Dakota	......	......	872	457	370	......
Tennessee	38,540	30,803	19,696	17,984	11,812	15,864
Texas	509	5,650	4,318	3,993	4,656	4,548
Utah	......	9	......	974	1,430	2,691
Vermont	1,002	151	148	363	570	611
Virginia	47,391	32,764	34,227	23,546	22,043	23,772
Washington	......	......	300	1,271	1,556	1,209
West Virginia	......	128	185	......	......	......
Wisconsin	2,252	2,462	2,295	2,278	2,251	2,157
Wyoming	......	17	320	301	122	108
Totals	355,537	297,242	228,999	249,411	354,942	465,139

Source: Bureau of the Census.

errors for individual states, the totals are of some value in giving a rough picture of the general trend of state debts. Before considering this point further, however, it is well to note two movements which were responsible for considerable amounts of borrowing in the latter part of the period under consideration.

Contingent Debt

Beginning in 1888 Massachusetts incurred a large contingent debt for the benefit of the Metropolitan District, which includes Boston and its suburbs. The funds were used to provide sewer, park, and water systems, and to assist in eliminating grade crossings. The bonds are direct obligations of the state, but are serviced by the cities within the District. "Amortization of this debt is provided for by the state as agent for the municipalities concerned, and the interest upon it is met by the municipalities."[61] This debt amounted to $76,110,954 in 1916. The cities of the District have always met their obligations promptly. Rhode Island also has used this arrangement to a limited extent.

Borrowing for Highways

The development of the automobile caused a growing demand for improved highways, and the years immediately preceding the World War witnessed the beginning of the highway debts which have since grown to large proportions. Massachusetts was the only state to borrow for this purpose before 1900; it authorized a highway loan of $300,000 in 1894. Other states soon joined the ranks; and by 1913 the total of state highway bonds outstanding, issued chiefly by New York, Massachusetts, Maryland, and California, amounted to over $50,000,000.[62] The growth continued at an accelerated pace, and in 1916 the Bureau of the Census stated the total debt incurred for "State roads" at $111,649,917 and for "other highway purposes" at $132,060,995. The latter category, however, included the $118,000,000 canal debt of New York. The principal issues for state roads were: New York, $65,000,000; California, $18,-000,000; Maryland, $14,760,000; and Massachusetts, $9,597,250.[63]

61. *Financial Statistics of States*, 1916, p. 58.
62. Edna Trull, *Borrowing for Highways* (New York, 1937), pp. 3-6, 25-26.
63. *Financial Statistics of States*, 1916, p. 122.

General Trends

The period from 1870 to 1890 was one of steady and fairly rapid debt reduction. In the South two factors—Reconstruction borrowing and the accumulation of unpaid interest—tended to increase the debts, but they were largely offset by the repudiations and adjustments enacted by the different states. The Northern and Middle Western states reduced their debts steadily, largely from tax revenues. The largest reductions were made in Connecticut, Illinois, Maine, Maryland, Massachusetts, Missouri, New York, and Pennsylvania. The only increases of any importance, outside the South, occurred in the District of Columbia, Indiana, and Michigan. There was a distinct tendency, however, for states which had no debt in 1870 to incur small debts. This was probably because of current deficits and the fact that the Bureau of the Census counted outstanding current warrants as indebtedness.

From 1890 to 1902 most states continued to reduce their debts, although more slowly, but two states—Massachusetts and New York—increased their debts so much that the total of net debts rose by about $20,000,000. The increase in New York was for canals, while Massachusetts borrowed heavily for the Metropolitan District, grade crossing elimination, highways, and for the construction of a state house. Massachusetts also borrowed $1,500,000 to cover costs of equipping troops for the Spanish-American War. Michigan and Ohio also incurred debts of $500,000 and $200,000, respectively, for this purpose. At some time between 1890 and 1902—probably about 1892 or 1893—the total net debt of the states reached its low point at about $225,000,000, when it was lower than it had been at any time since 1840.

After 1902 the total of debts rose steadily, and by 1913 the increase amounted to more than $100,000,000, in spite of the fact that some states continued to reduce their debts. The increasing rate of growth is shown by the fact that in the four years from 1912 to 1916 the total increased by about as much as it has risen in ten years before 1912. Four states—California, Maryland, Massachusetts, and New York—were responsible for almost all of the increase.

Concentration of Debt, 1916

In 1916 the total gross debt of all states, not including the District of Columbia, was $603,343,226. Of this amount, $322,071,889, or 52.4 per cent, was owed by New York and Massachusetts. The five states with the largest debts included the above two and California, Virginia, and Maryland. They owed $406,229,404, or 67.3 per cent of the total. With the net debt the story was essentially the same. The total, exclusive of the District of Columbia, was $459,661,269. New York and Massachusetts owed $234,783,156, or 52.2 per cent of the total, while the first five states owed $308,506,509, or 67.1 per cent of the total.[64] Thus, two of the forty-eight states were responsible for over one half of all debts, while five accounted for about two thirds.

Per capita net debts averaged $4.59 for the country as a whole, and ranged from $23.52 in Massachusetts to $0.04 in New Jersey and nothing in six other states. By sections, the figures varied from a high of $15.70 in New England to a low of $0.73 in the West North Central states. The South Atlantic states were near the national average with $4.88.

Forms and Purposes of Obligations

Because of poor reporting and poor state accounting systems before the World War, the Bureau of the Census was not able to make satisfactory analyses of state obligations. Such analysis as the data for 1916 will permit is given below. The total gross debt, exclusive of the District of Columbia, was $603,343,226, divided as follows: current (warrants, revenue bonds and notes, and obligations to trust funds), $52,324,007; floating, $43,151,028; and funded, $507,868,191. The analysis as to purpose was particularly incomplete, since large amounts were grouped under "miscellaneous" and "combined and unreported." Making the analysis under this handicap, however, we find that the percentage distribution of the gross debt was as follows: canals (New York State), 19.56; highways, 20.84; funding, 5.32; refunding, 3.74; public service enterprises, 3.75; charities, hospitals, and correction, 2.88; government buildings, 3.63; schools, 1.60; current debt, 8.67; combined and unre-

64. *Ibid.,* p. 120-121.

ported, 12.08; and miscellaneous, 17.95.[65] The total for canals and highways was approximately 40 per cent. If the railroad aid bonds and bonds issued to refund them could have been segregated, the total for transportation would undoubtedly have been above 50 per cent.

Interest Rates

An analysis of the $569,613,490 of funded and floating debt shows that $181,913,395 of obligations bore 4 per cent interest, while $99,-012,049 bore 3½ per cent, $91,250,701 bore 3 per cent, and $85,411,-376 bore 4½ per cent. Thus 82.33 per cent of the obligations bore 4½ per cent interest or less. The amount reported at 6 per cent was $33,303,401, while small amounts were reported at 7 and 8 per cent. A large majority of the 3 per cent bonds were issued by Massachusetts, New York, and Virginia, while Massachusetts, Maryland and Connecticut largely accounted for the 3½ per cent bonds. Most of the states had 4 per cent bonds outstanding, but New York, California, Maryland, and Connecticut had issued the bulk of them. A majority of the bonds issued by Alabama, North Carolina, and Tennessee also fell in this group.

In the 4½ per cent classification New York, Louisiana, Tennessee, and South Carolina were the leaders, in the order named. Michigan and Wisconsin were responsible for most of the 7 per cent bonds, while Alabama, Louisiana, and Georgia had outstanding small amounts of bonds bearing 8 per cent.[66] Thus it can be seen that the bonds with low rates of interest—4 per cent or less—were issued by states with very good credit, such as New York, Massachusetts, Maryland, Connecticut, and California, or by Southern states which had scaled down interest rates. North Carolina, it is true, had, in 1910, refunded $3,427,000 of adjustment bonds at 4 per cent after some difficulties and with the assistance of local banks and tobacco companies, but this was exceptional. As a rule, Southern states were not yet able to sell bonds on a 4 per cent basis.

Conclusion

As the World War approached, state debts were showing signs of another boom. The demand for improved highways was as

65. *Ibid.*, pp. 122-123.   66. *Ibid.*, p. 124.

strong as the demand for railroads, canals, and banks had been eighty years earlier. Between 1902 and 1916 the total of net debts almost doubled, and fully half of the increase came in the four years following 1912. In 1916 state debts were greater than they had ever been before and were growing at a steadily increasing rate.

CHAPTER X

TWO DECADES OF POST-WAR BORROWING

AFTER 1910 several factors, the most powerful of which was the development of the automobile, impelled states to borrow. In each of the years 1910, 1911, 1913, and 1914, state borrowing set new high records for the period since Reconstruction. In the latter year the total was over $70,000,000. After declines in 1915 and 1916 the total rose again in 1917 to over $50,000,000. During the World War the Federal Government exercised a practical monopoly in the loan market, and state loans dropped in 1918 to the lowest point since 1912, with a total of less than $40,000,000.

After the war the rapidly growing demand for highways, together with new demands arising out of the war, quickly increased state borrowing to amounts far above any ever known before. In many states the necessity of submitting borrowing proposals to popular referenda or of amending constitutions delayed borrowing for a time, so that the full force of the movement was not felt until 1921. In that year the states borrowed, chiefly for highways and soldiers' bonuses, more than $270,000,000. This total was more than three times as great as any prewar total and, with the exception of the year 1934, has not been exceeded since that time. After a sharp drop in 1922 the total again rose to high levels in 1923 and 1924. Then for the five years 1925-29 it was comparatively stable, fluctuating between $130,000,000 and $170,000,000 per year. The onset of the depression in 1930 brought new financial demands upon the states, especially for unemployment relief, and again the total of borrowing rose, this time to a new record of over $300,000,000 in 1934. Since that year, probably because of generous financial assistance from the Federal Government and the completion of many highway construction programs, borrowing has declined steadily

and fairly rapidly, reaching in 1938 the lowest total in more than
ten years.

It is the purpose of this chapter to give a brief general survey of
state borrowing from 1919 to 1938. During those twenty years the
states borrowed several times more than they had borrowed in the
preceding one hundred and thirty years. Attention will be given primarily to the purposes of the borrowing and the technical features
of the debts, such as form, maturities, and the interest rates at which
the bonds were sold. Later chapters will deal with borrowing for
particular purposes and evaluate experience. The figures used in
this study are not complete for several reasons. In the first place,
complete information is not available. The great majority of state
loans are sold at public sale and are thus reported in the financial
journals, but a few, especially those placed with federal or state
agencies, are not sold publicly and thus may go unreported. The
figures for this survey were taken from sales reported in the *Bond
Buyer* and the *Commercial and Financial Chronicle,* checked with,
and sometimes supplemented by, or modified according to, the
figures given in Moody's *Governments and Municipals.* In this way
at least 90 per cent, and probably 95 per cent or more, of all state
bond sales were covered, even though in some cases the information
obtained was not sufficient for a complete analysis or classification.
Thus while the coverage is not complete, it is sufficient to give
reliable information as to trends.

The second reason why the figures are not complete is that short-
term financing has been eliminated. The dividing line for this purpose was arbitrarily set at three years, and only those loans running
for three years or more are included. Of course, serial bonds maturing in less than three years which constitute a part of a large issue
are included in the total.

A third element excluded is revenue financing; that is, the totals
include only full faith and credit obligations of the states. In some
instances exclusions, with the information available, have been difficult to make, but the total error is not large. The two exceptions
to the above rule are the highway obligations of Mississippi and
New Mexico. Those, even though revenue obligations, are so sim-

ilar to the general highway bonds of other states that it has been considered best to include them for the sake of uniformity.

The total of state bonds included in the first table, in which the coverage is more complete than in the other two, is $3,717,060,000. If allowance is made for sales which were not reported, this would indicate that the total of state borrowing in this period was close to four billion dollars.

PURPOSES OF BORROWING

In order to discover the purposes for which states borrowed in this period, all loans reported were classified according to the categories given in Table 21. In most cases the title of bonds indicated definitely the purpose for which the proceeds were to be spent, but

TABLE 21

ANALYSIS OF STATE BORROWING ACCORDING TO PURPOSE, 1919-38

Year	Total Analyzed (in thousands of dollars)	PERCENTAGE DISTRIBUTION								
		Funding	Refunding	Highways and Bridges	Rivers, Harbors, and Waterways	Unemployment Relief	General Government	Soldiers' Bonuses and Loan Funds	Loan Funds	Miscellaneous
1919.............	71,410	0.44	0.39	48.38	19.61	......	4.99	4.20	15.32	6.67
1920.............	94,478	......	15.00	38.60	0.13	0.30	4.18	22.76	18.79	0.24
1921.............	273,526	0.96	1.06	48.90	5.05	......	4.57	30.16	5.78	3.52
1922.............	132,090	0.40	......	51.52	0.87	......	6.03	30.89	8.08	2.21
1923.............	234,846	......	0.59	42.90	......	......	5.96	39.18	9.61	1.76
1924.............	245,164	......	......	47.49	2.45	......	6.20	29.39	13.98	0.49
1925.............	169,733	5.90	4.13	70.52	0.53	......	8.05	3.92	6.43	0.52
1926.............	129,186	2.45	1.53	61.22	3.17	......	11.10	3.10	10.00	7.43
1927.............	136,953	2.19	6.31	62.38	5.11	......	10.21	9.49	3.51	0.80
1928.............	165,890	1.87	2.74	56.45	2.26	......	20.45	7.23	4.91	4.09
1929.............	167,430	1.54	......	78.89	3.76	......	4.02	......	7.09	4.70
1930.............	215,832	0.85	2.24	68.62	0.46	0.09	17.45	0.92	6.80	2.55
1931.............	255,576	1.52	0.70	56.87	0.68	0.08	24.60	5.81	4.29	5.44
1932.............	198,844	5.67	9.52	42.87	1.32	20.45	10.58	4.38	4.32	0.89
1933.............	201,464	11.19	6.36	23.00	0.68	36.68	18.66	0.40	2.36	0.67
1934.............	312,899	10.69	2.05	12.20	0.16	48.29	6.67	16.53	3.02	0.39
1935.............	249,087	4.09	21.09	17.03	......	41.17	11.44	2.00	2.97	0.20
1936.............	173,582	1.26	11.09	25.15	0.40	39.49	7.83	5.76	4.76	4.27
1937.............	153,623	1.48	9.96	44.60	......	19.85	14.01	5.85	......	4.32
1938.............	135,334	12.19	23.89	24.68	0.14	......	30.51	2.40	......	6.15
Totals............	3,717,060	3.48	5.52	44.42	1.76	12.59	11.43	12.16	6.05	2.57
Totals (in millions of dollars)..		129.5	205.2	1,651.2	65.3	467.9	424.8	452.8	224.8	95.5

where the title was vague or general or where an issue included bonds for several different purposes, attempts were made to learn the circumstances surrounding the issue in order to permit more accurate classification. The categories are generally self-explanatory, but a few comments may be made. The third column, "Highways and Bridges," includes also the large expenditures made for grade-crossing elimination in New York State. During the worst years of the depression several emergency or special highway issues were motivated largely by the desire to provide unemployment relief; these were included under highway issues. The category "General Government" includes bonds issued for educational institutions, hospitals, prisons, public buildings, and other similar purposes. The bonds included under "Loan Funds" were issued mainly for the rural credit systems.

Highway Borrowing

A study of Table 21 shows that the financing of highway construction was by far the most important cause of borrowing during the twenty years. In spite of its dominant position as the principal cause of borrowing, however, transportation was not as important relatively in this period as it was in the past century when states were borrowing to build canals and railroads. Nevertheless, from 1919 to 1938 highways were almost four times as important as the next two causes of borrowing—unemployment relief and soldiers' bonuses—and accounted for almost one half of the total. These three causes taken together were responsible for almost 70 per cent of the total.

But even these figures and comparisons do not show the full importance of highways as a factor in state indebtedness. As will be pointed out in the following chapter, the states have incurred several forms of debts for highways not included in these figures. If such debts were included, it would be safe to say that highways and bridges were responsible for well over one half of the borrowing for this period.

The total borrowed for highways and bridges during the period was approximately $1,651,000,000, with thirty-one states participating at one time or another. Eight states borrowed $100,000,000 or more each. Illinois led with $160,000,000, followed in order by New Jersey, Missouri, Louisiana, New York, West Virginia, North Carolina, and Pennsylvania. Together the eight states borrowed $1,016,000,000, or approximately 60 per cent of the total.

Bonus Borrowing

For five years beginning in 1920, loans for the purpose of paying bonuses to, or creating loan funds for, World War veterans were a major factor in state borrowing, accounting for nearly one third of the bonds sold in those years. Several states which had not borrowed for any other purpose for fifty years borrowed and opened their purses to the veterans. The peak was reached in 1923, when $92,000,-000 was borrowed for the purpose; thereafter the amount declined rapidly and soon was negligible. The small amounts which continued year after year represented mainly California's borrowing for its loan fund, as more fully described in Chapter XII. The large figure for 1934 represents Pennsylvania's long-delayed bonus payment.

Twenty states borrowed a total of $452,810,000 for bonuses and loan funds. Four states—California, Illinois, Pennsylvania, and New York—accounted for $226,000,000, or 50 per cent of the total.

Relief Borrowing

Borrowing for unemployment relief, although concentrated in a comparatively few states and confined almost entirely to six years, ranked second in this period. First attaining importance in 1932, such borrowing rapidly increased to a peak of $151,000,000 in 1934, or 48 per cent of the total for that record year. Thereafter, as federal relief appropriations increased and the depression eased somewhat, the states reduced their relief borrowings, and by 1938 had stopped them entirely. Only thirteen states contributed to the total of $467,-924,000 borrowed for relief. Of this amount New York borrowed $205,000,000, or 42 per cent. Five states—New York, Illinois, New Jersey, California, and Massachusetts—accounted for $354,000,000, or 75 per cent of the total.

Borrowing for Other Purposes

Compared with those discussed above, other purposes were un-important. Loans for general governmental purposes fluctuated widely, reaching their greatest relative importance of 30 per cent in 1938, a year when total borrowing was low. Borrowing for loan funds was important in only four years: in 1919 and 1920, when North and South Dakota were establishing their rural credit systems, and in 1924 and 1926, when Minnesota was doing likewise. The large amount of funding loans after 1932 reflects the difficulties experienced by the states in balancing their budgets during the depression years. The large figure for 1938 represents Connecticut's funding of a large deficit which had accumulated over several years. The comparatively large figures for refunding loans after 1932 are the result of two factors: first, those few states which had callable bonds outstanding called them and replaced them with bonds bearing lower rates of interest; second, several states which had built up large debts in the preceding years found it difficult or impossible to meet the heavy principal payments which fell due in the depression years, and thus were forced to refund. The large figure for 1938 is caused largely by Mississippi's refunding of a large amount of highway notes issued in the previous two years.

INTEREST RATES

The rates of interest which the states paid on the nearly four billion dollars which they borrowed in this period are shown in Table 22. The tremendous change which has taken place in the prevailing rates is evident at a glance. It was not feasible, in dealing with such a large total and with so many states over a long period of time, to use an exact or accurate measure of interest. Rather, the procedure followed was to classify all bonds sold, if the price or yield basis was given, into one of the ten groups given in the table. The effective yield basis, determined by the coupon rate and the sale price of the bonds, was taken in preference to the nominal or coupon rate, since it is a more accurate index of the true interest cost. Smaller class intervals than those used both as to yields and as to time, would have given a more accurate picture of the trends,

TABLE 22

ANALYSIS OF STATE BORROWING ACCORDING TO YIELDS AT WHICH
BONDS SOLD, 1919-38

Year	Total Analyzed (in thousands of dollars)	PERCENTAGE DISTRIBUTION									
		% 2 and under	% 2.01-2.50	% 2.51-3.00	% 3.01-3.50	% 3.51-4.00	% 4.01-4.50	% 4.51-5.00	% 5.01-5.50	% 5.51-6.00	% Over 6
1919...	46,406					27.09	18.96	36.04*	17.91		
1920...	42,011						13.09	54.32*	23.07	9.52	
1921...	219,514						18.58	36.13*	25.98	18.85	0.46
1922...	109,456					3.30	76.23*	20.47			
1923...	226,197					0.96	71.23*	27.43		0.38	
1924...	239,353					6.36	85.76*	6.63	1.25		
1925...	161,118					35.07	64.62*	0.31			
1926...	124,190					42.48	54.97*	2.55			
1927...	109,918					51.53*	46.65	1.82			
1928...	154,235					38.74	54.88*	2.28	0.49	3.61	
1929...	149,999					2.67	49.94*	43.12	0.77	1.50	2.00
1930...	214,285					31.67	36.16*	30.08		0.74	
1931...	233,589			0.43	36.29	30.62*	28.59	1.71	2.36		
1932...	178,612				22.24	10.50	43.51*	16.47		6.16	1.12
1933...	162,228			16.39	24.56	21.08*	12.05	14.33	0.49	8.02	3.08
1934...	266,096	15.50	1.97	32.24	30.86*	12.47	5.79	0.96	0.21		
1935...	244,268	9.39	45.82*	19.09	8.19	11.22	3.40	2.86			
1936...	163,473	50.42*	29.33	6.77	3.85	9.61					
1937...	156,318	10.16	37.27	20.25*	12.35	19.95					
1938...	135,334	44.91	8.27*	5.66	34.80	6.31	0.04				
Totals..	3,336,601	6.69	7.03	6.30	10.20	17.13	34.56*	12.74	2.60	2.38	0.33
Totals (in millions of dollars)....		223.3	234.6	210.4	340.5	571.6	1,153.4	425.3	86.8	79.7	11.0

*Median group.

but considerations of time and space were against the more detailed study. The total analyzed in this table is not as large as the total in the preceding table because in some instances sale prices or yields were not given. The total, however, covers more than 80 per cent of all borrowing and is therefore adequate to give an accurate picture of trends.[1]

The large movements of the rates are clearly discernible in the table. During the three post-war years—1919-21—the states paid the highest rates during the period and probably the highest since Re-

1. It is possible that there is a slight downward bias in the figures in the table due to the fact that in some instances the price or yield was not given because of difficulty in negotiating the sale or because the bonds were sold at a private sale after they had failed to receive acceptable bids at a public sale. Usually these were bonds of a comparatively poor credit rating on which the yield would be high.

construction days. From 1922 through 1926 there was a remarkable concentration in the 4-4½ per cent group, with the general tendency downward, although at no time were any bonds sold below 3½ per cent. After a still further drop in 1927, yields rose sharply in 1928 and 1929 because of the tight credit situation. Considering the large number of states that were borrowing in this period and their great diversity of debt burdens, financial administration, and ability to pay, it is remarkable that practically all bonds were sold within a range of 1 per cent. Perhaps it was another manifestation of the lack of discrimination characteristic of the New Era.

The declining interest rates of 1930 and 1931 are clearly shown in the table, as are the banking difficulties of 1932 and 1933. The sharp decline after 1932 was probably due to several factors. The most important, of course, was the great decline in interest rates generally. But the sharp increase in federal income tax rates, which increased the value of the tax-exemption feature of state bonds, was also a contributing factor, although it would be impossible to express it exactly. It is also probable that the shift toward shorter maturities, to be noted in the next table, had some small effect on yields. The full extent of this fall in rates can be realized when it is noted that before 1930 not a single sale of state bonds was reported below 3½ per cent, while in 1936 and 1938 nearly all sales were below this figure. From this table we cannot accurately compute averages, but it is safe to say that in 1929 the average rate was not far from 4½ per cent, while in 1936 it was close to 2 per cent. This represents a decline of more than 50 per cent within seven years.

There is little apparent connection between interest rates and the amount of bonds sold. The heavy sales of 1921 came at a time of high interest rates. From 1924 through 1927 interest rates declined slowly, but so did sales. Total sales were higher in 1928 and 1929 in spite of higher rates. In 1930, 1931, and 1932, volume and interest rates moved in opposite directions, although probably other market factors had more influence than interest rates. The record sales of 1934 came in a year of comparatively low interest rates, but sales dropped off substantially in 1935 and 1936, although interest rates continued to decline. In the same way, the very low sales of

1938 came in a year when interest rates were about as low as they have ever been. Inasmuch as it takes time for states to prepare plans, to authorize bond issues, and to present the bonds for sale, the proper procedure may be to compare the bond sales of one year with the interest rates of a previous year or two. Since we have no accurate average of interest rates, this is hardly feasible with the present material, but a study of the table indicates that such procedure would hardly yield any significant result.

FORM AND MATURITIES OF BONDS

Term v. Serial Bonds

Before the World War the states had almost exclusively used term bonds; that is, bonds, the whole issue of which mature on the same date. This involved, if the bonds were to be paid at maturity, the accumulation and management of a sinking fund. The use of this method presents several troublesome problems in state finance. First, legislatures must be persuaded to make the annual appropriations regularly. If there is difficulty in balancing the budget and if the maturity date of the bonds is fifteen or twenty years in the future, legislators are likely to be indifferent on this point. Second, after the fund has been accumulated, the legislature, in difficult years, may be tempted to "raid" it; that is, borrow from it and fail to repay the loan. Third, the administration of a sinking fund requires much routine clerical work and a considerable degree of financial judgment to insure a fair return, to protect the principal, and to maintain a sufficient degree of liquidity so that cash will be available when needed. Finally, since these funds are outside the stream of current funds and are accumulated in large sums, they present a greater temptation to public officials who might be dishonest.[2] For these reasons there has been, in the past thirty or forty years, a growing tendency to use serial bonds, which do not require sinking funds. In addition to the administrative considerations mentioned above, serial bonds may have a selling advantage in that they give the investor a greater choice of maturities; some investors may wish

2. For a further discussion of this point see Carl H. Chatters and Albert M. Hillhouse, *Local Government Debt Administration* (New York, 1939), pp. 18-19.

to make long-term commitments, while others prefer medium or short-term commitments. With serial bonds all may be satisfied.

This period of heavy state borrowing coincided with the strong shift toward serial bonds; consequently, a large majority of the bonds which the states issued in these twenty years were of this kind. It is very difficult to make an accurate division between term and serial bonds. An issue may be serial in name and form but really be more akin to term bonds in substance. For example, a so-called serial issue may provide for only nominal maturities for the first twelve or fifteen years and may concentrate the bulk of the payments into three or four years at the end.[3] On the other hand, individual issues may be term bonds, but the total effect may be that of serial maturities. For example, a state may be engaged in a program of borrowing over a period of several years. Each year comparatively small amounts of term bonds may be issued, but their maturities may be so spaced that the whole debt will mature over a period of time in uniform instalments. For these reasons, no attempt is made to give exact figures showing the division between term and serial bonds. In the early years of this period, however, the division was roughly one-third term to two-thirds serial. In the later years serial bonds gained in preference and in some years accounted for more than 90 per cent of the total. For the whole period about 85 per cent of the bonds issued were serial, at least in form.[4]

Callable Bonds

Undoubtedly the greatest administrative error made in the sale of state bonds during this period was the failure to make use of the call feature. In private finance this feature has long been recognized as valuable and almost indispensable, since it gives the borrower the right to readjust his debt structure as need arises and to take advantage of lower interest rates. Although twenty states used this

3. Louisiana sold a $2,500,000 issue of highway bonds on December 7, 1938, which approached this description. For the years 1942 through 1949 maturities will be small, but in the five years 1956-60 total maturities will be $1,448,000 (*Bond Buyer*, Dec. 10, 1938, p. 54).

4. There are indications that in some instances states made the bonds serial in form, but arranged the maturities so as to make them substantially term bonds in order to defer the burden of repayment as long as possible and at the same time meet the popular preference for serial bonds.

feature in their bonds at one time or another during the period, in most cases they used it only with small and occasional issues. An analysis of all the bonds on which sufficient information could be obtained indicates that only about 4 or 5 per cent of them were callable—or about $150,000,000 out of a total of over $3,500,000,000. In 1934-35 two states—Delaware and Wyoming—had the call feature in all their outstanding bonds; two others—Montana and Virginia—had it in more than 50 per cent of their obligations; and eight others had used it in more than 20 per cent of their bonds.[5]

Several states which did use the device have been able to reap large returns in the form of lower interest costs. In 1936 Colorado refunded more than $3,500,000 of bonds bearing 4 and 5 per cent into bonds bearing 1¾ and 2 per cent, while Delaware sold over $3,000,000 of bonds bearing from 2¼ to 2¾ per cent, to replace others bearing 4 per cent or more. In 1936 Mississippi refunded over $2,500,000 of 4½ and 5 per cent bonds into 2¼ to 2¾ per cent bonds. In 1935-36 the Kentucky Highway Commission refunded all outstanding bridge revenue bonds bearing 4 and 4½ per cent interest with 3 and 3½ per cent bonds. Even South Dakota, which has a very heavy debt burden, was able recently to refund old 5 and 6 per cent bonds with new bonds bearing from 2¾ to 4 per cent.

Some idea of the importance of this point may be gained from a brief consideration of the debt structure. In 1931, just as the era of low interest rates was beginning, the bonded debts of the states amounted to about $2,250,000,000. Most of these bonds carried nominal interest rates of 4 per cent or more.[6] It would be safe to estimate that the average coupon rate was not far from 4¼ per cent.[7] By 1936 these bonds, had they been callable, could have been refunded by issuing new bonds at an average interest rate of 2½ per cent or less (see Table 22 for yields of bonds sold that year). This would have meant a reduction in interest costs of about 40 per cent. Even allowing for the fact that some of these bonds would

5. Committee on Municipal Debt Administration, *The Call Feature in Municipal Bonds* (Chicago, 1938), p. 104.

6. *Financial Statistics of States,* 1931, pp. 106, 114.

7. This estimate is confirmed by the fact that in 1931 the states, on total interest-bearing indebtedness of about $2,590,000,000, paid interest amounting to $110,820,000 (*ibid.,* pp. 52, 114).

have been paid before 1936 and for the premiums and expenses connected with calling the old bonds, it is still evident that the states could now be realizing an annual saving of well over $30,000,000 if they had had the foresight to make their bonds callable.

It is difficult to assign a convincing reason for this great error. That state financial officials were aware of this elementary principle is shown by the fact that twenty states used it at one time or another. The argument that bonds including this feature would not have sold well is not borne out by the experience of the states which did use it. The pattern of interest rates realized by such states is not noticeably different from the general pattern. A study of this feature in the bonds of local governments showed that callable bonds sold at prices to cost the borrowers only 0.086 per cent more per year than noncallable bonds,[8] which was certainly a small price to pay for the potential benefits offered. The most logical explanation of the whole matter is that state financial officials were indifferent and took the advice of underwriting bankers who did not wish to have the feature included.

Even the object lessons afforded by those states which have been able to affect large savings by the use of the call feature does not seem to have influenced practice on this point; the relative amount of callable bonds issued has not increased in recent years. It is true that most bonds sold recently have borne low interest rates and that the call feature is of little value with such bonds. But Louisiana, which has continued to sell bonds bearing more than 3 per cent interest, has made no move to use it. After using the device profitably several times, Mississippi, in a large issue of 3¼ and 3½ per cent refunding bonds sold in 1938, omitted the feature. In this case, the investment firm heading the underwriting syndicate for the bonds was known to be in close touch with those writing the authorizing act. Undoubtedly the call feature should receive more attention than has been accorded it in the past. It should be an invariable rule that, whenever a bond issue is being prepared, careful consideration should be given to the use of the call feature and

8. Committee on Municipal Debt Administration, *op. cit.*, p. 12.

that, in general, it should be used with all bonds bearing more than 3 per cent unless there are definite reasons to the contrary.[9]

Forced Redemption

In the recent period of low interest rates two states were so eager to avail themselves of the privilege of redeeming their bonds that they attempted to force bondholders to surrender for redemption bonds which did not contain the call feature. One state succeeded, but the other did not. Missouri has outstanding a large amount of bonds, many of them bearing interest at from 4 to 4½ per cent. The state code contains a section, originally enacted in 1891, which created a Board of Fund Commissioners and empowered them to "refund any part of the bonded indebtedness of the state whenever they can do so to the advantage of the state."[10] In 1935 the House of Representatives instructed the board to refund certain parts of the state debt. The attorney-general of the state held that all outstanding bonds had been sold subject to the above section, which should be read into the contracts of such bonds. When the board ordered certain bonds to be surrendered for redemption, a case was brought before the state supreme court, which decided that the power of the board conferred in the section in question was meant to apply only to optionable or callable bonds and that the state's definite promise to pay interest for a specified time was not to be defeated by such power.[11]

North Dakota was more successful in a similar attempt. The state had shifted to the Farm Credit Administration a large number of rural credit loans and thus had on hand a large amount of cash which could earn very little return. A large amount of bonds was outstanding, maturing in the years from 1941 to 1949 and bearing 6 per cent interest; they contained no call feature and in a preliminary contract concerning them the Industrial Commission had specified that they should be "without option." But Chapter 154, Laws of 1919, which created the commission and authorized the bonds, specified that the bonds should "be payable at any time after five

9. See the work cited above for a full consideration of the problem and for a discussion of the factors determining how and when the call feature should be used.

10. *Revised Statutes of Missouri,* 1929, sec. 11500.

11. *State* v. *Smith,* 339 Mo. 202, 213, 214 (1936).

years from the date of their issue, upon public notice (of not less than one year) given by the Industrial Commission." In June, 1936, the commission called for redemption on July 1, 1937, $3,617,000 of the bonds. In a case brought before it, the supreme court of the state decided that there was no necessity that the option conferred in the 1919 law should "be referred to in the bonds themselves. A reference to the Statute is sufficient. There is no reason why, and so no requirement that, the option shall be exercised prior to the issuance of the bonds. . . . In short, the option cannot be exercised in advance. Neither can the right to exercise it be waived."[12] The power of the commission to redeem the bonds was upheld, and the bonds were redeemed as called.

Bond Maturities

The length of time which bonds run is a factor of importance in debt administration. This feature of state borrowing is analyzed in Table 23. In order to make serial bonds comparable with term bonds and also to show the full term of the debt, serial bond issues were classified according to their longest maturities; that is, if a $10,000,000 issue of serial bonds matured over a period ranging from five to twenty-five years, the whole amount was placed in the 20-25-year column. Thus the figures in Table 23 indicate the time which, at the time of issue, would have to run until the entire debt would be extinguished. The average maturities of the bonds would be considerably less; probably from 35 to 40 per cent less.

A large majority of the bonds fell, as would be expected, into the groups between ten and thirty years. The median was found in the 15-20-year group; the maximum concentration, in the 20-25-year group. There is little evidence of any definite trends in the maturities, nor does it seem that maturities were arranged to take advantage of prevailing interest rates. In fact, the sharp decline in maturities in the 1933-36 period came at a time of low interest rates, when a lengthening of maturities might have been expected if interest rates alone had been considered. This decline, however, was probably due to the unsettled condition of the market rather than to interest rates. The large spread between long-term and short-

12. *Catholic Order of Foresters* v. *State*, 67 N. D. 228, 232, 233 (1937).

TABLE 23

ANALYSIS OF STATE BORROWING ACCORDING TO MATURITIES
OF BONDS, 1919-38

Year	Total Analyzed (in thousands of dollars)	PERCENTAGE DISTRIBUTION									
		3.1–5.0 years	5.1–8.0 years	8.1–10.0 years	10.1–15.0 years	15.1–20.0 years	20.1–25.0 years	25.1–30.00 years	30.1–40.0 years	40.1–50.0 years	Over 50 years
1919...	69,740	1.03	2.29	2.45	5.74	24.57	9.37	19.49*	30.52	2.87	1.67
1920...	78,867	3.80	5.64	22.32	2.54	33.06*	16.65	0.90	4.48	10.61	......
1921...	270,075	1.12	0.85	4.24	12.29	32.76*	12.42	17.15	5.04	14.13	......
1922...	131,490	3.80	0.14	9.01	17.19	22.38*	10.89	22.11	14.10	0.38	......
1923...	234,796	1.49	2.56	2.66	7.33	41.95*	18.87	8.23	11.10	5.81	......
1924...	246,307	......	0.81	....	11.94	29.35	29.21*	11.09	13.56	3.23	0.81
1925...	169,683	0.59	0.35	6.62	10.88	14.59	12.43	40.77*	13.03	0.74	......
1926...	125,986	0.40	2.38	7.04	22.48	19.08*	14.94	14.35	2.86	16.47	......
1927...	133,547	0.07	......	2.40	25.36	14.22	30.61*	10.13	5.35	11.11	0.75
1928...	165,775	2.81	......	0.35	18.39	10.11	26.03*	33.48	6.33	2.05	0.45
1929...	166,849	3.33	1.20	10.00	17.48	17.30	13.77*	21.10	14.68	0.36	0.78
1930...	215,115	2.31	1.81	14.60	11.12	21.45*	34.53	3.34	9.41	1.39	......
1931...	253,354	1.22	1.02	2.68	3.50	18.30	42.80*	1.47	16.85	12.13	......
1932...	195,204	4.45	8.92	5.75	23.90	10.66*	30.34	3.51	9.22	2.61	0.64
1933...	190,448	4.35	27.22	20.31*	13.42	7.59	16.78	1.93	......	8.40	......
1934...	290,666	4.08	10.73	31.87	11.10*	20.47	17.03	1.80	......	2.75	0.17
1935...	246,343	4.25	10.02	21.82	22.05*	9.97	15.43	9.64	1.05	5.68	......
1936...	162,473	10.96	2.86	37.59*	8.49	18.05	8.74	12.76	0.09	......	0.43
1937...	153,626	3.74	2.49	21.07	22.42	9.75*	22.29	......	1.95	16.27	......
1938...	135,334	14.35	2.32	1.36	14.85	2.58	34.07*	28.58	......	1.69	0.14
Totals..	3,635,780	3.23	4.54	11.53	13.99	19.39*	21.63	12.03	7.45	5.92	0.25
Totals (in millions) of dollars......		117.5	165.4	419.2	508.7	705.0	786.8	437.7	271.1	215.6	8.9

*Median Group.

term interest rates in these years was probably an important factor also. The longer maturities issued in 1937 and 1938 represent an adjustment to the lower interest rates and a return to the normal pattern of the twenties.

All of the bonds running for more than fifty years were issued by California for improvements in the San Francisco Harbor. A majority of those in the 40-50-year column were issued by New York, chiefly for grade-crossing elimination. The figure in the 3-5-year column for 1938 represents a large issue by Massachusetts to cover hurricane and flood damage in the fall of 1938. Maryland is required by a constitutional provision to retire all bonds within fifteen years. It would seem that the states, with a few exceptions, have been sound in their practice on this point.

DEBTS BY STATES

Table 24 shows the total and per capita net debts of the different states for four years during the period under consideration. The selection of the years was determined partly by the availability of comparable figures.[13] The method used by the Bureau of the Census in computing debts is not the same as that described above, but either method will show the general trends in the growth of debts.

In the census figures some, but not all, revenue bonds are included. Apparently only those revenue obligations issued directly by the state or some regular state department are regarded as state indebtedness. Some revenue bonds were included in Colorado, Indiana, Kansas, Kentucky, Mississippi, Montana, New Hampshire, New Mexico, and Ohio, but important issues were excluded in Alabama, Maryland, and other states. Such inclusions and exclusions affect the figures for 1931 only to a slight extent, but greatly affect the 1937 figures. Obligations under reimbursement agreements apparently are not included in any of the figures except those for South Carolina in 1931 and those for states in which the agreements have been formally incorporated into the state debt.

For states which have loan or credit systems, the assets of such systems are deducted in arriving at the net debt, even though the systems may be heavily subsidized from tax revenues. This procedure greatly reduces the debt figures for California, Minnesota, and South Dakota, and leaves North Dakota with no net debt at all. In the same way, the debt incurred by Massachusetts for the Metropolitan District is deducted in computing net debt; this fact accounts for the small figure shown for that state.

The figures for 1937 cover only net funded debt, thus excluding warrants, tax-anticipation notes, and other forms of floating or unfunded debts. This is the same procedure followed in the analysis in this chapter, but it should be noted that there were, in 1937, substantial amounts of unfunded debt in California, Kentucky,

13. The series *Financial Statistics of States* was discontinued with the year 1931 and was not resumed until 1937, and then with some changes. The figures given in the decennial financial censuses of 1922 and 1932 are not strictly comparable with those given in the annual publication.

TABLE 24
Net Debts of the States for Selected Years, 1922-37
(Totals in thousands of dollars)

State	1922 Total	1922 Per Capita	1927 Total	1927 Per Capita	1931 Total	1931 Per Capita	1937* Total	1937* Per Capita
Ala......	14,494	$ 6.05	41,554	$16.34	66,534	$24.97	72,591	$25.14
Ariz.....			433	0.96	270	0.61	1,598	3.91
Ark.....	2,530	1.41	3,017	1.58	156,849	84.33	163,859	80.44
Calif....	76,244	20.93	105,876	24.20	132,463	22.88	106,332	17.40
Colo.....	9,509	9.75	11,414	10.64	7,038	6.76	30,056	28.12
Conn....	6,045	4.21	3,078	1.90	605	0.37		
Del.....	5,798	25.39	8,878	36.84	3,240	13.56	3,118	11.19
Fla......	485	0.47			580	0.39		
Ga......	5,382	1.81	9,249	2.92	9,448	3.25	23,492	7.61
Idaho...	5,516	12.08	4,783	9.01	3,770	8.45	2,204	4.49
Ill.......	12,737	1.91	140,159	19.33	195,517	25.43	200,539	25.50
Ind.....	426	0.14	1,649	0.52	3,101	0.95	4,458	1.29
Iowa....	185	0.08	20,195	8.33	14,817	5.99	6,458	2.53
Kan.....			24,837	13.62	21,892	11.60	21,467	11.46
Ky......	2,477	1.01	2,503	0.99	2,295	0.87	14,929	5.14
La......	13,679	7.45	16,459	8.51	73,313	34.50	126,325	59.25
Me......	12,654	16.36	21,568	27.27	24,171	30.25	29,969	35.05
Md.....	21,929	14.76	23,873	14.99	31,198	18.99	50,787	30.27
Mass....	75,968	19.12	22,103	5.21	17,266	4.04	22,772	5.15
Mich....	49,206	12.80	74,909	16.86	60,971	12.44	34,123	7.10
Minn....	19,476	7.96	11,715	4.39	14,221	5.53	62,559	23.66
Miss....	12,343	6.89	17,143	9.57	32,722	16.17	51,460	25.53
Mo......	30,308	8.83	69,958	19.93	103,005	28.25	119,215	29.89
Mont....	4,313	7.29	4,751	8.66	2,986	5.55	9,850	18.41
Neb.....					237	0.17	530	0.39
Nev.....	1,602	20.70	1,650	21.32	798	8.68	662	6.56
N. H....	3,018	6.77	1,818	4.00	6,005	12.89	13,901	27.31
N. J.....	16,349	4.98	63,275	17.03	56,872	13.92	86,905	20.04
N. M....	4,561	12.37	3,321	8.52	9,491	22.28	15,243	36.12
N. Y....	186,515	17.52	244,295	21.50	307,284	24.20	525,900	40.62
N. C....	33,326	12.59	147,981	51.44	169,400	52.92	136,420	39.25
N. D....	5,614	8.49	4,519	7.05	2,693	3.94		
Ohio....	29,584	4.96	19,128	2.87	6,208	0.92	10,427	1.55
Okla....	3,526	1.68	3,075	1.30	1,578	0.65	11,936	4.70
Ore.....	38,927	48.12	36,155	40.76	31,138	32.27	26,389	25.82
Pa......	48,994	5.45	92,400	9.56	78,636	8.13	121,670	11.98
R. I.....	9,338	15.05	18,385	26.15	16,722	24.16	26,966	39.60
S. C.....	5,225	3.03	29,567	16.03	69,430	39.83	40,771	21.83
S. D....	14,421	22.27	15,015	21.67	13,050	18.75	2,511	3.63
Tenn....	17,554	7.41	17,222	6.96	86,450	32.87	91,007	31.60
Texas...	4,102	0.85	4,364	0.81	4,446	0.75	26,649	4.33
Utah....	9,020	19.26	6,595	12.73	4,982	9.75	3,901	7.53
Vt......	2,112	5.99	1,694	4.81	9,182	25.51	7,843	20.74
Va......	21,205	8.96	26,637	10.52	25,335	10.44	23,892	8.88
Wash....	12,260	8.72	12,912	8.25	10,799	6.87	12,547	7.62
W. Va...	24,181	15.97	51,536	30.60	82,353	47.27	76,019	41.11
Wis.....	2,164	0.80	1,664	0.57	1,264	0.43	1,184	0.41
Wyo....	3,776	18.37	1,613	6.72	4,216	18.49	3,215	13.68
Totals...	879,076	$ 8.12	1,444,927	$12.32	1,976,844	$16.04	2,424,648	$18.90

*Net funded debt only.   Source: Bureau of the Census, *Financial Statistics of States*.

New York, Oklahoma, Pennsylvania, Texas, and a few other states. The net amount of such debts was probably over $200,000,000.

On the basis of the figures as they stand it is apparent that the net debts of the states increased from approximately $460,000,000 (see Table 20) in 1916 to nearly $2,425,000,000 in 1937, or roughly fivefold in twenty-one years. In the same period average per capita net indebtedness increased from $4.59 to $18.90, or approximately fourfold. If the various forms of indirect and contingent debts, most of which represent a greater or less burden on state finances, were included, the increases would be substantially greater.

SUMMARY

We may summarize or characterize the developments of this period as follows: the states borrowed mainly for highways, which accounted for nearly one half of all loans. Unemployment relief and soldiers' bonuses and loan funds each accounted for about one eighth of the total. The remainder—about 30 per cent—was divided among a great variety of purposes. From 1919 through 1929 no bonds were sold at an interest cost of less than 3½ per cent, while most of them sold at prices to yield from 3½ to 4½ per cent. After 1932 interest rates declined sharply, and from 1935 through 1938 a large majority of the bonds were sold at a cost of less than 3½ per cent. During the twenties, when the states were selling large amounts of bonds at comparatively high interest rates, they included the call feature in less than 5 per cent of them. As a result, the states are now paying out annually many millions of dollars in interest which might have been saved. No logical or defensible explanation of this practice is apparent. Most of the debts had maximum maturities of less than thirty years, but a few states have issued bonds running for as long as fifty years to finance improvements which would not last nearly that long. Between 1916 and 1937 the net debts of all states increased by fivefold and per capita debts, by fourfold.

CHAPTER XI

BORROWING FOR HIGHWAYS

BEFORE 1900 the construction and maintenance of highways were almost exclusively functions of local governments, principally counties and townships. It is true that before 1860 several states experimented with turnpikes and plankroads, six of them with borrowed funds. Kentucky and Pennsylvania borrowed about $2,500,000 each, Indiana over $1,000,000, and Virginia, Tennessee, and North Carolina smaller sums.[1] But the railroad soon outmoded overland travel by coach and wagon and made highways a matter of purely local concern. Several states had extended aid by buying the stocks of turnpike companies, expecting to realize a return from tolls. The decline of traffic ruined the companies, and the states lost their investments. Agitation for state participation in road building did not become general again until around 1900.

The first factor which revived interest in better rural roads was the development of the bicycle between 1875 and 1900. In 1880 the bicyclists organized the League of American Wheelmen, which did much to arouse public sentiment in favor of better roads. Rural roads were again becoming a matter of concern to adjoining towns and counties. New Jersey set precedents by providing, in 1891, advice and limited financial aid to counties in the building of roads and by establishing, in 1894, a state highway commission. Soon other states followed, and by 1900 seven states were aiding road construction. Massachusetts set another precedent in 1894 by borrowing $300,000 for highways.[2]

1. See Table 7 and Chapter V.
2. Edna Trull, *Borrowing for Highways* (New York: Dun and Bradstreet, Inc., 1937), pp. 5-6; A. F. Macdonald, *Federal Aid* (New York, 1928), pp. 85-86. In writing this chapter I have drawn heavily upon Miss Trull's excellent book. For a more complete treatment of many of the points discussed in this chapter the reader would do well to consult her work.

The major factor in the demand for better roads was, of course, the development of the automobile. While only about a hundred thousand motor vehicles were registered in 1906, by 1912 the number was approaching a million. Car owners, automobile manufacturers, oil companies, builders of road-building equipment, and contractors all joined in the agitation for better roads. By 1909 twenty-one additional states were providing state aid to roads, and by 1917 the remaining twenty had joined their ranks. But road conditions had now become a matter of concern, not only to adjoining towns and counties, but even to adjoining states. Thus arose a demand for federal aid in the construction of important interstate highways. After long debate, Congress, in 1916, enacted a law appropriating $25,000,000 annually to be apportioned among the states, partly on the basis of area, partly on the basis of population, and partly on the basis of road mileage. To obtain federal funds, states were required to spend equal amounts of their own money. Later acts raised annual appropriations considerably and modified the basis of allocation. As a qualification for receiving federal funds a state was required to have a highway department or commission adequate to manage a state highway system and to supervise the expenditure of funds. By 1917 all states met this requirement.

Thus by the time of the World War, the movement for state control and state financing of highways had gained much momentum. The machinery had been set up, but most of the states had not yet decided whether they would restrict themselves entirely to supervision and control, give limited financial assistance to local governments, or take over a system of state highways for which they would assume all financial responsibility. The war intervened to direct attention to other matters for a time, so it was not until the immediate post-war years that this matter came up for decision in most states.

In reality there were two questions to be decided: the first was that of state versus local financing of highways, while the second was the problem of how the state should finance its activities if it did assume an active part. The latter was a question of borrowing or pay-as-you-go. Over these questions each state had its own struggle, influenced by local conditions and local politics. The stories of those campaigns, if written, would be significant contributions to local history.[3] All states eventually set up state highway systems for which they assumed full financial responsibility, and over the years they have gradually increased the mileage included in such systems. Ultimately, too, more than half the states borrowed for highways, but only about fifteen of them placed their principal reliance upon borrowing; the others borrowed primarily to supplement current revenues.

MOVEMENTS IN STATE BORROWING

Prewar Borrowing

By 1918 only eleven states had borrowed for highways, and four of them—New York, Massachusetts, California, and Maryland, in that order—owed more than 90 per cent of the approximately $134,-000,000 of highway debts outstanding in that year. New York alone owed more than half the total. In the ensuing years each of the four states followed a different policy in financing highways. Massachusetts issued only one small loan in 1919 and then borrowed no more. California continued to borrow through 1924 and then ceased, while New York has continued to borrow intermittently, chiefly for grade-crossing elimination. Maryland borrowed small sums almost every year until 1936, when the State Roads Commission embarked upon a program of revenue financing.

1919-1922

Since the war there have been three distinct periods in which states have launched highway loan programs. The first and most important included the years 1919-22, when the states were feeling the strong post-war demand for highways. Michigan and Pennsylvania initiated large loan programs in 1919, while Delaware and South Dakota embarked upon less ambitious projects. After 1920 had passed without the launching of any large new programs, the year 1921 set an all-time record when Illinois, New Jersey, North Carolina, and West Virginia started important borrowing

3. For an interesting, complete, accurate, and colorful account of the campaign in one state see C. K. Brown, *The State Highway System of North Carolina* (Chapel Hill, 1931).

programs, while Colorado and Wyoming floated smaller initial loans, and Oregon, which had borrowed small sums in previous years, first appeared as a major borrower. Alabama and Missouri brought the first movement to a close in 1922, when they sold their first highway bonds. Altogether, thirteen states had opened highway loan programs in those four years, and eight of them were among the heaviest borrowers in the following decade.

Those states were leading the way at a time when comparatively little was known about highway construction and finance. It should be noted particularly that they were borrowing mainly upon the basis of general state revenues, because special highway revenues were small. The motor vehicle tax, while increasing rapidly, brought in only $64,697,000 in 1919 and $152,048,000 in 1922. The little-known gasoline tax yielded only $12,000,000 in 1922, and only three of the thirteen borrowing states had levied such a tax.[4]

1926-1927

In the years 1923-25, while the above states continued to borrow heavily, not a single new state began a highway borrowing program. In 1926 Virginia departed from its program of current financing to sell one small loan. In 1927 three states which were to be heavy borrowers—Arkansas, Louisiana, and Tennessee—sold their first highway bonds. By that time the gasoline tax had become established as the source of generous and stable revenues so that it was possible to borrow large sums, giving a pledge of such revenues with a fair assurance that the general revenues of the state would not be burdened with the service of the bonds. All three of the above states gave such pledges. Arkansas' action was practically forced by the breakdown of its system of local highway finance,[5] and this factor was probably of importance in the other two states. Another common characteristic of these states was that they were relatively poor Southern states with low credit ratings. It is doubtful whether they could have found purchasers for large amounts of bonds except on the pledge of the lucrative revenues of

4. Finla G. Crawford, *The Gasoline Tax in the United States, 1936* (Chicago, 1937).   5. See Chapter XV, below.

the gasoline tax and until the New Era philosophy of perpetual prosperity had induced a more optimistic attitude toward all state bonds.

1929-1931

Between 1929 and 1931 four states negotiated initial loans for highways. New Hampshire and Montana began in 1929 and 1931 respectively, but were never large borrowers. Minnesota and South Carolina opened their programs in 1930. In South Carolina two factors were probably responsible for the change. The first was dissatisfaction with the state's system of indirect borrowing; that is, the system whereby counties and special districts borrowed with a promise of reimbursement from the state. The second factor was the discovery of a device, explained more fully below, whereby the state could incur debts without the approval of two thirds of the voters, as required by the constitution. The first factor may also have been responsible for Minnesota's action.

Since 1931 only one state has begun a borrowing program for highways. Mississippi lagged far behind most other states in road building. As part of a program to attract industry and tourists and also to qualify for a large grant of federal funds, that state, in 1936, began to borrow and build, and within about two years had incurred a highway debt of over $30,000,000.

Yearly Variations

As might be inferred from the sporadic action of the states in launching their programs, the amounts borrowed for roads each year varied widely. An initial peak was reached in 1921 with over $133,000,000. In the ten years from 1923 through 1932 the totals never fell below $75,000,000 and often were over $100,000,000. The record years were 1930 and 1931 with figures approaching $150,-000,000. After 1932 the amounts declined sharply and exceeded $50,000,000 in only one year—1937. The 1938 figure—$33,403,000— was the lowest in the whole twenty-year period. It is quite likely that after 1932 new loans were less than the bonds retired and that the total highway debt declined; certainly the bonds sold in 1938 did not equal the bonds maturing that year.

Types of Programs

Two distinct methods of procedure were followed by the states in their highway borrowing. The first method was to map out and carry through a definite and limited program of borrowing in order to build a designated road system. When that goal was accomplished the state would maintain the roads, reduce the debt, and construct new roads or replace old ones out of current revenues. This procedure is more likely to be followed in those states where popular approval of all loans is required. States which have followed this method are: Alabama, California, Illinois, Michigan, Minnesota, New Jersey, North Carolina, Pennsylvania, and several smaller states. Perhaps Louisiana, Missouri, and New York should be placed in this group, too, although their borrowings have been spread over a considerable period of time. The sequence of events in Arkansas and Tennessee would seem to place them in this group also, but financial embarrassments interrupted their plans before any definite program could be completed.

The second method of procedure is for the state to borrow regularly to supplement current funds as the need arises. This can be accomplished more easily if the legislature does not have to secure popular approval of each loan. If this method is followed for a considerable time the new loans come to have much of the nature of refunding loans, even though they may not be designated as such. States which have followed this method are: Delaware, Maine, Maryland, New Mexico, and West Virginia. The use of this method in West Virginia depends upon the particular wording of a constitutional amendment. Two amendments were approved, one in 1920 for $50,000,000 of highway bonds and the other in 1928 for $35,000,000. The first specified that "the aggregate amount outstanding . . . at any one time, shall not exceed fifty million dollars." From time to time the legislature has authorized the issue of additional bonds as bonds of this first issue were retired.[6] Constitutionally, this can continue indefinitely, and the bonds thus issued are, in effect, refunding bonds.

While each of these methods has its advantages, the first is

6. Cf., for instance, *Acts,* 1297, c. 39; *ibid.,* 1931, c. 1.

more in keeping with sound debt management. The second is likely to lead to an increasing debt which finally becomes permanent or stable at a high level. In such a situation a state pays liberally for the exercise of its credit at the very time when it is unable to enjoy the benefits which the use of credit should afford.

TYPES OF HIGHWAY BONDS

Out of the extensive experience of the states with highway debts there have evolved several types of obligations. Some have been devised to avoid constitutional restrictions, while others have been developed to meet administrative needs. While there are almost numberless variations in details, all obligations fall within two broad groups: general obligations secured by the full faith and credit of the issuing state, and limited obligations or revenue issues resting exclusively upon designated sources of revenue.[7] Only the general obligations are discussed here; the limited obligations will be considered below.

Bonds Based on General Revenues

All early highway bonds were general obligations serviced from existing sources of state revenue. In some cases a definite part of the property tax levy was designated to pay principal and interest. As highway finance increased in importance and as special highway revenues grew rapidly, there arose a general demand that those revenues should be segregated and used exclusively for highway purposes, including the service of highway bonds. In keeping with this, many states began, as a matter of administrative policy, to transfer to general funds sufficient highway revenues to service such bonds. The bonds remained general obligations, but they were no longer a burden on general revenues so long as highway revenues were adequate.[8]

7. See Trull, *op. cit.,* chap. v, for a more detailed consideration of this topic.

8. California had some difficulty in making this change. There the voters refused to sanction a proposal to make the service of highway bonds a charge against highway revenues. After an extensive consideration of technical devices the legislature, in 1935, enacted a special motor vehicle license tax, entirely apart from the usual registration fee, to be paid into the general fund for highway debt service. In other states the change was made with less difficulty, the legislature merely appropriating a

General Obligations Based on Highway Revenues

Another type of general obligation bond, however, is fundamentally different in legal status and security. In order to sell
their bonds on more favorable terms, many states offered bondholders a definite pledge of all or part of their highway revenues
in addition to the full faith and credit of the state. The pledging
of particular revenues has often been used outside the United
States to bolster the credit of weak governments. Some states used
it for the same purpose, while others used it as an inducement to
voters to gain their approval of highway bond issues on the ground
that such bonds would not be a burden on general state revenues.

Two types of pledges are used. In the first, there is a general
provision that the bonds will be serviced from all or some designated part of highway revenues. Under such a pledge the bondholder's position is somewhat uncertain, since other charges, such
as collection costs and road maintenance, may rank on a parity
with debt service and, unless the pledge is quite specific, the state
may be able to vary the amount of highway revenues by changing
tax rates or transferring funds. In the second type of pledge, however, debt service is made a first claim on all or certain parts of the
highway revenues. The state may promise to maintain certain minimum tax rates or yields. Tennessee, for instance, pledges two
cents of the seven-cent gasoline tax for debt service, and Louisiana
has a similar arrangement. Missouri specifies that debt service
is a first claim against highway revenues, and that only after the
year's requirement has been fully provided for may the surplus be
transferred to highway operating funds.[9] In Arkansas all highway
revenues in excess of certain specified deductions for maintenance
and other costs are available for debt service. The state cannot
reduce the rate of the gasoline tax rates except under specified conditions.

While the legal significance of the first type of pledge is uncertain, since it has not been before a court for adjudication, the second type definitely strengthens the bondholder's position and gives

---

certain amount of highway funds for transfer to the general fund. Such changes do
not in any way affect the legal status or security of the bonds.

9. Trull, *op. cit.*, pp. 39-40.

him an additional remedy. In fact, under it he can, in effect, sue a state.[10]

Classification of Bonds

Miss Trull "cautiously" offers the following classification of general obligation bonds with the notation that no classification can be exact:

I. General obligations serviced from general revenues.
II. General obligations serviced from highway revenues as a matter of administrative policy.
III. General obligations, debt service for which is pledged from all or part of highway revenues.
IV. General obligations, debt service on which is a first charge on all or part of highway revenues.[11]

She then gives a tentative grouping of the borrowing states under this classification, with the warning that "the groupings are not authenticated by exhaustive legal research into statutes or court decisions but are based on accepted conclusions and the statements or opinions of officials." This grouping applies only to general obligations; some states have both general and limited obligations outstanding, and may have two or more types of general obligations.

I	II	III	IV
Colorado	Delaware	Alabama	Arkansas
Idaho	Maine	California	Louisiana
New York	Maryland	Illinois	Minnesota
Wyoming	Massachusetts	New Jersey	Missouri
	Michigan	Oregon	Tennessee
	New Hampshire	Virginia	Utah
	New Jersey	Wyoming	West Virginia
	New Mexico		Wyoming
	Pennsylvania		

New Jersey appears in two columns and Wyoming in three, because they have issued different types of bonds. North Carolina apparently belongs in Column III and South Carolina in Column IV, although, as explained below, the latter presents a peculiar situation.

10. For further discussion and illustration of this point, see Chapters XV and XX, below.   11. Trull, *op. cit.,* p. 42.

defend the state. The supreme court of the state, by a four-to-three vote, held the proposed bill unconstitutional.[15]

Later the voters approved a constitutional amendment which required the payment of all automobile and gasoline taxes into a special fund *not available for general purposes*. In the case just cited, the decision of the court had hinged on this point, since it held that the debentures would be a charge upon funds which were, or might be, available for general state purposes. Following the amendment, the 1935 legislature authorized the highway department to issue up to $25,000,000 of "revenue anticipation warrants" payable solely from highway funds and having a first lien on such funds. Taxes and fees charged by the state were not to be lowered below the amount necessary to service the warrants, which were not obligations of the state and which were to carry on their face a statement to that effect.[16] In a case challenging this act, the court held that since the highway funds, by constitutional provision, were no longer available for general purposes, the act was valid. Again the vote was four to three.[17] The full amount of the "warrants," with maturities ranging from 1939 to 1954, was issued.

Kansas

Developments in Kansas were similar to those in Colorado, but with a different background. The Kansas constitution not only forbids state borrowing but, before 1920, provided that "the state shall never be a party in carrying on any works of internal improvement."[18] In 1920 and 1928 amendments were adopted allowing the state to levy highway taxes and to adopt and maintain a state highway system, provided that "no general property tax shall ever be laid nor bonds issued by the state for such highways." In 1933 the legislature enacted a law very similar to the above Colorado act.[19] The state supreme court held that since the framers of the

15. *In re Senate Resolution No. 2*, 94 Colo. 101 (1934).
16. *Laws*, 1935, c. 181.
17. *Johnson* v. *McDonald*, 97 Colo. 324 (1935).
18. In 1917 the state appropriated $5,000 to aid counties, at the rate of $100 per mile, in improving roads. This was held to be a violation of the above constitutional provision. *State* v. *Knapp*, 99 Kan. 852 (1917). There was a similar decision in Minnesota in 1909. *Cooke* v. *Iverson*, 108 Minn. 388 (1909).
19. *Laws, Special Session*, 1933, c. 98.

constitution "regarded property as the basis of taxation," the constitutional prohibition of borrowing referred only to "debts to be paid by a general property tax. This is clear from the reading of the sections." It held that when the people (by the 1920 and 1928 amendments) permitted the state to engage in internal improvements, which had been responsible for the original debt limit, they also meant to permit borrowing, which was necessary to acquire the improvements.[20] This, in spite of the fact that the provision read that no bonds should "be issued by the state for such highways"! But the act was held valid, and "warrants" to the amount of $3,435,000 have been issued.

Other States

Early in the 1920's New Mexico began to issue highway "debentures" similar to the "warrants" of Colorado and Kansas. At first they ran for short periods—three to five years—but in recent years the volume has increased and the terms have been lengthened to from ten to twelve years. The total of such obligations outstanding in 1938 was $18,350,000. In 1933 Maryland authorized the State Roads Commission to issue revenue bonds for highway purposes, pledging a certain part of the revenue from the gasoline tax as security. Other highway funds may be used to service the bonds if necessary. In 1938 the commission sold $6,000,000 of term bonds maturing in 1968; the Maryland constitution forbids the issue of bonds running for more than fifteen years. In November, 1938, bonds of the commission were outstanding to the amount of $11,-358,000.

When Mississippi began to borrow in 1936, it sold revenue bonds instead of general obligations. All of the highway bonds outstanding, amounting to $32,817,000, are of this type and are secured by the specific pledge of $1\frac{1}{4}$ cents of the gasoline tax plus any further amount from such tax as may be necessary to service the bonds.

20. *State* v. *State Highway Commission*, 138 Kan. 913 (1934). On each point, logic and the English language would seem, to the author, to point to a conclusion exactly opposite to that reached by the court. Considering a similar statute enacted by the Oklahoma legislature in 1937, the Oklahoma Supreme Court held that the revenues so pledged were a part of the general revenues of the state which might be used for any public purpose desired by the legislature. It held that such revenue obligations must be a debt "in any sense." *Boswell* v. *State*, 181 Okla. 435 (1937).

Louisiana and Montana have outstanding small amounts of highway revenue bonds for which limited revenues are pledged without any provision for additional funds. Alabama has sold one issue of short-term gasoline tax revenue warrants to the amount of $1,750,000.

South Carolina

The South Carolina Highway "Certificates of Indebtedness" are a unique type. The South Carolina constitution forbids the creation of debt except with the approval of a two-thirds majority of the voters. One proposal to borrow for highways was defeated by the voters in the early 1920's, and the state proceeded under the county reimbursement plan. A 1929 law authorized the governor and treasurer to sign and issue bonds with a special lien on highway revenues but with a pledge of the full faith and credit of the state as additional security. Although the voters had not approved this act, the supreme court of the state held it to be constitutional.[21] Thus these should perhaps be classed primarily as revenue bonds supported by the full faith and credit of the state pledged in direct violation of the state constitution, but with the approval of the state supreme court.

The state used this method of financing highways for a number of years, but in 1936 new difficulties developed. After the legislature had passed, over the governor's veto, an act providing for the issue of $8,000,000 of highway "certificates," the governor refused to sign them. The legislature then empowered the treasurer to sign them alone and also made provisions for raising additional funds by a return to the county reimbursement plan. Certificates to the amount of $12,600,000 have been issued since 1936, and a total of $39,874,000 was outstanding in 1938.

Summary

A more detailed evaluation of revenue bonds and their uses will be given later, but a few pertinent comments may be offered here. First, the costs of borrowing are higher with revenue bonds

21. *State* v. *Moorer*, 152 S. C. 455 (1929). See the discussion of revenue bonds in a later chapter for a further consideration of this case.

than with general obligations. In every case where comparison is possible the revenue bonds have sold on a distinctly higher yield basis.[22] Second, there are no constitutional restrictions on the issue of revenue bonds; the states may sell as many bonds as they wish, with such features as they desire, if they can find buyers in the market. Third, the bondholder is in a favored position. He has a stronger legal position than the holder of a general obligation without a specific pledge, because if the pledged funds are collected he can take legal action to prevent the state from defeating his claim. If the pledged funds are inadequate, and the general credit of the state is good, it is quite likely that the state will protect the bondholder from loss. In other words, the holder of revenue bonds is protected by the moral obligation of the state plus pledged funds, while the holder of a general obligation has only the moral obligation, although it may be a little stronger.

STATE SERVICE OF LOCAL HIGHWAY DEBTS

In addition to the direct and indirect borrowing described above, many states have assumed, wholly or partly, definitely or indefinitely, varying amounts of highway obligations originally created by counties or special road districts. The legal responsibility assumed by the states varies from those cases in which the state has, by statutory or constitutional action, formally assumed the burden of paying the principal or interest, or both, of certain local debts to those cases in which the state returns to local governments certain revenues from the gasoline or motor vehicle tax with the direction that the service of highway debts shall have first claim on such funds. There are many gradations between these two extremes, and it is impossible, except arbitrarily, to draw a line to indicate where state

22. In 1935 Colorado sold general obligations to yield less than 2 per cent; in 1936, when general interest rates were lower, its revenue bonds with slightly longer maturities, sold on a 2.64 per cent basis. In early 1936 Mississippi sold general refunding bonds with maturities up to eight years at 2.16 per cent; the next month and throughout the remainder of the year it sold highway revenue bonds with maturities to twenty-four years at prices to yield from 3.67 to 4.00 per cent. In the same year Maryland sold general obligations at a cost of about 1.90 per cent, while bonds of the State Roads Commission with equal maturities sold at 2.14 per cent. Moody's ratings for the revenue bonds of Colorado, Kansas, and Mississippi are one rank lower than for general obligations; for Maryland, Montana, and New Mexico the ratings are the same.

assumption begins. In this section state assumption is recognized where the state's responsibility, legal or actual, can be calculated with a fair degree of accuracy.

Origin

The obligations for which the states have recognized responsibility in this field grew out of the peculiar development of the methods of financing highways. As noted above, financial responsibility for highways originally rested exclusively upon local governments. When the states took over certain roads for inclusion into state highways systems, local governments claimed that the recognition of responsibility should be retroactive to the extent of state assumption of debts incurred in building those roads. Many states allowed such claims in whole or in part; thus arose a part of the obligations. The other part arose after the states had taken over the roads. Some states could not or did not secure the necessary popular approval of state highway borrowing. They encouraged counties which could borrow to do so, and either to construct, under state supervision, roads in the state highway system or to turn the funds over to the state highway commission on the promise of reimbursement out of highway funds when available. In some instances highway commissions instituted such programs on their own initiative without statutory authorization.

North Carolina used the reimbursement plan at the time when it was borrowing most heavily. Some counties were not satisfied with their share of new highway mileage as allocated by the highway commission. An act passed in 1921 authorized the commission to make reimbursement contracts with the counties. If one county borrowed, it increased its allotment by that amount and "made it quite imperative for additional counties to advance money, for the county that advanced the most money got the most roads . . . the practice resulted in a very inequitable distribution of state funds, since it discriminated in favor of the counties which were willing to advance money to the state."[23]

In some states the reimbursement plan presented the unusual situation of two debts, neither of which existed, according to the

23. Brown, *op. cit.,* p. 183.

interpretation of state constitutions by the courts. Most courts hold that the promise of the state or of the highway department to reimburse counties out of highway construction funds, if and when they became available, does not constitute a debt within the meaning of the constitution.[24] On the other hand, the bonds issued by counties do not fall within constitutional debt limits, since they are to be repaid from a special fund and are not a charge upon the taxpayers of the county.[25] The state commitment is not a debt because payment is not definitely promised; the county bonds, although general obligations, are not a debt because they are to be paid from the proceeds of that indefinite promise!

Most of the local debts serviced by states fall within the groups described above. They were incurred for the construction of roads which are now parts of state highway systems. In a few instances, however, states have assumed, or provided funds for servicing, all local highway debts, regardless of whether the roads built were later included in state highway systems. In order to show the great variety of practices in the different states, the experiences of several states are discussed briefly below.

Arkansas

Before 1927 special road improvement districts in Arkansas had incurred large debts serviced from property taxes. When the state undertook its extensive program to equalize and improve road facilities, it assumed $83,136,477 of special district bonds and appropriated $6,500,000 annually to service them. The Arkansas constitution provides (art. 12, par. 12) that the state shall "not assume or pay the debt liability of any county, town, city, or other corporation whatever" unless such debt was incurred "to repel invasion, suppress insurrection or to provide for the public welfare and defense." The state supreme court held that the road improvement districts had been declared, in the acts creating them, to be bodies corporate

24. See, for instance, *Board of Supervisors* v. *Bibb,* 129 Va. 638 (1921); *McLeland* v. *Marshall Co.,* 199 Iowa 1232 (1925); *Faves* v. *City of Washington,* 159 Ga. 568 (1925); *State* v. *Moorer,* 152 S. C. 455 (1929), and cases cited. For opposite rulings, however, see *Crick* v. *Rash,* 190 Ky. 820 (1921), and *Berry* v. *Fox,* 114 W. Va. 513 (1934).

25. See *Briggs* v. *Greenville Co.* 137 S. C. 288 (1926), and cases cited.

for the purpose of their creation, but that really they were quasi-governmental or state agencies of special and limited powers. It also held that the state's action might be justified under the public welfare clause since highways "are for the public welfare in a sense."[26] It, therefore, held the act constitutional. These bonds were refunded in the 1934 refunding program and are now outstanding in the amount of more than $39,000,000.

Florida

Florida incurred no highway debts on its own account but proceeded under a reimbursement plan. Later (when the local units met with acute financial difficulties) the state extended aid to cover *all* road and bridge bonds, even though they had not been incurred to build parts of the state highway system. Many of the units were in default. If the state turned funds into their treasuries, they might be seized by creditors other than holders of road and bridge bonds, who had obtained judgments. The state wished to restrict its aid to road and bridge bonds. A state board of administration was created to supervise the road and bridge debts of all counties and special districts; it received all state funds allocated to the local units and also all tax funds raised by the local units for the service of road and bridge debts. The state treasurer was made "County Treasurer Ex-Officio" for the counties, and remitted all funds for debt service directly to the paying agents.

A 1929 act levied a three-cent gasoline tax for the benefit of the counties, the proceeds from one cent to be allocated according to collections, from another cent according to road and bridge debts outstanding, and from the third on a different basis for schools and roads. The board was to compute debt service requirements on road and bridge bonds for each county and to allocate state funds; if there was a deficiency, the county was to levy taxes sufficient to cover it. In a test case the state supreme court held: (1) if the gasoline tax was regarded as a state tax, the act was invalid, since the state could not levy a tax for county purposes; (2) if it was regarded as a county tax, the allocation was invalid, since the legis-

26. *Bush* v. *Martineau*, 174 Ark. 214 (1927); reaffirmed in *Tapley* v. *Futrell*, 187 Ark. 844 (1933).

lature could not take money "from the citizens of one county and divert it to the benefit of the citizens of another county." It held that all funds would have to be allocated according to collections.[27]

In 1931 the law was revised. The gasoline tax levy was definitely made a state tax, but the payments to counties and district were stated to be reimbursements for costs incurred in the building of roads which "was, is, and will be a legitimate proper state expense incurred for a general and state purpose and should be wholly borne by the State." On this basis the court upheld it, stating that the primary purpose of the act was not to pay the debts of the local units but to repay them for costs incurred in building state roads.[28] Since that time the disbursement of state funds has proceeded, but with much legislation and litigation over allocation and uses of the funds. Some counties are permitted to use the funds to buy in their obligations at a discount instead of to pay interest and principal as due, while others have not. Also,

In Aug., 1935 the State Supreme Court ruled that gasoline tax money held by the State Board of Administration may be mandamused for the payment of past-due obligations, exactly the same as ad valorem tax money; . . . that where the gasoline tax money had been appropriated by resolution for the payment of principal and interest, such allocation, in effect, made the gas tax money take the place of ad valorem taxes, and therefore, was available to legal action by bondholders just the same as any other moneys collected by direct taxation.[29]

On September 30, 1938, the gross highway indebtedness of the counties amounted to $127,630,344. Against this sum the board of administration held cash and securities amounting to $17,228,813, leaving a net debt of $110,401,531. Receipts from the gasoline tax for the fiscal year 1937-38 were $8,028,942, or 67.8 per cent of the total receipts available for debt service. On the basis of these figures the state's "share" of the debt may be stated as 67.8 per cent of the total, or $74,852,238.[30]

27. *Amos* v. *Mathews*, 99 Fla. 1 (1930).
28. *Carlton* v. *Mathews*, 103 Fla. 301 (1931).
29. Moody's *Governments and Municipals*, 1939 (cited hereinafter as *Moody's*).
30. *Reports of the Board of Administration*, 1938, pp. 6-7, 12. This is only an approximation, but it seems to be the only method available under the conditions; its validity is increased by the fact that the proportion of total receipts represented by receipts from the gasoline tax has changed little in recent years.

Georgia

Beginning in 1919 Georgia proceeded under the reimbursement plan, and counties and special districts borrowed considerable sums. In 1932 the voters approved a constitutional amendment formally assuming the local debt. Non-interest-bearing certificates were issued to the local units to the amount of the actual cost of road construction, as evidenced by certificates issued by the highway department. Payments on those certificates are made, solely out of special highway funds, at the rate of 10 per cent per year beginning March 25, 1936. Local units may sell the certificates at a discount not exceeding 5 per cent per year, in which case the proceeds must be devoted first to the discharge of debts incurred to build the roads in question.[31] The certificates were issued to the amount of $26,331,333.32, of which $18,672,237 were outstanding in the latter part of 1938.

Iowa

Iowa counties borrowed heavily for highways, issuing general obligations serviced from property taxes. In 1927 the state appropriated a part of the highway revenues to service the county primary road bonds, relieving the counties of the necessity of levying further property taxes for this purpose. In 1928 the legislature proposed a constitutional amendment to allow the issue of $100,000,000 of bonds for repaying the counties and providing additional highway funds. This amendment was approved by the voters, but the state supreme court held it invalid on procedural grounds.[32] Another amendment was proposed in 1931, and a special election was set for June 16, 1931. Before that date the matter was again brought before the court, which held that the second proposal was not in the proper form.[33] Following two defeats at the hands of the court, the legislature, in 1934, directed the state highway commission to supervise a refunding of the county primary road bonds so that annual debt service charges might be smoothed out and assumed entirely by the primary road fund. This was done at a great saving in interest costs,

31. *Laws*, 1931, Part I, Title IV, No. 152; *ibid.*, 1933, Part I, Title III, No. 126.
32. *State* v. *Executive Council*, 207 Iowa 923 (1929).
33. *Matthews* v. *Turner*, 212 Iowa 424 (1931).

and with such a rearrangement of maturities that annual charges approximate $8,000,000. Previously annual charges had varied from $18,116,404 in 1931 to $14,513,823 in 1934. The total amount of primary road bonds thus assumed was over $96,000,000; the amount outstanding November 1, 1938, was $79,790,000.

Tennessee

A Tennessee law enacted in 1919 gave the highway commission power to *require* any county in which a road was to be built to contribute a fair proportion of the necessary funds, not to exceed 50 per cent. A 1927 law, amended in 1931, provided for reimbursement to the counties of amounts equal to outstanding debts incurred to build roads later incorporated into the state road system. The state paid 5 per cent interest on unpaid balances, and the proceeds from one cent of the gasoline tax were placed in a reimbursement fund. The state supreme court held that this arrangement did not violate the constitutional provision forbidding the loaning or giving of the state credit "to or in aid of any person, . . . corporation or municipality."[34] The reimbursement obligations are treated, for all practical purposes, as part of the regular state debt and are being refunded under the debt reorganization plan adopted in 1937. The debts provided for in this way originally amounted to approximately $38,000,000, of which $31,997,824 were outstanding in 1938.

Texas

Under the original state-aid act passed in 1917 Texas left full responsibility for building and maintaining roads to the counties, subject to state supervision. State aid was limited to one fourth of the cost on not more than ten miles in any one county in one year. Under acts passed in 1923 and 1925 the state assumed full maintenance of a system of state roads, assumed full responsibility for finances on federal aid projects, and increased state aid to one half the costs on other projects. In 1932, in response to demands of local taxpayers for relief and reimbursement, the state created a board of county and district road indebtedness and turned over to it the

34. *Baker* v. *Hickman Co.*, 164 Tenn. 294 (1932).

proceeds from one cent of the gasoline tax.[35] This board found that local units had outstanding road debts of about $202,000,000, parts of which had been incurred in building state roads, and that the state's "share" of this debt was approximately $110,000,000. Under a plan similar to that used in Florida, the board has administered these local debts, using the state funds to pay first the interest and then, to the extent of remaining funds, the maturing principal on the state's share of the bonds. The local units are responsible for any deficiency. State funds have covered interest requirements in full from the beginning and have paid proportions of the principal requirements varying from 30 per cent in 1934 to 100 per cent in 1938. Total state aid in 1938 amounted to $8,751,590, divided into $4,305,524 for interest and $4,446,066 for principal. The state's "share" of the outstanding debts at the end of 1938 was $81,208,192.

In response to a legislative resolution, a consulting firm made a survey of this debt in 1938 and recommended that the state assume all county and district road debt, withholding certain highway revenues which had formerly been returned to the local units. It was estimated that, because of lower interest rates and more efficient handling of funds, the total saving over the next twenty years would be more than $50,000,000.[36] The 1939 legislature took no action on the report.

Other States

Several other states are providing funds in one way or another for servicing local highway bonds, but their arrangements do not present peculiarities sufficient to justify extended comment. Those

35. In order to avoid running afoul of the constitution, which prohibits the legislature from making any grant "to any . . . municipal or other corporation whatsoever," the act stated that the state had realized a "great benefit" from the county expenditures and that "both a legal and a moral obligation rest upon the state" to repay the local units. Hence the policy was to take over and "purchase the equity" of the counties and districts in roads which were part of the state system. The provisions of the act were declared to be fair and equitable repayment and fully discharged "the legally implied obligations of the State. . . ." (Laws, 4th Called Session, 42d Legislature, c. xiii). The act was upheld by the court. Road District No. 4 v. Allred, 123 Tex. 77 (1934).

36. Norman S. Taber and Company, Report on a Survey of the Highway Indebtedness of the State of Texas (New York, 1938). This report is summarized in Moody's, 1939, pp. 1518-1519.

states, together with approximate amounts of the debts, are given in Table 25. Minnesota, South Carolina, and Wisconsin have followed the usual reimbursement plan. The North Carolina Highway Commission borrowed $16,799,576 from counties for construction purposes, but the major part of this was repaid from the proceeds of a bond issue in 1927, leaving $6,828,136, which has gradually been reduced since that time. The amount outstanding on June 30, 1938, was $1,152,843. Recently Connecticut has provided for the servicing from state highway revenues of certain bonds issued for the Merritt Highway by Fairfield County and for the Middlesex and Portland Bridge by Middlesex County. Delaware has made no formal agreement to care for local highway bonds, but since 1927 the legislature has regularly included in the budget of the state highway department funds to meet the charges on county highway bonds. Alabama indirectly assumed responsibility for the bridge revenue bonds of the Alabama State Bridge Corporation following a default in 1934. The state highway department leased all the bridges of the corporation for an annual rental of $300,000, which was sufficient to meet the debt charges. The bridges were then made free.

Certain other states contribute funds which may or may not be used for debt service. In the typical case the state returns to the counties a certain part of the highway revenues, specifying that such funds may be used for any one of several purposes. Examples of this practice are found in Illinois, Michigan, and Mississippi. Since the funds may be used for different purposes in different counties, depending upon the local situation, it is not feasible to estimate the extent to which such funds are used for debt service nor the amount of bonds serviced in this way.

Reimbursement Plans Invalidated

In contrast with the numerous reimbursement or assumption plans which are in operation as described above, similar plans have been invalidated on constitutional grounds in a few states. In Kentucky the supreme court held that the highway commission could not constitutionally incur obligations in the form of reimbursement agreements with counties to an extent greater than the funds available for that purpose from current appropriations. To do so, it was held, would be to create a debt in violation of the constitution. The court definitely rejected the idea, accepted by most courts, that the reimbursement agreements were not debts falling within the constitutional prohibition.[37] A reimbursement plan enacted by the New Jersey legislature of 1930 was held to be unconstitutional by the state attorney-general.

A West Virginia act of 1933 appropriated funds to meet the charges on local bond issues to build roads which had been taken into the state road system and schools which had been included in the state free school system. The state constitution provides that the credit of the state shall not be "granted to or in aid of any county, city, township, corporation or person" nor shall the state assume the debts of such parties. The court held that

Unless plain and simple words have lost their meaning . . . our present constitution prohibits the Legislature from . . . assuming debts or liabilities such as are in said section indicated, whether such assumption be done directly and unequivocally or by indirection.

. . . .

. . . the state has not taken the county-district roads away from the communities which built them. . . . The school houses, also, . . . remain permanently for the use of the communities which brought them into being.[38]

The court further held that the act violated the due process clauses of the United States and West Virginia constitutions, since it taxed some citizens to pay the debts of others.

An Ohio act of 1935 levied a special motor vehicle tax, a part of the proceeds from which was to go into a fund to be used to service local road bonds. The Ohio Supreme Court held the act invalid on the grounds that it was inequitable, arbitrary, and discriminatory.[39]

Other Debts for Roads and Bridges

Several states have indirectly provided funds for the construction of roads and bridges through the borrowing of regular or special commissions or "authorities." The Kentucky Highway Com-

37. *Crick* v. *Rash*, 190 Ky. 820 (1921).
38. *Berry* v. *Fox*, 114 W. Va. 513 (1934).
39. *State* v. *Thrasher*, 130 Ohio 434 (1936).

mission has sold more than $16,000,000 of bridge revenue bonds. In other states special bridge commissions or districts have incurred large debts. Some of the commissions operate throughout the state, while others were created to build one or two bridges, perhaps of only local importance. The Pennsylvania Turnpike Commission was created to build a special toll highway and now has outstanding $35,000,000 of bonds. In 1933 the Florida legislature created the Overseas Road and Toll Bridge District to build a road from Key West to the mainland. The district has a debt limit of $20,000,000 and has borrowed heavily from the P.W.A., but no figures have been made public. The use of special agencies of this kind is increasing rapidly, but it is impossible at present to obtain comprehensive figures on their finances. One study of bridge revenue bonds lists the amounts issued in recent years as follows: 1934, $18,214,000; 1935, $23,512,800; 1936, $60,303,000; 1937, $65,631,000; 1938, $42,120,000.[40] Even this is not a complete list, for there are no public records of many bonds sold privately. The amount of bonds of this kind now outstanding which have been issued for road and bridge purposes is probably as high as $300,000,000.

TOTAL BORROWING AND NET HIGHWAY DEBTS

It is impossible to state exactly the amount of debts incurred by states for roads and bridges. As indicated in the preceding chapter, complete information on the placing of loans is not available. Further, it is extremely difficult in some cases to determine the extent to which a state's responsibility for local highway debts should be considered a state debt. Despite these limitations an attempt is made, in Table 25, to show, as nearly as available figures will permit, the total obligations incurred by states for road and bridge purposes for the years 1919-38. The figures for direct borrowing and revenue bonds were compiled in the manner described in the preceding chapter and are, therefore, subject to the qualifications stated there. The data for local debts assumed or serviced were determined by a study of each state concerned. In a majority of instances they are only approximations.

40. Robert Klaber, *Bridge Revenue Bonds* (New York: 285 Madison Avenue, privately mimeographed, 1939), p. 3.

TABLE 25

STATE BORROWING FOR ROADS AND BRIDGES, 1919-38, AND
AMOUNTS OUTSTANDING, 1938

(In thousands of dollars)

State	GROSS BORROWING, 1919-38				NET ROAD AND BRIDGE DEBT, 1938			
	Direct Borrowing	Local Debts Assumed or Serviced and Revenue Bonds	Total	Per Capita (on 1930 population)	Direct Debt	Local Debts Assumed or Serviced and Revenue Bonds	Total	Per Capita (on 1937 population)
Ala.........	$ 55,000	$ 5,000	$ 60,000	$ 22.67	$ 35,800	$ 3,000	$ 38,800	$ 13.43
Ark........	91,500	70,556	162,056	87.09	154,182	†	154,182	75,69
Calif.......	46,890	....	46,890	8.26	45,200	....	45,200	7.40
Colo.......	9,500	25,000	34,500	33.31	3,667	25,000	28,667	26.82
Conn.......	....	19,000	19,000	11.82	....	15,716	15,716	9.04
Del........	11,201	6,290*	17,491	73.37	2,550	6,225	8,775	33.75
Fla.........	....	107,495*	107,495*	73.22	....	74,852§	74,852§	45.17
Ga.........	....	26,575	26,575	9.14	....	18,672	18,672	6.05
Idaho......	2,800	....	2,800	6.29	445	....	445	.91
Ill.........	160,000	....	160,000	20.96	125,529	....	125,529	15.96
Iowa.......	....	96,445*	96,445*	34.96	....	79,790	79,790	31.31
Kan........	....	3,435	3,435	1.82	....	2,780	2,780	1.48
La.........	129,587	....	129,587	61.66	101,273	....	101,273	47.50
Me.........	36,614	....	36,614	45.91	26,712	....	26,712	31.24
Md.........	32,712	11,358	44,070	27.00	7,373	11,358	18,731	11.16
Mass.......	500	....	500	0.12	37	....	37	0.08
Mich.......	48,450	6,744*	55,194*	11.40	16,047	5,265	21,312	4.43
Minn.......	40,150	34,782	74,932	29.22	32,903	6,479	39,382	14.89
Miss.......	....	36,503	36,503	18.16	....	31,862	31,862	15.80
Mo.........	130,000	....	130,000	35.81	96,601	....	96,601	24.22
Mont.......	....	4,500	4,500	8.37	....	2,568	2,568	4.80
Nev........	1,800	188	1,988	21.83	300	188	488	4.83
N. H.......	10,580	....	10,580	22.73	7,132	....	7,132	14.01
N. J.......	143,000	....	143,000	35.38	38,101	....	38,101	8.79
N. M.......	....	25,679	25,679	60.66	100	18,350	18,450	43.72
N. Y.......	128,641	....	128,641	10.21	138,529	....	138,529	10.70
N. C.......	116,800	6,828	123,628	39.00	76,261	1,153	77,414	22.27
Ore........	47,822	....	47,822	50.13	18,606	....	18,606	18.20
Pa.........	100,000	....	100,000	10.38	52,077	....	52,077	5.13
R. I.......	4,500	....	4,500	6.54	4,289	....	4,289	6.30
S. C.......	39,874	38,000*	77,874*	44.76	39,874	22,625	62,499	33.46
Tenn.......	48,000	35,056	83,056	31.74	46,330‡	25,569	71,899	24.96
Tex........	....	110,000*	110,000*	18.88	....	81,208	81,208	13.19
Utah......	5,000	....	5,000	9.84	125	....	125	0.24
Va.........	8,400	....	8,400	3.47	2,628	....	2,628	0.98
W.Va......	118,948	....	118,948	68.78	71,846	....	71,846	38.86
Wis........	....	26,562*	26,562*	9.03	....	23,358	23,358	8.00
Wyo........	5,700	....	5,700	25.27	3,049	....	3,049	12.97
Totals...	1,573,969	695,896	2,269,965	....	1,147,566	456,018	1,603,584	....

*Approximate. †Included in preceding column.
‡Approximate; allocation of sinking fund estimated.
§Computed; see text for method of computation.

While the states borrowed directly only about a billion and a half dollars, total obligations incurred exceeded two and a quarter billions. In other words, obligations incurred through the sale of revenue bonds and the assumption of local debts amounted to more than 40 per cent of direct borrowing. Much of the 40 per cent was incurred because of the peculiar development of highway finance. It is not likely that further large amounts will be incurred through the assumption of local debts. The use of revenue bonds, however, may increase.

Only thirty-eight states appear in this table; the other ten[41] did not incur any measurable obligations for highways during this period. Kentucky might have been included in the table because of the bridge revenue bonds issued by its highway department, but the state was excluded on the ground that the bonds are to be serviced from bridge tolls and not from taxes levied by the state.[42] Of the thirty-eight states, eleven incurred obligations of $100,000,000 or more each and accounted for $1,413,695,000, or more than 60 per cent of the total. Twenty-four states accounted for more than 90 per cent of the whole. At the other extreme are twelve states which, altogether, were responsible for less than $90,000,000, or less than 5 per cent of the total. From this it is evident that borrowing for highways was heavily concentrated.

The second part of Table 25 shows the net highway debts outstanding in the latter part of 1938. The direct debt was computed by taking all general obligations issued for roads and bridges and deducting sinking funds held against such bonds.[43] Revenue bonds were treated in the same way. Local debts were taken without adjustment except in Minnesota, since the states do not generally maintain sinking funds against such obligations. This part of the table is more accurate than the first part, since these obligations are now stated fully in most instances. In computing per capita debts, estimates of population for 1937 were used.

41. Arizona, Indiana, Kentucky, Nebraska, North Dakota, Ohio, Oklahoma, South Dakota, Vermont, and Washington.

42. Further, to have taken notice of the bridge revenue bonds in this case would have raised difficult questions concerning similar bonds issued in many other states.

43. Only bonded indebtedness is considered here.

Much the same degree of concentration noted above is evident in this part of the table. Four states have net highway debts of more than $100,000,000 each, and, together, account for 32.4 per cent of the total. On the other extreme are four states with only nominal debts which total only a little more than $1,000,000.

Repayments

A comparison of total borrowings with net highway debts in 1938 will give some indication of the extent to which the states repaid their debts during this period. The states which started borrowing first, had made substantial repayments: New Jersey had accomplished most by repaying more than two thirds of its debt, Maryland and Michigan had repaid more than half, while Alabama, North Carolina, Pennsylvania, and West Virginia had repaid a third or more. Illinois and Missouri had repaid somewhat less than a third. The figures for West Virginia are slightly deceptive, since a part of its borrowing was, in effect, refunding, as noted above. New York ended the period with a net debt larger than the gross borrowing during the period, because of a large debt at the beginning, and California showed only a very small reduction for the same reason. Maryland's constitutional limit of fifteen years for debts forced a rapid reduction in that state.

The states which began their borrowing after 1926—principally Arkansas, Louisiana, South Carolina, and Tennessee—had made relatively little progress in repayment. Between 1927 and 1932 Arkansas repaid fairly large amounts of local debts, but under the 1934 readjustment large amounts of interest were funded. Thus the total had changed little. South Carolina made some progress in reducing its county reimbursement obligations, but paid nothing at all on the direct debt. Similarly, Minnesota had repaid the bulk of its obligations to counties, but had reduced the direct debt only a little. All the states together showed repayments of $665,815,000, or 29 per cent of total borrowing.

CAUSES AND EFFECTS OF HIGHWAY BORROWING

Since nearly half of all state borrowing in this period was for highways, it is of some interest to consider the characteristics of those states which borrowed and those which did not borrow for this purpose, and the changes which were going on in the two groups. For this comparison two groups of states were selected; the first is composed of the fourteen states which borrowed—directly, indirectly, or by assumption—the largest amounts for highways in this period, while the second is composed of the ten states which borrowed nothing and the four which borrowed least. These will be referred to as the borrowing and the nonborrowing states.[44] The first group borrowed $1,536,497,000, or 68 per cent of the total, while the nonborrowing states accounted for only $8,723,000, or less than 0.4 per cent.

In area the two groups are practically equal, each including 28 per cent of the total area of the United States. Perhaps the topography within the borrowing group is a little more unfavorable to highway construction, since it includes West Virginia, Pennsylvania, North Carolina, and Tennessee. This group also includes many of the highly industrialized sections of the East in which highway construction costs are high because of high labor costs, high costs of rights-of-way, and the necessity of wider and heavier construction.

Population and Manufactures

The borrowing group includes almost exactly one half of the total population of the country, while the other group includes only a little over a fifth. Since the areas are about the same, the density of population in the borrowing states is more than twice as great as in the nonborrowing states. But the trends of population in the two groups are of more significance. Between 1910 and 1920 population increased in the nonborrowing states at a rate almost twice as great as in the borrowing states, but from 1920 to 1937 this situation was almost reversed; the rate of growth dropped sharply in the former group and rose sharply in the latter. It is impossible to say whether this change was a cause or an effect of highway borrowing, but it does indicate that the two are associated to a significant extent.

44. The borrowing states in the order of their borrowing are: Arkansas, Illinois, New Jersey, Missouri, Louisiana, New York, North Carolina, West Virginia, Texas, Florida, Pennsylvania, Iowa, Tennessee, and South Carolina. The nonborrowing states are: Arizona, Indiana, Kentucky, Nebraska, North Dakota, Ohio, Oklahoma, South Dakota, Washington, Vermont, Massachusetts, Nevada, Kansas, and Idaho.

TABLE 26

COMPARISON OF STATES WHICH BORROWED MOST AND STATES WHICH BORROWED
LEAST FOR ROADS AND BRIDGES, 1919-38

Item Compared	Fourteen States Which Borrowed Most					Fourteen States Which Borrowed Least				
	1920	%of U.S.	1937	%of U.S.	% Change	1920	%of U.S.	1937	%of U.S.	% Change
Area (thousand square miles).............	861	28.4	861	28.4	....	852	28.1	852	28.1	......
Population (thousands)	51,781	49.0	63,892	49.8	+ 23.4	23,887	22.6	27,733	21.6	+ 16.6
Increase, 1910-20...	....	....	....	....	+ 13.8	....	....	....	....	+ 25.6
Average Density per Square Mile........	60.1	....	74.2	....	....	28.0	....	32.6	....	....
Value Added by Manufacture (millions)...	$12,875*	51.4	$12,438	49.4	— 3.4	$ 5,733*	22.9	$ 5,007	19.9	— 12.7
Increase, 1909-19...	....	....	....	....	+184.1	....	....	....	....	209.2
Total Income (millions)..........	$32,756*	50.8	$35,408†	50.1	+ 8.1	$14,286*	22.1	$14,147†	20.0	— 0.9
Motor Vehicle Registration (thousands) .	3,829	41.5	12,927	43.5	+237.6	2,510	27.2	6,647	22.4	+164.8
Surfaced Road Mileage‡										
High type......	6,683	42.6	59,912	52.7	+796.5	3,416	21.8	22,803	20.1	+567.2
Low type......	26,386	38.4	54,979	31.3	+108.4	15,899	23.2	55,795	31.8	+250.9
Totals.......	33,069	39.2	114,873	39.7	+247.4	19,315	22.9	78,598	27.2	+306.9
Gross Borrowing for Roads and Bridges, 1919-38 (thousands)§....	$1,536,497	68.0						$ 8,723	0.4	
Federal Funds Received for Highways, 1924-37 (thousands)......	$ 913,118	39.4						$ 616,092	26.6	
Net Collections from Gasoline Tax, 1919-35 (thousands)**..........	$1,998,202	42.4						$1,145,265	24.3	
Average Rate of Gasoline Tax (1936).................	4.46 cents	per	gallon					4.14 cents	per	gallon
Average Registration Tax per Vehicle†† (1935)...............	$12.35	....						$ 8.96	....	

*These data are for 1919. The estimates for total income are from Maurice Leven and W. I. King, *Income in the Various States* (New York, 1925).

†These data are from Robert R. Nathan and John L. Martin, *State Income Payments, 1929-37* (Washington: U. S. Department of Commerce, 1939), p. 2.

‡These figures include only roads in the various state highway systems. Figures in the 1920 column are for the end of 1921, while those in the 1937 column are for the end of 1936. All are compiled from reports of the U. S. Bureau of Public Roads.

§This includes both direct borrowing and obligations incurred through the assumption or servicing of local debts, as explained above.

**F. G. Crawford, *The Gasoline Tax in the United States, 1936* (Chicago, 1937), pp. 4-5.

††This is an average of state averages as computed by Henry J. Bitterman, *State and Federal Grants-in-Aid* (Chicago, 1938), p. 110.

Perhaps the two are both results of common causes; the same factors which make a state "progressive" as evidenced by an increasing population may also impel it to borrow in order to improve its highways.

The figures for value added by manufacture were used as a

rough measure of the industrialization of the two groups.[45] In this series the trends were very much the same as in population; the borrowing states accounted for about half of the total for the whole country and the nonborrowing states for about a fifth, and the latter group, which had shown a more rapid growth from 1909 to 1919, showed the greater loss between 1919 and 1937. Both groups, however, lost ground relatively in the latter period, for the country as a whole showed an increase of 0.52 per cent in these years.

Income and Motor Vehicle Registration

Estimates of income received in the different states are available for 1919 and 1937. Between those years, income for the country as a whole increased by 9.5 per cent. The borrowing states fared somewhat better than the nonborrowing states, enjoying an increase of 8.1 per cent compared with a decline of 0.9 per cent. This may have been due in part to the fact that the nonborrowing states were more dependent on agriculture, since agricultural prices declined more than prices in general. Again it is impossible to say which is cause and which effect, but it is of some significance that the states in the borrowing group fared a little better than those in the other group in the matter of income.

It is natural to expect that motor vehicle registration would increase more rapidly in those states which have made the greatest outlays for highways, and this proved to be true. The increase from 1920 to 1937 was 237.6 per cent in the borrowing states compared with an increase of 164.8 per cent in the nonborrowing states. The difference, however, was not as great as the difference in outlays in the two groups. In both groups the absolute increase in registrations was slightly more than the absolute increase in population.

Funds for Highways

The states have received most of their funds for highway construction from three important sources: borrowing, federal subsidies, and special highway taxes. It is not possible to give a complete sur-

45. These figures show large fluctuations, due in considerable part to price fluctuations. Since the different states were affected more or less equally by the price changes, it was not considered necessary to deflate the figures to the basis of a unit of uniform purchasing power.

vey of the funds received from those sources by the states in the two groups, but data are available on each of the three important sources for certain years. We have already noted that the borrowing states borrowed about a billion and a half dollars, while those in the other group borrowed practically none. From 1924 through 1937[46] the borrowing states received as federal highway subsidies, $913,118,000; nonborrowing states received $616,092,000, or about two thirds as much. In the distribution of federal funds special provision was made for states containing large amounts of public lands; several nonborrowing states benefited from this provision.

The gasoline tax is the most important of the special highway taxes. In the years 1919-35 the borrowing states received as net collections from this tax $1,998,202,000, while the nonborrowing states received $1,145,265,000. The latter group received a larger proportion of the collections than would be indicated by its population, income, or motor vehicle registration despite the fact that the average rate of the tax in the states of this group was consistently lower than in the borrowing states.[47] This is explained largely by the fact that the important states of New York, Illinois, and New Jersey were relatively late in adopting the tax. Collections for the two groups for 1935 were in approximately the same ratio as the motor vehicle registration, but the proportion of collections in the nonborrowing states was still higher than the proportion of population or income.

If we add these three samples of available highway funds, we find that the total for the borrowing states is $4,447,817,000 and for the nonborrowing states, $1,770,080,000. It must be noted, of course, that the borrowed funds do not constitute, for the whole period, a net addition to the funds available since they required large payments of principal and interest, most of which came from the special

46. These are the only years for which figures are available at present, but they account for a very large proportion of all the funds, since they include the years in which the largest grants were made.

47. The average rates for the two groups in selected years, in cents per gallon, were:

	1924	1928	1932	1936
Borrowing states	2.4	3.3	4.3	4.5
Nonborrowing states	1.9	3.1	4.1	4.1

Crawford, op. cit., Preface.

highway revenues. It is true also that in several states highway revenues have been diverted to nonhighway purposes. Even after making allowances for those factors, however, it is evident that the funds available for highway construction purposes in the borrowing states were much larger than in the nonborrowing states; it is probable that they were nearly twice as large.

Highway Construction

It would be enlightening to know exactly the number of miles of roads built by the states in the two groups and to compare this with the funds available for highway purposes. Such figures, however, would not have any great significance because of great variations in the extent to which local governments financed construction and to wide variations in construction costs because of differences in types of roads built, costs of rights-of-way, and costs of grading. Within these limitations, however, it may be of some significance to note the progress which the states in the two groups have made in road construction.

From reports of the United States Bureau of Public Roads we can determine the surfaced mileage in state highway systems[48] at the end of 1921 and at the end of 1936. At the end of 1921 the borrowing states had a total surfaced mileage of 33,069, of which 6,683 were high type and 26,386 were low type.[49] By the end of 1936 they had a total surfaced mileage of 114,873, of which 59,912 were high type and 54,979 were low type. During the fifteen years they added, by construction or acquisition, 53,229 miles of high type roads and 28,593 of low type.

The nonborrowing states had, at the end of 1921, total surfaced mileage of 19,315, of which 3,416 were high type and 15,899 were low type. At the end of 1936 the total was 78,598, of which 22,803 were high type and 55,795 low type. In the same fifteen years they acquired 19,387 miles of high type road and 39,896 of low type.

48. This does not include all rural roads, but only those roads designated as parts of "primary systems of rural State highways."

49. As classified by the Bureau of Public Roads, low type includes top-soil, sand-clay, gravel, chert, shale, waterbound macadam and low-cost bituminous roads; high type includes bituminous macadam, bituminous concrete, sheet asphalt, portland cement concrete, and block pavement roads.

It is safe to assume that a large majority of the mileage acquired by both groups was either constructed by the states or acquired from local governments in return for the assumption or servicing of local debts. Total surfaced mileage added by the borrowing states was 81,804; by the nonborrowing states, 59,283. But the significant difference was in the type of mileage acquired. The nonborrowing states acquired only 19,387 miles of high type surfacing, while the borrowing states acquired 53,229, or more than two and a half times as much. Thus, it would appear that the mileage acquired by the two groups, after allowances for types of construction, was in keeping with the funds available as indicated by the samples considered above. The borrowing states, however, will have to continue to provide funds for some years yet to pay interest and principal. As an offset against this fact, they got their roads, at least some of them, earlier than the nonborrowing states and have been able to enjoy them longer. The inexactness of our measures and the inherent difficulties of the problem are so great that we would not be justified in attempting to say whether the borrowing states realized a net advantage in this respect.

SUMMARY

Between 1919 and 1938 the states borrowed far more for highway purposes than they had borrowed for all purposes in the preceding one hundred and thirty years. There were three periods—1919-21, 1926-27, and 1929-31—in which states embarked upon highway borrowing programs. About 70 per cent, or approximately $1,575,-000,000 of the obligations, were incurred through the issue of general state obligations, while the other 30 per cent, or approximately $685,000,000, represented revenue bonds and local highway debts assumed or serviced. The trend in recent years has been toward the increased use of revenue bonds, but the states are not likely to accept responsibility for large additional amounts of local debts in the future. Revenue bonds have been used in several instances as a means of evading constitutional restrictions on borrowing, and the county reimbursement plan was quite generally used for this purpose.

About 70 per cent of the total borrowing occurred in fourteen states which cover 28 per cent of the total area of the country, have about half of the population and manufactures, and receive about half of the total income of the country. Although these fourteen states had shown, between 1910 and 1920, a slower growth in population and manufactures than the fourteen states which borrowed little or nothing for highways, this trend was reversed between 1920 and 1938; in this latter period the borrowing states showed a distinct advantage over the nonborrowing states in the growth of population and manufactures and in income received. The borrowing states also showed a substantially greater increase in motor vehicle registration and in surfaced road mileage, particularly in the mileage of roads with high types of paving. In relation to motor vehicle registrations, population, and income received, the nonborrowing states have realized larger net collections from the gasoline tax than the borrowing states, although their average gasoline tax rate, in 1936, was lower. The average registration fee per motor vehicle in the borrowing states was $12.35 in 1935 compared with only $8.96 in the nonborrowing states, although the latter group included Vermont with the abnormally high figure of $24.17. If the latter figure were eliminated the average would drop to $7.79, or more than a third below the average for the other group. Thus, while motorists in the nonborrowing states do not enjoy as many nor as good roads as those in the borrowing states, the special highway taxes they pay are distinctly lower.

CHAPTER XII

BORROWING FOR WORLD WAR VETERANS

IN THE YEARS immediately following the World War the states borrowed more money for the benefit of war veterans than for any other purpose except highways. In fact, for the states involved, that purpose was at times even more important than highways. Altogether, twenty-four states provided for bonus payments or loan funds, but in two of those the courts held the acts invalid and the legislation never became effective.

The payment of rewards for military service was, of course, no innovation in the field of state finance. As already noted, many states paid bounties, often from borrowed funds, to stimulate enlistment during the Civil War. After that war many of the Northern states, particularly in New England, provided supplements to federal pensions or disability payments. All Southern states eventually paid pensions, even though meager, to Confederate veterans.[1] But the states had never before attempted to pay, in a lump sum, such large amounts to so many veterans. The result was state borrowing on a scale never before seen for any other purpose except transportation.

DEVELOPMENT OF THE MOVEMENT

The forerunners of the bonus movement came in 1917, when New Hampshire and South Dakota provided payments to national guard troops who served in the Mexican border campaign. New Hampshire supplemented federal pay to the extent of seven dollars a month, while South Dakota paid a bonus of seventy-five dollars to each soldier for services rendered and for the "purpose of encouraging military service."[2]

1. See B. U. Ratchford and K. C. Heise, "Confederate Pensions," *Southern Economic Journal*, V (Oct., 1938), 207-217.
2. N. H., *Laws*, 1917, c. 38; S. D., *Laws*, 1917, c. 51.

Confusion over Methods

Early in 1919, when the troops were returning home, there was a great wave of enthusiasm to "do something for the boys." State legislators were perplexed as to how they could best express state gratitude. The result was chaotic laws appropriating money to pay for celebrations, to erect memorials, to establish rehabilitation funds, to provide vocational training, and to care for unemployed veterans. The epitome of this confused enthusiasm is shown by the Washington law which created a Veterans' Welfare Commission and appropriated $500,000 for its use. The Commission was to spend the money "in such manner and for such purposes as in its judgment will best facilitate and promote the return of such veterans . . . to civil life . . . or expend such funds in any manner whatsoever for such persons. . . . the manner in which such funds shall be expended shall be entirely in the discretion of the Commission."[3]

Educational and Farm Aids

Out of the confusion there emerged four types of benefits worthy of notice. The first was aid to enable veterans to continue their education. Almost all the states eventually provided some form of educational benefits, such as free tuition in state institutions, or funds to cover room rent, textbooks, and transportation. In a few states, such as California, Minnesota, and Wisconsin, there were provisions for a monthly cash allowance of thirty or forty dollars.

The second general type of benefit was the land settlement program. This was reminiscent of earlier days when the government had millions of acres of public land and donated them to veterans with a free hand. The plans of this kind provided that the state should, usually in co-operation with the Federal Government, acquire suitable agricultural lands, develop, improve, and subdivide them (as well as any public lands already owned) and make them available to veterans on easy terms. Among others, Maine, Minnesota, Montana, and South Dakota had plans of this kind.

The first two types of benefit did not involve borrowing except in rare instances. Loan funds to aid veterans in acquiring farms and

3. *Laws,* 1919, c. 9.

homes—a third type of benefit—were closely related to the aid programs. These funds are discussed separately below.

Generally, the aid plans were failures. It is true that several thousand veterans took advantage of them to pursue their education for
a few years or to acquire farms. But considering the age and educational training of the average discharged soldier, it is obvious that
only the exceptional one would be in a position to take advantage
of the educational benefits. Then, too, the experiences of modern
warfare are hardly conducive to the development of either scholars
or farmers. At any rate, it was soon apparent that only a few veterans would claim the benefits offered by these two programs, and
thus there arose a demand for state action which would provide
benefits for all veterans.

Cash Bonuses

During 1919 seven states led the way by voting cash bonuses—the
fourth type of benefit. Vermont had a general statute providing for
supplementary pay of ten dollars a month to residents of that state
who were in federal service as volunteers or members of the militia
or national guard. In March, 1919, this was extended to cover those
who had been drafted.[4] North Dakota, by a law approved March 6,
1919, was the first state to grant a cash bonus. The other states
taking similar action in 1919 were, in order: Vermont, New Hampshire, Wisconsin, Massachusetts, Minnesota, and Maine. New
Hampshire first voted a flat thirty dollars, but later in the year
provided an additional seventy dollars.

In 1920 only five states, compared with the seven of 1919, initiated
bonus legislation, partly because the original wave of enthusiasm
had waned and partly because relatively few state legislatures were
in session that year. The five states were: New Jersey, New York,
Rhode Island, South Dakota, and Washington. In 1921, however,
ten states took first action toward paying a bonus or creating a loan
fund: California, Illinois, Iowa, Kansas, Michigan, Missouri,
Montana, Ohio, Oregon, and Pennsylvania. The renewed impetus
of the movement in that year may be ascribed to the facts that
more legislatures were in session, an acute depression was at its

4. *Laws,* 1919, c. 165.

worst, and hopes for an early federal bonus had received their
first reverse. After 1921 only two states—Maryland in 1922 and
North Carolina in 1923—initiated action to pay bonuses or to create
loan funds.

Constitutional Complications

Although the first legal action to provide benefits was taken in
the different states in the years indicated, the benefits were not, in
all cases, legalized in those years. In a majority of the states a vote
of the people was required, which accounted for some delay. In
several instances there were other delays, and in two states—Maryland and Montana—the benefits were never realized.

The greatest delay occurred in Pennsylvania. In that state, borrowing must be authorized by a constitutional amendment, which
requires action by two consecutive sessions of the legislature and a
vote of the people. Also, a particular section of the constitution may
not be amended more often than once in five years. In 1921 and
1923 the legislature passed a resolution submitting to the people an
amendment to borrow $35,000,000 for bonuses and calling for a vote
in 1924. But constitutional amendments were voted in 1923. In the
past, amendments had been voted every two or three years without
regard to the five-year limitation. But in 1924 the matter was
brought before the state supreme court, which ruled that the amendment might not be voted upon until 1928.[5]

In 1925 the legislature again passed the resolution. In 1927 the
measure was approved by the House, and received two readings in
the Senate, but for some reason it was sidetracked before the third
reading. The matter thus could not come before the people in
1928. Perhaps it did not make any difference, for the people defeated all the bond proposals before them in that year, totaling
$138,000,000. In 1929 the legislature again proposed an amendment
to the constitution, this time to borrow $50,000,000 to pay bonuses
not only to World War veterans but also to veterans of the Spanish-
American War, the Boxer Rebellion, and the Philippine Insurrection. The measure was again passed in 1931 and approved by the

5. *Armstrong* v. *King,* 281 Pa. 207 (1924).

people in 1933. The bonus was paid in 1934. Thus thirteen years elapsed between the first action and the final payment of the bonus.

Original acts were held invalid by the courts in New York and North Carolina. The New York act was approved by a large majority in a popular referendum. After the court had declared it invalid, the voters amended the constitution, and the bonus was paid in 1924. The North Carolina act providing for a loan fund was submitted to the voters, although such action was not required by the constitution. It was approved by a large majority of those voting in 1924, but the terms of the act required that it be approved by a majority of registered voters. The latter requirement was not met, so the wording of the act was changed and the proposal was submitted to the voters again in 1926. It was again approved, but by a smaller majority than in 1924.

Of the twenty-two states which provided either bonuses or loan funds for veterans, nineteen paid bonuses; two—California and North Carolina—established loan funds; and one—Oregon—granted either a bonus or a loan at the option of the veteran. It may be of interest to note the result of the options exercised in the latter state. Up to June 30, 1936, Oregon had paid 24,081 bonuses, amounting to $4,991,749, and had granted 13,060 loans, totaling $30,716,825.[6]

Bonus Plans Defeated

In at least five states well-developed movements for bonuses were defeated: in four, by popular vote, and in the other, by a governor's veto. Montana voters first approved, by a referendum vote, a proposal to issue $4,500,000 bonds to pay a bonus. After the state supreme court had held the action invalid, they then defeated, by a very narrow margin, a proposed constitutional amendment to accomplish the same purpose. Oklahoma voters rejected an ambitious plan to issue $55,000,000 in bonds to finance a bonus and loan plan. Colorado voters defeated an $8,000,000 bonus bond issue, and Ken-

6. Oregon World War Veterans' State Aid Commission, *Eighth Biennial Report* (Salem, 1936), pp. 9-11. The average bonus was approximately $207 and the average loan approximately $2,352. The average bonus was for approximately sixteen months of service. It is probable that those who were in service longest, and hence were entitled to larger bonuses, took the cash, while those who had served for shorter periods chose the loans.

tucky voters, a $10,000,000 issue. The governor of Indiana vetoed a proposed measure to issue $20,000,000 of bonds for the payment of bonuses. These actions prevented the sale of $97,500,000 of additional bonds for veterans. Undoubtedly there were many other proposals which did not reach such an advanced stage.

PROVISION OF BONUS PLANS

Nature of Bonus

It is difficult to determine, from the enabling statutes, the exact legal nature of the bonus payments or the particular purpose for which the legislators intended them. Preambles to the various acts mention the recognition of heroic services, the adjustment of compensation between soldiers and civilians, the stimulation of patriotism, the promotion of the defense of the state, and the alleviation of the needs of disabled and unemployed veterans. To the extent that the payments were made for one or the other of those purposes they might be considered as gratuities, payments for services rendered, expenditures for defense, or charitable contributions. No doubt the legislators themselves were not always clear as to their purpose, although most of them probably considered the bonus a gratuity. Constitutional restrictions on state spending and uncertainties regarding court interpretation, however, often required that the real purpose be concealed or left vague. As will be noted below, the courts frequently contradict each other regarding what are and what are not proper state expenditures. Since most of the laws were enacted before the courts had considered this particular type of expenditure, the lawmakers had to tread warily, and, even so, a few of the laws came to grief in the courts.

Persons Eligible for Benefits

The definitions of persons eligible to receive bonuses show a high degree of uniformity in the different states. The first requirement was service in the armed forces of the United States between April 6, 1917, and November 11, 1918. A few states specified an initial date earlier by some weeks than April 6, 1917, and South Dakota placed the final date at October 1, 1919. Five states— Minnesota, Montana, New Hampshire, South Dakota, and Washington—included service in the forces of allied nations. Most laws provided that persons who did essentially civilian work and received civilian pay should not be eligible, even though inducted into the military or naval service. Nurses of the regular army and navy corps were eligible, but Massachusetts excluded yeomen (F). Seven states required a minimum service of sixty days, and the proposed Maryland law specified ninety days. The other states had no minimum requirement.

The second requirement was that the person should have been a resident of the state at the time of enlistment. Nineteen states required no previous period of residence, but South Dakota specified ninety days, Maryland, Massachusetts, and Rhode Island, six months, and Missouri, twelve months.

Groups regularly excluded were: conscientious objectors, those who evaded or tried to evade service, and those dishonorably discharged. New Hampshire excluded all commissioned officers and Ohio barred all officers above the rank of captain. Six states—Iowa, Oregon, Missouri, Rhode Island, South Dakota, and Washington—excluded those who had received a bonus from other states. In Oregon this applied to those who received a bonus from the United States, but both Oregon and Washington allowed the veteran to collect the difference if the other bonus was not as much as was due him under the law in question.

In all cases provisions were made for payments due to veterans who had died, although several of the original laws had to be amended for this purpose. As originally worded they had completely omitted any reference to dead veterans. Nine of the states specified that the bonus should go to certain relatives or any lawful heir, while eleven provided that payment should be made only to dependents or to groups that would normally be dependent. Several of the laws provided that if death occurred in service the maximum amount should be paid, regardless of the time served.

Amount of Benefits

Table 27 shows the amounts of benefits allowed in the different states. In New England the usual amount was a flat one hundred dollars. Elsewhere the usual rate was a stated sum per day or per

TABLE 27

STATE LOAN FUNDS AND BONUS PAYMENTS TO WORLD WAR VETERANS

State	Laws Authorizing (Year and Chapter Number)	Test Case	Type and Amount of Benefit	Amount Borrowed by State
Calif...	1921, 578; 1925, 430; 1929, 659; 1933, 686.	*Wel. Bd.* v. *Riley,* 188 Calif. 607; also 189 Calif. 124.	Loan; Max. $5,000 for homes, $7,500 for farms; Optional education bonus. $1,000 Max.	$77,000,000
Ill.....	1921, H.B. 127, pp. 66-70.	*Hagler* v. *Small,* 307 Ill. 460.	Bonus; 50¢ per day, $300 Max.	55,000,000
Iowa...	1921, 332.	*Grout* v. *Kendall,* 195 Iowa 467.	Bonus; 50¢ per day, $350 Max.	22,000,000
Kan....	1921, 255; Sp. Sess., 1923, 5, 6..........	*State* v. *Davis,* 113 Kansas 584.	Bonus; $1 per day, 4/6/17 to 6/30/19.	31,250,000
Me.....	Sp. Sess., 1919, 264; Const., IX, 19.	....	Bonus; $100.	3,300,000
Md....	1922, 448; 1924, 327; Const., III, 34.	*Brawner* v. *Supervisor,* 141 Md. 586.	Bonus; $10 per Mo., plus 25% for combat service.	Act held unconstitutional
Mass...	1919, 283, 307, 342, 346.	....	Bonus; $100.	None except short-term; see text.
Mich...	1921, J.R.1; Ex. Sess., 1921, 1; Const., X, 20.	....	Bonus; $15 per Mo., 4/6/17 to 8/1/19.	25,000,000
Minn. .	Ex. Sess. 1919, 49; 1931, 405.	*Gustafson* v. *Rhinow,* 144 Minn. 415.	Bonus; $15 per Mo., 4/6/17 to peace; Min. $50; Span. War Vets. included.	21,050,000
Mo....	First Ex. Sess. 1921, pp. 197-198; 2 Ex. Sess. 1921, pp. 6-17; 1923, pp. 388-391; Const., IV, 44b, 44c.	*Fahey* v. *Hackman,* 291 Mo. 351.	Bonus; $10 per Mo., $250 Max.	18,600,000
Mont. .	1921, 162.	*State* v. *Dixon,* 66 Mont. 76.	Bonus; $10 per Mo., $200 Max.	Act held unconstitutional
N. H...	1919, 140; Sp. Sess., 1919, 1.	....	Bonus; $100.	1,500,000
N. J...	1920, 159.	....	Bonus; $10 per Mo., $100 Max.	12,000,000
N. Y...	1920, 872; 1924, 19; Const., VII, 13.	*People* v. *West. Nat. Bank,* 231 N.Y. 465.	Bonus; $10 per Mo., $150 Max.	45,000,000
N. C...	1923, 190; 1925, 155; 1927, 97.	*Pat.* v. *Ev't.,* 189 N.C. 828; *Hinton* v. *St. Treas.,* 193. N.C. 496.	Loan; $3,000 Max.	2,500,000
N. D...	1919, 206; 1923, H.B. 275, pp. 109-110.	*Bauernfiend* v. *Nestos,* 48 N.D. 1218.	Bonus; $25 per Mo., 4/6/17 to 11/1/19.	None
Ohio...	1921, S.J. Res. 6; Const., VIII, 2a.	....	Bonus; $10 per Mo., $250 Max., officers above Capt. excluded.	25,000,000
Ore....	1921, 201; Const., XI-c.	*Boyd* v. *Olcott,* 102 Ore. 327.	Bonus; $15 per Mo. less 60 days $500 Max.; or loan, $3,000 Max.	32,850,000
Pa.....	Sp. Sess., 1933-34, 53; Const. IX, 16.	*Arms'g.* v. *King,* 281 Pa. 207; *Taylor* v. *King,* 284 Pa. 235.	Bonus; $10 per Mo. less 60 days; $200 Max.; Span. War Vets. included.	50,000,000
R. I...	1920, 1832.	....	Bonus; $100.	2,500,000
S. D. ..	1917, 51; Sp. Sess., 1920, 36; 1921, 363; Const., XIII, 18.	*State* v. *Handlin,* 38 S.D. 550.	Bonus; $75 for Mex. Campg.; $15 per Mo. for Span. and World War; $400 Max.	6,000,000
Vt.....	1919, 165.	....	Bonus; $10 per Mo.; $120 Max.; Officers excluded.	1,500,000
Wash. .	Ex. Sess., 1920, 1.	*State* v. *Clausen,* 113 Wash. 793.	Bonus; $15 per Mo., 4/6/17 to 11/11/19.	12,500,000
Wis....	1919, 667; Sp. Sess., 1919, 5.	*State* v. *Johnson,* 170 Wis. 218, 251.	Bonus; $10 per Mo.; $50 Min.; Opt. Ed. Bonus, $1,080 Max.	None;Approx. 21,000,000 paid.

month with a fixed maximum or a limit to the time period for which compensation could be claimed. While the veteran must have entered service before November 11, 1918, he could claim payment, except in Oregon, for service after that date. Various dates in 1919 were specified as the end of such periods of service, the latest being November 11, 1919, in Washington. The lowest and the most usual rate of pay was ten dollars per month, which was used by nine states. The highest was one dollar per day, paid by Kansas. The maxima varied widely, ranging from $100 in New Jersey to $500 in Oregon. Minnesota and Wisconsin set $50 as the minimum payment. Oregon prescribed that the first sixty days of service should be excluded, presumably on the grounds that these were covered by the federal bonus of $60 paid at the time of discharge.

The proposed Maryland law contained one unique feature. Each veteran who had actually been in combat should have his payment increased by 25 per cent. If legislators in other states had really been interested in rewarding "heroic" service, as they claimed to be, this feature offered interesting possibilities. A proposed initiative measure in Oklahoma would have paid either $30 per month in cash or $50 per month in the form of aid in acquiring a home, with maxima, respectively, of $250 and $500. The home aid feature would have been used in connection with a loan fund from which the veteran could borrow up to $1,500. A bond issue of $55,000,000 was proposed to finance both benefits, but was defeated.

North Dakota was the only state to impose restrictions on the use of bonus funds. At first the veteran could use them only in the purchase of a home or farm or to pursue his education. Later the number of uses was increased so that the restrictions lost much of their significance, but the funds still had to be used within the state except by special permission.[7]

Sources of Funds

Only three states financed their payments to veterans from taxes; the others borrowed all or substantially all of the funds used for this purpose. North Dakota levied a special mill tax on all taxable

7. *Supplement to Compiled Laws, 1925,* sec. 3787c2.

property and provided that the veterans should be paid, in the order in which their applications were filed, as funds became available. The adjutant-general was empowered to change the priority of claims.[8] Evidently there was some dissatisfaction with this arrangement, for soon there was a plan to speed up payments. The adjutant-general and the Industrial Commission entered into an agreement with a finance company whereby the former would purchase veterans' certificates at 82 and hold them as security for notes to be given to the finance company, which was to advance the funds. The purchased certificates were then to have priority in payment. The scheme involved borrowing to the amount of $6,500,000. The court held that the adjutant-general and the Industrial Commission were acting beyond their powers, and invalidated the whole procedure.[9] Later the law was amended to give the Industrial Commission power to borrow for this purpose, but this power apparently was never exercised.[10] Approximately twenty-six thousand claims were filed, and the tax was levied each year through 1927. By 1930 the state had collected $8,896,822 for the bonus.

Massachusetts levied several special taxes to raise funds for its bonus. They were: an additional poll tax of three dollars for the years 1920-23; a tax of $660,000 on cities and towns for 1919-22; an additional personal income tax of ½ per cent on dividends and interest for 1919-22; an increase of 25 per cent in the inheritance tax for one year; and an income tax of 1 per cent on corporations for one year. The poll tax produced $12,315,042 of the total, $22,687,515. The state borrowed $14,000,000 on tax-anticipation notes. By 1924 the state had collected all taxes, paid $18,219,344 in bonuses and $1,918,939 in expenses and interest, set aside about $500,000 as a reserve against future claims, and refunded about $2,000,000 to the cities and towns.[11]

Wisconsin raised the funds for its bonus by a three-mill levy on property for 1919 and an income surtax, ranging from 1¾ per cent to 6 per cent, on 1918 incomes. To provide for the educational

8. Laws, 1919, c. 206; Laws, Spec. Sess., 1919, c. 55; Laws, 1921, c. 103.
9. Bauernfeind v. Nestos, 48 N. D. 1218 (1922).
10. Laws, 1923, H. Bill No. 275, p. 109.
11. National Tax Association, Proceedings, 1924, pp. 128-129.

bonus, an income surtax of from 0.35 per cent to 1.2 per cent was levied on incomes for 1918 and for four years thereafter, and a tax of one mill was placed on property for five years.[12] Altogether, those taxes produced slightly less than $22,000,000. The original act provided that counties might, if they wished, borrow funds for the bonus, in which case they would be exempt from the property tax levy. Under this provision ten counties, in 1920 and 1921, borrowed over $800,000.

All other states borrowed the funds used to pay benefits. By the end of 1938 the total of such borrowing was $444,800,000. California had borrowed $77,000,000; Illinois, $55,000,000; Pennsylvania, $50,-000,000; and New York, $45,000,000. Serial bonds or certificates were used in almost all cases, with final maturities ranging from twelve years in Minnesota to from twenty-five to thirty years in Kansas and New York. If payments from current revenues are added to the amounts borrowed, the total outlays of the states for the purpose discussed here amount to approximately $497,000,000.

THE OPERATION OF LOAN FUNDS

California

California has put more money, by far, into its loan fund than have the other two states with similar plans, and has scored the only success in the field. The fund, managed by the Veterans' Welfare Commission, operates on the principle of purchasing homes and farms and reselling them to veterans, allowing about twenty years for payment. The Commission retains title until all payments have been made. The total value of properties may not exceed $5,000 with homes or $7,500 with farms; in the former case an initial payment of 5 per cent is required, and in the latter, 10 per cent. An administrative charge of 5 per cent is made on each transaction; the interest rate is 5 per cent. The fund has sold bonds to the amount of $77,000,000. To 1934 the average interest cost of the bonds was 4.285 per cent, but large issues of low-interest bonds in 1935-38 reduced this somewhat.

While the fund finances both farms and homes, the great majority of financing has been for homes. To 1934 the fund had

12. *Laws*, 1919, c. 667; *Laws*, Spec. Sess., 1919, c. 5.

invested $2,380,746 in 428 farms at an average cost of $5,562, and $53,969,192 in 11,401 homes at an average cost of $4,733. The marked success of the fund is shown by the fact that to 1934 it had sustained a net loss on repossessed properties of only $5,491 and delinquent accounts at that time amounted to only $271,006. The operating profit on June 30, 1934, was $2,317,633.[13]

Several factors have been responsible for the success of the fund. In the first place, properties must be appraised by a banker independent of the board. In the second place, the fund is run on a strictly business basis; great pains are taken to weed out poor risks. Loans are not granted merely because the applicants are veterans. The fund has had far more applications than it could fill, and thus has been able to pick the best risks. Finally, the administrators of the fund have exerted their influence and bargaining power to keep contractors' charges for building and repairing homes at a minimum. In this way they have been able to secure building values for veterans which no other private individual could obtain. In the light of its own experience the board is justified when it states that "the lending of State credit for the purpose of funding farm and home purchases through the medium of self-liquidating bonds has been definitely established as superior to any plan yet devised which involves the gift of cash bonuses or other rewards."[14]

Oregon

The other two states which have loan funds, however, present a different picture. To June 30, 1936, the Oregon fund had loaned $22,881,400 on city property, and $7,835,425 on farm property. Until 1933 the loan rate was 4 per cent, and the loans might not exceed 75 per cent of the value of the property. In 1933 these were changed to 6 per cent and 40 per cent, respectively. In 1935 the loan rate was reduced to 5 per cent, and in 1937, to 4 per cent; in the latter year the maximum loan was again made 75 per cent. All loans must mature by 1958. No brokerage or administrative charge is made on loans. On June 30, 1936, the fund held foreclosed properties which had cost it $5,450,651, and showed an operating deficit

13. *Report of Veterans' Welfare Board as of June 30, 1934* (Sacramento, 1934), pp. 30-32, 35, 38.   14. *Ibid.*, p. 11.

of $723,436, even after including the tax revenues mentioned below. Two excerpts from the 1936 report are revealing:

From a loan organization concerned primarily with the appraisal of property and the allotment of funds to veterans, this department has developed into one of the principal real estate operators of the State.

. . . .

Most of the loans outstanding are returning 4% on the money which the Commission has loaned. This money, raised through the sale of bonds, has cost the State an average of approximately 4½%. It is for this reason that the World War Veterans' State Aid Commission cannot become self-supporting.[15]

The state levies an annual tax which covers administrative expenses, reimburses the Commission for cash bonuses paid, and makes up the differer ce between interest paid on bonds and interest received on loans. In 1935-36 this tax yielded $494,645.

North Carolina

The North Carolina fund also makes its advances in the form of loans on mortgages. The state sold $2,500,000 of bonds to provide funds for this purpose at a yield of about 4.2 per cent. The fund loans at 6 per cent and makes only an appraisal fee for placing the loans. Loans may not exceed 75 per cent of the value of the property. In 1935 there was an investigation of the fund by a legislative committee, which made no public report. About that time the commissioner originally in charge of the fund was replaced. The fund makes no public report, but on June 30, 1938, it showed a cash overdraft of $573,681. Total assets of the fund on the same date amounted to $1,931,949.[16]

From the above considerations it is evident that the successful operation of a fund of this kind is dependent primarily on two factors: (1) sound, reasonable operating rules prescribed by the legislature, and (2) able and honest administration. In California both factors have been favorable, except for the fact that sales had to be made on a very small equity. In spite of this, vigorous and capable administration has made a success of the operations of the fund. In Oregon the terms prescribed by the legislature are not

15. World War Veterans' State Aid Commission, *op. cit.*, pp. 4, 6.
16. *The Budget of the State of North Carolina, 1939-41*, pp. 76-77, 588-589.

such as to permit the fund to support itself, but this is offset by the tax subsidy. Thus the deficit in the fund must be laid to the administration. The enabling regulations in North Carolina are sound enough, and the failure of the fund there must be ascribed to poor administration.

OTHER ASPECTS OF BENEFITS

Benefits for Other Veterans

The wave of legislation for the benefit of World War veterans stimulated demands for similar benefits for other veterans. In Michigan, $50,000 was appropriated to pay claims of Civil War veterans who were entitled to bounties but who had never received them.[17] The original South Dakota bonus act included veterans of the Spanish-American War and the Philippine Insurrection. In Kansas and Maine proposals to pay bonuses to Spanish War veterans were defeated by popular votes.[18] Colorado voters in 1924 defeated a proposition to pay bonuses to veterans of the Civil War, the Indian Wars, the Spanish-American War, the Philippine Insurrection, and the World War.[19] After paying the World War veterans in 1919-20, Minnesota, in 1931, voted to extend the payment to veterans of the Spanish, Philippine, and Chinese campaigns.[20] The belated Pennsylvania bonus also included such veterans. The Oregon loan fund act was amended to include the Spanish War veterans, and the California loan fund is available to all veterans.

Borrowing for Confederate Pensions

Although differing somewhat from the benefits discussed above, two other instances of state payments to veterans should be mentioned here. All Southern states pay pensions to Confederate veterans. During the 1920's Arkansas and Louisiana, anticipating that their pension payments would soon decline sharply and wishing to pay liberal pensions to the veterans in their old age, conceived the idea of funding the pensions for a number of years into

17. *Laws*, 1st Extra Sess., 1919, c. 3.
18. Kansas, *Laws*, 1923, c. 211; *Chronicle*, CXIX (1924), 2671; Maine, *Laws*, 1921, c. 189; *Chronicle*, CXIII (1921), 1270.
19. *Laws*, 1923, c. 86; *Chronicle*, CXIX (1924), 2908.
20. *Laws*, 1931, c. 405.

the future in order to be able to pay larger pensions for a few years. For this purpose Arkansas borrowed $9,450,000 and Louisiana, $5,589,260.[21] These bonds should properly be classed as funding bonds, since they were issued to fund a normal expenditure.

Regional Grouping

The states which have provided veterans' benefits fall into definite geographical groups. All the New England states except Connecticut paid bonuses, the amount of which was usually a flat $100. Connecticut provided a substitute by setting up an "endowment" of $2,500,000, the income from which is used to care for needy and disabled veterans.[22] The North Atlantic states, New Jersey, New York, and Pennsylvania, paid bonuses, as did all the Mid-Western states except Indiana and Nebraska. The three Pacific states provided either bonuses or loan funds. But North Carolina, with its small loan fund, was the only Southern state to provide benefits, while not a single state in the Rocky Mountains or Southwestern regions granted bonuses or loans.

The reasons for this sharp geographical division on the question are not apparent in all cases. For the Southern states there are three possible explanations. One is their comparative poverty, although this has not prevented many of them from borrowing for other purposes. The second is the fact that all of them are paying pensions to Confederate veterans, and this adds a considerable burden to their limited finances. The third, and most important, explanation is the presence of a large number of Negro veterans. Undoubtedly most Southern states would hesitate to borrow large sums of money with which to pay bonuses, many of which would go to colored veterans. Negroes could not constitutionally be excluded from a cash bonus, but a loan fund might be administered in such a way as to exclude them. This probably accounts for the North Carolina fund.

21. Ark.; Public Act No. 20, 178, 1927; La.; Act 23, 1928; Act 7, Ex. Sess. 1930; Act 82, 1934.

22. In fact, the $2,500,000 of "deficiency bonds" issued by Connecticut in 1920 might well be listed as bonus bonds, since the proceeds were used indirectly to establish this fund (*Public Acts,* 1919, c. 336, 367).

For the Rocky Mountain and Southwestern states the only explanation which suggests itself is a difference in the attitude of the people on the matter—perhaps a survival of the "pioneer spirit." This is exemplified in the vigorous language used by the Montana Supreme Court when it held the bonus law of that state unconstitutional.[23]   A subsequent vote of the people of that state on a constitutional amendment to pay a bonus sustained the court by a very small margin, although the voters had, by a referendum vote, approved the original act.

COURT DECISIONS

Table 27 shows that most of the acts conferring benefits on veterans were contested in the courts. Two facts account for this unusual amount of litigation. First, many taxpayers were strongly opposed to bonus payments. Second, bond dealers and underwriters were not familiar with such bonds and many of them doubted the constitutional power of the states to borrow and spend for this purpose. Consequently, they insisted on test cases in most states. The technical and superficial issues presented in many of the suits indicated very clearly that they were purely test cases, involving no real controversy. In fact, this went so far that in 1927 a bond attorney protested. He pointed out that in the first North Carolina case, counsel for an American Legion post had represented the plaintiff taxpayer; he insisted that in the second case there should be "at least the semblance of an actual controversy."[24] Other cases which were decided on the basis of technical or procedural considerations were those in Kansas, Maryland, Missouri, Oregon, and Pennsylvania.

Issues Considered

In no two cases were the same combination of issues presented, and decisions on particular issues differed considerably when they were considered in different states. Perhaps the one consideration which, more than any other, marked the decisions was the extent to which the courts relied upon customs, usage, and precedent.

23. *State* v. *Dixon*, 66 Mont. 76 (1923).
24. *Chronicle*, CXXIV (1927), 135.

The courts usually pointed out that the states had made payments of this kind almost from the beginning of their history and that it was now too late to argue that they were unconstitutional. Thus, the Supreme Court of Iowa said that the history of that state was "besprinkled with soldier legislation, Soldier bounty, soldier exemption, soldier preference, soldiers' homes and soldier memorials." Hence, according to usage, the court reasoned, expenditures for this purpose were proper.[25]

War Powers

In at least three states attempts were made to justify borrowing for bonus payments under the war powers. State constitutions usually impose no restrictions on borrowing when it is necessary to "repel invasion" or "defend the state."[26] The Minnesota court held that for a proper military purpose debts "may be legally contracted in time of war, without reference to a state of invasion or insurrection. Conditions may exist . . . which call for active military operations of various kinds, though no hostile invasion be imminent or even probable. [Such debts] must be for some legitimate military or naval purpose pertaining to the existing state of war."[27] The court offered no reasoning to show that the payment of a bonus constituted "a legitimate military or naval purpose pertaining to the existing state of war," but held that the bonus law was constitutionally justified under the war powers of the state. The South Dakota court reached a similar decision in regard to the bonus paid in 1917,[28] but the Illinois court decided to the contrary.[29] Perhaps the fact that the Minnesota bonus was authorized in 1919 while the Illinois payment was voted in 1921 may partly explain the difference in the opinions of the two courts.

Public Purpose

Another issue frequently presented to the courts was whether the payment of a bonus is for a public purpose. This is a vital

25. *Grout* v. *Kendall*, 195 Iowa 467, 479 (1923).
26. See Chapter XVII for a discussion of these powers.
27. *Gustafson* v. *Rhinow*, 144 Minn. 415, 418 (1920).
28. *State* v. *Handlin*, 38 S. D. 550 (1917).
29. *Hagler* v. *Small*, 307 Ill. 460 (1923).

issue, since all constitutional government implies that public funds will be spent only for "public purposes." This concept, however, is not at all definite. In Iowa, Minnesota, New York, North Carolina, and Washington the courts held that bonus payments and loan funds are for a public purpose, usually relying upon custom and usage for justification. The Montana court, however, denied this, at least so far as the state is concerned, and said that the obligation to provide for veterans rested, if anywhere, upon the United States Government.

Payment of Moral Claims

Other questions presented to the courts concerned the power of states to give gratuities, or to recognize and pay moral claims. The New York decision turned on the first point. The court admitted that the veterans might have some kind of a moral claim on the state. But, the court reasoned, a moral obligation, when applied to the spending of public funds, must be more than a mere desire to compensate someone to whom gratitude is due; an individual may pay his benefactor, but a state may not. The veterans had not been in the service of the state, and hence they had no legal claim against the state. Article VII, Section 1, of the New York Constitution provides that "The credit of the State shall not in any manner be given or loaned to or in aid of any individual, association or corporation." The court held that the payment of a bonus would constitute lending of the state's credit; hence it was unconstitutional.[30] The courts in Iowa, North Carolina, and Washington, however, held that the veterans did have a moral claim on the state which the latter could legally recognize and pay. The North Carolina court even went so far as to say that the veterans had a legal claim against the state, at least to the extent of the payment of pensions and compensation to the disabled and the widows.[31] The Montana court, on the contrary, denied the existence of any claim, stating: "There rests no legal duty on the state to reward those who battled for the preservation of the nation; the legal

30. *People* v. *Westchester National Bank,* 231 N. Y. 476-479 (1921).
31. *Hinton* v. *State Treasurer,* 193 N. C. 496, 509 (1927).

obligation runs the other way.   The individual owes a duty to society to come to the defense of his country in time of war."[32]

In three states there were particular variations of this problem. The constitutions of California, Illinois, and South Dakota contain provisions forbidding the legislature to grant extra compensation to any public officer, agent, servant, or contractor after the service has been rendered or the contract made.   The Illinois court held that "the recipients of the compensation . . . do not stand in the relation of public officer, agent, servant, or contractor of or with the State and that section has no application here."[33]   The positions of the California and South Dakota courts were similar.

In connection with this point, opinions frequently waxed eloquent on the heroism of the veterans.   Pages were covered with glowing tributes.   None of these exceeded the praise of the Montana justice who stated that he was a veteran himself, and that the veterans, more than anyone else, were opposed to placing the service of the soldiers on a commercial basis by a cash payment.

Other Issues

Several other issues were raised in the different cases.   In California, Illinois, North Carolina, and South Dakota the courts held that the laws might be upheld on the grounds that they stimulated patriotism and encouraged the defense of the state.   The Illinois and Iowa courts held, contrary to the New York decision, that the payment of a bonus did not constitute the lending of state credit. The South Dakota court also held that the bonus law did not violate the constitutional provision forbidding class legislation and special favors to particular groups.   A unique point was presented when it was argued, in the second North Carolina case, that the exclusion of conscientious objectors from the benefits constituted a violation of the constitutional guarantee of religious liberty.   The court ruled that the objection was not pertinent.[34]

In connection with the Louisiana bonds issued to pay Confederate pensions, the question was raised whether they violated the

32. *State* v. *Dixon,* 66 Mont. 76, 86 (1923).
33. *Hagler* v. *Small,* 307 Ill. 460, 467.
34. *Hinton* v. *State Treasurer,* 193 N. C. 496, 505-506.

section of the Fourteenth Amendment to the Federal Constitution which forbids the states to pay any debt incurred in aid of the rebellion. The attorney-general ruled that the pensions were not paid to the veterans because of their services, but because of their status as needy citizens.[35] Since the pensions are not paid to all needy citizens, it is a moot question whether the courts would sustain this opinion, and, if so, whether they would regard the pension law as class legislation.

SUMMARY

Since the World War twenty-two states have borrowed approximately $445,000,000 and twenty-four states have spent nearly $500,-000,000 to pay bonuses to, or establish loan funds for, World War veterans. Approximately $110,000,000 was loaned and the remainder was paid in bonuses. The usual benefit was a bonus of from $10 to $30 per month of military service, although the uniform $100 bonus was typical in New England. No benefits were provided by Rocky Mountain, Southwestern or Southern states (except North Carolina), but the practice was general in other regions. The movement gained so much momentum that in a few states benefits were extended to veterans of the Spanish-American War, the Boxer Uprising, and the Philippine Insurrection. In a majority of the states the bonus or loan acts or amendments were tested in the courts, but in only five cases did the courts hold them invalid. Three of these were re-enacted to make the benefit available. Except when the cases turned upon technical or procedural points, the courts usually upheld the acts on the grounds that the payment of bonuses was for a public purpose and had long been an accepted practice with the states. Bonus proposals were defeated by popular vote in four states, in one of them—Montana—after it had been approved in a referendum but held invalid by the court. The California loan system has been successful, but those in North Carolina and Oregon have had unprofitable records.

35. *Opinions of the Attorney-General of Louisiana, 1930-32*, pp. 79-82.

CHAPTER XIII

BORROWING FOR RURAL CREDIT SYSTEMS

THE PROBLEM of providing proper credit facilities for farmers has long been a difficult one in the United States. While most of the farmers' troubles have been too deep-rooted to be cured by easy credit, yet, in many regions, farmers have been handicapped by high interest rates and the onerous terms under which they had to borrow. As land prices rose and farmers came to use more machinery, the credit problem became more acute. Demands were made upon both federal and state governments for better credit facilities. About a third of the states responded by making provision for the investment of state trust and endowment funds in farm mortgages.[1] The Federal Government, after long deliberation and study, finally established the Federal Farm Credit System in 1916, and has extended it greatly since that time.

Farmer dissatisfaction was especially strong in the northern states of the Middle West, where mortgage debts were large and interest rates high. The movement to establish state rural credit systems centered in the Dakotas. South Dakota made provision for a state system before the establishment of the federal system. In North Dakota the movement encountered constitutional obstacles, but had progressed so far that it was carried to completion even after the federal system had been set up. Minnesota established its system in 1923 after the drastic decline in farm prices, largely to relieve embarrassed banks of doubtful farm mortgages. This chapter deals with the farm-loan experience of these three states.

1. E. S. Sparks, *History and Theory of Agricultural Credit in the United States* (New York, 1932), pp. 198-206.

In 1916 the voters of South Dakota approved, by a vote of 57,569 to 41,952, a constitutional amendment to allow the state to establish a rural credit system and to pledge the faith and credit of the state in raising funds. In 1917 the legislature passed the necessary enabling laws, creating the Rural Credit Board and authorizing it to issue bonds payable primarily from the assets and income of the board but further secured by the taxing power of the state. The board consisted of the governor and four other members appointed by him and removable by him at will.[2] The legislature appropriated $200,000 for the establishment and maintenance of the board.

Provisions of Bonds and Loans

The bonds bore not more than 5 per cent interest and could not be sold below par. They ran for periods "not exceeding twenty years" and were callable after five years. The board was required to have on hand at all times mortgages and cash equal to the face amount of bonds outstanding. Loans were made in amounts from $500 to $10,000 for the purpose of purchasing farm lands, equipment, fertilizers, livestock, buildings and other improvements, or for liquidating debts incurred for such purposes. They were amortized over periods of from five to thirty years; in certain cases principal payments might be omitted for the first five years. The interest rate on loans was to be not less than $\frac{3}{4}$ per cent nor more than $1\frac{1}{2}$ per cent above the rate paid on the bonds. No filing or administrative fees were charged. Loans could not exceed: (1) 70 per cent of the appraised value of land plus 40 per cent of the value of improvements, nor (2) the average assessed valuation of property for the three preceding years.

Amendments in 1919

In 1919 several significant changes were made in the provisions. Bonds might be made noncallable and could be sold "bearing such rates of interest as may be fixed by said board"; this removed the limitations on both interest rate and price. Further, the board

2. Laws, 1917, c. 333 and 334.

might "prescribe a reasonable time within which the purchase money, for bonds and warrants, may be drawn by the treasurer from the purchasing bank." The board was required to maintain, in mortgages and cash, an amount equal to only 95 per cent of outstanding bonds. The interest rate on loans might be from ½ per cent to 1½ per cent above the rate paid on bonds.[3]

Progress in Financing

The first bonds were sold in August, 1917, and the first loan was made in October. Thereafter borrowing and lending proceeded at a rapid pace. By the end of 1919 the board had sold bonds with a face value of $20,425,000 and had made loans amounting to $19,139,213. Until December, 1921, one Chicago bank bought, at private sales, all bonds sold, amounting to $36,500,000. Several issues were sold below par, one as low as 93½. The total discount on the $36,500,000 of bonds was $530,715. Beginning in December, 1921, $11,000,000 of bonds were sold at public sales, and the state realized premiums of $91,320. Doubtless this favorable result was due in part to the great change which had taken place in the money market.

By the end of 1924 total bond sales amounted to $47,400,000. The average interest rate was 5.174 per cent; adjusted for the discounts, the average effective interest cost was 5.22 per cent. Before January, 1920, loans were made at 5½ per cent; from January, 1920, to June, 1922, at 7 per cent; and thereafter, at 6 per cent. The average rate on all loans was close to 6 per cent. In the early years the average loan per acre was slightly above $16.00, but this declined after 1919; the average on all loans made to July 1, 1924, was $14.71. To December 31, 1924, approximately twelve thousand loans had been made, aggregating $46,126,250.

Management

Petty graft, partisan politics, and secrecy marked the early years of the board's operations. It made no public report until 1922 and then only in response to a court order. Even after that the reports were incomplete, vague, inaccurate, and so arranged as to conceal

3. *Revised Code, 1919*, secs. 10151, 10153, 10162, 10165, 10170.

losses which had already occurred. Always optimistic in tone, these reports, even as late as 1924, indicated that the board was operating at a profit. The 1923 report estimated annual net earnings at $150,000, and the 1924 report stated that "The net earnings of the Board will average $100,000 annually, and this surplus will create a fund far beyond any loss that will be sustained in lands, taken over by foreclosure." Although three hundred and forty-seven loans had been foreclosed, "The Board does not anticipate that any permanent loss will result to the state in any of the cases foreclosed."[4]

As rumors of irregularities in the board spread, demand arose for an investigation by the legislature. A legislative committee made a brief investigation in 1925, and an interim committee carried on the work and reported to the 1927 legislature.[5] A brief summary of those two reports will give a good appraisal of the work of the board up to June 30, 1926.

Bank Balances and Favoritism

The chief source of trouble was the board's independent treasurer, president of a large bank in the state capital and an influential politician, who handled millions of dollars of the board's funds as he pleased, with little regard for law or the rules of the board.

The financial affairs of the Rural Credit Board were so intermingled with the affairs of the bank [of which the treasurer was president], . . . that it is difficult to tell where the records of the one institution starts and the other leaves off. . . . Mr. Ewert has been Treasurer of, and in practically full control of, the moneys of the Board since the System was inaugurated in 1917. During that time . . . his accounts, so far as the same have been kept at or carried through the National Bank of Commerce, have never been examined, audited or supervised. . . . Other instances could be cited to show the hopeless confusion into which the affairs of the Board have been thrown because of the manner in which its funds were handled by Mr. Ewert. . . .[6]

4. *Annual Report of the Rural Credit Board*, 1924, p. 7.
5. "Report of Joint Committee of Senate and House; South Dakota Rural Credit Board," *Senate Journal*, 1925, pp. 673-748 (hereinafter cited as "1925 Report"); "Report of the Interim Commission to the State of South Dakota and Members and Officers of the Legislature of South Dakota at Its Twentieth Session, 1927," *Senate Journal*, 1927, pp. 85-199 (hereinafter cited as "1927 Report").
6. "1925 Report," p. 682.

He maintained for the board a cash balance which varied from about one million to about seven million dollars, averaging perhaps two millions or more.[7] The rules of the board provided that such funds should be deposited only in banks approved by the board, to an extent not greater than 40 per cent of the capital and surplus of any given bank, and be fully protected by pledged securities or surety bonds. The treasurer flagrantly disregarded the rules, especially in dealing with his own bank. On December 31, 1924, funds were deposited in 74 approved banks, of which 23 were closed, and in 177 nonapproved banks, of which 65 were closed. The treasurer used these funds, it was charged, "and the power derived therefrom, in times of financial distress to advance the political interests of himself and those to whom he was specially responsible for it."[8] In addition to the loss of interest, the carrying of large balances greatly increased the danger of loss through bank failures. Early in 1925 funds of the board in closed banks amounted to $972,722, of which it was estimated that at least $500,000 would be lost. The amount in the treasurer's own bank, which closed, was put at $425,000. "The fact that Mr. Ewert was persistently violating the law was called to the attention of the other members of the Board and nothing was done to stop the practice. In August, 1922, the Supreme Court ordered the Board to stop making excessive deposits and that order was ignored."[9]

The treasurer refused to appear before the legislative committee until subpoenaed and then did not bring the data ordered. The next day his bank failed to open. He was later convicted of stealing more than $200,000 of the board's funds.[10]

Bond Sales

As noted above, all bonds sold up to December, 1921, were sold to one Chicago bank. The sales were private, and in each case only one bid was offered, and that bid usually included terms favorable to the bank. For instance, a bid in January, 1921, specified that

Proceeds of bonds sold by us over and above the same prices are to be retained by and belong to us for our services in selling said bonds.

7. *Ibid.*, pp. 190-191.   8. *Ibid.*, p. 689.
9. *Ibid.*, p. 705.   10. "1927 Report," p. 180.

Any of said bonds delivered to us and not sold by us by April 1st., 1921, will be returned to you immediately after said date.[11]

Also the bids frequently specified that certain parts of the proceeds should be left on deposit with the purchasing bank, without interest, for periods of time varying from two weeks to eight or nine months. If the state withdrew such funds it would pay interest at the rate of 2 or 3 per cent. On several occasions the Chicago bank thus had the use of several million dollars for several weeks or months without any interest cost, while the state paid interest on its bonds without having the funds.

Nature and Purpose of Loans

Two sections of the 1925 report, taken together, form a striking commentary on the loans made by the board. The first:

Many loans were made on over-liberal valuations and in many sections of the State where privately owned farm loan agencies would not operate. . . . The larger percentage of delinquencies was explained by the Rural Credit Commissioner by the statement that the Rural Credit Board acquired the poorer classes of loans and that but few loans which would have been acceptable to the privately owned farm loan agencies were acquired by the Board.[12]

The second section quotes an analysis made by a special committee in 1922 concerning the purposes of the loans made as follows:

Payment of indebtedness:

Mortgages	53.3%
Other than mortgages	22. % [sic]
Total for indebtedness	75.5%
Buildings and improvements	4.3%
Purchase of equipment and livestock	.1. % [sic]
Purchase of land	19.2%
	100.0%

. . . .

These figures would indicate that the main purpose for which Rural Credit loans have been granted has been for the payment of indebtedness. This has been increasingly true. . . . approximately 40% of the indebtedness liquidated by Rural Credit loans represents notes and mortgages held by banks.[13]

11. Ibid., p. 104.

12. "1925 Report," p. 705. 13. Ibid., p. 686.

Privately owned loan agencies would not operate in certain districts nor make certain loans *at the time* the Rural Credit Board was lending. But they had made loans there earlier and were no doubt glad to have the board "bail them out." The figures show unmistakably that funds provided by the board were used mainly to repay private agencies. The banks, or at least the "right" ones, were favored in two ways: they secured the repayment of many poor loans and at the same time enjoyed the use of the large balances deposited with them by the board—or Mr. Ewert. It was also charged that favoritism was shown in the placing of loans.

Results of Operations

The loan account of the board on June 30, 1926, was as follows:[14]

	No. of Loans	Acreage	Original Amount	Principal Unpaid	Book Value
Current Loans	5,532	1,338,325	$19,643,925	$17,884,378	
Delinquent Loans.	4,065	1,141,088	16,384,500	15,645,289	
Foreclosures	689	202,513	2,826,725	2,777,454	$3,751,856
Real Estate	531	167,801	2,300,175		2,928,292
	10,817	2,849,727	$41,155,325	$36,307,121	$6,680,148
Satisfactions	1,062				
Cancellations	239				
	12,118				

Thus within ten years after operations began, approximately one half of all loans were delinquent, while over 10 per cent had been foreclosed or were in process of foreclosure, representing a total investment of more than six million dollars. The operating loss to June 30, 1926, was $2,265,120, while the total deficit at that time was $3,740,695.[15]

Liquidation Begun

Following the revelations by the investigating committee, the 1925 legislature repealed the original rural credits law and provided for the liquidation of the system. It abolished the office of treasurer, limited the total amount of bonds outstanding to $50,000,000, pro-

14. "1927 Report," p. 122.   15. *Ibid.*, pp. 107, 111.

vided for the sale or lease of lands acquired through foreclosure, prohibited new loans with minor exceptions, and provided for refunding outstanding bonds.[16] The figures in Table 28 show the progress of liquidation. It would have been a long and slow process at best, but the Great Depression and several years of drought greatly increased the difficulties. Thus far liquidation has largely been a process of acquiring land through the foreclosure of defaulted mortgages. The payment of taxes on such land has added considerably to the board's expenses.

In 1927 the board estimated the annual deficit at from $560,000 to $860,000 and stated that an annual tax-levy of $1,000,000 would be necessary for debt service. Under a law enacted that year, the board ordered such a levy.[17] In 1931 the board was reorganized and empowered to make renewal loans to include the old loans plus delinquent interest and taxes. Land acquired by the board

TABLE 28

FINANCES OF THE SOUTH DAKOTA RURAL CREDIT SYSTEM, 1921-38

(In thousands of dollars; years ending June 30)

Year	Interest Receipts	Receipts from Tax Revenues	Interest Payments	Taxes Paid	Operating Deficit Shown	Loans Out-standing	Real Estate Owned†	Total Debt
1921.......	.....	.....	.....	.....	.....	32,700	.....	36,500
1922.......	5,811*	.....	5,423*	.....	.....	35,942	.....	41,500
1923.......	1,820	.....	2,236	.....	.....	40,431	.....	44,500
1924.......	1,817	.....	2,307	.....	.....	40,879	.....	47,500
1925.......	2,315	.....	2,308	.....	.....	40,471	522	46,500
1926.......	2,072	.....	2,386	1,328	2,764	36,392	2,819	45,500
1927.......	2,319	.....	2,396	515	.....	30,782	7,065	45,900
1928.......	2,059	.....	2,290	2,062	5,345‡	26,705	9,443	45,900
1929.......	1,801	305	2,280	139	.....	23,757	11,755	45,900
1930.......	1,769	963	2,175	139	.....	21,488	16,204	44,556
1931.......	1,269	962	2,295	241	.....	20,023	17,944	42,675
1932.......	493	926	2,158	207	10,214	16,610	21,218	42,275
1933.......	317	1,086	2,272	181	.....	15,570	23,869	46,009
1934.......	339	3,619	2,133	214	.....	14,017	26,112	44,469
1935.......	480	2,870	2,115	231	.....	10,932	29,469	43,419
1936.......	560	2,987	2,057	400	16,117	6,375	33,337	40,269
1937.......	374§	2,230	1,796	330	17,622	5,562	34,155	38,869
1938.......	646§	2,497	1,731	370	18,846	4,238	34,025	38,069
1939.......	784§	2,565	1,640	446	19,860	3,522	35,544	36,869

*Accumulated totals since 1917.
†Investment or book value: includes original loan, accrued interest, taxes paid and other expenses incurred.
‡On Dec. 31, 1927.
§Cash receipts of interest plus income from leases on land.
  Source: Rural Credit Board, *Annual Reports.*

16. *Laws*, 1925, c. 266.   17. *Annual Report*, 1927, pp. 9-11.

was to be subject to local taxation for county and school purposes only, limited to four mills and fifteen mills, respectively.[18]   Interest payments and repayment of principal on mortgages fell from $1,-302,231 in 1930-31 to $570,248 in 1931-32.   On June 30, 1931, the 12,116 loans originally made were divided as follows: paid, 2,211; active, 1,154; delinquent, 4,674; foreclosed, 4,967; in litigation, 10. The director estimated at that time that it would be necessary, to balance the Rural Credit budget, to levy $5,000,000 in taxes annually in addition to the $1,000,000 already levied.[19]

In response to a legislative resolution, the state attorney-general made another investigation of the Rural Credit System in 1932.[20] He added little of importance to the findings of the two previous investigations, upon which he relied heavily. He concluded that probably not more than $19,700,000 would be realized from the $36,640,077 of assets reported by the department on June 30, 1932, "which means that the people of the state will have to make additional payments of about $38,000,000 rised [sic] by general taxation to make up the loss resulting from the South Dkota [sic] rural credit venture."[21]

Refunding

Beginning in 1926 the state, partly because it was unable to meet maturing obligations and partly to take advantage of lower interest rates, began to refund the Rural Credit bonds. Since 1931 refunding has progressed steadily, the state offering one or more large issues almost every year. In 1932, when the state's financial outlook was most discouraging, one issue was sold with an interest rate of 6½ per cent. This, however, was soon retired. In the same year the governor tried to sell large amounts of "baby bonds" to citizens of the state but disposed of only $150,000. The low interest rates of recent years have enabled the state to reduce its interest costs considerably; one small issue was sold with a 2¾ per cent rate in 1937, and two others bear 3 per cent. By 1938 approximately $23,-000,000 of the $38,000,000 bonds outstanding were refunding bonds

18. *Laws*, 1931, c. 222, 223, and 257.   19. *Annual Report*, 1931, pp. 6, 10.
20. *Report of an Investigation of the Rural Credit Department of the State of South Dakota made by the Attorney General* ([Pierre?], 1932).
21. *Ibid.*, p. 53.

and had an average rate probably near 4 per cent compared with an average of over 5 per cent for the original bonds.

Liquidation Continued

In 1933 the state faced a financial crisis. Funds were not available to meet principal and interest requirements, and trust funds "not properly applicable thereto but borrowed temporarily for such purposes" were used to avoid default. One half of the proceeds of the gasoline tax was allocated to the board for debt service, and the tax commission was authorized to levy sufficient taxes to cover any deficit. The board was declared to be a public corporation and was authorized to borrow any amounts needed for refunding. It was further stated that "in all matters arising under this chapter the state of South Dakota may sue and be sued as a private individual."[22] Evidently the state hoped to gain a better credit standing by waiving its immunity from suit. The interest rate on mortgages was reduced to 3 per cent, and the board was allowed to extend, up to a maximum of thirty years, the loans of delinquent borrowers, including delinquent taxes and interest, provided the total did not exceed the original loan.

About the same time the state moved to dispose of several projects which had been set up at the time the Rural Credit System was established. These included a bonding department for public employees, a hail insurance system, and a coal mine, all of which had been unprofitable. Three other projects, parts of the same program, were successful and were retained. They were plants for the manufacture of cement, license plates, and twine. The cement plant, for which the state borrowed $2,000,000 in 1921 and 1923, was a consistent profitmaker and by 1938 had accumulated a sinking fund larger than the amount of bonds outstanding.

In 1937 the legislature replaced the allocation of one half the proceeds from the gasoline tax by a two-mills property tax. From time to time in recent years other tax revenues have been assigned to the board to make up the totals shown in Table 28. Through

22. *Laws,* 1933, c. 167. See also c. 170, 188, and 189, and *Annual Report,* 1934, p. 14.

June 30, 1939, the taxpayers of South Dakota had contributed $22,-339,543 to the Rural Credit System and succeeded in reducing the debt by less than $10,000,000. In 1938 the state treasurer estimated that before all bonds were retired the system would have cost the taxpayers $60,000,000. A deficit of about $23,000,000 would be realized in liquidating the assets of the board, which added to the $17,000,000 the taxpayers had already paid and an estimated $20,-000,000 to pay future interest, made up this sum.[23]

The 1939 legislature appropriated additional tax revenues of approximately $2,500,000 per year to the system, and the board entered upon an aggressive program to sell the land held. On June 30, 1939, it was able to report, *"For the first time in the history of the Department, we are selling more land than we are acquiring."* (Italics in original.)   At that time the system held 6,583 tracts of land, aggregating 1,731,711 acres. Over 87 per cent of this was rented, yielding $635,965 in 1938-39. Taxes, however, amounted to $446,010, leaving less than $200,000 as net return on a book investment of over $35,000,000. At the end of the 1939 fiscal year, only 1,281 of the original 12,116 loans remained in force; the unpaid principal on these amounted to $3,522,160. The director was considering a plan for the voluntary refunding of the rural credit bonds which might substantially reduce the $1,640,492 paid in interest in 1938-39. Receipts of the board for that year included $147,451 in interest, $636,092 in land rent, and $2,564,594 from taxes.[24]   The treasurer estimated that the taxpayers would have to pay about two thirds of the principal of the bonds then outstanding. Current income of the board is sufficient to pay only about half of the annual interest. Therefore, about 60 per cent of the debt service may be considered as a burden on the general fund.

NORTH DAKOTA

Agrarian discontent in North Dakota grew out of high interest rates on mortgages and poor facilities for marketing wheat. For many years farmers had railed at the commercial wheat buyers, largely from the Minnesota mills, charging collusion in fixing

23. *Chronicle*, CXLVI (1938), 1287.
24. *Annual Report of the Rural Credit Board*, 1939, *passim*.

prices, improper grading and weighing, and other abuses.[25] Beginning in 1907 the state took several steps to provide better facilities for the marketing of wheat and "the state had by 1915 committed itself definitely to state-owned terminal facilities."[26] A conservative governor and an unfavorable committee report prevented any action in 1915, and conditions were ripe for a political revolution. An astute organizer capitalized on this situation by organizing the Non-Partisan League, which, by the end of 1915, had enrolled some twenty-six thousand members in a program calling for state-owned and operated elevators and flour mills, state hail insurance, fair grading of grain, and rural credits at cost.[27] The League won a victory in the 1916 election but failed to gain control of the state senate. The opposition in the senate blocked the League's program in 1917, and it was not until 1919 that action was taken to carry out the promised program.

Organization

The system established in 1919 centered in a state bank—the Bank of North Dakota—which was a combination central and mortgage bank. The state supplied its $2,000,000 of capital by issuing to it that amount of bonds. The bank performed many of the usual central bank functions. No law required commercial banks to affiliate with it, but other pressure was exerted upon them to do so. A requirement that all public funds in the state be deposited in the bank assured it of substantial funds in the beginning. All deposits were guaranteed by the state. During the first year private deposits were not received. The bank could make loans on real estate up to 50 per cent of the appraised value and transfer the mortgages, in blocks of $100,000, to the state treasurer who would issue state bonds up to a limit of $10,000,000 in return. Provision was also made for the issuance of state bonds to finance a system of state-owned elevators and flour mills. All of the above

25. For a good description of prevailing conditions and farmer attitudes see Alvin S. Tostlebe, *The Bank of North Dakota: An Experiment in Agrarian Banking,* in "Columbia University Studies in History, Economics and Public Law," Vol. CXIV, No. 1 (New York, 1934), chap. ii.

26. *Ibid.*, p. 56.   27. *Ibid.*, p. 59.

bonds were general state obligations and were payable from tax revenues if profits from the various projects were inadequate.

An ex-officio Industrial Commission managed this system of enterprises, with the governor having almost dictatorial powers. "Most of the policy, to say nothing of detail" was left to the judgment of this political commission. The laws were hastily drawn and gave the commission wide powers.[28] The commission decided to make mortgage loans to be amortized over thirty-four years at 7 per cent, of which 1 per cent would be repayment of principal.

Early Operations

The bank opened in July, 1919, and soon had deposits of nearly $20,000,000. Other operations got under way soon thereafter. Litigation and doubt as to the success of the state's program delayed bond sales in the early years.[29] In the meantime the bank could make real estate loans only from deposits. Further difficulties developed in the form of a crop failure (1919), a sharp decline in wheat prices, widespread bank failures, and the repeal of the law requiring that public funds be deposited in the bank. The latter move deprived the bank of about one half of its deposits.

The Non-Partisan program encountered severe criticism and opposition from the beginning. The political character of the Industrial Commission made that body especially vulnerable to attack. Political considerations affected especially the management of the bank, in which minor scandals occurred. However, there was "good reason to believe that farm loans were made impartially and on reasonable security."[30] But the whole program was hampered by the inability to raise funds. The disturbed market conditions in 1920-21 and the state's questionable credit made it impossible to sell state bonds on favorable terms. The bank began to solicit private deposits and disposed of some of its state bonds at discounts. It was charged that this latter move violated the law

28. For copies of the laws setting up this system see *Laws,* 1919, c. 147-154. The acts establishing the bank and the Industrial Commission were approved by the voters in a special election in June, 1919, by votes of 61,118 to 50,271 and 61,495 to 48,239, respectively (*Laws,* 1919, p. 509).

29. The Supreme Court of the United States approved the constitutionality of the various bond issues in 1920. *Green* v. *Frazer,* 253 U. S. 233 (1920).

30. Tostlebe, *op. cit.,* p. 113.

prohibiting the sale of state bonds below par. Failing to get satisfactory bids from investment bankers, the administration tried to sell bonds directly to investors through the bank. The governor designated a "North Dakota Bond Selling Day," and bonds were offered on the instalment plan. Approximately $140,000 was spent promoting bond sales, but results continued to be unsatisfactory.

In the fall of 1921 the voters recalled the Non-Partisan state officials, but rejected a series of measures designed to end the industrial program. Thus the victorious candidates, although they had bitterly condemned the program, were forced to continue it. To the end of 1921 the state had issued $2,000,000 of bank bonds, $120,300 of mill and elevator bonds, and $2,500,000 of real estate bonds. Loans on real estate amounted to $2,760,332. The new administration raised the standards for mortgage loans. The Farm Loan Department was set up as a separate division of the bank to handle farm loans. All loans were to be amortized in twenty-six years, the gross interest rate was placed at 8 per cent (of which 1½ per cent was applied to the reduction of principal), and all lands were reappraised in the light of lower wheat prices. In 1923 an application fee of five dollars and an appraisal charge dependent upon costs were imposed. In 1922 the voters approved an additional $10,000,000 of real estate bonds. The 1923 legislature canceled part of the above amount but added $25,000,000 more. Additions in 1929 and 1931 raised the total bonds authorized for this purpose to $42,750,000.[31]

In another respect the new administration was less sound. It adopted a system of territorial allocation which discriminated against eastern counties and favored the dry, semiarid counties of the west. These western counties were favored both in the placing of loans and in collections and have been responsible for a disproportionate number of defaults.[32] The harder terms imposed, together with long delays, brought protests from the farmers, many of whom were unable to meet payments on loans made by private

31. *Laws,* 1923, p. 548 and c. 292; *ibid.,* 1929, c. 182; *ibid.,* 1931, c. 102.
32. Gilbert W. Cooke, "The North Dakota Rural Credit System," *Journal of Land and Public Utility Economics,* XIV (Aug., 1938), 282.

agencies and were turning to the state system for refinancing.[33] But gradually the volume of lending increased. As market conditions improved and the New Era developed, the state could sell bonds on better terms. In the ensuing ten years the state sold more than $35,000,000 of bonds and loaned the proceeds; the total of loans outstanding reached a peak of over $31,000,000 in 1931. The number of loans made and their amounts are shown in Table 29.

TABLE 29

FARM LOANS MADE BY NORTH DAKOTA INDUSTRIAL COMMISSION, 1919-33

Year	Number of Loans Made	Amount	Average Per Acre
1919-21	755	$ 2,760,332	$14.07
1922	1,077	3,470,691	12.66
1923	1,984	5,950,500	11.31
1924	2,213	6,382,600	11.14
1925	1,804	4,772,100	9.82
1926	1,330	3,169,150	9.42
1927	1,202	2,569,700	8.52
1928	808	1,767,700	8.44
1929	780	1,616,700	7.98
1930	1,257	2,546,800	7.74
1931	2,291	4,074,300	6.96
1932	928	1,384,400	6.08
1933	57	85,700	5.95
Totals	16,486	$40,549,973	9.66

Source: Industrial Commission, *Annual Reports.*

As in South Dakota, depression and crop failures have added to the inherent difficulties of the problem. In the early years the state levied property taxes to help service the real estate bonds, and every year since 1921 has levied a tax to pay a part of the debt service on one or more of the projects. Collections of interest and principal dropped from $1,156,853 in 1931 to $682,731 in 1932, and the state had to borrow $2,250,000 from the bank to meet debt

33. Tostlebe, *op. cit.,* pp. 168-172. It would appear that here, as in South Dakota, the bulk of the funds supplied by the state went to pay off or "bail out" private loan agencies. This assumption is supported by the fact that total mortgage debts of farms owned wholly by operators (about two thirds of all farms) in North Dakota decreased from $108,285,000 in 1920 to $82,411,000 in 1925 and to $60,444,000 in 1930 (*Statistical Abstract of the United States,* 1924, p. 560). On the latter date state loans constituted nearly half of the total. Under these conditions it is hardly likely that any large part of the state loans represented new financing.

service requirements. The tax levies for debt service bore heavily upon an agricultural state whose income was declining rapidly. In the years 1924-28 gross farm income averaged $260,542,000, while state and local taxes averaged $32,628,434. In 1931 gross farm income was $79,827,000, while taxes were $35,808,675, or 44.9 per cent of such income.[34]

Liquidation Started

In 1932 the North Dakota Governmental Commission reported that the cash deficit of the system, already incurred or imminent, was $3,816,163 and called attention to the large number of foreclosures and the large amount of land taken over. It concluded that the figures "conclusively demonstrate that the problem which has arisen . . . is an appalling one, which threatens disaster" and recommended that the system should be liquidated or other steps be taken to prevent further loss.[35] The 1933 legislature ordered that no further mill and elevator bonds be issued and limited the amount of real estate bonds outstanding at any one time to $35,000,000.[36] The system was placed in liquidation, and no new loans have been made since that time.

Refinancing with Farm Credit Administration

Comparatively, North Dakota was conservative in the placing of loans. The Industrial Commission profited by this fact when, in 1933-34, it refinanced approximately one half of its loans with the Federal Farm Credit Administration. Over 8,000 loans, representing original loans of $18,035,144, were refinanced. The total loss taken on those loans by the state was $4,489,007, composed of $1,747,550 of principal and $2,741,457 of accrued interest.[37] The receipt of funds from this refinancing left the commission embarrassed by an excess of cash. On June 30, 1935, the Real Estate Bond Payment Fund showed a balance of $11,727,409. Prevailing market rates of interest were quite low, while the real estate bonds outstand-

34. *Report of the Tax Commission of North Dakota*, 1932, Public Doc. No. 31, p. 2879.
35. Public Doc. No. 36, 1931-32, pp. 3468-3470.
36. *Laws*, 1933, c. 101, 102; *Report of the Industrial Commission*, 1933, p. 11.
37. *Report of North Dakota Industrial Commission*, 1935, pp. 22-23.

ing bore from 4¼ to 6 per cent interest, were nominally noncallable and matured, except for a few small blocks, in 1939 or later. The commission first bought bonds in the open market; the income statement of the bank for 1935 showed the item, "premiums paid on North Dakota bonds purchased during year, $594,427." A footnote explained: "The above premiums were paid on REAL ESTATE SERIES Bonds purchased on open market—maturing through July 1, 1948—so that it was possible to cancel $5,000,000 in Bonds on December 29, 1935, in advance of maturity dates of said bonds. The savings to the State on interest by canceling these bonds amount to $249,997.30 annually. The Bank of North Dakota absorbed the premiums paid from profits earned in the Bank."[38]

Evidently this method of retiring bonds became too expensive, and soon thereafter the commission decided to call some of the bonds, although they were nominally noncallable, as described in Chapter X. Approximately $3,600,000 of bonds bearing interest at 5½ and 6 per cent were retired in this way on July 1, 1937. On June 30, 1938, the balance in the bond repayment fund was below $3,000,000.

Results of Operations—Bank

The bank has been the most profitable—or the least unprofitable —of the three major ventures undertaken by the state. Because of the way accounts have been kept it is impossible to state definitely whether the bank, over its whole life, has operated at a profit or a loss. Between 1919 and 1930, tax revenues to the amount of $2,-201,362 were used to service the bank bonds. In this way one million dollars of such bonds were retired; the other million was retired from bank profits. The bank showed a net loss, up to September 30, 1925, of $253,930; thereafter, it showed a profit every year to 1932, the profit in the latter year being the largest in its history. Net operating profit to that time was $1,661,069, but losses charged off at that time amounted to $1,727,486, leaving a net loss of $66,017.[39] Since that time the bank has been prosperous: it paid

38. *Ibid.*, p. 7.
39. *Report of State Board of Auditors for North Dakota*, Public Doc. No. 33, 1932, p. 3137.

from profits nearly $600,000 as premiums on bonds purchased, and on December 31, 1938, it showed undivided profits of $507,984 and reserves of $239,693.[40]

Results of Operations—Mill and Elevator

The mill and elevator operations have shown a continuous deficit from the beginning. The first venture was the purchase of a small mill for about $100,000 "in order to demonstrate what could be done with a state-owned and state-operated flour mill." "Rapid breaks in wheat prices, an increase in the price of cotton sacks, and losses in consignments combined to produce, by the end of 1924, a deficit of $98,158, approximating a loss of $1.50 per barrel. Up to the time that the mill and machinery were sold for $2,550 on November 6, 1931, the interest accruals and the depreciation charges had increased the total deficit to about $120,000."[41]

In April, 1920, the Industrial Commission let the first contracts for a much larger venture, to consist of three plants. These were completed within three years at a total cost of $3,044,392.

After allowance for depreciation and interest . . . a loss was incurred in every period of operation; before allowance for these two items, an operating profit occurred in all except four periods.

. . . .

The sales in North Dakota varied between 106,697 and 209,186 barrels and composed from 13 to 44 per cent of the total sales.

. . . .

. . . it was the general practice to sell in eastern territory at a loss, and recuperate partly with a higher price for the flour sold in North Dakota; at times this differential reached a dollar.[42]

Up to June 30, 1932, the mill and elevator project showed a total operating loss of $2,229,545, or 41.8 cents per barrel of flour manufactured.[43] The State Mill had total fixed assets nearly three times the amount of the private-mill average per barrel of daily capacity, and these assets were represented, on the credit side of the ledger,

40. *Report,* Collection and Land Department, Bank of North Dakota, 1938, p. 1.
41. Gilbert W. Cooke, "The North Dakota State Mill and Elevator," *Journal of Political Economy,* XLVI (Feb., 1938), 27. This article gives an excellent summary and critical discussion of the project.   42. *Ibid.,* pp. 32, 40.
43. State Board of Auditors, *op. cit.,* p. 3159.

by fixed liabilities on which the interest charges averaged about 5¾ per cent.

The cost to the state government from the beginning of production until January 4, 1937, is listed . . . as "accrued interest on construction bonds paid by taxation," $1,890,152; "interest on operating bonds paid by taxation," $549,189; "bonds paid by taxation," $1,168,552. These three items total $3,607,894; since the recorded total deficit at that date was $3,684,804.31, this indicates that up to then the Mill failed to earn its depreciation charges by some $77,000.

.   .   .   .

. . . the State Mill would have had to have been operated better than were 60 per cent of the private mills in America (who reported to the Millers' Federation) in order to have earned its interest charges.[44]

Results of Operations—Loans

The results of the system's loan operations to December 31, 1938, were as follows:[45]

Total loans made $40,505,450*

Principal repaid .... 23,756,501†
Unpaid principal—
   Open loans .... $ 4,936,708
Foreclosures 893,368
   Land owned 10,918,793   16,748,949

Total as above $40,505,450

  * The total is not the same as given in Table 29 because the Bank of North Dakota assumed a small number of loans.
  † Includes $1,873,721 discount or loss taken on settlements.

On the surface this is a comparatively good showing, since more than one half of the principal had been repaid. Approximately 80 per cent of those repayments, however, represent refinancing with the Farm Credit Administration. The loans which remain are presumably the poorer ones which could not be refinanced. On these the state will suffer heavier losses.

Of the original 16,482 loans, there were outstanding at the end of 1938 only 3,024, aggregating $4,936,708. Of these, 2,324 were delinquent, while only 461 were in good standing. Delinquent pay-

44. Cooke, "State Mill and Elevator," *op. cit.,* pp. 50-51.
45. *Report,* Collection and Land Department, Bank of North Dakota, 1938, pp. 7-8.

TABLE 30

DATA ON NORTH DAKOTA RURAL CREDIT SYSTEM FOR
SELECTED YEARS, 1921-38

(In thousands of dollars; years ending December 31)

Year	Loans Outstanding	Real Estate Owned	Collections of Principal and Interest	Real Estate Bonds Outstanding
1921	2,568	......	......	2,500
1922	6,231	......	......	3,270
1926	24,751		1,648	22,059
1927	25,181	1,764	1,968	26,858
1928	25,690	2,221	2,227	......
1929	26,365	2,466	2,145	......
1930	28,016	2,813	1,589	31,357
1931	31,185	3,436	1,157	35,297
1932	30,754	5,024	683	36,348
1933	28,898	6,565	1,002	39,062
1934	16,462	6,738	12,760	37,412*
1935	11,250	6,558	4,683	27,412
1936	8,396	8,697	......	27,064
1937	6,706	11,836	422†	21,544
1938	4,937	13,655	416†	19,566

*June 30, 1934.
†Includes farm rents and receipts from sale of farms.

ments amounted to $1,450,569. The state owned 1,214,963 acres of land, representing a total investment of $13,655,182. On loans repaid and farms sold the state had received $18,693,610, and had taken a loss of $4,810,343. Of the total amount of bonds sold, amounting to $39,573,000, $19,729,000 had been redeemed, leaving $19,844,000 outstanding.[46]

By the end of 1936 the taxpayers of the state had contributed to aid the system as follows:[47]

Motor vehicle tax transfers.............................$2,941,718.62
Beer revenue transferred................................. 1,015,000.00
General tax levy collected............................... 4,033,274.70

    Total Additional Revenue.........................$7,989,993.32

It is certain that they will have to make substantial contributions for some years to come. Cooke estimated total deficits after 1936 at $12,000,000, making the total $20,000,000, but in the light of collections in 1937 and 1938 this appears to be far too low. Total collec-

46. Ibid., pp. 2, 4, 6, 22.
47. Cooke, "The North Dakota Rural Credit System," op. cit., p. 282.

tions in these years averaged only a little over $600,000, or about half enough to pay interest on outstanding bonds, before deducting any expenses. From this it would appear that approximately 75 per cent of the real estate bonds outstanding, or roughly $15,000,000, should be considered as a burden on general revenues. Of course, all the mill and elevator bonds, amounting to $2,500,000, will have to be serviced from tax revenues.

Conclusion

North Dakota's industrial program has been, with the partial exception of the bank, a complete and costly failure. To June 30, 1938, it had cost the taxpayers of the state over $15,000,000 and is certain to cost many millions more before it is finally completed. A part of the blame for the failure may be attributed to the unfortunate time at which it was begun and to mismanagement in the early years, but even without these it is doubtful whether it could have been a success. The bulk of the funds went into the real estate credit system, which was essentially a rescue project and as such doomed to failure, barring the intervention of a miracle. Further, the successful management of enterprises of this type requires talent of a kind which few states have been able to command.

MINNESOTA

Unlike the Dakotas, Minnesota took no action to establish a farm loan system until after the decline of farm prices in 1920-21. During the years of high land prices, private loan agencies, including commercial banks, had loaned heavily on the sparsely settled lands in the northern parts of the state. The drop in the prices of farm products created an "emergency" in which these agencies faced heavy losses on their loans. They campaigned for a state loan system which would relieve them of their bad loans.[48]

48. One who is intimately acquainted with the system and its history writes: "Knowing that the Federal Land Bank System at that time was in a position to extend all credit necessary to those who could properly qualify, I fail to see any need for a state agency. Consequently, it is my opinion that the underlying reasons for the creation of this Department were primarily political. I do know that one gubernatorial campaign was waged on a platform of Rural Credit and since then the Department has been a target for political exploitation to the extent of making it

Organization

After the voters had approved the necessary constitutional amendment in 1922, the 1923 legislature created the Minnesota Rural Credit Bureau and authorized it to issue general state obligations, bearing interest at not over 5 per cent, up to $40,000,000. The bureau was to make loans to farmers, varying from $500 to $15,000, to be amortized within forty years, up to 60 per cent of the value of land and one third of the value of improvements. If the bureau lacked funds to pay interest, it could issue certificates of indebtedness up to $500,000; if sufficient funds could not be obtained within this limit, the bureau could issue tax-levy certificates to cover the deficiency. The state auditor was then required to levy upon all taxable property to retire the latter certificates.[49] A special act provided for more lenient loans to disabled World War veterans.[50]

Early Operations

The speed with which the bureau made loans in its first two years was in keeping with the "emergency" which brought the system into being. Loans were made as rapidly as possible, and few questions were asked. The bureau issued bonds bearing from 4 to 4¾ per cent interest and loaned at 5¼ per cent plus a nominal application fee. "The greatest exploitation took place during the first two or three years of the Department's existence. Very little attention was given to the security offered. Although the law set a definite loanability, many of the grants of credit resulted in outright sales to the states."[51]

The freedom with which loans had been handed out, aroused criticism and prompted an investigation by a legislative committee in 1925. The committee found that there had been many abuses

---

possible for banks in territories where other agencies were reluctant to extend credit to unload their frozen assets on the state" (letter to the author from T. H. Arens, Conservator, Department of Rural Credit, May 17, 1937). See also "Report of the Committee Appointed to Investigate the Rural Credits Bureau," *Journal of the Senate,* 1925, pp. 581-588.

49. *Laws,* 1923, c. 225.　　　　　　　　50. *Ibid.,* c. 253.

51. Letter from T. H. Arens cited above. After reading the above, Mr. Arens added: "In most cases on the early loans the appraisals were made in the back room of the bank involved. Appraisals, on which credit was extended, compared with current appraisals, clearly indicates that the first appraisers never saw the security."

and unsound practices, but tended to excuse the bureau on the ground that it had to meet an emergency. By February 1, 1925, the bureau had received 10,298 applications for $59,778,946 and had approved 7,550 aggregating $37,338,100. Forty-three foreclosures had been made and 235 other loans were delinquent, mostly in the northern part of the state.

The committee severely criticized the method used in appraising land.

The appraisal is done by a local man, in some cases by men directly or indirectly interested in banks who profit greatly by the State's loan, if one were made, to the extent of shifting the burden of carrying certain loans from the bank to the State. While the local appraiser is acquainted with the land in question he is also subject to tremendous pressure from the owner of the land, in many cases from the local banks, often from local business men . . . and consequently . . . the strong tendency has been to overestimate the value of land. . . . Some of the appraisers . . . admitted that the appraisals were too high in many instances, but seek to justify themselves on the grounds that an emergency existed which required heroic measures. . . . appraisers were appointed without due regard to proper qualifications and . . . in most instances . . . the Bureau made no attempt to verify the appraiser's figures although the appraisal was made by a person whose qualifications were wholly unknown to the Bureau. . . .

. . . .

. . . in several instances the owner of the land not only refused to pay the first installment and interest on the loan, but actually, after the loan was made, abandoned the land.[52]

The committee also directed special criticism against the loans to veterans, who had been exploited through land sales at outrageous prices. "Poor land located in an unattractive locality was selected for these ex-service men by the Veterans' Bureau and sold to them at about four times its real value. . . . A 'hard bargain' is a mild expression when applied to the treatment these boys received."[53]

The recommendations of the committee were: (1) supplemental appraisals should be supplied by having state or district appraisers check all appraisals by local men; (2) the loan limits should be reduced to 50 per cent of land and 30 per cent of improvements,

52. "Report of the Committee . . . ," op. cit., pp. 582-583.
53. Ibid., pp. 586-587.

with a maximum of $12,000 for individual loans; (3) the bureau should be permitted to take chattel mortgages for additional security and should have wider powers to dispose of land taken in through foreclosure.

Changes in 1925

The 1925 legislature acted favorably on all the recommendations except that it did not reduce the maximum for individual loans. It also increased the total authorization of bonds to $70,000,000 and increased the application fee to five dollars per $1,000.[54]

Later Operations

Under the changes made in 1925, lending proceeded more slowly and more conservatively, while delinquencies mounted steadily, as shown in Table 31. From July 1, 1925, to the end of 1928 "only about one third of the total amount of the loans was placed on farms in the sections where the great bulk of the old loans were

TABLE 31

DATA ON FINANCES OF MINNESOTA RURAL CREDIT SYSTEM, 1923-38

(All dollars in thousands; years ending December 31)

Year	Number of Loans Closed	Amount of Loans Closed	Loans Outstanding	Real Estate and Sheriff's Certificates Owned	Deficit in Interest Account	Bonds and Certificates Outstanding
1923	786	$ 4,370	$......	$......	$......	$ 9,000
1924	5,568	28,241	......	......	......	36,125
1925	1,346	6,144	......	......	......	38,125
1926	1,501	5,922	......	......	......	43,390
1927	971	3,787	44,536	......	......	47,200
1928	839	3,600	44,985	5,074	521	50,250
1929	597	2,523	......	......	......	52,825
1930	648	3,164	43,583	11,462	935	57,050
1931	616	2,681	43,480	......	......	......
1932	423	1,102	36,944	22,972	3,694	63,317
1933	257	699	35,139	25,141	5,701	64,250
1934	8	34	32,708	27,525*	7,545	63,199
1935	1	1	27,390	30,724*	9,472	64,074
1936	1	2	21,465	34,246*	10,800	65,820
1937	3	17	12,223	38,591*	12,180	59,728
1938	1	2	8,681	38,543*	13,606	59,542†
	13,566	62,290				

*Includes sales contracts.
†Gross debt less $1,452,000 bonds and certificates held in treasury.

54. Laws, 1925, c. 191, 226, 244, and 270.

made. The balance has been made in the older communities of the west central and southern sections of the state where land values are higher and farming conditions more stable. . . . The law enacted in 1925 providing for a double system of appraisals has been very helpful in sifting out undesirable loan risks. . . ."[55]

On December 31, 1928, Rural Credit Bonds outstanding amounted to $50,250,000, bearing an average interest rate of 4.36 per cent. Mortgage loans outstanding amounted to $44,984,775, of which $9,313,300, representing 1,667 loans covering 278,272 acres, were delinquent, while 1,179 loans covering 226,158 acres had been foreclosed. The 1928 report was optimistic, pointing out that 97 per cent of the foreclosures had resulted from loans made during the first two years and predicting: "Whatever losses there may be in connection with foreclosed farms will, we believe, be absorbed by the net interest earnings of the Department which now amount to $823,326.82 and accumulations at the rate of about $223,000 a year."[56] In the same year, however, the department issued its first certificates of indebtedness. The first tax-levy certificates were issued in 1931. Use of the latter certificates meant that tax levies had to be made each year to pay them. After they had been issued to the amount of $4,606,354, the state changed its policy, increased the authorization for certificates of indebtedness, and thus elected to allow the deficit to accumulate rather than to pay it currently. Tax levies for the retirement of the tax-levy certificates were as follows: 1931, 0.18 mill; 1932, 1.04 mill; 1933, 1.25 mill; 1934, 1.00 mill.

By the end of 1930 foreclosures amounted to approximately $12,000,000. They increased rapidly in the next two years as the depression deepened, and by the end of 1932 the state owned real estate with a book value of approximately $23,000,000, while the total rural credit debt was $63,317,500. The legislature then decided that it was time to stop the costly experiment.

Liquidation Started

The 1933 legislature placed the system in liquidation by a series of acts which (1) ordered that no further loans should be made

55. *Report of the Department of Rural Credit*, 1928, p. 3.
56. *Ibid.*, pp. 4, 8.

except those already approved;[57] (2) appointed, to replace the former bureau, a single conservator whose duty it was to "collect all moneys due the State under this act and to sell all property acquired by it . . . with a view to the complete and speedy liquidation of the business of the Department";[58] (3) established a three-year moratorium for those mortgagors who could not meet their payments and at the same time pay their taxes and insurance, provided they paid the taxes and insurance and maintained the property.[59] The conservator was given power to issue certificates of indebtedness to any amount necessary to meet debt service requirements, and was instructed to sell tax-levy certificates only in case it was impossible to raise the necessary funds by sale of certificates of indebtedness. These powers were increased in 1935 by provisions allowing the conservator to make composition settlements with mortgagors and to contract for land sales on a crop-payment plan. Under the latter plan he would accept, for five years, one third of the crop produced on a farm in satisfaction of the interest and principal payments due during that period provided the debtor would pay taxes and insurance and keep the farm in good repair.[60]

Progress of Liquidation

The conservator took charge of the system on July 1, 1933, and has followed an aggressive policy of liquidation. His task was to make collections on active loans, to foreclose on delinquent loans, and to dispose of land acquired through foreclosure as rapidly as the best interests of the state would permit. Progress in this program was delayed by additional concessions to debtors:

. . . In 1934, many foreclosures were withheld pending outcome of efforts of defaulting borrowers to refinance with the Federal Land Bank. In 1935, Ch. 341 of the State Laws renewed the indulgence granted delinquent borrowers by Ch. 403 of the 1933 laws. In 1937, the Legislature enacted Ch. 465 which endorsed both interest and principal delinquencies back into the mortgage and reamortized them over the life of the loan. All these measures had the effect of postponing delinquencies, and forestalling the time when conversion of the loans

57. *Laws*, 1933, c. 386.
58. *Ibid.*, c. 429.   59. *Ibid.*, c. 403.
60. *Ibid.*, 1935, c. 367; 1937, c. 409. If the crop payment is less than the interest requirement, the principal payment is not canceled.

and revaluations of the farms would otherwise have been consummated. It has been the experience of the Department that such extensions did not benefit the delinquent borrowers materially, and that the ultimate effect was to continue them in uncertainty only to have them eventually lose title to their farms.[61]

Income was further reduced by a 1937 law which reduced the interest rate on all mortgages to 4 per cent.[62]

Refinancing with the Farm Credit Administration was delayed by the inability of the conservator to make compromise settlements before 1935. To the end of 1935, 733 mortgages had been refinanced, the system receiving $3,274,247 and taking a loss of $300,416, or 8.5 per cent. During 1936, 883 additional loans were refinanced, producing receipts of $3,691,221 and a loss of $1,539,935, or 29.4 per cent. After this, no figures for F.C.A. refinancing are given, but total refinancing dropped sharply and a major portion of the funds came from private agencies.[63]

The conservator's biggest problem has been the management of acquired land. Sales were pushed as rapidly as possible without demoralizing the real estate market; from July, 1933, to the end of 1938, nearly four thousand farms were sold for $16,413,820. The loss on such sales to the end of 1937 was about 38 per cent. Few of the sales, however, were for cash; most of them were "standard contract" sales with down payments averaging about 14 per cent, while some were crop-payment sales with down payments averaging about 4 per cent. Such sales do not represent the end of the conservator's troubles. Many of the contract sales become delinquent, and the land has to be resold or the contracts rewritten. At the end of 1938, 890 of 2,537 contract sales outstanding were delinquent. The crop-payment sales have been fairly successful; in 1938 the conservator realized a gross return of 5.3 per cent on the total purchase price of lands sold in this way, but the results varied widely between the different districts of the state.

Pending sale, the conservator rents the land to which he holds title. Income from this source has been substantial; from $133,018

---

61. *Liquidator* (published by the Department of Rural Credit), VI (Dec. 31, 1938), 43.　　　　62. *Laws*, 1937, c. 465.
63. *Liquidator*, V (Dec. 31, 1937), Foreword.

in 1929 it increased to a peak of $1,008,246 in 1937 and dropped to $852,703 in 1938. The latter sum represented a return of somewhat less than 4 per cent on the state's investment of approximately $26,000,000 in such lands.[64]

By the end of 1938 the conservator was able to report that

> By far the major portion of the work of liquidation has been completed. Out of the 13,566 original mortgage loans, 9,476 have been completely liquidated, or revalued and readjusted to the extent where they require only the minimum of service and expense. Of the 9,476 units, 3,186 have been completely liquidated, . . . 3,353 remain as active and practically current loans, and 2,937 are carried as contracts for deed.
>
> .   .   .   .
>
> Title by foreclosure or deed has been acquired to 7,769 farms, representing more than two-thirds of the $62,290,000.00 originally loaned. Of these, 4,090 remain unsold.[65]

The following figures show the progress of liquidation from July, 1933, to December, 1938:[66]

	July 1933	December 1938
Active mortgage loans	9,290	3,353
Sheriff's certificates	310	204
Sales contracts	377	3,206
Real estate owned	3,062	3,886
Complete liquidation	562	3,233
	13,601	13,882

Attempts at Refunding

On December 31, 1938, rural credit bonds and certificates outstanding amounted to $60,990,000, the major portion of which will mature in the years from 1941 to 1949 with one large block maturing in 1954. Part of the certificates bear 4.25 per cent interest, while the $50,000,000 of bonds bear from 4.01 to 4.75 per cent. All are non-callable. The State Board of Investment holds $21,195,000 of bonds and certificates. The legislature has tried at different times to find

---

64. *Ibid.*, VI (1938), 82, 83.   65. *Ibid.*, Foreword.

66. *Ibid.*, p. 66. The figures represent numbers of loans; the totals differ from each other and from the figure for loans originally made, because some loans were divided in the process of liquidation.

a way of refunding these obligations at lower interest rates. It empowered the conservator to issue refunding obligations and specifically directed him to request the Investment Board to surrender the obligations which it holds. The board has refused to do so. Were refunding possible, it would permit a saving of 30 per cent or more on annual interest costs, but apparently it is impossible.

Results of Operations

The following figures summarize the system's loan experience from 1923 to December 31, 1938:[67]

		Number	Original Loan Amount
Loans paid in full		1,431	$5,420,950
Loans paid by compromise settlement		1,013	5,910,550
Loans foreclosed or deeded:			
Farms subsequently sold	3,679	$19,726,000	
Farms held as real estate or sheriff's certificates	4,090	21,301,100	7,769	41,027,000
Loans still active		3,353	9,931,500
Total		13,566	$62,290,000

The conservator's consolidated balance sheet for December 31, 1938, may be summarized as follows:[68]

ASSETS		LIABILITIES	
Cash and investment	$ 3,796,729	Bonds and certificates	$60,990,000
Mortgage loans	8,680,900	Reserves	5,717,810
Sales contracts	12,285,507	Tax levy certificates (already redeemed from taxes)	4,606,354
Sheriff's certificates and real estate	26,257,612	Other liabilities	758,736
Other assets	104,172	Deficit	—20,947,980
	$51,124,920		$51,124,920

The sales contracts, sheriff's certificates, and real estate represented 1,136,160 acres of land, while mortgage loans covered 446,792

67. *Ibid.*, p. 38.   68. *Ibid.*, pp. 2-3.

acres. The conservator pointed out that, as of December 31, 1938, "there were $23,283,196.00 in mortgage loans and contracts drawing interest for the Department as contracted to $60,990,000.00 in bonds and certificates of indebtedness on which it was paying interest. The interest loss caused by this differential during 1938 was $1,630,000.00. The average interest loss from this source for the past seven years has been $1,706,000.00."[69] He estimated that the deficit for the biennium 1939-41, including principal maturities, would be about $5,144,000.

Thus far the taxpayers of the state have subsidized the system only by the payment of the $4,606,354 of tax-levy certificates. Deficits above this amount have been met by issuing certificates of indebtedness or by using principal repayments on the mortgages to cover interest rather than to repay bonds and certificates. But the drain on tax revenues will be heavy in the future. A recent committee reported: ". . . the state faces a definitely known loss of $14,000,000 on the principal plus an anticipated additional principal loss of $16,-000,000. Interest deficits will require an estimated $10,000,000 additional amount and a total of not less than $5,000,000 will be required for administration during the period while the bureau's affairs are being settled. Thus the loss and expense to the taxpayers may eventually reach $50,000,000."[70] In 1938 the conservator recommended that a start be made on the task of repayment by levying a tax of $2,000,000 per year.

From the estimates of funds to be realized from the liquidation of assets and from the figures on collections and payments of interest we may estimate that approximately 60 per cent of the total rural credit debt will eventually have to be serviced from tax revenues.

OTHER STATES

Two other states have made minor ventures into this field. In 1917 Oregon sold $450,000 of rural credit bonds and loaned the proceeds. The bonds were retired gradually, leaving only $84,000 outstanding in 1938. So far as it is known, the fund has been self-

69. *Ibid.*, VI, "Comment."
70. *Report of the Legislative Tax Commission of Investigation and Inquiry,* 1937, p. 33.

supporting. Assets held by the fund on June 30, 1938, were valued at $141,999.[71]

In 1931 the Arkansas legislature "in response to urgent appeals, hurriedly passed" an act creating the State Agricultural Credit Board and authorizing it to issue $1,500,000 of general obligations of the state. The purpose was to finance, through loans to individuals, the formation of local credit corporations which would secure loans for farmers through the Federal Intermediate Credit Banks. There were some irregularities in the sale of bonds, but $1,296,000 of them were sold and proceeds loaned in the amount of $1,032,255.[72] Repayments to December 1, 1934, amounted to $206,734. Although a tax of one-half mill was provided to service the bonds, this has never been levied. Receipts of the fund were adequate for debt service requirements until 1937, when an unspecified amount was transferred from general revenues. Bonds outstanding on December 31, 1938, amounted to $345,000.

CONCLUSION

There can be no question as to the failure of the rural credit system in Minnesota and the Dakotas. Several factors contributed to those failures. Many of the loans were made on the basis of the abnormally high land prices prevailing during the war period. These values were drastically deflated during the depression which has beset agriculture almost continuously since 1920.[73] The Great Depression and droughts in 1934 and 1936 completed the ruin of the systems. Each of the systems had two or more years of gross mismanagement at the beginning, from which it would have been difficult to recover even under favorable conditions. A majority of the loans made by each system was used to refinance loans made by private loan agencies; that is, each was a rescue project, directly

71. *Moody's*, 1939, p. 1334.
72. *Biennial Report of the State Comptroller*, 1934, pp. 22-26.
73. The extent of this deflation is indicated by the decline in the value of farm land and buildings between 1920 and 1935, as reported by the Bureau of the Census:

	1920	1935	Per Cent Decline
Minnesota	$3,301,168,000	$1,383,072,000	58.1
North Dakota	1,488,521,000	707,139,000	52.5
South Dakota	2,472,894,000	691,863,000	72.0

Statistical Abstract of the United States, 1938, p. 588.

or indirectly. South Dakota had the poorest management and has fared worst. North Dakota has had fairly good management except in the early period and has fared best. Minnesota had poor management in the beginning, mediocre management in the middle period, and the best since the beginning of liquidation.

The following figures indicate the extent of the failure of the loan systems:

	Total Loans Made	Bonds Sold (Exclusive of Refunding)	Estimated Total Cost to Taxpayers
South Dakota	$41,155,325	$47,500,000	$60,000,000
North Dakota	40,505,450	39,573,000	25,000,000
Minnesota	62,290,000	66,000,000 (approx.)	50,000,000
Totals	$143,950,775	$153,073,000	$135,000,000

Eventually the taxpayers will pay almost as much as the total amount loaned; in South Dakota, considerably more.

These experiments are examples of the rather general practice of prescribing easy credit facilities for those in economic distress. This usually leads to the making of loans according to need rather than according to ability to repay. Unless the distress is purely temporary, or unless something else is done to remove it, this practice is disastrous, for it merely piles larger debts on those in distress. Credit, which is merely another name for debt, is never a final solution for any basic economic problem. There is grave danger that any state loan system will make matters worse by increasing debts in an effort to alleviate an acute situation. The demonstrated dangers of mismanagement and political manipulation increase the odds against such a system to a point where only an exceptional one can succeed.

CHAPTER XIV

BORROWING FOR UNEMPLOYMENT RELIEF
AND OTHER PURPOSES

THE GOVERNMENTAL functions discussed in the three preceding chapters were the most significant causes of state borrowing in the period 1919-38 and were responsible for more than 60 per cent of the total debts incurred in that period. The states, however, have incurred debts for a great variety of other purposes. Some of the more important of these are discussed briefly in this chapter.

UNEMPLOYMENT RELIEF

Before 1930 the task of providing relief for the unemployed was almost exclusively a local government function. As the number of unemployed increased in 1930 and 1931, and as many local units became financially embarrassed, it became apparent that some other agency would have to provide funds. It was natural that the first demand should be upon the states. Most states were slow to act, some because they hesitated to assume the responsibility for this function, others because they faced financial difficulties themselves. While the states delayed, it became evident that the problem was too large even for the state governments, and the Federal Government began to appropriate large amounts for relief. This early intervention of the national government was responsible for the fact that the states borrowed no more than they did for relief.

State Borrowing for Local Units

The reluctance of some states to accept the relief function was responsible for a feature which characterized several relief loans; that is, state borrowing for local account. The need for funds was urgent, and local governments were unable to provide them. While accepting the necessity of providing funds at the time, several states wished to avoid establishing a precedent and also to be reimbursed by the local governments later. Three different types of procedure were followed to accomplish this end.

Two states borrowed funds and reloaned them to local governments. California sold $20,000,000 of bonds in 1933 and reloaned the proceeds to local units, which paid the state the same rate of interest borne by the bonds. Repayments were to be made in ten annual instalments in the form of deductions from the counties' share of the motor fuel tax. A county's consent was necessary before any of its cities or towns could borrow.[1] A move to cancel the county obligations was defeated in the state legislature in 1937. In February, 1938, the state comptroller withheld, as payments on these bonds, $1,526,606 of the $4,085,245 apportioned to the counties from the motor fuel tax.[2]

A Massachusetts act authorized state bonds up to $30,000,000 for a similar purpose. During 1933 cities and towns could borrow, with the approval of the Emergency Finance Board, amounts equal to the excess spent for relief in 1932 over the amount spent in 1929; for 1934 the limit was 40 per cent of the maximum allotment for 1933. They were to give their notes or bonds to the state treasurer, who might, in order to pay principal and interest on the state bonds, order a levy of taxes in such units or withhold funds due to them from the state or from the relief funds of the Federal Government.[3] Exclusive of refunding, the state borrowed $7,453,000 under this act. On November 30, 1938, $1,583,000 of such obligations remained outstanding.

A second method of relief borrowing was for the states to borrow and spend the money themselves, but to apportion the costs of servicing the bonds to the counties. The $50,000,000 which Illinois borrowed is serviced by deductions from the counties' share of the motor fuel tax.[4] One New Hampshire loan is serviced in the same way. In Nevada, also, the counties are required to contribute to the service of relief bonds,[5] but their contributions are not adequate to cover total requirements.

1. Statutes and Amendments, 1922, c. 207.
2. Moody's, 1939, p 168.   3. Acts, 1933, c. 307.
4. Illinois Revised Statutes, 1937, c. 23, secs. 396, 403.
5. Laws, 1935, c. 97.

A third form of state aid was state guaranty of local bonds. A New Hampshire act of 1933 authorized the governor and his council, within their discretion and for a period of six years, to guarantee, in the name of the state, the bonds and notes of local units which were financially embarrassed on account of inability to collect taxes or of heavy relief demands, provided they could not sell their obligations on reasonable terms through regular banking channels. The governor and council act as agents in selling the bonds, and the governor may appoint a fiscal agent and require him to sign all warrants drawn against the borrowed funds.[6] On June 30, 1938, $6,127,000 of such obligations bearing the state guarantee were outstanding. A Connecticut act provided for similar guarantees, but apparently no action has been taken under it.[7]

Ohio, in 1932, authorized the issue of relief bonds which are on the border line between state and local obligations. Counties could, with the approval of the State Relief Commission and the Tax Commission, borrow funds for relief, issuing bonds to be serviced from the proceeds of a 1 per cent gross receipts tax on all public utility companies. The proceeds of the tax are apportioned among the counties according to a complicated formula, and are to be held by them in a special fund and applied solely to the payment of the principal and interest of the relief bonds, except that any excess may be used for other relief purposes. The state treasurer was designated as paying agent for the counties, and remits debt service funds directly to the trustee or fiscal agent.[8]

Total Relief Bonds Issued

The above were new and unusual forms of state borrowing, but the bulk of state debts incurred for relief was of the ordinary type with no unusual characteristics. Table 32 summarizes, so far as available information permits, the total borrowed for relief by the different states, the amounts of such debts outstanding in 1938, and the principal sources of funds for debt service. The total shown there is somewhat larger than the total for relief borrowing given in

6. *Laws*, 1935, c. 63.   7. *Laws*, 1933, c. 276.
8. *Laws*, Spec. Sess., 1932, p. 17. The amount of such bonds issued is not available.

Chapter X because the sale of some of the bonds was not publicly reported at the time; the guaranteeing of local obligations was never so reported. The amounts outstanding in 1938 are gross amounts, since it was possible in only a few cases to ascertain the amount of sinking funds held against relief bonds. Almost all of them, however, are serial bonds against which no sinking funds are held.

R.F.C. Loans

The totals in Table 32 do not include the relief loans made to the states by the R.F.C. in 1932-33. The Relief and Construction Act of 1932[9] directed the R.F.C. to lend $300,000,000 to states and local governments for work relief at 3 per cent interest, state loans to be repaid in five annual instalments from future highway grants-in-aid. All except six states—Connecticut, Delaware, Massachusetts,

TABLE 32

STATE BORROWING FOR UNEMPLOYMENT RELIEF

State	Bonds Sold or Obligations Incurred	Amounts Outstanding, 1938*	Date of Final Maturity	Principal Sources of Funds for Debt Service
Calif...	$ 44,000,000	$ 42,000,000	1949	General Fund; counties' share of motor fuel tax.
Ill......	50,000,000	40,900,000	1954	Counties' share of motor fuel tax
Md....	20,500,000	15,796,000	1949	General fund
Mass...	37,453,000†	17,833,000	1945	Gasoline tax; payments from local units
Minn...	10,524,300‡	19,198,000	1941	Ad valorem tax
Nev....	405,000	153,000	1952	General fund and contributions from counties
N. H...	9,127,000§	8,377,000§	1942	General fund; local units' share of highway funds
N. J....	35,000,000	17,500,000	1943	Motor fuel tax; liquor tax
N. Y...	210,000,000	155,070,000	1947	General fund
Pa.....	25,000,000	15,000,000	1943	General fund
R. I....	8,000,000	4,600,000	1939	General fund; highway fund
Tenn...	750,000	500,000	1939	General fund
Tex....	20,000,000	13,539,000	1943	General fund
Vt.....	500,000	500,000	1947	General fund
Wash. .	10,000,000	9,206,000	1952	Gasoline tax
Totals..	$481,259,000	$360,172,000		

*Gross amounts; see text. †Includes $7,453,000 of Municipal Relief Bonds.
‡Incomplete; an additional $10,000,000 or more were sold without public report of sale.
§Includes $6,127,000 of local government bonds guaranteed by state.

9. 47 *Statutes at Large* 709.

Nebraska, Vermont, and Wyoming—received such loans, the amounts varying from $176,000 in Maryland to nearly $40,000,000 in Illinois. "In 1934, however, the states were relieved of the obligation of repayment from highway grants-in-aid, so that $280,026,000 may be regarded as an outright grant to the borrowing states."[10]

States Which Borrowed Most

Only fifteen states borrowed for relief, and two of them—New York and Illinois—borrowed more than one half of the total. The six states which borrowed most heavily accounted for more than 75 per cent of the total. Those six states are highly industrialized and rank near the top in per capita wealth and income. It was natural that those states should be the ones to borrow most, since the industrial areas were the ones most affected by unemployment and since the relatively high level of income gave rise to the demand for, and the means of providing, adequate relief. With the exception of Texas, all states which borrowed for relief are states which have frequently appeared in the loan market. "What borrowing did take place occurred in these States in which borrowing had previously been established as an acceptable fiscal practice. It is noteworthy that the 12 states which borrowed for emergency relief account for half of the combined indebtedness of all State governments."[11]

It has been pointed out that there was a tendency for those states whose constitutions forbid borrowing to make relatively small contributions for relief.[12] This was true, but the reason probably lay deeper than the constitutional provision. In almost every case those states which contributed least were poor states; borrowing for relief would have increased the handicap of their poverty. Of the six states which borrowed most, one had to amend its constitution, while four others had to secure the approval of the voters in referenda.

In this connection Washington resorted to an unusual procedure by invoking the emergency or defense provisions of the constitution to issue relief bonds. The Washington constitution

10. Bitterman, *op. cit.*, p. 157.
11. L. László Ecker-R, "State Relief Borrowing," *Monthly Report Federal Emergency Relief Administration*, Aug., 1935, p. 11.
12. *Monthly Report*, F.E.R.A., May, 1936, pp. 131-132.

requires that the voters approve all debts with certain exceptions, including bonds "to suppress insurrection." The legislature, in order to justify the issuance of bonds without a vote of the people, wrote a long preamble to the enabling act, including these excerpts:

World wide economic depression has brought about unemployment of and distress to the citizens of the state. Their savings and reserves are becoming depleted. Hunger marches. Discontent, social unrest, and incipient insurrection exist. Acts of insurrection are occurring. The moral resistance of the people is declining. Government itself is imperiled and must be protected and preserved.

. . . .

A critical emergency, calling for constructive action is presented; otherwise catastrophe impends. Pauperizing relief is unsatisfactory and inadequate. It is imperative that existing unemployment and distress be in some measure allayed. The citizenry of the state must have opportunity for self-support. So, only, is democracy safe. This obligation is upon the state. Legislation is essential for its fulfillment.[13]

When the court was called upon to consider this act, it held that under a reasonable interpretation the term "suppress insurrection" would include action designed to *prevent* insurrection, and that under conditions then existing, the issuance of bonds for relief might reasonably be expected to prevent insurrection. It specifically condemned the idea that the legislature would have to wait until violence or bloodshed developed before it could act to suppress insurrection. There was a strong dissenting opinion.[14] Apparently, this was the only case in which relief borrowing was permitted under such a provision. Michigan voters refused to approve an issue of "incipient insurrection" bonds for relief purposes.

Forms and Maturities

All relief bonds except the small amounts issued by Nevada and Tennessee were serial in form. This was due, no doubt, both to the popularity of serial bonds and to the fact that many of the bonds were of comparatively short duration. It is proper that bonds of this type should have short maturities since they are used to meet a temporary emergency which may recur before many years. Seven

13. *Laws,* 1933, c. 65.
14. *State* v. *Martin,* 173 Wash. 249 (1933).

of the fifteen states have adhered to this principle and have so arranged their maturity schedules that all relief bonds will mature by 1943. The others, however, have spread maturities over longer periods, and in three states the last bonds will not mature until after 1950. It is quite probable that unemployment may again become a serious problem before those bonds are finally paid. By 1938 approximately 25 per cent of all relief bonds sold had been retired.

Source of Debt Service Funds

When the states were issuing relief bonds, they were hard pressed for revenues. Such new revenue sources as could be discovered were needed to meet current expenditures. For this reason the tendency was to provide for servicing the bonds from the general fund or from the proceeds of some existing tax. The gasoline or motor fuel tax was one of the most productive and stable taxes levied by the states, and several pledged it for debt service. In some instances there was an additional reason for this action in that relief projects were designated to improve highways. This was also a convenient way in which to place the burden of the debts upon local governments in case they received a part of the highway funds. Approximately $96,000,000 of the bonds outstanding in 1938 were serviced from highway funds.

AID TO LOCAL GOVERNMENTS

On several occasions in recent years various states have used their credit for the benefit of local governments, usually by borrowing funds and reloaning them to such units. Typically, such action has been taken to give aid in emergencies, to encourage some activity by the local units, or to solve administrative problems rather than for the sole purpose of obtaining lower interest rates for the local units. The more important examples of such borrowing are discussed below.

Massachusetts

Massachusetts has borrowed over a longer period of time, more continuously, and in larger amounts for this purpose than any other state. Beginning in 1889, the state borrowed large sums to finance water, sewer, and park projects in the area covered by forty-three cities and towns in the vicinity of Boston. Bonds have been sold also for the building and improvement of the Cambridge Subway and the development of the Charles River Basin. In 1919 several boards were consolidated into the Metropolitan District under the supervision of one commission.[15] Bonds sold for the benefit of this district make up most of the "Contingent Debt" of the state, which in recent years has constituted from two thirds to four fifths of the total gross debt of the state. In 1931 the gross direct debt was $22,179,575 and the gross contingent debt, $98,657,287; in 1938 the figures were $45,288,646 and $113,892,766, respectively. The contingent debt is serviced from taxes levied on property within the Metropolitan District.

Recently Massachusetts has borrowed funds and reloaned them to local units for several other purposes, including relief, as noted above. To aid units which had been forced to take title to property for delinquent taxes, a 1933 act authorized the treasurer to issue up to $25,000,000 of state notes and to loan the proceeds against such titles. Subject to the approval of the State Emergency Finance Board, local units could borrow up to the full amount of such titles to meet current expenditures, giving one-year notes in return. Collections on the titles are remitted to the state, and any excess of interest earned over interest paid by the state is distributed to the borrowing units in proportion to amounts borrowed.[16] For the past several years the state has issued annually $17,000,000 of one-year notes for this purpose.

North Carolina

Between 1921 and 1928 North Carolina borrowed $17,500,000 and reloaned it to the counties, at the rate of interest borne by the bonds, to encourage the building of better schoolhouses. On June 30, 1938, $10,085,000 of such bonds remained outstanding, while the state held county notes amounting to $7,330,429. Sixteen counties were delinquent on principal payments to the amount of $235,417, and thirteen counties were delinquent on interest payments in the amount of $76,541.

15. *Acts,* 1919, c. 350.   16. *Acts,* 1933, c. 49.

Mississippi

In 1928-29 Mississippi sold $1,961,000 of bonds bearing 4½ per cent interest and with the proceeds bought a similar amount of bonds bearing the same rate of interest issued by four counties in the Delta region of the state. The purpose was to aid the counties in repairing the damage wrought by the 1927 flood. Maturities and interest payments on the county bonds were synchronized with those of the state bonds, and it was not expected that the state would have to provide any funds for servicing the bonds. One of the counties defaulted on several payments and in 1934 was allowed to refund its bonds into 4 per cent term bonds maturing in 1959. The state bonds mature serially to 1953. One other county has defaulted for short periods of time on small payments, but the other two counties have met their obligations promptly. On June 30, 1938, $1,503,000 of the Delta Rehabilitation Bonds were outstanding.[17]

Oregon

In 1919 Oregon voters approved a constitutional amendment permitting the state to pay the interest on bonds of irrigation and drainage districts for the first five years. Some fifteen districts were formed, and almost all of them experienced financial difficulties; thirteen defaulted on their obligations. Before the amendment was repealed in 1930 the state had paid interest, through issuing state bonds, to the amount of $2,172,760. In 1933 the legislature authorized the cancellation of this debt of the districts to the state if they could reach agreements with their other creditors which would reduce their debts to amounts which they could carry.[18] It is estimated that the venture will eventually cost the state a total of $4,327,876.[19]

Minnesota

In 1927 and 1929 the Minnesota legislature passed special acts permitting distressed municipalities to refund their debts. As further aid, a 1933 act authorized the State Board of Investment to

17. *Mississippi's Public Debt History, 1798-1938* (an unpublished MS by P. L. Guyton), pp. 72-74, 91; *Laws*, 1928, c. 88.

18. *General Laws*, 1933, c. 242.   19. *Moody's*, 1939, p. 1512.

purchase up to 50 per cent of such refunding bonds, issuing state certificates of indebtedness to provide funds.[20] The municipalities were authorized to issue special bonds to be purchased by the board. Such bonds might bear a rate of interest lower than those sold on competitive bids, but from ¼ per cent to 1 per cent higher than the rate on the state certificates sold by the board. State certificates outstanding on January 1, 1938, amounted to $2,314,500. No detailed statement of the fund's experience is available, but its receipts are running slightly below expenditures.

Conclusion

The above are the only examples of this type of borrowing on which information is available. The governor of New Jersey, in 1931-32, proposed the establishment of a state fund of $20,000,000 to aid the many municipalities in that state which could not meet debt service requirements, but the plan failed. Except for Massachusetts the states have been sparing in the use of their credit for the benefit of local governments, and have confined their aid to special and emergency situations. This is perhaps desirable, for extensive use of the device would create grave dangers of abuse and would require the states to extend their control over the finances of local units far beyond the present scope and perhaps farther than would be desirable. In their limited experience the states have been fairly successful, especially in view of the unfavorable conditions which prevailed in most cases.

HARBOR IMPROVEMENTS

Several states have incurred debts for the construction of docks, piers, wharves, and other harbor improvements, but only three states have borrowed on a scale to justify mention. The harbor debts of these three are discussed briefly in this section.

Alabama

In 1923 Alabama voters amended their constitution to permit the issue of $10,000,000 of bonds for harbor improvements at Mobile. The bonds are payable out of the receipts from the state docks, but

20. *Laws*, 1933, c. 389.

general revenues may be used if such receipts are inadequate. In recent years they have been serviced from the general fund. The full amount of bonds was issued, of which $9,325,000 were outstanding in September, 1938. During the past ten years net receipts from the docks have not been sufficient to service the bonds, and the state has had to provide for an average annual deficit of approximately $200,000.[21] Since annual debt service requirements were approximately $500,000, this means that approximately 40 per cent of the debt is a charge on the general funds of the state.

California

Between 1919 and 1938 California borrowed $10,450,000 for improvements at the port of San Francisco. The port is operated by the Board of State Harbor Commissioners, which "derives its income from charges for tolls, dockage, demurrage, rentals, switching, etc. The current expense of the port and the State Belt Railroad, and interest on outstanding bonded indebtedness, are paid out of income; and provision is also made therefrom for the redemption of the bonds at maturity."[22] In recent years the board has had an income of approximately $2,750,000 per year, but apparently before the deduction of depreciation charges. The income has been sufficient to cover all expenses and debt service charges and leave a small surplus. Harbor improvement bonds outstanding in July, 1938, amounted to $19,303,000, against which a sinking fund of $2,428,548 had been accumulated.

Louisiana

The Board of Commissioners of the Port of New Orleans operates the port of New Orleans and has the power to issue general obligations of the state of Louisiana. As a subsidy the board receives the proceeds from 0.45 of one cent of the gasoline tax. Receipts from the source, in 1937 and 1938, averaged about $1,000,000 per year. A constitutional amendment adopted in 1928 empowers the board to create industrial districts and to raise funds therefor

21. *Moody's*, 1939, pp. 111-112.
22. *State of California Budget for the Biennium July 1, 1937, to June 30, 1939*, p. 688.

by the issue of revenue bonds. Apparently none of the latter has been issued. From 1919 through 1938 the state sold $25,000,000 of bonds for the benefit of the board; the total of such bonds outstanding on December 1, 1938, was $36,110,000.

After receipt of the gasoline-tax subsidy and before depreciation charges, the board showed a deficit, after debt service payments, of $237,833 in 1937 and a surplus of $5,026 in 1938. Since interest and principal payments on the debt were about $2,500,000 and the tax subsidy about $1,000,000, the board earned, before depreciation charges, only about two fifths of the debt service requirements. But since any reasonable depreciation charge on the $47,000,000 of depreciable assets would amount to more than $1,500,000, the board actually operated at a loss before debt service charges, and hence the whole debt should be considered as a charge on the general revenues of the state.[23]

WARRANTS AND FUNDING BONDS

Most state debts are incurred according to definite plans authorized either by the voters or by the legislature. Occasionally, however, substantial debts are created by the practice of allowing current deficits to accumulate either in the form of unpaid warrants, which may or may not bear interest, or in the form of funding bonds which are issued periodically to cover the deficits. The more important examples of such debts are discussed in this section. While the constitutional aspects of warrant debts are treated more fully in a later chapter, the question cannot be entirely avoided here.

Kentucky

Kentucky has had a substantial warrant debt for about thirty years. In 1909 warrants outstanding amounted to $550,539. In the ensuing years expenditures increased more rapidly than revenues, with the result that outstanding warrants rose to $5,451,689 in 1918. Thereafter steps were taken to increase revenues, and for the next ten years the amount of warrants fluctuated widely from a low of about $3,500,000 in 1919 to a high of about $11,325,000 in

23. *Moody's,* 1939, pp. 560-561.

1925.[24] When the treasurer did not have sufficient funds to pay warrants as they were presented, he stamped them, and thereafter they bore interest at 5 per cent until paid.

The Kentucky constitution provides that the state may not incur a debt in excess of $500,000 without the approval of the voters. In 1916, however, the legislature attempted to fund the warrants without such approval. The act provided that the Board of Sinking Fund Commissioners might sell one-year tax-anticipation certificates up to 100 per cent of estimated revenues and also call in all warrants having no maturity dates and issue new 5 per cent, five-year warrants to be sold to the highest bidder at public sale. The state supreme court ruled that, while ordinary warrants were not debts within the meaning of the constitution, the proposed certificates and warrants would be, and hence that the act was unconstitutional.[25]

In 1922 the voters rejected a proposal to issue a total of $75,-000,000 of bonds, including $6,000,000 to fund the warrants. Another proposal, including $4,000,000 of funding bonds, was defeated in 1926.[26]

After 1930 the volume of warrants increased rapidly because of a sharp decline in state revenues, reaching a peak of over $21,-000,000 in 1935. Undeterred by previous reverses, the legislature in 1932 attempted again to fund the warrants without a vote of the people.[27] The enabling act stated that outstanding warrants were "valid debts" of the state which might be funded according to constitutional provisions without a vote of the people, and authorized the treasurer to issue $14,000,000 of serial bonds for that purpose. The court faced a difficult dilemma; if it ruled that the warrants were debts and thus fundable without a popular vote, it would logically be forced to rule that all above $500,000 were invalid because they had been issued in violation of the constitution. On the other hand, if it held that they were not debts, it would logically follow that the state was not obligated to pay them. The court

24. Allen B. Edwards, *A History of the Kentucky State Debt* (an unpublished thesis in the Duke University Library, Durham, N. C., 1939), p. 68.

25. *Stanley* v. *Townsend*, 170 Ky. 833 (1916).

26. Edwards, *op. cit.*, pp. 38-39.   27. *Acts*, 1932, c. 20.

cut the Gordian knot by holding that the warrants were "valid assignments of . . . appropriations, or orders on the treasury . . . valid evidences of casual deficits" but that they were not debts.

"Debt" or "debts" as used [in the constitution] mean an obligation entered into in strict accordance with the provisions of those sections binding the Commonwealth to pay it by the levy and collection of general taxes. . . . A contingent liability is not within the meaning of the Constitution, . . . nor are "casual deficits" debts within such limit. . . . the warrants . . . are orders on the treasury of the state and are both valid and collectible and are to be paid . . . whenever sufficient funds are in the treasury for that purpose. . . . It is an inexorable duty of the Legislature to provide . . . for the payment . . . of the warrants.[28]

Defeated by both the people and the courts, the legislature took no further action, and the warrants continued to accumulate. In December, 1935, the Chandler administration took office, pledged to tax reform and a refinancing of the debt. After many difficulties, tax revenues were increased, and the state initiated a program of refunding the 5 per cent warrants into new 3 per cent warrants to be sold to the highest bidder at public sale. The court approved the program,[29] and the new warrants were easily sold at handsome premiums. By March 15, 1937, all old warrants had been refunded into new warrants at a substantial saving in interest to the state. This reduction in expenditures, together with increased tax revenues, permitted the state to reduce the amount of warrants. By May, 1939, the amount outstanding had been reduced to $6,-310,700.[30]

California

California's warrant debt grew out of the depression. When the treasurer became unable to pay warrants as they were presented, the legislature authorized him to register such warrants and pay interest on them at the rate of 5 per cent.[31] The court upheld this act, stating that the issuance of warrants did not "create an indebted-

28. State Budget Commission v. Lebus, 244 Ky. 700, 710-711 (1932).
29. Bankers Bond Co. v. Buckingham, 265 Ky. 712 (1936).
30. Edwards, op. cit., pp. 47-48, 69.   31. Statutes, 1933, c. 605.

ness or liability within the meaning of the debt limitation clause."[32] The net warrant debt of the general fund increased rapidly, reaching $22,168,337 in 1935 and $46,577,887 in 1936. In an effort to provide a cheaper and more orderly system of financing, the legislature, in 1935, proposed a constitutional amendment allowing the state to borrow on one-year tax-anticipation notes up to 50 per cent of the revenues of the preceding year, but the voters rejected it.

In 1937 the state initiated a program, similar to Kentucky's, of paying old 5 per cent warrants from the proceeds for new warrants sold at public sale at much lower rates of interest. The new warrants ran from three to six months, and the state offered several issues every month. As the system became established, the interest rate declined from $1\frac{1}{4}$ per cent to as low as $\frac{1}{2}$ per cent about the middle of 1938, representing a large saving to the state. In September, 1938, however, Mr. Downey, who advocated liberal old-age pensions, won the nomination for United States Senator, and the interest rate on warrants suddenly jumped to 3 per cent. It has remained comparatively high since that time. On July 3, 1938, outstanding warrants amounted to $37,178,077. The outbreak of the European war and the "Ham and Eggs" campaign in the fall of 1939 raised the interest rate on the warrants to 4 per cent and for a time almost completely stopped the sale of refunding warrants. Such incidents illustrate the dangers and the expense of maintaining a floating debt in this form.

Montana

On two occasions Montana has issued bonds to fund warrants, and each time the state supreme court had to face the same question that was raised in Kentucky. In 1925 the court upheld an act of the legislature authorizing the issue of $3,750,000 of treasury notes to fund warrants, stating that "These warrants evidence a valid outstanding indebtedness of the State, both morally and legally binding upon us, and must be paid in some manner." In meeting the contention that if the warrants were debts they were invalid because they had been issued in excess of the constitutional limit of $100,000, the court probably came as near as any court ever

32. *Riley* v. *Johnson,* 219 Calif. 513, 520-521 (1933).

came to declaring that it was reversing the constitution. It stated: "This is the interpretation of our constitution 'by the spirit which vivifies and not by the letter which killeth.' "[33]

A $4,500,000 issue of funding bonds were authorized and sold in 1933, to fund warrants which had been accumulating for about ten years. The court upheld this act by the same reasoning used in 1925.[34] In 1938, $3,696,000 of these bonds were still outstanding. This position of the court allows the state to borrow any amount that it wishes, without a vote of the people, merely by allowing the debt to accumulate first in the form of warrants.

Other States

In 1935 the Oklahoma legislature authorized the issue of two series of bonds to fund outstanding warrants. Series A bonds were to be exchanged directly for warrants, while Series B bonds were to be sold for cash and the proceeds used to pay warrants. Series A amounted to about $7,000,000, while Series B totaled $3,100,000. The court approved the act on the ground that the issuance of the bonds did not increase the debt of the state but merely exchanged one form of debt for another.[35] A similar issue of approximately $18,000,000 was approved and sold in 1939.[36]

For many years Texas has had outstanding large amounts of warrants on which no interest is paid. On August 31, 1936, the gross amount was $17,738,687; two years later it had increased to $24,605,130. The net amount in 1938—the gross amount less cash held in the funds issuing warrants—was $18,269,835. A large majority was issued by the General Fund, and almost all the remainder by the Confederate Pension Fund. A call by the state treasurer on December 5, 1938, indicates the delay experienced in the redemption of state warrants. He called for payment at that time a part of the general fund warrants written between August 31, 1937, and August 31, 1938. Warrants against the Confederate Pension Fund written before March, 1938, were to be paid if they had not been discounted; those which had been discounted were to be

---

33. *Toomey v. State Board of Examiners*, 74 Mont. 1, 23 (1925).
34. *State v. Erickson*, 93 Mont. 466 (1933).
35. *In re State Funding Bonds of 1935, Series A*, 173 Okla. 622 (1935).
36. *In re State Treasury Note Indebtedness*, 90 P. (2d) 19 (1939).

paid only if they were written before March, 1937.[37] Those who receive payments from the two funds have the choice of waiting several months for their money or of selling their warrants for what they will bring. In this way the state forces its employees, pensioners, and other payees to pay interest on the state debt.

Along with several other states, Texas owes a fairly large debt to various trust funds. From time to time as funds have accrued to state agencies and institutions, the state has taken the funds and given in return its promise to pay. In Texas the promises have frequently taken the form of manuscript bonds. The state has been negligent about servicing such bonds. On August 31, 1938, the amount of such obligations outstanding was $4,102,000, of which $787,500 were past due; accrued interest amounted to $540,567.[38]

Georgia has developed a unique system of short-term borrowing based upon an unusual type of warrant or certificate. The state owns the Western and Atlantic Railroad, which is now leased for a net monthly rental of $45,000. A law enacted in 1921 enables the governor to anticipate or discount receipts from this source by writing warrants against future monthly rentals, depositing them with a trustee, and then issuing and selling certificates representing full ownership of the warrants. The certificates are not full faith and credit obligations of the state, but rest entirely upon the rental income. The state supreme court has held that such action by the governor does not create a state debt nor does it violate the constitutional provision requiring that the proceeds from the sale of state property be used to pay the state debt.[39] In November, 1938, $5,985,000 of certificates were outstanding, representing the discounting of all state rental income through the year 1949. On December 5, 1938, the R.F.C. held $3,240,000 of such warrant certificates.

Funding Bonds

Several other states have issued substantial amounts of funding bonds in order to cover deficits. In 1934 Alabama sold $16,765,750 of such bonds to pay a deficit which had accumulated over several

37. *Moody's*, 1939, p. 1530.   38. *Loc. cit.*
39. *Wright* v. *Hardwick*, 152 Ga. 302 (1921).

years. Between 1919 and 1938 North Carolina sold $26,180,531 of funding bonds, most of them in 1934 and 1935 to cover a depression deficit. From 1932 to 1937 Tennessee experienced a deficit every year and had to borrow $18,318,000. Mississippi, too, had many deficits and borrowed, during the twenty years, a total of $13,-731,500 on funding bonds. Connecticut sold $15,000,000 of such bonds in 1938. Louisiana and South Carolina borrowed $4,000,000 and $5,730,000, respectively, to cover deficits. Several other states borrowed small amounts, but the above represent a large majority of all deficit funding.

CHAPTER XV

ARKANSAS, A STATE THAT BORROWED TOO MUCH

ARKANSAS WAS the only state which defaulted on its debt during the Great Depression. The developments which led to that default, the measures taken by the state to readjust its debt, and the subsequent management of the debt provide abundant material for a case study of state borrowing. This chapter provides an outline and a brief discussion of that material.

ORIGIN OF THE PROBLEM

Arkansas borrowed principally for highways. The origin of its debt troubles is found in the system of local highway finance which prevailed before 1927. The state was slow to assume the burden of highway finance which consequently devolved upon local governments. But the state constitution prohibited counties from borrowing except for refunding. As a result, local "improvement" districts were created to perform those functions which required borrowing.

The Alexander Road Law

After many road districts had been created by special acts, a general statute, known as "The Alexander Road Law," was enacted in 1915 providing uniform procedure for the formation of road improvement districts without legislative action.[1] A district could be formed only on the petition of landowners representing a majority in number, acreage, or land value in the region affected. Assessments had to be in proportion to benefits, and debts could not exceed 30 per cent of assessed land values. Means were provided for hearing protests and appeals against either the formation of districts or assessments. County courts passed upon petitions and chartered the districts. By the end of 1916, one hundred and twenty districts had been formed under the act.

1. *Acts*, 1915, Act 338.

Special Charters in 1919-20

The procedure of the Alexander Law did not suit some individuals who had ulterior motives or ideas different from those of their neighbors. Such persons persuaded the legislature to pass a large number of special acts creating road districts. The regular 1919 session created 133 new districts, and a special session filled two thick volumes with charters. A court decision, however, held void all the acts passed at the special session. Another special session in 1920 created 140 districts and amended many other acts. From 1913 to 1920, 504 special acts were passed, creating 312 districts, exclusive of the invalid acts of 1919.[2]

Those acts were passed without the consent, and sometimes without the knowledge, of property owners in the districts being created. One act was passed over the protests of 90 per cent of such owners. District commissioners were given dictatorial powers; they could create debts and levy assessments as they chose. They were not liable for mistakes or negligence, but only for wilful misconduct. Provisions for hearing protests and appeals were inadequate. Some districts overlapped, subjecting property owners to two road assessments. The commissioners were not bonded and kept few, if any, records of the funds which passed through their hands.[3] "Even when they were honest, intelligent citizens, as most of them were, they knew nothing of the problems of road building or of road financing. When they were dishonest or incompetent, as too frequently they were, the affairs of the district suffered, poor construction resulted, bad financing took place, costs ran into excessive figures, and graft took its share."[4]

There was little state supervision, so the commissioners built roads as they chose, of varying width and quality. If roads in the different districts connected, it was largely accidental. Maintenance was left to the counties which usually spent "available revenue on roads in worse condition than those of the road improvement dis-

2. R. Murray Havens, *History of Financing of Public Highways in Arkansas* (an unpublished thesis in the University of Kansas Library, Lawrence, 1933), p. 46.
3. *Chronicle,* CXII (1921), 21; T. H. MacDonald, "The Arkansas Road Finance Situation," *American City,* XXIV (May, 1921), 494-495.
4. Havens, *op. cit.,* p. 26.

tricts." Excessive fees were paid to engineers and lawyers, and road costs were often exorbitant. Concerning the sale of bonds by one district, the state comptroller reported at a later date that "From the evidence at hand one would be justified in concluding that Orthwein and his associates (if any) [who handled the bonds] were the ones issuing the bonds, and that the district was receiving small commissions."[5] The governor, in 1921, described it as "the most vicious system of special taxation ever enacted in any State in the Union."[6]

Reaction, 1920-21

There was a pronounced reaction in 1920-21. Heavy taxes to service district bonds were levied just when cotton prices and land values collapsed. Rumors of extravagance and graft were circulating. Several districts defaulted on their bonds. In one district, property owners used their shotguns to force road commissioners to resign. In 1921 the legislature abolished many districts, but none which had incurred debts. The Secretary of Agriculture ordered an investigation, charging incompetency, inefficiency, and unsatisfactory maintenance. He threatened to suspend federal aid unless better maintenance was provided and state supervision increased. The legislature adjourned without taking any action to meet the Secretary's criticisms.

The Harrelson Act

In January, 1923, the Secretary of Agriculture suspended federal aid until certain conditions were met. Again the legislature adjourned without acting to correct the situation. The governor called a special session which met in September, 1923, and enacted a new road law, known as the "Harrelson Act." The highway commission was reorganized with increased powers and charged with the construction and maintenance of state highways. A state highway fund was established, to receive the proceeds from the automobile and gasoline taxes, which were increased substantially. From this fund $3,000,000 was to be distributed to local units.[7] More than half of

5. *Report*, 1934, p. 17.
6. *Chronicle, loc. cit.*   7. *Acts*, Ex. Sess., 1923, Act 5.

this sum went to the districts for debt service, while less than half went to the counties for maintenance and construction. The districts had to meet maturing obligations of about $6,000,000 per year. In 1926 and 1927 the state spent about $1,500,000 per year on construction. The highway fund was showing a steady increase, and with good management the state would have had a decent road system in time.

There were, however, several dissatisfied groups in the state. One of these was the property owners in the districts, who wished to be relieved of highway taxes. As other states developed special highway revenues, it became apparent that the districts had acted too hastily in trying to build roads on the basis of property taxes. Another dissatisfied group comprised those who lived in counties where no roads had been built by improvement districts. These and other interested groups soon forced the state to increase the scope of its highway activities. A measure requiring the state to assume all district road debts was defeated by a narrow margin in 1925. In 1927 such a measure passed easily as part of a more ambitious program by the state.

THE BORROWING PROGRAM

Probably no state ever embarked upon a more ambitious borrowing program, in relation to its resources, than did Arkansas in 1927. The debt was to be incurred primarily for two purposes: highways and Confederate pensions.

The Highway Program

The first step in the highway program was to assume the debts of the road districts. The section of the act relating to those debts was loosely drawn and was several times amended. It did not formally assume the bonds, but merely appropriated from the highway fund $6,500,000 per year to be allocated to the districts, which were required to reduce their road taxes proportionately.[8] The amount of bonds assumed under this section and its various amendments was $70,556,000.

----

8. *Acts*, 1927, Act 11, sec. 3. This act is commonly known as the "Martineau Act."

The second step in highway financing was to authorize the sale of $13,000,000 of bonds per year for four years to provide construction funds. Construction was to begin in those counties in which few roads had been built by the districts in order to bring them up to "parity" before proceeding with a state-wide program. The gasoline tax was raised from four to five cents per gallon, and all highway revenues were pledged as security for the bonds. The state promised that the laws levying those taxes would never, so long as the bonds were outstanding, "be repealed or amended so as to in any manner reduce the revenue therein provided for." It further pledged to maintain highway revenues at a minimum of $7,500,000 and that it would not sell more highway bonds than could be serviced by such sum.[9] Another act empowered the highway commission to issue bonds, without any stated limit, to build toll bridges, while still another provided for aid to municipal improvement districts in the construction of streets which formed parts of the state highway system.[10]

Confederate Pensions

For several years prior to 1927 Arkansas had levied a two-mill property tax for Confederate pensions, which had yielded about $1,150,000 per year. In its orgy of borrowing, the legislature approved $14,000,000 of bonds to raise additional funds in the declining years of the veterans and dependents. The bonds were to be sold in amounts declining from $3,000,000 in 1927 to $750,000 in 1933; they did not begin to mature until 1934.[11] They were to be serviced from the proceeds of the two-mill tax.

Resources and Credit Rating

Excluding the bridge bonds, these acts committed Arkansas to the creation or assumption of a debt of $126,000,000 within six years, or approximately 5 per cent of the total estimated wealth of the state as of 1922. Arkansas has long been a poor state; it ranked forty-second in per capita wealth in 1922 with $1,439, and forty-sixth in

9. *Ibid.*, secs. 4 and 5.
10. *Acts*, 1927, Acts 104 and 184.   11. *Ibid.*, Acts 20 and 178.

per capita income in 1929 with $279.[12] This program alone would create a state debt of approximately $69 per capita.

For the five years 1923-27, average state revenues from all sources had been $14,200,000, while highway revenues in those years had averaged $5,288,000. In 1926, for the first time, highway revenues exceeded $7,000,000.[13] Now the state was embarked upon a program which would require the highway fund to pay interest on a debt of $52,000,000 and to remit to the road districts $6,500,000 per year for several years, while the general fund was servicing an additional debt of over $15,000,000. The proposed new debt was nearly nine times the average gross revenues of the state for the preceding five years.

The credit rating of the state is indicated by an analysis which appeared just about the time the state was starting its program. It concluded that the state was trying to

. . . get along without paying enough taxes to cover its expenses and using every financial expedient they can find in order to "get by." The debt provisions of its constitution look very conservative but because of their impracticability they have encouraged a type of "high finance" which is most objectionable.

.   .   .   .

It has had and continues to have a somewhat hectic financial career. Its record of repudiation is not reassuring nor are its financial practices during the last half century. The State has consistently spent more money than it raised by taxation resulting in funding operations as well as in the use of money from the various educational trust funds for general state purposes. Its people have an apparent horror of paying interest but are not willing to pay taxes sufficient to furnish what they demand without borrowing. . . . The people are trying to follow a pay-as-you-go policy without paying. . . . There is nothing to be proud of in this record. . . . Nothing but a fairly complete revolution in financial policy will correct the situation.[14]

12. Robert R. Doane, "The Geographic Distribution of the Physical Wealth of the United States," *Annalist,* XLVI (Nov. 15, 1935), 676; Robert R. Nathan and John L. Martin, *State Income Payments, 1929-37* (Washington: Department of Commerce, 1939), p. 6.

13. *Comptroller's Biennial Report,* 1932, p. 21.

14. National Association of Mutual Savings Banks, *Critical Analysis of State Debts* (New York, 1927), p. 14.

8

ARKANSAS' DEBT 389

The report characterized the attitude of the people as "a somewhat cynical regard for ordinary good faith."

Bond Sales

With such a background, it was small wonder that the bonds did not sell readily. A banking syndicate bought the first $13,000,000 of 4½ per cent bonds on March 17, 1927, and offered them to the public to yield from 4.05 to 4.10 per cent. They were later repriced to yield 4.25 per cent. In early August the syndicate was dissolved with $8,000,000 unsold; the bonds were again repriced to yield 4.40 per cent.[15] Before this issue was finally sold, however, the highway commission was requesting an increase in the amounts authorized, stating that otherwise it could not undertake any new projects before March, 1928.

As the state began to spend freely, additional demands for funds came from many quarters. A special session of the legislature met in September, 1928, and increased the amount of highway bonds which might be sold to $18,000,000 per year, set $7,500,000 as a limit for toll bridge bonds, and amended the section assuming the district bonds.[16] A 1929 act entirely removed the limit on highway bonds except for the provision that they should not exceed an amount which could be serviced by $7,500,000 per year. It was estimated that this would allow the state to incur a highway debt of about $105,-000,000. This meant that the state was contemplating an eventual debt of approximately $177,000,000 as follows: highway debt, $105,-000,000; district debt, $47,000,000; toll bridge bonds, $7,500,000; Confederate pension bonds, $14,000,000; old and miscellaneous debt, $3,500,000. This would have amounted to about $95 per capita.

In May, 1928, $13,000,000 of highway bonds bearing 4½ per cent were sold at a small premium, but thereafter all bonds bore 4¾ or 5 per cent. By May, 1931, a total of $91,500,000 highway and bridge bonds had been sold. On $49,000,000 of highway bonds sold through 1929, the state realized a total premium of $389,000, but on the $35,000,000 sold thereafter it took discounts of $627,000 disguised as fiscal agents' fees.[17] In the meantime the Confederate pension bonds

15. *Chronicle*, CXXVII (1927), 712-713.
16. *Acts*, Ex. Sess., 1928, Acts 5, 6, 8.   17. Havens, *op. cit.*, p. 101.

were being sold at about the same rates of interest. Only $9,450,000 of the authorized $14,000,000 had been sold when the state's credit collapsed in 1931 and rendered further sales impossible. Table 33 shows the increase in the debt.

Assumption of District Debts

The assumption of the road district debts was the occasion of much trouble and many shady transactions. The legislature passed so many amendments and special acts affecting the districts that it is impossible to describe clearly the course of events. Under certain conditions, districts in or near towns or cities could continue to operate and be reimbursed for half of their expenses by the county or state. An act of 1929 provided for payment by the state of un-funded claims against districts incurred before January 1, 1927.[18] Considering the conditions of the district records, this was almost an open invitation to graft. In 1934 the state comptroller reported that "To what extent the Highway Fund was preyed upon in con-sequence of Act 153 of 1929, could only be determined by making a detailed audit of scores of transactions," but that $691,604 had been paid on claims which, it had been estimated, would not exceed $178,000.[19]

Many suburban improvement districts were primarily real estate development projects, with power to pave streets, to lay gutters and sidewalks, and to construct and operate utilities. The Commissioner

TABLE 33

SUMMARY OF THE ARKANSAS STATE DEBT, 1926-38

(In thousands of dollars)

Description	June 30, 1926	June 30, 1928	June 30, 1930	Dec. 1, 1932	Nov. 30, 1934	Dec. 31, 1936	Dec. 31, 1938
Highway Bonds	$......	$ 26,000	$ 58,000	$ 84,000 ⎫			
Toll Bridge Bonds	....	....	5,000	7,220 ⎬	$152,963	$148,267	$141,895
Road District Bonds	....	....	48,305	46,017	53,489 ⎭		
Confederate Pension Bonds	....	3,000	7,600	9,442	9,284	8,724	8,029
School Revolving Loan Bonds	....	....	500	1,000	1,000	1,000	925
Agricultural Credit Bonds	....	....	....	1,375	981	581	345
Miscellaneous Bonds	3,126	3,253	3,352	3,770	5,329	3,970	3,988
Totals	$ 3,126	$ 80,558	$120,469	$160,294	$168,019	$163,280	$155,280

18. Acts, 1927, Acts 184 and 359; ibid., 1929, Act 153.
19. Report, 1934, p. 16.

of Highways had used such districts in developing his suburban properties near Little Rock. Of seventeen such districts, which had issued over $2,000,000 of bonds, only one had any part of its construction included within the state highway system, but the state assumed nearly all of the bonds. "Six of the districts were organized so shortly before the passage of the act authorizing the assumption of road improvement district obligations that there was considerable doubt as to their right to participate in state aid."[20] In several cases the bonds had not been printed on the date specified for assumption, although the districts had acknowledged their receipt. The affairs of the districts and of the corporations which directed their financing and construction were all handled together under the direction of the commissioner.

The service of the assumed bonds was the largest expense of the highway fund, amounting to $34,068,707 for the years from 1928 through 1932. Because of the heavy maturities of such bonds in this period the highway bonds sold by the state did not begin to mature until 1935.

Administration of the Program

The state financial officers seem to have been intoxicated by the large amount of money suddenly placed at their disposal. Carelessness and extravagance were general, and petty graft was all too frequent. The *Comptroller's Report* for 1934—a remarkable document in several respects—contains many vague and general charges of inefficiency and dishonesty and a few specific examples of petty thievery. For example: "In most matters of this kind, there is a little inside ring of shady sharpshooters who have contact with the actors. If you are a member of this soulless symphony there is prompt consideration. If outside the happy circle or a stranger to the 'touch' you get the glassy stare of silence; nothing more. But, at that period in the State's progression, money came from bonds, and bonds there were in plenty. It was an era of prodigality, an interlude of fortune."[21] In one specific instance "There was the impressive payment of $21,714.13, four hundred dollars of which was honestly administered, while $21,300 went haywire. Proper pay-

20. Havens, *op. cit.*, p. 127.   21. *Report*, 1934, p. 17.

ments were 1.8 per cent of the warrant; 'cut-ins' were 98.2 per cent."[22]

A special audit of highway affairs was ordered by the legislature in 1931. The audit committee severely criticized the method used by the highway commission in placing contracts and estimated that "had these contracts been awarded as provided by law there would have been a saving of four million dollars." It also estimated that the state had, under the 1929 act, paid questionable claims against the districts to the amount of more than $500,000.[23] Apparently, however, no action was taken against any individual on any of the charges.

Additional Loans Authorized, 1931

Although storm clouds had begun to gather on the state's financial horizon by early 1931, the legislature of that year continued to authorize new loans. New bond issues approved amounted to $7,010,000 as follows: armories, $400,000; agricultural credit board, $1,500,000; educational institutions, $2,050,000; state hospital, $3,060,-000.[24] Also, the highway commission was directed, if sufficient funds were available, to assume the debts of street improvement districts within cities and towns, estimated at about $6,000,000.[25] In addition, an unspecified amount of notes was authorized, the proceeds from which were to be loaned to local units to assist in the payment of teachers' salaries. The amount sold was $2,000,000.

By these acts the state provided for an increase in its debt of over $14,000,000 at a time when the debt structure was already beginning to topple. Not all of the bonds were issued before the state's credit collapsed, but additional obligations incurred amounted to over $10,000,000.

THE CRISIS AND DEFAULT

Through the year 1930 the state faced no difficult financial problem. Gross revenues increased from $18,358,286 in 1926-27 to $22,-458,777 in 1929-30. A major part of the increase was in highway revenues. After 1930, revenues declined to $20,413,015 in 1930-31

22. Ibid., p. 74.   23. Havens, op. cit., pp. 124-125.
24. Acts, 1931, Acts 10, 14, 19, 34, 57, and 70.
25. Ibid., Act 248. The amount eventually assumed was $6,341,584.

and to $17,448,516 in 1931-32. Those amounts were not available for state spending, however, since distributions to counties amounted to $3,794,313 in the former year and $1,283,170 in the latter, leaving, net, approximately $16,600,000 and $16,165,000, respectively.[26]

The Highway Fund

The finances of the highway fund were of particular significance, since most of the debt rested upon it. Roughly speaking, the state was using current highway revenues to pay debt service and borrowing funds for construction. Increasing revenues were adequate to meet the increased debt service requirements through 1930, but when the current revenues began to decline, disaster threatened. Not all highway revenues were available for state purposes, since substantial amounts were returned to the counties. After this and other deductions, the net amounts available to the commission have been computed as follows:

	Gasoline Tax	Auto License Tax	Totals
1927	$4,338,737	$3,524,575	$ 7,863,313
1928	5,578,698	3,666,802	9,245,500
1929	6,617,131	4,055,357	10,672,488
1930	6,761,907	4,139,918	10,901,825
1931	5,686,019	3,369,840	9,055,859
1932	4,660,899	2,747,626	7,408,525

In the same years the interest requirements on highway bonds (there were no maturities in those years) were, respectively: $292,-500, $861,250, $1,712,500, $2,287,500, $3,598,700, and $3,992,500.[27] In addition were the payments on district bonds, averaging about $7,000,000 per year and, in later years, the deficiency on toll bridge bonds which was about $250,000 per year. In the fiscal year 1931-32 debt service payments from the highway fund amounted to $11,111,-508 divided as follows: interest on highway bonds, $3,973,700; payments on district bonds, $6,643,058; toll bridge bonds and interest, $494,750. In late 1932 the comptroller estimated highway debt service

26. *Comptroller's Report*, 1932, pp. 21, 28.
27. *Hubbell* v. *Leonard*, 6 Fed. Supp. 145, 148. The computations were for calendar years.

requirements for the calendar year 1933 at $8,459,573.[28] Revenues
fell far below this figure.

Attempt to Refund District Bonds

In an effort to relieve the strain caused by the heavy maturities
of the district bonds, the legislature in 1932 authorized the refunding
of the district bonds into revenue bonds. The new bonds would
bear 4½ per cent interest compared with an average of 4¾ per cent
paid on the old bonds, and would have a lien on highway revenues
junior only to the highway and toll bridge bonds. Their lien would
rank ahead of road maintenance and operating expenses of the
highway commission. Service on old district bonds not exchanged,
however, would rank eighth. The refunding act pledged the state
to levy sufficient highway taxes to service the bonds at all times, but
did not pledge the faith and credit of the state. Each revenue bond
issued would have a maturity date ten years later than the district
bond for which it was exchanged. The old bonds were not to be
canceled, but were to be held as collateral for the revenue bonds and,
in case of default on the latter, might be reclaimed.[29]

Near the end of 1932 the comptroller reported that $13,000,000
of the district bonds had been exchanged and that $7,000,000 more
were "in sight" for refunding.[30] It was reported in February, 1933,
however, that only $15,000,000 out of $47,000,000 of the district bonds
had been exchanged.[31] Shortly thereafter all highway obligations
were in default.

Defaults

As early as August, 1932, the state defaulted on the payment of
certain district bonds. On March 1, 1933, it defaulted on all highway
obligations by failing to pay $770,500 in interest. No further interest
was paid until 1935. By January 1, 1934, total accrued interest

28. *Comptroller's Report,* 1932, p. 10. The drop from the 1931-32 figures is
explained by the omission of any allowance for principal payments on district bonds.
See the refunding plan described below.

29. *Acts,* 2d Ex. Sess., 1932, Act 15. This act admitted that there was some question about the validity of certain district bonds assumed by the state and provided
that *taxpayers* might bring suit to prevent their exchange for revenue bonds. Apparently the state itself would raise no question concerning their validity.

30. *Report,* 1932, p. 5.   31. *Chronicle,* CXXXVI (1933), 2279.

amounted to $9,174,415 as follows: highway bonds, $4,470,000; toll bridge bonds, $435,835; and district bonds, $4,250,000.[32]

READJUSTMENT

Legislation

When the 1933 legislature met, the state was in the depth of depression. The spending program had come to an abrupt halt. Highways were not being properly maintained, and automobile owners were clamoring for a reduction in the license tax. One of the first acts of the legislature was to reorganize the highway commission, providing for a chairman with a salary of $5,000 per year instead of the $3,000 previously paid. It then proceeded to violate its pledge to holders of highway obligations by: (1) reducing the license tax on automobiles and light trucks by 50 per cent; (2) appropriating $1,000,000 for highway maintenance and placing it ahead of debt service; (3) insuring to counties the proceeds from one cent of the gasoline tax, even though total highway revenues fell below $7,500,000 per year; and, finally, (4) appropriating $16,000 from the highway fund to pay legislators, after making several futile attempts to find the funds elsewhere.[33]

The Ellis Refunding Act

When it became apparent that the state would not be able to service its debt without some adjustments, the legislature authorized the refunding of all highway obligations.[34] The act provided for the refunding of all highway, toll bridge, and district bonds into Arkansas State Bonds bearing 3 per cent interest and payable in twenty-five years. The new bonds would have no specific pledge of, or lien on, any revenues, but were "direct obligations of the state, for the payment of which, principal and interest, the full faith and credit of the State, and all its resources are hereby pledged." Beginning January 1, 1934, the state treasurer was to set aside $125,-000 every three months into a "Bond Refunding Fund" to be used

32. *Comptroller's Report*, 1934, p. 9.

33. *Acts*, 1933, Acts 4, 6, 19, 48, and 73. On all cars over four years old, there was an additional 25 per cent reduction in the license tax.

34. *Ibid.*, Act 167. This was known as the Ellis Act; it was signed by the governor on March 28, 1933.

in the purchase of bonds. A later act appropriated $4,380,000 of highway revenues per year to pay interest and $500,000 per year for the purchase of bonds.[35]

Constitutional Amendments

This session of the legislature proposed two constitutional amendments. The first prohibited any increase in the tax rates then in effect without the approval of the voters or, in emergency, by three fourths of the members of the legislature and limited appropriations in any biennium, for all purposes except highways, Confederate pensions, and debt service, to $2,500,000. The second prohibited the issue of bonds by the state, except for refunding existing debt or valid district bonds, unless approved by the voters.[36] The two amendments were approved in 1934.

Litigation

Bondholders objected strenuously to the refunding act for several reasons: (1) the average interest rate was reduced by more than 35 per cent; (2) the new bonds were not secured by the pledge of any specific revenues; (3) district bonds were placed on a parity with other highway obligations; (4) maturities were extended, in most instances, by several years. A host of suits was begun, involving various phases of the problem. In several cases bondholders requested that receivers be appointed for toll bridges to impound revenues for their benefit, in accordance with the terms of the bonds. The state supreme court ruled that such were suits against the state which could not be maintained.[37] The same court approved the refunding act and dismissed other suits on the grounds that they were actions against the state.[38] Bondholders then sought relief in the federal courts and were successful in obtaining a receiver for at least one of the toll bridges.

35. *Ibid.*, Act 183. An act passed about the same time, however, reappropriated $250,000 of the $500,000 to state hospitals (*ibid.*, Act 270).

36. *Ibid.*, S. J. Res. 1 and 2, pp. 877-880.

37. *Watson* v. *Dodge*, 187 Ark. 1055 (1933). The court had previously ruled that the legislature could not give permission allowing the state to be sued. *Highway Commission* v. *Dodge*, 181 Ark. 539 (1930).

38. *Leonard* v. *Smith*, 187 Ark. 695 (1933).

The states of Connecticut, Nevada, and Pennsylvania protested against the refunding act because of Arkansas bonds which they held for trust funds. Pennsylvania secured permission from the Supreme Court of the United States to bring suit and announced that it would bring action to compel the state to raise the gasoline and motor vehicle tax rates to yield a minimum of $7,500,000 per year, according to its pledge. A special session of the legislature hastily appropriated $60,000 to enable the Refunding Board to "compromise, discharge and adjust any obligations" to be refunded under the act.[39] The state then offered to pay in full all interest on bonds held by other states.

Private bondholders brought other suits in the federal courts, and on November 1, 1933, a federal district court issued an interlocutory injunction restraining the state treasurer from disbursing highway funds except for maintenance. The final decision in this case was rendered shortly afterward. It not only changed the whole refunding policy of the state, but set a precedent which may be of great significance to other states.

Hubbell v. Leonard

The plaintiffs cited the various acts of the state which gave holders of highway obligations a prior lien on highway revenues and the acts of the 1933 legislature which violated those pledges, especially the act which appropriated highway revenues to service the new refunding bonds. They contended that all the latter acts were unconstitutional because they impaired the obligation of the contract in the highway bonds, and asked that the state treasurer be restrained from disbursing highway funds under color of those invalid acts. The defendant state treasurer admitted that the 1933 acts had impaired the obligation of contracts, but contended that the court had no jurisdiction to consider that question until it had decided whether this was a suit against the state. If it was such a suit, the court would have to dismiss the case and could not determine any other question or issue.[40] The court did not agree with

39. *Acts,* Ex. Sess., 1933, Act 12.
40. *Hubbell* v. *Leonard,* 6 Fed. Supp. 145, 151 (1933). By a coincidence, the

this contention, holding that it would first have to determine the validity of the laws in question. If they were unconstitutional "they furnish no protection for the acts of the officer, and hence a suit to enjoin such acts could not be said to be a suit against the state." The court then pointed out that the plaintiffs were not asking for any affirmative action against the state, which would clearly be unconstitutional under the Eleventh Amendment, but were merely seeking to prevent a state official from acting to their detriment under the alleged powers of unconstitutional statutes. Quoting from another case, the court held: "Where state officials, purporting to act under state authority, invade rights secured by the Federal Constitution, they are subject to the process of the federal courts in order that the persons injured may have appropriate relief."[41]

The court then held that when the acts of state officers represent the sovereign will of the state, a suit against them may not be maintained because the state is then the real party, but when such acts are in violation of the sovereign will they may be controlled by injunction or mandamus. It distinguished between the state and the state government, holding that when the government acts within the constitution it represents the state; when it does not so act it is a "lawless usurper."[42] It then ruled that this was not a suit against the state, that the 1933 acts were unconstitutional, and hence that there had been no lawful appropriation of the highway funds to service the new bonds. The state treasurer, accordingly, was forbidden to pay out funds for that purpose.

The state did not choose to appeal the case. Thus private individuals were able, in effect, to sue a state and to tie up its funds. The state faced a grave emergency. Practically none of the old bonds had been exchanged, and obviously no more of them would be exchanged for the state could not now pay interest on them. A special session of the legislature was called to enact another refunding law.

---

judge who heard this case was Judge Martineau, author of the highway act of 1927 under which the bonds had been issued.

41. *Ibid.*, p. 153. The case quoted was *Sterling* v. *Constantin*, 287 U. S. 378 (1932).   42. *Loc. cit.*

The Second Refunding Law

This law was drafted in conference with committees representing bondholders and ran to fifty printed pages, in striking contrast with the simple, five-page law enacted in 1933.[43] Under it all highway obligations were to be refunded. Old highway and toll bridge bonds were to be exchanged par for par, into refunding bonds, "Series A," bearing the same rate of interest and maturing ten years later than the original bonds. Until April 1, 1937, cash payments of interest were to be at the rate of only 3½ per cent, and from April 1, 1937, to April 1, 1939, at the rate of 4 per cent. The difference, together with accrued interest to January 1, 1934, was to be paid in "Series B" bonds, which bore 3¼ per cent interest, were dated at issue, and were to mature in not less than fifteen years. After April 1, 1939, the full interest rate was to be paid in cash.

The assumed district bonds did not receive quite such favorable treatment. The principal was to be refunded into Series A bonds maturing January 1, 1949, and bearing 3 per cent interest, payable entirely in cash. Accrued interest to January 1, 1934, was funded into Series B bonds bearing no interest and maturing January 1, 1949.[44]

In all cases the old bonds were not to be canceled, but were to be held by the state treasurer as collateral and might be reclaimed by the holders of the new bonds in case of default. All new bonds were callable at par and accrued interest on any interest date.

The highway fund, completely reorganized, was to provide the funds to service the new bonds. It was to receive funds from three principal sources. (1) The gasoline tax was raised to 6½ cents per gallon, and 92.3 per cent of the proceeds were appropriated to the highway fund, the other 7.7 per cent going to the county highway fund. (2) Proceeds from the motor vehicle license tax, the rates of which were changed only slightly from those established in 1933, were also devoted to the highway fund. (3) Bridge tolls were to be paid into the highway fund. The state promised not to reduce the rates of the gasoline and automobile taxes so as to reduce the revenues below $8,537,000 per year, and to raise the rates or to levy additional

43. *Acts,* 2d Ex. Sess., 1934, Act 11.   44. *Ibid.,* secs. 6 and 7.

taxes if necessary to keep the yield up to that figure. It also promised
not to sell more bonds than could be serviced from such sum. If revenues of the fund exceed $10,000,000 in any year, the Refunding
Board may determine the definite amount by which the gasoline
tax may be reduced (not exceeding ½ cent per gallon) without
reducing revenues below that figure. The board may then reduce
the rate by one half of such amount; the revenues from the other
half must be transferred to the county highway fund.[45]

The first charge upon the highway fund is 25 per cent, or a
minimum of $2,100,000 per year, for the maintenance of roads
and bridges. The second charge is the interest payments on refunding bonds, including a computed 3 per cent on the non-interest-
bearing Road District Refunding Bonds, Series B. Amounts remaining after those charges go into bond redemption accounts for
the various issues. When certain amounts accumulate in such
accounts, the state treasurer must invite tenders and purchase for
retirement bonds of the respective issues which are offered at lowest prices.[46] The integrity of the highway fund is protected by
the following provision: "The transfer or appropriation of any
money from the State Highway Fund, or from the State Highway
revenues . . . to or for any purpose other than as specified in this
Act, and expenses of collection shall be deemed to be an immediate default on the part of the State with respect to the obligations
authorized to be issued hereunder."[47]

Refunding

This plan was quickly approved by the state supreme court.[48]
It was acceptable to most bondholders, and refunding proceeded
rapidly. By the end of 1936 more than 99 per cent of all issues
except two had been deposited for refunding. The two exceptions
were: one toll bridge issue involving less than $500,000, of which
90.9 per cent had been deposited; and road district bonds, amounting to $46,805,075, of which 94.8 had been deposited.[49]

The debt structure resulting from this refunding spread the

45. *Ibid.*, secs. 48 and 51.   46. *Ibid.*, secs. 37 and 38.
47. *Ibid.*, sec. 2.
48. *Sparling* v. *Refunding Board*, 189 Ark. 189 (1934).
49. *Comptroller's Report*, 1936, p. 12.

burden of debt service over a period of about forty years. There will be no maturities until the fiscal year 1943-44. Before that time annual cash interest requirements rise from about $2,500,000 in the years 1934-37 to $6,016,327 in 1939-43. From 1944 to 1958 total debt service requirements will vary between $6,000,000 and $6,500,-000 except for three years; in the years 1943-44, 1948-49, and 1953-54 heavy maturities will raise them to $12,055,200, $51,620,796, and $16,559,794, respectively. Undoubtedly large issues will have to be refunded in those years, which, in turn, will raise the debt service requirements of later years, as now calculated. From 1959 to 1968 total requirements will be only a little below $6,000,000 per year. From 1969 through 1972 they will be a little over $5,000,000 per year, and thereafter they decline rapidly to $1,325,100 in 1976-77.[50] The total to be paid in principal and interest from 1936 through 1977 is $288,211,960.

RECENT DEBT MANAGEMENT

Revenues

After 1933 highway revenues rose slowly but steadily. Collections from the gasoline tax rose from $7,100,317 in 1934-35 to $8,544,-270 in 1936-37. Other highway revenues increased in proportion, and the total rose from $9,709,913 to $12,047,123 in the same period. After the necessary deductions, amounts available for debt service were $7,266,134, and $9,019,142, respectively. In September, 1934, the treasurer made the first purchases of bonds for retirement. Purchases were made on two occasions in 1935, and since then have been made at intervals of about three months. The average offering price on the early tenders was quite low, and the state was able to purchase bonds at an average discount of over 30 per cent, but in recent years the prices have risen. By the end of 1937 the average discount was not much over 10 per cent.[51] To July 30, 1938, the state had purchased obligations with a par value of $16,-539,934 at a cost of $13,331,425 to effect a saving of $3,208,508.[52] In June, 1939, the par value of all bonds retired by purchase was reported at $19,270,000.

50. *Ibid.,* p. 115.
51. *Financial Analysis State Bonded Indebtedness,* Dec. 31, 1937, p. 13.
52. *Comptroller's Report,* 1936, p. 123; *Moody's,* 1939, p. 147.

Table 34 shows the changes which have taken place in the highway debt in recent years. By devoting approximately 75 per cent of all highway revenues to debt service, the state, aided by the large discounts at which it was able to buy in its bonds, was able to reduce its highway debt by about $16,000,000 from 1934 to 1938.

TABLE 34

CHANGES IN THE ARKANSAS HIGHWAY DEBT, 1934-38

Description	Retired, 1934-36	Outstanding, Dec. 31, 1936	Outstanding, Dec. 31, 1938
Highway Refunding Bonds, Series A .	$1,797,000	$ 82,203,000	$ 79,843,000
Highway Refunding Bonds, Series B .	88,865*	9,067,185	8,715,510
Toll Bridge Refunding Bonds, Series A	867,000	6,353,000	6,097,000
Toll Bridge Refunding Bonds, Series B	41,204*	876,969	842,832
Road District Refunding Bonds, Series A.....................	4,659,800	42,145,275	39,412,825
Road District Refunding Bonds, Series B.....................	1,558,690	2,808,713	2,343,971
Other Obligations.................	550,742	6,719,687	6,517,594
Totals...................	$9,461,632	$150,173,828†	$143,772,732†

*Includes unmatured scrip attached to "A" bonds for which "B" bonds would have been issued.
†The totals do not agree with the figures given in the previous table because of the fact that the amounts given for the "B" bonds include bonds to be issued through 1939.

Attempts to Refund

Under the 1934 refunding plan, no part of highway revenues is available for road construction. Further, taxpayers of the state are irked by the high interest rates paid on the refunding bonds compared with the low rates enjoyed by other states on current borrowing. Impelled by those two considerations, state officials have, since 1936, tried desperately to find some way of refunding the highway debt at lower rates of interest and thus to release some funds for construction. The 5 per cent highway bonds rose rapidly to near par in 1936, and since then have fluctuated between about 87 and 99; apparently, they have never been above par.

The legislature has passed several acts authorizing refunding. It has petitioned Congress to allow the Social Security Board to invest in Arkansas bonds an amount equal to payments from that state. State officials have negotiated with the R.F.C. in an attempt to get its aid in carrying through a refunding plan. In March,

1937, the state signed a contract with an underwriting syndicate, making a tentative refunding agreement, but no successful plan was devised.[53]

All refunding plans have been attacked in the courts. Some have been held invalid, while others could not be carried through. In the fall of 1938 the voters rejected a constitutional amendment which would have guaranteed a fund for the service of highway bonds with a minimum of $8,985,000 and a maximum of $10,985,-000. If necessary, the state would have been bound to levy ad valorem and other taxes to provide this fund. The proposal also provided for refunding the highway debt at reduced rates of interest and the assumption by the state of some $4,136,600 of additional district bonds.[54] Another amendment guaranteeing a minimum fund of $8,500,000 was defeated in 1940.

In July, 1939, the state supreme court disapproved a refunding plan which the governor had framed under the power given him by the legislature. The court rejected the plan because: (1) the proposed bonds were noncallable; (2) highway funds were pledged to service them; (3) it proposed to issue interest-bearing bonds in exchange for the non-interest-bearing Road District Refunding Bonds, Series B; and (4) it proposed to pay interest on the old bonds for a period after the new bonds began to draw interest.[55] The governor immediately called the legislature to meet in special session and to enact another refunding law. According to the plan he proposed, the proceeds from 5¾ cents of the gasoline tax, together with other highway revenues, would make up the highway fund. Proceeds from ¾ cents of the gasoline tax would go to the counties. The first $13,000,000 of the highway fund would be allocated as follows: the first $7,500,000 would go for debt service, the next $3,000,000 for road and bridge maintenance, and the next $2,500,000 for construction. From $13,000,000 to $16,000,000, funds could be used by the legislature for any highway purpose; any funds above $16,000,000 would be used 50 per cent for debt retirement and 50 per cent at the discretion of the legislature. In com-

53. Bond Buyer, March 27, 1937, p. 3.
54. Ibid., Oct. 15, 1938, p. 47; Nov. 12, 1938, p. 6; Nov. 19, 1938, p. 9.
55. Ibid., July 15, 1939, p. 6.

municating the plan to the legislature the governor said that he had received a promise from the R.F.C. to buy 50 per cent of the refunding issue.[56]

During the time it was trying to work out a refunding plan, the legislature passed several bills contradictory to the terms of the 1934 refunding plan. Some would have reduced the gasoline or automobile taxes, diverted highway funds, put additional maintenance funds ahead of debt service, or assumed additional district bonds. Some were so clearly in violation of the 1934 act that the governor vetoed them, although several which he signed appear to be obvious violations. In 1938 the legislature enacted, on the recommendation of the governor, a law to make all toll bridges free in order that the state could qualify for a grant of $3,000,000 from the United States which might be used for road construction.[57] This reduced the revenues of the highway fund by about $600,000 per year, and was considered by many a violation of the state's agreement.

In order to facilitate refunding, the 1939 legislature enacted a law which practically allows the state to "rig the market" for its own securities. An ex-officio State Investment Board was created and given power to invest one half of the state's average daily cash balance in state securities. With those as collateral, the board might borrow from banks up to $6,000,000 and buy additional securities.[58] This would have given the board a total fund of approximately $9,000,000, but the "pyramiding" section was held invalid by the courts.[59]

The above developments are merely examples of activities which are going on all the time. They indicate, however, that the taxpayers of the state have not yet resigned themselves to the hard and disagreeable task of repaying the debt; they are still seeking an "easy way out." They apparently are not willing to heed the advice given by the leading newspaper of the state in March, 1938:

The people of Arkansas should know the facts about the State's debt situation and they should realize that Arkansas suffers morally and financially from its present credit standing. Anything which

56. Ibid., July 22, 1939, p. 3. 57. Acts, Ex. Sess., 1938, Act 11.
58. Acts, 1939, Act 223. 59. Bond Buyer, June 17, 1939, p. 52.

further impaired that standing would make Arkansas suffer still more, both morally and in money out of pocket.

· · · · · · · · · ·

With the highway bonds at their present prices they cannot be refunded with bonds bearing lower interest. . . . If another high market comparable to that of the last quarter of 1936 should develop, refunding might be revived. The best way to prepare Arkansas to take advantage of such an opportunity is to make protection and strengthening of the State's credit standing our constant and determined purpose.[60]

In 1938 the state collected tax revenues of $22,501,085 and paid $5,772,489, or a little more than 25 per cent of revenues as interest on its debt. Adequate provision for the repayment of the principal of that debt would require an additional 15 to 20 per cent, meaning that the state would have to devote over 40 per cent of its total revenues to debt service. Even if the interest rate should be reduced to 3 per cent, adequate debt service would still require over 30 per cent of state revenues. For a state such as Arkansas, that is too high for safety.[61]

CONCLUSION

Arkansas' experience illustrates the dangers of borrowing in a poor state with inadequate financial administration and a relatively low level of political morality. Before 1927 the state fiscal officers had never handled large amounts of money and so had never developed proper controls. Administrators and engineers had never spent large sums of money and so were not trained in planning outlays. Political leaders were not accustomed to "easy money" and could not resist the temptations of extravagance and petty graft. The sudden transition from poverty to riches placed too great a strain on the financial and administrative machinery of the state. The exhilaration of the sudden enrichment led also to demands

60. *Arkansas Gazette*, March 13, 1938, as quoted in *Bond Buyer*, March 26, 1938, p. 13.
61. On Feb. 27, 1941, the state refunded its entire highway debt by selling to the R.F.C. $136,330,557 of 3 and 3¼ per cent bonds at an effective yield of 3.2 per cent. A large syndicate of private bankers withdrew from the negotiations just before the sale because of the low interest rates (*New York Times*, Feb. 28, 1941, p. 30).

which forced borrowing beyond the original plan and greatly accentuated the state's troubles in later years.

Another evil of the situation was the division of financial responsibility for highways between the state and the districts. Local districts of this kind are by nature conducive to inefficiency and political manipulation. When the division of responsibility is vague and there is a general feeling that debts can be shifted to the state, irresponsible financing is likely to develop. Arkansas would have fared better if it had abolished, finally and completely, all road and street districts in 1921, when their evils were first exposed, and assumed their debts then.

Finally, the experience illustrates the need for a constitutional debt limitation. Until 1934 the Arkansas legislature could borrow without limit. Even with a constitutional limitation it is quite possible that the state would have borrowed much—probably too much. But a limitation would have forced state officials to formulate some kind of a plan, however crude, and to submit it to the voters for consideration over a period of weeks or months instead of acting on a momentary whim in the midst of a hectic legislative session. Further, it would have required the state to proceed more slowly in its borrowing, which, in the final analysis, is probably the chief merit of any constitutional debt limitation. It is quite unlikely that the voters could have been persuaded to approve a debt of $175,000,000 or $180,000,000 at one time or even over a short period of time. If action could have been delayed for a year or two, much of the debt would never have been incurred and the money which was borrowed would have been spent more efficiently. A debt limitation such as that described in Chapter XXV, stated in terms of average revenues, would certainly have exerted a healthy restraint on Arkansas' borrowing and averted much of the state's present difficulty.

CHAPTER XVI

THE TENNESSEE DEBT: A CASE STUDY IN DEBT ADMINISTRATION

NEXT TO Arkansas, perhaps Tennessee has had more difficulty with its debt during recent years than any other state. While Tennessee was not so reckless as Arkansas in regard to amounts borrowed, the management of its debt was particularly inept and brought the state to the brink of default. Certain parts of Tennessee's debt history illustrate how a state debt should *not* be managed. No attempt is made here to present the complete story; consideration will be given only to the peculiar problem which developed and to the solution which was finally reached. The three phases of financial administration which were primarily responsible for the difficulties and which will be stressed below were: (1) a poorly arranged schedule of maturities, (2) defective provisions for debt service, and (3) the absence of any effective budget system for the control of current expenditures.

HOW THE DEBT WAS INCURRED

In 1915 Tennessee's debt was $11,781,000. In that year the state refunded its old debt of $10,781,000, composed principally of the residue remaining from the 1882 settlement of the pre-Civil War and Reconstruction debts, several times refunded. A funding issue of $1,000,000 made up the total of $11,781,000.[1] For the next ten years there were no important additions to the debt.

General Fund Debt

Until 1927 there was no division of the debt, all of which was serviced from the general fund. Beginning in 1917, small amounts

1. Norman S. Taber and Company, *State of Tennessee; Reorganizing the Debt Structure* (New York, 1937), p. 8.

of bonds were issued from time to time to aid state institutions, to cover current deficits, or to refund maturing obligations.

Operations affecting the general fund debt and its status at the end of 1936 have been summarized as follows:

As of January 1, 1937, there was outstanding $15,545,000 in bonds serviced by the general fund of the State. This was the remainder of a total of $24,497,000 issued to be serviced from this fund since July 1, 1915.

Of this total of $24,497,000, $14,621,000 was issued for refunding purposes, and $3,500,000 represented bonds issued to fund deficits, leaving only $6,376,000 which might be called productive debt since 1915. Principal retired from the general fund has totalled $8,952,000, an amount less than half the unproductive debt created in or carried over into this period from this fund alone.

While some of the bonds serviced from the general fund are serial in form, the larger issues are term or semi-term bonds. No sinking funds have been established, and the maturity schedule is such as to offer difficulties even if the general fund were in a position to make modest annual provisions for debt retirement.[2]

Highway Debt

The highway debt is the largest single component of the total and the one which has caused the most trouble. The state entered upon a program of highway building in 1925 and began to borrow in large amounts in 1927. "The legislature of 1929 . . . increased the three cent gas tax by two cents and designated that the proceeds from one cent of this be applied toward the payment of highway bonds, to take effect January 1, 1931, and an additional cent be applied after January 1, 1935. Through a process of issuing short term notes which were refunded into long term bonds, the highway debt had increased to $47,200,000 by 1933."[3]

The greatest mistake of the whole borrowing program was made in arranging the maturities of the highway bonds. In the early years, all borrowing was by short-term notes. No long-term bonds were issued in 1927, when interest rates were comparatively low. In 1928 and 1929 interest rates were higher, which may have been a factor in delaying the funding of the debt into long-term bonds.

2. *Ibid.*, pp. 11, 15.   3. *Ibid.*, p. 18.

But the increasing size of the debt and the necessity of constant refunding made it imperative that some more permanent arrangement be made. So in 1929 and 1930 two issues of "Highway Notes" and one issue of "Highway Bonds" were sold bearing 4½ and 4¾ per cent interest. They totaled $35,000,000, were not callable, and all matured in a single year—1939. "Evidently little consideration was taken of the amounts that could be paid off at maturity, for . . . even with the largest gas collections in Tennessee history, it is estimated that there will be on hand cash amounting to only approximately $10,000,000 by 1939. This would have made it necessary to refund at that time some $25,000,000 in an uncertain bond market."[4]

Another issue of highway bonds was sold in 1932 at 6 per cent, maturing in 1946 and 1947. A part of it represented the refunding of $2,000,000 of notes which had been sold in 1927 at 3¾ per cent, refunded in 1928 at 5.3 per cent, refunded again at 5¾ per cent, and now finally refunded at 6 per cent.[5] A worse arrangement could hardly be imagined. "There has been actual refunding of nearly every highway issue in part or in whole. Although the proceeds of one cent of the gas tax have been set aside since 1931, and two cents since 1935, few bonds have been directly retired."[6]

Bridge Bonds

Between 1927 and 1930 the state sold $13,850,000 of bridge bonds for the construction of sixteen toll bridges. All were term bonds maturing in the years 1942-45, and only $4,000,000, maturing in 1942-43, were callable. They were to be serviced from tolls, supplemented as needed by general revenues of the highway department. To the end of 1936 it was stated that toll income "has not covered even interest requirements, at $629,437.50 annually, and no provision whatever has been made toward the retirement of principal. . . . Income from toll bridges has had a steady increase, . . . but the increase has not prevented a steady drain against the Highway Department operating expenses."[7]

4. *Ibid.*
6. *Ibid.*, p. 18.
5. *Ibid.*, p. 20.
7. *Ibid.*, p. 22.

County Reimbursement Debt

In 1927 the legislature provided that, beginning in 1929, the state should reimburse the counties for expenditures made on roads later incorporated into the state highway system, with interest at 5 per cent. The repayments were to be completed by 1949, and revenues from one cent of the gasoline tax were appropriated for that purpose. "However, in order to assure the State's meeting its obligation to the Counties within a reasonable period, the legislature provided that if, in 1939, it is apparent that a continuance of the one cent gasoline tax will not be sufficient to discharge the entire debt by 1949, such additional amount as may be necessary is to be paid by the Highway Department."[8]

The amount finally assumed under this act was $35,341,605.57. To the end of 1936 interest payments on such obligations amounted to $13,595,550, while $3,726,070 of principal had been repaid, leaving $31,615,535 outstanding. On the basis of tax collections in 1935-36, it was estimated that revenues from one cent of the gasoline tax would fail to retire the county obligations by 1949 by the amount of $20,287,972, which would have to be repaid from general highway revenues. The latter contingency, however, "would not only eliminate allowance for construction, essential to receive regular federal aid, but would cripple highway maintenance."[9]

Funding Bonds

Beginning in 1930 there were large deficits in the general fund. Since the state was unable to sell funding bonds based merely upon its general credit, the legislature pledged the proceeds from one cent of the gasoline tax to service such bonds. Through 1936, $15,945,000 of such bonds bearing 5½ and 6 per cent interest, were sold, each issue having a different lien on the pledged revenues. After the interest on all issues was paid, any excess funds were allocated to a sinking fund for the issue having first lien. When that sinking fund was sufficient to cover principal and *all interest payments until maturity,* excess funds were placed in a sinking fund for the issue having second lien, and so on.

8. *Ibid.,* p. 28.   9. *Ibid.,* p. 29.

On December 31, 1936, the sinking fund for the $1,000,000 of first lien bonds—to mature in 1941—contained $1,305,783 in cash. "This amount is sufficient to pay the interest on these bonds and the principal at maturity. Thus, we find the State paying interest of $60,000 a year for the next five years whereas the money is on hand now to pay off the entire debt . . . this money cannot be used to pay off bonds coming due prior to 1941 nor can it be put to work in investments to reduce interest cost [because of limitations in the law governing sinking funds to be noted below]."[10]

It was estimated in 1937 that the pledged revenues were adequate to service the funding bonds; in fact, more than adequate, for the sinking funds would all be filled several years before the maturity of the bonds, and the state would have to hold idle cash for several years while continuing to pay interest on the bonds. In the meantime, while the sinking funds were being filled up more rapidly than necessary, the state was deprived of the funds which it needed very much. Thus the act authorizing those bonds contained three costly mistakes: (1) the bonds were not callable; (2) the amount appropriated to sinking funds was too large; (3) the terms governing the use of the sinking funds were too rigid.

Other Bonds

Between 1927 and 1931, Tennessee sold $1,000,000 of bonds to aid in the building of rural schools and $2,500,000 for the state university. Both issues were serviced from the proceeds of the tobacco tax and were known as "Tobacco Tax Bonds." The rural school bonds received $82,000 of such proceeds annually, and the university bonds, $225,000. Both sums were adequate to pay interest and leave liberal amounts to be added to sinking funds.

In 1929 the state sold $1,500,000 of bonds to purchase land for the Smoky Mountain National Park and pledged for their service the revenues from one tenth of a cent of the gasoline tax. Such revenues were adequate for interest and sinking fund requirements.

Summary

Table 35 gives a summary of bond sales and retirements in Tennessee for the years from 1915 through 1936. It does not in-

10. *Ibid.*, p. 16.

clude transactions affecting the county reimbursement obligations.
On January 1, 1937, the total funded debt of the state was $129,-
015,534.56, composed of $47,200,000 highway bonds, $13,850,000
bridge bonds, $31,615,534.56 county reimbursement obligations,
$15,945,000 funding bonds, and $20,405,000 general fund, and miscellaneous bonds.

ADMINISTRATION OF THE PROGRAM

During the great expansion of financial activity between 1927
and 1931 the state lost heavily because of corruption and inadequate financial facilities. Most of the losses can be traced directly
to the depredations of the powerful, far-flung, and unscrupulous
financial system headed by Luke Lea and Rogers Caldwell. These
men controlled several newspapers, a chain of banks, several insur-

TABLE 35
SUMMARY OF THE SALE AND RETIREMENT OF STATE BONDS
IN TENNESSEE, 1915-36
(In thousands of dollars)

Year	Productive Debt	Refunding Bonds	Deficit Bonds	Bonds Retired	Debt Outstanding at End of Year
1915......		10,781	1,000		11,781
1916......					11,781
1917......	1,380			150	13,011
1918......				170	12,841
1919......				170	12,671
1920......	625			240	13,056
1921.....	1,340			170	14,226
1922.....				220	14,006
1923.....	250	617		170	14,703
1924.....				205	14,498
1925.....	1,650			285	15,863
1926.....				291	15,572
1927.....	22,500	1,000		1,341	37,731
1928.....	3,500			560	40,671
1929.....	9,760	6,000		6,341	50,090
1930.....	29,050		2,500	359	81,281
1931.....	1,031			2,879	79,433
1932.....		11,500	7,500	9,359	89,074
1933.....		2,635	10,000	7,045	94,664
1934.....		360		774	94,250
1935.....	750	6,106	1,950	6,106	96,950
1936.....	450	11,560		11,560	97,400
Totals..	72,286	50,559	22,950	48,395	97,400

Source: Norman S. Taber and Company, *op. cit.*, p. 34.

ance companies, many investment and financial concerns, and a host of other enterprises in Tennessee and adjoining states. When Henry Horton became governor of Tennessee, on the death of Governor Peay in 1927, Lea and Caldwell became influential figures in the management of the state's finances. They lost no time in turning their influence to their personal gain.

Space is lacking for a full account of the many and complicated transactions by which Lea and Caldwell robbed the state, but a few of the more important ones will be mentioned briefly.[11]

Sale of Bonds

Lea and Caldwell insisted that the state borrow liberally and sell the bonds in large blocks. They frequently attended meetings of the funding board when terms and amounts of the bonds to be issued were under consideration. The state treasurer opposed the large issues, holding that the state did not need the funds immediately and that the state's financial machinery was not adequate to handle the large amounts of cash. Lea and Caldwell had their way and then bought the bonds, either without competition or in collusion with other bidders. They bought a large issue of bonds in June, 1929, on a bid which contained this provision: "After the various State depositories shall have been fully supplied with funds, first from other sources and then from proceeds of these sales, . . . the surplus proceeds shall be deposited with such good and solvent banks of the State of Tennessee, and in such amounts as we may designate—the said deposits to be withdrawn from said banks proportionately and only as funds are needed to pay for the highway and bridge projects contemplated in the issuance of said securities."[12] This explains the large issues of 1929 and 1930. "Political

11. For detailed accounts see: "Interim Report of the Special Investigation Committee," *House Journal*, 1931, pp. 454-483; "Second Report of the Special Legislative Committee," *ibid.*, pp. 643-812; "Unanimous Report of the Special Committee of the House . . . Relating to the Impeachment of the Governor," *ibid.*, pp. 873-936, 958-1049.

12. "Second Report of the Special Legislative Committee," *House Journal*, 1931, p. 716.

"The bid was accepted under the conditions stated and the syndicate in turn sold the bonds to a New York Syndicate headed by Lehman Brothers. As a matter of fact, the bonds were signed in New York by the proper state officials and delivered

friends of the present governor . . . desired the use of these millions through financial institutions being manipulated by them for their own benefit, and requiring more and more additional funds to prevent their collapse."[13] According to state law, these funds should have been deposited pro rata in the various depositories designated by the funding board, no bank receiving an amount greater than 25 per cent of its capital stock. Actually the provisions of the law were almost entirely disregarded.

Depositing the State's Funds

Lea and Caldwell were conducting a vast speculation, aided by the millions of state funds deposited in their various banks. They controlled four "banks" in Tennessee which received a majority of all state deposits, especially of highway funds. Lea first prepared the way by securing the appointment of a friend as superintendent of banks. Then from time to time, as his various enterprises needed funds, he ordered state funds transferred to his banks. When the need was urgent, the banks did not wait for mail delivery but sent special messengers to state offices for the vouchers. The commissioner of highways later admitted that he made such transfers on Lea's orders "in an unguarded moment," and that he had no legal right to make them.[14] In several instances such funds were used immediately to pay bills owed by Caldwell's various companies.

The largest deposits of state funds were made in the Bank of Tennessee, which "was but an adjunct to and a creature of . . . Caldwell and Company . . . it consisted only of an upper story room, with no vault or safe, and, in fact, with none of the provisions made for a banking house, save, perhaps, a table and a few chairs. Its directors and operators were the same as those who controlled and operated the stock and bond company of Caldwell

---

directly to Lehman Brothers. The commissions from the sale of the bonds totaled $169,894, of which Caldwell and Company received only $7,417.

"The real gain to Caldwell and Company from the issue was the deposits of the State that were placed in the Bank of Tennessee" (John B. McFerrin, *Caldwell and Company*, Chapel Hill, 1939, p. 109).

13. "Second Report . . . ," *op. cit.*, p. 717.   14. *Ibid.*, p. 673.

and Company."[15] It did not conduct a regular commercial banking business, yet it held from two to four millions of state funds. Although a member of the state funding board held, after May, 1930, a sworn official statement showing that the bank was insolvent, the board continued to make deposits in the bank until a few days before it closed in November, 1930.[16]

Another of the Lea-Caldwell "banks" was a trust company whose directors, by official resolution, had decided to receive no deposits. It received none except $252,509 of state funds. When the four Lea-Caldwell banks closed in November, 1930, they held $5,196,102 of highway funds out of a total of $7,775,918 on deposit in all banks in the state. Other state funds held by the four banks brought the total to $6,698,118. In contrast with the $5,196,102 lost in those four banks, the highway department lost only $23,688 by the failure of other banks. By June 30, 1937, the department had collected nearly all of the latter, but had received only $1,411,043, or less than 30 per cent, from the Lea-Caldwell banks.[17]

State law required that state deposits be protected by pledged securities or surety bonds. The deposits in the Bank of Tennessee were usually protected by surety bonds signed by Caldwell and several of his vice-presidents. Once in the bank, the funds were quickly transferred to Caldwell and Company through the bank's purchase of securities from the company. Such purchases were made in large volume under a repurchase agreement. Obviously the type of security, the price, and other terms would be such as would suit the convenience of the company. Securities were exchanged or substituted at will, and shortly before the bank closed, Caldwell and Company removed valuable securities in exchange for fifteen hundred shares of the bank's own worthless stock. Since the bank was merely a department of Caldwell and Company, the net result of the whole series of transactions was that the state was making unsecured advances to the company at 3 per cent, the rate paid on deposits.[18]

15. *Ibid.*, pp. 715-716.   16. *Ibid.*, p. 655.

17. Tennessee Taxpayers Association, *Sixth Annual Survey of the Government of the State of Tennessee* (mimeographed; Nashville, 1937), p. 26.

18. "Second Report . . . ," *op. cit.*, pp. 657-658; McFerrin, *op. cit.*, pp. 110, 123.

Highway Policies

About the time Tennessee began to borrow for highways, Lea and Caldwell secured control of the Kentucky Asphalt Company, expecting to sell its output on favorable terms for the construction of Tennessee roads. The commissioner of highways then incumbent refused to buy the asphalt on a noncompetitive basis, and was discharged by Governor Horton. His successor discriminated to some extent in favor of the Lea-Caldwell asphalt, but refused to waste the state's money by building certain roads and bridges necessary to promote the governor's political interests. He remained in office one year. The third appointee bought "Kyrock" from the Lea-Caldwell Company at an estimated extra cost to the state of about a million dollars and transferred highway funds according to Lea's orders in his "unguarded moments." The governor found his services more satisfactory.[19]

The Reckoning

When the Lea-Caldwell organization collapsed and its banks closed, there was a strong and widespread demand that all the participants in the manipulations be punished. A special legislative committee prepared impeachment charges against Governor Horton. The proceedings, however, were poorly handled; and the prosecution was handicapped by the popular belief that if Horton were removed, the control of the state would fall to the suspect Crump machine, considered as bad as, if not worse than, the Horton organization. Delays permitted Horton to reach an agreement with certain Republican representatives who held the balance of power, the latter agreeing to "vote against impeachment in exchange for roads."[20] When the matter finally came to a vote, the House failed to sustain the charges. The governor bought his freedom "with pardons, jobs, and good roads."[21]

The proper officials were slow and reluctant to bring charges against Lea and Caldwell. Eventually, however, Caldwell was indicted on several counts in state and federal courts in both Tennessee and Kentucky. Lea was indicted in Tennessee and

19. "Second Report . . . ," *op. cit.*, pp. 660-676.
20. McFerrin, *op. cit.*, pp. 189-201.   21. *Ibid.*, p. 202.

North Carolina, while several other members of the organization were indicted in Tennessee. In Nashville, Caldwell was tried and convicted of violating trust agreements. He appealed to the Supreme Court of Tennessee, which ordered a new trial. The prosecuting attorney never set a date for the new trial, and the court's decision "had the effect of acquitting him of the charges."[22] As long as Horton was governor, he would not allow Caldwell to be extradited to Kentucky, and the charges there were eventually dismissed. Lea and his son were convicted in North Carolina and, after the most exhaustive legal fights, served short prison terms. Both were fully pardoned in 1937. They were never brought to trial in Tennessee. All other trials in Tennessee resulted in acquittals. "Of all the indictments returned, only those in Asheville against Luke Lea, Luke Lea, Jr., and Wallace B. Davis resulted in prison terms which were even partially served. The net result of all the criminal prosecutions appears little short of a travesty on justice."[23]

DEBT PROBLEMS

By the end of 1931 the financial plight of Tennessee was indeed desperate. The state had no budget system worthy of the name and no executive control over expenditures. The legislature had voted appropriations in excess of *estimated* revenues, and collections had dropped far below estimates. Unpaid obligations mounted rapidly, and the general fund faced a growing deficit of more than $5,000,000. In addition, over $10,000,000 of short-term funding notes would soon mature. Millions of dollars of state funds were tied up in closed banks. A special session of the legislature late in 1931 authorized the special funding bonds and pledged the proceeds from one cent of the gasoline tax for their service. Early in 1932 Governor Horton made a desperate effort to rearrange the finances of the state and to provide sinking funds for certain parts of the debt.

In the meantime local and New York banks saved the state from default by extending loans when notes could not be sold in the open market. Finally the state was able to sell its bonds, although

22. *Ibid.*, p. 213.   23. *Ibid.*, p. 221.

on onerous terms. In 1932, $20,000,000 of funding and highway bonds, maturing between 1941 and 1947, were sold bearing 6 per cent interest. This was part of the price the state paid for poor debt management.

Arrangement of Maturities

One of the important factors which impaired the state's credit was the schedule of maturing obligations through 1939. As the situation stood in 1932, the state could not possibly hope to redeem obligations maturing through 1939 under the terms then prevailing. Table 36 shows the schedule of maturities at that time. The fact that the state would have to depend upon refunding a part of those obligations in an uncertain market created the possibility of default and made investors reluctant to buy its bonds.

As soon as the 1932-33 crisis was over, attention was given to a rearrangement of the debt structure. A 1935 law empowered the funding board to refund a large part of the debt and to adjust maturities so as to give a schedule more in keeping with the state's ability to pay.[24] The board offered to exchange new highway bonds bearing 3.5 and 3.9 per cent, maturing in 1955 and 1958, for those maturing in 1939. Certain general fund bonds were also refunded at a considerable reduction in interest. Even those exchanges and refundings, however, still left the state with a schedule of maturities which it could not meet; $29,515,000 of bonds matured in the three years 1937-39, and $28,033,000, in 1939 alone. Table 36 shows the complete maturity schedule as it stood in 1936.

Problems of the Sinking Fund

Sinking fund provisions for the different parts of the debt were noted above. In brief, certain parts of the debt had no sinking funds, other parts had inadequate funds, while still others had funds which were accumulating faster than needed. But those funds were separated into watertight compartments; transfers could not be made from one to the other, no matter how great the need. Further, the state law provided that money in the sinking funds could not be invested at a yield below 4 per cent. Those provisions did not

24. *Public Acts*, 1935, c. 147.

TABLE 36

SCHEDULE OF MATURING OBLIGATIONS IN TENNESSEE, 1932 AND 1936

(In thousands of dollars)

Obligations Maturing in–	1932	1936
1932-33..................	$ 6,103	$......
1934-36..................	5,772	....
1937-39..................	36,473	29,515
1940-42..................	6,476	9,876
1943-45..................	15,905	27,611
1946-48..................	12,365	14,450
1949-51..................	1,865	2,225
1952-54..................	1,657	1,657
1955-57..................	621	8,270
1958-60..................	705	1,214
1961....................	1,010	1,010

Source: *Reports of the Comptroller of the Treasury.*

cause any great difficulties until about 1935, because sinking fund revenues were comparatively low and state bonds could be bought to yield 4 per cent or more. But in 1935 the proceeds from an additional one cent of the gasoline tax were turned into the highway sinking fund, all revenues rose with an improvement in economic conditions, and the price of state bonds rose to a point where the yield was below 4 per cent. Cash which could not be invested began to accumulate in the sinking funds. Banks paid only 1½ per cent on deposits, while the state sold funding and refunding bonds bearing from 3 to 4 per cent. By June 30, 1936, all sinking funds held $5,546,863 of cash and only $1,921,500 of investments; a year later cash had risen to $12,038,370, while investments had not changed.

The total amount going into sinking funds was larger than was necessary, in the long run, to pay interest and discharge the principal of the debt. But in the meantime the state was being deprived of badly needed current revenues, was forced to hold millions of dollars in sinking fund cash at a very low yield, and at the same time sell funding and refunding bonds at high rates of interest.

The Situation in 1936

By 1936 the above factors and the necessity of providing for the heavy maturities of 1939 made a readjustment of the debt imperative. Highway maintenance and construction were almost paralyzed. For the year ending June 30, 1936, the seven-cent gasoline tax produced a total revenue of $15,648,726, which was allocated as follows:[25]

	Cents per Gallon	Gross Yield
County Road Aid Fund	2.0	$4,420,166
Highway Bond and Note Fund	2.0	4,420,166
Funding Bond Fund	1.0	2,210,083
County Reimbursement Bond Fund	1.0	2,210,083
Maintenance and Construction	0.9	1,989,075
Smoky Mountain Park Bond Fund	0.1	221,008
General Administration		178,143

Approximately 58 per cent of total proceeds was devoted to debt service, 28 per cent was returned to the counties, leaving about 14 per cent for administration, construction, and maintenance. Further, there were no prospects for early relief, for no part of the tax pledged for debt service would be released before 1944; some parts would remain pledged until 1959.

It was estimated that unless some change were made, about $13,500,000 of the highway bonds maturing in 1939 would have to be refunded. Further, large amounts of general fund and bridge bonds would have to be refunded from time to time, and the state would either have to borrow or raise additional revenues to discharge the county reimbursement obligations by 1949. It did not seem feasible either to raise the highway taxes—the gasoline tax was already seven cents per gallon—or to raise the funds from other taxes. It was estimated that "if the present method of handling the State's debt is continued, some $60,000,000 of bonds will have to be refunded in the next few years. . . . The cost of additional interest, therefore, can be conservatively estimated to be some $24,000,000."[26]

FINANCIAL REORGANIZATION

The financial difficulties of the state focused attention upon the need for improvement in financial practices and a reorganization of the debt. In the 1933-35 biennium total expenditures were reduced

25. Tennessee Taxpayers Association, *Fifth Annual Survey of the Government of the State of Tennessee* (mimeographed; Nashville, 1936), p. 220.

26. Norman S. Taber and Company, *op. cit.,* p. 34.

by over $10,000,000 compared with the previous biennium; even so, the deficit was more than $5,000,000. The 1935 legislature provided for a modern system of accounting and laid the foundation for improved budgetary control. The governor, within his limited powers, worked to improve budgetary practice and in 1935 went as far as he could in preparing an executive budget. Following a survey of the state's fiscal system in 1936,[27] the 1937 legislature strengthened the budget law by providing for a director of the budget with adequate powers to formulate and administer a real executive budget. Under it the state was able, in the year ending June 30, 1938, to keep expenditures below revenues for the first time in several years.

Debt Survey

But the debt was the most pressing problem and the phase of the state's finances most in need of reorganization. In 1936 the state engaged the services of a firm of financial consultants to make a survey of the debt and to recommend a plan of reorganization. The report was made to the 1937 legislature, which acted upon the recommendations.

Prerequisites of the Plan

After a survey of the debt history and an analysis of the different parts of the debt, the report stated the minimum essentials of a debt reorganization program as follows:

1. The meeting of all maturing obligations when they become due.
2. Reimbursement to the Counties which will permit the meeting of their obligations promptly.
3. Attainment of these two objectives without the necessity of providing additional funds for debt service.
4. Liberation of excess funds to aid in balancing the State's operating budgets in order that its credit may be strengthened by sound current operations.
5. Provision for release from debt service requirements as soon as possible, of gas tax funds needed for highway maintenance and construction, or for a reduction in the high gas tax levy.
6. Accomplishment of these several points without violating in any way existing contractual relations with creditors.

27. Tipton R. Snavely, *A Study of the Fiscal System of Tennessee* (Nashville, 1936).

Only the most casual scrutiny of the outlined replanning essentials is necessary to show that the ordinary methods of reorganization and refinancing will not meet the requirements òf this involved situation. . . .

Close analysis of the problem leads inevitably to the conclusion that the State has not been employing its available debt service funds as flexibly or as economically as it should. The key to the solution lies in the employment to best advantage of the idle cash which is building up in the sinking funds. . . .

The major problem, that of providing adequate service for the entire State debt from present revenues, lends itself to ready solution if available funds are directed to the purpose with their full potentialities for flexibility and effectiveness. The revenues now being used to service part of the State's obligations will be pooled and used to service the entire debt.[28]

The Plan of Reorganization

The unique plan recommended in the report for the reorganization of the debt was enacted into law by the legislature.[29] Its unusual nature will perhaps justify extended consideration of its features. The best summary of the principal features of the plan is found in the report which recommended it:

It is first necessary to fulfill contractual obligations arising from the specific allocation of revenue. To this end there will be issued Sinking Fund Retirement Certificates equal in amount to the bonds now outstanding in the hands of the public, namely $91,502,500. . . . these certificates will be credited to the various sinking funds and will have maturities which will come due prior to the maturities of the corresponding bonds.

Such action, by providing investments to the full extent needed by each sinking fund, will release all assets now held in the sinking funds amounting to over $10,000,000, as well as some $11,000,000 annually now pledged for the payment of only a portion of the State's debt.

These "investments" or certificates issued to fill up the several sinking funds will be held by a State Board of Liquidation, will be non-negotiable, cannot be sold to the public, will cause no additional cost to the State, and will not increase the State's indebtedness. They will merely constitute a mechanism through which the State will provide for the payment at maturity of its existing bonds and interest.

Adequate provision will be made for meeting the maturities on the

28. Norman S. Taber and Company, op. cit., pp. 42-43.
29. Public Acts, 1937, c. 165.

certificates. Not only will all the revenue now used for debt service be pledged, but in addition other present highway revenues will be available. Five cents of the gasoline tax, . . . inspection fees on volatile substances, bridge tolls, one-half automobile registration fees, franchise tax and $307,500 of the tobacco tax will be pledged for payment of the debt. Of the $17,700,000 a year thus available, however, only $10,300,000 will be needed. . . . "Consolidated Bonds" issued to take up the old sinking fund investments, callable bridge bonds, and County reimbursement debt . . . will also be paid from the above revenue.[30]

In addition to the $91,502,500 provided for above, there were other debts of $37,327,500, consisting of $4,000,000 of callable bridge bonds, which were called for redemption on July 1, 1937; $1,827,500 of other state bonds held in sinking funds; and approximately $31,500,000 of county reimbursement obligations. To pay the first two categories and also to cover any deficit existing on July 1, 1937, new "Consolidated Bonds" were to be sold immediately. The State Board of Claims was to administer the liquidation of the reimbursement obligations and should pay to the counties at once, from the proceeds of the sale of consolidated bonds, any excess "between the principal amount to be reimbursed to any County by the State and the principal amount of any outstanding net indebtedness incurred for the purpose on account of which such reimbursement is to be made."

After paying in cash this excess, if any, the Board of Claims shall proceed to liquidate the balance of the indebtedness, as rapidly as possible, in any or all of the following ways:

A. As the County bonds, subject to reimbursement, mature, consolidated bonds will be sold to provide the payment thereof.

B. Wherever County bonds subject to reimbursement, are callable prior to maturity, they shall be called and consolidated bonds will be sold to provide the payment thereof.

C. Wherever unmatured County bonds, subject to reimbursement, can either be purchased for cash or exchanged for consolidated bonds on terms advantageous to the State, consolidated bonds will be issued and sold or exchanged as required.

D. Beginning in 1939 the Board of Claims will set aside in separate sinking funds . . . ten per cent per annum, of the unpaid balance due the Counties. Such payment will be made by the deposit of con-

30. Norman S. Taber and Company, *op. cit.*, p. 45.

solidated bonds having a market value equal to the principal payment and shall constitute a discharge of that amount of the State's obligation so that by 1949 the entire indebtedness of the State to the counties will be discharged.[31]

Other Details

The above summary covered the first six sections of the reorganization act, which contained the most important features of the plan. Certain significant provisions, however, were included in later sections. Sections seven and eight pledged for debt service the proceeds of the taxes and fees mentioned above and provided that the state treasurer should make monthly payments from such proceeds to the Sinking Fund Board adequate to meet debt service. Further, "In making such payments out of said fees and taxes the full amount of the annual proceeds of a tax of five cents (5c) per gallon on gasoline or other motor vehicle fuel shall be paid to the State Sinking Fund Board before any payments are made out of such other fees and taxes, excepting the net receipts from toll bridges. . . ." In case of default the treasurer was to pay to the Sinking Fund Board, "out of the first monies received from such fees and taxes the amount required for the payment of the obligations of the State" without further authorization. "Whenever there shall have been paid into the hands of the State Sinking Fund Board the amount certified by them as necessary to meet the monthly requirements . . . the remainder of the revenue pledged and accruing during such month may be applied to such other purposes as may be provided by law."[32]

The effects of these two provisions were: first, to place the burden of servicing the entire debt upon gasoline tax revenues and toll bridge collections to the extent that they were able to bear it; and, second, to liberate for current use the excess of the proceeds from the various taxes and fees pledged for debt service and not needed for that purpose. The latter feature was an essential part of the plan and was widely urged as one of its outstanding advantages, but the former received little attention. Almost all the funds for servicing the entire

31. *Ibid.*, p. 47.   32. *Public Acts,* 1937, c. 165, sec. 8.

debt are coming from special highway revenues, as is shown by the receipts of the sinking fund for the year ending June 30, 1938. Of total receipts of $11,270,172, $10,325,000 came from the gasoline tax, $654,591 from bridge tolls, and only $290,221 from the tobacco tax.[33]

Other details may be summarized briefly. The Sinking Fund Board was empowered to invest cash in the sinking fund "with such interest yield as such Board shall deem satisfactory" (Sec. 11). This, of course, removed an unsound provision which had previously caused heavy losses to the state. The state promised not to reduce the rates of the various taxes and fees pledged for debt service unless the Sinking Fund Board should certify that "Such fees and taxes at lower rates . . . will be sufficient to provide funds adequately to meet all payments required . . . as well as to provide for the other obligations and expenses of the State . . . in which event the State of Tennessee shall be under no obligation to charge or levy . . . fees or taxes in excess of the rates so certified by the . . . Board" (Sec. 12). This restores to the state some control over tax rates by making possible tax reductions in future years if revenues are adequate.

The same section declares that bondholders have "A vested right in the performance of the covenants and pledges contained in this Act, and the performance of the duties imposed upon any officer or agency of the State by the provisions of this Act may be enforced by the holder of any bond of the State . . . by appropriate proceedings." A later section, however, provides that "Nothing in this Act shall be construed as either waiving the immunity of the State of Tennessee from suit or as extending its consent to be sued, any other portions of this Act to the contrary notwithstanding" (Sec. 15). In the light of the latter section, the former means nothing, and its inclusion might be interpreted as an attempt to deceive bondholders.

The Sinking Fund Board is authorized to issue refunding bonds, and new bonds without limit so long as revenues from pledged taxes and fees are equal to 150 per cent of all debt service requirements (Sec. 13).

33. *Annual Report of the Comptroller of the Treasury,* 1938, p. 14.

Appraisal of the Plan

The plan freed the state from the restrictions of previous sinking fund contracts by filling sinking funds with newly created state obligations. It was contended that this violated no contractual obligation of the state. The bondholders have suffered no serious wrong, and it is possible that in the long run they may profit from the reorganization; nevertheless, it would seem that, technically, the state violated its promise. In case of a future default, bondholders would have for their protection only the retirement certificates which, it is true, have a first claim on more revenues than were pledged for the original bonds. But in the meantime several millions of dollars which would otherwise have been impounded for the benefit of bondholders will have been spent for current operations or will never have been received because of tax reductions. The plan was a brilliant one and, on the basis of experience to the present, seems to be a definite success in this particular case. It may be a dangerous precedent, however, if states and other governments adopt the practice of discharging all sinking fund obligations by creating new bonds for that purpose.

Some of the benefits claimed for the plan were: (1) the release of over $1,000,000 a year to the highway department; (2) the release of over $1,500,000 a year to the general fund which can be applied as needed; (3) the improvement of the financial position of the state and lower rates of interest on refunding and new financing; (4) yearly reductions in the state debt, with retirement of over $100,-000,000 in fourteen years, if no new bonds are sold; (5) total savings in interest of between $20,000,000 and $30,000,000 because of the elimination of future refunding; (6) the progressive release of or reduction in gasoline taxes—by 1951 only one-half cent of that tax will be needed for debt service instead of four and one-tenth cent in 1936.[34] All in all, it was a most ingenious plan which went far to rehabilitate the state's financial position. With the other financial reforms, it re-established the state's credit on a sound basis.

34. Norman S. Taber and Company, *op. cit.*, p. 48.

Operation of the Plan

Soon after the plan went into operation several large bond issues were sold to meet maturing obligations, to fund the 1937 deficit, and to make payments to counties. By the end of 1938, $6,310,000 of county reimbursement obligations had been funded into consolidated bonds. The pooling of sinking fund assets gave the state sufficient funds, together with current revenues, to meet the heavy maturities in 1939. In January, 1939, it paid $13,601,000 of bonds and had on hand or in sight funds to retire approximately $10,000,-000 more in December of that year.[35]

During the year ended June 30, 1938, the general fund was "relieved of over $1,359,695.25 of expenditures, while the Highway Department, in addition to nine-tenths of one cent of the gasoline tax, received $396,058.21 more than it would have received under the old plan of debt administration. Therefore, it is evident that some $1,700,000 a year less money is being used for debt service than heretofore, even though all bonds are being retired out of current receipts. . . . It is contemplated that over $120,000,000 of the State's debt will be paid off by 1953."[36]

The improvement in the state's credit position is shown by the decline in the yields at which its bonds sold. In June, 1937, the yield on two large issues was approximately 3.35 per cent; by December, 1938, the yield had declined to 2.45 per cent, and by June, 1939, to a little below 2 per cent.

On June 30, 1938, the total debt of the state, including $25,571,961 of county reimbursement obligations, was $132,480,461, against which were held sinking fund assets of $17,666,446. On December 1, 1939, after payment of the bonds maturing in that month, the debt was as follows: direct bonded debt, $88,652,500.00; county highway reimbursement debt, $21,563,437.32; total, $110,215,847.23.[37] Sinking funds had been drained of nearly all liquid, available assets, but the gross debt of the state was reduced by approximately $22,-000,000 in eighteen months.

35. *Bond Buyer*, March 11, 1939, p. 39.
36. *Report of the Treasurer*, 1938, pp. 9-11.
37. Tennessee Taxpayers Association, *Reduction in the Bonded Debt of the State of Tennessee under the 1937 Debt Reorganization Act* (mimeographed; Nashville, 1939). p. 5.

CONCLUSION

Practically all of Tennessee's troubles were caused by inefficient financial administration and poor debt planning. If the financial reforms adopted in 1935-37 had been adopted ten years earlier, the state would have saved the millions of dollars which were lost in bank failures and the large sums lost through graft and collusion. Further, the state would have been largely saved from the crises of 1931-33 and would not now be paying the excessive rates of interest on the bonds sold during those years. This experience illustrates again the dangers which may develop when a state with inadequate financial controls and which has been accustomed to dealing in relatively small sums of money suddenly enlarges its financial transactions by heavy borrowing.

CHAPTER XVII

CONSTITUTIONAL PROVISIONS GOVERNING STATE BORROWING

IN PRECEDING chapters we have noticed that from time to time voters in the various states have imposed constitutional limitations on the power of their lawmakers to incur debts. In some instances the restrictions have been too rigid and have seriously embarrassed legislative bodies in times of financial stress. In other instances there have been no limitations at all or only very lax ones, and legislatures have recklessly incurred large debts. Often excessive borrowing has resulted in action by the electorate to increase its control over borrowing.[1] The purpose of this chapter is to analyze the limitations on state borrowing as they exist in present constitutions and to offer some appraisal of their effects.[1a]

CONSTITUTIONAL PROVISIONS

Table 37 exhibits the constitutional provisions governing the more important uses of state credit. For purposes of analysis, the states may be divided into three groups according to the methods used to regulate borrowing. States in the first group have constitutional provisions which, with certain minor exceptions, forbid the legislature to incur any debt. Under such a condition each project involving borrowing must be authorized by a constitutional amend-

1. Recent examples are found in Arkansas and North Carolina. Before 1934 the Arkansas legislature could borrow without any quantitative limit. In that year the voters approved a constitutional amendment which required that, with minor exceptions, all proposals to incur debts should be approved by popular referenda. Before 1936 the North Carolina legislature could borrow without limit so long as the debt did not exceed $7\frac{1}{2}$ per cent of the assessed value of property in the state. In that year an amendment was adopted to limit the amount which the legislature could borrow in any biennium, without a vote of the people, to two thirds of the amount of the debt which was retired in the previous biennium.

1a. The substance of this chapter appeared as an article under this same title in the *American Political Science Review*, XXXII (Aug., 1938), 694-707.

TABLE 37
Provisions of State Constitutions Limiting State Borrowing

State	Citation: Article and Section of Constitution	Limitations on the Electorate	Limitations on the Legislature	Exceptions to Limitations on the Legislature
		Code: Authorization of loan by voters requires: C.A.—constitutional amendment; Ref.—referendum; Int.—provision for tax to pay interest; Pay.—provision for repayment.	Code: N.L.—no limit; N.B.—Leg. may not borrow; Int.—Leg. must levy tax to pay interest; Pay.—Leg. must levy tax for repayment.	Code: 1—To cover casual deficit; 2—To refund; 3—To repel invasion; 4—To suppress insurrection; 5—To defend state.
Ala.	IV,93,94;XI,213; XIII,253;XX;XX-A.	C. A.	N. B.	1($300,000)2,(3,4 by ⅔ vote.)
Ariz.	VII,13;IX,5,7.	C.A. (vote limited to real prop. taxpayers.)	N. B.	1($350,000)3,4,5.
Ark.	XII,7,12;XVI,1; XX;XXIX.	Ref.	N. B.	2.
Calif.	IV,31;XII,13;XVI, 1-10.	Ref.;Int.;Pay.(75 years).	$300,000	3,4.
Colo.	XI,1-5.	C. A.	N. B.	1($100,000)2,3,4,5; to erect pub. buildings.
Conn.	No provisions.	No provisions.	No provisions.	
Del.	VIII,3,4.	Legislature borrows.	¾ vote each house.	1,2,3,4,5.
Fla.	IX,6,10.	C. A.	N. B.	3,4.
Ga.	VII,3-5,8,12-14.	C. A.	N. B.	1($500,000)2,3,4,5; ($3,500,000 to pay public school teachers).
Idaho	VIII,1,2; XII,3.	Ref.;Int.;Pay.(20 years).	$2,000.000	3,4.
Ill.	IV,18-20.	Ref.;Int.	N. B.	1($250,000)3,4,5.
Ind.	X,5,6;XI,12.	C. A.	N. B.	1,3,4,5.
Iowa	VII,1-6;VIII,3.	Ref.;Int.;Pay.(20 years).	N. B.	1($250,000)3,4,5.
Kan.	XI,6-9.	Ref.;Int.;Pay.(when due).	$1,000,000	3,4,5.
Ky.	Secs.49,50,176-178.	Ref.;Int.;Pay.(30 years).	N. B.	1($500,000)2,3,4,5.
La.	IV,2,12;VI,16,22; XVIII,3.	C. A.	N. B.	2,3,4.
Me.	IX,14-21.	C. A.	$36,000,000(exceptions) 4% Int.;15-year serial bonds.	3,4,5.
Md.	III,34.	Leg. borrows except for veterans' bonus.	N.L.;Int.;Pay.(15 years).	1($50,000)5.
Mass.	LXII,1-3.	Legislature borrows.	⅔ vote each house.	3,4,5 and tax anticipation loans.
Mich.	III,4;X,10-14,20A.	C.A. (vote limited to prop. taxpayers and spouses.)	N. B.	1($250,000)3,4,5.
Minn.	IX,5-7;10,14a;XVI, 1,4;XVII,1.	C. A.	N. B.	$250,000;3,4, rural credits; to prevent forest fires; $75,000,000 for highways.
Miss.	XIV,258.	No provisions.	No provisions.	
Mo.	IV,44-46,48,49; XII,25.	C. A.	N. B.	1 and emergencies, ($250,000 each year) 2.
Mont.	V,38;XIII,1-4; XX,12.	Ref.;Int.;Pay.(when due).	$100,000;Int.;Pay.	3,4.

TABLE 37 *(Continued)*

State	Citation: Article and Section of Constitution	Limitations on the Electorate	Limitations on the Legislature	Exceptions to Limitations on the Legislature
		Code: Authorization of loan by voters requires: C.A.—constitutional amendment; Ref.—referendum; Int.—provision for tax to pay interest; Pay.—provision for repayment.	Code: N.L.—no limit; N.B.—Leg. may not borrow; Int.—Leg. must levy tax to pay interest; Pay.—Leg. must levy tax for repayment.	Code: 1—To cover casual deficit; 2—To refund; 3—To repel invasion; 4—To suppress insurrection; 5—To defend state.
Neb.	XIII,1,3.	C. A.	N. B.	1($100,000)3,4,5.
Nev.	VIII,9;IX,3,4.	C. A.	1% ass'd. value Prop.; Int.;Pay.(20 years).	3,4,5; to preserve natural resources.
N. H.	No provisions.	No provisions.	No provisions.	
N. J.	IV,Sec.VI,3,4.	Ref.;Int.;Pay.(35 years).	$100,000	3,4,5.
N. M.	IX,7-9,14,16;XXI,3.	Ref.(limited to 1% ass'd. value prop.);Int.;Pay. (50 years).	N. B.	1($200,000)4,5; for necessary expenses.
N. Y.	VII,1-5,11-15;VIII,9.	Ref.(and approval of Leg.) Pay.(50 years); serial.	N. B.	3,4,5; to suppress forest fires; tax anticipation loans.
N. C.	I,6;II,14,30;V,4.	Ref.	⅔ amount debt reduced previous biennum.	1,2,3,4; tax antic. loans to 50% revenues.
N. D.	XII,182,185.	C. A.	$2,000,000; Int.; Pay. (30 years).	3,4,5; funds to lend on real estate; $10,000,000 for state enterprises.
Ohio	VIII,1-5,7-11; XII,4,6,11.	C. A.	N. B.	1($750,000),2,3,4,5.
Okla.	X,4,14-16,23-25.	Ref.;Int.;Pay.(25 years).	N. B.	1($400,000) 3,4,5.
Ore.	XI,6-8;XI-a - XI-d.	C. A.	11% ass'd. value prop. for specified purposes.	3,4,5.
Pa.	IX,4-6,9,16,17,19.	C. A.	N. B.	1($1,000,000) 2,3,4,5.
R. I.	IV,13.	Ref.	$ 50,000	3,4,5.
S. C.	X,6,11.	Ref.;(⅔ majority) Int.;Pay.(40 years).	N. B.	1.
S. D.	VIII,13;XIII,1-3, 11,13-18.	C. A.	Int.;Pay.(10 years); for rural credits,½% ass'd. value prop. and ⅔ vote.	1($100,000) 2,3,4,5; to provide funds for coal, cement and electric enterprises.
Tenn.	II,31,33.	No provisions.	No provisions.	
Tex.	III,49-50;51-a.	C. A.	N. B.	1($200,000) 2,3,4,5.
Utah	XIII,2;VI,31; XIV,1,2,5,6.	C. A.	1-½% ass'd. value prop; Int.;Pay.(20 years).	1,2,3,4,5.
Vt.	No provisions.	No provisions.	No provisions.	
Va.	XIII,184,184a,185, 187.	Ref. (limited to 1% value taxable real estate).	N. B.	1,2,3,4,5.
Wash.	VIII,1,2,5; IX,5.	Ref.;Int.;Pay.(20 years).	N. B.	1($400,000) 3,4,5.
W. Va.	X,4,6;XV.	C.A.; Pay. (not less than than 20 years).	N. B.	1,2,3,4,5; $50,000,000 for roads.
Wis.	VIII,3,4,6,7,10.	C. A.	N. B.	1($100,000) 3,4,5.
Wyo.	XVI,1,2,6,9.	Ref. (limited to 1% ass'd. value taxable prop.).	Amount tax revenues for current year.	4,5.

Source: *Constitutions of the States and United States* (Albany: New York State Constitutional Convention Committee, 1938).

ment, with such formality and delay as that procedure entails. Voters are duly warned of the seriousness of the proposed step by the fact that it involves a change in the organic law of their state. In some states with the "amending habit," however, the solemnity of the procedure has been greatly reduced, and constitutions have been extended to great lengths by many provisions authorizing specific debts.[2]

Authorization by Referenda

States in the second group have constitutions which require that every law authorizing borrowing, again with minor exceptions, shall be submitted to a popular referendum.[3] Under such provisions the people still have the final decision, but the procedure is not so elaborate as in the first case. Again, the effectiveness of the restrictions may depend upon the solemnity with which the electorate regards the referendum procedure.

Borrowing by the Legislature

The third group is composed of states in which the legislature exercises the borrowing power without any immediate check by the electorate. Such a situation may result from either of two conditions. First, the constitution may not mention the subject of debt at all, in which case the legislature derives its power from the generally

2. For example, Louisiana has a very long constitution. Between 1921 and 1936, 127 amendments were proposed and 118 adopted, many of which authorized borrowing and made detailed provisions for the sale of bonds and the use of the proceeds. "Ease of amendment in Louisiana is not due to the language of the article itself, but rather results from extraneous factors not found in the written document. . . . In fact, it seems probable that the amending clause of any American constitution . . . would not be a barrier to amendment in Louisiana at the present time" (Allen L. Powell, "Amending the Louisiana Constitution," *Southwestern Social Science Quarterly*, XVIII, June, 1937, 30, 31).

3. A typical provision of this kind is found in the Oklahoma constitution (Art. X, sec. 25). It reads in part: ". . . no debts shall hereafter be contracted by or on behalf of this State, unless such debts shall be authorized by law for some work or object, to be distinctly specified therein, and such law shall impose and provide for the collection of a direct annual tax to pay, and sufficient to pay, the interest on such debt as it falls due and also to pay and discharge the principal of such debt within twenty-five years from the time of the contracting thereof. No such law shall take effect until it shall, at a general election, have been submitted to the people and have received a majority of all the votes cast for and against it at such election. On the final passage of such bill in either house of the Legislature, the question shall be taken by yeas and nays, to be duly entered on the journals thereof. . . ."

accepted constitutional principle that the legislature has all law-making powers not denied to it by the constitution.[4] Second, the constitution may impose such a general limitation on the borrowing power of the legislature that for all practical purposes that body may be said to exercise control of borrowing. Obviously, it is impossible to lay down any definite principle for determining when the limitation is so liberal as to place the significant and effective control of debts in the hands of the legislature. Perhaps the most practical test is to determine, on the basis of present conditions, whether the legislature has the power to incur a substantial additional debt for such purposes as it chooses, before being checked by the constitutional limitation. Table 38 shows the division of the states according to such a test.

TABLE 38

Location of the "Effective" Borrowing Power of the States

In the Electorate		In the Legislature
I By Constitutional Amendment	II By Referendum	III Without Quantative Limit
Alabama	Arkansas (since 1934)	(Arkansas before 1934)
Arizona	California	Connecticut
Colorado	Idaho	Delaware
Florida	Illinois	Maryland
Georgia	Iowa	Massachusetts
Indiana	Kansas	Mississippi
Louisiana	Kentucky	New Hampshire
Maine	Montana	South Carolina
Michigan	New Jersey	Tennessee
Minnesota	New Mexico	Vermont
Missouri	New York	With Remote Quanti-
Nebraska	North Carolina	tative Limit
Ohio	(since 1936)	Nevada
Oregon	Oklahoma	(North Carolina before
Pennsylvania	Rhode Island	1936)
Texas	Virginia	North Dakota
West Virginia	Washington	South Dakota
Wisconsin	Wyoming	Utah

Grouping of the States

There are a number of problems connected with the classification of states as described above. For example, Oregon is placed in Class

4. "All power to incur indebtedness for public purposes, unless given by the constitution to some other body politic or individual, rests in the legislature; and the power of the legislature, in the absence of constitutional limitation, is plenary" (59 *Corpus Juris* 213).

I and New York in Class II. The legislatures of those states have power to incur large debts, but only for purposes specified in constitutional amendments. Those two states were classified according to the normal method of borrowing which prevails.[5] Nevada and Utah are placed in Class III, even though the absolute amount of the indebtedness which their legislatures can incur is not large. The purposes for which such indebtedness might be incurred, however, are unrestricted. South Carolina is placed in Class III in spite of constitutional provisions to the contrary. The legislature and the courts of that state, between them, have almost completely nullified those provisions.[6] Arkansas and North Carolina are named in two groups because they have recently shifted from the third to the second, after incurring large debts.

The states are fairly evenly divided among the three methods of limitation. There seems to be no definite geographical or other logical basis for the grouping, although four of the six New England states give their legislatures unlimited powers. The only other states in which such powers are found are in the Middle Atlantic group—Delaware and Maryland—and in the South—Mississippi, South Carolina, and Tennessee.

At the other extreme are those states in which every bond issue requires a constitutional amendment. This procedure varies somewhat from state to state, but generally requires that the legislature approve the proposed amendment by a two-thirds vote before submitting it to the people. In some states the proposed amendment must be passed at two consecutive sessions of the legislature.

5. In this connection it should be noted that in all the states in Classes II and III the amendment of the constitution is an alternative method of authorizing borrowing which may be used in special cases. New York has used it on several occasions. In Montana a constitutional amendment was proposed to authorize bonds to pay veterans' bonuses when the court rejected a measure approved in a referendum. In the same way, states in Class III may submit proposals to popular vote, even though such action is not required. Maryland and North Carolina took such action on proposals to issue bonds for veterans' bonuses and loan funds. On the other hand, there may be a limit even on borrowing approved by popular vote. New Mexico and Virginia limit the debt which may be incurred in this way to 1 per cent of the assessed value of property.

6. Cf. 36 *Statutes of S. C.* 670; *Briggs* v. *Greenville Co.*, 137 S. C. 288 (1926); *State* v. *Moorer*, 152 S. C. 455 (1929). This point was discussed briefly in Chapter XI and will be considered further in the following chapter.

Pennsylvania probably has greater constitutional obstacles to borrowing than any other state in the Union, for in addition to the above two requirements, its constitution may not be amended oftener than once in five years.[7] Arizona and Michigan have recently limited the vote on bond issues to taxpayers.

Voting

There is considerable variation in the specific rules governing voting in those states which authorize borrowing by referendum. In some states the vote must be at a general election, while in others special elections are allowed. As a rule, a simple majority of those voting on the proposition is sufficient to decide the question, but a few states require a majority of those voting for governor or members of the legislature. South Carolina, which would be in this group if its constitution were observed, requires the approval of two thirds of those voting on the question. The only bond proposition put before the people of that state since the World War—a $10,000,000 issue in 1924—was defeated.

A Maryland case provides an unusual commentary on the location of the borrowing power in certain circumstances. In 1922 the legislature desired to pay a bonus to World War veterans, but thought it best to have an expression of opinion on the matter from the people. A law was enacted providing for the bonus and a $9,000,000 bond issue to raise the funds, to become effective only when approved by popular vote.[8] Before the time for the election the matter was brought before the state supreme court, which held the act unconstitutional on two grounds: first, the people having

7. Cf. Pa. constitution, Art. 18; *Armstrong* v. *King,* 281 Pa. 207 (1924); and *Taylor* v. *King,* 284 Pa. 235 (1925). Before 1924 this provision was disregarded and amendments were approved every two or three years; i.e., in 1909, 1911, 1913, 1915, 1919, and 1923. In June, 1937, the state supreme court reverted to its earlier position and held that there was "no absolute bar to amendment of the Constitution oftener than once in five years" but that "the same subject matter should not be dealt with by amendment until a lapse of five years." *Commonwealth* v. *Lawrence,* 326 Pa. 526 (1937). This apparently did not relax the restriction on borrowing, since the court implied that any proposal to borrow would be considered "the same subject matter" if any other proposal to borrow had been considered within the five previous years. In November, 1937, the voters rejected an amendment to eliminate the five-year "time-lock" clause. This restriction on borrowing has, without doubt, been an important factor in keeping Pennsylvania's debt low, especially during the Democratic administration of Governor Earle.   8. *Laws,* 1922, c. 448.

delegated the power to make laws to the legislature, the latter could not redelegate the power back to the people; second, the people had prescribed the manner in which laws should be enacted, and the legislature could not prescribe any different method.[9]

Payment of Interest and Principal

In addition to prescribing the procedure which must be followed in authorizing borrowing and/or limiting the amount of debt which may be incurred, constitutional provisions may also regulate other phases of debt administration. Several constitutions require the levying of taxes for debt service. As may be noted from Table 37, seventeen constitutions require that taxes be levied to pay interest and nineteen require that provision be made for repayment of principal. It is doubtful whether such provisions have ever been very effective, and with the decline in the use of property taxes by states they have even less meaning. The property tax rate may be arrived at by adding up several rates for specific purposes, but it is hardly feasible to levy income, license, and excise taxes in this fashion. In several instances constitutional provisions state that the law levying a tax for interest is irrepealable so long as any of the bonds remain outstanding. While this may seem to afford greater protection to the bondholders, it may introduce an undesirable rigidity into the tax system and hamper legislatures in their efforts to meet difficult financial situations.

Usually the provisions regarding repayment of debts are so vague and general as to destroy any significance that they might otherwise have. Such provisions can never mean as much as they imply, for a state can always divert funds to debt redemption which would otherwise be spent for capital outlays, and then borrow to finance the capital expenditures. Further, there is always the danger that the maximum term allowed for repayment may become the usual term. But the provisions are probably worth while, for they may have some effect in preventing irresponsible legislatures from interfering too much with the financial affairs of the third and fourth generations, and in making the present generation more keenly aware of the true burden of a large debt. A limit of not

9. *Brawner* v. *Supervisor,* 141 Md. 586 (1922).

more than thirty years is probably desirable for state debts; certainly a limit of more than forty years can have little significance. Maryland's limit of fifteen years is the lowest in the country. In the absence of other restrictions, it has probably been an important factor in holding that state's debt to reasonable proportions. The West Virginia constitution contains a unique provision requiring that "the payment of any liability other than that for the ordinary expenses of the state shall be equally distributed over a period of at least twenty years."[10] Regardless of the conditions which dictated this provision, it obviously has no economic justification.

Emergencies and Refundings

All constitutions which impose restrictions on borrowing contain exceptions for emergencies. Thus, most of them allow borrowing to cover casual deficits. This is desirable, since such deficits occur in every state at some time or other, and a state government might well be paralyzed at a critical time if it could not borrow to cover current expenditures without the delay involved in a referendum. But such borrowing is often limited to specific amounts, set fifty, sixty, or one hundred years ago to fit the conditions then current. The usual amount is $500,000 or less. In view of the size of modern state budgets, these amounts are far too small. The limit should be stated as a per cent of revenues.

Provisions allowing the refunding of debts are both necessary and dangerous. They are necessary in order to allow a state to work out of an embarrassing financial position or to take advantage of lower interest rates. They are dangerous because they may be relied upon to extend the debt as a substitute for raising the funds for repayment.

The necessity for the war exceptions is obvious. South Carolina and Arkansas are the only states with limitations on the borrowing power which do not except loans for defense. One of the problems connected with war exceptions is the question of when they may be invoked. When the United States is at war, are all the states automatically at war with the enemy nation and thus free to invoke

10. Art. X, sec. 4.

the war powers? It seems to be the general opinion that they are, and during the World War several states authorized war loans and gave governors wide powers in the use of the proceeds. Some of the purposes specified were: provision for dependents of soldiers, purchase of equipment, loans to farmers, and aid to the United States. A brief survey indicates that nine states, four of them in New England, borrowed about $8,500,000. Michigan was first with $3,500,000. In view of the responsibility of the national government for defense at the present time, the expediency of such borrowing by the states is questionable.

The war exceptions usually include borrowing to "suppress insurrection." The interpretation of this phrase may also offer difficulties. During the recent depression at least four states attempted to invoke this power, to justify borrowing for relief. Legislatures were called into special sessions to "allay . . . widespread public discontent and social unrest . . . to prevent disaster . . . and to defend the state." Asserting that the "public peace, order, tranquility, and safety are seriously affected and endangered, and the processes of orderly government itself imperiled" and that "acts of insurrection have occurred," the legislatures authorized bond issues. In Michigan, contrary to the wishes of the governor, the "incipient insurrection" bonds were submitted to a vote of the people and defeated by a large majority.[11] In Colorado and Kansas the bonds were highway revenue bonds, the details of which were given in Chapter XI. In the first decision on the Colorado bonds, the court held that constitutional provisions were not to be put in abeyance by a simple declaration of the governor. "Such a construction, once adopted, breaks the barrier, and future legislatures, protected by the precedent, might pile up mountains of debts on future generations."[12] The Washington bonds were for unemployment relief and were upheld by the court, as described in Chapter XIV.

Indirect or Contingent Debts

In addition to the provisions which deal with the direct debts of the states, there are other constitutional provisions which govern

11. *Chronicle,* CXXXVIII (1935), 3131.
12. *In re Senate Resolution No. 2,* 94 Colo. 101, 116 (1933).

the indirect use of the state's credit. Forty-three states are forbidden to lend or pledge their credit to or for the benefit of individuals, private enterprises, and/or local governmental units. Twenty-five constitutions forbid state ownership of stock in private corporations. These provisions are necessary to prevent the evasion of debt limits by indirection; they reflect the states' disastrous experiences with railroad, canal, and banking companies during the nineteenth century. Within the past ten years, several states have been employing "authorities" or other similar arrangements in order to borrow indirectly, as will be more fully discussed below. It is quite probable that such devices will eventually have to be brought under constitutional limitations.

Assumed Debts

It would seem that the ordinary provisions regarding borrowing and the creation of debts should cover the situation which arises when a state contemplates assuming a debt which has already been created by some state agency or local governmental unit. But the courts have been so narrow and legalistic in their interpretations of constitutional provisions in cases of this kind that nineteen states have included in their constitutions separate provisions to cover this particular problem.[13] Such provisions usually forbid the state to assume the debts of any individual, private corporation, or local unit. In some instances, donations, grants, or gifts to any of these are forbidden. With many local governments in financial distress and appealing to the states for aid, these limitations have received considerable attention in recent years. Various methods of evasion have been attempted. A common practice has been to provide that highway commissions shall assume local road bonds or service them from state highway funds, as described in Chapter XI. Another is for states to reimburse counties for highway expenditures. In most states the courts have been exceedingly lenient, even to the extent of rendering decisions directly contrary to any reasonable meaning of

13. Some states inserted provisions of this kind to prevent state assumption of local government bonds issued to aid railroads (A. M. Hillhouse, *Municipal Bonds*, Chicago, 1936, p. 179).

the words of the constitution.[14] A few courts, however, have adhered closely to the terms of the constitutional provisions.[15]

EFFECTS OF CONSTITUTIONAL LIMITATIONS
Total Debts

As one measure of the effectiveness of debt limitations we may compare the total debts of the states in the different groups. In 1938 the totals for the different groups, computed as described in Chapter XXII, were as given below. The totals for gross direct debts were: Class I, $865,051,420; Class II, $1,353,538,509; Class III, $856,938,836. The situation regarding net direct debts was as follows: in Class I, five of the eighteen states had no direct debts, and the other thirteen had a total of $745,316,209; in Class II, one state had no net debt, and the other fourteen had a total of $1,094,625,347; in Class III, the fifteen states had total net indebtedness of $785,735,181. In each group, however, there was one state which had such a large debt that it distorted the total for that group. These states were: Louisiana in Class I, New York in Class II, and Arkansas in Class III.[16] Eliminating those states, the totals for the three classes were: Class I, $585,955,729; Class II, $553,326,189; Class III, $632,083,453. Class III includes three of the four smallest states in the Union from the point of view of population.

Per Capita Debts

A more significant, though still rough, measure of debts is the per capita debts in the different states. Considering only those states which had debts in 1938, the average per capita net debts for the different groups were: Class I, $22.75; Class II, $17.95; Class III, $29.63.[17] This, however, is not a fair test of the effectiveness of con-

14. A few of such decisions are: *Bush* v. *Martineau*, 174 Ark. 214 (1927); *Tapley* v. *Futrell*, 187 Ark. 844 (1933); *Amos* v. *Mathews*, 99 Fla. 1 (1930); *Carlton* v. *Mathews*, 103 Fla. 301 (1931); *Mitchell* v. *Lowden*, 123 N. E. 566 (Ill.); *Baker* v. *Hickman Co.*, 164 Tenn. 294 (1932); *Road District No. 4* v. *Allred*, 123 Tex. 77 (1934).

15. Cf. *Crick* v. *Rash*, 190 Ky. 820 (1921); *Berry* v. *Fox*, 112 W. Va. 513 (1932).

16. For this purpose Arkansas and North Carolina are placed in Class III, since they were in that group when they incurred their debts.

17. The population figures used were estimated for 1937 made by the Bureau of the Census. These were the last estimates made before the 1940 census.

stitutional limitations since it does not consider their restraining effects upon those states which had no net debts. A fairer test is to consider the different groups as a whole by dividing the total net indebtedness of each group by the estimated population of that group. The figures for such a comparison are: Class I, $13.03; Class II, $22.89; Class III, $33.79.[18]

Even more than with total debts, the figure for the state with the largest debt in each group distorts the average for the group. If such states are eliminated, the averages for those states which had debts are: Class I, $17.00; Class II, $14.96; Class III, $26.35. The same comparison, dividing total net indebtedness by total population, gives these results: Class I, $10.61; Class II, $15.81; Class III, $29.72.

Debt Burdens

The most significant measure of state debts is to be found in the relationship between per capita debts and the ability of the people of a state to pay; that is, in the debt burden. In Chapter XXII an attempt is made to develop a means of measuring debt burdens. Taking the figures as computed in that chapter, we find that the averages for the different groups are: Class I, 128; Class II, 82; Class III, 209.[19]

The above comparisons indicate that constitutional debt limitations have some effect in restraining borrowing. By any significant method of measurement, the states in which the legislature has had wide discretion in determining borrowing policies have larger debts than the states in the other two groups, despite the fact that the

18. A study of state debts as of 1915, when they were much smaller than in 1938, showed substantially similar results. In that study, the states were divided into seven groups. While this classification differs from that given above, the groups were such that comparisons may be made with some degree of validity. Two groups, covering twenty-four states, were comparable to Class I above; they had per capita net debts of $2.32 and $2.80 respectively. Two other groups included fifteen states and were comparable to Class II above; they had per capita debts of $2.94 and $3.83. Three other groups, comprising nine states, were comparable to Class III above and had per capita debts of $4.65, $5.70, and $5.87 respectively. Commonwealth of Massachusetts, *Bulletins for the Constitutional Convention*, Bulletin No. 15 (Boston, 1918), pp. 578-580.

19. These are unweighted averages of the figures for the debt burdens of the individual states in each group.

former group includes five of the poorest states in the Union—
Arkansas, Mississippi, North Carolina, South Carolina, and Tennessee—and four of the New England states which have been quite
conservative in their borrowing. It is significant, too, that the two
states which have had most trouble with their debts in the past ten
years—Arkansas and Tennessee—imposed no limitations on their
legislatures while they were incurring their debts.

Votes on Bonds

As another test of the effectiveness of the different methods of
debt limitation, we may note the results of popular votes on bond
proposals. No complete figures are available on such elections, but
a survey of the data given in *The Commercial and Financial Chronicle* and Moody's *Governments,* which undoubtedly cover a large
majority of the cases, shows that between 1919 and 1938 the voters
in thirty-five states were asked to decide on proposals involving
some $4,384,587,000 of state bonds (excluding propositions submitted
a second time without a change in the result). In some states—including Iowa, Louisiana, Maine, Minnesota, Missouri, New York,
and West Virginia—all proposals were approved. New York voters
alone approved the issue of bonds to the amount of $1,134,000,000—
more than a third of all bonds approved—and rejected none. On
the other hand, several states, including Arizona, Kentucky, Nebraska, Oklahoma, and Virginia—rejected all proposals to borrow.
California voters defeated the largest single proposal by twice
refusing to approve the issue of $500,000,000 to finance electric power
developments.

Highway and bridge bonds were most frequently voted upon.
The survey indicates that $1,413,200,000 were approved and $340,-
300,000 were rejected. Bonds to provide veterans' bonuses and loan
funds were next, with $441,450,000 approved and $78,500,000 defeated. Bonds for unemployment relief were approved to the
amount of $361,000,000, while only approximately $40,000,000 were
defeated.

By groups, states in Class I approved $992,850,000 and defeated
$504,104,000, states in Class II approved $1,974,563,000 and rejected

$972,520,000, while states in Class III approved $21,500,000 and defeated $19,050,000. The total approved amounted to $2,988,913,000 and the total defeated, $1,395,674,000. Thus it appears that the voters disapproved nearly a third of all bond proposals submitted to them and that the ratio of bonds rejected was almost as high in the states which require referenda as in the states which borrow only by constitutional amendment.

Evasion

Other testimony to the restraining power of the popular vote is afforded by the lengths to which legislators sometimes go to avoid it. Several times it has happened that legislators, in states requiring a popular vote on bond proposals, have taken great pains to devise a scheme whereby they might issue bonds without submitting the question to the people. If the courts held the method unconstitutional, the next step was usually either to drop the matter or to attempt to devise an alternative method which, it was hoped, would win the approval of the court.[20] Submission of the question to the people was exceptional in such instances.

Rigid or severe debt limitations stimulate evasion of the type mentioned above. In 1928 Iowa voters approved a proposal to have the state issue $100,000,000 of bonds, largely to repay counties for outlays made in building roads. The state supreme court held the proposal invalid on procedural grounds.[21] Again the legislature, after passing it twice, provided for submitting the question to the people. But before the date for the vote the matter was again brought before the court, which held that the proposed amendment was not in the form required by the constitution in that it covered more than "one object or purpose."[22] After more than five years of fruitless effort, the project was abandoned, and the legislature proceeded, indirectly, to assume the debt by appropriating to the counties sufficient funds each year to service the bonds.

Other evidence of this tendency to evasion is shown in Table 25.

20. Cf., for example, *In re Senate Resolution No. 2*, 94 Colo. 101 (1934); *Johnson v. McDonald*, 97 Colo. 324 (1935); *Stanley v. Townsend*, 170 Ky. 833 (1916); *State Budget Commission v. Lebus*, 244 Ky. 700 (1932).

21. *State v. Executive Council*, 207 Iowa 923 (1929).

22. *Mathews v. Turner*, 212 Iowa 424 (1931).

444   AMERICAN STATE DEBTS

The states which have gone fartherest in assuming or servicing local highway debts and in issuing revenue bonds are those with rigid debt restrictions. The states in Class I had, in 1938, $237,834,000 of such contingent or indirect highway debt, while states in Class II had $85,138,000 and states in Class III, only $82,837,000. There are various other ways of evading constitutional debt limitations, as will be discussed below. Incomplete figures show that the totals for all forms of contingent or indirect debts, including the highway debts mentioned above, were as follows in 1938: states in Class I, $301,-636,000; states in Class II, $120,299,000; states in Class III, $91,173,000.

When debt troubles develop, the usual procedure is for the voters to curtail the borrowing power of the legislature. This was true during the nineteenth century and more recently has been true in Arkansas and North Carolina. In such cases the voter evidently feels that his judgment on matters of borrowing is better than that of his legislator. This may well be, since the voter is not beset by questions of shortsighted expediency in getting or holding votes. The politician may be tempted to gain favor by giving the taxpayer much and taxing him little. Borrowing offers the means of doing this for a time.

CONCLUSION

In several constitutions the provisions relating to debts are sadly in need of redrafting. The Louisiana constitution has already been mentioned; its provisions relating to borrowing are voluminous, scattered, vague, and ambiguous. Very much the same is true of the Minnesota constitution, which contains numerous exceptions to the established limitations and gives the legislature wide powers along certain lines. The constitutions of the two Dakotas are badly in need of clarification and more definitely restrictive provisions. The Oregon constitution permits the legislature to incur a ruinous debt for certain purposes if it should so decide.

In most of the states in Class III the legislatures are under no restraints except such as those imposed by their own wills and the refusal of investors to buy bonds. Mississippi and Tennessee urgently need strong constitutional restrictions, for their legislatures have shown that they may not safely be intrusted with unlimited borrowing power. Maryland has kept its debt within reasonable limits, thanks mainly to the provision requiring the payment of debts within fifteen years. Without that provision the story might have been different. The legislatures of Connecticut, Delaware, New Hampshire, Massachusetts, and Vermont have shown ability to exercise the borrowing power wisely, and there is no reason to recommend that their powers be curbed at the present time.

In several respects the rigid provisions which restrict borrowing in some states should be relaxed. It was suggested above that legislatures should be allowed more freedom in borrowing to cover casual deficits. The same would apply to borrowing in anticipation of tax revenues. Before going further with a discussion of the constitutional provisions necessary to insure an effective and yet flexible control of borrowing, however, we must first give attention to court interpretations of present provisions and to the ways in which those provisions are being evaded.

CHAPTER XVIII

COURT INTERPRETATIONS OF CONSTITUTIONAL PROVISIONS; THE SPECIAL FUND DOCTRINE

CONSTITUTIONAL debt limitations mean little until they have been interpreted by the courts. On first consideration it would seem that there is little room for disagreement regarding the comparatively simple provisions governing state borrowing. But the courts have been called upon scores, and even hundreds, of times to interpret those provisions, and considerable differences have arisen between different courts in their interpretations. Most frequently the courts have been asked to decide the meaning of the word *debt* as used in the various constitutions; that is, whether certain obligations incurred by a state or some one of its agencies or departments is a debt within the meaning of the constitution. Over a long period of years the courts have evolved what has come to be known as the "Special Fund Doctrine," which is applied in many cases. In some states the application of this doctrine has greatly modified and weakened constitutional provisions; in a few, it has practically nullified them. This chapter is devoted to a consideration of that doctrine.

ORIGIN AND DEVELOPMENT

New York

Arguments in favor of the special fund doctrine were first advanced in New York in 1852, at which time the constitution prohibited state borrowing without a vote of the people. The constitution also provided that revenues from state canals should be applied each year: first, to cover maintenance and debt service; next, to the extent of $200,000, to the general fund of the state; and, finally, to the completion of the canal system. When the system was completed, all surplus revenues were to accrue to the state. In

1851 the legislature, without a vote of the people, passed an act authorizing the sale of $9,000,000 of bonds to complete canal construction in three years. The bonds were to be serviced exclusively from the surplus funds available for canal construction without "any other liability, obligation, or pledge on the part of this state."[1]

The court held the act to be unconstitutional because: (1) according to it, surplus revenues could not be applied to the completion of the canals each fiscal year as required by the constitution; (2) it applied a part of the revenues to the payment of interest instead of to the completion of the canals; (3) it would defer the transfer of surplus revenues to the general fund beyond the completion of the canals.[2] In its opinion the court stated that it made "no difference whether the debt is contracted on the general credit of the state or on the credit of a fund belonging to the state. When the interest on the loan is raised by a tax, it comes from the pockets of the people individually. When it is paid out of a fund belonging to the people, it is paid out of their common purse. [The purpose of the constitutional debt limit] was to protect the people against the exhausting burthen of paying interest."[3]

The court felt that the bonds would impose a moral obligation upon the people if the funds pledged for their service proved insufficient. But the court's greatest concern was for the possible future of such practice. It believed that if a debt could be created "in regard to one source of revenue, we see no reason why the same thing may not be done in regard to every other source of revenue of the state, including not only all revenue which may arise from property, but also all which may be realized by the exercise of the power of taxation. Such an anticipation of revenue would no more create a debt than this bill does."[4] Here the court indeed spoke with prophetic vision.

Regarding the nature of the obligations, the court pointed out that the act provided "a promise to pay interest semi-annually and an appropriation to pay that interest. If this does not make a complete and perfect obligation, I am at a loss to conceive what would."[5]

1. *Newell* v. *People*, 7 N. Y. 9, 12 (1852).
2. *Ibid.*, pp. 92-93.   3. *Ibid.*, p. 86.
4. *Ibid.*, p. 103.   5. *Ibid.*, p. 105.

The vote of the court was four to one, with one concurring and one dissenting opinion. The latter held that there could not be a debt within the meaning of the constitution unless the obligation involved, directly or indirectly, "taxation or . . . the application of funds of which the state has the unlimited control and disposition."[6]

This case was remarkable in that the court saw and dealt with many implications of the question. The basic principles were stated, and in the many years since that time little that is significant has been added to those principles.

Colorado

There were no further developments of the special fund doctrine for forty years after the above case. This is reasonable in view of the fact that there was little state borrowing for twenty-five or thirty years after the Civil War. Between 1890 and 1920, however, there were several developments, almost all of them in the Far West, which marked the beginning of court recognition of the doctrine.

In 1889 Colorado authorized the building of certain canals to reclaim state and other lands and to supply labor for convicts, and appropriated, altogether, $100,000 toward expenses. Proper officials were empowered to issue interest-bearing certificates and use them in lieu of cash to pay for materials and labor. The certificates were to be paid, principal and interest, only from canal revenues and receipts from land sales. The court ruled that they did not constitute a state debt since they had no claim on general state revenues.[7] Thus was the first step in the development of the doctrine achieved when a court permitted the issue of bonds to be serviced by the income from property which had been purchased partly by state funds.

Obligations Based on Land Grants

The next group of cases involved obligations issued by states to be paid from the income from public lands. When the various Western states entered the Union, it was a custom for Congress to set aside certain public lands to be used by the state for public pur-

6. *Ibid.*, p. 125.
7. *In re Canal Certificates*, 19 Colo. 63 (1893).

poses, such as public buildings and state universities. In most, if not all, of the university grants it was provided that the funds derived from land sales should constitute an endowment, the principal of which could not be used. In some cases the interest could not be used until the fund attained a specified size.

In 1897 Montana authorized the issue of $450,000 of bonds to be serviced exclusively by income from land grants; $100,000 to finance the construction of buildings at the state university and $350,000 to build a state capitol. In a case involving the university bonds the court ruled that the land fund was a trust fund of which the state was agent and that claims against the fund could not be considered a state debt.[8] A few years later the Supreme Court of North Dakota reached an opposite decision on a similar case.[9] Another similar issue of bonds was ruled invalid in Utah in 1909. There the court pointed out that the state supported the university by appropriations, that all university property was held in the name of the state, and that the state would have to replace it if it were destroyed. It held that any debt of the university was a debt of the state and that "These notes, therefore, both in law and fact, are state obligations."[10]

The Montana case represented the second step in the development of the doctrine. There the court permitted the issue of bonds which were to be serviced wholly from a fund which was received by the state but which had to be used for restricted purposes.

Obligations Based on Earmarked Revenues

Minnesota contributed the next important development in the special fund doctrine. In 1909 the legislature authorized, to finance the construction of a prison, an issue of $2,250,000 of "certificates of

8. *State* v. *Collins,* 21 Mont. 448 (1898). The court added that the expenditure of such funds was not subject to the examination and approval of state board of examiners, as were the expenditures of regular state funds. In connection with the Capitol Building Bonds it was provided that, if at any time no funds were available to pay interest, 6 per cent warrants should be drawn and registered, "and by reason of the delivery of said warrants to the holders of said bonds and the surrender of the interest coupons, there shall be no default in the payment of interest" (*Laws,* 1897, pp. 170-171).

9. *State* v. *McMillan,* 12 N. D. 280 (1903).

10. *State* v. *Candland,* 36 Utah 406, 428 (1909).

indebtedness" to be serviced from the proceeds of a tax to be levied each year for ten years. They were to be paid only from the special tax fund and were not general obligations of the state.[11] The court ruled that the certificates did not constitute a state debt but were "mere evidence of the holder's right to demand and receive . . . the proceeds of the tax authorized by the act to be levied and collected."[12] The court reached its decision through the misinterpretation of an earlier decision upholding an act which had appropriated the proceeds of a tax levied for building purposes but which had not authorized the issue of certificates. The court held that the latter point was not an important difference.[13]

For several years no other court was willing to follow the Minnesota court. In 1913 the Iowa court rejected an act essentially similar to the one above,[14] and the Washington court held invalid the part of an act which added a pledge of the state's general credit to an issue of Capitol Building Bonds based upon the income from public lands.[15] In 1915 the Washington legislature tried to finance the construction of a capitol through the issue of $4,000,000 of bonds, the principal to be paid from land income and the interest from a special tax. The interest payments were to be considered a loan from the general funds of the state, to be repaid from land income later. The court ruled that the bonds would be a state debt and "The act upon its face bears unmistakable evidence of a studied effort to circumvent the constitution. [To approve it] would be to give judicial approval to a subterfuge."[16] Ten years later the legislature passed an essentially similar act except that the special tax revenues were not earmarked for interest payments; they were still to be repaid from the

11. *Laws*, 1909, c. 27.
12. *Brown* v. *Ringdall*, 109 Minn. 6, 12-13 (1909). A dissenting opinion stated that the act in question "opens wide the door and renders the constitution meaningless."
13. The earlier case was *Fleckton* v. *Lamberton*, 69 Minn. 187 (1897). We have here another example of the development of important court doctrines through the misinterpretation of earlier court decisions. Probably the most important example is the doctrine of the immunity of state and local obligations from federal taxation, and vice versa, which developed largely through the misinterpretation, by later courts, of Marshall's decision in *McCulloch* v. *Maryland*.
14. *Rowley* v. *Clarke*, 162 Iowa 732 (1913).
15. *State Capitol Commission* v. *State Board of Finance*, 74 Wash. 15 (1913).
16. *State* v. *Lister*, 91 Wash. 9, 17 (1916).

land fund when all bonds had been retired. The court rendered a favorable opinion, holding that the tax funds might be kept separate and not be used to service the bonds: thus, "In no possible way is the credit of the state involved."[17]

In 1921 the Kentucky court rejected the special fund doctrine as applied to county reimbursement agreements. The legislature had passed an act permitting the highway commission to accept advances from counties for road construction, to be repaid later from the proceeds of special highway taxes. The court accepted the special fund doctrine in its strict sense, but held that the legislature might not "specialize a fund" and create a debt against it.

> Under this contention the legislature, or the debt contracting authority, could divide the public revenue into numerous sub-divisions . . . almost without limit. Debts could then be contracted in unlimited amounts and payable in the far distant future and still be immune from attack as violating constitutional provisions . . . provided each debt was payable out of some one of the specially designated funds into which all of the revenue collected by taxation from the people had been divided. A mere statement of the proposition carries with it, it seems to us, its own refutation.[18]

This case, however, is an exception, since reimbursement agreements are in force in many states. Few, if any of them, have been contested in the courts. The South Carolina case noted below is the only other case found on the point.

The Minnesota and Washington courts achieved the third step in the development of the doctrine and accomplished what the New York court had feared in 1852 by designating the proceeds from certain taxes as special funds for the servicing of bonds. This was an important and crucial point and marked a definite beginning of the process of undermining constitutional limitations by court interpretation.

Other Cases

Before proceeding to a consideration of the latest developments in the special fund doctrine, we should note two other cases. In 1912 New Jersey enacted a law authorizing the State Water Supply Com-

17. *State* v. *Clausen*, 134 Wash. 196, 202 (1925).
18. *Crick* v. *Rash*, 190 Ky. 820, 836 (1921).

mission to issue bonds for the purchase of land to protect the water supply. The bonds were to be secured only by the holdings of the commission. The court held the act unconstitutional on the grounds that the commission was merely a state agency and that the sinking fund to retire the bonds was to come from state appropriations. It held that the argument that the indebtedness was not a state debt because it was to be paid from a special fund was "an illogical argument that carries with it its own refutation."[19] The Ohio court upheld an act empowering the Superintendent of Public Works to issue bonds for the construction of flood control and power dams and reservoirs. The bonds were to be serviced exclusively from the revenues of the various projects and were not to be a liability of the state.[20]

Latest Development

South Carolina has contributed the cases which have carried the special fund doctrine to its absurd extreme. In 1926 the supreme court of that state applied the doctrine to uphold a reimbursement arrangement.[21] In 1929 the legislature passed a long and complex act outlining two alternative methods of borrowing for highways, of which the highway commission was to choose one. Under the "District Plan" the state was to be divided into two large districts which were to borrow for highways under a reimbursement agreement with the commission. Under the "State Unit Plan" the governor and treasurer were to issue and sell "certificates of indebtedness" under the same procedure prescribed for the sale of state bonds. The certificates were to be paid from the proceeds of the gasoline tax but were further secured by a pledge of the full faith, credit, and taxing power of the state.[22] The highway commission chose the state unit plan, and the matter was brought before the supreme court of the state.

19. *Wilson* v. *State Water Supply Commission*, 84 N. J. 150, 158 (1915).
20. *Kasch* v. *Miller*, 104 Ohio 281 (1922).
21. *Briggs* v. *Greenville Co.*, 137 S. C. 288 (1926). The court depended for precedents upon the Colorado and Ohio cases cited above, which clearly were not relevant, and the Minnesota case which resulted from a misinterpretation.
22. 36 S. C. Statutes 670. The South Carolina constitution forbids the state to borrow except on approval of two thirds of the voters. There were no provisions for submitting this act to a popular vote.

To hear the case, the court sat *en banc;* that is, the twelve circuit judges were called in to sit along with the five justices of the supreme court. The case was bitterly contested and the decision of the court was long, confused, and, in places, almost incoherent. The court, by a vote of eleven to six and with three of the five supreme justices dissenting, upheld the act. It is difficult to follow the reasoning, but apparently the court applied the special fund doctrine, considering the gasoline tax revenues as the special fund. The *Briggs* case was cited as a precedent. In the eyes of the court, the purpose of a constitutional debt limitation was to "serve as a limit to taxation —as a protection to taxpayers, and especially those whose property might be subjected to taxation."[23] Since the certificates were to be serviced from the existing gasoline tax, the court reasoned that taxpayers could not be hurt.

The chief justice wrote a long and vigorous dissenting opinion. One argument of the counsel for the state aroused the wrath of the chief justice. It was:

Nor does such pledge [of the credit of the state] transform such special bonds . . . into a public debt, because such pledge merely assures that upon failure or inadequacy of the special taxes pledged, another special tax—namely, the *ad valorem* tax upon property— will be used.

This pledge of the faith, credit and taxing power of the State is merely a pledge of Honor, because the State cannot be sued for an enforcement thereof without its consent.[24]

The chief justice contended that the terms of the act "demonstrate that the real purpose of the act was the creation of a public debt, applying to the entire State and payable out of the resources of the State," and that the act was unconstitutional.

Since 1929 the court has held to the majority position in the above case. A later decision stated: "This court has also constantly held that bonds issued by the State which are payable out of special funds do not create debts of the State . . . although the full faith, credit, and taxing powers of the State . . . are pledged for the payment of the same."[25] The legislature has proceeded to divide up

23. *State* v. *Moorer*, 152 S. C. 455, 491 (1929).   24. *Ibid.*, pp. 526-527.
25. *Clarke* v. *S. C. Public Service Authority*, 177 S. C. 427 (1935). See also *Crawford* v. *Johnston*, 177 S. C. 399 (1935), and S. C. *Acts*, 1937, Act 339.

the revenues of the state into special funds and to issue certificates against them without a vote of the people. By 1938, $655,000 had been issued against a special hydro-electric tax and $1,350,000 against the income tax. In 1918 the debt of the state was approximately $7,500,000. In 1938 the debt of the state, exclusive of $22,625,000 of reimbursement obligations, was $47,531,652. The people had approved no part of the $40,000,000 increase.

South Carolina, although followed by no other state as yet, has accomplished the fourth and, presumably, the last step in the development of the special fund doctrine. The South Carolina debt limitation has been completely nullified by court interpretation and legislative action; it is difficult to see how the doctrine could go further than that.

PRESENT STATUS OF THE DOCTRINE

The special fund doctrine has grown during the past forty years, with first one state and then another contributing to its development. Let us now consider its present status. We shall analyze the leading cases on the subject, classified under several broad topics according to the purposes for which the bonds were issued or were intended to be issued. Frequently cases in the same category differ from each other in detail, as do the constitutional provisions under which they were decided. Such details will be noted where they are significant or important.

Highway Revenue Obligations

The courts are divided on the application of the special fund doctrine to obligations which depend solely upon the revenues from special highway taxes. In a given case the decision may depend upon whether the highway funds may be used for general state purposes. A further consideration of the Colorado case mentioned in Chapter XI may show how evenly balanced the arguments are in cases of this kind.

When the question of issuing revenue highway debentures first came before the Colorado court, it was defeated by a vote of four to three. The decision hinged on the fact that the highway revenues might be used for general state purposes if the legislature so ordered.

The majority ventured the opinion that the purpose of debt limitations was "to keep the state substantially on a cash basis, to prohibit the pledge of future fixed revenues, to forbid the contracting of debts which must be paid therefrom, and to make certain that one general assembly shall not paralyze the next by devouring the available revenues of both."[26]

After the above case, a constitutional amendment was adopted prohibiting the transfer of highway funds to other state funds. The legislature then authorized the issue of the highway debentures, and the matter was again brought before the court. The court pointed out that the amendment created a special fund which must be used exclusively for highways and thus was not available for general state purposes. It then upheld the act by a vote of four to three. Three of the former majority joined in a strong dissent.[27]

The Kansas case, also mentioned in Chapter XI, was similar but was decided upon different grounds. The court approved the issue of debentures on the ground that: (1) the constitutional debt limitation applied only to bonds to be serviced from property taxes; and (2) the people had authorized borrowing for highways when they approved an amendment allowing the state to spend money for highways.[28]

Among other states, Maryland and Mississippi have issued such revenue obligations, but these have not involved any constitutional question, since there are no quantitative limits on the legislatures in those states. They were probably used in Maryland to avoid the fifteen-year limit on state bonds. New Mexico has used obligations

26. *In re Senate Resolution No. 2*, 94 Colo. 101, 119 (1934). The tone of the majority opinion was more positive and dogmatic than the vote would support. In one place it was stated: "We venture the assertion that no man, able to read and understand ordinary English, however otherwise educated or uneducated, wise or foolish, would question for a moment that this bill was a plain violation of the constitutional prohibition, or find any reason to the contrary save by a resort to profound legal learning and doubtful application of judicial precedents" (*ibid.*, p. 114).

27. *Johnson* v. *McDonald*, 97 Colo. 324 (1935). The minority held that there was no real difference between this and the former act. One of them wrote: "I admire, while I deplore, the cunning logic that convinced the court that black is white and that there is no difference between heaven and hell" (*ibid.*, p. 335).

28. *State* v. *State Highway Commission*, 138 Kan. 913 (1934). The amendment contained a provision which stated that bonds should not be "issued by the state for such highways" (Art. XI, sec. 8).

of this kind extensively—almost exclusively—to finance its road program. Their use in South Carolina and the court's decisions have been noted above. The Kentucky court rejected the idea that revenues from highway taxes could be considered as a special fund for purposes of issuing revenue obligations. The Oklahoma court reached a similar decision on the ground that the revenues were part of the general revenues of the state which might be used for any public purpose.[29] The Montana court has also decided against such issues,[30] and on two occasions the people have approved revenue obligations by popular votes. Apparently the matter has never been brought before the court in Missouri, but if it should arise, the court's decision would probably be adverse since it has held, in another connection, that the money received in the highway fund "is as much public or state revenue as any money coming into the state treasury from any source."[31]

Bridge Revenue Bonds

Almost without exception the courts have approved the issue of revenue bonds to be serviced from bridge tolls, even though in some cases the projects involved the expenditure of general state funds to build approaches or to maintain the bridges. Generally the courts have regarded these as clear cases for the application of the special fund doctrine, although there have been a few dissenting opinions.[32] The California court summed up the prevailing opinion when it stated: "The overwhelming weight of judicial opinion in this country is to the effect that bonds . . . issued by states . . . secured by and payable only from the revenues to be realized from a particular

29. *Boswell* v. *State*, 181 Okla. 435 (1937).
30. *State* v. *State Highway Commission*, 89 Mont. 205 (1931).
31. *State* v. *Hackman*, 282 S. W. 1007 (1926).
32. Some representative cases are: *Alabama State Bridge Corporation* v. *Smith*, 317 Ala. 311 (1928); *In re California Toll Bridge Authority*, 212 Calif. 928 (1931); *California Toll Bridge Authority* v. *Kelly*, 218 Calif. 7 (1933); *Bloxton* v. *State Highway Commission*, 225 Ky. 324 (1928); *Estes* v. *State Highway Commission*, 235 Ky. 86 (1930); *Bates* v. *State Bridge Commission*, 109 W. Va. 186 (1930). In the Alabama case, which was one of the first of its kind, a dissenting justice wrote that "it seems, on principles of equity, that the state cannot avoid liability for the principal. Either this, or the state might aid in perpetrating the fraud to its own benefit," which was unthinkable. He reasoned that the corporation was a child of the state and all its benefits inured to the state, which would receive all its property at dissolution.

utility or property, acquired with the proceeds of the bonds . . . do not constitute debts of the particular state. . . ."[33]

Bridge bonds have been issued either by special state agencies or by highway commissions. The special agencies—usually bridge commissions or authorities—are usually composed of state officials acting ex-officio and are thus, for all practical purposes, a part of the regular state governments. In most instances the bridges will pass to the state and tolls will be removed when all bonds are retired.

The few cases in which courts disapproved bridge revenue bonds turned upon minor points. In 1935 an issue of refunding bridge bonds in Kentucky contained a provision that if toll revenues should be insufficient to cover debt service, the deficiency should be supplied by the highway commission. The court ruled that such a feature would make the bonds obligations of the general highway funds and hence unconstitutional.[34] The provision was eliminated, and the bonds were resold. The Rhode Island court held that bridge revenue bonds would not be constitutional if they were sold in the name of the state.[35] A Michigan act authorizing bridge bonds included a provision exempting them from taxation and making them lawful investments "in the same manner and to the same extent as other bonds of the State." The court stated that "these obligations are not bonds of the State and therefore cannot be lawful investments," as are other state bonds. If this section had not been separable, the court would have been forced to disapprove the whole act.[36]

Revenue Bonds of Educational Institutions

Several of the cases discussed in the development of the special fund doctrine involved revenue bonds issued by state universities. In the past ten years such bond issues have increased greatly. The advent of the New Deal with its search for suitable lending opportunities was an important factor in the increase. Almost without exception the courts now approve such borrowing.

33. *In re California Toll Bridge Authority*, 212 Calif. 298, 302 (1931).
34. *State Highway Commission* v. *King*, 259 Ky. 414 (1935).
35. *Opinion to the Governor*, 193 Atl. 503 (1937).
36. *Attorney-General* v. *State Bridge Commission*, 277 Mich. 373 (1936).

The details of the borrowing plans used by educational institutions vary considerably. The simplest and the one closest to the principle of revenue borrowing is for the institution to borrow to finance a building, pledging for debt service the net revenues from the building, which may be a dormitory, a dining hall, a stadium, a library, or other college building. Sometimes, but not usually, a mortgage on the structure is given. In many instances the institution promises to pay for light, heat, water, janitor service, and other operating expenses from its general funds, leaving debt service as the first and only claim on gross rentals or income. In other instances the institution pledges the income from other buildings already built to aid in debt service. If the structure is not income-producing, funds for debt service may be raised by levying a fee on all students.[37] Finally, the institution may promise to service the debt from any funds available.

As an alternative to direct borrowing, the institution may convey land to a nonprofit corporation (usually composed of university or state officials) which will borrow money and erect certain buildings. The university will then rent the buildings at a price adequate to cover debt service. The conveyance is usually limited in time and carries an agreement that when all bonds are retired, title to land and buildings will revert to the university.

The courts usually approve all the above forms of borrowing,[38] reasoning that there is no liability on the state and that tax revenues are not obligated. A Minnesota case is often cited as a precedent. In it the court, while recognizing that the property of the university was really state property, held that "the board could use campus rentals for the building of a dormitory without a legislative appropriation for such purpose and in spite of an appropriation for a

---

37. Several universities, including the universities of Montana and Wisconsin, have financed buildings by levying fees on students for the use of union buildings. The University of Virginia levies a fee of twenty dollars per year on each student to service library bonds.

38. Some typical cases are: *Hopkins* v. *Baldwin*, 123 Fla. 649 (1936); *McDonald* v. *University of Kentucky*, 225 Ky. 205 (1928); *Caldwell Bros.* v. *Board of Supervisors of L. S. U. and A. and M. College*, 176 La. 826 (1933); *Fanning* v. *University of Minnesota*, 183 Minn. 222 (1931); *Barbour* v. *State Board of Education*, 92 Mont. 321 (1932); *McLain* v. *Regents*, 124 Ore. 629 (1928); *Loomis* v. *Callahan*, 196 Wis. 518 (1928).

different one. . . . The legislature . . . assumed to give the university that which was its own . . . neither dormitory nor the land upon which it is built nor other property of the university or the state, saving the income mentioned, shall be security."[39] In a Florida case the court stated that "should any attempt be hereafter made to have the state appropriate for, or to divert any tax resources to, the retirement in whole or in part of the revenue certificates . . . appropriate relief . . . may be hereafter had in due course of legal procedure."[40]

The Wisconsin court refused to condemn borrowing by the university merely because the plan was a subterfuge devised to circumvent the constitutional limitation. A dissenting opinion in that case stressed the moral obligation involved and the fact that the university and the state were really one.[41]

The only case in this group which disapproved borrowing of this kind is from North Dakota and follows the precedent of the McMillan case cited above. The plan was to convey land to a building corporation. The court held that it allowed the conveyance of state property and the pledge of state property and income as security for the debt. The reasoning, as in the Candland case, was that all property belonged to the state. A further point was that the state constitution limited state debts to thirty years while the proposed debt was to run for fifty years.[42] The Georgia court upheld borrowing by the university, but the state government, in its opposition to the New Deal lending program, forestalled borrowing by enacting a law declaring the Board of Regents to be a governmental agency, the university property to be state property and members of the Board to be public officers.[43]

Obligations of Special Agencies

As the courts came to recognize the special fund doctrine, many states created special agencies or commissions with the power to issue revenue bonds or gave that power to existing agencies. Most

39. *Fanning* v. *University of Minnesota*, 183 Minn. 222, 228 (1931).
40. *Baldwin* v. *Hopkins*, 123 Fla. 649, 659 (1936).
41. *Loomis* v. *Caldwell*, 196 Wis. 524 ff.
42. *Wilder* v. *Murphy*, 56 N. D. 436 (1928).
43. *State* v. *Regents of the University System of Georgia*, 179 Ga. 210 (1934); *Georgia Laws*, 1935, Part I, Title IV, No. 20.

such agencies were composed of state officials acting ex-officio or of regular state departments or commissions organized under a new name. Court decisions on such borrowing have been divided, often depending upon whether existing state property or income was pledged to service the bonds.

The Montana court approved a plan allowing a state board to engage in irrigation and flood control work and to issue revenue bonds to be serviced from the income of such projects.[44] The Oklahoma court, in approving a similar plan, stated that it recognized the special fund doctrine in a "restricted sense." It continued with a statement which is a good summary of the elements of the strict doctrine: "The project is purely self-liquidating. The act does not pledge any existing revenues of the state or of the Authority, and does not pledge any revenues derived from taxation, either on an ad valorem basis or by special taxes. . . . In the event of the failure of revenues from the properties to be acquired by the district, the state is under no obligation to make up the loss."[45] In Oregon, revenue bonds to finance a state office building were approved. A Washington court approved the issue of revenue bonds by the Liquor Control Board to be paid from liquor revenues and by the Director of Conservation and Development to be secured by obligations of local governments.[46] The Rhode Island court refused to allow the issue of revenue bonds which involved the pledge or transfer of state property as security.[47] In Louisiana, however, the court approved revenue bonds issued by a state institution and secured exclusively by a pledge of certain state revenues. It held that the "dedication" of taxes to the institution was not an "appropriation" and hence not forbidden by the constitution; that debts of state agencies "which are separate and distinct legal entities are not debts or liabilities of the State."[48]

44. *State* v. *Cooney*, 100 Mont. 391 (1935). Other similar cases are: *Brown* v. *The Arkansas Centennial Commission*, 194 Ark. 479 (1937); *Christman* v. *Wilson*, 187 Ky. 644 (1920); *Hughes* v. *State Board of Health*, 260 Ky. 228 (1935).
45. *Sheldon* v. *Grand River Dam Authority*, 182 Okla. 24, 29 (1938).
46. *Eastern and Western Lumber Co.* v. *Patterson*, 124 Ore. 112 (1928); *Ajax* v. *Gregory*, 177 Wash. 465 (1933); *State* v. *Yelle*, 183 Wash. 380 (1935).
47. *Re Opinion to the Governor*, 169 Atl. 748 (1933).
48. *State* v. *Charity Hospital*, 182 La. 268, 275 (1935).

The Alabama court disapproved two plans for the issue of revenue bonds to be secured by pledges of state appropriations.[49] The Florida court also disapproved two plans, one involving transfer of property by a state board to a nonprofit corporation and the other including a mortgage on property to be acquired and a pledge of state appropriations. In the latter case the court held that the mortgage would be "an express contract lien and charge upon the corpus of the property of the state" and that the proposed pledge of appropriations was "without authority of law and ineffectual." It hinted that the proposal would have been approved if it had included only a pledge of revenues from the project.[50]

An Idaho proposal which apparently involved no pledge of existing state property or income was disapproved by the court, which stated, in part: "Though disclaiming state liability, it is clearly the intention of the act to place the credit of the state, morally and in some degree financially, back of this enterprise . . . this so-called agency of the state is authorized to 'create' a 'debt or debts' . . . which *somebody, some agency or some fund must eventually pay;* and that, *under the authority, command and administration of this Board*. [Italics in original.]"[51] An essentially similar Kansas case was decided in the same way.[52] An Ohio plan was held invalid on the grounds that existing state revenues were included in the pledge of funds for debt service.[53]

Two important Pennsylvania cases show how close decisions in cases of this kind may be. In 1935 Pennsylvania created the General State Authority to construct buildings for state departments and institutions. The state was to convey land to it and to lease the buildings, after they had been erected, at a price sufficient to cover expenses and debt service. Revenue bonds issued by the authority would be retired within thirty years, after which the property would revert to the state. The court held the act invalid on the ground

49. *In re Opinion of the Justices*, 225 Ala. 356 (1932); *In re Opinion of the Justices*, 227 Ala. 289 (1933).
50. *Sholtz* v. *McCord*, 150 So. 234 (1933); *Brash* v. *State Tuberculosis Board*, 124 Fla. 167, 175 (1936).
51. *State Water Conservation Board* v. *Enking*, 56 Idaho 722, 734 (1936).
52. *State* v. *Atherton*, 139 Kan. 197 (1934).
53. *State* v. *Griffith*, 22 N. E. (2d) 200 (1939).

that bonds payable from a special fund are proper and outside the constitutional limitation only when issued for self-liquidating projects and that the contemplated projects were not self-liquidating because the funds were to come from state appropriations. It also ruled that the proposed transactions were contracts for instalment purchase rather than true leases.[54]

Some changes were made in the lease agreements, and a year later the case was brought before the court for a rehearing. The court granted the rehearing because of certain new facts which were brought to its attention, namely: (1) land of the state or authority had been exempted from execution; (2) it was shown that the state would pay less rent to the authority than it was then paying; and (3) "the new leases will be 'straight' leases to the commonwealth, and, at the end of the thirty year period, the title and ownership of the project and ground will be in the General State Authority. There is no provision for re-conveyance to the state."[55] Debt service was to be a first claim on any funds available to the various institutions. The court defined a self-liquidating project as "one wherein the revenues received are sufficient to pay the bonded debt and interest charges over a period of time. The source of the receipt is not important." The court then upheld the act, making the following points: (1) no property but only income was pledged to service the bonds. "This difference between a pledge of property and a pledge of income merely has been said to distinguish a transaction which creates a debt within the constitutional limitation from one creating a debt not within it." (2) The lease agreements were only lease agreements and not contracts to purchase property; "if this were an outright purchase of property to be paid for in the future, it would undoubtedly be within the constitutional limitation." (3) "The fact that the proposed plan might be termed an evasion of the constitution would not condemn it unless such evasion was illegal. It is never an illegal evasion to accomplish a desired result, lawful in itself, by discovering a legal way to do it." (4) The legislature had the power to exempt the bonds of the

54. *Kelly* v. *Earle,* 320 Pa. 449 (1936).
55. *Kelly* v. *Earle,* 325 Pa. 337 (1937).

Authority from taxation. "The legislature may exempt from taxation the bonds of governmental instrumentalities."

Of the "new facts" mentioned by the court, it appears that the only significant one was that the state would not get its land back, with the buildings erected thereon, when the bonds were retired. The land would continue to be held by a state agency, which is practically indistinguishable from the state itself. Under the principle that the source of debt service funds is not important, any state debt is self-liquidating so long as the state raises the necessary revenues and makes sufficient appropriations to the various departments and institutions. On that basis a general fund debt is self-liquidating until the state defaults.

Revenue Obligations of States

Several states have, at different times, proposed to issue revenue bonds directly. The Iowa legislature proposed an issue of $20,-000,000 such obligations to repay public deposits lost in bank failures, the bonds to be serviced from interest payments on deposits, proceeds from bank liquidations, and certain taxes. The court held it unconstitutional.[56] Oregon issued, with the approval of its court, bonds for unemployment relief to be serviced from profits of the state liquor store system.[57] New Mexico issued revenue bonds to finance the construction of a supreme court building, secured by the proceeds from a fee of $2.50 on every civil action in the state. The court approved the bonds on the grounds that the constitutional debt limitation applied only to debts to be paid from a property tax.[58] The unique form of borrowing practiced in Georgia, whereby the state discounts the rentals from a leased railroad, also received approval.[59]

At least three states have issued revenue obligations of the tax-anticipation type. In 1935 the Pennsylvania legislature authorized $45,000,000 of such obligations to be repaid from tax revenues collected during that biennium. The amount was increased to $60,000,-

56. *Hubbell* v. *Herring,* 216 Iowa 728 (1933).
57. *Moses* v. *Meier,* 148 Ore. 185 (1934).
58. *State* v. *Connelly,* 39 N. M. 312 (1935).
59. *Wright* v. *Hardwick,* 152 Ga. 302 (1921).

ooo in the next biennium and to $100,000,000 in 1939. Provisions for repayment are made by setting aside large amounts from tax revenues in the last few months of the biennium. The court held that such obligations did not come within the constitutional limitation.[60] An Illinois act of 1931 authorized the issue of tax-anticipation notes up to 75 per cent of taxes already levied, the notes to state "the particular State tax against and in anticipation of which they are issued" and to be payable "solely from said tax when collected and not otherwise." The court held that the notes did not constitute a debt in the constitutional sense because a tax becomes an asset of the state when levied.[61] In 1937 Alabama sold $1,750,000 of warrants to be repaid from the proceeds of the gasoline tax.

Classification of States

Apparently the courts in all states recognize the special fund doctrine in some form. On the basis of the above cases it is possible to make a tentative classification of some of the states into two groups. In one group the doctrine is applied strictly, while in the other it is applied loosely. The classification must be tentative because in some states borderline cases have not arisen and because courts may change their position, as did the Pennsylvania court. With these qualifications the states covered by the cases discussed above may be divided as follows: (1) states in which the doctrine is applied strictly: Alabama, Florida, Idaho, Iowa, Kentucky, Montana, North Dakota, Ohio, Oklahoma, and Utah; (2) states in which the doctrine is applied loosely: Arkansas, Kansas, Louisiana, Minnesota, New Mexico, Oregon, Pennsylvania, South Carolina and Washington.

APPRAISAL

In the development and application of the special fund doctrine, most courts have shown an almost complete disregard for, or ignorance of, the economic factors involved. Decisions have been made more often on the basis of narrow, legalistic reasoning than on a broad consideration of economic effects. The courts have taken a

60. *Kelly* v. *Baldwin,* 319 Pa. 53 (1935).
61. *The People* v. *Nelson,* 344 Ill. 46, 50, 52 (1931).

term from the field of finance and around it have developed an attenuated legal doctrine which bears little resemblance to the original meaning of the term. It is a standard rule of constitutional law that constitutional provisions should be interpreted in the light of their meaning at the time they were framed, but it would be absurd to contend that the framers of the various state constitutions, or the voters who approved them, contemplated the exclusion of the various kinds of indebtedness which many courts have exempted under the special fund doctrine. Several important court decisions have resulted from the misinterpretation, or irrelevant application, of earlier decisions.

In the field of state finance, there is no economic justification for the special fund doctrine. If a state has a reasonable debt limitation it can borrow directly, and, by proper adjustments, realize all the advantages offered by revenue borrowing while avoiding its disadvantages. The disadvantages of revenue borrowing by states and state agencies are discussed in a later chapter, but it may be noted here that two of them are: a higher rate of interest and a weakening of state control over the management and use of the proceeds. Direct borrowing would avoid both of these. On the other hand, a state could finance any project directly and, by the appropriate rules and regulations, make it self-supporting to the same extent as under revenue borrowing.

The principal cause of the development of revenue borrowing has been the existence of strict constitutional debt limitations. Some of those limitations appear to be too rigid and severe, and should be modified. Perhaps many courts thought that they were merely making the constitutions flexible and practical when they recognized the special fund doctrine, but in several instances they have practically nullified the limitations by a liberal interpretation of the doctrine. South Carolina affords an outstanding example of such nullification. It is not possible to specify definite rules, but obviously there are boundaries beyond which courts may not go in the interpretation of constitutions if the will of the people is to be observed. In some cases, at least, the courts have gone beyond any reasonable boundaries in the application of the special fund doctrine.

One final point should be noted. When the courts permit a certain type of borrowing under the special fund doctrine there is then no constitutional limitation whatever on such borrowing. The only remaining safeguard arises from the discretion of the men in control and the investors who buy, or refuse to buy, the bonds.

CHAPTER XIX

OTHER COURT INTERPRETATIONS OF
CONSTITUTIONAL PROVISIONS

NEARLY ALL the cases considered in the previous chapter involved long-term bonds or certificates. Since those obligations were in the form of true debts, the courts could not logically rule that they were exempt from constitutional provisions on the ground of form; they were exempted only by invocation of the special fund doctrine. Most of the other problems related to state borrowing which have been presented to the courts for decision have involved forms of obligations and nature of claims. For example, when and to what extent do warrants, treasury notes, appropriations, and contracts constitute state debts? Many state constitutions forbid the state to assume the debts of local governments. Yet states may share taxes with, or grant subsidies to, local governments for the purpose of servicing debts, and it is extremely difficult to say exactly where state assumption, as contemplated by the constitution, begins. The same is true of the prohibition, found in many constitutions, against the state's lending its credit. Leading cases involving the above questions are briefly discussed in this chapter.

WARRANTS AND TREASURY NOTES

Warrants are used in the ordinary conduct of state business very much as individuals and business firms use checks. A party with a claim against the state files the necessary information about the claim with the proper state official—usually the auditor. When the auditor has ascertained the validity of the claim and the appropriation under which it is to be paid, he issues an order or warrant on the treasury for its payment. In the ordinary course of business the average modern state has warrants outstanding at any given time amounting to hundreds of thousands or even millions of dollars. When revenues fall below appropriations the treasury becomes unable to pay the warrants as they are presented. In the absence of proper budgetary control, the auditor may continue to issue warrants. Under such conditions they may accumulate until they amount to many millions, as they have in California and Kentucky in recent years. In most states the treasurer is required to stamp warrants which he is unable to pay, and thereafter they draw interest at a rate prescribed by statute. The question which the courts have had to answer is: When, if ever, are warrants to be considered as debts within the meaning of constitutional provisions?

Issuance of Warrants

Without exception the courts hold that the issuance of warrants against cash in the treasury does not create a debt. Obviously this is both sensible and necessary; otherwise a state with a strict debt limitation would be unable to carry on its daily business. The difficulties arise when warrants are drawn against anticipated revenues. Several early California cases held that warrants which were endorsed by the treasurer for want of funds became a part of the state debt as contemplated by the constitution.[1] But a later Nevada case, which has since been widely cited, was to the contrary. The warrants in the latter case were issued to pay legislators and bore interest at the rate of 15 per cent. The court reasoned: (1) without question, ordinary warrants are not debts; (2) warrants against revenues already provided for are essentially the same as current warrants; (3) the payment of interest makes no difference, but is merely a statutory allowance for delay; and (4) the legislature is an essential component of the state government and its activities must be provided for. The conclusion was that the warrants were a debt "but not a debt repugnant to the constitution, as it is only contingent—a debt existent, but payable only upon the collection of revenues."[2]

Generally the courts seem to have followed the Nevada case, and most of them now, in the absence of statutory or constitutional pro-

1. *People* v. *Johnson*, 6 Calif. 499 (1856); *Nougues* v. *Douglass,* 7 Calif. 65 (1857); *State* v. *McCauley*, 15 Calif. 429 (1860).
2. *State* v. *Parkinson*, 5 Nev. 17, 27-28 (1869).

visions to the contrary, allow the issue of warrants against the collection of taxes already levied.[3] The theory was accurately and fully stated by the Oklahoma court as follows: "When a warrant was issued for the payment of money, by the proper officer by virtue of an appropriation where the money was already within the treasury ... or where a tax levy had already been made, and provision made for the collection of the same, and such warrant was issued on such fund in the treasury as would be supplied by such tax, the issuance of such warrant did not create an indebtedness within the terms of the constitution. . . ."[4] The California court used the same reasoning to justify the registration of warrants which could not be paid immediately, and the payment of interest thereon.[5]

Alabama, in 1931, attempted to masquerade bonds as warrants by authorizing the issue of $15,000,000 in "warrants" to pay outstanding warrants, claims, and accounts owed by the state. The new "warrants" were to be in denominations from $100 to $1,000, payable at fixed dates from 1932 to 1941, and to carry coupons for interest at the rate of 5 per cent. Obviously these were to be true bonds, and the court so decided.[6] A second Alabama proposal was to allow the auditor to issue, to the holders of two or more warrants, one warrant for the total sum and to enter on the new warrant the date when funds would be available to pay it. The court approved this plan.[7] The Kentucky court rejected a plan which would have allowed the state to sell five-year, 5 per cent warrants and to use the proceeds for the retirement of outstanding warrants.[8] Later, however, as described in Chapter XIV, it approved an essentially similar issue of warrants.

3. Some typical cases are: *In re the Incurring of State Debts,* 19 R. I. 610 (1896); *In re State Warrants,* 6 S. D. 519 (1895); *Bryan* v. *Menefee,* 21 Okla. 1 (1907); *Rowley* v. *Clarke,* 162 Iowa 732 (1913); *State* v. *Eagleson,* 32 Idaho 276 (1919); *Stanley* v. *Townsend,* 170 Ky. 833 (1916).

4. *Bryan* v. *Menefee,* 21 Okla. 1, 9. Cf.: "Warrants issued in anticipation of taxes are held not to constitute a debt on the theory that moneys, the receipt of which is certain from the collection of taxes, are regarded as for all practical purposes already in the treasury and the contracts made upon the strength thereof are treated as cash transactions" (59 *Corpus Juris* 224 n.).

5. *Riley* v. *Johnson,* 219 Calif. 513 (1933).

6. *In re Opinion of the Justices,* 223 Ala. 130 (1931).

7. *In re Opinion of the Justices,* 225 Ala. 360 (1932).

8. *Stanley* v. *Townsend,* 170 Ky. 833 (1916).

Treasury Notes

At least two state courts have applied the theory governing warrants to the issue of treasury notes[9] in anticipation of tax revenues. The Idaho court held that the rule "applies to treasury notes with equal force as to state warrants,"[10] while the Oklahoma court has stated: "We find no wrong in providing a means of taking up properly issued warrants by use of notes of less burden, payable out of the same revenues from which the warrants ultimately would be payable."[11] Such notes are, of course, closely related to the revenue notes issued by Alabama, Illinois, and Pennsylvania, as discussed in the previous chapter. The position of the Idaho and Oklahoma courts, however, does not appear to be generally accepted; no other supporting cases are found. In 1935 California voters rejected a proposed constitutional amendment to allow the state to borrow in anticipation of revenues up to 50 per cent of the previous year's revenues.[12] In Minnesota the prohibition against borrowing has been evaded without a decision of the court.

The attorney-general's office has ruled that certificates of indebtedness, maturing up to ten years, can be issued outside the constitutional restrictions on borrowing providing that the law authorizing the debt also provides for an annual levy for its retirement. In such instances the state is held to be merely anticipating the future receipt of revenue and is not creating a debt. This policy, which is one of doubtful validity, has not been passed upon by the Minnesota Supreme Court.[13]

Funding of Warrants and Treasury Notes

In several instances states with large amounts of interest-bearing warrants outstanding have attempted to fund them into bonds without the approval of the people as required by constitutional provisions. The attempts were made under provisions, found in almost

9. Treasury notes are short-term, interest-bearing obligations. They may be used for any kind of short-term borrowing, but states use them principally to anticipate tax collections and bond sales.

10. *State* v. *Eagleson,* 32 Idaho 276, 280 (1919).

11. *In re State Treasury Note Indebtedness,* 90 P. (2d) 19, 26 (1939). This case, however, is not strictly comparable with the Idaho case, since the Oklahoma court, as noted below, held in recent years that both warrants and notes are debts.

12. *Resolutions and Amendments,* 1935, c. 128.

13. Arthur Borak, "Minnesota Changes Its Tax System," *Bulletin of the National Tax Association,* XXIII (1938), 213.

all constitutions, allowing the legislature to refund existing debts without a vote of the people. If the courts held that warrants were debts, it would be proper to fund them without popular approval. This could be repeated indefinitely to build up a large debt. If the courts found that warrants were not debts, they would have to find some special category in which to put them if the legislatures were to be required, or even allowed, to pay them. As explained above in Chapter XIV, the Kentucky court took a middle course, holding that the warrants were not debts and hence could not be refunded without popular approval, but were "valid evidences of casual deficits" or "orders on the treasury of the state . . . both valid and collectible" and that it was "an inexorable duty of the Legislature to provide" for their payment.[14]

The Montana court reached a different conclusion in a similar case. In response to the contention that if the warrants were debts they were invalid because they had been issued in amounts far larger than allowed in the constitution, the court fell back upon a plea of expediency and concluded: "This is the interpretation of our constitution 'by the spirit which vivifies and not by the letter which killeth.' "[15] Eight years later the same court approved a larger issue for the same purpose.[16]

In 1935 the Oklahoma court approved an issue of funding bonds of approximately $10,000,000 to retire warrants on the ground that the warrants were "valid and existing obligations of the state . . . subject to being funded," and that the funding bonds "neither create any debt nor increase the debt of the state."[17] In 1939 it was called upon to approve another issue, this time for over $18,000,000 for the same purpose. The decision bears evidence that the court regrets its former decisions and would like to reverse its position but does not dare do so. "Whatever construction might be placed upon the above constitutional provision if its interpretation were before us for the first time, we are not willing to depart from the construction placed thereon, and necessarily relied on, in the long-standing opinions of

14. *State Budget Commission* v. *Lebus*, 244 Ky. 700, 710-711 (1932).
15. *Toomey* v. *State Board of Examiners*, 74 Mont. 1, 23 (1925).
16. *State* v. *Erickson*, 93 Mont. 466 (1933).
17. *In re State Funding Bonds of 1935, Series A*, 173 Okla. 622, 625 (1935).

this court above cited. Under the rule of stare decisis, we follow them."[18]

As the matter now stands, the legislatures of Montana and Oklahoma may borrow any amounts they wish (assuming willing lenders) by issuing tax-anticipation notes and funding those notes into long-term bonds bearing the full faith and credit of the state. The courts of those states have applied the special fund doctrine strictly, but have left another loophole wide open.

The Kentucky court has affirmed the power of state officials to contract for the sale of both new and refunding warrants at rate of interest, agreeable to the purchaser, below the statutory rate provided for warrants which are not paid on presentation.[19] California accomplished the same result by a change in the statute, and both states have taken advantage of this power to reduce the rate of interest on their warrants and have issued and refunded warrants very much as though they were short-term notes. As previously noted, California sold warrants in 1938 bearing interest at a rate as low as ½ per cent.

Appraisal

Regarding warrants, the position taken by the California court in 1860 is economically sound. Certainly the average individual does not consider that he has created a debt when he writes a check against funds in his bank. But when he gives a check without having on deposit sufficient funds to cover it, he is in debt. So it should be with the state. To prevent the haphazard accumulation of a warrant debt, the auditor should be forbidden to issue warrants

18. *In re State Treasury Note Indebtedness,* 90 P. (2d) 19, 26 (1939). Three justices wrote specially concurring opinions, all protesting against the accepted rule. One wrote: "I am of the opinion that [our prior] decisions should now be overruled so that in the future no debt will be created in violation of our Constitution. By the foregoing decisions the provisions of our Constitution . . . have, under the guise of judicial construction, been rendered nugatory. . . . The result is that now we have a debt of some $25,000,000 incurred without a vote of the people for 'casual deficits or failures in revenue or expenses not provided for' in the face of plain language . . . that 'such debts . . . singly or in the aggregate, shall not, at any time, exceed four hundred thousand dollars.' " Another said: "[I believe] that the constitutional provisions should be . . . interpreted as the people understood it at the time of adoption, notwithstanding local ingenious judicial decisions holding that a debt is not a debt" (*ibid.,* pp. 27-28).

19. *Bankers Bond Co.* v. *Buckingham,* 265 Ky. 712 (1936).

whenever there are not sufficient funds in the treasury to pay them. This might be accomplished by forbidding the issuance of warrants, (1) whenever outstanding warrants exceed cash in the treasury, or (2) so long as the treasurer is unable to pay warrants as they are presented.[20] This would place the burden of providing the funds necessary for the operation of the state government upon the policy-determining officers of the state, where it properly belongs, rather than upon the auditor.[21] The policy-determining officers, in turn, should be empowered to provide the needed funds by borrowing at short term in reasonable amounts, as suggested below. Such arrangements would provide a more orderly and systematic method of finance.

Treasury and other tax-anticipation notes should definitely be treated as debts. They are evidence that the state has incurred obligations beyond its present ability to pay. The fact that taxes have been levied which will probably retire them does not change the nature of the notes. Estimates of tax yields are doubtful at best. Legislators in a hurry to adjourn may arbitrarily increase revenue estimates in order to balance the budget. Sudden changes in economic conditions may drastically reduce revenues. The proper arrangement in this connection would be to provide in the constitution that tax-anticipation notes are to be considered as debts, and to give to the proper state officials the power to issue such notes up to 25 or 30 per cent of the previous year's revenues. Any amount remaining unpaid at the end of the fiscal year should be considered as a casual deficit, to be funded and retired from tax revenues over the ensuing four or five years. Such arrangements would definitely limit such financing and place the responsibility on the proper officials, while still allowing them ample means of providing funds in the periods within the fiscal year when receipts are low. Under the interpretations used by most courts now, funds may be borrowed up to 100 per cent of the vague and uncertain estimates of future tax revenues.

20. These provisions would apply separately to each fund against which warrants are drawn.

21. It would also prevent the injustice of forcing state employees and others who receive the warrants to pay the interest on the state's debt.

APPROPRIATIONS AND CONTRACTS

Appropriations

The courts adopt much the same attitude toward legislative appropriations as toward warrants, and several of the above cases affirm the legislature's power to appropriate funds in advance of their receipt.[22] Obviously this is the only practical view, since a legislature could not wait until all revenues were collected before making appropriations. Such appropriations, however, may extend only until the next regular meeting of the legislature and revenues must be provided to cover them. "If the appropriations or other obligations assumed during any fiscal year, aside from government expense, exceed the revenues of that year, such excess has been held to constitute an indebtedness within the meaning of the constitution."[23] The California court has held that the legislature cannot, after warrants have been issued, repeal or modify an appropriation act so as to defeat the payment of the warrants from "such moneys as would otherwise accumulate in such fund."[24]

Contracts

States and state agencies often find it desirable and convenient to enter into long-term agreements or contracts, especially regarding the rental of property. Where payments are to be made over a period of years as services are rendered, it is not proper to consider such contracts as debts to the full amount of the payments to be made. Yet if such contracts are considered binding on the state, they have much the same effect as debts in that they definitely allocate future expenditures and place them beyond the control of the legislature. Courts have frequently been called upon to decide whether and to what extent contracts are debts within the meaning of constitutions.

An early California decision approved a long-term lease contract by the state to pay $10,000 per month for the use of certain property on the ground that "Until the services are rendered there can be no

22. *In re the Incurring of State Debts,* 19 R. I. 610 (1896); *In re State Warrants,* 6 S. D. 519 (1895); *State* v. *Eagleson,* 32 Idaho 276 (1919).

23. 59 *Corpus Juris* 223-224. On the other hand, however, the Alabama court approved the action of a state board in borrowing money for buildings, to be repaid from appropriations of later years. *In re Opinion of the Justices,* 220 Ala. 539 (1930).

24. *Riley* v. *Johnson,* 219 Calif. 513, 521 (1933).

debt on the part of the state. . . . The state only became indebted as the services were each month performed."[25] In Kentucky the highway commission entered into certain contracts extending over several years. It contended that it could incur obligations so long as the payments to be made in any one year did not exceed revenues for that year. The court pointed out that the commission received appropriations every two years and could not be sure of funds beyond the end of any given biennium. Since the state may not impair the obligation of a contract, if the commission could make valid contracts extending beyond the biennium it could bind the state, defy the legislature, and nullify its power. Hence it held that the commission could not make contracts beyond the period covered by existing appropriations.[26] The Florida court went further and refused to allow the road department to borrow up to 20 per cent of estimated revenues for the current year, in accordance with an act of the legislature. It held that a debt incurred by the department pursuant to lawful authority was a state obligation, whether for a long or a short time, and refused to sanction any borrowing at all.[27]

Appraisal

It is, of course, necessary to allow appropriations to be made in advance of the receipt of revenues. But under a proper system of budgetary control, appropriations are never debts or liabilities of the state; they are made subject to the condition that they will be paid only if, and to the extent that, revenues are adequate to cover them. The director of the budget is given power to reduce all appropriations to the extent necessary to keep expenditures within the limits of revenues. Under such a system there would be no cause for considering appropriations as debts.

The situation regarding contracts is somewhat more complicated. If a given legislature authorizes or approves a contract, that contract would, to the extent that it is considered valid, bind future legislatures despite the generally accepted rule that one legislature may

25. *State* v. *McCauley*, 15 Calif. 429, 455 (1860). The Pennsylvania case which approved the revenue bonds of the General State Authority ruled the same way. *Kelly* v. *Earle*, 325 Pa. 337 (1937).

26. *Billeter and Wiley* v. *State Highway Commission*, 203 Ky. 15 (1924).

27. *Advisory Opinion to the Governor*, 94 Fla. 967 (1927).

not bind another. Since this subject has many ramifications and must be fitted into a larger constitutional system, it would seem that it is one which could and should be governed by court interpretations rather than by specific constitutional provisions. It would be proper and fitting for the courts to develop a constructive doctrine which would integrate the controlling law on this point with the specific provisions of the existing constitution. Thus, in states where the legislature is forbidden by the constitution to incur debts, the court might well hold that all long-term contracts are made with the implied condition that they are subject to future appropriations, since state officials and the legislature are without power to bind the state further.

ASSUMPTION OF LOCAL DEBTS

In recent years many states have been importuned to assume, or to help in servicing, the debts of local governments. One reason for such agitation has been the widespread financial embarrassment of local governments. Another has been the growing recognition by states of their responsibility for the financing of highways. Since many of the local debts were incurred to finance the construction of roads, the local units feel that when the state assumes the maintenance of the roads, they should also assume the service of the bonds which were sold to build them. Action by the state to provide relief for the local units has frequently posed troublesome problems for the courts.

Many state constitutions contain specific provisions forbidding the state to assume the debts of local governments.[28] Some prohibit grants or payments to such units. The generally accepted rule of interpretation is that such limitations, even if municipal and political subdivisions are specifically mentioned, do "not apply to the assumption of debts for state purposes incurred by an agency of the state or under state authority."[29]

In most states the courts have been liberal in their interpretations

28. For example, the Arkansas constitution provides that the state "shall never assume or pay the debt or liability of any county, city, or other corporation whatever" unless such debt was incurred "to repel invasion, suppress insurrection, or to provide for the public welfare and defense" (Art. XII, par. 12).
29. 59 *Corpus Juris* 210.

of such provisions. The Arkansas court, as noted in Chapter XV, approved the assumption by the state of the large debts of road districts, holding that the districts were corporations for the purpose of their creation, but were really quasi-governmental or state agencies. It held further that the assumption might be justified under the public welfare clause, since highways "are for the public welfare in a sense."[30] The Florida constitution forbids the levying of any state tax or the use of any state funds to pay local debts. The court's interpretation of this provision partially invalidated the first act to service local road bonds from the highway fund. In a second case the court approved an essentially similar act on the ground that the primary purpose of the act was not to pay the debts of counties and districts but to reimburse them for expenditures made on state roads.[31] In Georgia the court ruled that an act authorizing the highway commission to reimburse counties for road expenditures did not violate the provision prohibiting the assumption of local debts.[32]

The Oregon court has approved acts whereby the state paid the interest and sinking fund requirements on rehabilitation bonds issued by a city after severe fire damage, and paid the interest on bonds issued by counties to build interstate bridges.[33] The Texas constitution provides that "The Legislature shall have no power to make any grant . . . of public money to any individual, association of individuals, municipal or other corporations whatsoever" except as reimbursement for aid given in time of public calamity. The court upheld the act appropriating highway funds for the service of county and district road bonds on the ground that it was "The settled law of this State that the above quoted constitutional provision does not prevent the appropriation or granting of State funds to municipal and political corporations when the money is granted to be used for a governmental purpose."[34]

30. *Bush* v. *Martineau,* 174 Ark. 214 (1927). See also *Tapley* v. *Futrell,* 187 Ark. 844 (1933).
31. *Amos* v. *Mathews,* 99 Fla. 1 (1930); *Carlton* v. *Mathews,* 103 Fla. 301 (1931).   32. *Faves* v. *City of Washington,* 159 Ga. 568 (1925).
33. *Kinney* v. *City of Astoria,* 108 Ore. 514 (1923). *Stoppenback* v. *Multonah,* 71 Ore. 493 (1914). In the latter case the court held that the constitutional prohibition applied only to debts "in contracting which the state originally had no part."
34. *Road District No. 4* v. *Allred,* 123 Tex. 77, 89 (1934).

The few instances in which courts have prevented assumption of local debts are illustrated by the two cases below. The Indiana Board of Agriculture proposed to convey certain properties to the state on condition that the state assume the debts resting on the property. The state was to levy a property tax to retire the debts. The court held the act invalid.[35] A West Virginia act of 1933 appropriated "so much moneys as may be required" to service certain local road and school bonds issued to finance construction of properties later incorporated into the state road and school systems. The court pointed out that the local communities still received the same benefits as before from the schools and roads and held that "Unless plain and simple words have lost their meaning . . . our present constitution prohibits the Legislature from . . . assuming debts or liabilities such as are in said section indicated, whether such assumption be done directly and unequivocally or by indirection."[36] The court further held that the act would violate the due process clauses of both the United States and West Virginia constitutions, since it would tax some citizens to pay the debts of others.

THE LENDING OF STATE CREDIT

Constitutional provisions concerning the lending or giving of state credit are similar to those governing the assumption of local debts and are equally difficult to interpret and apply. In general the position of the courts is that

In the use of its credit, the state cannot do indirectly what it cannot do directly. A limitation on the power of the legislature to lend or give the credit of the state should, it has been held, be construed liberally to effect its purpose; thus, any plan or scheme, by which, in effect, the credit of the state is given or loaned, is prohibited, regardless of the particular form of the transaction.

[Such limitation, however,] does not apply to a loan or gift of the state's credit for the state's purposes or for the common good.

. . . .

The specific grant of power to do a particular thing, which may involve the use of the state's credit, controls with respect to such special matter as against a general prohibition.[37]

35. *Scott* v. *Indiana Board of Agriculture,* 192 Ind. 311 (1922).
36. *Berry* v. *Fox,* 114 W. Va. 513, 519 (1934). 37. 59 *Corpus Juris* 207-208.

Most of the acts which have been challenged under the above provisions have been upheld by the courts. The Arkansas court approved a plan whereby the state would borrow money and loan it to school districts, stating that the constitutional inhibition was against the lending of state credit and not against the use of it.[38] It also upheld the Agricultural Credit Act under which the state borrowed money and reloaned it to farmers' organizations in a time of severe drought. It added, however, "The doctrine announced in this case has no application except in cases where the calamity is certain and irremediable in its nature and general in its scope."[39] An Iowa act of 1925 authorized the highway commission to contract with counties and pledged "The good faith of the state . . . to cause to be made available, each year, sufficient funds to equal the total of any sums now or hereafter apportioned to the state for road purposes by the United States Government." The effect was to assure the counties that they could borrow for highways, knowing that funds would be available from state highway taxes to service the bonds. The court held that the act did not lend the credit of the state.[40] The Tennessee act to reimburse counties for highway expenditures was held not to involve a lending of state credit.[41] The North Carolina court has interpreted the words "any person, association, or corporation" to mean private individuals or corporations,[42] and has ruled that the purchase of land by a state commission to be donated to the Federal Government for a park does not constitute a lending of state credit.[43]

The Massachusetts court has rejected two proposals involving state credit. The first was to have the state guarantee the bonds of a privately owned bridge corporation, the state to manage the corporation until the bonds were repaid. The court stated: "Scarcely anything can be a more direct giving or loaning of credit than the guaranty of the payment of principal and interest upon obligations

38. *Ruff* v. *Womack,* 174 Ark. 92 (1927).
39. *Cobb* v. *Parnell,* 183 Ark. 429, 445 (1931).
40. *McLeland* v. *Marshall Co.,* 199 Iowa 1232 (1925).
41. *Baker* v. *Hickman Co.,* 164 Tenn. 294 (1932).
42. *Lacy* v. *Bank,* 183 N. C. 373 (1922).
43. *Yarborough* v. *Park Commission,* 196 N. C. 284 (1928).

of another as they fall due."[44] The other plan which the court rejected involved a state-owned corporation along the lines of the H.O.L.C. which would lend money on home mortgages and insure private corporations against loss on such loans.[45]

The New Hampshire constitution contains no specific provisions relating to state credit, but its court was called upon to decide a case on that point. It was proposed to have the state guarantee the bonds of the Water Resources Board, which was to develop the water supply for a certain area. The court pointed out that taxes may not be levied for the benefit of private persons or for private uses and that the same principle applies to the use of the state's credit to guarantee bonds. The validity of the plan would depend on the facts, but from the facts presented the court did not believe the bonds could properly be guaranteed. "If particular users of water are to be the beneficiaries of the project, with the public deriving only indirect advantages from it, it would not be within the agency's power to execute . . . so as to permit you to pledge the state's credit for any of its obligations."[46] If, however, it was shown that the public benefit was uppermost, then the state might properly guarantee the bonds. Evidently the proper officials were able to show that the public benefit was uppermost, for the bonds were guaranteed.

Appraisal

The constitutional provisions regarding assumption of local debts and the lending of state credit could hardly be more definite and specific than they are. Strict provisions are desirable, since the knowledge that the state is ultimately liable or the general feeling that the state will assume debts is likely to breed irresponsibility. The danger is greater because the state usually does not have the same control over borrowing of this kind as it does over direct borrowing. In other words, power and responsibility are to some extent divided.

Most of the courts have been somewhat lenient despite the

44. *In re Opinion of the Justices,* 276 Mass. 617 (1931).
45. *In re Opinion of Justices,* 291 Mass. 567 (1935).
46. *Opinion of the Justices,* 88 N. H. 484, 490 (1937).

definite terms of the provisions. Of the comparatively few cases which have arisen on these points, those in Arkansas and Tennessee involved the largest sums. It is doubtful whether the net result of the actions taken under those decisions was beneficial to all concerned. Admittedly, the courts could easily have reached opposite conclusions by strict constructions.

On one point in particular some courts have been guilty of a fallacy. The general rule is that limitations on assuming debts and lending state credit do not apply to projects involving a state purpose or the common good. But the limitations on direct borrowing, where they exist, certainly apply to borrowing for such projects. Thus to allow the state to assume debts or to lend its credit, in such cases, even for a state purpose, is to allow it to "do indirectly what it cannot do directly." The Oregon and Texas cases cited above illustrate this point.

It would seem to be a fair conclusion that the net result of court interpretation has been to weaken the force of constitutional debt limitations and to obscure and disperse responsibility for borrowing. In some states a more liberal debt limitation is needed, but when it is attained by court interpretation it opens up methods of borrowing which are entirely beyond constitutional control. The diffusion and obscuring of responsibility weaken state control over finances and lead to lax financing without giving any advantage in return.

CHAPTER XX

THE ENFORCEMENT OF STATE BONDS

THE VALUE of private bonds rests largely upon the readiness of the courts to enforce contractual obligations. When an investor purchases a state bond, he enters into a contract with the state. A study of state debts would not be complete without some consideration of the means whereby the holder of a state bond can enforce that contract.

This question involves many technical details on which the best legal experts disagree. In this chapter we shall note briefly the general controlling principles as found in constitutions and court decisions. This must be almost exclusively a study of federal constitutional law for two reasons: first, a state may not be sued in its own courts without its consent; second, even if a plaintiff secured a judgment in a state court, it is doubtful whether it could be enforced if the executive branch of the state government refused to heed it.

JURISDICTION OF FEDERAL COURTS

Before a bondholder can enforce the terms of his contract he must bring action in a court which has jurisdiction over the state which issued the bond. The Constitution of the United States provides that in all suits involving states, the Supreme Court of the United States shall have original jurisdiction,[1] but the Eleventh Amendment of that Constitution provides further that "The judicial power of the United States shall not be construed to extend to any suit in law or equity, commenced or prosecuted against any one of the United States by citizens of another State, or by citizens of any Foreign State."[2] This means that an individual or private company

1. Art. III, sec. 2.
2. This amendment was adopted in 1795, almost immediately after the court had ruled, in *Chisholm* v. *Georgia*, that a state was liable to be sued by a citizen of another state. It was the first amendment to be adopted after the first ten, embodying

may not bring action directly against a state, but it does not necessarily mean that they have no legal remedy at all. In certain circumstances, depending upon the terms of the contract, they may bring action against state officials or state agencies and obtain limited protection.

Actions Dismissed

Actions nominally against state officials which would really involve the state will not be heard by the court. " 'The question whether a suit is within the prohibition of the Eleventh Amendment is not always determined by reference to the nominal parties on the record,' but is determined by a consideration of the nature of the case as presented on the whole record. A suit nominally against individuals, but restraining or otherwise affecting their action as State officers may be in substance a suit against the State which the Constitution forbids."[3]

The *Jumel* case, discussed in Chapter IX, was dismissed on the ground that it was a suit against the state. The plaintiff asked for a mandamus requiring certain state officials to collect taxes and to pay out certain funds as promised in the bond contract. The Court held that a mandamus as requested would require the officers "to act contrary to the positive orders of the supreme political power of the State, whose creature they are."[4] In the *Christian* case a bondholder asked the Court to enforce a lien, contained in his bond, against certain railroad bonds owned by the state and held by the state treasurer. The Court dismissed the action as a suit against the state, but intimated that if the plaintiff had been a true pledgee, the common law right of a pledgee to sell out a defaulting pledgor might have been invoked to make the action one in *rem* against the property alone, and not a suit against the state.[5] The Court has also refused to take jurisdiction in a case to compel a state official to

---

the bill of rights, had been adopted as a group (*The Constitution of the United States*, annotated, Washington, 1938, pp. 37, 727).

3. *Ibid.*, p. 729, and cases cited.

4. *Louisiana* v. *Jumel*, 107 U. S. 711 (1882). See also *Hans* v. *Louisiana*, 134 U. S. 1 (1890).

5. *Christian* v. *Atlantic and N. C. R. R. Co.*, 133 U. S. 233 (1890).

exercise the state's power of taxation where it was clear that the state was an indispensable party.[6]

Actions Upheld

On the other hand, the Court has taken jurisdiction in many cases involving state officials. In all of the Virginia Coupon cases discussed in Chapter VIII, state officials were required to accept coupons in payment of taxes, as promised in the contract. On several occasions state officials have been required to accept bank notes which had been designated as legal tender for the payment of taxes.[7] In another case state officials were forbidden to issue certain bonds in violation of a refunding agreement on the ground that such action would impair the obligation of the contract with bondholders who had already exchanged their bonds.[8] The general position of the Court seems to be: (1) a mandamus or injunction will lie against a state official to compel or to enjoin a purely ministerial, nondiscretionary act when requested by one who is threatened by irreparable injury; (2) if the official pleads the authority of an unconstitutional law, that will not prevent the issuance of the writ, for such a law will be treated by the courts as null and void.[9]

The application of these principles is clearly illustrated in the Arkansas case discussed in Chapter XV. The state had issued certain bonds, pledging as security the proceeds from certain taxes. The state later proposed to divert such proceeds to service an issue of refunding bonds in an effort to compel the bondholders to accept new bonds on unfavorable terms. A district court pointed out that the proposed action was a violation of the contract, and enjoined the state treasurer from paying out the pledged funds in any way contrary to the terms of the contract.[10] The court stated that the plaintiffs did not ask for an order requiring any affirmative action

6. *Cunningham* v. *Macon and Brunswick R. R. Co.*, 109 U. S. 446 (1883).
7. *Woodruff* v. *Trapnall*, 10 How. 190 (1850); *Furman* v. *Nichol*, 8 Wall. 44 (1868); *Keith* v. *Clark*, 97 U. S. 454 (1878).
8. *Board of Liquidation* v. *McComb*, 92 U. S. 531 (1875). The officials were acting under a law enacted by the legislature.
9. *Ibid.*; *In re Ayers*, 123 U. S. 443 (1887). See also the discussion in *The Constitution*, pp. 730-733.
10. *Hubbell* v. *Leonard*, 6 Fed. Supp. 145 (1934).

on the part of state officials, which would have been contrary to the Eleventh Amendment.

It will be seen, therefore, that the relief which bondholders may be able to get in the courts will depend primarily on two factors: (1) the attitude of the court and (2) the terms of the contract. The court must determine what are "purely ministerial acts" and also whether the laws under which officials claim to be acting are constitutional. On both points there is considerable room for the exercise of judgment by the court. The terms of the contract will determine whether the bondholders will be able to get a court order, and, if so, whether it will be of such a nature as to exert pressure on the state to make it act favorably on the bondholders' demands.

It is difficult to see how the court could issue any order which would help the bondholders in the case of a general credit obligation without the pledge of any specific funds. Further, even with such a pledge, if the state should repeal the law which produces the pledged funds, it is doubtful if the courts would take any effective action, since they have repeatedly ruled that they may not exercise the taxing power.[11] In Arkansas the special taxes could not be repealed since the proceeds were necessary for road maintenance. It should be noted in this connection that one of the advantages of revenue bonds over general credit obligations is that they always carry a lien on certain specific revenues which the issuing bodies are pledged to maintain. No doubt this has been an important cause of their growing popularity in recent years.

State Consent

Unless prohibited by its constitution, a state may waive its immunity and consent to be sued, in which case, of course, the Eleventh Amendment would no longer be a bar. If a state is determined on repudiation, such consent would not be forthcoming, and even in other cases it may be difficult or impossible to obtain. In some states

---

11. On one occasion the North Carolina legislature repealed certain tax levies which had been pledged for debt service. The Supreme Court refused to issue a mandamus ordering the auditor to continue to levy and collect the taxes as originally promised. *North Carolina* v. *Temple,* 134 U. S. 22 (1890).

the constitution provides that the state shall never be a defendant,[12] while in at least one state it has been held that "an act giving to an individual the right to sue the State is unconstitutional as special legislation."[13] But even if such consent is given, it is not a contract, and the consent may be withdrawn or the conditions under which suits may be maintained may be changed, even after a suit has started, without impairing the obligation of a contract.[14] Thus, it can be seen that it is difficult for an individual to obtain a state's consent to be sued, and even if he succeeds, it may be taken from him at any moment without any remedy whatsoever. Finally, even if an individual succeeds in obtaining a judgment against a state, there remains the important problem of enforcing the judgment, which is discussed below.

Suits by Other States

Beyond question, the Supreme Court has jurisdiction to hear a case brought by one state to collect a debt owed to it by another state.[15] In such a case, however, the state must be a bona fide creditor and may not act merely as a collecting agency for claims held by its citizens.[16] Nor may the Supreme Court entertain a suit

12. *Kansas City Bridge Co.* v. *Alabama Bridge Corp.*, 59 Fed. Rep. 48 (1932); *Stewart* v. *Commission*, 185 S. E. 567 (Va., 1936). In the former case the court held that, even though the act creating the Bridge Corporation stated that it might sue and be sued, the corporation was an agency of the state and that this was a suit against the state in violation of the constitutional provision that the state should "never be made a defendant in any court of law or equity."

13. *Chick Springs Water Co.* v. *Highway Department*, 159 S. C. 481 (1931). In this case the court held that the highway department was an agency of the state and that an action against it was an action against the state itself.

14. Charles K. Burdick, *The Law of the American Constitution* (New York, 1922), p. 456; Benjamin F. Wright, *The Contract Clause of the Constitution* (Cambridge, 1938), pp. 229-234; *Baltzer* v. *North Carolina*, 161 U. S. 240 (1896); *Beers* v. *Arkansas*, 20 How. 527 (1858); *Bank of Washington* v. *Arkansas*, 20 How. 530 (1858). In 1925 an outstanding authority on constitutional law stated that "It is well settled that 'the laws which subsist at the time and place of the making of a contract and where it is to be performed, enter into and form a part of it, as if they were expressly referred to or incorporated in its terms'" (Lawrence B. Evans, *Leading Cases on American Constitutional Law*, Chicago, 1925, p. 469, quoting from *Von Hoffman* v. *Quincy*, 4 Wall. 535, 1866). The exception is made on the ground that a state's immunity from suit is an element of sovereignty which may not be contracted away.

15. *South Dakota* v. *North Carolina*, 192 U. S. 286 (1904); *Virginia* v. *West Virginia*, 206 U. S. 290 (1907), and ensuing cases cited in Chapter VIII.

16. *New York* v. *Louisiana; New Hampshire* v. *Louisiana*, 108 U. S. 76 (1893).

brought by a state to which one of its citizens is a party.[17] This means that individuals may not benefit from a suit by one state against another except in so far as such a suit exerts pressure upon the defendant state to compromise with individual bondholders, as happened in the South Dakota suit against North Carolina. In 1933-34 the threats of Nevada and Pennsylvania to bring suits on Arkansas bonds held by them in trust funds probably had some effect in inducing Arkansas to enact a new refunding act more satisfactory to individual bondholders. It is doubtful, however, whether there will be any more suits of the South Dakota type, since there is a pronounced feeling among states that they should have more respect for the principle of "comity between states" than to accept defaulted bonds of a sister state for the purpose of bringing suit thereon.

It is well settled that the United States may bring suit against a state upon bonds issued by the state.[18]

Suits by Foreign States

The right of a foreign state to sue one of the United States was long in doubt. Early thought seems to have been that the Supreme Court could entertain such a suit. In *Chisholm* v. *Georgia* it was stated, as an *obiter dictum,* that "as every nation is responsible for the conduct of its citizens towards other nations, all questions touching the justice due to foreign nations, or people, ought to be ascertained by, and depend on, national authority."[19] In *Cherokee Nation* v. *Georgia* "The Supreme Court decided as a judicial question that the Cherokee Nation was not a foreign State, but the justices were in agreement upon the major premise, to wit, that the Supreme Court had original jurisdiction over controversies between a State and foreign States."[20] Thereafter leading jurists assumed this position in their writings, and one of them made a categorical statement to this effect.

17. Burdick, *op. cit.,* p. 96. Further, it will be remembered that in *South Dakota* v. *North Carolina* the court dismissed that part of the action which involved two individual defendants.

18. *United States* v. *North Carolina*, 136 U. S. 211 (1890).

19. 2 Dall. 419, 476.

20. J. S. Reeves, "The Principality of Monaco v. The State of Mississippi," *American Journal of International Law*, XXVII (1934), 740.

488   AMERICAN STATE DEBTS

There was no case on this point until 1934, when the Principality of Monaco applied for permission to bring suit against Mississippi on bonds repudiated before the Civil War. Mr. Chief Justice Hughes wrote the opinion for an undivided Court, pointing out that the Constitution was not explicit on the point. States, he held, are immune from suit without their consent except where there has been "a surrender of this immunity in the plan of the Convention," and he did not believe that the framers of the Constitution intended that states should be sued by a foreign state without their consent. By accepting the Constitution, the states consented to suits by the United States and other states of the Union, but a foreign state "lies outside the structure of the Union"; it is without the coercive jurisdiction of the Supreme Court and may not be sued by one of the United States without its consent. Hence, he concluded that "the Principality of Monaco, with respect to the right to maintain the proposed suit, is in no better case than the donors of the bonds, and that the application for leave to sue must be denied."[21]

Certain interested parties in England have charged that the position of the United States on this question is not in keeping with accepted international law on the responsibility of a federal state for the conduct of its constituent states. They allege that the Federal Government will neither accept responsibility for state actions nor allow foreign states or individuals to bring action for redress in the federal courts.

That Government, in fact, seems to vary its attitude according to whether a dispute lies between its own nationals and a foreign State or between foreign nationals and its own States. It is alone in the world to adhere in theory and practice to the amazing thesis that its own subsidiary (and increasingly subsidized) "sovereign States" can find sanctuary from just debts behind a national aegis, interposed, not only between their foreign creditors and direct diplomatic intercourse, but also between those debtor "sovereign States" and the bar of their own national Supreme Court, while the National Government ingenuously divests itself of all responsibility attaching to such interposition.[22]

21. *Monaco* v. *Mississippi*, 292 U. S. 313, 322, 330 (1934).
22. Council of the Corporation of Foreign Bondholders, *Annual Report* (1930), p. 48.

There is an hiatus in our federal structure here. The states are free to enter into fiscal contracts with the governments or citizens of foreign states, yet the latter are barred from recourse against the states through either diplomatic or federal judicial channels. The situation results from the ever troublesome division of power between the Federal Government and the states. Reeves is of the opinion that "International law does not appear to confer a right upon a State to sue a political subdivision of another State in the courts of the latter. Whether or not such a right exists is purely a matter of the constitutional law of the State and is, therefore, wholly permissive. The fact that the State's organization is federal would seem to make no modification as to its duties in international law."[23]

He does state, however, that the above decision of the Supreme Court closed one door to foreign plaintiffs and at the same time opened the whole question of federal responsibility in international law for the conduct of constituent states. He concludes: "The route of diplomatic reclamation has its terminus in an international court. That the United States would consent to have an international court pass upon the delinquencies of States of the Union, for which the United States might be responsible, is hardly likely."[24]

IMPAIRMENT OF THE OBLIGATION OF CONTRACTS

Practically all actions brought against state officials by bondholders have involved state laws which were alleged to be unconstitutional because they impaired the obligation of the bond contract. Article I, Section 10, of the Federal Constitution, provides that "No State shall . . . make any . . . law impairing the obligation of contracts." Obviously an outright repudiation of its debts by a state would violate this section. "But outright repudiation has been less frequent than some indirect, partially concealed attempt to change the remedy, impose a tax on the obligation, or in some way reduce the value of the instrument of indebtedness."[25] In this section we shall examine several cases to see what kind of action the Court considers to be an impairment of the obligation of a contract.[26]

23. Reeves, op. cit., p. 741.
24. Ibid., p. 742.   25. Wright, op. cit., p. 224.
26. For more extensive treatments of this subject see ibid., chap. x; Burdick, op. cit., pp. 453-457; Evans, op. cit., pp. 527-530; 12 Corpus Juris 998-999.

All of the numerous Virginia Coupon cases were brought on the ground that the state was attempting to impair the obligation of the contract contained in the coupons by taxing them, refusing to accept them in payment of taxes and fees, prescribing unusual and difficult methods for proving their validity, and otherwise discriminating against them. In a great majority of the cases the federal courts held that the state acts were invalid.[27] In 1874 Louisiana entered into an agreement with bondholders to refund certain debts. A later act provided that certain additional debts not included in the original agreement should be refunded. The Supreme Court held the act invalid on the ground that it would weaken the security of the bondholders who had already exchanged their bonds.[28] As noted in Chapter IX, the Minnesota court approved a refunding plan on the ground that the constitutional amendment which repudiated the bonds impaired the obligation of a contract.[29] Previously the Supreme Court of the United States had strongly intimated that the amendment was unconstitutional. On several occasions the Court has held that states must accept bank notes and other obligations which had been designated as receivable for taxes.[30]

On other occasions the Court has found that certain state acts impaired the obligation of contracts, but was unable to give the bondholders the relief they sought because to do so would have involved direct action against the state. Such were the *Jumel* and *Christian* cases, discussed above. A North Carolina law of 1869 authorized the issue of certain bonds and the levy of a tax to service them. Subsequent acts of the legislature repealed the tax levy. The acts clearly impaired the obligation of the bond con-

27. See the cases cited in the first section of Chapter VIII. Regarding attempts to reduce the interest rate indirectly through taxation of interest payments, the Court has said: "A change of the expressed stipulations of a contract, or the relief of a debtor from strict and literal compliance with its requirements, can no more be effected by an exertion of the taxing power than it can be by the exertion of any other power of the State legislature." *Murray* v. *Charleston*, 96 U. S. 432 (1878).

28. *Board of Liquidation* v. *McComb*, 92 U. S. 531 (1876).

29. *State* v. *Young*, 29 Minn. 474 (1881).

30. *Briscoe* v. *Bank of Kentucky*, 11 Pet. 257 (1837); *Woodruff* v. *Trapnall*, 10 How. 190 (1850); *Furman* v. *Nichol*, 8 Wall. 44 (1869); *Keith* v. *Clark*, 97 U. S. 454 (1878). The case of *Hagood* v. *Southern*, 117 U. S. 52 (1886) also involved script which had been made receivable for taxes, but in that instance the Court ruled that the action was a suit against the state.

tract, but when bondholders asked the federal courts for an order requiring the auditor to levy and collect the tax they were refused on the ground that it was a suit against the state.[31] Other such cases could be cited, but the principle is clear; even when a state act clearly impairs the obligation of a contract, the federal courts will not interfere to protect a private bondholder where such protection would require a positive, affirmative intervention in the affairs of the state government. In other words, under certain conditions a private bondholder may maintain, in the federal courts, an action to protect himself from loss which would result from a state's impairing the obligation of its contract, but under other conditions the Eleventh Amendment is an effective bar against such action.

On the other hand, the Court has ruled that certain changes in the remedy or procedure for enforcing the contract do not constitute an impairment of the obligation.[32] As noted above, the consent of a state to be sued is not a contract, and its withdrawal does not constitute impairment. Even the power given to a state court by a state constitution is not part of a contract. When certain bonds were issued by North Carolina in 1868, the state supreme court had jurisdiction to hear claims against the state, but could not issue a judgment against the state. It could only make recommendations to the legislature, which was free to accept or reject them. A later amendment repealed the recommendatory power of the court and repudiated certain bonds. The Supreme Court of the United States ruled that the state court had never been able to take action constituting a remedy and that the removal of its recommendatory power did not constitute impairment of the obligation of a contract.[33]

The Court has ruled further that a contract to pay interest is not to be implied when a state fails to pay obligations when they become due. On one occasion the United States held certain North Carolina bonds which were not paid at maturity. Later the state

31. *North Carolina v. Temple*, 134 U. S. 22 (1890).

32. On this point Burdick states: "By the obligation of a contract must be meant the legal obligation—the obligation of the parties to adhere to their agreement, which, at the time of contracting, the law recognized and made enforceable . . . it has been held that where the statute deals only with remedy, if a reasonably adequate remedy is left the obligation of the contract has not been impaired" (*op. cit.*, pp. 453-454).

33. *Baltzer v. North Carolina*, 161 U. S. 240 (1896).

offered to pay the principal and all interest coupons, but the United States demanded, in addition, interest from the date of maturity to the date of payment. The matter was brought before the Court which held that "Interest . . . is not to be awarded against a sovereign government unless its consent to pay interest has been manifested by an act of legislature, or by a lawful contract of its executive officers . . . the state, unless by or pursuant to an explicit statute, is not liable for interest even on a sum certain which is overdue and unpaid."[34]

From the above it can be seen that despite the constitutional prohibition, states may, under certain conditions, impair the obligations of contracts with impunity. If only private parties are injured and if the conditions are such that the federal courts may not enjoin state officials without positively interfering with state policy, the courts are, under their present doctrine, powerless to entertain a suit. It has been suggested by interested British parties that the Federal Government should assume a more aggressive position in this matter and should, on its own initiative, take positive steps to prevent the states from violating the Federal Constitution.[35] The argument is that in many instances only private individuals are injured by state action, that they are barred by the Eleventh Amendment from seeking relief and that, therefore, the Federal Government should act to protect them from illegal state action. Such action would represent a fundamental change in our present theory of federal government and is not likely to occur in the near future.

ENFORCING JUDGMENTS AGAINST STATES

The extent to which, and the methods by which, federal courts may enforce a judgment against a state have been and still remain moot questions. Since the courts will not entertain any action by private parties which would require direct action against a state, the powers and methods which the courts may employ in such cases are distinctly more limited than in cases brought by the United States or by other states. The two types of cases will be discussed separately.

34. *United States* v. *North Carolina,* 136 U. S. 211, 221 (1890).
35. Council of the Corporation of Foreign Bondholders, *Annual Reports* (1929, 1930, and 1931), *passim.*

Actions by Individuals

Since the courts will allow private parties to proceed only against state officials, and not against the state itself, the chances of securing an execution of the judgment in such cases are better than in cases which would require affirmative action by the state. Where the judgment against officials is negative or restraining, the courts may proceed directly against such officials personally. If they disregard the court order, they may be adjudged in contempt of court and may be imprisoned or fined. Thus by physical coercion they may be prevented from taking the action forbidden by the court.[36] If they resign from office to escape the court order, the office would be left vacant and the forbidden act would not be committed. Thus, it would appear that in cases of this kind the federal courts, if they choose to exert their powers to the limit, may enforce their judgments with certainty and assure plaintiffs such relief as they find appropriate.

Where the judgment requires state officials to take some affirmative, although ministerial and nondiscretionary, action, enforcement of the judgment may be more difficult. In such a case the court may issue a writ of mandamus ordering an official to take a specified action. If he refuses, the court may fine or imprison him, but that does not insure that the action will be taken. The official may resign or remain in prison indefinitely without complying with the order. No cases of this kind involving state officials are found, but between 1870 and 1890 and again in 1932 there were several instances in which local government officials defied federal court orders and remained in prison for long periods.[37] In cases of this kind, then, the judgment of the court may be defeated by the determined resistance of state officials.

36. It will be remembered that the Attorney-General of the State of Virginia was imprisoned in 1887 on such an order by a district federal court. The Supreme Court granted him a writ of habeas corpus on the ground that the action against him was a suit against the state. *In re Ayres,* 123 U. S. 443 (1887).

37. A. M. Hillhouse, *Municipal Bonds* (New York, 1936), pp. 92, 285. In some instances the officials remained in hiding to escape the service of court orders.

Actions by Other States

Judgments arising from cases against a state brought by other states or by the United States are likely to be more difficult of enforcement and may fully test the power of the Court, since they may require some affirmative action by the state itself. Early decisions indicated definitely that the Court did not consider itself competent to force a state to act against its will. The case of *Kentucky* v. *Dennison* was long considered as controlling. In it the Court stated: "If the Governor of Ohio refuses to perform his duty, there is no power delegated to the General Government, either through the Judicial Department or any other department, to use any coercive means to compel him."[38] Some years later the Court held that the taxing power "belongs in this country to the legislative sovereignty, State or National. . . . It certainly is not vested . . . in any Federal Court. . . . It is not only not one of the inherent powers of the Court to levy and collect taxes, but it is an invasion by the judiciary of the Federal Government of the legislative functions of the State Government."[39] Another case decided at the same term stated the same conclusion and held further that if local government officials should resign rather than obey a mandamus ordering a tax levy, the power of the Court was exhausted; that the Court could not levy a tax itself.[40]

In *South Dakota* v. *North Carolina* the Court reviewed these and other decisions and stated further: "The public property held by any municipality, city, county, or State is exempt from seizure upon execution, because it is held by such corporation, not as a part of its private assets, but as a trustee for public purposes. As a rule no such municipality has any private property subject to be taken upon execution."[41] On the other hand, it pointed out the clear statement of the Court's jurisdiction over "controversies between two or more States," and the "necessity of some way of ending controversies between States, and the fact that this claim for the payment of money is one justiciable in its nature."

38. 24 How. 66 (1861).
39. *Heine* v. *The Levee Commissioners,* 19 Wall. 655, 661 (1873).
40. *Rees* v. *Watertown,* 19 Wall. 107 (1873).
41. 192 U. S. 286, 318.

In this case the Court was able to reach a decision without having to deal with the levying of taxes or the seizure of public property. The bonds on which the suit was brought carried a lien on certain railroad stocks owned by North Carolina. The Court concluded: "And surely if, as we have often held, this court has jurisdiction of an action by one State against another to recover a tract of land, there would seem to be no doubt of the jurisdiction of one to enforce the delivery of personal property." The Court then ordered that the stocks be sold unless North Carolina paid before a designated day. North Carolina paid, and the Court was spared the necessity of going further into the question of coercing a state.

In the long controversy between Virginia and West Virginia the Court was forced, by West Virginia's recalcitrance, to examine the question further. One of West Virginia's arguments was that the Court had no jurisdiction over the case because it did not have the power to enforce a judgment. In the last of the several decisions the Court turned back for a consideration of the circumstances surrounding the framing of the Constitution and the adoption of the Eleventh Amendment, and concluded that it was the intention of all concerned, by giving the Court jurisdiction over controversies between states, to give it also the power to enforce its decisions. It pointed out that without such power in the Court, one state might wrong another with impunity and thus destroy the Union. It therefore held that it had "the duty to enforce the judgment by resort to appropriate remedies . . . , even although their exertion may operate upon the governmental powers of the State."

It then proceeded to examine methods of enforcement and mentioned four: (1) legislation by Congress; (2) a mandamus ordering the legislature of West Virginia to levy a tax to pay the judgment; (3) "the levy of a tax adequate to pay the judgment and [provision] for its enforcement irrespective of state agencies"; and (4) "such other and appropriate equitable remedy, by dealing with the funds or taxable property of West Virginia or the rights of the State, as may secure an execution of the judgment."[42] The Court invoked none of these methods, but preferred to allow West Virginia time

42. *Virginia* v. *West Virginia*, 246 U. S. 565 (1918).

to act without further coercion. West Virginia met its obligation, and again the Court was relieved of the necessity of implementing its judgment.

In recent decisions the Court has definitely abandoned its earlier position and indicates that it is now ready, although reluctant, to take steps sufficiently drastic to compel a state to respect its judgments.

SUMMARY

Since the Eleventh Amendment prevents private parties from suing a state, the individual holder of a state bond must rely principally on the good faith of the issuing state. In exceptional circumstances he may get some relief by bringing suit against state officials if he can show that they are performing, or failing to perform, to his detriment, some ministerial, nondiscretionary duty under color of an unconstitutional law. The extent of the relief that can be obtained in this way will depend largely upon the terms of the bond contract. Other states or the United States may sue a state directly to enforce the collection of a bond, but such action is unlikely to benefit private bondholders; in rare cases it may induce the defaulting state to offer private bondholders a more satisfactory compromise.

States may adopt various indirect means of reducing the burden of their obligations and inflicting loss on bondholders. The courts have been diligent in protecting bondholders in such cases if the latter are able to maintain action in the courts.

Judgments rendered in the type of cases which individuals may bring against state officials can usually be enforced by the courts. Determined resistance by the officials, however, may render a writ of mandamus impotent. Judgments directly against a state that require some affirmative action by the state are more difficult of enforcement. The Supreme Court has not yet been forced to choose a specific method of enforcing such judgments, but it has indicated that it will, if necessary, secure compliance with its decrees by proceeding directly against the state government or by exercising the taxing power itself.

CHAPTER XXI

STATE REVENUE AND LIMITED OBLIGATION BONDS

IN PRECEDING chapters attention was directed primarily to the direct debts of the states; that is, obligations pledging the full faith and credit of the states and issued through regular state channels. From time to time, however, reference has been made to revenue bonds and other indirect or contingent obligations issued either by the states themselves or by various state departments, agencies, or institutions. Chapter XVIII showed how most state courts have come to consider such obligations as special issues, the sale of which can be justified under the special fund doctrine, without the approval normally required by constitutions. It is now appropriate that we should examine in some detail these obligations, which are rapidly increasing in volume.

NATURE AND PURPOSES OF REVENUE BONDS

The Concept

In general usage the term "revenue bond" does not have a definite or uniform connotation. The various instruments which have been given this label vary widely in their features and in the revenues or income pledged for their service. In the broad, general sense, such as has been employed in previous chapters, the term means all obligations of political units or their agencies, institutions, or departments which do not bear the full faith and credit of any political unit but which are payable from certain designated sources of revenue, whether such sources be tax revenues, fees, or earnings of proprietary enterprises. Roughly, the term includes all bonds issued under the special fund doctrine.

In sharp contrast with the above is the strict or scientific meaning of the term. The best statement of this concept is given in a recent study as follows: *"Revenue bonds are all those bonds of political units that are payable as to principal and interest exclusively from the earnings, or (in case of a sale of the property) from other non-contributed assets, of a specified revenue-producing enterprise, for the acquisition, construction, improvement, or operation of which enterprise the bonds were issued.* [Italics in original.]"[1] The author points out that this definition excludes all bonds bearing the full faith and credit of any political unit and also bonds which are payable in the first instance from specified earnings but which may, if such earnings are inadequate, be paid from other sources. The term also excludes "obligations, the principal and interest of which are payable from some other enterprise than the one for which the funds are borrowed, or obligations that are payable from excise taxes, although the taxes may be closely related to the financed enterprise."[2] It thus excludes bonds which are to be paid from "automobile registrations, liquor and other licenses, penalties, forfeitures, and land grant funds."

On two points this concept is not definite. First, it does not specify whether the "earnings" from which the bonds are to be paid are gross or net. A state might assist an undertaking by exempting it from taxes, by providing repairs, maintenance, and administration, or by rendering other services. Such aid might be so extensive as to place the real burden of the debt on the taxpayers of the state. In another place Knappen states that the pledging of gross income "is contrary to the revenue bond theory which is bottomed on the idea of fully self-supporting enterprises."[3] Presumably, then, "earnings" are to be interpreted to mean "net earnings." Second, the concept does not indicate the source of the revenues or earnings. If they come entirely or in large part from state appropriations, either directly or indirectly, there is always the possibility that the earnings may be artificially produced and that the state may be using the project merely as a screen for indirect

---

1. Laurence S. Knappen, *Revenue Bonds and the Investor* (New York, 1939), p. 1. A substantially similar definition is given in Federal Emergency Administration of Public Works, *Revenue Bond Financing by Political Subdivisions: Its Origin, Scope, and Growth in the United States* (Washington, 1936), p. 1. As its title indicates, this study is concerned exclusively with revenue bonds of local governments.

2. Knappen, *op. cit.*, p. 2.   3. *Ibid.*, p. 52.

borrowing. In most instances the state is not dealing with the project at arm's length, and the appropriations made by the state are frequently determined by debt service requirements of the so-called revenue bonds. If the state promises, before the bonds are sold, to make such appropriations, the obligations are not true revenue bonds.

It matters little which concept of revenue bonds is used if the differences between them are kept clearly in mind. Perhaps the greatest danger arises from the fact that arguments in favor of true revenue bonds may be advanced to justify the issue of obligations which are not revenue bonds at all, but merely disguised state obligations. This was noted in nearly all the cases which marked the development of the special fund doctrine.

In the realm of state finance there have been few obligations which meet the specifications of the strict concept of revenue bonds. A few state agencies and institutions have issued such obligations, but Knappen states that "not one single state revenue bond, as strictly defined here, has been discovered despite much searching."[4] For lack of a better term and in keeping with popular usage, the term "revenue bond" will continue to be used here in its broad and general concept, despite the inaccuracy. Most of the evaluations, criticisms, and recommendations given below depend upon the fact that nearly all such obligations are not true revenue bonds.

Difficulties and Limitations

There are two major difficulties in dealing with revenue bonds in relation to state finance. The first is the difficulty of determining whether certain revenue bonds fall within the sphere of state or of local finance. Some revenue bond projects are purely local and are sponsored by local units, while others are just as clearly state projects. But others, usually administered by special agencies created by the state, fall between these two categories. In this chapter the attempt is made to limit consideration to those projects falling clearly within the sphere of state finance.

The second difficulty is the absence of comprehensive data. The regulations governing the issue and sale of direct state obligations

4. *Ibid.*, pp. 75-76.

usually do not apply to revenue bonds. The latter may be sold at private sale, and no public report may be made. Some state officials seem intentionally to suppress information about revenue bonds, evidently fearing that the giving of information might be construed as state recognition of responsibility.[5] As a result, there are no comprehensive and accurate statistics on the sale of revenue bonds or amounts outstanding.

Highway Revenue Bonds

Six states have issued revenue bonds directly to finance highway construction, and in 1938 had outstanding $92,106,000 of such obligations. Fourteen other states had assumed or were servicing from highway revenues $363,912,000 of local government road bonds.[6] All of these are clearly in the sphere of state finance, since they were issued or assumed for state purposes and are serviced from the proceeds of state taxes. However, they do not meet any of the tests of a revenue bond. The highway projects do not produce any net revenue, since no direct charge is made for their use. On the other hand, thousands of car owners who use their cars only on city streets may help to pay the service on the bonds, although they never use the roads for which the bonds were issued.

Logically there is no valid reason for classifying such obligations as revenue bonds except that they do not carry the full faith and credit of the state and that the courts have approved their issue under the special fund doctrine. They depend for their service upon the exercise of the state's taxing power and are paid from the proceeds of the states' most lucrative tax.

Revenue Bonds of State Educational Institutions

Revenue financing by state educational institutions has grown rapidly in recent years. As noted in a previous chapter, such financing had its origin in the past century. Only within the past fifteen years, however, has it assumed important proportions. The New Deal's lending programs of 1933-35 and 1938, accompanied by liberal

5. Cf. Frederick L. Bird, "The Problem of Revenue Bonds," *Bond Buyer*, Nov. 27, 1937, p. 2.
6. The states, with amounts outstanding in each, are shown in Table 25.

grants, were primarily responsible for the large growth in recent years. An analysis of the very incomplete data at hand shows total issues of $60,203,625 distributed by years as follows:[7]

Before 1934	$9,152,000	1936	$ 3,649,500
1934	8,176,000	1937	8,082,500
1935	9,680,500	1938	21,463,125

Amounts given by *Moody's* as outstanding in 1938 total $55,207,101,[8] but the figures were incomplete at the time of publication. Further large issues were sold in November and December, 1938, in order to take advantage of federal offers which were to expire at the end of the year. The states in which the bulk of such financing has occurred are Indiana, Kentucky, Louisiana, Michigan, Montana, Oklahoma, Texas, and Virginia.

TABLE 39

REVENUE BONDS OF STATE EDUCATIONAL INSTITUTIONS OUTSTANDING IN 1938*

State	Amount	State	Amount
Arizona	$ 1,267,000	North Carolina	$ 1,520,000
Arkansas	2,852,000	Ohio	1,105,000
Colorado	2,000,101	Oklahoma	2,460,500
Florida	202,000	Oregon	1,377,000
Idaho	798,000	Pennsylvania	1,400,000
Indiana	5,504,000	South Carolina	596,000§
Iowa	615,000	Texas	8,736,000
Kentucky	1,601,000	Virginia	4,278,500
Louisiana	11,002,000†	Washington	376,000
Michigan	2,862,500‡	West Virginia	1,387,500
Montana	1,550,000		
New Mexico	1,717,500	*Total*	$55,207,101

*This tabulation is not complete, but it includes all issues listed in Moody's *Governments and Municipals* for 1939.
†Includes an issue of $6,000,000 sold by the Louisiana State Board of Education in August, 1938, for the benefit of various educational and charitable institutions.
‡Does not include several large issues sold in November and December, 1938.
§Does not include $1,522,000 issued by the state, and bearing its full faith and credit, for the benefit of educational institutions, of which $150,000 are payable from tuition fees of the State Medical College.

The bonds have been issued primarily to finance the construction of dormitories, student union buildings, dining halls, libraries, and athletic facilities. In a majority of cases P.W.A. grants covered from 30 to 45 per cent of total costs. If the projects were revenue-

7. The figures were derived from *Moody's* and a collection of circulars issued by bond houses.
8. The amounts for each state are shown in Table 39.

producing, net or, more frequently, gross revenues were pledged for debt service; in other cases the usual procedure was to levy a fee on all students. Only rarely were bondholders given a mortgage lien on property of any kind; the usual security was a pledge of revenues together with a promise of the issuing agency to keep the facilities fully used in so far as possible and to charge rates adequate to produce sufficient funds for servicing the bonds. In some cases this means that if there are not sufficient students to fill all dormitories, students must be placed first in those for which revenue bonds were issued, leaving vacant those which are free of debt.

Among the issues examined in detail, not one was found which met all the tests of a revenue bond. The most usual features which prevent such classification were subsidies from the issuing institution in the form of free heat, water, power, or, in some instances, all operating expenses. Quite often revenues from buildings already in existence, constructed from general funds, were pledged for debt service. In many cases student fees ranging from $2.50 to $20.00 per year were levied to provide all or a part of the funds required for debt service. Such fees were most frequently used in connection with student buildings, libraries, auditoriums, and administration buildings. In a few instances no specific funds were pledged; the bonds were to be serviced from the general funds of the issuing institution.

A sample of thirty issues from ten states was analyzed in detail with results as stated below. All except three issues were sold in the years from 1936 to 1938. The thirty issues amounted to $12,284,000, or approximately $400,000 per issue. Only three contained a mortgage lien on real estate, while twenty-two were callable. In regard to nominal or coupon rates of interest they were divided as follows:[9]

3	per cent, 4	4	per cent, 13
3½	per cent, 7	4½	per cent, 2
3¾	per cent, 5	5	per cent, 1

9. Two of the issues were split between different rates of interest. The effective yield would be a more accurate measure of the true interest cost, but this was not available in many instances. The indications are, however, that most issues were sold near par. Of fourteen issues for which prices are available, eight were sold at par, two at 98½, and four at 97.

This would indicate that the average nominal rate was slightly below 4 per cent. The issues were to be serviced, in whole or in part, from the following sources: student fees, 18; net income from the project, 9; gross rentals or income from the project, 6; income from other properties, 7. In at least thirteen cases the institution promised to subsidize the project by supplying free water, heat, power, or other services. In several issues this point was not mentioned specifically, but it is possible that such a subsidy was contemplated. All issues except one were serial in form with final maturities distributed as follows:

1946-50	2	1961-65	2
1951-55	11	1966-70	6
1956-60	9		

The average final maturity was not far from twenty years.

The institutions which issued these obligations are supported by the state, their property is state property, and their finances are regulated by the state. In many cases subsidies out of state appropriations or income from state property were pledged for debt service. In a majority of cases compulsory student fees, which operate as a tax on all students, were so pledged. Clearly these obligations are in the sphere of state finance, and just as clearly they are not true revenue bonds. Since there is nothing approaching a complete list of such obligations, the total cannot be determined. We know only that it is substantially greater than the total of the figures given by *Moody's*. Probably an estimate of $75,000,000 would be reasonable.

Toll Bridge Revenue Bonds

The financing of costly bridges has been handled in several different ways by the states. In some, such as Arkansas, Maine, New Hampshire, Tennessee, and perhaps a few others, general state obligations were issued, and the proceeds from tolls set aside into special funds to service the bonds. In others, such as Kentucky and West Virginia, regular highway or road departments have issued revenue bonds which depend entirely upon tolls for their service. In several other states special commissions or authorities have been created to sell revenue bonds. Often such authorities are ex-officio bodies and for all practical purposes are parts of the regular state governments.[10] Some are incorporated and others are not. Often it is difficult to determine whether the authorities are meant to be state-wide in their operations or whether they are of only local significance. If they are purely local they should not be considered as operating in the sphere of state finance. The bonds selected for consideration in this section were chosen on the basis of the personnel of the issuing body. Information in this field, however, is so incomplete that there might well be other issues which should be included.

Most toll bridge obligations are true revenue bonds, although several of the projects are subsidized by highway departments, as noted below. Table 40 shows the amounts of toll bridge revenue bonds outstanding in 1938 issued by state agencies, departments or

TABLE 40

CERTAIN TOLL BRIDGE REVENUE BONDS OUTSTANDING IN 1938

State	Issuing Agency		Amount
Ala...	Ala. Bridge Authority, Inc.	$ 2,118,700	
	Ala. State Bridge Corp.	3,000,000	
	Ala. Bridge Commission	950,000	$ 6,068,700
Calif..	Calif. Toll Bridge Authority		$ 73,000,000
Ky...	State Highway Department		13,522,000
Mich..	State Bridge Commission		2,300,000
N. Y..	N. Y. State Bridge Authority		1,953,000
Ohio..	Ohio State Bridge Commission		5,500,000
Pa...	Del. River Joint Commission of Pa. and N. J.	37,520,000	
	Del. River Joint Toll Bridge Commission	2,500,000	40,020,000
Vt...	Missisquoi Bay Bridge Commission		200,000
W.Va.	W. Va. State Road Commission		2,743,000
	Total		$145,306,700

Source: *Moody's*, 1939.

10. For example: "The California Toll Bridge Authority consists of important state officials, such as the governor and the heads of departments concerned with public works. At the recommendation of the Department of Public Works, the Authority is authorized to issue its bridge revenue bonds and direct the Department of Public Works to build and operate the bridges financed, collect the tolls thereon, and turn the money over to the State Treasurer" (Robert Klaber, *Bridge Revenue Bonds,* p. 26).

commissions, according to the data available. It cannot be regarded as complete because of the inadequacy of data and the uncertainty of separating state from local projects.

In Alabama three agencies have issued bridge revenue bonds. The Alabama State Bridge Corporation issued $5,000,000 of bonds, but defaulted in 1934. The state highway department leased all bridges and removed all tolls; the $3,000,000 of bonds now outstanding are serviced from the lease payments. The Alabama Bridge Authority, Inc., has outstanding $2,118,700 of bonds which are serviced from highway revenues; it charges no tolls on the bridges which it built. Neither of the above issues are true revenue bonds, but merely limited obligations serviced from state funds. The Alabama Bridge Commission has outstanding $950,000 of bonds which are serviced from tolls.

The $73,000,000 of bonds of the California Bridge Authority were issued for the construction of the Oakland-San Francisco Bridge and are serviced from tolls. The Kentucky State Highway Commission has issued all of that state's $13,522,000 bridge bonds outstanding in 1938. They are serviced from tolls, but the state pledged its good faith "to give its moral support to the payment of both principal and interest on the bonds. All the cost of operating, maintaining, repairing and insuring the bridges shall be paid from other State funds."[11]

All the other bridge bonds shown in the table were issued by special bridge commissions, except those in West Virginia, which were issued by the State Road Commission, and all are serviced from tolls. The issue of the Missisquoi Bay Bridge Commission in Vermont has certain unusual provisions. The $200,000 of bonds outstanding in 1938 were regular revenue obligations with first claim on net revenues. But an additional issue of $100,000 was to be issued and to be "sold to State of Vermont for purpose of defraying part of bridge construction costs. This issue is to be junior to $200,000 serial 4s (above), and no interest or principal on this issue of 2½% bonds shall be payable until the issue of 4% bonds has been fully paid and cancelled."[12]

11. *Moody's*, 1939, p. 536.   12. *Ibid.*, p. 1624.

It appears that of the approximately $145,000,000 of bridge revenue bonds issued by state agencies and considered here, only a little over $5,000,000 are serviced from state funds. The others are serviced entirely from tolls, although in several cases the state highway department pays for repairs, maintenance, and/or insurance.

Other Revenue Bonds

The states and their agencies have issued a considerable volume of revenue bonds for a variety of other purposes. Some are true revenue bonds, some are supported entirely by state taxes or other state funds, while others are mixed in nature. The amounts are shown in Table 41.

TABLE 41

MISCELLANEOUS STATE REVENUE BONDS OUTSTANDING IN 1938

State	Issuing Agency or Nature of Bonds		Amount
Ark...	State Board of Education, Revolving Fund Bonds		$1,040,000
Ga....	Western and Atlantic Warrants		5,985,000
Ill....	Ill. Armory Board		1,150,000
Ind...	State Board of Agriculture	$ 490,000	
	Armory Bonds	1,122,000	1,612,000
Ky....	Board of Health	$ 192,000	
	State Board of Agriculture	124,000	
	Ky. Children's Home Association	64,000	380,000
La....	Charity Hospital		$8,820,000
Mont..	Water Conservation Board		1,316,000
N. H..	Water Resources Board		*1,400,000
N. M.	Capitol Addition Bonds		714,647
N. Y..	Saratoga Springs Authority		3,200,000
N. C..	State Board of Health		160,000
N. D..	Capitol Building Certificates	$ 418,000	
	Water Conservation Commission	150,000	568,000
Wash.	Department of Conservation and Development		$ 333,000
	Total		$26,678,647

*Does not include $900,000 Series B bonds guaranteed by the State of New Hampshire.
Source: *Moody's*, 1939.

The $1,040,000 of bonds in Arkansas were issued by the State Board of Education and are secured by obligations of local school districts. The Georgia obligations are the railroad warrants discussed in a previous chapter. Both Illinois and Indiana have sold revenue bonds to finance the construction of armories. National Guard units rent the armories and pay the rent from state appropriations. In both cases the bonds are in reality state obligations. The Kentucky bonds issued by the State Board of Health and the Children's Home Association are paid only from state appropriations.

The bonds issued by the Charity Hospital of Louisiana are serviced entirely from a certain portion of the state franchise tax on corporations. Thus they are limited state obligations payable from a specified tax. Nevertheless, the court justified their issue under the special fund doctrine. The New Mexico bonds were issued directly by the state and are payable from the rentals of public land and from a special fee on all civil actions in state courts. The North Carolina State Board of Health receives its income partly from state appropriations and partly from fees. Its bonds are payable from all funds under its control. The North Dakota Capitol Building Certificates are payable from a special tax levy, but they have been justified under the special fund doctrine. The bonds of the Washington Department of Conservation and Development are secured by the bonds of local reclamation districts in the state.

The above-mentioned bonds issued by Georgia, Illinois, Indiana, Kentucky, Louisiana, New Mexico, North Carolina, and North Dakota, are not true revenue bonds. They total over $18,000,000, or more than two thirds of all bonds considered here.

TECHNICAL AND INVESTMENT ASPECTS

Legality of Issue

Since the bonds under discussion do not bear the full faith and credit of the state, they are usually issued without the constitutional approval required in many states. Hence the legality of their issue usually depends upon the extent to which the courts of the particular state recognize the special fund doctrine. For this reason bond dealers and underwriters generally insist that the legality of each issue be tested in the courts, unless similar bonds have already been approved. This precaution has forestalled the sale of many proposed issues and has apparently insured the validity of all issues sold to the public, for the records show no instance of the invalidation of an issue after it has been sold. In the field of local revenue bonds, however, the courts have held two Texas issues to be invalid, and bondholders have lost everything.[13]

Negotiability

Under the Uniform Negotiable Instruments Law revenue bonds are nonnegotiable because they do not carry an unconditional promise to pay. In many instances, however, they are made negotiable by statute. Investors and dealers usually prefer negotiable bonds because they are protected when they acquire title innocently and in good faith, regardless of the title of the person from whom they acquired the bond. On the other hand, if they intend to hold the bond and have taken the proper precautions at the time of purchase, a nonnegotiable bond offers an advantage in that they would still have a claim against the issuer in case the bond were stolen. To the issuer a nonnegotiable bond is dangerous in that it might be presented for payment by one who did not have a good title. If the issuer should pay him, the rightful owner of the bond could still demand payment.[14]

Legality as Investment

One of the reasons why state bonds command a ready market is that they qualify, almost without exception, as legal investments for commercial and savings banks, insurance companies, trustees, and other similar parties. In this respect revenue bonds are at a considerable disadvantage. As a class, revenue bonds are not eligible for purchase by banks which are members of the Federal Reserve System, but most of them are eligible in that they meet the requirements prescribed by banking authorities for bonds in general. This means, however, that a bank's purchases of one issue are limited to 10 per cent of its capital and surplus. Revenue bonds are frequently designated as legal investments for savings banks in the state in which they are issued, but "correspondence with most of

13. Knappen, *op. cit.*, pp. 115-118. The bonds in question were sold by Cross Plains and Hamlin, Texas.

14. For a further discussion of this point see *ibid.*, pp. 63-65, and John F. Fowler, Jr., *Revenue Bonds* (New York, 1938), pp. 107-108.

the superintendents of banking in the northeastern states has not revealed a single instance in which the law has been interpreted in a way to allow savings banks to buy revenue bonds—barring express statutory authority."[15] Again, particular issues may meet the requirements or be designated as legal investments, but revenue bonds issued in most of the states will have some difficulty in gaining access to the savings banks of the Northeastern states. Further, in New York "no bonds that are issued after 1938 and that are not supported, to some extent, at least, by the faith and credit of the issuing body, will be eligible for savings bank investment."[16]

Since insurance companies are not subject to such strict regulation as savings banks, nearly all of the former are free to purchase revenue bonds. "The slightly higher income available on revenue bonds has caused them to be looked upon with favor by some of the life insurance companies," and in recent years the amount of such bonds held by insurance companies has increased considerably. Revenue bonds are frequently legal for trust funds, but it depends entirely upon state law. Pennsylvania is one important state in which they are not legal.[17]

Tax Status

Revenue bonds and the income from them are invariably exempted from local property and income taxes, and in the past the income has been exempt from the federal income tax. In recent years, however, the Supreme Court of the United States has shown an inclination to narrow the scope of tax exemption by declaring that salaries paid, and activities engaged in, by state agencies and institutions are subject to federal taxes if the activity is not an essential one, or if such taxation will not impose a burden upon the state.[18] These decisions have raised serious questions concern-

15. Knappen, op. cit., p. 104.   16. Ibid., p. 105.

17. For further discussion of this topic see ibid., pp. 102-109, and Fowler, op. cit., pp. 140-146.

18. Helvering v. Gerhardt, 304 U. S. 405 (1938), and Allen v. Regents of the University System, 304 U. S. 439 and 590 (1938). The latter point made by the Court puts the proponents of revenue bonds in a rather paradoxical situation. To justify the issue of the bonds, they had to argue that the bonds could not, in any way, impose a burden upon, or a claim against the state. To justify exemption from

ing the future tax status of revenue bonds. Federal revenue authorities have held that bonds of the Marine Parkway Authority are liable for the federal stamp tax. In 1939 President Roosevelt requested Congress to extend the federal income tax to cover salaries and interest paid by state and local governments. Congress complied to the extent of taxing salaries; the trend is definitely toward the inclusion of interest. Knappen states: ". . . revenue bonds occupy the more precarious position, and, where issued in connection with non-essential functions, it may even be that they will be singled out for taxation while general obligation bonds are left untouched."[19]

Mortgage Liens

Few revenue bonds carry a mortgage lien on any property, and there is considerable debate as to whether such a lien is a desirable feature for the bondholder. Most of the projects financed with revenue bonds are public in nature, and in case of default public convenience would require that they continue in operation. If bondholders foreclosed, there would be troublesome problems connected with a franchise and also the possibility that private operation would be subjected to taxation while public operation was tax free. There is also the possibility that, in some cases, the inclusion of a mortgage feature would make the bonds full credit obligations and remove them from the category of revenue bonds. For these and other reasons some argue that a mortgage lien does not strengthen the bondholder's security. Others, however, take a different position and argue that a mortgage, especially if it carries a conditional franchise to operate the property, is a valuable element in the bondholder's security.[20]

---

federal taxation, they must argue that such taxation will be a burden upon the state. See *The Tax Exempt Status of State and Municipal Bonds,* an opinion prepared by Thomas, Wood, and Hoffman and printed by Brown Harriman and Company (New York, 1937), pp. 24-27. Knappen sums it up slightly differently: "Apparently revenue bonds are not obligations of issuing municipalities when it comes to eligibility for savings bank investment or when it is a question of what constitutes 'indebtedness' within constitutional debt limits, but they are obligations of the municipality when it comes to tax exemption!" (*op. cit.,* p. 105 n.).

19. *Op. cit.,* p. 112.   20. Cf. *ibid.,* pp. 30-33.

Creditors' Remedies

In the absence of a mortgage and the right to foreclose, the holder of a revenue bond has three possible remedies in case of default. First, if trustees, public officials, or others, have not performed their duties as prescribed in the contract, he may ask a court for a mandamus ordering them to do so. Thus he may ask that the proper officials fix rates or charge prices sufficient to produce enough revenue to service the bonds.[21] Second, he may ask for an injunction to stop acts or policies which are contrary to the contract and detrimental to his interests. Third, he may ask for the appointment of a receiver. In general, he has this right even without specific statutory authority, but many revenue bond statutes expressly authorize the appointment of receivers and outline their duties.[22]

Investment Merits

Knappen sums up the advantages and disadvantages of revenue bonds as follows:

The strong points in regard to revenue bonds are: (1) the pledging of a type of income that may be surer than taxes, (2) the possibility of giving preferred status to a limited amount of bonds, whereas general obligation bonds are usually all equally secured, and (3) the provision of a better remedy than is accorded general obligation bonds.

On the other hand, the dangers include (1) invalid issuance in this comparatively new field, (2) use in connection with promotional projects, (3) obsolescence of the project before the bonds can be retired, and (4) too large issues relative to the total cost of the project.[23]

The last advantage cited is of special significance in the field of state finance. A state may repudiate a general obligation bond which carries no pledge of specific revenues, and creditors will be powerless to maintain suit. But if a state or one of its agencies pledges as security for a debt a specific source of revenue and thereafter attempts to repudiate the debt, creditors can maintain action

---

21. Frequently the duties of trustees and others are vague and indefinite, so that their legal obligations are difficult to determine. One authority advocates the more extensive use of indentures so that such duties may be more clearly stated. John Pershing, "Revenue Bond Remedies," 22 *Cornell Law Quarterly* 64 ff. (Dec., 1936).

22. For a further discussion of remedies see Knappen, *op. cit.*, pp. 57-63; Fowler, *op. cit.*, pp. 111-130; Pershing, *loc. cit.*   23. *Op. cit.*, p. 276.

in the federal courts to compel the proper officials to allocate the funds as prescribed in the contract.

APPRAISAL OF STATE REVENUE BONDS

There are outstanding, in the sphere of state finances, some $700,000,000 or more of bonds which do not carry the faith and credit of any state. Except for the highway bonds of Mississippi and New Mexico and a few other small issues, these bonds are not usually included in the tabulation of state debts. Yet over $500,-000,000 of them depend upon and are payable from state funds, directly or indirectly. In this section an attempt is made to appraise the use of revenue bonds by states and state agencies as a matter of public policy and to indicate some of the groups which favor and some which oppose such financing.

Advantages of Revenue Bonds

In view of the rapid growth of revenue bond financing in recent years it is natural to ask what features of this method of financing have been responsible for the growth. Perhaps the outstanding feature is its flexibility in that it is not subject to constitutional restrictions. In states with rigid debt limitations, an issue of revenue bonds can be authorized and sold quickly, while an issue of general state obligations might require several months or even two years or more, with the ultimate outcome uncertain. In recent years it has sometimes been necessary for states and their agencies to act quickly in order to take advantage of federal grants and loans. The use of revenue bonds permit quick action.

In addition to this short-run advantage, it is claimed that the use of revenue bonds permits governmental units to overcome the "obstacle" imposed by constitutional debt limitations and thus emancipates "public borrowers from the shackles imposed by archaic laws."[24] This is based upon the assumption that constitutional debt limitations are an evil to be overcome and disregarded if possible. It is true that several states have constitutional provisions which make state borrowing a slow, tedious, and uncertain proce-

24. Fowler, *op. cit.*, p. 42. It should be noted, however, that Fowler's attention is devoted primarily to the issue of revenue bonds by local governments.

dure. If the voters of those states, however, after they have had
adequate opportunity to express themselves, do not choose to change
such provisions nor to authorize specific borrowings, it is difficult
to see how the use of revenue bonds as a subterfuge can be recon-
ciled with the principles of democratic government. Debt limitations were adopted as a result of experience; in principle they are
not so "archaic" as the financial methods which brought them into
being. The use of revenue bonds is not an attempt to adjust those
limitations to present needs, but rather to render them impotent by
avoiding them entirely. Such action is a confession that we are
not willing to learn from experience.

Another advantage claimed for revenue bonds is that they assure
"a more equitable distribution of the costs of a public enterprise
among the persons benefited than any other plan for financing
which has been devised."[25] This is not necessarily true. Unless
political expediency prevents it, the same distribution of costs can
be applied with the use of general obligations as with the use of
revenue bonds. The same fees, charges, or tolls could be levied
and used to service general obligations as are now used to service
the revenue bonds. The only question would be whether the
political considerations in a given situation would allow it. Further, this contention rests upon the benefit doctrine of the distribution of governmental costs. Fowler continues: ". . . as far as
possible, the costs of a public service should be paid for only by
the users, and only in proportion to the use which they actually
make of the service, as is provided in revenue-bond financing."[26]
Most students of governmental finance accept the benefit doctrine
as valid within a limited scope, but do not accept it as a satisfactory theory for the distribution of the costs of all or most governmental services. Many of the so-called revenue bonds in the field
of state finance, however, do not distribute costs according to benefit; they are serviced from special taxes, compulsory fees, or state
appropriations which may have little or no relation to services.
This is a good example of the fallacy of applying the arguments
for a true revenue bond to the pseudo revenue bonds issued by
many states.

25. *Ibid.*, p. 167.   26. *Idem.*

Disadvantages of Revenue Bonds

The most definite and tangible disadvantage of revenue bonds in comparison with general state obligations is their greater interest cost. Relatively few direct comparisons are available, since it is not often that both kinds of bonds are sold in the same state at or near the same date in comparable amounts and with comparable maturities. In so far as comparisons can be made, however, there are definite indications that the interest cost of revenue bonds is higher by amounts ranging from ¼ per cent to nearly 2 per cent; in no case is there any evidence that revenue bonds had a lower interest cost than general obligations. In Table 42 a few comparisons are

TABLE 42

COMPARISON OF YIELDS, GENERAL OBLIGATIONS AND REVENUE BONDS OF STATES

Date		Nature of Obligation	Maturity (in years)	Interest Cost (%)
		LOUISIANA		
Jan.	1937.	Highway Bonds—Gen. Obligations........	4–23	3.61
Jan.	1937.	L. S. U. Rev. Bonds.....................	1–18	3.95
Oct.	1938.	Highway Bonds—Gen. Obligations..........	4–23	3.4
July	1938.	Charity Hospital Rev. Bonds.............	4–30	3.85
Sept.	1938.	State Board of Education Rev. Bonds......	4–28	4.73
Oct.	1938.	L. S. U. Rev. Bonds.....................	3–20	4.25
		WEST VIRGINIA		
May	1937.	Road Bonds—Gen. Obligations............	1–25	2.42
July	1937.	Road Bonds—Gen. Obligations...........	1–25	2.33
June	1937.	Bridge Rev. Bonds......................	1–15	2.82
Oct.	1937.	Road Bonds—Gen. Obligations............	1–25	2.55
Nov.	1937.	Bridge Rev. Bonds.....................	2–15	3.47
		NORTH CAROLINA		
May	1937.	Gen. Obligations.......................	3–11	2.83
Dec.	1937.	State Board of Health Rev. Bonds........	2–20	4.50
Oct.	1938.	Gen. Obligations.......................	2–11	2.07
Oct.	1938.	University Rev. Bonds..................	2–21	3.72
		MARYLAND		
June	1938.	Gen. Obligations.......................	1–15	1.58
July	1938.	Gen. Obligations.......................	3–15	1.48
Sept.	1938.	Road Comm. Rev. Bonds................	1–12	2.91
		PENNSYLVANIA		
Oct.	1938.	Turnpike Comm. Rev. Bonds.............	9–30	4.01 - 4.25

Source: *Municipal Bond Sales, passim.*

given. In all cases the issues are large enough to insure a fair expression of the interest cost. No comparison is available for Pennsylvania, but obviously general obligations of the State of Pennsylvania, of comparable maturities, would have had a far lower interest cost than that realized on the Turnpike Revenue Bonds in October, 1938.

The difference in the interest costs of the two types of obligations was vividly demonstrated in North Carolina in September and October, 1938. On September 21, 1938, the Treasurer of North Carolina sold $287,000 of University revenue bonds at an interest cost of 3.72 per cent. Six days later he rejected all bids on $4,620,000 of general state obligations because the best bid represented an interest cost of 3.16 per cent; the market was badly upset on account of the European war crisis. On October 21, he sold $444,000 more of University revenue bonds at a cost of 3.72 per cent. Six days later he sold the general obligations at a cost of 2.073 per cent.[27] The revenue bonds had longer maturities than the general obligations, but the difference was not nearly enough to account for the difference in interest cost.

Another disadvantage of revenue bonds is the absence of effective state control over the disposition of the proceeds. Since the state is not supplying the funds, it will not supervise their spending as closely as if they were state funds. In some cases the bond proceeds are handled in the same way as state appropriations, but in others they are not.[28] Of course, irregularities and scandals may and do occur in ordinary state departments, but with special agencies conducting their financing independently of the state government, the

---

27. *Bond Buyer*, Jan. 3, 1939, p. 3.

28. The scandal which occurred at Louisiana State University in the summer of 1939 grew out of the revenue bonds which the institution had been selling for several years. An example of how inefficient the special agencies which issue revenue bonds may be was afforded in Ohio in the spring of 1939. The legislature had created The Public Institutional Building Authority and had empowered it to issue bonds to finance improvements and extensions to state hospitals. On April 4, 1939, the Authority invited proposals, to be submitted by April 10, "embodying complete, comprehensive and detailed plans for financing the construction or acquisition of said hospital buildings." The proposals were to include an offer to supply funds needed in such plans and "shall set forth in detail the plan of financing and describe fully all leases, deeds, securities or other documents incident thereto" (*Bond Buyer*, April 8, 1939, p. 14). This would indicate that the Authority was not competent to formulate its own plans of operations and finance, but left them to prospective underwriters who were expected, in six days, to submit complete plans for extensive changes affecting state hospitals!

chances of such irregularities are doubled or perhaps more than doubled, since the financial machinery of the agencies will be hastily assembled and not subject to the usual financial controls. In this connection it should be noted that the use of revenue bonds makes it more difficult to determine the true financial position of a state— to the confusion of the public, the worry of credit-rating agencies, and the exasperation of students of public finance.

Still another, and potentially the greatest, disadvantage of revenue bonds is the absence of any constitutional restrictions. Since they are issued under the special fund doctrine, constitutional debt limitations do not apply. There is not likely to be any organized opposition to new issues, since there are no groups which are immediately threatened. In the past it has been comparatively easy for an institution or agency wishing to expand, to secure authority for issuing revenue bonds. In many respects the situation is similar to that affecting internal improvements between 1825 and 1838. Unless some form of control is found, the results may be comparable.

One legislative committee has summarized the dangers of state-created public authorities in the following points. (1) "Authorities are performing a governmental function and yet are not responsible to the people, nor are the members generally removable by the appointing officer except for cause." (2) There is doubt and uncertainty concerning the "ultimate financial liability should an authority be unable to meet its obligations." One case is cited in which the court imposed upon the state the liability for certain revenue bonds.[29] (3) In several acts the state comptroller was authorized "to invest funds of the State in the bonds of such authorities." "Where the Comptroller purchases substantially all of the bonds of an issue, the authority system is, in effect, an evasion of the constitutional prohibition against the incurring of indebtedness by the State except with the approval of the people."[30] The latter point is well illustrated by an absurd scheme which failed of passage. The proposed bill would have authorized the comptroller to invest state funds in the revenue bonds of the World War Memorial Authority,

29. *Williamsburgh Savings Bank* v. *State*, 243 N. Y. 231 (1926).
30. *Report of the Joint Legislative Committee on State Fiscal Policies* (New York), Legislative Doc. (1938) No. 41 (Albany, 1937), pp. 83-85.

which could issue $10,000,000 of bonds. The Department of Public Works was to lease the entire memorial at a rent of $650,000 a year, to be paid from a state appropriation, and the state was to maintain the buildings and grounds.

The Moral Responsibility of States

Revenue bonds are issued on the theory that the states are in no way responsible for their payment. In reality, however, state finances may be affected in several ways. Assume that important state institutions and agencies have issued large amounts of revenue bonds and that both they and the state suffer sharp declines in revenues so that it becomes necessary for the state to reduce appropriations. The fact that the agencies have heavy fixed charges to meet will make it necessary for them to make disproportionately heavy reductions in their other expenditures and may so impair their services that it will be necessary for the state to come to their aid. That, in turn, may mean either that taxes will be increased or that other state services will be impaired still more. The economic effects of the indebtedness will be the same as if the state had incurred the debts except that the effects may be more localized. If the distress in the affected areas becomes sufficiently acute, the state may be compelled to assume the burden and generalize the distress to some extent.

There are other reasons why the state may intervene. If an important agency is affected, the state may be unwilling to see its own credit standing impaired by a default, even though it has given no specific promise in regard to the bonds. In the same way, it may feel impelled to act to prevent innocent investors who may have been deceived. All revenue bond projects are at least tacitly approved by the state, since they are carried out under special laws. Almost always the bonds bear the name of the state in large letters and usually they are signed by important state officials. Quite often they are sealed with the great seal of the state. Several states have designated revenue bonds as legal investments for trustees. Under such conditions it would not be surprising if the uninitiated investor thought that he was buying obligations of the state when he purchased revenue bonds.

If the agency which issued the revenue bonds was one performing an important state function, it is doubtful whether, as a matter of broad general policy, the state's refusal to give aid in time of stress would be thoroughly honest. Citizens have a right to expect their governments to conduct their financial affairs on a plane of honesty and integrity above that found in the market place and beyond the letter of the law. The state is morally obligated to finance its functions in a manner which is safe and sound for all parties concerned. If it should induce investors to provide the funds to finance those functions under a scheme which later proved to be unprofitable and then refused to lend assistance, it would render itself vulnerable to charges of sharp practice which would be beneath the dignity of a government.

As an indication of what might be expected if trouble develops with revenue bonds, we may consider a significant New York case which dealt with special-assessment bonds issued by an improvement district.[31] The state had created and sponsored the district, which failed. The legislature had appropriated some funds to aid the district and had authorized the court of claims to hear proceedings based upon the moral obligation of the state to investors. Both the bonds issued by the district and the statute authorizing them stated expressly that the state was not liable for the payment of interest or principal.

In its opinion the court stated that the courts of New York have recognized that the state "may be honorable and voluntarily recognize just obligations which it fairly and honestly ought to pay even though they do not constitute purely legal claims such as in the case of an individual could be enforced under the compulsion of judgment and execution."[32] It was necessary only that the procedure for ascertaining such claims be correct and constitutional, as they were in this case. The court continued: "The State approved and started on its disastrous course the improvement plan. . . . It committed the duty of prosecution to an agency composed of State officials and authorized this body to procure money by the sale of bonds and certificates. . . . The agency of the State . . . represented

31. *Williamsburgh Savings Bank* v. *State*, 243 N. Y. 231 (1926).
32. *Ibid.*, p. 240.

that the value of the benefited lands would be ample to sustain assessments with which to pay the obligations which were issued."[33]

It was not necessary, the court reasoned, to hold that between private parties, there would have been a cause of action because of misrepresentation or lack of consideration. "It is sufficient, in connection with the other facts, that the State has permitted one of its agencies to gather into its treasury moneys of its citizens with assurance of repayment under a plan indorsed and put forth by it, but which, owing to its inherent defects, has lamentably failed with threat of resultant loss to the moneys thus invested."[34]

The court concluded that in similar circumstances an honorable businessman would feel impelled to recognize his responsibility and that the state should not be less conscientious than one of its citizens.

The above considerations, among others, indicate that, in spite of legal provisions, if the revenue bonds considered in this chapter should ever be defaulted in considerable volume, pressure would be brought to bear upon the states to render financial assistance. The procedure in two cases in which revenue bonds have suffered default substantiates this view.

Revenue Bonds in Default

The Alabama State Bridge Corporation issued $5,000,000 of bonds in 1929. Between 1930 and 1934 the Alabama Highway Commission contributed from $250,000 to $450,000 annually to help service the bonds. Bonds maturing after December 1, 1934, were not paid, and interest payments were defaulted after December 1, 1935. In 1935 the state legislature authorized the Highway Department to lease all bridges from the Corporation, to free them of tolls, and to pay as rent an amount sufficient to service the bonds. This was conditioned upon bondholders agreeing to an extension of maturities and accepting a reduction in interest to 4 per cent. Ultimately over 75 per cent of the bondholders accepted the terms, and the agreement became effective.[35] The supreme court of the state approved this act.[36] In 1937 the state secured assistance from the Federal Gov-

33. *Ibid.*, p. 245.
34. *Ibid.*, pp. 246-247.   35. Klaber, *op. cit.*, pp. 64-65.
36. *Scott* v. *Alabama State Bridge Corporation*, 233 Ala. 12 (1936).

ernment under an act permitting the Secretary of Agriculture to aid any state which removed tolls from bridges up to 50 per cent of the cost of the bridges. At present the Highway Department is paying as rent approximately $275,000 per year, which is just adequate to cover debt service on the $3,000,000 of bonds outstanding.[37]

The second default occurred in Montana. Beginning in 1909 the state issued $725,000 of revenue bonds to finance the building of a state capitol. The bonds were payable from the income from land grants. After 1932 the income from land declined sharply, and by 1939, $62,371.15 of unpaid interest had accrued on the $574,252.50 of bonds then outstanding. The outstanding bonds were not owned by private investors, but were held by a state trust fund for the benefit of public schools and educational institutions. The trust fund was established by the state constitution, which required the state to guarantee all investments.

The 1939 legislature authorized the refunding of all outstanding capitol bonds and accrued interest into general obligations of the state.[38] When the act was brought before the state supreme court, it ruled that the fact that the bonds were held in a trust fund "was obviously the inspiration for such legislation" and that the trust fund was "inviolate and sacred" since investments therein were guaranteed by the state against loss. "It seems too plain for quibble that under the explicit wording of the Constitution the defaulted bonds in which the trust funds were invested automatically, but nevertheless certainly, became obligations of the state—in the beginning perhaps contingent liabilities, but upon subsequent and appropriate recognition by the legislature of loss, that contingency gave

37. A similar default by the Port of New York Authority on bonds issued for the Staten Island bridges was narrowly avoided in 1931. The states of New York and New Jersey transferred to the Authority the Holland Tunnel in return for revenue bonds of the Authority. Revenues from the Tunnel were sufficient to allow the Authority to pool the revenues from all projects and to meet the payments on the Staten Island bonds (Klaber, op. cit., p. 65). This illustrates another way in which states can give indirect aid to revenue bond projects. Still another way would be for highway authorities to design highway systems, traffic routes, and bridge approaches in such a way as to force motorists to use certain bridges or tunnels. New York has made appropriations to the Saratoga Springs Authority and to the Niagara Frontier Bridge Commission to prevent defaults (Report of Joint Legislative Committee on State Fiscal Policies, pp. 85-86).   38 Laws, 1939, c. 133.

way to certainty, and recognized, absolute, and liquidated liability came into the transaction."[39]

Since the state guarantee of the school funds was written into the constitution, the court held that "it follows as the night the day that the investments made thereof must likewise be protected." The court also stated that the investment of the school funds in the revenue bonds was proper and legal. Since the state's obligation arose automatically under the constitution as soon as the bonds were defaulted, no new debt was created by the issuance of the general state obligations; rather, the refunding was merely a changing of the form of that obligation.

In this case the coincidence that the bonds were held in a state-guaranteed fund enabled the state to assume the revenue bonds without raising the question of its power generally to pay bonds issued under the special fund doctrine.

A third default occurred in Iowa. In 1929 the Athletic Council of the State University of Iowa sold $500,000 of revenue bonds to finance the construction of a stadium. By March, 1938, only $20,000 of the bonds had been redeemed, and unpaid interest to the amount of $135,000 had accrued.[40] Apparently no move has been made to refund or adjust the debt.

Proponents of Revenue Bonds

The impetus for the great increase in the use of revenue bonds in the state domain in recent years has come largely from three sources. First, the Federal Government, through the P.W.A., has sponsored and encouraged the use of revenue bonds in connection with its lending programs in order to circumvent rigid constitutional limitations. P.W.A. officials have been active in suggesting to state officials methods of using revenue bonds in order to qualify for federal grants, and on one occasion President Roosevelt threatened to stop the flow of federal funds to Georgia unless that state found means of avoiding its "archaic" debt limitation.[41] Second, ambitious

39. *Lodge* v. *Ayers*, 91 P. (2d) 691 (1939).
40. *Moody's*, 1939, p. 470.
41. It should be noted that while the Federal Government, through P.W.A., has been encouraging "self-liquidating" projects which involve tolls and other charges, it has, through the Secretary of Agriculture, been active in trying to persuade states

officials of states and state agencies have seized upon the use of revenue bonds as a means of expanding physical facilities despite rigid debt limitations. Perhaps the outstanding example of this was the Earle administration in Pennsylvania, which created the Pennsylvania General State Authority and the Pennsylvania Turnpike Commission. Third, though less conspicuous, have been the bond dealers. In recent years they have been searching almost frantically for new bond issues. If general obligations are available only in limited quantities, they are not averse to taking revenue bonds and making them as palatable as possible to the investing public.[42]

Opponents of Revenue Bonds

So far there has been little organized opposition to the use of revenue bonds. Motorists are showing signs of resentment. In the summer of 1939 motorists' organizations in New York protested against the growing use of tolls on roads and bridges around that city, and the Automobile Club of New York advised automobile owners to boycott Connecticut when a toll was imposed on the Merritt Parkway.[43] Another group expressed the sentiment that "Toll roads, whether sponsored by the Federal Government, the states, or local communities, are definitely repugnant to American concepts of freedom of the highways."[44] On the whole, however, as Knappen states, "the consumer's complaints have been conspicuous by their absence."[45] Taxpayers have looked askance at revenue bonds, lest they be asked eventually to pay the bill, but have thus far shown little active opposition.[46] Academic students and representatives of credit-rating agencies have looked on with interest, have noted the need for the exercise of control and discretion, and have approved the use of revenue bonds, as strictly defined,

to remove tolls from bridges, even to the extent of offering special grants of highway funds for that purpose.

42. Fowler, in his book, presents the general viewpoint of the financial world on the matter. He shows a distinct tendency to emphasize the merits and to gloss over the weaknesses of revenue bonds.

43. *New York Times,* June 23, 1939, p. 7.

44. National Highway Users Conference, *Highway Transportation Remakes America* (Washington, 1939), p. 28.

45. Knappen, *op. cit.,* p. 275.   46. *Idem.*

when properly used.[47] They have generally condemned the kind of revenue bonds usually issued by states and their agencies.

SUMMARY

The use of revenue bonds by states and state agencies has increased greatly in recent years, chiefly on account of the need of local governments for assistance in meeting payments on highway obligations, and the federal lending program. Incomplete data indicate that in 1938 approximately $680,000,000 of such obligations were outstanding, of which over $500,000,000 were serviced, directly or indirectly, from state funds. Thus a majority of the obligations are not true revenue obligations, but represent merely a device used by the states to avoid constitutional debt limits. The only real advantage of such obligations is their flexibility in that they can be issued quickly without conforming to the procedure prescribed by constitutions for incurring debts. The dangers or disadvantages are a higher interest cost, the absence of any quantitative limit, and the absence of any effective state control over the disposition of the proceeds. The absence of constitutional restrictions on the issue of such obligations is likely to be of special danger because taxpayers are told that the bonds will never be a charge against general state revenues. The states, however, have a definite moral responsibility for the bonds, which is likely to be invoked if and when they are defaulted. In two of the three cases of default which have occurred thus far, the states concerned have assumed full responsibility for the defaulted bonds.

47. Cf. *ibid.*, pp. 276-277, and Bird, *op. cit.*

CHAPTER XXII

STATE DEBTS AND DEBT SERVICE IN 1938

PRECEDING CHAPTERS have shown that it is difficult to make an accurate compilation of state debts. It is often impossible to indicate exactly where state liabilities begin and end. The formal statement of indebtedness as issued by many states gives little indication of the debt burden resting upon taxpayers. In some instances direct state obligations represent no burden to taxpayers, while in others obligations which were never issued by the state and for which the state has never acknowledged any legal responsibility may be serviced entirely from state revenues. It is obvious, therefore, that any statement of indebtedness or of debt service representing charges against tax revenues would require a rather intimate knowledge of the particular situation in each state—probably a greater knowledge than any one person has at the present time. Despite the difficulties, however, an attempt is made in this chapter to compile such a statement.

STATE DEBTS IN 1938

Table 43 provides data on various phases of state indebtedness. In order to show the effects of regional influences, the states have been arranged in certain groups according to Odum's plan in his regional studies.[1] It is believed that his arrangement brings out more clearly than any other the effects of regional influences.

Gross Debts

In this table and throughout this chapter consideration is confined to bonded indebtedness. The figures listed in Table 43 in the column headed Gross Direct Debt include all bonded indebtedness of the state which carries the full faith and credit of the state as well as state guarantees of other obligations. The figures were derived

1. Howard W. Odum, *Southern Regions of the United States* (Chapel Hill, 1936), chap. iii.

TABLE 43
State Debts, 1938
(All except per capita figures in thousands of dollars)

Date and State	Gross Direct Debt	Net Direct Debt	Per Capita	Self-Supporting or Contingent Direct Debt	Net Tax-Supported Direct Debt	Per Capita	Revenue and Local Government Bonds Based on State Funds	Total Net Debt	Per Capita
12- 5 Conn..	25,000	25,000	14.38	....	25,000	14.38	15,716	40,716	23.39
7- 1 Del....	3,462	3,402	13.03	....	3,402	13.03	6,225	9,627	36.88
12-31 Me....	28,972	28,250	33.04	2,975	25,275	29.56	....	25,275	29.53
8-31 Md....	48,247	48,247	28.75	....	48,247	28.75	11,358	59,605	35.50
11-30 Mass..	159,181	99,708	22.53	59,022	40,685	9.19	....	40,685	9.19
6-30 N.H...	18,629†	16,501	32.42	8,141‡	8,360	16.42	1,400	9,760	19.14
6-30 N.J...	167,536	70,513	16.26	....	70,513	16.26	......	70,513	16.26
6-30 N.Y...	681,823	541,299	41.81	....	541,299	41.81	......	541,299	41.81
10-31 Pa....	129,942	110,653	10.90	....	110,653	10.90	1,400	112,053	11.01
6-30 R.I....	33,420	27,306	40.10	....	27,306	40.10	......	27,306	40.10
6-30 Vt.....	7,718	7,272	19.04	....	7,272	19.04	......	7,272	19.04
7- 2 W.Va..	81,127	81,127	43.88	....	81,127	43.88	1,387	82,514	44.24
Northeastern States.....	1,385,058	1,059,278	26.56	70,138	989,139	24.80	37,486	1,026,625	25.74
9-30 Ala....	68,100	68,100	23.58	5,595§	62,505	21.64	5,119	67,624	23.36
12-31 Ark. ..	154,182	153,652	75.43	1,220	152,432	74.83	2,852	155,284	75.82
Fla....	....	....	......	....	....	......	75,054	75,054	44.94
6-30 Ga....	3,809	3,318	1.08	....	3,318	1.08	24,657	27,975	9.07
7- 1 Ky....	2,481	....	......	....	....	......	1,981	1,981	0.68
11-15 La....	159,360	159,360	74.75	....	159,360	74.75	19,802	179,162	84.03
12- 1 Miss..	32,944	32,944	16.28	1,503‖	31,441	15.54	31,862	63,303	31.29
6-30 N.C...	155,012	139,003	39.99	8,330¶	130,672	37.59	2,833	133,505	38.23
12- 1 S.C...	47,532	46,626	24.96	296	46,330	24.80	23,221	69,551	37.09
6-30 Tenn..	132,582	116,355	40.40	8,000**	108,355	37.62	....	108,355	37.62
6-30 Va....	22,108	16,696	6.21	....	16,696	6.21	4,278	20,974	7.75
Southeastern States.....	778,111	736,054	26.53	24,944	711,109	25.64	191,658	902,768	32.55
11- 1 Ill.....	188,682	188,682	24.00	....	188,682	24.00	1,150	189,832	24.10
6-30 Ind....	340	....	......	....	....	......	6,626	6,626	1.91
6-30 Iowa..	5,500	5,500	2.16	....	5,500	2.16	80,405	85,905	33.66
7- 1 Mich..	72,419	22,789	4.74	....	22,789	4.74	8,127	30,916	6.40
6-30 Minn..	127,066	122,714	46.27	32,217††	90,479	34.12	6,479	96,958	36.56
10-31 Mo....	114,317	106,529	26.71	....	106,529	26.71	....	106,529	26.71
12-31 Ohio..	5,542	....	......	....	....	......	1,105	1,105	0.16
7- 1 Wis. ..	1,184	....	......	....	....	......	23,358	23,358	7.98
Middle States.....	515,050	446,214	12.74	32,217	413,979	11.82	127,250	541,229	15.49
6-30 Colo...	3,667	3,667	3.43	....	3,667	3.43	27,000	30,667	28.63
10- 1 Idaho.	1,685	1,641	3.34	....	1,641	3.34	798	2,439	4.95
7- 1 Kan...	16,500	16,500	8.80	....	16,500	8.80	2,780	19,280	10.34
10- 1 Mont .	4,831	4,831	9.03	....	4,831	9.03	4,118	8,949	16.60
Neb....	....	....	......	....	....	......	....	....	....
6-30 N.D...	25,462	22,098	31.34	4,671‡‡	17,427	24.72	418	17,845	25.28
6-30 S.D...	46,069	39,670	57.37	15,194§§	24,505	35.41	......	24,505	35.41
7- 1 Utah..	7,955	2,642	5.10	....	2,642	5.10	......	2,642	5.10
9-30 Wyo..	3,050	3,049	12.97	....	3,049	12.97	......	3,049	12.97
Northwestern States.....	109,220	94,128	12.58	19,865	74,262	9.92	35,114	109,376	14.62
7- 1 Ariz...	1,284	1,284	3.14	....	1,284	3.14	1,267	2,551	6.19
6-30 N.M...	2,669	2,351	5.57	....	2,351	5.57	20,782	23,133	54.82
6-30 Okla...	8,434	8,434	3.32	....	8,434	3.32	2,460	10,894	4.28
8-31 Tex...	17,642	10,769	1.75	....	10,769	1.75	89,944	100,713	16.32
Southwestern States.....	30,029	22,838	2.39	....	22,838	2.39	114,453	137,291	14.37
7- 3 Calif. .	187,008	179,998	29.46	78,187	101,811	16.66	......	101,811	16.66
7- 2 Nev....	729	729	7.22	....	729	7.22	188	917	9.08
6-30 Ore....	43,661	20,277	19.84	‖ ‖	20,277	19.84	1,377	21,654	21.08
9-30 Wash..	10,031	10,031	6.09	....	10,031	6.09	376	10,407	6.28
Far Western States.....	241,430	211,035	23.61	78,187	132,848	14.86	1,941	134,789	15.08
United States	3,058,894	2,569,547	19.88	225,351	2,344,175	18.14	507,903	2,852,078	22.07

*Toll bridge bonds.
†Includes $7,027,000 of local government and revenue bonds guaranteed by the state.
‡Guaranteed bonds and net toll bridge debt amounting to $1,113,791.
§60% of Harbor Improvement Debt. ‖ Delta Rehabilitation Bonds.
¶$7,330,429 represented by county obligations held by state and $1,000,000 of Veterans Loan Debt.
**Estimated amount of toll bridge debt which is self-supporting.
††40% of net rural credit debt plus $2,500,000 of municipal aid bonds.
‡‡25% of net rural credit debt. §§40% of net rural credit debt. ‖ ‖Included in sinking fund.

in most cases from *Moody's* and the Chronicle's *State and Municipal Compendium.*

Net Debt

In order to arrive at net direct indebtedness, two deductions were made from the gross debt. First, sinking funds were deducted. It is possible that in some cases small sinking funds were not listed by the two sources mentioned, but it is not likely that these would be large enough materially to affect the result. Such omissions are especially likely in cases where reserves are held for debt service in current accounts which are not labeled as sinking funds. Since a large majority of state bonds are serial in form, however, sinking funds and similar reserves are maintained in only a few states, outstanding among which are Massachusetts, Michigan, New Jersey, New York, North Carolina, and Pennsylvania.

The second item deducted was debts owed to state trust funds. In the past, several states have received, particularly from the Federal Government, certain funds to be used or held in trust for certain specific functions. If suitable investments were not available the states have at times used the funds for current purposes and issued their obligations to the proper trust funds. Such obligations are in reality debts owed by one part of the state government to another. Such nominal indebtedness is the only direct debt of Indiana, Kentucky, Ohio, and Wisconsin. The deduction of such indebtedness leaves those states without any net direct debt.

The figures thus arrived at resemble very closely the figures which are most frequently quoted as the net debts of the states. The per capita figures were found by dividing the figures for net debt by the population estimates for 1937.[2]

Self-Supporting Debt

In order to determine the part of the direct debt which is supported from tax revenues, self-supporting or contingent debts which do not represent a charge against tax revenues were deducted from the net direct debt. In most instances these figures are estimates

2. These estimates were made by the Bureau of the Census and were the last ones made before the 1940 census.

and should not be considered as definitive. Generally, they represent debts incurred for harbor improvement or rural credit projects. The extent to which such projects are believed to be self-supporting has been indicated in previous chapters.[3] The deduction of these self-supporting elements from the direct net debt leaves the net tax-supported direct debt.

Total Net Debt

The previous chapter has shown that the states are supporting a large indebtedness not directly issued by the states. When such debts are added to the figures representing net tax-supported direct debt, they give the total net debt, which is perhaps the most significant figure representing the total indebtedness serviced from state revenues.

Regional Analysis

On any basis of measurement, the total debts of the Northeastern states were, in 1938, greater than those of any other region, largely because of New York's huge debt, which represented approximately one half of the total for the region. The direct debts of the Northeastern states were more than 30 per cent higher than those of any other region. Because there were relatively few self-supporting debts and many revenue obligations in the South, however, the total net debts of the Southeastern region approached those of the Northeast. The totals for the two Eastern regions comprised approximately two thirds of the total for the whole country. The total debts of the four Western regions were substantially less than those of the Northeastern states and only slightly greater than those of the Southeastern states. Quite curiously, the total net indebtedness of the Middle states was almost exactly equal to that of New York.

The per capita debts of the different regions varied widely but not so much as did total debts. For net direct debts, the per capita figures of the Northeastern and Southeastern states were almost identical at slightly above $26.50. The figure for the Far Western states approached this, but for the Middle and Northwestern states the figures were less than half as much, while in the Southwest the

3. See Chapters XIII and XIV.

figure was less than one tenth. The per capita total net debt in the Southeast was substantially higher than in any other region because of the small amount of self-supporting debt and the large issues of revenue obligations. The way in which the per capita figures for the four Western regions clustered around $15.00—less than one half the figure for the Southeast—is indeed striking. The large highway revenue issues serviced by New Mexico and Texas were primarily responsible for raising the figure in the Southwest, while the deduction of the large debts incurred for the veterans' loan fund and harbor improvements in California reduced the figure for the Far West.

Analysis by States

New York had by far the largest debt of any state, its total net debt being approximately 19 per cent of the total for the whole country. The five states with the largest total net debts—New York, Illinois, Louisiana, Arkansas, and North Carolina—owed a total of nearly $1,200,000,000, or approximately 42 per cent of the total. Five other states—Pennsylvania, Tennessee, Missouri, California, and Texas—had debts of over $100,000,000. The total for those ten states was slightly over $1,800,000,000, or approximately 64 per cent of the total. Nebraska was the only state which had no funded debt of any kind, but Kentucky, Nevada, and Ohio had only nominal debts.

Louisiana had the highest per capita debt with $84.03, while Arkansas was second with $75.82. Both figures were more than three times the national average of $22.07. No other figure was close to the first two, but New Mexico was third with $54.82. All Southern states except Georgia, Kentucky, and Virginia had per capita debts well above the national average. Except for Nebraska, Ohio and Kentucky had the lowest per capita debts. Indiana, Oklahoma, and Idaho also had per capita debts of less than five dollars.

THE BURDEN OF STATE DEBTS

The figures for total debts or even for per capita debts are poor measures of the burden of state indebtedness to taxpayers. Debt burdens can best be weighed in relation to revenue possibilities. In the past it has been customary to indicate burdens by relating debts to the assessed value of property subject to taxation. This had some validity so long as the states depended heavily upon the property tax for their revenues. Recently, however, the states have largely relinquished the property tax to local governments, and the assessed value of property has come to be recognized as a poor indicator of true value. For these reasons it has been deemed desirable to construct a new measure of debt burdens. That measure is described below.

Construction of the Measure

The new measure is constructed on the assumption that debt burdens can best be measured primarily in terms of the various forms of income upon which the states may draw for their revenues. The means of measuring income by states are still crude and approximate, and the following figures must be interpreted in the light of this fact.

The measure, as shown in Table 44, is a composite of four series which supply information concerning income produced or received or wealth located in the various states. One of the series is itself a composite. All figures have been reduced to a per capita basis. For each state the figures of each series are converted into relatives which indicate the position of that state in relation to the national average. The average rank or relative for each state is an unweighted arithmetic average of the relatives for each of the four series.

The first series reveals income payments in 1937.[4] The figures are estimates intended to cover a large majority of all income received in the different states for the year indicated. They indicate the size of the total fund from which nearly all state revenues must be drawn. The second series shows per capita retail sales in 1935.[5] These figures are significant for two reasons. First, in conjunction with the figures showing size of income, they give some clue to income distribution, since a larger proportion of a given income is

4. Robert R. Nathan and John L. Martin, *State Income Payments, 1929-37* (Washington: Bureau of Foreign and Domestic Commerce, 1939), p. 2.
5. Bureau of the Census, *Census of Business: 1935,* "Retail Distribution," Vol. I, *United States Summary* (Washington, 1937).

TABLE 44

INDEX OF THE BURDEN OF STATE DEBTS, 1938

State	Income		Retail Sales		Estimated Wealth		Output of Primary Industries		Average Rank	Per Capita Net Debt	Debt Rank	Index of Debt Burden
	Per Capita	Rank	Per Capita	Rank	Per Capita	Rank	Per Capita	Rank				
Connecticut.........	$ 767	140	$ 324	126	$1930	140	$ 422	146	138	$23.39	106	77
Delaware...........	923	169	286	111	1593	115	292	101	124	36.88	167	135
Maine.............	494	90	273	106	969	70	249	86	88	29.53	134	152
Maryland...........	650	119	269	105	1570	114	309	107	111	35.50	161	145
Massachusetts......	668	122	340	132	1710	124	300	103	120	9.19	42	35
New Hampshire......	503	92	301	117	1170	85	246	85	95	19.14	87	92
New Jersey..........	623	114	284	111	1960	143	343	118	121	16.26	74	61
New York...........	859	157	355	138	2370	172	286	99	141	41.81	189	134
Pennsylvania........	580	106	248	96	1590	116	349	120	109	11.01	50	46
Rhode Island.......	692	127	319	124	1994	145	367	127	131	40.10	182	139
Vermont............	445	82	262	102	905	66	251	87	84	19.04	86	102
West Virginia........	409	75	182	71	957	70	295	102	79	44.24	200	253
Northeastern States ..	688	126	302	118	1560	113	310	107	116	25.74	117	101
Alabama...........	233	43	118	46	652	47	138	48	46	23.36	106	230
Arkansas...........	212	39	120	47	639	46	107	37	42	75.82	344	819
Florida............	483	88	261	102	906	66	150	52	77	44.94	204	265
Georgia............	288	53	160	62	698	51	139	48	52	9.07	41	79
Kentucky...........	295	54	136	53	866	63	156	54	56	0.68	3	5
Louisiana..........	367	67	161	63	676	49	225	78	64	84.03	381	595
Mississippi.........	207	38	88	34	452	33	142	42	37	31.29	142	384
North Carolina......	285	52	135	53	859	62	213	73	60	38.23	173	288
South Carolina......	261	48	134	52	625	45	151	52	49	37.09	168	343
Tennessee..........	298	54	171	67	729	53	161	55	57	37.62	170	298
Virginia............	358	65	178	69	1305	95	184	63	83	7.75	35	42
Southeastern States...	295	54	147	57	764	56	161	56	56	32.55	147	262
Illinois.............	643	118	266	104	1773	129	373	129	120	24.10	109	91
Indiana............	494	90	226	88	1400	102	390	134	103	1.91	9	9
Iowa..............	427	78	255	99	1596	116	295	102	99	33.66	153	155
Michigan...........	675	123	293	114	1338	97	505	174	127	6.40	29	23
Minnesota..........	521	95	311	121	1550	113	277	96	106	36.56	166	157
Missouri...........	461	84	236	92	1358	99	215	74	87	26.71	121	139
Ohio..............	625	114	252	99	1535	112	416	143	117	0.16	1	1
Wisconsin..........	565	103	299	116	1466	107	356	123	112	7.98	36	32
Middle States.......	577	105	274	107	1502	109	372	128	112	15.49	70	62
Colorado...........	568	104	278	108	1484	108	252	87	102	28.63	130	127
Idaho..............	486	89	291	113	1090	79	345	119	100	4.95	22	22
Kansas............	435	80	237	92	1392	101	292	101	93	10.34	47	51
Montana...........	590	108	356	139	1797	131	341	118	124	16.60	75	60
Nebraska...........	424	78	236	92	1430	104	214	74	87			
North Dakota.......	316	58	214	83	1321	96	151	52	72	25.28	115	160
South Dakota........	314	57	211	82	1463	106	177	61	76	35.41	160	211
Utah..............	483	88	255	99	1117	81	296	102	92	5.10	23	25
Wyoming...........	616	113	354	138	1950	142	405	140	133	12.97	59	44
Northwestern States..	453	83	261	102	1449	105	259	89	95	14.62	66	69
Arizona............	577	105	287	112	1357	99	365	126	110	6.19	28	25
New Mexico........	417	76	207	81	905	66	240	83	76	54.82	248	326
Oklahoma..........	323	59	171	67	743	54	230	79	65	4.28	19	29
Texas..............	411	75	212	82	1262	92	264	91	85	16.32	74	87
Southwestern States..	395	72	202	79	1067	78	258	89	79	14.37	65	82
California..........	837	153	385	150	2280	165	352	121	147	16.66	75	51
Nevada............	911	167	432	168	2460	179	561	193	177	9.08	41	23
Oregon............	570	104	333	130	1400	102	292	101	109	21.08	96	88
Washington.........	614	112	321	125	1425	104	292	101	110	6.28	28	25
Far Western States...	766	140	362	141	1891	138	336	116	134	15.08	68	51
United States........	547	100	257	100	1375	100	290	100	100	22.07	100	100

Sources: See text.

likely to be spent at retail if it is equally divided than if it is concentrated. Second, they indicate the size of the base for the many
sales taxes which the states are now levying.

The third series shows the per capita figures for estimated taxable
wealth in 1936.[6] These are significant because they furnish a rough
check on the income figures and because some states still levy
property taxes. The last series shows the per capita value of the
output of certain primary industries. It is composed of cash farm
income for 1937, value of mineral production for 1936, and value
added by manufacture for 1937.[7] These supply an additional rough
check upon the general income figures and also indicate the size of
the base for certain business or severance taxes.

These series provide a rather broad base for the measurement of
income and taxpaying ability. They are not all for the same year,
but for the purpose at hand that is perhaps an advantage, since the
final figure is not likely to be distorted by temporary developments. In general, the different series agree with each other to a
striking degree, which tends to corroborate their validity. In most
cases the exceptions—such as Delaware and Florida—can be explained on a logical basis.

Analysis of the Measure

The average rank or relative for the states may be considered as
a fairly reliable index of taxpaying ability. A figure above 100 indicates an ability above the average for the country as a whole, while
a figure below 100 indicates less than average ability. As a region,
the Far Western states ranked first with a figure of 134. The Northeastern states were second with 116. Southern states, with an
average of 56, showed an ability far below that of the nation as a
whole.

6. Edna Trull, *Resources and Debts of the Forty-eight States, 1937* (New York,
1937), p. 98. Concerning these figures the author states: "In order to secure greater
comparability, an effort has been made to adjust assessed valuation statistics to full
value. The figures, however, are presented with trepidation. Although state tax commissions and boards of equalization have been consulted, it must be said that the
statistics are estimates and are not always official" (*ibid.*, p. 96).

7. The sources are cash farm income (*Statistical Abstract of the United States,
1938*, p. 618), value of mineral production (*ibid.*, 714), and value added by manufacture (Bureau of the Census, *Census of Manufactures, 1937*, preliminary figures
by states).

The sparsely settled states of the West with large per capita natural resources—Nevada, Wyoming, and Montana—ranked high, with Nevada leading the nation with an average of 177. California was second with 147. In the East, New York, Connecticut, and Rhode Island showed the highest averages. Mississippi, with an average of 37, had the lowest figure, followed by Arkansas, Alabama, and South Carolina.

Application of the Measure

In order to compare debts with ability to pay, the figures for per capita total net debt were converted into relatives by the same method used on the income and wealth series. The results are given in the column headed Debt Rank. Those figures show the per capita debt of each state as a relative of the national average. The index of debt burden was then computed by dividing the average relative of taxpaying ability *into* the relative of per capita debt, multiplied by 100. That figure thus expresses the debt relative as a per cent of the relative showing taxpaying ability; it shows the debt burden only in relation to the national averages of ability and indebtedness.

The Far Western states had the lowest debt burden by a substantial margin, followed by the Middle states. This was mainly due to their high ability, especially in the Far West. The Northeastern states had an average burden, since both per capita debts and ability were somewhat above average. In spite of the low figures for Kentucky and Virginia, the Southeastern states had a debt burden more than two and a half times the national average. This resulted both from their high per capita debts and their very low ability.

Among the individual states, Arkansas had by far the heaviest debt burden with a figure of 819, while Louisiana was second with 595. Other states with burdens more than three times the national average were Mississippi, South Carolina, and New Mexico. West Virginia, with a figure of 253, had the heaviest burden in the Northeast. Nebraska, Ohio, Kentucky, Indiana, Idaho, and Michigan had the lowest burdens. Pennsylvania had the lowest burden in the Northeast.

Debt burdens were more unevenly distributed than per capita

indebtedness because the poor states have borrowed heavily. Arkansas, with the second lowest index of ability, had the second largest per capita debt, while all four states with ability indexes below 50 had per capita debts above average. The six poorest states according to this measure, had an average[8] index of ability of 47 and an average index of per capita debts of 133. Of the twenty-five states with indexes of ability below average, fifteen had per capita debts above average. On the other hand, the six richest states, according to this measure, had an average ability of 144 and average per capita debts of 101. Of the twenty-two states with indexes of ability above average, fourteen had per capita debts below average. The Southeastern states, as a group, had an ability index 46 per cent below average and per capita debts 47 per cent above average, while the Far Western states had an ability index 34 per cent above average and per capita debts 32 per cent below average. This would indicate that the poor states had slightly larger per capita debts, absolutely, than the rich states.[9] It is also evident that the old states of the East had substantially larger per capita debts than the new states of the West. Only four of the seventeen states in the three Western regions had per capita debts above average. One state had no debt, and five others had per capita debts less than one third of the national average.

DEBT SERVICE IN 1938

No complete figures are available for debt service requirements on the debts as computed in the previous sections. Two series are available, however, which will convey some idea of the size of interest and principal payments which the states must make annually. These are presented and discussed below.

The first series is that compiled by the Bureau of the Census showing interest payments by the states for 1937. These figures include interest paid on current or short-term debt as well as on funded debt. However, interest on funded debt constitutes approx-

8. These are arithmetic averages of the state figures.

9. The coefficient of correlation between the ability index and the debt index is —.042. The standard deviation of the ability index is 30.34 and of the debt index, 84.09.

imately 95 per cent of the total.[10] Interest on contingent obligations is not included if the state received the funds from local governments. Interest on some revenue bonds, such as those in Mississippi and New Mexico, is included, but in general such interest is not covered. No distinction is made between interest paid from self-supporting enterprises and that paid from tax revenues.

In some respects interest payments constitute a more accurate index of debt burden than total debt service requirements. Interest payments cannot easily be manipulated, whereas principal repayments will depend upon the debt structure, the length of time the bonds run, and provisions for the accumulation of sinking funds. Thus a state with a large debt might, for several years, make no provision for repayment, while another state with a much lower debt might be repaying its debt so rapidly that its total debt service requirements might be heavier than those of the first state.

The Burden of Interest Payments

In order to facilitate comparisons between states, the 1937 interest payments have been expressed as per capita amounts and as percentages of total revenue receipts of the different states. According to this computation, the Far Western states made the highest per capita interest payments, only because the large payments on the self-supporting debts of California and Oregon were included. With these excluded, the figure would be much lower. The figures for the Northeastern and Southeastern states were almost identical, as were their per capita net direct debts. The figures for the other three sections were considerably below the national average of 95 cents per capita.

South Dakota had the highest figures for any state—$3.11— largely because of the inclusion of the heavy payments on its partially self-supporting debt. Louisiana was second with $2.83 and Arkansas, third with $2.45. This order would probably have been reversed had not Arkansas been able to reduce its interest rates by its refunding in 1934 following the default. Florida was the only state which made no interest payments, but per capita amounts were only nominal in Nebraska, Georgia, Wisconsin, Indiana, and Ohio.

A more accurate index of the burden of interest payments is a comparison of such payments with total revenue receipts. The third column of figures in Table 45 gives such a comparison. The Southeastern states definitely had the heaviest burden in this comparison, with a figure of 5.4 per cent. The Northeastern states were second with 3.3 per cent; the Far Western states, third with 3.0 per cent, which was also the national average.

Among the individual states, Arkansas was far in the lead with a figure of 15.2 per cent, or more than five times the national average. Tennessee was second with 9.6 per cent, and South Dakota, even with the inclusion of payments on its self-supporting debt, was third with 9.5 per cent. The states with the lowest per capita payments were also the states with the lowest payments in relation to revenue receipts.

Moody's Computations for Total Debt Service Requirements

For most states, Moody's *Governments and Municipals* gives advance estimates of the requirements for interest and principal payments. The 1939 edition of this volume gives computations for the fiscal year 1938-39. These are shown in the fourth, fifth, and sixth columns of Table 45. The figures are incomplete and unofficial. For several states no figures at all were given; attempts were made to supply estimates for them on the same basis as the computations for other states. In all cases the computations were made for the funded debts as formally reported by the different states. Thus they do not include payments to be made on floating or current debts, payments to be made on debts of local governments, nor, generally, the payments on revenue obligations, although in the cases of Mississippi and New Mexico such payments are included. Payments on self-supporting debts are included.

These figures are likely to be inaccurate or misleading in several respects. First, they are amounts, as nearly as can be estimated, of payments which were scheduled to be made; they were not necessarily made in every case. For example, Minnesota had $14,135,000

TABLE 45
The Service of State Debts, 1937 and 1938-39
(All dollar figures except per capita in thousands)

State	Bureau of Census Data			Moody's Computations for 1938-39					Per Cent of Per Capita Retail Sales 1935
	Interest Payments 1937	Per Capita	Per Cent of Revenue Receipts	Interest	Principal	Total	Per Capita	Per Cent of Revenue Receipts 1937	
Conn.........	$ 291	$0.17	0.5	$ 391*	$ 1,250	$ 1,641	$0.94	2.8	0.3
Del.........	88	0.34	0.7	83	155	238	0.92	2.0	0.3
Me.........	1,175	1.37	4.0	1,028	1,966	2,994	3.50	10.1	1.3
Md.........	1,912	1.14	3.9	1,598	4,271	5,869	3.50	12.0	1.3
Mass........	737	0.17	0.5	588	8,647	9,235†	2.09	6.6	0.6
N. H........	513	1.01	2.8	367	1,645	2,012	3.95	10.9	1.3
N. J........	7,655	1.76	5.3	6,719	14,244	20,963	4.83	14.6	1.7
N. Y........	23,126	1.78	4.7	19,864	35,537	55,401	4.28	11.4	1.2
Pa.........	5,427	0.53	1.4	4,927	4,500	9,427	0.93	2.5	0.4
R. I........	1,008	1.48	4.6	1,170	1,011	2,181‡	3.20	9.9	1.0
Vt.........	297	0.78	2.5	256	677	933	2.44	7.9	0.9
W. Va.......	3,681	1.97	6.1	3,681	4,560	8,241§	4.46	13.6	2.5
Northeastern States.....	45,910	1.15	3.3	40,672	78,463	119,135	2.99	8.4	1.0
Ala.........	3,223	1.11	6.4	2,828	1,594	4,422††	1.53	8.7	1.3
Ark.........	5,017	2.45	15.2	5,803	790	6,593	3.24	20.0	2.7
Fla.........									
Ga.........	24	0.01	0.1	154	215	369	0.12	0.9	0.1
Ky.........	1,384	0.47	2.2						
La.........	6,032	2.83	7.7	7,131	5,131	12,262‡‡	5.75	15.7	3.6
Miss.......	2,317	1.15	5.7	2,654	4,270	6,929	3.43	17.1	3.9
N. C.......	7,044	2.02	7.5	6,335	7,200	13,535	3.89	14.5	2.9
S. C.......	1,722	0.92	4.7	1,722	927	2,649§	1.42	7.3	1.1
Tenn.......	4,730	1.63	9.6	4,920	5,377	10,297	3.58	21.0	2.1
Va.........	955	0.35	1.5	530	1,295	1,825	0.68	2.8	0.4
Southeastern States.....	32,448	1.17	5.4	32,077	26,799	58,856	2.12	9.8	1.4
Ill.........	8,654	1.10	4.5	7,373	11,800	19,173	2.44	9.9	0.9
Ind.........	170	0.05	0.2						
Iowa........	337	0.13	0.4	198	1,100	1,298	0.51	1.5	0.2
Mich.......	4,388	0.91	2.3	3,533		3,533	0.73	1.8	0.2
Minn.......	4,311	1.63	4.1	4,751	14,135	18,886	7.14	18.0	2.3
Mo.........	4,856	1.22	5.6	4,198	6,713	10,911	2.74	12.5	1.2
Ohio.......	483	0.07	0.2						
Wis........	83	0.03	0.1						
Middle States.....	23,282	0.66	2.1	20,053	33,748	53,801	1.54	4.8	0.6
Colo.......	347	0.32	0.9	**83	304	388	0.36	1.0	0.1
Idaho......	107	0.22	0.6	52	333	385	0.78	2.0	0.3
Kan........	982	0.53	2.3	723	1,000	1,723	0.92	4.0	0.4
Mont.......	470	0.87	2.1	193	420	613**	1.15	2.7	0.3
Neb........	17	0.01	0.1						
N. D.......	1,305	1.85	6.6	1,159	337	1,496††	2.12	7.5	1.0
S. D.......	2,155	3.11	9.5	2,022	4,225	6,247††**	9.03	27.6	4.3
Utah......	469	0.90	1.9	353	594	947*	1.83	3.9	0.7
Wyo........	141	0.60	1.0	124	166	290‡‡	1.24	2.1	0.4
Northwestern States.....	5,993	0.80	2.5	4,709	7,379	12,088	1.62	5.1	0.6
Ariz.......	111	0.27	0.5	40	30	70	0.17	0.3	0.1
N. M.......	569	1.35	2.3	755	1,181	1,936	4.59	8.0	2.2
Okla.......	561	0.22	0.7	183	1,031	1,214	0.48	1.5	0.3
Tex........	1,111	0.18	0.6	‡‡480	2,289	2,769	0.45	1.6	0.2
Southwestern States.....	2,352	0.25	0.8	1,458	4,531	5,989	0.63	2.0	0.3
Calif.......	9,088	1.48	3.2	7,205	9,062	16,267††	2.66	5.8	0.7
Nev........	43	0.43	0.6	29	64	93*	0.93	1.3	0.2
Ore........	2,233	2.17	5.4	1,842	3,223	5,065	4.96	12.2	1.5
Wash.......	680	0.41	0.9	394	845	1,239	0.75	1.7	0.2
Far Western States.....	12,044	1.35	3.0	9,470	13,194	22,664	2.54	5.6	0.7
United States	122,029	0.95	3.0	108,439	164,114	272,553	2.11	6.7	0.8

*Not given by *Moody's*; full year's requirement computed by author.　†Direct debt only.
‡Actual disbursements, 1937-38; allocation estimated.　§Partly estimated.
||Includes service of self-supporting debt.　‡‡Estimated.
**Not given by *Moody's*; estimated by author.

of obligations falling due in this year, but it is quite likely that a large part of them was refunded rather than redeemed in cash. The same is true of South Dakota. On the other hand, Arkansas had only $790,000 of obligations falling due, but the state was obligated to devote all highway revenues above certain amounts to debt retirement. During the calendar year 1937 the state paid out some $4,150,000 for such retirements. If such an amount were added for 1938-39 the total would amount to well over 30 per cent of the state's revenue receipts. The same principle would hold in other states where the yield of certain specified taxes rather than definite amounts are pledged for debt service, but such provisions are not common except in the service of local government debts.

In the second place, the figures do not include any allowance for the service of bonds issued during the year.

In the third place, the figures include the service of self-supporting debts, which should be deducted if the aim is to state the burden of debts on state revenues. The total debt service funds received from self-supporting projects were probably from $14,000,-000 to $16,000,000 and were received chiefly by California, Minnesota, Oregon, and South Dakota.

Finally, the figures do not include funds for the service of revenue bonds and local government debts which are serviced from state funds. The total of such funds was probably between $40,000,-000 and $50,000,000 and was paid principally by Texas, Iowa, Florida, Colorado, Georgia, Wisconsin, South Carolina, and Connecticut.

Even with these limitations, however, the figures are valuable since they give a rough and approximate idea of the total outlay of the states for debt service. The total funds which must be raised from state revenues may be calculated by deducting approximately $15,000,000, representing contributions of self-supporting projects, from the total of $272,553,000 and then by adding approximately $45,000,000, representing payments on revenue obligations. This total of between $290,000,000 and $295,000,000 may be considered a fairly accurate estimate.

Comparisons by Regions

In order to facilitate comparisons by regions and by states, total debt service requirements as computed by *Moody's* have been stated in terms of revenue receipts in 1937 and in terms of per capita retail sales in 1935. In terms of revenue receipts, the Southeastern states had, in 1938-39, the heaviest burden with 9.8 per cent, although their lead over the Northeastern states in this respect was less than it was in the case of interest alone. This indicates that the Southeastern states were not retiring their debts as rapidly as the Northeastern states, and is in keeping with the impression gained by a study of particular states. If the amounts devoted to debt retirement in Arkansas were added, the burden would have been heavier and the comparative standing of this group in regard to debt retirement would have been improved, but it would still have been below the Northeastern states. The lowest burden was found in the Southwestern states with 2.0 per cent, but this would be increased—in fact, more than doubled—if Texas' contributions to local debt service were included. Other regions showed debt service requirements not far from 5 per cent of revenue receipts. The comparison with per capita retail sales of 1935 showed results in line with the above.

Comparison by States

As the table stands, South Dakota had the heaviest burden in relation to revenue receipts, with a figure of 27.6 per cent. This should be reduced, probably by a third, for funds received from self-supporting projects. If the funds devoted to debt retirement in Arkansas were included, that state would have had, by far, the heaviest burden with a figure of 33 or 34 per cent. Tennessee ranked third with a figure of 21.0 per cent and was the only other state with a figure above 20 per cent. Other states with heavy burdens were Minnesota, Mississippi, Louisiana, New Jersey, North Carolina, and West Virginia. South Carolina would also have been placed in this group by the inclusion of payments on local government debts. All of the above states had burdens more than twice as heavy as the national average of 6.7 per cent of revenue receipts. The same was true when the burden is stated in terms of per capita retail sales in 1935.

Six states—Florida, Kentucky, Indiana, Ohio, Wisconsin, and Nebraska—had only nominal direct debts or none at all, so that no charges were computed for them in Table 45. Of these, however, Florida and Wisconsin made large payments on local road debts. Other states with very low burdens, including both direct and indirect debts, were Arizona, Nevada, Oklahoma, Washington, Michigan, Idaho, and Wyoming.

For the country as a whole, the burden of state debt service was not heavy. It was represented by 6.7 per cent of 1937 revenue receipts and by 0.8 per cent of 1935 per capita retail sales. If payments on revenue obligations were added, these figures would probably have been increased to about 7.5 per cent and 1.0 per cent, respectively. They would still, however, be quite moderate. But for the few states in which debt service required more than 20 per cent of revenue receipts and 3 per cent or more of retail sales, they were a serious problem and threatened the ability of the states to provide the necessary governmental services to their citizens.

SUMMARY AND CONCLUSION

Per capita state debts were, in 1938, distinctly larger in the Eastern regions than in the Middle or Western regions. Considering total net debts which were serviced from state funds, the figure for the Southeastern states was considerably higher than those for other regions; it was more than twice as large as the figure for any other region except the Northeast. Variations between individual states were very great, ranging from more than seventy-five dollars in Arkansas and Louisiana to nothing in Nebraska and only nominal sums in Ohio and Kentucky.

On the other hand, indexes of wealth and income indicate the greatest taxpaying ability in the Far Western states, followed by the Northeastern and Middle states. The Southeastern states were lowest by a wide margin. Variations between individual states were not so great in respect to ability to pay as in respect to debt; nevertheless, they covered a range from 37 for Mississippi to 177 for Nevada.

There are no complete data on the interest and principal payments which states make on account of their debts. However, such data as are available indicate that such payments were heavier in the Southeast than in any other region, both in relation to the revenue receipts of the states and in relation to the incomes of taxpayers. This was true despite the fact that Southern states were making smaller payments on principal than were other states. In a few instances debt payments exceeded 20 per cent of total revenue receipts of states.

It is difficult to find any logical explanation for the prevalence of state borrowing. The two regions which have borrowed most—the Northeast and the Southeast—are almost opposites in regard to wealth and income, industrialization, and density of population. The same is true of certain individual states, such as New York and Illinois on the one hand and Arkansas and Louisiana on the other. The one characteristic which is common to the Eastern regions is that they are a little older and perhaps a little more mature than the regions of the West. It may be that in an old and more settled state, the government is not so able to raise a large amount of additional funds to meet demands for new services as would be the case in a new and growing state.

It is quite likely that the explanation for the large debts of the Southeast, which are farthest out of line with the national average, lies in the poverty of that region. Since the Southern states borrowed neither for soldiers' bonuses, relief, nor rural credit systems, it is evident that they borrowed primarily for highways. This is confirmed by a quick inspection of their debt statements. The demand for highways came suddenly in the post-war years. The Southern states were handicapped generally by poor systems of financial administration, limited revenue possibilities, and remnants of their pre-Civil War and Reconstruction debts. When the halcyon days of the twenties presented the possibility of acquiring highways through borrowing they did not hesitate to grasp it. Generally they attempted to justify their expenditures for roads as investments which would bring prosperity and repay the debts many times over. In some states there was much truth in this contention, but it is probable that most of the roads would have been built regardless of this justification.

A third possible explanation for the variations in state borrowing lies in the attitudes and prejudices of voters and variations in state politics. Popular attitudes toward public borrowing may vary greatly, even within two adjoining states with essentially similar economic conditions. Such a contrast is afforded by North Carolina and Virginia. In the same way, and perhaps of greater importance, the political organization may vary greatly from state to state. If the "machine" in one state is well established and controlled by competent and fairly honest politicians, state borrowing, if it is practiced at all, will likely be kept within moderate limits. But if there are frequent shifts of control between conflicting machines or if those in control are weak, incompetent, or dishonest, borrowed funds may be used to purchase votes or to line the pockets of the insiders.

A final explanation might lie in constitutional provisions. This, however, is likely to be temporary and superficial rather than basic and fundamental. Such provisions can be changed. They may exert a restraining influence for a time, and such delay may save the state from mistakes. But if popular demand or the influence of politicians is strong enough, they will ultimately give way.

CHAPTER XXIII

THE ECONOMIC EFFECTS OF STATE
BORROWING

THE INCURRING, servicing, and repaying of debts on a large scale must necessarily have far-reaching economic effects. The states have borrowed nearly four billions of dollars since 1918, have paid large amounts as interest for several years, and have repaid several hundred millions of dollars. It is difficult, for several reasons, to isolate or measure the economic effects of such policies. First, state financial policies have been only a minor factor among the many forces affecting the general economic situation. The financial policies of the Federal Government, of local governments, and of private industry have overshadowed those of the states because of the size of the sums involved. Second, the economic effects of the debt policy of a given state may be widely scattered in space. Some, and perhaps most, of the effects may be confined to the borrowing state, but others may occur at distant points, especially if funds are borrowed and materials are bought in other states. Third, the initial effects will vary considerably according to the use to which the funds are put. Borrowing to pay soldiers' bonuses or to finance relief payments would likely have its initial effect upon the consumer goods industries, while borrowing for highways would likely affect at first the heavy goods industries. Of course, the affected industries will, to a greater or less extent, transmit the initial effects on to other industries through wage payments and purchases of materials.

The above considerations and the scarcity of relevant data limit the quantitative analysis of the problem. Consequently, this chapter must be primarily deductive in its approach, although the limited factual material available will be used to test the conclusions reached by deduction.

THE EFFECTS OF INCURRING DEBTS

At the time when debts are being incurred certain economic tendencies are set in motion, only to be reversed when borrowing ceases and the payment of interest and the repayment of principal begin. These two situations will be discussed separately.

Political Effects

When a state embarks upon a program of borrowing, it is able, for a time, to render to its citizens services with a value greater than the value of taxes paid.[1] During such time the taxpayers get a large return for their money. The utility or satisfaction which they realize from the governmental services is personal, but they are not likely to have a keen feeling of personal responsibility toward the debt, especially if it is to mature in the distant future. Such a situation may affect the conduct of state government in that it is likely to redound to the advantage of the particular political group in power at the time. When taxpayers are realizing a large return for the money which they pay in taxes, they are likely to be favorably inclined toward the public officials who produce those results. Borrowed funds, even though properly applied, tend to entrench in office those who lead the borrowing program. Because of this, inefficient and careless officials may, by irresponsible borrowing, have an advantage over more efficient and conscientious candidates who try to replace them.

Effects upon Administration of Expenditures

More specifically, borrowed funds will probably be expended less efficiently than tax revenues for three reasons. In the first place, legislators and taxpayers are likely to be less critical of the amounts and purposes of appropriations. As one study has expressed it: "While theoretically there should be no distinction in treatment, the fact remains, and for self-evident reasons, that as a

1. The increased services may be realized not only in the field for which the state is borrowing, but in state services generally. If before borrowing begins the state is financing capital improvements from current funds, it may stop all such appropriations and finance the improvements exclusively from borrowed funds. This may ease the fiscal problem all around and permit the state to enlarge its program of current services. Thus in 1905, when it began to borrow for highways, New York ceased to appropriate current funds for highway construction. See p. 251.

practical matter appropriations from the proceeds of the sale of bond issues are subjected to far less critical administrative, legislative and public scrutiny than appropriations which are financed from current tax revenues."[2]

Another writer has expressed it more succinctly: "Public borrowing is conducive to extravagance because it dissociates the pleasure of public expenditures from the pain of paying taxes."[3] It is highly doubtful whether, in 1927, Arkansas legislators and taxpayers would have agreed to treble the amounts that they were paying to Confederate veterans if it had been necessary to raise the funds by taxation. No doubt many of the bonuses paid to World War veterans would have been less if the funds had been raised by taxation rather than by borrowing.

The second reason for the reduced efficiency in the spending of borrowed funds lies in the nonadjustment of state agencies to an increased rate of spending. A borrowing program usually entails a considerable expansion in the state's activities. Especially if the borrowing is to meet a new need, the agency charged with spending the funds will be new and small. It probably will be so engrossed in expanding its personnel, planning spending programs, and supervising construction that it will fail either to investigate existing techniques or to devise better ones. When the borrowing comes in the early stages of the development of the technique, such mistakes may be costly. For example, North Carolina borrowed heavily for highways at a time when highway engineering was relatively poorly developed. Instead of designing and building adequate motor highways, the state merely paved the existing narrow, crooked roads with their weak, dangerous bridges. No attention was given to avoiding congested areas or to banking curves. In recent years the state has spent millions of dollars in straightening roads, building by-passes around congested areas, and correcting other early mistakes. In some cases long stretches of road have been entirely relocated. Some of the mistakes would have been avoided if construction had been undertaken more slowly. Another

2. *Report of the Joint Legislative Committee on State Fiscal Policies*, New York Legislative Doc. (1938) No. 41, p. 70.
3. Harold M. Groves, *Financing Government* (New York, 1939), p. 674.

example is afforded by the railroad and canal building in the 1830's. Borrowing was begun for canals. When the railroad appeared, its future was so uncertain that canal building continued and in some cases duplicate facilities were provided for the same areas. Millions of dollars were spent on canals which soon became obsolete. If the building had proceeded more slowly until the possibilities of the railroad had been demonstrated, much waste would have been avoided.

On the other hand, in certain types of activity it is more economical to proceed on a fairly large scale. In the construction of highways and buildings there is an optimum size for the working unit and an optimum speed at which to proceed so that funds, facilities, and public property will not be tied up too long in the process of construction and so that parts of the project will not deteriorate before the whole is completed. Today most, if not all, of our states are able, out of current revenues, to finance a scale of operations which will meet these technical requirements. But there is a larger aspect of the problem. For example, to get the most use from its highways, a state must build a network or system of highways; work must be carried forward in many different parts of the state at the same time. There is also the political problem, for if limited funds are used in only certain parts of the state "the remainder of the state will be left entirely unprovided for. Such a practice gives opportunity for corruption and favoritism and is capable of producing political difficulties of the first magnitude. Taxpayers supplying the funds will not look with favor upon the expenditure in favored localities of funds collected from the entire state. . . . by means of bond issues it is possible to build roads everywhere over the state within a short period and to connect them quickly into a *system* capable of giving genuine service to the motoring public."[4]

This latter point is certainly true and is one of the real advantages of the borrowing method. But it, in turn, creates a problem, since it means that for a short period of time certain of the state's resources will be used intensively and then will be abandoned or will have to be shifted to other uses—if they can be found. Since

4. C. K. Brown, *The State Highway System of North Carolina*, p. 218.

the construction industry is subject to wide fluctuations anyway, such a policy will aggravate the problem unless care is taken to time state spending so as to offset those fluctuations.

A third factor tending to lower the efficiency with which borrowed funds are used is their administration. A borrowing program will impose upon the accounting and treasury departments the task of handling large amounts of money for which they may not be prepared. Accounting systems designed to handle normal revenues may be swamped, and depositary systems may be unable to handle the large balances which are usually carried when activities are expanded. The resulting confusion and the feeling of affluence which fiscal officers experience with large amounts of funds under their control may promote waste, favoritism, and graft. Shortly after North Carolina started its program of heavy borrowing in 1921, the state's accounts were so badly confused that the state, the governor claimed, had a surplus of $2,500,000 while the Commissioner of Revenue contended at the same time that there was a deficit of $5,000,000.[5] After it had required a leading accounting firm six months to determine the true state of affairs, a new accounting system was installed. In previous chapters we have seen that inadequate provisions for safeguarding state deposits led to the loss of large amounts of borrowed funds in South Dakota and Tennessee. It is true, in one sense, that such difficulties are not the result of borrowing but of administrative weaknesses. But the large amounts of borrowed funds accentuate the weaknesses and tend to make fiscal officers careless about the funds which they handle. These considerations, together with the fact that the public tends to be less critical about the use of borrowed funds, provide a situation in which graft may flourish. It is no accident that many of our worst scandals have developed in times of heavy borrowing. The Louisiana situation which was revealed in the summer of 1939 is merely one illustration of that fact.

Effects upon Purposes of Expenditures

It is probable also that borrowing may cause a change in the pattern of state expenditures. In providing services to its citizens

5. News and Observer (Raleigh, N. C.), Jan. 10; Feb. 2, 6, 7, 8, 1923.

a state must divide its funds between payments for physical plant and materials and payments to personnel; i.e., salaries. So long as a state makes all payments from current revenues the balance between these two types of payments will probably be maintained fairly well. Changes will be made slowly, and if one type of payment gets out of line, as shown by existing needs, it can be corrected before it has gone far. But in a period of prosperity and optimism the state may begin to borrow in order to expand its services rapidly. Borrowed funds are usually used to expand physical facilities; rarely, if ever, to expand personnel or to raise salaries. When the borrowing period has ended and optimism has turned to pessimism, the state may find that it has expanded beyond its means and that curtailment is necessary. But it has already purchased its physical facilities for the larger program, and they must be maintained at all costs. The fixed charges on the debt cannot be reduced save by default. The result is that the personnel—usually underpaid even at best—is forced to bear the total burden of adjustment. State employees must suffer for the sins of overexpansion in the field of physical facilities. The university professor may have his salary reduced to $2,000, but he continues to teach in a million-dollar building. The combination of factors may be so uneconomical that the state's efficiency will be reduced in the long run.

Effects upon State as a Whole

The effects of state borrowing upon private incomes and economic activity are different from the effects of national borrowing for two reasons. In the typical case the state borrows outside its own boundaries. The funds are imported and thus will tend to raise interest rates and lower bank reserves in the state where the funds are borrowed, but to have opposite effects in the borrowing state. In this respect the borrowing will probably have more of a stimulating effect than if it were carried out entirely within the state. In the second place, part of the expenditures will take place outside the borrowing states. It is almost certain that at least a part of the materials and supplies will be bought outside the state. In this way a part of the stimulating effects will be lost to the borrowing state. This analysis is limited to the effects which take place within the state that borrows.

Effects of State Spending

As a state spends within its own borders, it will tend to raise wages and the prices of materials and to increase money incomes and profits. If there are no idle factors of production within the state at the beginning, the state will have to bid against other employers for men and materials. The competition for labor and materials will tend to raise wages and prices. To the extent that this is true, total production will not be increased, but the character of the production will be changed. State lines, however, are not economic frontiers, and if there exist elsewhere factors of production which are idle or less well paid, they may be attracted to the state and will increase total production.

If the factors of production within the state are not fully employed at the beginning of the borrowing period, the state's payments to laborers and to the sellers of materials and supplies will increase incomes and total production without causing any pronounced rise in prices and wages. The recipients of the payments will, in turn, spend a large part of their increased incomes, thereby increasing the incomes of others and bringing into operation the familiar "multiplier."[6] The process will continue until a substantial portion of the economic system has felt the stimulating effects of the state's expenditures.

Effects of the Borrowing

The funds which a state borrows may come from any one of three sources. They may come from savings within the state. To get such funds, the state would have to bid against other borrowers within or without the state. As a result, interest rates would tend to rise.

If banks within the state buy the state bonds through an expansion of bank credit, the money supply will be increased and interest rates will be little affected unless the banks are forced to

6. For a good discussion of this principle see J. M. Keynes, *The General Theory of Employment, Interest, and Money* (New York, 1936), pp. 13-31.

curtail credit in other directions or to build up their reserves by rediscounting or borrowing. The increased volume of bank credit will tend to accentuate the stimulating effects of state spending.

The third and most usual source of funds for borrowing states is one of the large financial centers outside the state. In such borrowing the funds are usually transferred through the banking system and thus come into the borrowing state as reserves of the banks which serve as state depositories. Except as they must use such funds to pay for purchases outside the state, those banks have their reserves increased and are thus enabled, as a group, to make loans to several times the amount of the new reserves. This will tend to reduce interest rates and/or to make the banks inclined to lend more freely. Such developments should provide funds to finance the expansion started by state spending.

Effects upon Incomes

The effects of state spending may be offset or more than offset by the financial policies of other governments or of private business. It has been noted above that the volume of state financial transactions is small, relative to the total of such transactions. For what it may be worth, however, let us note the behavior of income payments in those states which increased their debts most during the depression of the 1930's. Between 1930 and 1937 nine states increased their net debts by more than ten dollars. They were, in descending order of their increases: Louisiana, Minnesota, New York, Colorado, Rhode Island, New Mexico, New Hampshire, New Jersey, and Maryland.[7] Index numbers, showing the variations in total income payments in those nine states and in the whole of the United States, are:[8]

	1929	1930	1931	1932	1933	1934	1935	1936	1937
Nine states	100	94	83	65	62	72	77	88	93
United States	100	92	78	61	57	66	72	83	88

7. Edna Trull, *Resources and Debts of the Forty-eight States, 1937*, p. 27. It will be noted that those states had few other characteristics in common.

8. Nathan and Martin, *op. cit.*, p. 3. This source gives index numbers for total income payments in each state based upon 1929 as 100. The figures given above in the nine states are simple arithmetic averages of the figures for each of those states; the figures for the United States are relatives of the totals for the whole country.

On the average, total income payments in the nine states were maintained at a higher level, in relation to 1929, than in the country as a whole. The margin was not large, but it was distinct and consistent.[9] Too much weight should not be attached to this single piece of evidence, but since it lends definite support to the deductive theory it is worthy of note.

It may be ventured, then, that state borrowing tends to expand business activity, to increase income payments, and perhaps to increase profits in the borrowing states. If tax rates are not raised when borrowing is begun, the burden of taxes within the state may decrease because of the higher incomes and larger profits. For the same reason tax revenues may increase; that is, existing taxes may produce more revenues without any increase in rates. This is especially true in a state which is borrowing for highways and depending heavily upon the gasoline tax. The use of gasoline, especially by cars from outside the state, may increase because of the better roads. Under such conditions the taxpayer comes to believe that borrowing is true magic; he feels that his tax burden is less and at the same time that business is better and that he is enjoying more governmental services than ever before. With the taxpayer converted and the administrator and politician pleased with the additional patronage to be distributed and many advantages, proper or improper, to be derived from handling large amounts of state funds, the demand for more borrowing may become so strong that original borrowing plans are revised upward unless there are strong and effective limits. In brief, the local inflation created by state borrowing and spending may conceal the rising debt burden and create a demand for continued borrowing.

9. Two criticisms have been made against this conclusion. The first is that the higher incomes may have been the cause and not the result of the borrowing; that is, those states which had high incomes may have been more free in their borrowing. This is possible, but there is no basis for it in the American experience. As noted elsewhere, the poor states have probably been more persistent in borrowing than the wealthy states. The second criticism is that the figures prove too much—that the relatively small volume of state borrowing could not possibly have produced the effects shown. The nine states were chosen solely on the basis of the changes in their debts. The operation of no other selective factor is apparent. It is not claimed that the whole effect was produced by state borrowing, for obviously our measures are crude and inaccurate. The results do lend some support to the theory.

THE EFFECTS OF REPAYING DEBTS

When debts have been incurred the interest charges on them must be paid. In addition, it has been customary for our states to make periodical payments toward the retirement of principal. The effects of these two types of payments will be discussed together.

Political Effects

The effects upon state governments of the repayment of debts are the opposite of those caused by the incurring of debts. States must now collect in taxes more than they can spend on services to their citizens. If the borrowed funds were used to pay bonuses, to cover operating deficits, or for other similar purposes, taxpayers will have no tangible benefits to show for them, but will still have to pay the increased taxes. If they were used to provide permanent improvements, it may be that taxpayers, as a group, will have increased incomes from which to pay the heavier taxes. Even in this instance, however, the individual is likely to regard the increased income as the result of his own efforts and will have little relish for the increased taxes. In any case, taxpayers will have become accustomed to the higher level of services during the period of borrowing and will now take them for granted. After the stimulation caused by the spending of borrowed funds has worn off, taxes will remain high or even go higher. From any point of view, the taxpayer does not receive, during the period of debt payment, as large a return for his tax dollar as he does during the period of borrowing. Since all value appraisals are relative, the taxpayer now thinks that he is not getting a bargain—is not getting his money's worth—from the dollars paid in taxes.

The burden of meeting interest and principal payments will intensify the whole fiscal problem of the state. New services cannot be provided so easily. If the state meets reverses, the state's personnel, as already noted, may have to bear the full brunt of making the necessary adjustments. Taxpayers are likely to be critical and ill-tempered. Officials must tread carefully to avoid losing their political heads. In such times investigating committees flourish and past records are brought out and examined. The backwash from periods of heavy borrowing may easily sweep many officials from office.

Effects upon State Fiscal Policies

The most important effect of a heavy debt burden is to rob the state of its freedom of movement and its ability to meet new emergencies. The great advantage of the credit or borrowing system— the "funding" system it was formerly called—is the freedom and flexibility that it gives to a state in meeting emergencies and new needs. When a state has borrowed heavily, it forfeits this advantage for a time. Heavy fixed charges mean that the way in which a state must spend a substantial part of its funds is determined in advance. If new needs arise, the state is less able to meet them than if it had not borrowed. At the time when a state is paying most heavily for the privilege of borrowing it is least able to borrow. When a state borrows, it gives hostages to the future and takes the chance that there will not arise, during the life of the debt, a pressing need which will require the use of that part of its credit. The group which incurs the debt, imposes its will and its wishes upon the groups of future years, which must repay the debt.

Effects of Taxation

In analyzing the economic effects of the repayment of state debts we must consider primarily two factors: the way in which the funds are raised and those to whom they are paid. In regard to the latter point, interest payments must be considered apart from repayments of principal, since they may be regarded differently by the recipients.

Most states derive a large majority of their revenues from taxes which are regressive in effect. For all states together, the gasoline tax is the most important source of revenue, accounting for about 16 per cent of the total. Other important sources are gross receipts and general sales taxes, income taxes, and motor vehicle license taxes. Income and inheritance taxes are the only ones which are progressive, and their progression is usually mild. The two taxes together contribute only about 9 per cent of all state revenues.[10]

Since state taxes as a whole are distinctly regressive, funds raised

10. *Financial Statistics of States, 1937*, pp. 46-47.

by such taxes come primarily from the middle and lower income classes. Those classes ordinarily spend most of their incomes for consumer goods. The payment of taxes means a reduction in private spending, which, in turn, must mean a reduction in business activity and profits unless it is offset by the spending of those who receive the funds. In other words, there is a net reduction in the purchasing power of the taxpayers as a group, and such a reduction must have an effect on the economic system unless it is offset by the increase in the purchasing power of the bondholders. It is, therefore, pertinent to determine where the bondholders are located and how they will use the funds which they receive.

Effects of Payments

In the typical case the state sells its bonds in one of the large financial centers, and a large part of them are bought and held by parties residing outside the borrowing state.[11] In such cases the funds paid as service on the debt, whether as interest or repayment of principal, are lost to the state and represent a net reduction in its purchasing power. In other words, to the extent that payments are made to bondholders outside the state the purchasing power lost by taxpayers cannot be offset by the increase in purchasing power realized by the bondholders. In such a case the multiplier works in reverse and will tend to produce falling prices, lower profits, and unemployment.[12]

To the extent that bonds are held within the state, there is a

11. Of course, it may be true that such bonds are bought by funds which came originally from the borrowing state in the form of insurance premiums or other similar payments. To the extent that this was true and to the extent that insurance and other payments came back into the state as debt service payments were made, the effect would be the same as if the bonds were held inside the state. Of course, to the extent that deductions were made because of the "loading" or overhead expenses of insurance companies and others, this effect would be lost.

12. My colleague, Professor J. J. Spengler, points out that there may be an exception to this line of reasoning. If state A pays interest to people in state B, the latter may spend it in such ways that, directly or indirectly, state A may regain some of the purchasing power, in which case the deflationary effect of the multiplier would be reduced. This is true, but the probability is that state A would be able to regain only a small part of such purchasing power. Professor Spengler further points out that the important point is the comparative wealth of those who pay taxes and those who receive the interest and principal payments. If the latter are the richer, the velocity of circulation will probably be reduced, and the reverse effect of the multiplier will be felt.

chance that the purchasing power lost by taxpayers may be offset by that gained by bondholders. The bonds, however, will be held by those who enjoy a higher level of income than the taxpayers generally, and who will save a larger part of their income. Bondholders probably will regard interest received as part of their regular income and spend it for consumer goods in the same proportion as they spend all regular income. But since they ordinarily save a larger part of their income than do taxpayers generally, the net result will be a reduction in the demand for consumer goods. Principal repayments will almost surely be regarded not as income but as a return of principal, and will be reinvested. Thus the part of tax revenues which go to repay principal will represent a reduction in the demand for consumer goods.

It seems safe to conclude that, in general, the repayment of debts by states, including the payment of interest, is deflationary. This is true of all the funds which are paid to bondholders outside the state and of principal repayments to bondholders inside the state. Interest payments to the latter are deflationary only to the extent that they are saved.

Effects upon Bank Credit

The effects of debt repayment upon the banks of the debtor state are the opposite of the effects caused by the creation of the debt. Funds which are sent out of the state are remitted through the banking system and act to reduce the reserves of the banks within the state. If the banks have expanded their credit up to the limit allowed by their reserves, the loss of such funds will force them either to curtail loans or to build up their reserves by rediscounting or other means. The effects of payments made to bondholders within the state may not be so serious. Interest payments may be spent locally or held as bank balances. In either case the bank's reserve situation is not changed. If interest or principal payments should be saved and invested outside the state, the banks would have to make the remittances and reduce their reserves accordingly. If a state is reducing its debt, and other investment opportunities are not expanding in proportion, it is quite probable that some of the funds will be sent outside the state for reinvestment. The depressing effect of the state's debt repayment upon business generally may have an influence toward reducing investment opportunities within the state.

The deflationary effect of debt repayment upon the banks may be accentuated by the fact that the state, as a rule, will carry smaller bank balances in a period of debt reduction than in a period of borrowing. There will be less need for large balances, and the state will probably have more difficulty in keeping an adequate supply of cash on hand. If the state is in a strained financial position it will reduce its balances to a minimum or even overdraw. Since this is most likely to happen in a time of economic stress, the additional pressure thus placed upon the banks may be the cause of additional bank failures. In 1931-32 North Carolina banks complained that the state's policy in reducing its balances contributed to the widespread bank failures.

When banks have their reserves reduced and find it difficult to raise the funds which must be sent out of the state, they will have to curtail their lending operations. Interest rates will tend to rise, and a tight credit situation will accentuate the deflationary effects of the taxes which are levied to raise the funds for debt service.

Effects upon Incomes

As one check on the operation of this theory we may apply the same test as was used above to measure the effects of borrowing. Between 1930 and 1937 the reductions in state debts were considerably less than the increases, but five states reduced their per capita net debts by eight dollars or more in those years. The states, in the descending order of their decreases, were: North Dakota, Oregon, South Dakota, Delaware, and North Carolina.[13] Averages of index numbers of total income payments in those states and the index for the United States as a whole were:[14]

	1929	1930	1931	1932	1933	1934	1935	1936	1937
Five states	100	87	71	51	53	65	72	85	90
United States	100	92	78	61	57	66	72	83	88

13. Trull, *op. cit.*, p. 29.   14. Nathan and Martin, *op. cit.*, p. 3.

Income in the five states fell more, in relation to 1929, than in the country as a whole, reached the low point a little earlier, and thereafter rose faster, so that in 1936 and 1937 it was slightly higher than in the remainder of the country. During the downswing, income behaved as indicated by the theory, but its behavior in the later years indicates either that the theory is incomplete or that other factors than the repayment of state debts were dominant.[15] In view of the relatively small size of state financial transactions, as previously noted, and of the extensive activities of the Federal Government directed toward relief, the latter alternative was quite possible.

Further Comparisons

In order to compare the behavior of income payments under conditions of increasing and of decreasing debts, it may be well to place the figures used in the two previous comparisons side by side. Also, lest the samples chosen may have been too small, it may be well to compare the figures for all states in which debts increased with the figures for all states in which debts decreased.

Between 1930 and 1937 per capita net debts increased in twenty-five states and decreased in twenty-one states, but the decreases were considerably less than the increases. The increases ranged from twenty-four cents in Indiana to $34.59 in Louisiana and averaged $9.44, while the decreases ranged from six cents in Wisconsin to $16.82 in North Dakota and averaged $4.56.[16] Averages of the index numbers of total income payments for the states in the two groups are presented in Table 46, together with the figures used in the previous comparisons. Two series are given for the United States. The first is taken from the income study cited and is based upon the total income payments for the whole country. It is thus automatically weighted according to the payments made in each state. But the figures for the various groups are unweighted aver-

15. The sample of states used was not satisfactory for several reasons: first, it was too small; second, the agricultural situation was dominant in the Dakotas; and, third, in North Dakota, which achieved the greatest debt reduction, there was little debt liquidation but rather a transfer from state to other agencies, particularly federal agencies.

16. Trull, *Resources and Debts of the Forty-eight States, 1937*, pp. 27-29.

TABLE 46

The Behavior of Total Income Payments in States Which Increased and
States Which Reduced per Capita Net Debts, 1930-37

Group	1929	1930	1931	1932	1933	1934	1935	1936	1937
States in Which Debts Increased:									
Nine states.....................	100	94	83	65	62	72	77	88	93
Twenty-five states...............	100	90	77	61	59	70	75	87	92
United States—as a whole........	100	92	78	61	57	66	72	83	88
United States—average of states*..	100	90	77	59	58	69	75	87	93
States in Which Debts Decreased:									
Five states.....................	100	87	71	51	53	65	72	85	90
Twenty-one states...............	100	90	75	56	55	66	74	86	92

*See text for explanation of this series and reasons for its use.

ages of the index numbers for the different states.[17] Because of the
wide variations in the volume of payments in the different states,
this procedure gives the paradoxical result that in 1935, 1936, and
1937 the averages for both the twenty-five states and the twenty-one
states are above the index number for the country as a whole. For
this reason it was considered desirable, for comparative purposes, to
construct another series for the country as a whole by making an
unweighted average of the index numbers of the forty-eight states
and the District of Columbia. This is the reason for the second
series, which is perhaps more useful for the present comparison
than the figures based upon the total income payments of the whole
country.

In general, the figures for the larger groups confirm the conclusions indicated by the two smaller samples previously used. In
the earlier comparisons, the states with the largest increases or decreases were taken. The average increase or decrease of debts for the
whole groups was considerably less than for the selected states. We
should, therefore, expect that income payments in the larger groups
would be affected less than in the smaller, selected groups. This is
what the figures reveal. The figures for the states with the largest
increases and the largest decreases are farther apart than are the

17. It was considered not feasible, for purposes of this study, to engage in the
elaborate and laborious task of weighting the figures for each state for each of the
years according to the volume of income payments.

figures for the two groups as a whole. The difference in income payments between the nine states which increased debts most and the five states which decreased debts most was greatest in 1932, when it was 21.5 per cent, and least in 1937, when it was 3.2 per cent. The figures for the larger groups show that the states which increased debts had consistently higher levels of income, in relation to 1929, than the states which decreased debts except in 1930 and 1937, when they were the same.

Again, it must be noted that this evidence is not conclusive, but it contributes reasonable support to the theory which has been discussed above. Limitations of time and space and the scarcity of relevant data preclude a further exploration of the problem here.

SUMMARY AND CONCLUSION

The creation and repayment of state debts will have economic repercussions, directly or indirectly, upon both the state government and the citizens of the borrowing state. Substantial borrowing will tend to ease the whole fiscal problem of the state, enable the state to expand its services, and generate a feeling of opulence on the part of state officials. Appropriations and expenditures are likely to be scrutinized less carefully by both legislators and taxpayers. Waste, extravagance, and graft are thus more likely to develop. Spending agencies may be so burdened with planning and administering spending programs that they may not be able to learn or develop the most efficient methods of spending funds. Faced with the problem of handling large amounts of new funds, state fiscal officials may not be able to protect them properly nor to adjust accounting systems to keep the necessary records.

State borrowing tends to increase private incomes and stimulate business activity within the state in two ways. First, increased state expenditures will tend to increase employment and incomes directly. Second, the borrowing tends to increase the volume of bank credit, thus increasing the effective money supply. The latter effect will be greatly increased if the funds are borrowed outside the state and are brought in as reserves of depository banks. Purchases outside the state will reduce the effects of both of these factors.

The effects of the payment of interest and of the repayment of principal will, in general, be exactly the opposite of the effects of borrowing. The state will be forced to curtail services, taxpayers will demand retrenchment, all expenditures will be examined carefully, and the whole governmental machinery may be studied in an effort to eliminate waste, inefficiency, and graft. The increased expenditures during borrowing periods are usually for materials and physical equipment; payments for those appear in later years as fixed charges on the debt, which cannot be reduced save by default. Thus, when it becomes imperative to reduce total expenditures, payments for personal services will usually have to bear the brunt of all adjustments. This may result in an uneconomic and inefficient combination of factors.

The payment of debt service charges exerts a deflationary effect on production and private incomes. Purchasing power is taken from taxpayers and turned over to bondholders; the demand for consumer goods is reduced, while the volume of savings is increased. This, in itself, is likely to disturb the equilibrium between consumption and savings, and if there should not be sufficient investment opportunities to absorb the savings there would be a strong deflationary effect. If debt service funds have to be remitted outside the state, the deflationary tendency will be accentuated by the depletion of bank reserves.

State finances are only a minor factor in the total movement of funds within a state. Nevertheless, the data which are available on income payments by states between 1929 and 1937 lend some support for the above theory. They show that in the states which increased their debts substantially between 1930 and 1937, income payments were maintained at appreciably higher levels, in relation to 1929, than in the country as a whole, while in those states which reduced their debts, income payments declined more than in the whole nation. The contrast was even more marked in the comparison of those states which increased their debts most with those states which reduced their debts most.

The findings of this chapter also lend support to the much discussed and often recommended policy that governmental units should plan their finances and activities so that they would borrow little in periods of prosperity and concentrate their borrowing in periods of depression. In addition to alleviating the economic effects of booms and depressions, it would frequently enable such units to get more for their money, because they could take advantage of low prices. More time for planning might also enable spending agencies to use funds more wisely. Because of these real advantages, the policy is to be commended to states. There are, however, at least two important practical obstacles which may prevent the states from following it. First, the needs which are the cause of much state borrowing—highways, buildings, and the like—arise and become acute in periods of prosperity. Citizens are not willing to postpone such important projects for years, and such delay may be uneconomical in many cases. Second, voters must approve most state borrowing. When they are feeling prosperous they are willing to approve bond issues, but when depression comes and they see the havoc wrought by heavy debts they are likely to be less favorably disposed toward borrowing. These two problems must be dealt with before states will be free to plan their borrowing in such a way that it will accomplish most in promoting the steady use of their resources.

CHAPTER XXIV

THE ADMINISTRATON OF STATE DEBTS

ONE OF THE most important features of a borrowing program and the one which has been most neglected by the American states is that of administration. It is not the purpose of this chapter to give an exhaustive discussion of the technique of debt administration—such would require a volume in itself—but rather to vindicate some of the general principles which should be observed in the incurring and management of state debts.[1] Many of these principles are mere truisms of sound financial management, the present repetition of which would not be justified save that they have often been violated by the states.

THE FORMULATION OF A DEBT PLAN

The first step in sound debt administration is the formulation of a plan to govern borrowing and debt repayment. It should be obvious that a state cannot expect successfully to incur and repay a large debt without careful preparation and planning in advance. Yet debt planning has been the exception rather than the rule among American states. It is probably true that no state which has borrowed according to a thorough, carefully prepared plan has ever had serious difficulties with its debt.

Several factors militate against careful debt planning by states. State fiscal officials—who alone can plan with authority—are usually not specially trained for their work. They must wage a political campaign to gain the favor of voters and they hold office for only short periods. Again, the political group which is responsible

---

1. For a comprehensive, detailed, and lucid discussion of debt administration see Chatters and Hillhouse, *Local Government Debt Administration* (New York, 1939). This is a manual designed to guide local government officials in the administration of their debts, but most of it will apply equally to state problems. It has been of great assistance in the writing of this chapter.

for the borrowing knows that it will not have to provide for repayment and is likely to be inclined to let successors worry about that problem. Finally, legislators or voters are the ones who ultimately determine what the state's debt will be; they are likely to be swayed by the needs and the emotions of the moment rather than the provisions of a plan which they do not fully understand. In spite of these considerations, competent, honest officials who command the respect of their constituents can exert much influence if they will formulate a sound debt policy, demonstrate its strength, and defend it vigorously.

Objectives of Borrowing

Before there can be sound debt planning there must first be a decision on the objectives to be accomplished, in the long run, by borrowing. This is the most basic decision involved in debt planning, yet most state officials avoid it or never realize that the problem exists. It requires a long-range perspective—a view that embraces decades rather than months or years.

One possible objective is that of a permanent debt. Under such an objective the state, whenever it incurs an operating deficit or wishes to make an outlay which current revenues will not cover, borrows the amount, never repays it, and continues to pay interest on it indefinitely. The debt, and with it interest payments, would continue to mount with the passing years until the state could no longer borrow. Probably no state would admit of such an objective, yet many states are acting in accordance with it by continued refunding and by scheduling debts to run the full life of the improvement financed by the borrowing. By this method the state realizes an advantage at the time of the borrowing, but continues to pay for it indefinitely. Most important, it loses the principal advantage to be derived from borrowing—the ability to meet new emergencies when they arise.

Another possible objective of borrowing is to reduce the fluctuations of the business cycle. Many national governments have borrowed for this purpose in recent years. The theory is that, in depressions, public borrowing will, by putting private savings to work and by creating new funds, create employment and stimulate private business. In periods of prosperity heavy taxation to retire public debts will reduce spending and prevent overexpansion. Regardless of the merits of the theory, the states are not now in a position to subscribe to it. It would involve an amount of long-range planning and a degree of co-ordination with the other states and with the Federal Government which are as yet impossible. In general, the states and the local governments have accentuated rather than alleviated the swings of the business cycle by borrowing heavily in prosperous years and reducing their borrowing in years of depression.

Still another, and probably the most usual, objective of state borrowing is to meet large, nonrecurrent outlays. In a given situation the people may wish to make a large immediate outlay to provide a system of highways or to pay soldiers' bonuses. It may be more convenient to spread the cost of such projects over several years, on the assumption that the need will not recur for a period of years, during which the debt will be repaid. Such action is logical and proper, provided the cost of the nonrecurrent outlay is not confused with the transition to a higher level of government spending. The outlays are usually made at a time when the state is entering upon new activities requiring permanently larger expenditures. There is a temptation for the state to capitalize all the increased expenditures and thus to fund, for a time, what is really an operating deficit.[2] When borrowing stops, the state will have to increase revenues, not only to pay debt service, but also to cover the increased normal expenditures. The maintenance and replacement of the assets acquired by borrowing will add considerably to normal expenditures. Those demands plus debt service requirements are likely to reach a peak a few years after borrowing stops, and that is the critical time in a debt program. To avoid this sudden strain and to eliminate some of the deceptive prosperity caused by borrowing, it would be well to require that some stated proportion of all capital outlays—say 10 or 15 per cent—should be contributed from current revenues. All borrowing under a program of this kind

2. For example, before 1905 New York annually appropriated current revenues for highway construction, but when the state began to borrow for highways it stopped the current appropriations. See above, p. 251.

should be carried out under a capital budget which should provide for the repayment of the debt incurred for the nonrecurrent outlay within twenty or twenty-five years at most. Debt service payments plus the increased normal expenditures should be equalized from year to year as nearly as possible.

A final objective of borrowing is to meet emergencies. Under this philosophy the state would never borrow as a normal policy but only to meet unpredictable emergencies caused by a sharp decline in revenues or some urgent new demand for expenditures, such as that for unemployment relief or the relief of destitution caused by a catastrophe. Debts would run for short periods of time and would probably never be large in amount. This would be the most conservative possible use of state credit and would make borrowing dependent upon developments beyond the control of the state.

Purposes of Borrowing

The immediate purposes for which a state will borrow will depend upon the objective which it is pursuing. For a time it may borrow to cover operating deficits, but if such practice is persistent, it will ultimately lead to such a large debt that the state can no longer borrow. If it is to avoid a permanent debt and the difficulties of a debt which is too large, a state should borrow only for capital or nonrecurrent outlays and for them only to such an extent as will enable it to spread its expenditures more smoothly over a period of twenty or twenty-five years. In most instances the states have borrowed for proper purposes, but they have not always been correct in the amounts which they have borrowed for those purposes nor in the duration of their debts.

Amounts to Be Borrowed

One of the primary purposes of debt planning is to control the amounts to be borrowed. Here a distinction should be made between the amount which it is *safe* to borrow and the amount which it is *proper* to borrow. Obviously, it is not good policy to borrow beyond the limit of safety; it may be the best policy to borrow only small amounts or not at all, depending upon the conditions in a given situation. It will be advisable to borrow, within the limits of safety, if borrowing offers the best method of spreading over several years the costs of a project which the people decide upon. If the project can be carried forward gradually, it may be best to finance it on a cash basis, since the total costs will be less. If the costs are large and the project must be completed within limited time, borrowing may be best.

In the discussion of the amounts to be borrowed, most attention has been given to the limits of safety, and most debt limitations are framed with that in view. The maximum amount which can be safely borrowed will depend upon the amounts which the state can collect and pay as debt service without seriously interfering with the state's services or the functioning of the economic system. This means that the maximum safe debt will depend upon estimates of future economic conditions, the state's revenue system, and the nature of its expenditures. Economic conditions are important because they will greatly influence tax collections. The revenue system will also influence revenues because it will determine the extent to which revenues vary with business conditions. The nature of the expenditures are significant because some are more flexible than others and thus can be reduced in time of stress.

It has generally been accepted that debt service requirements should not exceed from 20 to 25 per cent of total expenditures. The logic of this principle is that debt service requirements are a rigid, inflexible item in the budget. If revenues decline, debt service must be maintained at the cost of heavy cuts in other items. For example, suppose debt service takes 50 per cent of the total budget. Then suppose that revenues decline 25 per cent. The other, more flexible, items in the budget would have to be reduced 50 per cent to balance the budget. The validity of this rule will depend in part upon the relative flexibility of other items in the budget. If there are many other inflexible items, debt service should be kept lower. It is probably true that governmental costs of states are becoming less flexible for two reasons. First, states are spending more and more in the form of grants to local governments and pensions and other aids to the aged and the needy; these can be reduced in times of depression only with the greatest difficulty.

Second, depression periods now impose new demands upon the state in the form of unemployment relief so that amounts saved in one quarter are required in another. The difficulty of the problem is increased by the fact that as states develop revenue systems based upon ability to pay, revenues are more sensitive to business conditions and drop off sharply in depressions.

If debt service requirements are to be kept within 20 or 25 per cent of the total budget, the debt must not exceed two and a half or three times annual expenditures. If the debt were three times expenditures, principal repayments (assuming the debt to run for twenty years) would take 15 per cent of all expenditures. If the average interest rate were 4 per cent, interest payments would require another 12 per cent, or a total of 27 per cent. If the interest rate were 3 per cent, the total would be 24 per cent.[3] In calculating the maximum, however, some margin of safety should be allowed for emergency borrowing, for the growing inflexibility of governmental costs, and for the increased normal costs of government.

Form of Bonds

In planning the debt, the form of bonds must also be decided. It must first be decided whether they will be term or serial bonds. The merits of these two kinds of bonds have already been discussed and will not be further considered here.[4] In general, serial bonds are used almost exclusively by the states at the present time, and this seems to be sound unless there are definite and substantial reasons to the contrary. The inclusion of the call feature is another question to be decided.[5] The states have lost heavily by not using it in the past. Unless there are good reasons to the contrary, states should make all bonds callable after a period of, say, five years. It is doubtful whether the inclusion of such a feature would have any appreciable effect upon the sale price of the bonds, but if there is doubt on the point, alternate bids might be asked. The proper officials could then decide whether the difference in price justifies the inclusion of the feature.

3. The recommendations concerning debt limitations, given below in Chapter XXV, are based upon these principles.
4. See above, pp. 268-269. See also Chatters and Hillhouse, *op. cit.*, pp. 17-23.
5. This question has been discussed earlier. See pp. 269-272.

Maturity Schedule

A final feature of importance in the debt plan is the schedule of maturities. Where serial bonds are used, it is usual to have them mature in equal annual instalments. Since interest payments will decline with the debt, total debt service requirements will slowly and regularly decrease. This is desirable since it will reduce costs and give opportunity for borrowing to meet future needs.[6] It is possible to use serial annuities, in which principal payments increase as interest payments decline, thus giving a uniform total for debt service from year to year. Such an arrangement increases total interest costs and is not easily adjusted for new borrowing. In some cases it may be desirable to use deferred annuities, in which principal payments do not begin for several years after the bonds are issued.[7]

The important principle in regard to maturities is to prevent an arrangement whereby large amounts mature in one year unless provisions are made for sinking funds to meet them. Tennessee's violation of this principle was costly and troublesome.

THE AUTHORIZATION OF BORROWING

States must borrow only under definite and specific mandates or grants of power from either the legislature or the voters. The exact procedure to be followed in securing the authorization involves highly complicated and technical questions and varies from state to state. All pertinent constitutional provisions and court rulings must be strictly observed lest the bonds be declared invalid. Since these vary widely from state to state, the most that can be done here is to mention a few general principles which apply in many states.

If the legislature has the power to incur debts, the constitutional provisions governing the passage of finance bills must be followed exactly. In many states the passage of finance bills must follow a different and more specific procedure than ordinary bills. For example, in North Carolina such bills must be passed three times in each house on separate days and the yeas and nays must be recorded

6. See Chatters and Hillhouse, *op. cit.,* pp. 23-26, 294, 358-361.
7. For further discussions of serial annuities and deferred serials see *ibid.,* pp. 20-22.

on the second and third readings.[8] In certain other states, bills to authorize borrowing must receive more than a mere majority vote to be valid.

If borrowing is authorized by the voters, either in a referendum or in a constitutional amendment, the submission of the proposition and the voting thereon must be exactly as prescribed by the constitution. Many constitutions provide that the bonds voted upon must be "for a single object or purpose." Several issues of bonds approved by the people have been held invalid by the courts because one proposition attempted to authorize bonds for several purposes.[9] Other constitutions require that the bond authorization must levy a direct tax to pay interest and to retire the bonds. An Iowa amendment proposed to levy a direct tax only in the event that revenues from certain indirect taxes were not adequate for debt service. The court ruled the amendment invalid.[10] In the same way provisions regarding the frequency with which amendments may be voted upon, the elections at which they may be submitted, and the clarity and completeness with which the proposition is stated to the voters must be carefully observed. Because of the highly technical nature of these considerations, underwriters usually insist, before they will buy state bonds, that all matters affecting validity be passed upon by competent and experienced bond attorneys. In cases of doubt a test case will be carried to the supreme court of the state.

THE SALE OF BONDS

Once bonds have been properly authorized, the next problem is to sell them on terms most advantageous to the state. This will involve decisions as to when, how, and in what amounts the bonds will be sold.[11]

8. *The Constitution of North Carolina*, Art. II, sec. 14.

9. See, for instance: *Allen v. Cromwell*, 203 Ky. 836 (1924); *Herrin v. Erickson*, 90 Mont. 259 (1931); *Mathews v. Turner*, 212 Iowa 424 (1931). In the Iowa case all the bonds were to be used for highways, but the proposed amendment contained other propositions affecting highway finance. The court declared that the amendment must not only be for "one object or purpose" but must also be one proposition.

10. *State v. Executive Council*, 207 Iowa 923 (1929). The court held that the amendment was invalid also because it was proposed to issue the bonds in instalments over a period of years and because the general assembly had no power to make an irrevocable and irrepealable pledge of the gasoline and automobile taxes.

11. For a more complete discussion of the technique of selling bonds see Chatters and Hillhouse, *op. cit.*, chap. iii.

Timing Sales

Two factors should determine the amount of bonds to be sold and the time of sale: the need for the funds and the condition of the bond market. If at a given time market conditions are not favorable for the sale of long-term bonds, expenditures should be postponed if such is feasible. If postponement is not feasible and if there is a prospect of improvement in market conditions in the near future, the bonds might be sold temporarily to some state fund which has the necessary cash, or short-term notes might be used. All bond sales should be planned to take full advantage of seasonal and temporary conditions in the bond market.[12] If market conditions should change drastically after a bond sale has been advertised, fiscal officers should not hesitate, if the need for funds permits, to reject all bids and to reoffer the bonds later.[13]

The Amount of Sales

The determination of the amount of bonds to be sold at a given time also presents a problem. On the one hand, funds must be available when needed, and the state should avoid frequent sales of small amounts which entail considerable work and expense and may not command the best price. On the other hand, the state should not sell large amounts of bonds a long time before the funds are needed. This would require the state to pay interest on unneeded funds and create a temptation to the improper use of funds. The most frequent abuse in connection with state borrowing has been the improper use of state funds which were borrowed before they were needed. Under present conditions, since banks are not allowed to pay interest on demand deposits and since short-term interest rates are very low, it might be best for the state to raise funds initially by the sale of temporary notes and to sell the long-term obligations

12. *Ibid.*, pp. 31-39.
13. For example, North Carolina advertised $4,620,000 of bonds to be sold on September 27, 1938. When the time arrived for the submission of bids, the Munich crisis practically paralyzed the bond market. As a result, the best bid received represented an interest cost of 3.16 per cent. All bids were rejected, and the bonds were sold a month later at an interest cost of 2.073 per cent (*Bond Buyer*, Jan. 7, 1939, p. 3). If war had developed, the bond market would have been "frozen" for some time, but even so it is probable that financing could have been arranged at a cost no greater than that represented by the first bids.

after most of the expenditures have been made. Such a policy involves some risk, but probably no more than the carrying of large,
unneeded balances.

Bids

A century ago the practice was for states to authorize and print
an issue of bonds, with all terms definitely fixed, and then entrust
the bonds to a committee to be sold, by private negotiation, in one
of the large financial centers at the best price possible. Such a policy
placed too much dependence upon the integrity and ability of the
committee members and did not insure the maximum of competition among bidders. Today the almost universal practice is for the
states publicly to advertise bond sales several weeks in advance,
stating all terms except the rate of interest, and to invite bids on the
interest rate and price. Usually a maximum interest rate is stated,
and most constitutions prohibit the sale of bonds below par. In
recent years split-rate bids have been much used. Such bids provide
that one part of the issue shall bear one rate of interest while the
other part shall bear a different rate.[14] If no acceptable bid is received at the public sale, some states allow the bonds to be sold
by private negotiation.[15] For several years West Virginia has followed the practice of granting to the successful bidder on an issue
of bonds an option to buy a specified amount of additional bonds
on the same terms within a limited time.[16] In some states, however,
such practice is prohibited.

Bidders are usually required to make a good-faith deposit at the
time they submit bids, to insure responsibility. Bids are usually on
an "all or none" basis.[17]

14. New Jersey has provided a variation on this practice. A recent offer of bonds
specified that one rate of interest should apply to the whole issue, but that the
arrangement of the maturities should vary, depending upon the rate bid (Bond
Buyer, Jan. 21, 1939, p. 23).

15. The Supreme Court of Kentucky, however, set aside a sale of bonds in which
the State Highway Commission had, in private negotiations, agreed to sell bonds on
terms different from those specified for the public sale. State Highway Commission
v. Veiling, 230 Ky. 381 (1929).

16. Bond Buyer, Feb. 25, 1939, p. 11. "In case the option is not exercised, the
additional bonds will not be offered for sale until the successful bidder has had a
reasonable opportunity to dispose of this issue."

17. "Bids, with but few exceptions, should be on an 'all or none' basis. Usually,
if a bidder knows that he will be able to have control over marketing the entire

Direct Sales

Few states have tried to sell their bonds directly to investors, and none of those attempts could, according to available information, be called successful. Usually the attempts have been made only after failure to receive acceptable bids from underwriters, and have been based upon patriotic appeals to citizens to rescue the state in time of stress.

With the organization and competition which prevail in the investment banking field today, it is doubtful whether the states can hope to effect any savings by the direct sale of bonds. The work, expense, and uncertainty which such efforts would entail would probably more than offset any savings which might be realized. In recent years there has been a considerable increase in the number of local investment firms and bond dealers interested in state bonds, and they are becoming an increasingly important factor in the market.

THE PROTECTION OF BORROWED FUNDS

Once funds have been borrowed, they must be protected until they are spent. With only a few exceptions the states have used commercial banks as depositories. Under such a system the sound principles which should govern have been definitely formulated and generally accepted.[18] They should be enacted into law and rigidly enforced. First, favoritism in the selection of depositories should be excluded by a comprehensive and impersonal procedure for the designation of such depositories. Standards should be prescribed which would eliminate unsafe banks. Second, funds should be further protected by requiring depository banks to deposit with the state treasurer either approved collateral or a surety bond sufficient to cover any state deposit. Third, steps should be taken to protect the state against the loss of interest. In the past it has been customary either to prescribe a rate of interest which depository banks must pay or to require depositories to bid against each other for deposits.

issue, he will be able to put in a slightly better bid. When only part of an issue is obtained, the bidder runs the risk of other parts being offered to the investing public at a lower price" (Chatters and Hillhouse, *op. cit.,* p. 48).

18. For a full discussion of this topic see M. L. Faust, *The Security of Public Deposits,* Public Administration Service, No. 51 (Chicago, 1936), and H. L. Lutz, *Public Finance* (3d ed.; New York, 1936), chap. xxxvii.

This is no longer feasible, since banks are not allowed to pay interest on demand deposits. If funds are not to be used for several months, the state may realize a return on them, either by placing them in a time deposit or by investing them in high-grade, short-term obligations. States cannot now expect to realize as large a return on temporarily idle funds as formerly, and for that reason they should be more careful in the timing of bond sales.

THE ADMINISTRATION OF DEBT SERVICE

Although not so spectacular as other phases of debt management, the long and tedious task of administering debt service is most important. It requires consistent, careful and prosaic work year after year, while taxpayers are performing the unpleasant duty of paying their debts. Sometimes fiscal officers must play the part of taskmasters to coerce unenthusiastic legislators to vote the necessary funds for debt service.

The first step is to prepare a complete and detailed schedule of interest and principal requirements over the life of the debt. When a budget is being prepared, the payments which will fall due during the budget period should be included and provided for. To guard against omissions it might be well, at the time the debt is incurred, to authorize the treasurer to make all payments necessary to service the debt from any funds in the treasury not otherwise obligated. In providing for debt service it is not sufficient for the legislature merely to appropriate the proceeds of some given tax or profit-making enterprise. Such revenue may be inadequate; hence such sources should be examined carefully every time a budget is prepared. If it appears that revenues will not be sufficient, other funds must be provided.[19]

The Management of Sinking Funds

Since the use of term bonds is declining, the management of sinking funds will soon cease to be a major problem. In a few states, however, it is still of considerable importance. The first task is to compute the size of the annual payments or contributions,

---

19. For a more detailed discussion of the problems involved in making interest and principal payments see Chatters and Hillhouse, *op. cit.*, chap. iv.

which, together with interest earnings, will provide the funds needed to retire the bonds at maturity. This is done on an actuarial basis.[20] Such payments should then be included in the regular budgets. It is preferable to make such payments from the general revenues of the state rather than to dedicate the entire proceeds of certain taxes to the sinking fund. Tennessee's predicament in 1935-39 illustrates the embarrassments which may arise from the latter practice.

The most difficult problem in the management of sinking funds is to keep all funds properly invested. Sinking fund investments must meet three specifications: (1) they must be safe, (2) they must be convertible into cash or its equivalent at the proper time without loss, and (3) they must yield a satisfactory return. Usually bonds of the issue for which the sinking fund is created are the best possible investment.[21] Administrative officials must be given some discretion in the investment of sinking funds, but the statutory requirements should be sufficiently definite and specific to protect the funds.

The existence of large sinking funds is always a temptation to administrators and legislators to use them for improper purposes. For example, if market conditions are unfavorable, the state may sell to sinking funds an issue of bonds maturing long after the bonds for which the fund was created. Or if local governments are in distress and the bond market is "frozen," pressure may be brought to bear on the state to invest its sinking funds in local government obligations, which are neither safe nor liquid. In 1939 state sinking funds in both Michigan and New Jersey held large amounts of local obligations. Many of the local units had defaulted or were in distress. In some cases maturities of the local obligations had been extended with the consent of state sinking fund officials. State obligations were soon to mature, requiring that investments be converted into cash. In both states proposals were made to refund the state obligations rather than to depress the bond market by liquidating the local obligations. Michigan sold large blocks of local obligations to underwriters in an effort to raise cash. New Jersey was prevented from redeeming several million dollars of

20. See *ibid.*, pp. 125-133, for the method to be used.
21. For further details see *ibid.*, pp. 134-164.

bonds because the sale of local government bonds to raise the necessary cash would have depressed the market for such bonds.[22]

The control of large sinking funds carries with it much power. It is doubtful whether the state should be denied the use of this power to tide itself over a difficult period or to help distressed local governments in periods of emergency. But such power must inevitably carry the risk of abuse. The work and the risk connected with the management of sinking funds probably more than offset the possibilities of good; so it is well that the states are turning to serial bonds.

DEBT ADJUSTMENTS

Voluntary Adjustments

During the life of a debt, conditions may arise which make desirable a reorganization of the debt structure. The first of these, which may be considered normal and desirable, is a pronounced decline in the market rate of interest. If the bonds have been made callable, as they should, it will be quite profitable for the state to call bonds bearing high rates of interest, say from 4 to 5 per cent, and refund them with bonds bearing from 2 to 3½ per cent. If the old bonds have a long time to run, the state may realize a substantial saving by such refunding, even though it redeems the old bonds at a premium. The decision as to the exact time at which to conduct such refunding in order to realize the maximum advantage will present a problem. Responsible officials should be familiar with interest rate cycles and should follow the market carefully. If conditions permit, the saving realized from refunding may be used to speed the retirement of the debt. If so, the maturities of the new bonds should be earlier than those of the old bonds.

A second condition requiring adjustment may be a bad arrangement of maturities. Because of poor planning a state may find that it will have to face heavy maturities in a given year and that no adequate provisions have been made for retirement. Such a condition faced Tennessee in 1939. Well in advance of the critical year, plans should be made to refund, at a favorable time, all the bonds which cannot be redeemed and to arrange the maturities so that the debt may be retired uniformly.

22. *Bond Buyer*, June 3, 1939, p. 2; July 1, 1939, p. 4.

Even though the debt was properly planned at the time that it was incurred, conditions may change so drastically that the state finds itself unable to meet its obligations. In order to avert default the state may find it desirable to refund the bonds which will mature over a period of years. If a comprehensive plan is presented to the bondholders, together with a frank explanation, they may agree to accept refunding bonds, although the state may have to give them a bonus in the form of higher interest rates or other desirable features. If such a plan is attempted, enough of the maturities should be refunded to insure against a repetition of the trouble; bondholders are not likely to look with favor upon a second request to refund. The important point in this connection is that the state should act, if possible, before trouble develops. If bondholders see that the state is taking energetic and intelligent steps to meet financial difficulties, they will be favorably impressed. If the state does nothing until after a default, with all of its unfavorable publicity, it may be impossible to refund on reasonable terms.

Involuntary Adjustments

More fundamental adjustments in the debt structure may be required after a state has defaulted. The extent of the adjustments and the methods to be used in such cases will vary widely, depending upon the size of the debt in relation to the state's ability to pay. If the causes of the default are essentially temporary, it may be necessary only to fund accrued interest and to refund the bonds which will mature over a period of five or six years. But if the state has incurred a larger debt than it can repay over a long period of time, it will be necessary for the bondholders to accept sacrifices in the form of a lower rate of interest or even, in more serious cases, reductions in principal. Since the procedure must depend largely upon the circumstances of a particular situation, few generalizations of value can be offered.

A thorough survey of the state's ability to pay should be made, preferably by an outside, impartial authority. In all negotiations with bondholders the state should be represented by a competent committee which represents all major political factions within the state. All reasonable efforts should be made to avoid antagonizing bondholders, since that would be fatal to successful negotiations. The state should take and retain the initiative in the effort to work out a suitable reorganization, since state officials know better than anyone else the effort of which the state is capable. The state should evince its sincerity by a willingness to introduce all sound economies and to rationalize its governmental organization as indicated by the best accepted practice. In so far as possible, the state should deal directly with bondholders or bona fide committees which represent them rather than with a third party who is trying to mediate between them for the sake of fees or profit. In planning the reorganized debt the sound principles of debt planning should be observed. In such a case as this, term bonds might be preferable to serial bonds with a proviso that all funds available for principal payments shall be used to purchase bonds on the market or directly from bondholders by tender. Such practice may enable the state to retire a part of its debt at a saving and at the same time insure bondholders of a market for their holdings.[23]

SHORT-TERM BORROWING

A complete debt plan should indicate the part to be played by short-term borrowing and provide for its control. Dollar for dollar, short-term debt is more dangerous than long-term debt because it must frequently be renewed and because a disruption of the money market may force the state to pay exorbitant rates of interest or even make refunding impossible for a time. It is dangerous also because in some states large debts may be built up through short-term borrowing and then be funded into long-term obligations without the approval of the people as required by constitutional provisions. Nevertheless, short-term borrowing has a legitimate and important place in a state's financial plan if it is properly used.

Borrowing in Anticipation of Revenues

Within limits it is proper for states to borrow for short periods in anticipation of revenues. If revenue receipts are heavily concentrated at certain dates while expenditures are spread evenly throughout the year, it may be necessary for the state to borrow during the

23. For a fuller discussion of debt adjustments see Chatters and Hillhouse, op. cit., chaps. n and xi.

two or three months immediately preceding the receipts. Such practice, however, is costly and subject to abuse; it should be avoided if possible. Since the states have relinquished the property tax, there is not so much excuse for anticipating taxes as formerly. Revenues produced by the gasoline tax, the sales tax, and most of the other taxes levied by states come in regularly every month and are rarely delinquent. Under such conditions, short-term borrowing is more likely to represent a deficit than delayed revenue collections. This should be prevented by proper budgeting and budgetary control. If receipts are not properly synchronized with expenditures, two remedies are available for reducing or eliminating short-term borrowing; either change the due date of the taxes so that revenues will come in earlier, or accumulate a cash balance to carry the state over the period of low revenues. In any case a definite limit—say 25 per cent of the preceding year's revenues—should be placed upon such borrowing.[24]

Borrowing to Cover Deficits

Even the best budgets may go awry on occasions, leaving the state with a deficit. To cover such casual deficits, the state should have the power to issue short-term obligations up to a limited amount—say 25 per cent of the budget. Proper budgetary control should prevent an accumulated deficit of more than that amount. While the obligations will be short-term in the beginning, they should be funded at the first opportunity, and provisions for retirement should be included in subsequent budgets.

Borrowing to Supplement Bond Issues

Short-term borrowing may be used to give flexibility to a program of long-term borrowing in two ways. As indicated above, it may be advantageous for a state to anticipate the proceeds of a

24. Warrants unpaid after presentation should be considered as part of the short-term debt. In fact, if the state has the proper budgetary control and limited power to borrow in anticipation of revenues and to cover deficits as recommended in the following chapter, fiscal officials should not be allowed to issue warrants unless funds are in the treasury to cover them. The issuance of warrants which cannot be paid is a costly and unfair form of borrowing; costly in the case of contractors and others who can fix a price which anticipates the delay or discount involved, unfair to state employees who must wait for their pay or accept exorbitant discounts.

bond sale by short-term borrowing. By such procedure the state may avoid the loss of interest on idle funds and may be able to choose a more advantageous time for the sale of the bonds. In the same way short-term borrowing gives flexibility near the maturity of long-term bonds. For example, interest rates may drop substantially a few years before the maturity of callable bonds. A considerable saving in interest may be realized by refunding the bonds into low interest-bearing notes.[25] Or at maturity the state may not have on hand the entire amount needed to retire the whole issue. If there is a reasonable prospect that the state will be able to raise the funds in the near future, it might well issue short-term notes to provide for the remainder.

SUMMARY

Careful and intelligent administration would have eliminated most, if not all, of the troubles which have attended state borrowing in the past. Before embarking upon a program of heavy borrowing a state should consider carefully the objective which it hopes to accomplish, in the long run, by credit operations. Probably the unformulated objective which most states have aimed at in the past was to spread the cost of heavy capital outlays over a period of years, but their practice has not always been consistent with such an objective. The amount to be borrowed should also receive careful consideration, and ample margins should be allowed for future declines in revenue, increased cost of government attendant on new activities, and emergency borrowing which may be forced upon the state. The form of the bonds and their schedule of maturities should be determined by prevailing conditions and estimates of future conditions.

The procedure for the sale of bonds and the protection of borrowed funds is now practically standardized. The only safeguards needed are provisions to guard against deviations from this procedure, motivated by favoritism or ignorance. The successful administration of debt service requires only the preparation of a complete and detailed schedule of requirements and the incorpora-

25. In July, 1935, West Virginia refunded $2,240,000 of 3½ per cent bonds maturing in 1936-39 into 1.4 per cent notes maturing in the same years (*Biennial Report of the Treasurer*, 1936, p. 7).

tion of the proper amounts into the budgets at the proper times. The management of sinking funds offers many opportunities for mistakes and irregularities, but with the growing use of serial bonds, sinking funds are rapidly disappearing.

Major or minor adjustments in the debt structure may be necessary in order to take advantage of lower interest rates, to correct a bad maturity schedule, to avert default, or to reduce an unduly heavy burden after a state has defaulted. In this phase of debt management careful and competent administration can do much to avert trouble for the state or to produce a positive saving. A limited amount of short-term borrowing is necessary, to allow fiscal official freedom of action, to keep the state's machinery from being halted in emergencies, and to provide flexibility in a program of long-term borrowing, but the practice must be restricted to avoid trouble and abuse.

Successful debt administration consists principally in the consistent, impartial, intelligent, and honest application of common-sense principles. Some technical knowledge of the money and bond markets and of the law and constitution of the particular state are necessary. In many instances the necessity of observing sound principles must be "sold" to legislators and voters. In the final analysis, probably our greatest hope for improvement in the field of state borrowing lies in the possibility of improved administration.

CHAPTER XXV

CONCLUSIONS AND RECOMMENDATIONS

FIVE DISTINCT periods are discernible in the debt history of the American states. Each of these periods has been marked by certain pronounced characteristics. In this concluding chapter it may be well briefly to evaluate the success which has attended state borrowing in each period.

REVIEW OF STATE DEBT EXPERIENCE

First Period

In the first period, roughly from 1820 to 1840, the states borrowed principally for canals, railroads, and banks. From almost every point of view this period of borrowing was a failure. With only a few exceptions the canals were soon obsolete and the state outlays were lost. State aid probably speeded up the building of railroads, but the haste resulted in the building of many poorly planned roads, and often those which were ultimately successful experienced initial failures in which the states lost their investments. No doubt some of the private fortunes made in railroads grew out of the forced sales of state-aided property. While some of the banks established with state aid were successful, others were poorly managed and only intensified the troubles which developed after 1840. Taxpayers finally paid most of the debts which had been incurred for canals, railroads, and banks.

Second Period

Between 1845 and 1860 the states borrowed chiefly for railroads. For a time these ventures were more successful than those of the previous period, and if the Civil War had not intervened, the states might have escaped without serious loss. As it was, however, losses were general and severe, and even to this day remnants of those debts, after considerable scaling down in the post-war days, are still imbedded in the state debts of North Carolina, Tennessee, and Virginia. State borrowing in this period was not a success.

Third Period

During the Civil War both Northern and Southern states borrowed to aid in financing the war. Generally the Northern states, aided by reimbursements from the Federal Government, repaid their debts promptly; from that point of view the experience may be termed a success. Doubts may arise, however, if consideration is given to the ways in which state funds were used and to the question of whether state borrowing promoted a sounder and more equitable method of financing the war.

Much of the borrowing in Southern states took the form of paper money and bank loans and thus contributed to the currency disorders which added to the difficulties of the war. At the end of the war all the debts were repudiated. It is highly doubtful whether state borrowing during this period resulted in any permanent good.

Fourth Period

During the Reconstruction period the credit of Southern states was used as an instrument whereby unscrupulous men enriched themselves and saddled a crushing burden upon a prostrate people. Obviously, this is not a fair or typical example of state borrowing, but it illustrates one of the dangers connected with the practice. When villains seize the government, they are likely to use for their own advantage all the customs and practices which have been developed. In this instance, the practice of state borrowing was corrupted and used with devastating effect upon all concerned.

Fifth Period

The fifth period of state borrowing began about 1910, and still continues. It is marked by borrowing for many purposes, but mainly for highways, veterans' bonuses, and unemployment relief. The volume of state loans has far surpassed the volume of all previous periods combined. It is still too early to formulate a final evaluation of this period, for most of the loans have yet to be repaid, but some tentative impressions may be recorded.

Highway borrowing, which accounts for nearly one half of the total in the present period, has been successful in the main. It has enabled the states to meet an insistent demand for large outlays and to spread the costs over a period of years. The economic and social advantages of a system of good roads has probably been worth the added cost involved in borrowing. But there have been exceptions. The ability to borrow has led some states to spend too much for roads, has caused heavy expenditures for roads which were poorly designed and badly located, and has provided opportunities for graft. Arkansas and Tennessee are two examples of states in which highway borrowing has been poorly managed. Only the future can tell whether Louisiana and Mississippi are going too far in their programs of borrowing for highways.

The relatively few states which have borrowed for unemployment relief have made advantageous use of their credit. Borrowing enabled them to relieve distress, to keep the machinery of government operating, and to make some contribution toward recovery at a time when revenues had been seriously reduced. The same might be said of some states which found it necessary to borrow in order to cover operating deficits during the worst years of the depression.

The benefits realized from other projects financed by borrowing are not so clear. The rural credit systems are definitely failures for all concerned, except the bankers who were able to unload their bad loans on the state. New York borrowed some $150,000,000 for canals whose worth is highly questionable. The debts incurred for bonuses did not make any constructive contribution toward the solution of the veterans' problem; instead, the whole idea of state bonuses only added confusion to the question and encouraged veterans' groups to persevere in the good old American custom of asking more and more from legislative bodies.

Final Evaluation

From the above it should be evident that it is not feasible to make any general statement as to whether the states have, on the whole, realized a net advantage from their borrowings. In some instances they have and in others they have not. For states, as for individuals and business firms, there is a proper place for borrowing, but it is not always easy to keep it in its place. To paraphrase an old proverb, debts are useful servants but hard masters. Successful borrowing requires good judgment, careful planning, and efficient administration. Unfortunately, some of the states have not always provided these essentials.

THE CONCENTRATION OF STATE DEBTS

From the beginning, state borrowing has been heavily concentrated in a relatively few states. Some borrowing movements have been general, but in all instances a few states have led the way to such an extent that they have accumulated a major portion of the total indebtedness. At any given time the five states with the largest debts have owed from 40 to 60 per cent of the total, while the top ten states have always owed from 60 to 80 per cent of the whole. Further, the states which, over the past one hundred years, have occupied the first ten positions, have generally come from a small group; in other words, the top ten tend to be repeaters, decade after decade. Table 47 shows, for selected years, the ranking of the top ten states and the proportion of the total which was owed by the

TABLE 47

THE TEN STATES WITH LARGEST DEBTS FOR SELECTED YEARS, 1841-1938

Rank	1841	1853	1860	1870	1880	1890	1902	1912	1922	1931	1938
1st	Pa.	Pa.	Pa.	Va.	Va.	Va.	Mass.	N.Y.	N.Y.	N.Y.	N.Y.
2d	La.	N.Y.	N.Y.	Tenn.	Tenn.	D.C.	Va.	Mass.	Calif.	Ill.	Ill.
3d	N.Y.	Ill.	Va.	N.Y.	La.	Tenn.	Tenn.	Va.	Mass.	N.C.	La.
4th	Ala.	Md.	Mo.	Pa.	D.C.	La.	La.	La.	Mich.	Ark.	Ark.
5th	Md.	Ohio	Tenn.	N.C.	Mass.	Ala.	Ala.	Ala.	Pa.	Calif.	N.C.
Total for five states as % of U. S.	57.8	58.3	58.9	50.4	43.8	44.6	53.7	60.4	49.7	48.6	42.0
6th	Ill.	Va.	Ohio	Mass.	Mo.	Mo.	N.Y.	Tenn.	Ore.	Mo.	Pa.
7th	Ind.	La.	Md.	La.	N.C.	Ga.	Ga.	Calif.	N.C.	Tenn.	Tenn.
8th	Miss.	Ind.	Ill.	Mo.	Pa.	Ark.	N.C.	N.C.	Mo.	W.Va.	Mo.
9th	Mich.	Miss.	Ind.	Md.	Ala.	Ind.	S.C.	Md.	Ohio	La.	Calif.
10th	Mass.	Mass.	N.C.	Conn.	Md.	Md.	Md.	Conn.	W.Va.	Ala.	Tex.
Total for ten states as % of U. S.	81.1	80.7	82.8	77.0	68.2	65.5	67.5	73.0	67.5	69.5	60.6
U. S. Total (in millions)	$190	$193	$257	$356	$297	$229	$249	$355	$879	$1,977	$2,852

The rankings are based upon figures for gross debts from 1841 through 1870; thereafter upon net debt figures. All figures are from the Bureau of the Census except those for 1938, which are taken from Table 43. The 1938 figures include sums for revenue bonds, debts of state agencies, and local debts assumed or serviced by the states.

first five and the first ten states. The table shows a slight, though irregular, tendency for the concentration in the top states to decrease. This may be accounted for in part by the fact that the number of states in the Union has increased considerably since the earlier years; in the later years, however, it has been accounted for by more widespread borrowing.

If a weight of 10 is assigned for each first place position, 9 for each second place, and so on, we find that the leading scorers are: New York, 79; Virginia, 60; Louisiana, 56; Tennessee, 53; Pennsylvania, 51; Massachusetts, 40; North Carolina, 35; Illinois, 34; Missouri, 31; Alabama, 28; Maryland, 24; California, 21; District of Columbia, 16; Arkansas, 14; Ohio, 13. These fifteen states account for 555 of the total of 605 points; they are the states which have most consistently owed large amounts. On the average their debts have, at any given time, been 60 per cent or more of the total of state debts.

The regional grouping of these states is worthy of note. Eight of them, including the District of Columbia, are in the Southeast, three are in the Northeast, three in the Middle West, and one in the Far West. The predominance of the Southeastern states with their low per capita wealth and income supplies a clue to much of the trouble which has developed in the field of state debts.

THE FUTURE OF STATE DEBTS

It is hazardous to attempt a forecast of the course of state debts, for no one can tell what lies ahead. On the basis of information available at present, however, it seems that we have entered a new phase in the development of public finance in which state debts are to play a more important part than in the past. Several factors point in this direction. Many new demands are being made upon all grades of government. In general, local governments are unable to meet those demands and are turning to the states for aid. As a result, the states are assuming or subsidizing the financing of public schools, highways, social security, and other functions to a great extent. Some of those functions will necessitate borrowing, but even if they do not, the states will be so hard pressed for funds that they will find it difficult to retire debts.

Perhaps a brief review of certain events in New York will illustrate the trend. In 1925, for the first time in its history, New York borrowed to finance the erection of state buildings. Between 1925 and 1936 it borrowed some $89,000,000 for that purpose. In 1926 a special legislative committee pointed with concern to the growing state debt, which at that time amounted to approximately $227,-000,000, and recommended that the state switch over to a policy of paying for improvements from current revenues as soon as possible.[1] In 1937 another joint legislative committee surveyed the situation and stated: "At some time, now or in the future, the policy of continuous borrowing must be halted and the State and its communities headed in the other direction. It is not easy to reverse directions; especially it is not easy to shift from the easy borrowing policy to the harder task of traversing the road back. . . . We believe the time has come now, when times are better, for people of this State to clench their fists and take a small dose of unpleasant medicine, because if they do not take it now they are going to have to take a far worse dose in the future."[2]

Yet in January, 1939, when the net debt was approximately $523,000,000, the governor stated that the funded debt of the state would undoubtedly be nearly, if not quite, doubled during the next few years. Total authorizations for new borrowing at that time amounted to $537,500,000, consisting of housing, $300,000,000; grade crossing elimination, $197,500,000; and State Institutional Building, $40,000,000. This was "aside from possible borrowing that may be desired for institutional and other public construction."[3]

Another factor which is likely to contribute to continued state borrowing in the future is highways. During the past century the states borrowed large amounts for canals and railroads, but those forms of transportation soon passed out of state ownership, and were turned over to private owners. It is hardly conceivable that this will happen with highways; rather the tendency is for the states to take over roads now maintained by local governments. The thousands of miles of highways under their control to be maintained

1. Special Joint Committee on Taxation and Retrenchment, *The Debt of the State of New York, Past, Present, and Future* (Albany, 1926), pp. 95-104.
2. *Report of the Joint Legislative Committee on State Fiscal Policies*, p. 66.
3. *Bond Buyer*, Feb. 4, 1939, p. 2.

and replaced will always furnish the states with an opportunity for borrowing.

The extensive use of serial bonds by states in recent years is not so conducive to refunding as were the term bonds formerly used. The effect of refunding can be obtained, however, by using current revenues to repay debts and then by borrowing to pay for current outlays and improvements. Outlays for the extension and replacement of the numerous public buildings and the extensive highway systems will always provide sufficient capital outlays to justify borrowing in amounts as great as the maturities of bonds.

While state debts are likely to increase, at least moderately, in the future, there are more definite limits to state borrowing than to national borrowing. These arise from the more limited revenue possibilities and from the fact that states cannot create money. The limit to the total of state indebtedness in the future will depend upon economic conditions, the development of new sources of state revenues, and the number of states which practice borrowing. Many states which now have only nominal debts, such as Ohio, Indiana, and Wisconsin, could borrow hundreds of millions of dollars if they chose. If states such as these, which have generally refrained from borrowing in the past fifty years, do not enter the field, the limit to total state indebtedness will be reduced considerably. For the states which are now important borrowers, the limit would probably be somewhat less than twice the present amount, since several of them, such as Arkansas, South Dakota, and Louisiana, now owe about as much as they can safely carry.

PRINCIPLES OF STATE BORROWING

It may be profitable to formulate, on the basis of the states' experiences with their debts, some general principles to guide future state borrowing. These are stated below rather categorically with only brief explanations or justifications. The considerations from which they are drawn are recorded in the preceding chapters.

No Loan Funds

States should not borrow to establish loan funds. Both experience and logic indicate that such funds do not have a reasonable chance to succeed. Apparently, California has operated its veterans' loan fund successfully, but nearly all other attempts have failed. During the Colonial period the loan funds in New England and the Carolinas were almost all failures, although some of the Middle Colonies operated them with fair success. In early New York State a similar attempt met with losses. Veterans' loan funds in North Carolina and Oregon have been distinctly unprofitable, while the rural credit systems of the Dakotas and Minnesota have been disastrous.

In view of the political conditions which exist in most states, it is hardly logical to expect such funds to succeed. Usually a fund is established only after a hard-fought political campaign which arouses emotions and creates factions. If the campaign is successful, it is only natural to expect that the successful faction will administer the fund and grant loans on the basis of political influence and need, rather than on the basis of ability to repay loans. Further, in most states the personnel organization and the salaries paid will not attract men capable of administering such funds successfully.

No Subsidies to Private Industry

States should not use their credit to subsidize private industry, either through the purchase or the guaranteeing of private securities. In addition to the considerations mentioned above, which apply fully here, the fact is that public officials must pass judgment upon the probable success of private ventures. Men who can make such decisions successfully will usually find more congenial work and greater rewards in private industry than in public service. State subsidies have all the evils of a tariff without one of its strongest justifications—that of defense. "Infant industries" are likely to remain infants and to keep calling for more and more aid. State subsidies promote state "nationalism" and encourage states to compete with one another for industries. The businessman is then able to play one state against another and to get a virtual guarantee of profits with the taxpayer footing the bill. In view of the abundance of investment funds now available in this country and the ease with which corporations can be organized to carry out ventures of any size, there is no longer any valid excuse for state subsidies to private industry.

Generally, state borrowing for highways has been successful, whereas in almost every instance state borrowing to aid railroads was a failure. Undoubtedly the difference in method was an important reason for the difference in results. The railroads were designed, built, and operated for the purpose of making a profit rather than for public service. If that profit came from state subsidies in the form of a profit on construction, it was no less acceptable to the owners; perhaps it was more acceptable in that it was quicker and more certain. Private enterprise and the state have quite different ends to serve when they undertake a venture, and it is not often that both can be served successfully.

Better Administrative and Financial Machinery

Before a state embarks upon a program of borrowing, it should take special precautions to see that its administrative and financial machinery is adequate to handle the increased business which borrowing will entail. Accounting and auditing methods and personnel should be adequate to keep records abreast of financial transactions. Depository arrangements should be adequate to handle the larger balances and to protect the state against loss. In the past many states have lost funds in the interval between borrowing and spending.

Planning

Except in emergencies, states should borrow only in accordance with a carefully prepared, long-range plan. Before a state starts to borrow, it should decide what it wishes to accomplish, in the long run, by the borrowing, prepare a plan to achieve that goal, and then abide by the plan. Once borrowing has started, perspectives change, and many groups will attempt to swerve the state from its plan. The local inflation produced by the borrowing will conceal the rising debt burden and produce demands for additional borrowing. The expansion of state services along certain lines will engender demands for expansion along other lines. Construction in certain sections of the state will produce charges of favoritism and give rise to demands for an equal amount of construction in other sections. Unless a definite plan is agreed upon in advance, it may not be possible to keep the debt within reasonable bounds. This is not to imply that the original plan should never be changed. Conditions may arise to warrant a change, but the changes should be considered as fully and as seriously as the original plan and with regard to the same objectives.

Borrow Slowly

The final, and perhaps the most important, principle is that states should proceed slowly in borrowing. Hasty borrowing intensifies many of the problems mentioned above; it increases the size of the balances which must be handled and protected; it multiplies the difficulties of accountants and auditors; it increases the technical problems of designing and administering spending programs and does not allow time for research and training in the best methods of construction; it intensifies the local inflation caused by the borrowing; it does not give taxpayers an opportunity to call a halt if the debt burden grows too heavy; and it does not give citizens generally time to judge whether the benefits of the borrowing program are sufficient to warrant its continuance. It will be noted that most of these considerations tend to encourage more borrowing or to weaken the resistance to it. Perhaps this explains why practically all troublesome state debts in the past have been those which were built up hurriedly. In general, much is to be gained and nothing to be lost by proceeding slowly.

RECOMMENDATIONS

Based upon, and supplementary to, the above general principles, certain specific recommendations for the administration of state debts are offered below. Their observance, within the framework of the above principles, would, it is believed, almost certainly prevent overborrowing and would greatly help to put state long-term finances upon a systematic basis. Recommendations concerning debt limitations are given in a separate section below.

Centralized Responsibility

States which have or expect to have large debts should centralize the responsibility for debt management in some one officer or board. This would not necessarily mean the creation of a new position, since some existing official might be charged with the duty. If the debt is large, however, it would be desirable to have a separate office for this function. In most states the treasurer is now responsible for the detailed work of debt administration. Depending upon his status in the organization of state government and upon his other duties, he might be designated as debt officer. In any case he should be a member of the advisory board or council. The recommended debt officer or board should be an executive planning agency directly under the supervision of the governor, very much like an executive budget board except that it would have no record-keeping or administrative duties; those would be left with the treasurer as now. The duties of such a board or officer should be to prepare, for the use of the governor and the legislature, a long-range plan for the debt, plans for the improvement of debt service, and to prepare and to have available at all times all pertinent data regarding the debt and debt service. It would, of course, have no power to shape policies, but its work, if well executed, would provide the data upon which such policy decisions could be formed and would carry much weight with both executives and legislators, just as a well-prepared budget now carries such weight.

A Capital Budget

In connection with its debt plan, a state should have a capital budget. Most states have found the current budget indispensable in the management of their current finances; the capital budget offers almost as many advantages in the field of long-term finances.[4] It is merely a plan of the capital outlays which the state expects to make during the ensuing six or eight years and the methods by which they will be financed. It gives perspective and method to capital spending and enables state officials and legislators to see the whole picture and thus to keep the various parts in correct proportion. That part of it beyond the usual appropriation period does not have the effect of law since one legislature cannot bind another, but its own reasonableness and logic and the publicity which goes with the plan give it considerable weight.

4. For a description of such a budget and the advantages which it offers, see *Report of the* [N. Y.] *Joint Legislative Committee on State Fiscal Policies*, pp. 49-60.

Parts of Outlays Financed from Current Revenues

As a matter of fixed policy, states should require that a certain part—say from 5 to 15 per cent—of the cost of all capital improvements should be financed from current revenues. This might well be incorporated into the debt limitations. There are several advantages to such a requirement. First, it would reduce the amount of funds which would have to be borrowed. Second, it would test the desire of the people for the improvement. They might be willing to approve a large program of outlays if they did not have to make any "down payment," but, if they had to submit to increased taxes immediately in order to raise the necessary 5 or 10 per cent, they might decide that they could get along with a less ambitious program. Third, it would be a test of their ability to carry the debt. If no payments are made from current revenues, taxpayers feel practically no change in their tax loan during the first year or two of a borrowing program. A contribution of 10 per cent of the cost of the outlay would be approximately equal to the amount needed annually for debt service after the improvement is completed, not to mention the cost of maintaining and operating the asset. If taxpayers cannot raise the 10 per cent without undue hardship, they will not be able to service the debt after it has been incurred. Three states—Massachusetts, New Jersey, and New York—have incorporated a requirement of this kind into their laws regulating local government debts.[5]

Limit Term of Bonds to Twenty-five Years

Regardless of the purpose of borrowing, states should not issue bonds running longer than twenty-five years. The life of the improvement financed by the borrowing, while it may properly be regarded as the outside limit for the bonds, is fallacious as a guide to the normal or usual term of the bonds. It would bind the state to a policy of a permanent debt, for as soon as the improvement was worn out, another debt would have to be incurred to replace it. It would be just as sensible for the individual to arrange the term of the debt on his house to run for the full time, the house was expected to last.

5. B. U. Ratchford, "A Formula for Limiting State and Local Debts," *Quarterly Journal of Economics*, LI (1936), 82.

The significant factor to be observed in arranging the term of the debt is the effect of the debt upon state finances. The existence of a debt lessens a state's freedom of action in financial matters and compels it to apportion a part of its revenues in a predetermined manner. It reduces a state's ability to meet new demands and new emergencies. New conditions may arise in which a state will need all possible freedom of action to change the disposition of its revenues. The longer its debts run, the longer a state will have to wait for such freedom. A state should not borrow for a period longer than that for which it can plan with some degree of certainty. Certainly this would not be more than twenty or twenty-five years. Wherever possible, the term should be shorter, since shorter terms will give greater flexibility to state finances.

DEBT LIMITATIONS

The question of a constitutional limitation for state debts is one on which there may be considerable variations of opinion. Some would abolish them entirely or liberalize them greatly, while others advocate limitations stricter than we now have. There is no magic in debt limitations, and we should not expect to solve all problems by writing a formula into the constitution. Nor should we expect the same considerations to apply equally to all states. Some states, such as Connecticut, Delaware, Massachusetts, and Vermont, do not now have limitations and apparently do not need them, since over the past one hundred years or more their legislatures have shown that they can exercise the borrowing power with discretion. So long as this condition continues, such states do not need to worry about constitutional limitations. On the other hand, there are states, especially in the South, in which the legislatures have repeatedly shown that they may not safely be entrusted with unlimited borrowing power. For such states definite and effective constitutional limitations are necessary.

Scope of Limitation

Before attempting to describe a limitation, let us first see what features a limitation should possess. First, it should include all obligations incurred by the state or any of its departments, whether payable from general or special revenues. This is necessary to prevent widespread evasion by the practice of labeling any given revenues as a special fund and then issuing revenue bonds against it. The present tendency of the courts is to allow such practice with very few restrictions.[6] Second, the limitation should include all obligations of state agencies, regardless of the funds from which they are payable, if such agencies receive, directly or indirectly, as much as 10 per cent of their revenues from state appropriations, or from the proceeds of taxes or fees levied by state law, or if they have received as much as 25 per cent of their assets from the state. This would include revenue bonds issued by educational institutions, hospitals, and special agencies, such as the General State Authority of Pennsylvania. Some bonds may be true revenue bonds which should be left outside the limitation, but most of them are merely concealed state obligations, and it appears impossible to separate the true from the pseudo revenue bonds without writing an elaborate cost-accounting formula into the constitution. The above provisions would leave outside the limitation the bonds of state agencies, such as bridge commissions, which are truly self-supporting and which do not depend upon the state either for construction or operating funds. The constitution should provide, however, that the state may never appropriate funds to support special agencies which have been established with unlimited borrowing power unless the debts of such agencies may be added to the existing state debt without exceeding the constitutional limit. The provision, found in many constitutions at present, forbidding the state to lend its credit to any private person or corporation should be retained.

Characteristics of Debt Limit

A debt limit should possess certain characteristics. First, it should bear some relationship to the wealth and income of the people of the state and to the revenues of the state government. For this reason a limit stated as a fixed sum is likely to be rendered obsolete in a short time. A few states have expressed debt limits in terms of the assessed value of taxable property, but assessed values are no

6. See Chapters XVIII and XXI.

longer, if they ever were, an accurate measure of wealth.[7] Since the states have generally abandoned the property tax as a source of revenue, the figures for assessed values now have even less significance than formerly.

Estimates of the wealth and income of states have not yet achieved sufficient accuracy or official recognition to warrant using them in a constitutional limitation. For these reasons the only measure of debt-paying capacity which may feasibly be used is the revenue receipts of the state, as described below. These probably bear some rough relationship to the wealth and income of the people, but, more important, they show how much of that income the people have been accustomed to pay to the state. As a test of the ability and willingness of the people to pay public debts, this is quite important. If, in order to pay their public debts, the taxpayers must substantially increase their tax payments there may be trouble, even though their income is high.

Other characteristics which a debt limit should possess are: (1) it should exert pressure gradually as the ultimate limit is approached; (2) it should not drop abruptly in a period of depression; (3) it should be definite and capable of being expressed in a short section of the constitution; (4) it should leave as little as possible to court interpretation; and (5) it should be strong enough to be effective. It is believed that the limitation proposed below will meet these specifications. After the formula has been described, we shall return to a discussion of this point.

A Proposed Limitation

In the light of the above considerations it is here proposed to limit the debts of a state in terms of average revenue receipts. The concept of "revenue receipts," however, is not sufficiently definite and specific for use in a constitutional provision, since a state might label all receipts of state institutions, agencies, and enterprises as revenue receipts. Therefore, revenue receipts would have to be defined as: (1) net collections from taxes and license and regis-

7. See the article, "A Formula for Limiting State and Local Debts," cited above, for a further consideration of this point.

tration fees levied by law; (2) donations and grants from the Federal Government; and (3) net receipts from state investments and enterprises. Receipts from these sources would include more than 90 per cent of all state revenue receipts as now defined by the Bureau of the Census, and for all practical purposes may be treated as synonymous with receipts as the term is now understood.

The basic limit would be as follows: the legislature could authorize borrowing so long as the net debt[8] incurred under such authorization did not exceed 100 per cent of average revenue receipts for the five preceding years. The electorate could, by a referendum vote, authorize borrowing to a similar amount. The normal or basic limit for the debt would thus be an amount equal to twice[9] the average revenue receipts, as above defined, for the preceding five years; it would be a moving limit to be recomputed each year. It would be desirable to keep the two parts of the debt separate to show: (1) the part of the debt authorized by the legislature and by the people and (2) the amount of additional indebtedness which each might authorize.

Advantages of the Limitation

We may now note briefly how this limitation meets the requirements discussed above. First, it is not rigid over time, but expands as the state's revenues increase. Increasing revenues are, in some measure at least, proof of an increasing ability to pay debts. Second, it exerts pressure gradually. Some limitations impose no restraint until the ultimate limit is reached; then all borrowing is prohibited. Under the proposed formula, the legislature may authorize borrowing at first by the enactment of a simple statute. In the second stage a vote of the people is required. Beyond that, no borrowing could be authorized except by constitutional amendment. Third, the debt limit would not decline sharply in a period of depression. Revenue receipts do not show a decline for several months

8. Net debt would be gross debt less sinking fund assets. Gross debt would include all bonds, judgments, and other obligations except current warrants. Sinking fund assets would include only cash, securities, and other assets approved for sinking investments; they would not include the assets of loan funds established by the state.

9. See above, pp. 565-566, for the reasons for this limit.

after the onset of the depression; and even after that, the five-year average of revenue receipts would not decline substantially for two or three years. In fact, if revenues were increasing before the depression, the debt limit would increase for a year or two after the beginning of the depression. Fourth, the concept is a simple one and can be easily expressed in the form of a short constitutional provision. Fifth, there is little room for court interpretation if the scope of the receipts is carefully stated. Finally, it is strong enough to keep the debt within safe bounds.[10]

Exceptions to the Limitation

Most constitutions which now impose restrictions on state borrowing allow unlimited borrowing for certain purposes. It would be desirable to continue to exempt borrowing to refund existing debts and to suppress insurrection. In view of the responsibility of the Federal Government for national defense at the present time it is doubtful whether borrowing "to repel invasion" and "to defend the state" should continue to be exempt. If they are retained, precautions should be taken to insure that the state does not engage in unrestricted borrowing merely because the Federal Government happens to be at war. This might be accomplished by providing that the war powers might not be invoked unless the state was actually threatened with invasion or unless the Federal Government requested financial aid from the state.

It has been customary also to exempt borrowing for casual deficits. This is generally desirable, but it opens the way to abuses. The same is true of borrowing to meet emergencies caused by depressions. If a state borrows up to its constitutional limit, it may be greatly embarrassed if it is unable to borrow further, to meet such emergencies. Of course, states should allow some leeway to cover such contingencies, but if they do not, it may be desirable to allow them to invoke an "emergency limit." One authority has suggested that "the supplementary debt limit, and the loans contracted under it, should probably be kept separate from the regular debt limit and the regular borrowings, with provision for the rapid amortization

10. See the article cited above for a further discussion of the proposal.

of the supplementary borrowings, so that the next emergency will find them wiped off the books."[11]

To meet this need, it is proposed that the constitutional limitation should allow, in addition to the borrowing covered in the basic limitation, emergency borrowing as follows: the legislature should be empowered to borrow, solely to cover casual deficits, to relieve distress, or to alleviate unemployment, an amount not to exceed 50 per cent of average revenue receipts of the five preceding years, provided that such indebtedness should not run for more than ten years. Such a provision would prevent the creation of any dangerous debt and might afford a much needed relief in an emergency.

One final exception would be borrowing in anticipation of taxes. The legislature should have the power to authorize short-term borrowing for such a purpose, in addition to all other debts, up to 25 per cent of the estimated receipts of taxes already levied. This would give fiscal officials the necessary freedom in arranging to meet regular expenditures from irregular sources of revenues. With such power, however, they should be prohibited from issuing warrants unless there are funds in the treasury to cover them. It would preclude the possibility of a net warrant debt. With all the above features included, the total net debt of a state, long-term and short-term, regular and emergency, could not exceed approximately 275 per cent[12] of the average revenue receipts, as specially defined above, for the five preceding years.

Summary of Proposed Limitation

It may be well to summarize briefly the features which should be included in the constitutional limitation. First, the state should be prohibited from lending its credit to any private person or corporation. Second, a small part—say 10 per cent—of the cost of all public improvements financed by borrowing should be raised from current revenues. Third, state bonds should not be issued with a term of more than twenty-five years. Fourth, the limitation should cover all debts and obligations of the states and of those state

11. J. M. Clark, *Economics of Planning Public Works* (Washington, 1935), p. 120.

12. See above, pp. 565-566, for a discussion of the reasons for this limit.

agencies which receive, directly or indirectly, as much as 10 per cent of their revenues from state funds. Fifth, the basic debt limit should be an amount equal to twice the average revenue receipts of the state, as specially defined, for the five years immediately preceding. One half of this amount would be subject to authorization by the legislature and the other half by a referendum vote of the people. Sixth, in emergencies the legislature could authorize additional borrowing, for special purposes and with a term of not more than ten years, to an amount equal to 50 per cent of average revenue receipts. Seventh, the legislature could authorize short-term borrowing in anticipation of taxes already levied to an amount equal to 25 per cent of the estimated yield of such taxes. Finally, borrowing to refund existing debts and to defend the state would be exempt from the limitation.

Evaluation of the Proposal

The above plan would allow a reasonable and prudent use of the state's credit, but would definitely prevent excessive borrowing. Borrowing could be authorized without undue delay, and the debt limit would rise with the increase of state revenues. If the state desired to make heavy outlays, it could, by increasing revenues, pay for a part of the outlays and at the same time raise the debt limit. Large revenues collected to retire a debt would increase the future margin of borrowing both by reducing the existing debt and by raising the debt limit. In emergencies the legislature could invoke additional borrowing power to a limited extent. These provisions would allow all the borrowing that is desirable under normal conditions. If an emergency should arise to make further borrowing necessary, the people always have the privilege of amending the constitution.

A rough survey of state finances for the past twenty years or more indicates that if the above provisions had been in effect, borrowing programs would have been drastically curtailed in Arkansas, Louisiana, Mississippi, North Carolina, North Dakota, South Carolina, South Dakota, Tennessee, and West Virginia. Smaller reductions would have been required in Alabama, Illinois, and Missouri.

On the other hand, it would not have interfered with the programs in such important states as California, Maryland, Massachusetts, New Jersey, New York, and Pennsylvania. On the basis of present information it would seem that the proposed limitation would have prevented nearly all of the indebtedness which has caused trouble and would not have seriously restricted those states which have borrowed prudently.

APPENDIX

Federal Taxation of State Bonds

It is appropriate to mention the doctrine of the immunity of state instrumentalities from federal taxation—a doctrine originated and developed by the federal courts. This is a highly controversial question which has been receiving increasing attention in recent years as federal authorities increase their efforts to repeal the immunity and as the Supreme Court of the United States gives indications of a disposition to reverse its traditional stand. The problem is not discussed here, because an adequate treatment would require several chapters or even a separate volume. Further, nondiscriminatory taxation of state bonds by the Federal Government would not in any way change the principles or philosophy of state borrowing. The only effect would be that states would have to pay slightly higher rates of interest on bonds issued in the future—probably from one quarter to one half of one per cent. Those states which levy income taxes would recoup a large part, if not all, of such loss by collecting income taxes on the interest of newly issued federal bonds, since it is contemplated that the repeal of the immunity will be reciprocal.

The present writer does not feel that he has anything of value to add to the voluminous literature on the question which has appeared in recent years. He feels, with the overwhelming majority of impartial students of the question, that the reciprocal immunity should be repealed. (See "Answers by American Professors of Public Finance to Questionnaire on Taxation. . . ," New York State Tax Commission, 1936). Below is given a selected bibliography of the literature so that those who are interested may pursue the matter further.

Selected Bibliography on the Taxation of Government Instrumentalities

Adams, T. S. "Tax-Exempt Securities," *Proceedings*, National Tax Association, 1922. Minneapolis, 1923.

Committee on Taxation of Municipal Obligations and Salaries, American Bar Association. *The Taxation of Municipal Obligations and Salaries*. Chicago, 1939.

Hardy, Charles O. *Tax-Exempt Securities and the Surtax*. New York. 1926.

HILLHOUSE, A. M. "Intergovernmental Tax Exemptions," in *Municipal Yearbook* (1939), pp. 345-381.

LUTZ, HARLEY L. *The Fiscal and Economic Aspects of the Taxation of Public Securities.* New York, 1939.

MAGILL, ROSWELL. "The Problem of Intergovernmental Tax Exemptions," *The Tax Magazine*, XV (December, 1937), 699-703.

MELLON, ANDREW W. *Taxation: The People's Business.* New York, 1924.

MILLS, OGDEN L. "Tax-Exempt Securities," *Proceedings*, National Tax Association, 1923. New York, 1924. Pp. 334-361.

ROSS, OGDEN J. "Intergovernmental Tax Immunity," *Proceedings*, National Tax Association, 1939. Columbia, S. C., 1940. Pp. 165 ff.

SHULTZ, WILLIAM J. "Tax Exemption of Governmental Securities," *Taxes*, XVII (June, 1939), 331-332, 359-362.

SIMONS, HENRY C. *Personal Income Taxation.* Chicago, 1938. Chapter VIII.

STUDENSKI, PAUL. "Federal Taxation of State and Municipal Securities," *Taxes*, XVII (January, 1939), 175-177.

TAX POLICY LEAGUE. *Tax Exemptions.* New York, 1939. Part III.

TUCKER, ROBERT H. "Some Aspects of Intergovernmental Tax Exemptions," *Southern Economic Journal*, VI (January, 1940), 273-290.

U. S. DEPARTMENT OF JUSTICE. *Taxation of Government Bondholders and Employees.* Washington, 1938.

U. S. SENATE. *Report No. 2140*, Part 2. 75th Cong., 3d Sess. Washington, 1940.

WENCHEL, JOHN P. "Federal Taxation of State and Local Bonds," *Taxes*, XVII (March, 1938), 134-136.

SELECTED BIBLIOGRAPHY

SELECTED BIBLIOGRAPHY

This is an attempt to list those sources which are definitely valuable and helpful in dealing with state debts. In addition, unusually good sources are marked thus (*).

I. PUBLIC DOCUMENTS

A. FEDERAL DOCUMENTS

Bureau of the Census
  Ninth Census: 1870, III.
  *Tenth Census: 1880, VII, "Valuation, Taxation, and Public Indebtedness."
  Eleventh Census: 1890, XV, "Wealth, Debt, and Taxation." Part I.
  *Wealth, Debt, and Taxation: 1902.
  *Wealth, Debt, and Taxation: 1913.
  Wealth, Public Debt, and Taxation: 1922. 5 vols.
  *Financial Statistics of State and Local Governments: 1932.
  *Financial Statistics of States (annual, 1915-19; 1921-31; 1937-).
  Census of American Business: 1935, "Retail Distribution."
  Statistical Abstract of the United States (annual).
  Biennial Census of Manufactures.

Congress
  American State Papers, Class III, Finance. 5 vols. 1832-61.
  The Debates and Proceedings in the Congress of the United States, 1834-56. 42 vols.
  House Documents: No. 227, 25th Cong., 3d Sess.; No. 179, 25th Cong., 2d Sess.; No. 145, 26th Cong., 1st Sess.; No. 111, 26th Cong., 2d Sess.; No. 197, 27th Cong., 3d Sess.; No. 40, 27th Cong., 3d Sess.; No. 254, 27th Cong., 2d Sess.; No. 136, 28th Cong., 2d Sess.; No. 263, 54th Cong., 2d Sess.
  House Executive Doc. No. 59, 40th Cong., 2d Sess.
  House Reports: No. 296, 27th Cong., 3d Sess.; No. 120, 27th Cong., 3d Sess.
  Senate Documents: No. 24, 20th Cong., 2d Sess.; No. 18, 26th Cong., 1st Sess.; No. 45, 26th Cong., 1st Sess.; No. 153, 26th Cong., 1st Sess.; No. 197, 26th Cong., 1st Sess.; No. 447, 26th Cong., 1st Sess.; No. 43, 26th Cong., 2d Sess.; No. 116, 27th Cong., 1st Sess.; No. 69, 27th Cong., 2d Sess.; No. 15, 27th Cong., 3d Sess.; No. 130, Pt. 5, 27th Cong., 3d Sess.; No. 181, Pt. 3, 27th Cong., 3d Sess.; No. 150, 29th Cong., 1st Sess.; No. 15, 34th

Cong., 1st Sess.; No. 250, 62d Cong., 2d Sess.; No. 432, 63d Cong., 2d Sess.

Senate Reports: No. 41, 42d Cong., 2d Sess.; No. 572, 44th Cong., 2d Sess.; No. 623, 53d Cong., 2d Sess.

Department of Commerce
Bureau of Foreign and Domestic Commerce
Long-Term Debts in the United States, 1937.
State Income Payments, 1929-37. 1939. (Compiled by Robert R. Nathan and John L. Martin.)

Federal Emergency Relief Administration
Monthly Reports.
Economics of Planning Public Works, 1935. (Prepared by J. M. Clark.)
Revenue Bond Financing by Political Subdivisions: Its Origin Scope, and Growth in the United States. 1936.

Library of Congress
The Constitution of the United States (revised and annotated, 1938).

B. STATE DOCUMENTS

No attempt is made in this section to list all the state documents which pertain to state debts nor all of those which were used in the preparation of this work; that would be a tedious and unnecessary task, since the documents are much the same in every state. As occasion demanded, the following sources were consulted for each state: the laws or acts of the legislature; the journals of the two houses of the legislature; the reports of the court of highest appeal; the annual or biennial reports of the treasurer, the auditor or comptroller, the tax commission, and other state officials and agencies. For those states which have good budget systems the budget report is one of the best sources of information concerning the debt and debt service. The documents listed below have been useful and may be overlooked unless special attention is directed to them.

Alabama. *Report of the Commissioners to Adjust and Liquidate the Indebtedness of the State of Alabama to the Governor.* Montgomery, January, 1876. December, 1876.

Georgia. *Report of the Committee of the Legislature to Investigate the Bonds.* Atlanta, 1872.

Illinois. *Constitutional Convention Bulletins.* Springfield, 1919.

Massachusetts. *Bulletins for the Constitutional Convention, 1917-1918.* Boston, 1918. 2 vols.

Minnesota. "Report of the Committee Appointed to Investigate the Rural Credits Bureau," *Journal of the Senate,* 1925, pp. 581-588.
Report of the Legislative Tax Commission of Investigation and Inquiry. 1937.
The Liquidator (Published annually by the Department of Rural Credit, 1934-).

New York. *The Invalid Bonds of Georgia.* 1885.
  *The Debt of the State of New York Past, Present, and Future.
  Legislative Document (1926), No. 70.
  Operation of Debt and Tax Rate Limits in the State of New York
  (Special Report of the State Tax Commission, No. 5), 1932.
  Constitutions of the States and United States. 1938.
  Problems Relating to Taxation and Finance. 1938.
  *Report of the Joint Legislative Committee on State Fiscal Policies.
  Legislative Document (1938) No. 41.
North Carolina. *Acts and Resolutions of the General Assembly Passed
  in Secret Session, 1861-64.* (Bound with N. C. *Laws,* 1864-65.)
  Report of the Senate Investigation Committee (Thomas Bragg,
  Chairman), 1870.
  *Report of the Commission to Investigate Charges of Fraud and
  Corruption* (W. M. Shipp, Chairman), 1872.
  *In the Matter of the Republic of Cuba vs. the State of North
  Carolina.* 1917.
North Dakota. *Reports, Farm Loan Department of the Bank of North
  Dakota.*
  Report of the North Dakota Governmental Commission. 1932.
  *A Report of the Tax Survey Commission on North Dakota's Tax
  System and Its Administration.* 1936
Rhode Island. *Report of the Board of Commissioners of the Sinking
  Fund to the General Assembly at January Session, 1885.* 1885.
South Dakota. "Report of Joint Committee of Senate and House; South
  Dakota Rural Credit Board," *Senate Journal,* 1925, pp. 673-
  748.
  "Report of the Interim Commission to the State of South Dakota and
  Members and Officers of the Legislature. . . ," *Senate Journal,*
  1927, pp. 85-199.
  *Report of an Investigation of the Rural Credit Department of the
  State of South Dakota, made by the Attorney-General.* 1932.
Tennessee. "Interim Report of the Special Investigating Committee,"
  House Journal, 1931, pp. 454-483.
  "Second Report of the Special Legislative Committee," *House
  Journal,* 1931, pp. 643-812.
  "Unanimous Report of the Special Committee of the House . . .
  Relating to the Impeachment of the Governor," *House Journal,*
  1931, pp. 873-936, 985-1049.
Virginia. Report of the Senate Committee on Finance on the Condi-
  tion of the State, January 28, 1865, *Senate Journal and Docu-
  ments,* 1864-65; *Senate Document* No. 11.
  Report of the Virginia Debt Commission, *House Document* No. 11,
  1922.

II. PERIODICALS AND PERIODICAL LITERATURE

A. GENERAL

Annalist (weekly, 1913-40).
*Bond Buyer (weekly, 1893-).
*Commercial and Financial Chronicle (weekly, 1865-).
Hunt's Merchants' Magazine and Commercial Review (weekly, 1840-70).
*Moody's Governments and Municipals (annual, 1918-).
*Municipal Bond Sales (published annually by the *Bond Buyer*, 1903-).
New York Times (daily, 1858-).
*State and Municipal Compendium (semiannual, 1928-).

B. SPECIAL ARTICLES

ANDERSON, BENJAMIN M. "State and Municipal Borrowing in Relation to the Business Cycle," *Chase Economic Bulletin,* June 10, 1925.

ANONYMOUS. "South Carolina's First Paper Money," *Sound Currency,* V (1898), 33-47. (Reprinted from *Statutes of South Carolina,* IX, 1841.)

BEALE, HOWARD K. "Reconstruction," *Encyclopedia of the Social Sciences,* XIII, 168-172.

BIRD, FREDERICK L. "The Problem of Revenue Bonds," *Bond Buyer,* Nov. 27, 1937, p. 2.

BORAK, ARTHUR. "Minnesota Changes Its Tax System," *Bulletin of the National Tax Association,* XXIII (1938), 209-213; 226-236.

BOYD, W. K. "Fiscal and Economic Conditions in North Carolina During the Civil War," *North Carolina Booklet,* XIV (1915), 195-219.

BROUGH, C. H. "History of Banking in Mississippi," *Publications of the Mississippi Historical Society,* III (1901), 317-341.

BROWN, C. K. "The Florida Investments of George W. Swepson," *North Carolina Historical Review,* V (1928), 275-288.

*COOKE, GILBERT W. "The North Dakota Rural Credit System," *Journal of Land and Public Utility Economics,* XIV (1938), 273-283.

*———. "The North Dakota State Mill and Elevator," *Journal of Political Economy,* XLVI (1938), 23-51.

COOPER, EVELYN N. "Federal Taxation of Obligations Issued by State Educational Institutions," *Legal Notes on Local Government,* III (1937), 1-9.

*[CURTIS, BENJAMIN R.] "Debts of the States," *North American Review,* LVIII (1844), 109-157.

FOLWELL, WILLIAM W. "The Five Million Loan," *Minnesota Historical Society Collections,* XV (1915), 189-214.

GRAY, MORRIS. "The Coupon Legislation of Virginia," *American Law Review,* XXIII (1889), 924-945.

HARLOW, RALPH V. "Aspects of Revolutionary Finance," *American Historical Review,* XXXV (1929), 46-68.

HOWLAND, C. P. "Our Repudiated State Bonds," *Foreign Affairs,* VI (1928), 395-407.

HUME, JOHN F. "Are We a Nation of Rascals?" *North American Review,* CXXXIX (1884), 127-144.

JENKS, W. L. "Michigan's Five Million Dollar Loan," *Michigan History Magazine,* XV (1931), 575-634.

*LESTER, RICHARD A. "Currency Issues to Overcome Depressions in Pennsylvania, 1723 and 1729," *Journal of Political Economy,* XLVI (1938), 324-375.

*———. "Currency Issues to Overcome Depressions in Delaware, New Jersey, New York, and Maryland, 1715-37," *Journal of Political Economy,* XLVII (1939), 182-217.

MacDONALD, T. H. "The Arkansas Road Finance Situation," *American City,* XXIV (1921), 494-495.

MORTON, R. L. "The Virginia State Debt and Internal Improvements, 1829-1838," *Journal of Political Economy,* XXV (1917), 339-373.

PERRY, AMOS. "Rhode Island Revolutionary Debt," *Publications, Rhode Island Historical Society,* IV (1897), 234-243.

*PERSHING, JOHN. "Revenue Bond Remedies," *Cornell Law Quarterly,* XXII (1936), 64-82.

POWELL, ALDEN L. "Amending the Louisiana Constitution," *Southwestern Social Science Quarterly,* XVIII (1937), 25-34.

*RANDALL, JAMES G. "The Virginia Debt Controversy," *Political Science Quarterly,* XXX (1915), 553-577.

RANDOLPH, B. C. "Foreign Bondholders and the Repudiated Debts of the Southern States," *American Journal of International Law,* XXV (1931), 63-82.

RATCHFORD, B. U. "A Formula for Limiting State and Local Debts," *Quarterly Journal of Economics,* LI (1936), 71-89.

———. "An International Debt Settlement: the North Carolina Debt to France," *American Historical Review,* XL (1934), 63-69.

———. "The Settlement of Certain State Claims Against the Federal Government," *Southern Economic Journal,* IV (1937), 54-75.

—— (with K. C. Heise). "Confederate Pensions," *Southern Economic Journal,* V (1938), 207-217.

REEVES, J. S. "The Principality of Monaco v. the State of Mississippi," *American Journal of International Law,* XXVIII (1934), 739-742.

SABY, R. S. "Railroad Legislation in Minnesota, 1849-1870," *Minnesota Historical Society Collection,* XV (1915), 1-188.

STILL, BAYRD. "An Interpretation of the Statehood Process," *Mississippi Valley Historical Review,* XXIII (1936), 189-204.

STUDENSKI, PAUL. "Repudiation of Public Debts," *Encyclopedia of the Social Sciences,* XIII, 321-324.

TURNER, RAYMOND. "Repudiation of Debts by States of the Union," *Current History,* XXIII (1926), 475-483.

WHTTE, HORACE. "New York's Colonial Currency," *Sound Currency* V, (1898), 49-64.

III. MONOGRAPHS, PAMPHLETS, AND SPECIAL WORKS

Anonymous. *Communication from Group of Alabama Bondholders to Commissioners to Adjust and Liquidate the Indebtedness of the State of Alabama.* New York, December 18, 1875.

——. *The Plough and the Sickle: or Rhode Island in the War of the Revolution of 1776.* Providence, 1846.

BEARD, CHARLES A. *An Economic Interpretation of the Constitution of the United States.* New York, 1936.

BEHRENS, KATHRYN L. *Paper Money in Maryland, 1727-1789.* ("Johns Hopkins Studies," XL.) Baltimore, 1923.

BETTERSWORTH, JOHN K. *Confederate Mississippi.* An unpublished thesis in the Duke University Library. (Typewritten.) Durham, 1937.

BITTERMAN, HENRY J. *State and Federal Grants-in-Aid.* Chicago, 1938.

*BOGART, E. L. *Internal Improvements and State Debt in Ohio.* New York, 1924.

BOYLE, JAMES E. *The Financial History of Kansas.* ("Bulletin of the University of Wisconsin, Economics and Political Science Series," V.) Madison, 1909.

BRADBEER, W. W. *Confederate and Southern State Currency.* Mount Vernon, N. Y. 1915.

*BRECK, S. *Historical Sketches of the Continental Paper Money,* Philadelphia, 1843.

*BRONSON, HENRY. *A Historical Account of Connecticut Currency, Continental Money, and the Finances of the Revolution.* ("Papers of the New Haven Colony Historical Society," I.) New Haven, 1865.

*BROWN, C. K. *A State Movement in Railroad Development.* Chapel Hill, 1928.

——. *The State Highway System of North Carolina.* Chapel Hill, 1931.

*BULLOCK, CHARLES J. *Historical Sketch of the Finances and Financial Policy of Massachusetts from 1780 to 1905.* ("Publications of the American Economic Association," 3d Series, III, No. 2.) New York, 1907.

*——. *The Monetary History of the United States.* New York, 1900.

*Burgess, John W. *Reconstruction and the Constitution, 1866-1876.* New York, 1903.

Caldwell, Joshua W. *Studies in the Constitutional History of Tennessee.* Cincinnati, 1907.

Caldwell, Stephen A. *A Banking History of Louisiana.* Baton Rouge, 1935.

*Chatters, Carl H., and Hillhouse, Albert M. *Local Government Debt Administration.* New York, 1939.

Clark, Evans (editor). *The Internal Debts of the United States.* New York, 1933.

Clark, W. A. *The History of the Banking Institutions Organized in South Carolina Prior to 1860.* Columbia, 1922.

Clayton, Powell. *The Aftermath of the Civil War in Arkansas.* New York, 1915.

Committee on Municipal Debt Administration. *The Call Feature in Municipal Bonds.* Chicago, 1938.

Crawford, Finla G. *The Gasoline Tax in the United States, 1936.* Chicago, 1937.

*Davis, A. Mc. *Currency and Banking in the Province of the Massachusetts Bay.* ("Publications of the American Economic Association," 3d Series, I.) New York, 1900.

Davis, W. W. *The Civil War and Reconstruction in Florida.* ("Columbia Studies," LIII.) New York, 1913.

Del Mar, Alexander. *The History of Money in America.* New York, 1899.

Dodd, Agnes P. *History of Money in the British Empire and the United States.* London, 1911.

Douglas, Charles H. J. *The Financial History of Massachusetts from the Organization of the Massachusetts Bay Colony to the American Revolution.* ("Columbia Studies," I.) New York, 1897.

Douglas, William. *A Discussion Concerning the Currencies of the British Plantations in America.* (Reprinted in "Economic Studies of American Economic Association," II.) New York, 1897.

Edwards, Allen B. *A History of the Kentucky State Debt.* An unpublished thesis in the Duke University Library. (Typewritten.) Durham, 1939.

Elliot, Jonathan. *The Funding System of the United States and of Great Britain.* Washington, 1845.

Evans, William C. *The Public Debt of Arkansas: Its History from 1836 to 1885.* An unpublished thesis in the University of Arkansas Library. (Typewritten.) Fayetteville, 1928.

Faust, M. L. *The Security of Public Deposits.* (Public Administration Service No. 51.) Chicago, 1936.

FELT, J. B. *An Historical Account of Massachusetts Currency.* Boston, 1839.

FICKLEN, J. R. *History of Reconstruction in Louisiana.* ("Johns Hopkins Studies," XXVIII.) Baltimore, 1910.

*FLEMING, WALTER L. *Civil War and Reconstruction in Alabama.* New York, 1905.

FOWLER, JOHN F. *Revenue Bonds.* New York, 1938.

GALLATIN, ALBERT. *Views of the Public Debt, Receipts, and Expenditures of the United States.* Second Edition. Philadelphia, 1801.

GARNER, JAMES W. *Reconstruction in Mississippi.* New York, 1901.

GOUGE, WILLIAM M. *A Short History of Paper Money and Banking in the United States.* 2 vols. Philadelphia, 1833.

GOULD, C. P. *Money and Transportation in Maryland, 1720-1765.* ("Johns Hopkins Studies," XXXIII.) Baltimore, 1915.

GREEN, FLETCHER M. *Constitutional Development in the South Atlantic States, 1776-1860.* Chapel Hill, 1930.

GRENOBLE, WILLIAM L. *A History of the Virginia State Debt.* An unpublished thesis in the University of Virginia Library. (Typewritten.) Charlottesville, 1937.

HAMILTON, J. G. DE R. *Reconstruction in North Carolina.* ("Columbia Studies," LVIII.) New York, 1914.

HANNA, H. S. *A Financial History of Maryland, 1789-1848.* ("Johns Hopkins Studies," XXV.) Baltimore, 1907.

*HAVENS, R. MURRAY. *History of Financing of Public Highways in Arkansas.* An unpublished thesis in the University of Kansas Library. (Typewritten.) Lawrence, 1933.

HICKCOX, J. H. *A History of the Bills of Credit or Paper Money Issued by New York from 1709 to 1789.* Albany, 1866.

*HILLHOUSE, ALBERT M. *Municipal Bonds.* New York, 1936.

JEWETT, F. E. *A Financial History of Maine.* New York, 1937.

KEARNY, JOHN W. *Sketch of American Finance, 1789-1835.* New York, 1887.

*KLABER, ROBERT. *Bridge Revenue Bonds.* (Privately mimeographed.) New York, 1939.

*KNAPPEN, LAURENCE S. *Revenue Bonds and the Investor.* New York, 1939.

LESTER, RICHARD A. *Monetary Experiments; Early American and Recent Scandinavian.* Princeton, 1939.

LEVEN, MAURICE, and KING, W. I. *Income in the Various States.* New York, 1935.

LEWIS, CLEONA. *America's Stake in International Investments.* Washington, 1938.

LONN, E. *Reconstruction in Louisiana after 1868.* New York, 1918.

*McCulloch, Albert J. *The Loan Office Experiment in Missouri, 1821-1836.* ("The University of Missouri Bulletin," XV.) Columbia, 1914.

MacDonald, A. F. *Federal Aid.* New York, 1928.

*McFerrin, John B. *Caldwell and Company: A Southern Financial Empire.* Chapel Hill, 1939.

*McGrane, Reginald C. *Foreign Bondholders and American State Debts.* New York, 1935.

Maclay, Edgar S. (editor). *The Journal of William Maclay, U. S. Senator from Pennsylvania, 1789-91.* New York, 1927.

*Miller, Edward T. *A Financial History of Texas.* ("Bulletin of the University of Texas," No. 37.) Austin, 1916.

*Million, John W. *State Aid to Railways in Missouri.* Chicago, 1896.

National Association of Mutual Savings Banks. *Critical Survey of State Debts.* New York, 1927.

National Highway Users Conference. *Highway Transportation Remakes America.* Washington, 1939.

*Nettels, Curtis P. *The Money Supply of the American Colonies before 1720.* Madison, 1934.

Nevins, Allan. *The American States During and After the Revolution, 1775-1789.* New York, 1924.

Patton, J. W. *Unionism and Reconstruction in Tennessee, 1860-1869.* Chapel Hill, 1934.

*Pearson, C. C. *The Readjuster Movement in Virginia.* New Haven, 1917.

Phelan, R. V. *The Financial History of Wisconsin.* ("Bulletin of the University of Wisconsin, Economics and Political Science Series," II.) Madison, 1907.

*Phillips, Henry, Jr. *Historical Sketches of the Paper Currency of the American Colonies Prior to the Adoption of the Federal Constitution.* Roxbury, 1865.

Ramsdell, Charles W. *Reconstruction in Texas.* New York, 1910.

Randall, James G. *The Civil War and Reconstruction.* New York, 1937.

Ratchford, B. U. *A History of the North Carolina Debt, 1712-1900.* An unpublished thesis in the Duke University Library. (Typewritten.) Durham, 1932.

Richmond, John W. *Rhode Island Repudiation: or the History of the Revolutionary Debt of Rhode Island.* Providence, 1855.

Ripley, William Z. *The Financial History of Virginia, 1609-1776.* ("Columbia Studies," I.) New York, 1893.

Rodney, R. S. *Colonial Finance in Delaware.* Wilmington, 1928.

*Royall, W. L. *History of the Virginia Debt Controversy.* Richmond, 1897.

RUSH, RICHARD. *Remarks on the Loan of a Million and a Half Dollars. . . .* London, 1829.

*SCHUCKERS, J. W. *A Brief Account of the Finances and Paper Money of the Revolutionary War.* Philadelphia, 1874.

*SCOTT, WILLIAM A. *The Repudiation of State Debts.* New York, 1893.

*SECRIST, HORACE. *An Economic Analysis of the Constitutional Restrictions upon Public Indebtedness in the United States.* ("Bulletin of the University of Wisconsin," No. 637.) Madison, 1914.

*SIMKINS, F. B., and WOODY, R. H. *South Carolina During Reconstruction.* Chapel Hill, 1932.

SINGEWALD, KARL. *The Doctrine of Non-Suability of the State in the United States.* ("Johns Hopkins Studies," XXVIII.) Baltimore, 1910.

SMITH, E. A. *History of the Confederate Treasury.* ("Publications of Southern Historical Association," V.) Washington and Harrisburg, 1901.

SNAVELY, TIPTON R. *A Study of the Fiscal System of Tennessee.* Nashville, 1936.

SNEED, JOHN L. T. *Tennessee and Her Bondage; A Vindication and a Warning.* Memphis, 1881.

SPARKS, E. S. *History and Theory of Agricultural Credit in the United States.* New York, 1932.

*SOWERS, DON C. *The Financial History of New York State from 1789 to 1912.* ("Columbia Studies," LVII.) New York, 1914.

STAPLES, T. S. *Reconstruction in Arkansas.* New York, 1923.

STOKES, JORDAN. *State Debt of Tennessee.* Nashville, 1880.

STUDENSKI, PAUL. *Public Borrowing.* New York, 1930.

*SUMNER, WILLIAM G. *The Financier and the Finances of the American Revolution.* 2 vols. New York, 1891.

*TABER, NORMAN S., AND CO. *Report on a Survey of the Highway Indebtedness of the State of Texas.* New York, 1938.

*———. *State of Tennessee: Reorganizing the Debt Structure.* New York, 1937.

THOMAS, DAVID Y. *Arkansas in War and Reconstruction, 1861-1874.* Little Rock, 1926.

*THOMPSON, C. M. *Reconstruction in Georgia.* ("Columbia Studies," LXIV.) New York, 1916.

THOMSON, WOOD and HOFFMAN. *The Tax Exempt Status of State and Municipal Bonds.* (Published by Brown, Harriman and Co.) New York, 1937.

*TOSTLEBE, ALVIN S. *The Bank of North Dakota; An Experiment in Agrarian Banking.* ("Columbia Studies," CXIV.) New York, 1924.

TROTTER, ALEXANDER. *Observations on the Financial Position and Credit of Such of the States of the North American Union as Have Contracted Public Debts.* London, 1839.

*TRULL, EDNA. *The Debts and Resources of the Forty-eight States.* New York, 1938.

*——. *Borrowing for Highways.* New York, 1937.

WEBSTER, PELATIAH. *Political Essays on the Nature and Operation of Money, Public Finances, and Other Subjects.* Philadelphia, 1791.

WHITE, ROBERT H. *Development of the Tennessee State Educational Organization, 1796-1929.* ("George Peabody College for Teachers Contribution to Education," No. 62.) Nashville, 1929.

WINKLER, MAX. *Foreign Bonds—An Autopsy.* Philadelphia, 1933.

WOOD, FREDERICK A. *The Finances of Vermont.* ("Columbia Studies," LII.) New York, 1913.

*WORTHINGTON, T. K. *Historical Sketch of the Finances of Pennsylvania.* ("Publications of the American Economic Association," II.) Baltimore, 1888.

WRIGHT, BENJAMIN F. *The Contract Clause of the Constitution.* Cambridge, 1938.

IV. REFERENCE AND GENERAL WORKS

ADAMS, HENRY (editor). *The Writings of Albert Gallatin.* 3 vols. London, 1879.

ADAMS, HENRY C. *Public Debts: An Essay in the Science of Finance.* New York, 1895.

ARNOLD, SAMUEL G. *History of the State of Rhode Island.* 2 vols. New York, 1860.

BADGER, RALPH E., and GUTHMAN, HARRY G. *Investment Principles and Practices.* Revised Edition. New York, 1936.

*BOLLES, ALBERT S. *The Financial History of the United States.* 3 vols. Second Edition. New York, 1884-86.

BOWERS, CLAUDE G. *Jefferson and Hamilton.* New York, 1928.

BREVARD, CAROLINE M. *A History of Florida.* 2 vols. Deland, 1924.

BURDICK, CHARLES K. *The Law of the American Constitution.* New York, 1922.

CHAMBERLAINE, LAWRENCE, and EDWARDS, GEORGE W. *The Principles of Bond Investment.* Revised Edition. New York, 1927.

COULTER, E. M. *A Short History of Georgia.* Chapel Hill, 1933.

Council of the Corporation of Foreign Bondholders. *Annual Reports,* London.

CURTIS, BENJAMIN R. (editor). *A Memoir of Benjamin Robbins Curtis, LL.D., with Some of His Professional and Miscellaneous Writings.* 2 vols. Boston, 1879.

DEWEY, DAVIS R. *Financial History of the United States.* Twelfth Edition. New York, 1934.

DODD, W. F. *The Government of the District of Columbia.* Washington, 1909.

DRAYTON, JOHN. *A View of South Carolina.* Charleston, 1802.

FISHER, E. J. *New Jersey as a Royal Province, 1738 to 1776.* ("Columbia Studies," XLI.) New York, 1911.

FLEMING, WALTER L. *Documentary History of Reconstruction.* 2 vols. Cleveland, 1906-1907.

GAYER, ARTHUR D. *Public Works in Prosperity and Depression.* New York, 1935.

GROVES, HAROLD M. *Financing Government.* New York, 1939.

HEPBURN, A. BARTON. *A History of the Currency in the United States.* New Edition Revised. New York, 1924.

HEWITT, A. *An Historical Account of the Rise and Progress of the Colonies of South Carolina and Georgia.* 2 vols. London, 1779.

LODGE, HENRY C. *Alexander Hamilton.* Boston, 1899.

LUTZ, HARLEY L. *Public Finance.* Third Edition. New York, 1936.

MOORE, J. W. *History of North Carolina from the Earliest Discoveries to the Present Time.* 2 vols. Raleigh, 1880.

PHELAN, JAMES. *History of Tennessee.* Boston and New York, 1889.

PIKE, JAMES S. *The Prostrate State.* New York, 1874.

RAMSAY, DAVID. *History of South Carolina from Its First Settlement in 1670 to the Year 1808.* Newberry, 1858 (2 vols. bound in one; originally written 1808.)

*SCHMECKEBIER, L. F. *The District of Columbia: Its Government and Administration.* Baltimore, 1928.

SCHWAB, J. C. *The Confederate States of America, 1861-1865.* New York, 1901.

SEMMES, JOHN E. *John H. B. Latrobe and His Times, 1803-1891.* Baltimore, 1917.

SHEPHERD, W. R. *History of the Proprietary Government in Pennsylvania.* ("Columbia Studies," VI.) New York, 1896.

*SHULTZ, WILLIAM J., and CAINE, M. R. *Financial Development of the United States.* New York, 1937.

SMITH, DAN T. *Deficits and Depressions.* New York, 1936.

SMITH, SYDNEY. *The Works of the Rev. Sydney Smith.* 2 vols. London, 1859.

STEVENS, W. B. *A History of Georgia.* 2 vols. New York, 1847, and Philadelphia, 1859.

STODDARD, F. H. *The Life and Letters of Charles Butler.* New York, 1903.

Tennessee Taxpayers Association. *Annual Surveys of the Government of the State of Tennessee.* Nashville.

Wallace, D. D. *The History of South Carolina.* 3 vols. New York, 1934.

Withers, William. *The Retirement of Public Debts.* New York, 1932.

V. Table of Cases

Carlton v. *Mathews*, 103 Fla. 301 (1931).

Catholic Order of Foresters v. *State*, 67 N. D. 228 (1937).

Cherokee Nation v. *Georgia*, 5 Pet. 1 (1831).

Chick Springs Water Company v. *Highway Department*, 159 S. C. 481 (1931).

Chisholm v. *Georgia*, 2 Dall. 419 (1793).

Christian v. *Atlantic and North Carolina Railroad Company*, 133 U. S. 233 (1890).

Christman v. *Wilson*, 187 Ky. 644 (1920).

Clarke v. *S. C. Public Service Authority*, 177 S. C. 427 (1935).

Clarke v. *Tyler*, 30 Gratt. 134 (1878).

Cobb v. *Parnell*, 183 Ark. 429 (1931).

Commonwealth v. *Lawrence*, 326 Pa. 526 (1937).

Cooke v. *Iverson*, 108 Minn. 388 (1909).

Craig v. *The State of Missouri*, 4 Pet. 410 (1830).

Crawford v. *Johnston*, 177 S. C. 399 (1935).

Crick v. *Rash*, 190 Ky. 820 (1921).

Cunningham v. *Macon and Brunswick Railroad Company*, 109 U. S. 446 (1883).

Eastern and Western Lumber Company v. *Patterson*, 124 Ore. 112 (1928).

Estes v. *State Highway Commission*, 225 Ky. 86 (1930).

Fahey v. *Hackman*, 291 Mo. 351 (1922).

Fanning v. *University of Minnesota*, 183 Minn. 222 (1931).

Faves v. *City of Washington*, 159 Ga. 568 (1929).

Florida v. *Anderson*, 91 U. S. 667 (1875).

Flecton v. *Lamberton*, 69 Minn. 187 (1897).

Furman v. *Nichol*, 8 Wall 44 (1868).

Grout v. *Kendall*, 195 Iowa 467 (1923).

Gustafson v. *Rhinow*, 144 Minn 415 (1920).

Green v. *Frazier*, 253 U. S. 233 (1920).

Hagood v. *Southern*, 117 U. S. 52 (1886).

Hagler v. *Small*, 307 Ill. 460 (1923).

Hans v. *Louisiana*, 134 U. S. 1 (1890).

Hartman v. *Greenhow*, 102 U. S. 672 (1881).

Heine v. *The Levee Commissioners*, 19 Wall. 655 (1873).

Helvering v. *Gerhardt*, 304 U. S. 405 (1938).

Herrin v. *Erickson*, 90 Mont. 259 (1931).

Highway Commission v. *Dodge*, 181 Ark. 539 (1930).

Hinton v. *State Treasurer*, 193 N. C. 496 (1927).

Holland v. *Florida*, 15 Fla. 455 (1876).

Hope and Company v. *Board of Liquidation*, 43 La. Ann. 741 (1891).

Hopkins v. *Baldwin*, 123 Fla. 649 (1936).

Hubbell v. *Herring,* 216 Iowa 728 (1933).

Hubbell v. *Leonard,* 6 Fed. Supp. 145 (1934).

Hughes v. *State Board of Health,* 260 Ky. 228 (1935).

In re Ayers, 123 U. S. 443 (1887).

In re California Toll Bridge Authority, 212 Calif. 298 (1931).

In re Canal Certificates, 19 Colo. 63 (1893).

In re Opinion of the Justices, 225 Ala. 356 (1932); 227 Ala. 289 (1933); 223 Ala. 130 (1931).

In re Opinion of the Justices, 276 Mass. 617 (1931); 291 Mass. 567, (1935).

In re Senate Resolution No. 2, 94 Colo. 101 (1934).

In re State Funding Bonds, 1935, Series A, 173 Okla. 622 (1935).

In re State Treasury Note Indebtedness, 90 P (2d) 19 (1939).

In re State Warrants, 6 S. D. 519 (1895).

In re the Incurring of State Debts, 19 R. I. 610 (1896).

Johnson v. *McDonald,* 97 Colo. 324 (1935).

Kansas City Bridge Company v. *Alabama Bridge Corporation,* 59 Fed. Rep. 48 (1932).

Kasch v. *Miller,* 104 Ohio 281 (1922).

Keith v. *Clark,* 97 U. S. 454 (1878); 106 U. S. 464 (1882).

Kelly v. *Baldwin,* 319 Pa. 53 (1935).

Kelly v. *Earle,* 320 Pa. 449 (1936); 325 Pa. 337 (1937).

Kentucky v. *Dennison,* 24 How. 66 (1861).

Kinney v. *City of Astoria,* 108 Ore. 514 (1923).

Lacey v. *Bank,* 183 N. C. 373 (1922).

Lee v. *Robinson,* 196 U. S. 64 (1904).

Leonard v. *Smith,* 187 Ark. 695 (1933).

Lodge v. *Ayers,* 91 P (2d) 691 (1939).

Loomis v. *Callahan,* 196 Wis. 518 (1928).

Louisiana v. *Jumel,* 107 U. S. 711 (1883).

Lynn v. *Polk,* 8 Lea's Tenn. 121 (1881).

McDonald v. *University of Kentucky,* 225 Ky. 205 (1928).

McLain v. *Regents,* 124 Ore. 629 (1928).

McLeland v. *Marshall County,* 199 Iowa 1232 (1925).

McGahey v. *Virginia,* 135 U. S. 662 (1890).

Mankser v. *The State,* 1 Mo. 452 (1824).

Matthews v. *Turner,* 212 Iowa 424 (1931).

Minnesota and Pacific Railroad Company v. *H. H. Sibley,* 2 Minn. 13 (1858).

Monaco v. *Mississippi,* 292 U. S. 313 (1934).

Moore v. *Greenhow,* 114 U. S. 338 (1885).

Moses v. *Meier,* 148 Ore. 185 (1934).

Murray v. *Charleston,* 96 U. S. 432 (1878).

New York v. *Louisiana; New Hampshire* v. *Louisiana*, 108 U. S. 76 (1883).

Newell v. *People*, 7 N. Y. 9 (1852).

North Carolina v. *Temple*, 134 U. S. 22 (1890).

Nougues v. *Douglass*, 7 Calif. 65 (1857).

Opinion of the Justices, 88 N. H. 484 (1937).

Opinion to the Governor, 54 R. I. 45 (1933); 58 R. I. 486 (1937).

Patterson v. *Everett*, 189 N. C. 828 (1925).

People v. *Johnson*, 6 Calif. 499 (1856).

People v. *Westchester National Bank*, 231 N. Y. 465 (1921).

Poindexter v. *Greenhow*, 114 U. S. 270 (1885).

Railroad Companies v. *Schutte*, 103 U. S. 118 (1880).

Rees v. *Watertown*, 19 Wall. 107 (1873).

Riley v. *Johnson*, 219 Calif. 513 (1933).

Road District No. 4 v. *Allred*, 123 Tex. 77 (1934).

Rowley v. *Clarke*, 162 Iowa 732 (1913).

Royall v. *Virginia*, 116 U. S. 572 (1886); 121 U. S. 102 (1887).

Ruff v. *Womack*, 174 Ark. 92 (1927).

Scott v. *Alabama State Bridge Corporation*, 233 Ala. 12 (1936).

Scott v. *Indiana Board of Agriculture*, 192 Ind. 311 (1922).

Secombe v. *Kittelson*, 29 Minn. 555 (1882).

Sheldon v. *Grand River Dam Authority*, 182 Okla. 24 (1938).

Sholtz v. *McCord*, 112 Fla. 248 (1933).

Smith v. *Greenhow*, 109 U. S. 669 (1883).

Smithee v. *Garth*, 33 Ark. 17 (1878).

South Dakota v. *North Carolina*, 192 U. S. 286 (1904).

Sparling v. *Refunding Board*, 189 Ark. 189 (1934).

Stanley v. *Townsend*, 170 Ky. 833 (1916).

State v. *Atherton*, 139 Kan. 197 (1934).

State v. *Candland*, 36 Utah 406 (1909).

State v. *Charity Hospital*, 182 La. 268 (1935).

State v. *Clausen*, 113 Wash. 570 (1921).

State v. *Collins*, 21 Mont. 448 (1898).

State v. *Cooney*, 100 Mont. 391 (1935).

State v. *Connelly*, 39 N. M. 312 (1935).

State v. *Davis*, 113 Kan. 584 (1923).

State v. *Dixon*, 66 Mont. 76 (1923).

State v. *Eagleson*, 32 Idaho 276 (1919).

State v. *Erickson*, 93 Mont. 466 (1933).

State v. *Executive Council*, 207 Iowa 923 (1929).

State v. *Griffith*, 135 Ohio 604 (1939).

State v. *Hackman*, 314 Mo. 33 (1926).

State v. *Handlin*, 38 S. D. 550 (1917).

State v. *Knapp*, 99 Kan. 852 (1917).

State v. *Johnson*, 170 Wis. 218, 251 (1919).

State v. *Johnson*, 25 Miss. 625 (1852).

State v. *Lister*, 91 Wash. 9 (1916).

State v. *McCauley*, 15 Calif. 429 (1860).

State v. *McMillan*, 12 N. D. 280 (1903).

State v. *Martin*, 173 Wash. 249 (1933).

State v. *Moorer*, 152 S. C. 455 (1929).

State v. *Parkinson*, 5 Nev. 17 (1869).

State v. *Regents of the University System of Georgia*, 179 Ga. 210 (1934).

State v. *Smith*, 339 Mo. 204, 213, 214 (1936).

State v. *State Highway Commission*, 138 Kan. 913 (1934).

State v. *State Highway Commission*, 89 Mont. 205 (1931).

State v. *Thrasher*, 130 Ohio 434 (1936).

State v. *Yelle*, 183 Wash. 380 (1935).

State v. *Young*, 29 Minn. 474 (1881).

State Budget Commission v. *Lebus*, 244 Ky. 700 (1932).

State Capitol Commission v. *State Board of Finance*, 74 Wash. 15 (1913).

State Highway Commission v. *King*, 259 Ky. 414 (1935).

State Highway Commission v. *Veiling*, 230 Ky. 381 (1929).

State Water Conservation Board v. *Enking*, 56 Idaho 722 (1936).

Sterling v. *Constantin*, 287 U. S. 378 (1932).

Stewart v. *Commission*, 117 W. Va. 352 (1936).

Stoppenback v. *Multonah*, 71 Ore. 493 (1914).

Tapley v. *Futrell*, 187 Ark. 844 (1933).

Taylor v. *King*, 284 Pa. 235 (1925).

The People v. *Nelson*, 344 Ill. 46 (1931).

Thomas v. *Taylor*, 42 Miss. 651 (1869).

Toomey v. *State Board of Examiners*, 74 Mont. 1 (1925).

The Civil Rights Cases, 109 U. S. 3 (1883).

U. S. v. *Cruikshank*, 92 U. S. 542 (1876).

U. S. v. *Harris*, 106 U. S. 629 (1882).

U. S. v. *North Carolina*, 136 U. S. 211 (1890).

U. S. v. *Reese*, 92 U. S. 214 (1876).

Veterans Welfare Board v. *Jordan*, 188 Calif. 602 (1922); 189 Calif. 124 (1922).

Virginia v. *West Virginia*, 206 U. S. 290 (1907); 220 U. S. 1 (1911); 222 U. S. 17 (1911); 231 U. S. 89 (1913); 234 U. S. 117 (1914); 238 U. S. 202 (1915); 241 U. S. 531 (1916); 246 U. S. 565 (1918).

Van Hoffman v. *Quincy*, 4 Wall. 535 (1866).

Watson v. *Dodge*, 187 Ark. 1055 (1933).

Wheelon v. *South Dakota Land Settlement Board*, 43 S. D. 551 (1921).
Whitney v. *Peay*, 24 Ark. 22 (1862).
Wilder v. *Murphy*, 56 N. D. 436 (1928).
Williamsburgh Savings Bank v. *State*, 243 N. Y. 231 (1926).
Wilson v. *State Water Supply Commission*, 84 N. J. 150 (1915).
Wise v. *Rogers*, 24 Gratt. 169 (1873).
Woodruff v. *Trapnall*, 10 How. 190 (1850).
Wright v. *Hardwick*, 152 Ga. 302 (1921).
Yarborough v. *Park Commission*, 196 N. C. 284 (1928).

INDEX

INDEX

Adams, Henry C., 81

Administration of debts, 89-92, 391-392, 408-409, 412-417, 543-546, 561-579, 588; responsibility for, 589-590

Advantages of borrowing, 545, 562, 563, 565

Aid to local governments, 371-374

Alabama, 99, 155, 469; bridge revenue bonds in, 505, 519-521; harbor improvement debt of, 374-375; Reconstruction debt of, 187

Amounts of debt to be incurred, 564-566

Amounts of debts outstanding, 24-25, 28, 45, 50-51, 88, 127, 151, 181-183, 253-255, 275-277, 524-528

Appropriations as debts, 474

Arkansas, 383-406, 528, 532; assumption of local highway debt by, 294-295; credit rating of in 1927, 388-389; defaults by, 98, 112, 392-395; lending of credit by, 479; Reconstruction debt of, 189-190; refunding of debt by, 189, 395-396, 399-400; repudiation of debt by, 111-112; rural credit debt of, 363

Assumption of local debts by states, 292-302, 386, 390-391, 410, 439-440, 476-478, 500

Astor, John Jacob, 74

Authorization of borrowing, 567-568

Bank of North Dakota, 344, 345, 349

Bank loans to states, 74, 97-98, 142-143

Banks, borrowing for, 84, 88, 105-106, 109, 111-112

Bidding for state bonds, 570

Biddle, Nicholas, 94

Bills of credit, amounts of outstanding, 24-25; attempts of English Government to restrict, 14, 16, 18; denominations of, 21; depreciation of, 13, 14, 15, 27-28; interest payments on, 11-12; legal tender provisions of, 12;

purposes of, 9, 10, 17, 18, 19; refunding issues of, 12; relation to sterling, 20; retirement of, 16, 17. *See also* Paper money

Bolles, Albert Sidney, 31-32, 57, 65

Bonds, methods of selling, 90-95, 132-134, 149-150, 335, 337, 338, 389-390, 413-414, 568-571; prices of, 120, 133, 178, 179

Bonus payments to World War veterans, 264, 313-332; amounts of, 319-331; borrowing for, 316-317, 321-323, 328-332; court decisions affecting, 328-332; development of movement for, 313-318; forms of benefits, 314-316; plans for defeated, 317-318; provisions of plans for, 318-321

Borrowing power, location of, 433, 435-436, 594-595

Bounties, borrowing for, 137-139

Bridge revenue bonds, 302, 456-457, 503-506, 519-520

Bronson, Henry, 38

Bullock, Charles J., 32

Burden of state debts, 528-539; index of, 530, 532; measure of, 529-532

Butler, Charles, 113, 113, 118

California, 139, 140, 366, 505; early debt of, 130-131; harbor improvement debt of, 375; highway debt of, 255, 280; loan fund for World War veterans, 323-324; special fund doctrine in, 456-457; warrant debt of, 378-379

Call feature in state bonds, 269-272, 348-349, 411, 423, 566, 574

Canals, borrowing for, 88, 123-124, 250-251

Capital budget, 563-564, 590

Causes of borrowing, 80-86, 124-126, 137-139, 152-153, 171-172, 250-252, 255, 260, 262-265, 278-280, 305-310, 318, 327-328, 333, 343-344, 353-354, 365-367, 371, 383-386, 407-412, 540-541. *See also* Purposes of borrowing

Revolutionary War debts, amounts of, 45, 50-51; balances of due to and from states, 61-66; certificate debt, 42-45, 69-70; effects of on adoption of Federal Constitution, 49-50; paper money, 33-34, 37-39; retirement of, 68-72

Rhode Island, 122; bills of credit in, 11, 13, 17, 22; loan funds in, 13, 22; paper money in, 48-49; retirement of Revolutionary debt in, 70-72

Richmond, John W., 71-72

Riddleberger Act, The, 207-208

Royall, William L., 198, 199, 201, 209, 210, 214

Rural credit systems, 333-364

Serial bonds, 268-269, 566

Short-term borrowing, 408-412, 576-578, 597

Shuckers, J. W., 33

Sinking funds, 127-128, 526, 567, 572-574; in Tennessee, 410-411, 418-419, 422-423, 425

Smith, Rev. Sidney, 99

South Carolina, 12, 13, 14, 42, 47, 68-69, 177, 182, 244-245, 282, 435; highway debt of, 291; paper money in, 36, 40; Reconstruction debt of, 185-186; special fund doctrine in, 452-454

South Dakota, 313, 314, 538; rural credit debt of, 334-343; suit against North Carolina by, 236-239

Special fund doctrine, 446-466; development of, 448-454; origin of, 446-448; present status of, 454-464

State consent to suit, 485-486

State finances, around 1820, 77-79; in Civil War, 136, 157-159; in Reconstruction, 163; in Revolutionary War, 31-33

State functions, 4-5

State investments, 77-79; 199-200, 223

Subsidies to private industry, 587-588

Suits against states, 214, 220-226, 232-241, 243, 396-398, 482-496

Tax-exempt status of state bonds, 509-510, 600-601

Tax-receivable coupons, 200-206, 208-215

Tennessee, 150 n., 407-428; debt adjustments by, 190-191, 420-425; debt of during Reconstruction, 180-181; railroad debt of, 125; service of local highway debt by, 298

Term bonds, 268-269, 576

Texas, 151, 158, 477; debt of during Republic, 128-130; service of local highway debt by, 298-299; warrant debt of, 380-381

Treasury notes, 470; in Colonial period, 16, 17; funding of, 470-472; in North Carolina, 75-76

Trull, Edna, 278, 286, 287, 531, 549, 556

Trust funds, state debts to, 381, 526

Turnpikes. See Highways

Unemployment relief, borrowing for, 264, 365-371; forms of, 365-367; extent of, 367-370

Utah, 449

Vermont, 136, 505

Virginia, 124, 149, 155-156, 150, 244; bills of credit in, 17; debt adjustment by, 197-218; paper money in, 33, 144, 149; suits against West Virginia by, 220-226

Voting on proposals to borrow, 435-436, 442-443

War borrowing by states, in Civil War, 137-139, 152-153; in Revolutionary War, 33-45; in Spanish-American War, 252; in War of 1812, 74-75; in World War, 438

War power, borrowing under, 329, 369-370, 437-438

Warrants, 376-382, 467-469; funding of, 470-472

Washington, 314; borrowing for unemployment relief by, 369-370; special fund doctrine in, 450-451, 460

Webster, Pelatiah, 25, 32, 54-55

West Virginia, 197-199, 220-226, 280, 283, 301, 437, 478, 505, 570; service of local highway debts by, 301; sued by Virginia, 220-226

Wisconsin, 136, 322-323

World War veterans. See Bonus payments

Worthington, T. K., 85